PIXEL
EXAM GUIDE

on

CIRCUITS AND NETWORKS

PIXEL

EXAM GUIDE

on

CIRCUITS AND NETWORKS

Mc Graw Hill Education

McGraw Hill Education (India) Private Limited

CHENNAI

McGraw Hill Education Offices

Chennai New York St Louis San Francisco Auckland Bogotá Caracas
Kuala Lumpur Lisbon London Madrid Mexico City Milan Montreal
San Juan Santiago Singapore Sydney Tokyo Toronto

McGraw Hill Education (India) Private Limited

Published by McGraw Hill Education (India) Private Limited
444/1, Sri Ekambara Naicker Industrial Estate, Alapakkam, Porur, Chennai 600 116

Circuits and Networks

1 2 3 4 5 6 7 8 9 D102739 22 21 20 19 18

Printed and bound in India.

ISBN (13): 978-93-5260-795-2
ISBN (10): 93-5260-795-3

Managing Director: *Kaushik Bellani*

Director—Science & Engineering Portfolio: *Vibha Mahajan*
Senior Portfolio Manager—Science & Engineering: *Hemant K Jha*
Portfolio Manager—Science & Engineering: *Navneet Kumar*

Senior Manager—Content Development: *Shalini Jha*
Content Developer: *Sachin Kumar*

Production Head: *Satinder S Baveja*
Assistant Manager—Production: *Anuj K Shriwastava*

General Manager—Production: *Rajender P Ghansela*
Manager—Production: *Reji Kumar*

Typeset at Text-o-Graphics, B-1/56, Aravali Apartment, Sector-34, Noida 201 301, and printed at

Magic International Pvt. Ltd., Plot No. 26E, Sector-31,(Industrial), Site-IV, Greater Noida 201306

RQLQCRYMDXXZR

Visit us at: www.mheducation.co.in

Preface

This book caters to the needs of first and second-year undergraduate students of EEE/ECE/EI/CSE pursuing course on Circuits and Networks. It will prove to be a great aid in preparation for semesterial examination of various universities. Readers who want to refresh, deepen and systemize their knowledge on subject matter will find this book as an ultimate resort.

Students often find Circuits and Networks a back-breaking course because of the mathematical complexity involved and importance that it enjoys in later semesters. The market is flooded with exhaustive and heavy volumes on Circuits and Networks but there is no individual textbook that provides holistic, simple yet concise and quality coverage on all the key topics. This further adds up to the challenge specially during "*the exam days*".

This book has a perfect blend of focused content coverage and key pedagogical aids following question-and-answer format based on the real questions that students ask. The pedagogical aids have been designed using ***5Es Approach: Engage, Explore, Explain, Elaborate and Evaluate***. Hence, this book fills the void in the market.

We may consider this book to be an attempt to supplement excellent comprehensive circuits and networks textbooks like Circuits and Networks (A Sudhakar, Fifth Edition, 2015), Engineering Circuit Analysis (William H. Hayt, Eighth Edition, 2013)

Highlights

- Focus on basic concepts
- **Just enough theory** with emphasis on theorems, transient response, network functions, techniques of analysis, etc., which are frequently asked in exams
- **Solutions to previous year questions** from universities such as AKTU, GTU, RGPV, RTU, GTU, PU, MU, AU, etc.
- **Summary** at the end of each chapter to quickly review the concepts
- Clearly labeled **illustrations** with proper notations
- Examination-oriented pedagogy:
  - **229** step-wise Solved Examples
  - **144** Practice Problems
  - **100** Multiple Choice Questions

Organization of the Book

The book is divided into 13 chapters.

Chapter 1 deals with the basic network concepts. It discusses the circuit elements, series and parallel combination of these elements, star-delta transformation and source shifting. **Chapter 2** on Methods of Analysing Circuits discusses the network topology, Kirchoff's law, mesh and nodal analysis. Then **Chapter 3** on Network Theorem discusses the various theorems beneficial for the analysis and determination of voltages and currents. Steady state AC analysis and transient response are discussed in **Chapter 4**. The chapter also deals with various theorems involved in the analysis.

Chapter 5 on Resonance explores the frequency response of circuits and evaluates the resonance frequency. It also talks about half power frequency, band width and quality factor. Then is **Chapter 6** on Coupled Circuits. This chapter discusses different types of coupling and analysis of coupled circuits. **Chapter 7** on Polyphase Circuits explains the analysis of three-phase 3-wire and 4-wire circuits, phasor diagrams and star-delta conversion. Transfer functions and driving-point functions are discussed in **Chapter 8** on Network Functions.

Chapter 9 on Two-Port Networks discusses about different parameters involved and also the relationship between the parameters. **Chapter 10** explains the Fourier method of waveform analysis. It also discusses Fourier transform. **Chapter 11** gives an introduction to Laplace Transform, and hence the name of the chapter. It highlights the different properties of the transform, nodal and mesh analysis and modelling of R, L, and C in s-domain and additional circuit analysis techniques in s-domain. **Chapter 12** on Network Synthesis defines Hurwitz polynomial and the methods to determine it. Finally, **Chapter 13** on Filters and Attenuator describes their design and analysis.

Web Supplements

The text is supported by additional content which can be accessed at *http://www.mhhe.com/exam_prep/cn.*

- *Solutions Manual (for Instructors and Students)*

Acknowledgements

The content was extensively reviewed from reviewers all across the country. Special thanks to the faculty members for providing their valuable suggestions and encouraging comments regarding the development of the manuscript.

Publisher's Note

McGraw Hill Education (India) invites suggestions and comments from you, all of which can be sent to *info.india@mheducation.com* (kindly mention the title and author name in the subject line). Piracy-related issues may also be reported.

Contents

Basic Network Concept

1

CHAPTER OUTLINE

- Circuit elements: Resistance, Inductance and Capacitance
- Series and parallel combination of resistors, inductors and capacitors
- Sources and source transformation
- Star-delta transformation
- Source shifting

1.1 INTRODUCTION

An electric network is defined as the interconnection of various electric components in a prescribed manner to form a closed path. Therefore, it is important to know the basic concepts of electric networks and the properties of the electric components to carry out computational analysis of networks.

1.2 CIRCUIT ELEMENTS: RESISTANCE, INDUCTANCE AND CAPACITANCE

University Question

1. State the limitation of Ohm's law. **[AU, 2013]**

1.2.1 Resistance

Resistance of a material is defined as its property to obstruct the flow of electric current through the material. Based on the value of resistance, materials can be classified into good conductors and bad conductors of electric current. It is denoted as R and the unit of resistance is Ohm (Ω). The symbol of resistance is as shown in Figure 1.1.

Figure 1.1

The resistance of a conductor depends on the resistivity of the material of the conductor (ρ), length of the conductor (l) and the area of cross section of the conductor (A). The relationship is given by

$$R = \frac{\rho l}{A}$$

Ohm's law states that the potential difference V between the two ends of a conductor is directly proportional to the current I flowing through the conductor at constant temperature and the constant of proportionality is the resistance of the conductor R. The mathematical expression of Ohm's law is given as

$$V = IR$$

When a current flows through a resistive material or a resistor, the electrical energy absorbed by the resistor is converted into heat energy. The amount of heat dissipated in the resistor or the power is denoted by the letter P and measured in units of Watts (W). It is given by

$$P = VI = I^2R$$

Note: Remember that while solving problems the basic quantities must be used in the formula, i.e. VOLTS, OHMS and AMPERES (not milli, kilo, etc).

Example 1.1

A bulb is rated as 230 V, 230 W. Find the rated current and resistance of the filament. ○○●

[AU, 2011]

Solution Given data: Voltage $V = 230$ V; Power $P = 230$ W

Required data: Current I = ? Resistance R = ?

$$\text{Power } P = \text{Voltage} \times \text{Current} = V \times I$$

$$230 = 230 \times I \quad \text{or} \quad I = 1 \text{ A}$$

Resistance of the filament $R = V/I = 230/1$ or $R = 230\ \Omega$

1.2.2 Inductance

An inductor is a device made of wire wound according to various designs that can store energy in a magnetic field. Inductance is the quantitative measure of the property of an inductor to oppose any sudden change in the current flowing in it. Inductance is developed by the voltage induced across the inductor from the electromagnetic field arising due to the current flowing in it. It is denoted as L and the unit of inductance is Henry (H). The symbol of inductance is as shown in Figure 1.2.

The current voltage relationship is given as

$$v = L\frac{di}{dt}$$

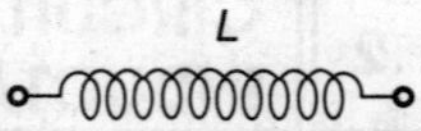

Figure 1.2

where, v is the voltage across inductor in volts, and i is the current through inductor in amps.

Inductance is also defined as the ratio of magnetic flux linking with the coil to the current producing the flux.

$$L = \frac{N\phi}{I}$$

where N is the number of turns in the coil, ϕ is the flux in weber and I is the current in the coil in amps.

Inductance of a solenoid, which is the most common configuration of coil of wire, is given as

$$L = \frac{\mu N^2 A}{l}$$

where μ is the relative permeability of the core, A is the cross-sectional area of the solenoid and l is the length of solenoid.

Note: Difficulty Level ⟶ ○○● — Easy; ○●● — Medium; ●●● — Difficult

The energy stored by inductor in the magnetic field is given as

$$W = \frac{LI^2}{2}$$

Example 1.2

An air cored solenoid 1 m in length and 10 cm in diameter has 5000 turns. Calculate the inductance and energy stored in the magnetic field when a current of 2 A flows in the solenoid. ○●●

[VTU, 2011]

Solution Given data: length of solenoid $l = 1$ m, diameter $\mu = 10$ cm $= 0.1$ m, air cored so $\mu = \mu_0 = 4\pi \times 10^{-7}$

Number of turns $N = 5000$, Current $I = 2$ A

Required data inductance $L = ?$ Energy stored $W = ?$

$$\text{Area of cross section } A = \frac{\pi d^2}{4} = 7.854 \times 10^{-3} \text{ m}^2$$

$$\text{Inductance } L = \frac{\mu N^2 A}{l} = \frac{4\pi \times 10^{-7} \times 50002 \times 7.854 \times 10^{-3}}{1} = 0.2467 \text{ H}$$

$$\text{Energy stored } W = \frac{LI^2}{2} = \frac{0.2467 \times 2^2}{2} = 0.4934 \text{ J}$$

1.2.3 Capacitance

A capacitor consists of two conducting surfaces or plates separated by an insulating material or dielectric. The property of a capacitor to store charge on its conducting surfaces, in the form of an electrostatic field when a steady voltage is applied across it, is called the capacitance. Capacitance is also the quantitative measure of the property of a capacitor to oppose any sudden change in the voltage across it. It is denoted as C and the unit of capacitance is Farad (F). The symbol of capacitance is as shown in Figure 1.3.

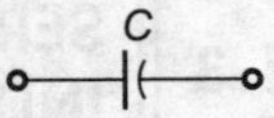

Figure 1.3

Capacitance is given by $C = \frac{Q}{V}$ where Q is the amount of charge on capacitor plate and V is the voltage across the plates. The capacitance is proportional to the area of plates A and inversely proportional to the distance between the plates d. It is also given as

$$C = \varepsilon_0 \frac{A}{d}$$

where ε_0 is the absolute permittivity.

The current voltage relationship is given as

$$i = C\frac{dv}{dt}$$

The energy stored by the capacitor in the electrostatic field is given by

$$W = \frac{CV^2}{2}$$

Example 1.3

When a dc voltage is applied to a capacitor, voltage across its terminals is found to build up in accordance with $v_C = 50\,(1 - e^{-100t})$. After 0.01s, the current flow is equal to 2 mA. (a) Find the value of capacitance in farad. (b) How much energy is stored in the electric field? ●●●

[AU, 2014]

Solution Given data: Applied voltage $v = 50\,(1 - e^{-100t})$, time = 0.01 s, current $i = 2$ mA $= 2 \times 10^{-3}$ A.

Required data capacitance C = ? Energy stored W = ?

(a) $i = C\dfrac{dv}{dt}$ or $i = C\dfrac{d}{dt}50\,(1 - e^{-100t}) = C \times 50 \times 100e^{-100t}$

At $t = 0.01$ s, $i = 2 \times 10^{-3}$ A.

Therefore $2 \times 10^{-3} = C \times 50 \times 100e^{-100 \times 0.01}$

$C = 1.089\ \mu\text{F}$

(b) $W = \dfrac{CV^2}{2}$

At $t = 0.01$ s, $v = 50(1 - e^{-100 \times 0.01}) = 31.6$ V

Therefore, $W = \dfrac{1}{2} \times 1.089 \times 10^{-6} \times (31.6)^2 = 0.543$ mJ

1.3 SERIES AND PARALLEL COMBINATION OF RESISTORS, INDUCTORS AND CAPACITORS

1.3.1 Resistors in Series

Consider the connection of resistors shown in Figure 1.4. The resistors are said to be connected in series. In a series circuit the current flowing through each element is same but the voltage drops are proportional to the values of resistors. So, the series circuit acts a voltage divider. The total voltage is given by the addition of the individual voltage drops. The total equivalent resistance of the combination is equal to the sum of the individual resistances.

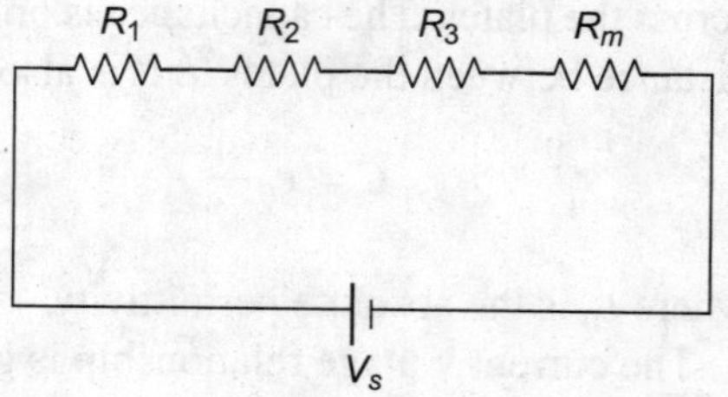

Figure 1.4

$$R_{eq} = R_1 + R_2 + R_3 + \cdots + R_m$$

The total power in the series circuit is the total voltage applied to a circuit, multiplied by the total current.

1.3.2 Resistors in Parallel

Consider the connection of resistors shown in Figure 1.5. The resistors are said to be connected in parallel. In a parallel connection, the total current entering the parallel branches is divided into the branches currents according to the resistance values. The voltage across each element is the same and equal to the applied voltage. So, the parallel connection acts as a current divider. The total equivalent resistance of the combination is given as

$$\frac{1}{R_{eq}} = \frac{1}{R_1} + \frac{1}{R_2} + \frac{1}{R_3} + \cdots + \frac{1}{R_m}$$

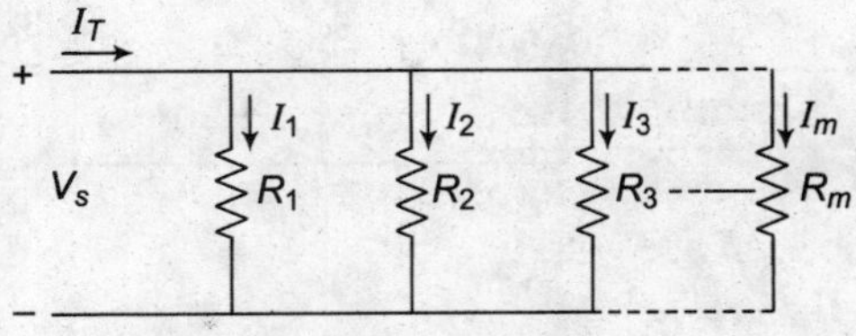

Figure 1.5

Example 1.4

Find the equivalent resistance between terminals *A* and *B* of the network shown in Figure 1.6. ○●●

[JNTU, 2006]

Solution

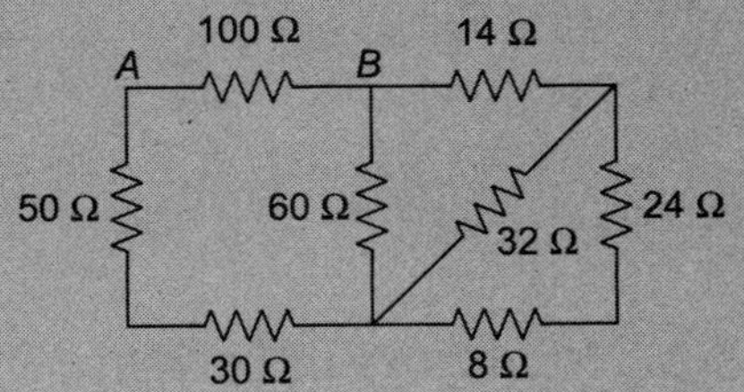

Figure 1.6

Step 1: The 50 Ω and 30 Ω are in series [Figure 1.7(a)(i)]. So the equivalent resistance is 50 + 30 = 80 Ω. Similarly, the 8 Ω and the 24 Ω are in series. The equivalent resistance will be 8 + 24 = 32 Ω.

Step 2: The 32 Ω and 32 Ω are in parallel [Figure 1.7(a)(ii)]. So the equivalent resistance is $\frac{32 \times 32}{32 + 32} = 16\ \Omega$.

Step 3: This 16 Ω and 14 Ω are in series [Figure 1.7(b)(i)]. So the equivalent resistance is 16 +14 = 30 Ω.

Step 4: This 30 Ω and 60 Ω are in parallel [Figure 1.7(b)(ii)]. So the equivalent resistance is

$$\frac{30 \times 60}{30 + 60} = 20\ \Omega.$$

Step 5: This 20 Ω and 80 Ω are in series [Figure 1.7(c)(i)]. So the equivalent resistance is 20 + 80 = 100 Ω.

Step 6: Finally both the 100 Ω are in parallel [Figure 1.7(c)(ii)]. So the equivalent resistance is

$$\frac{100 \times 100}{100 + 100} = 50\ \Omega.$$

The equivalent resistance between terminals *A* and *B* of the network is 50 Ω.

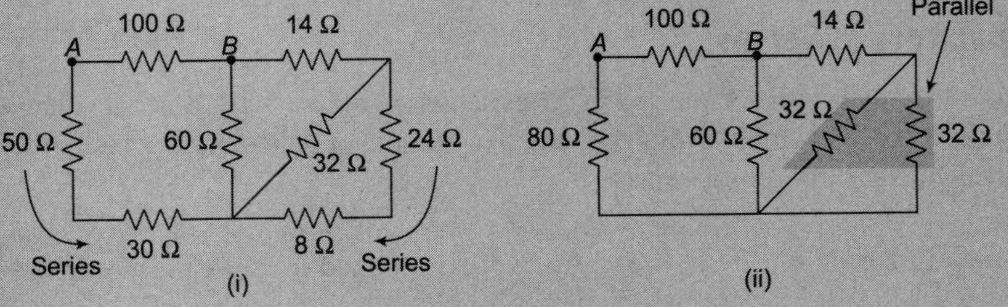

Figure 1.7(a)

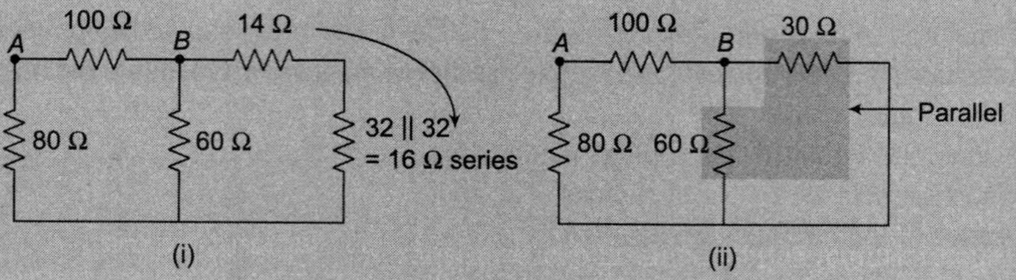

Figure 1.7(b)

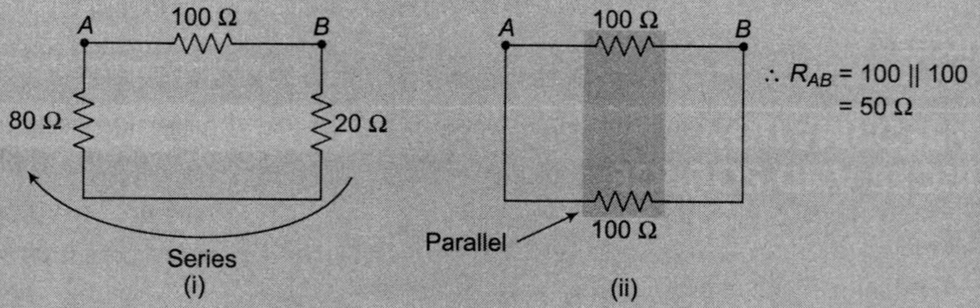

Figure 1.7(c)

1.3.3 Inductors in Series

Consider n number of inductors connected in series shown in Figure 1.8. When a voltage is applied to such a combination, the current passing through each inductor is the same. The total combined equivalent inductance of any number of inductors is the sum of the individual inductances. It is given as

$$L_{eq} = L_1 + L_2 + L_3 + \cdots + L_n$$

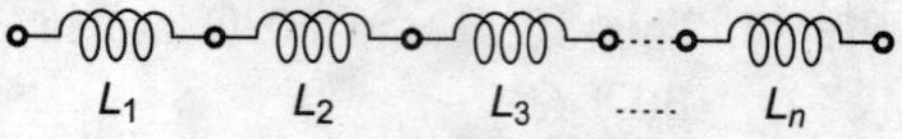

Figure 1.8

1.3.4 Inductors in Parallel

Consider n number of inductors connected in parallel shown in Figure 1.9. In a parallel connection, the current flowing in each inductor is different. The voltage across each inductor is same and equal to the applied voltage. The total equivalent inductance of the combination is given by

$$\frac{1}{L_{eq}} = \frac{1}{L_1} + \frac{1}{L_2} + \cdots + \frac{1}{L_n}$$

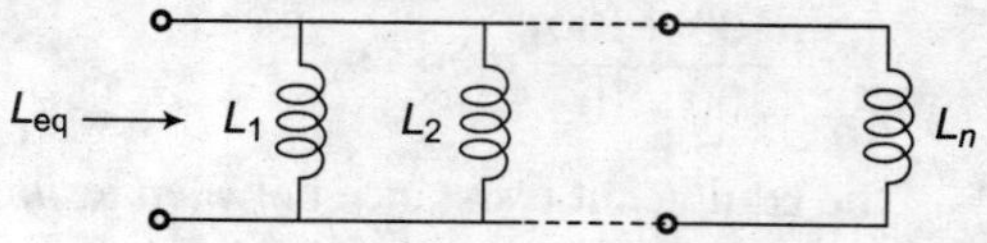

Figure 1.9

1.3.5 Capacitors in Series

Consider n number of capacitors connected in series shown in Figure 1.10. When a voltage is applied to such a combination, the total applied voltage is equal to the sum of voltages across individual capacitors. The total equivalent capacitance is given as

$$\frac{1}{C_{eq}} = \frac{1}{C_1} + \frac{1}{C_2} + \cdots + \frac{1}{C_n}$$

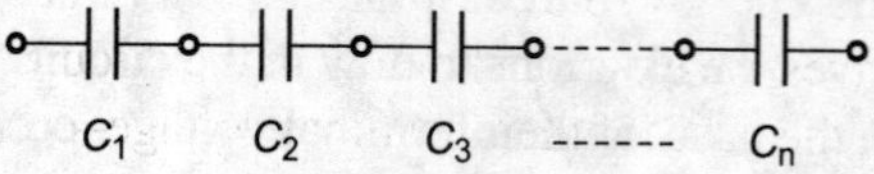

Figure 1.10

1.3.6 Capacitors in Parallel

Consider n number of capacitors connected in parallel. In a parallel connection, the current flowing in each capacitor is different. The voltage across each capacitor is same and equal to the applied voltage. The total equivalent capacitance of the combination is given as

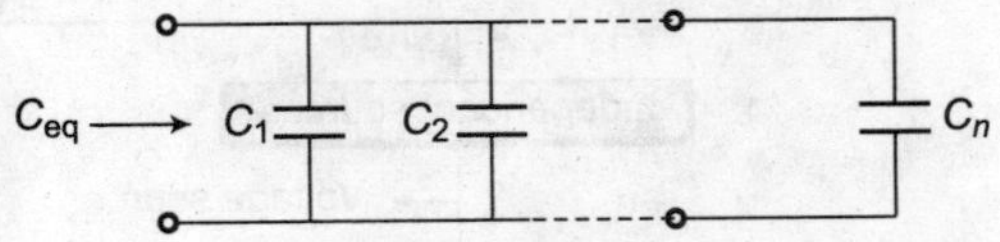

Figure 1.11

$$C_{eq} = C_1 + C_2 + C_3 + \cdots + C_n$$

Example 1.5

Find the total equivalent capacitance and total energy stored if the applied voltage is 100 V for the circuit shown in Figure 1.12. **[JNTU, 2010]** ○○●

Solution:

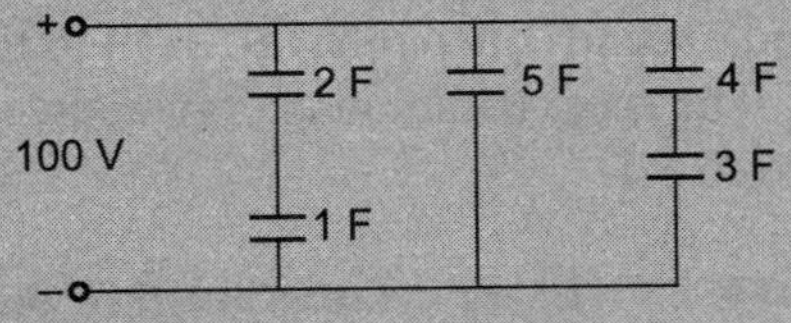

Figure 1.12

Step 1: 4 F and 3 F are in series. So the equivalent capacitance is $\dfrac{4\times 3}{4+3} = 12/7$ F

Step 2: This 12/7 F and 5 F are in parallel. So the equivalent capacitance is $\dfrac{12}{7} + 5 = 47/7$ F

Step 3: The 2 F and 1 F are in series. So the equivalent capacitance is $\dfrac{2\times 1}{2+1} = 2/3$ F

Step 4: The 2/3 F and the 47/7 F are in parallel.

So the total equivalent capacitance is $\dfrac{2}{3} + \dfrac{47}{7} = 155/21$ F or 7.38 F

Step 5: Applied voltage $V = 100$ V. Energy stored in the network is $W = \dfrac{1}{2}CV^2$

$$W = \frac{1}{2} \times 7.38 \times 100 \times 100 = 36900 \text{ J}$$

1.4 SOURCES AND SOURCE TRANSFORMATION

1.4.1 Sources

The energy source in an electric circuit is the one which drives the electrons to flow in the circuit. They are classified on the basis of their terminal voltage–current characteristics as shown in Figure 1.13.

University Questions

1. Explain about voltage source and current source. Include ideal, practical, independent and dependent sources in your explanation. **[GTU, 2010]**
2. Explain source transformation techniques with suitable circuits. **[JNTU, 2012]**

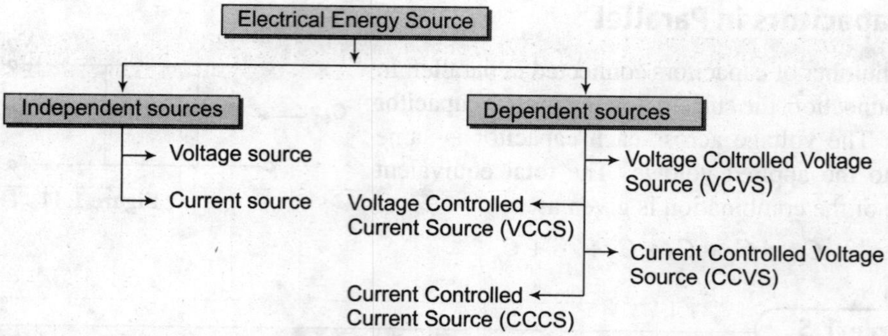

Figure 1.13

An independent source is the one in which the source voltage or current is independent and unaffected by any other part of the circuit whereas, in a dependent source, the source voltage or current is variable and depends on another element in the circuit.

The most common energy sources used in electric circuits, their features and symbols are given in Table 1.1.

Table 1.1 Energy sources and their properties

Type of Source	Important Feature	Symbol
Independent ideal voltage source with constant magnitude	Zero internal resistance	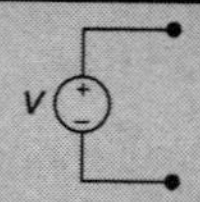
Independent ideal voltage source with time varying magnitude	Zero internal resistance	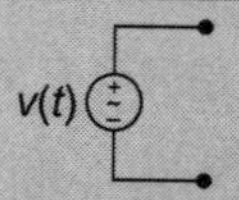
Independent practical voltage source with constant magnitude	Has an internal resistance which is represented in series with the source	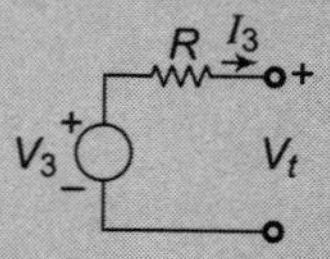
Independent ideal current source with constant magnitude	Infinite internal resistance	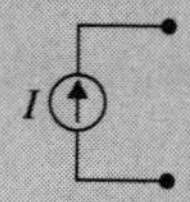
Independent ideal current source with time varying magnitude	Infinite internal resistance	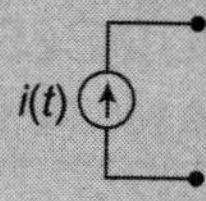
Independent practical current source with constant magnitude	Internal resistance is represented in parallel with the source	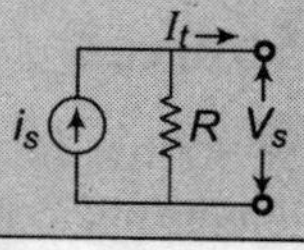

(Continued)

Table 1.1 *(Continued)*

Type of Source	Important Feature	Symbol
Dependent voltage source		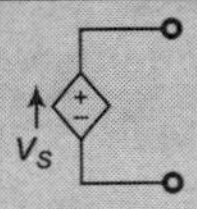
Dependent current source		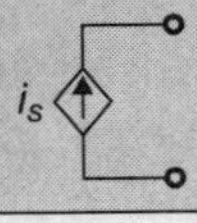

1.4.2 Source Transformation

Sometimes while solving a problem, it may be more convenient to transform a voltage source to a current source or vice versa to simplify the circuit. The thumb rule is that any practical voltage source represented by a voltage V and its internal resistance R in series can be transformed into an equivalent current source with the same resistance now connected in parallel, where the value of current source is given by $I = V/R$. Similarly, any practical current source represented by a current I and its internal resistance R in parallel can be transformed into an equivalent voltage source with the same resistance now connected in series, where the value of voltage source is given by $V = IR$. Remember, that the terminal conditions, voltage and current of the original and the transformed network must remain same before and after the transformation.

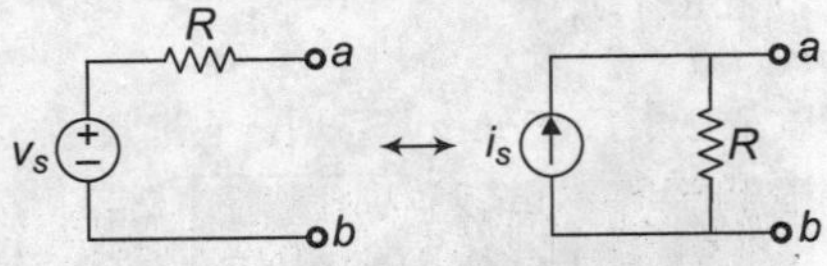

Figure 1.14

Note that the arrow of the current source is directed towards the positive terminal of the voltage source.

Example 1.6

Find the voltage and current source equivalent representation of the network (Figure 1.15) across *AB*. **[JNTU, 2010]** ○○●

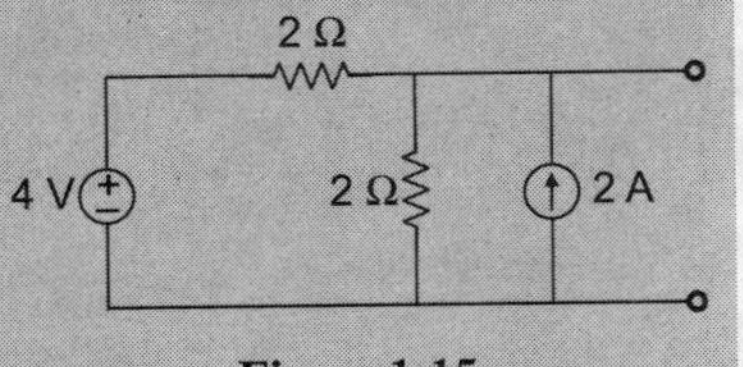

Figure 1.15

Solution

Step 1: Transforming the 4 V voltage source into equivalent current source of value = 4/2 = 2 A and connecting the 2 Ω we get the network shown in Figure 1.16 (a)

Step 2: Combining the current sources we get 2 + 2 = 4 A and combining the resistances in parallel we get $\frac{2 \times 2}{2+2} = 1\ \Omega$. So the current source equivalent representation is as shown in Figure 1.16 (b).

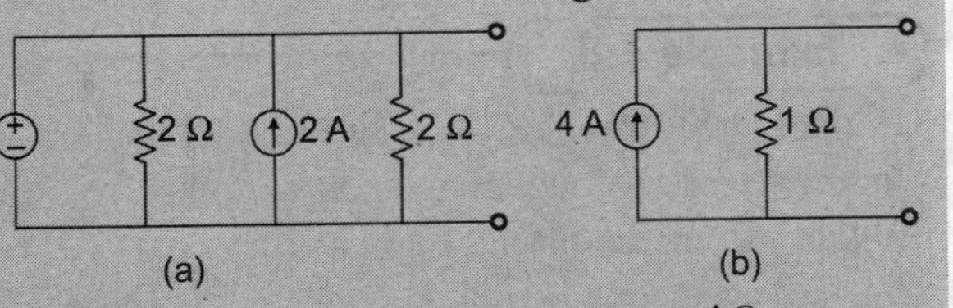

Step 3: We can find the voltage source equivalent representation from the circuit obtained in step 2. Transforming the current source of 4 A into voltage source of 4 × 1 = 4 V and connecting the 1 Ω resistance in series we get the voltage source equivalent representation as shown in Figure 1.16 (c).

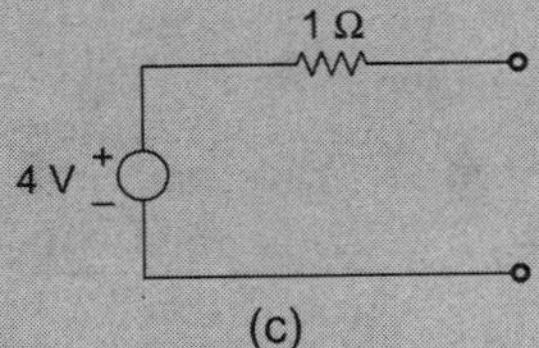

Figure 1.16

Example 1.7

Using source transformation, reduce the network, shown in Figure 1.17, between *A* and *B* into an equivalent voltage source.

[JNTU, 2006] ○●●

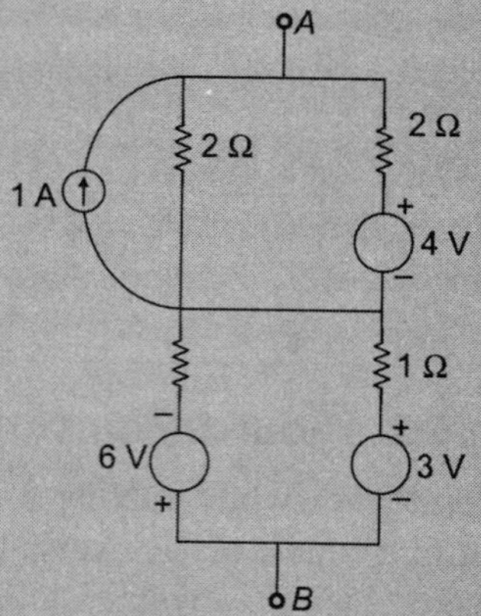

Figure 1.17

Solution

Step 1: Transforming all the voltage sources into respective current sources and connecting the corresponding resistances in parallel, the circuit becomes Figure 1.18 (a).

Step 2: Combining the current sources and the resistances in parallel, the circuit becomes as shown in Figure 1.18 (b).

Step 3: Transforming the current sources to respective voltage sources and connecting the corresponding resistances in series, the circuit becomes as shown in Figure 1.18 (c).

Step 4: Combining the voltage sources and the resistances in series, the reduced network is obtained as as shown in Figure 1.18 (d).

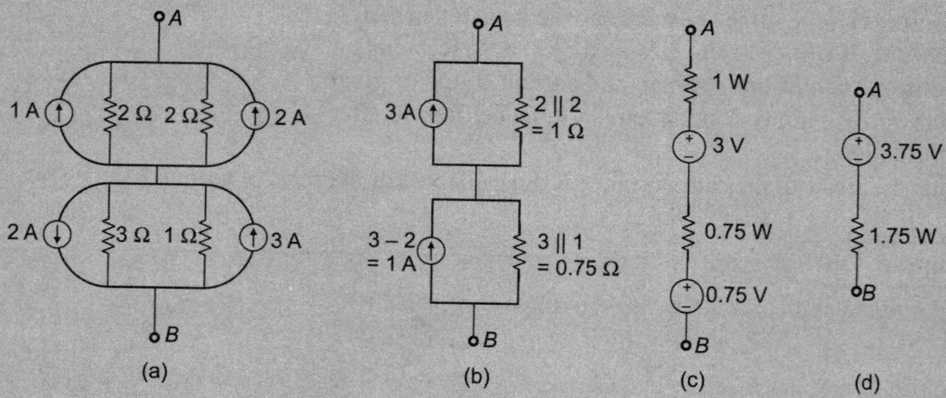

Figure 1.18

Example 1.8

Reduce the network shown in Figure 1.19 to a single loop network by successive source transformation, to obtain the current in the 12 Ω resistor. ○●●

[JNTU, 2006]

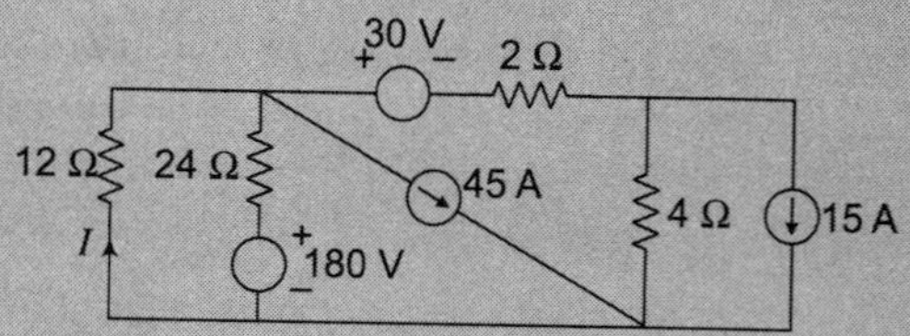

Figure 1.19

Solution

Step 1: Transform the 15 A current source into equivalent voltage source of value 15 × 4 = 60 V and connect the 4 Ω resistor in series. Also transform the 180 V voltage source into equivalent current source of value 180/24 = 7.5 A and connect the 24 Ω resistor in parallel. The circuit now becomes as shown in Figure 1.20 (a).

Step 2: Combine the 7.5 A and 45 A current sources [Net value = 45 – 7.5 = 37.5 A] and the resistors 12 Ω and 24 Ω in parallel. Also combine the 60 V and 30 V voltage sources and the resistors 2 Ω and 4 Ω in series. The circuit becomes as shown in Figure 1.20 (b).

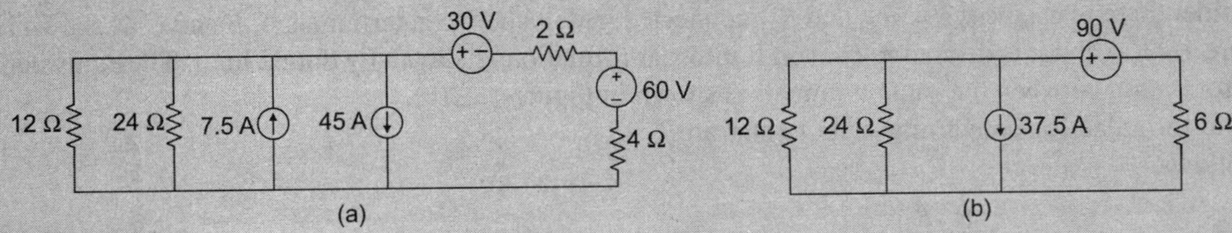

Figure 1.20

Step 3: Transform the 90 V voltage source into equivalent current source of value 90/6 = 15 A and connect 6 Ω in parallel as shown in Figure 1.20 (c).

Step 4: Keeping 12 Ω separate, as we need to find the current flowing in it, combine the current sources [37.5 – 15 = 22.5 A] and the resistors 24 Ω and 6 Ω in parallel as shown in Figure 1.20 (b).

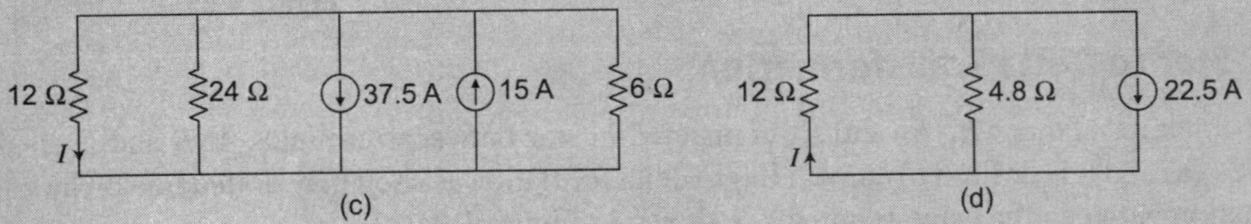

Figure 1.20

Step 5: Transform the 22.5 A source into voltage source of value 22.5 × 4.8 = 108 V and connect the 4.8 Ω in series. Apply Ohm's law to find the current I = 108/(4.8 + 12) = 6.428 A

1.5 || STAR-DELTA TRANSFORMATION

Star connection and delta connection are two different ways of connecting resistances. If three resistors are connected such that one end of each resistor is connected together to form a junction point then the resistors are said to be connected in star. The connection is shown in Figure 1.21.

If three resistors are connected such that they form a closed loop or path then the resistors are said to be connected in delta. The connection is shown in Figure 1.22.

University Question

1. Given a delta circuit having resistors, write the required expressions to transform the circuit to a star circuit. **[AU, 2012]**

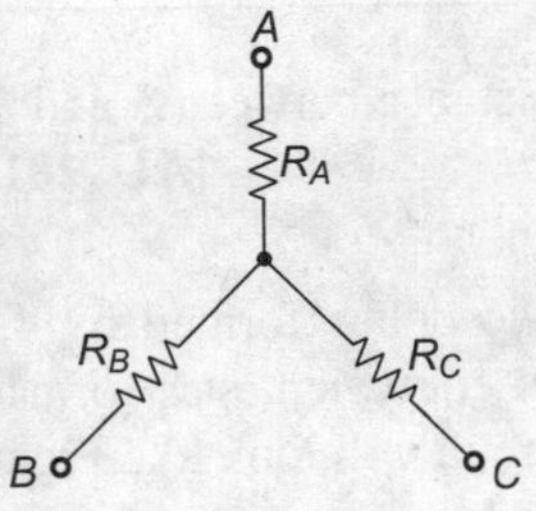

Figure 1.21

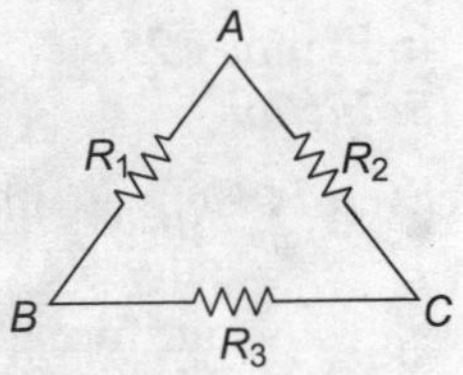

Figure 1.22

Both the connections can be transformed into each other and the transformation technique is useful in solving complex networks and reducing the number of equations.

1.5.1 Delta to Star Transformation

Consider three resistances R_{12}, R_{23} and R_{31} connected in delta between terminals A, B and C as shown in Figure 1.23(a) and it is desired to convert it into star formation as shown by dotted lines. The equivalent star formation between the same terminals is shown in Figure 1.23(b).

The formulae for converting delta to star are as follows.

$$R_1 = \frac{R_{12}R_{31}}{R_{12} + R_{23} + R_{31}}$$

$$R_2 = \frac{R_{12}R_{23}}{R_{12} + R_{23} + R_{31}}$$

$$R_3 = \frac{R_{23}R_{31}}{R_{12} + R_{23} + R_{31}}$$

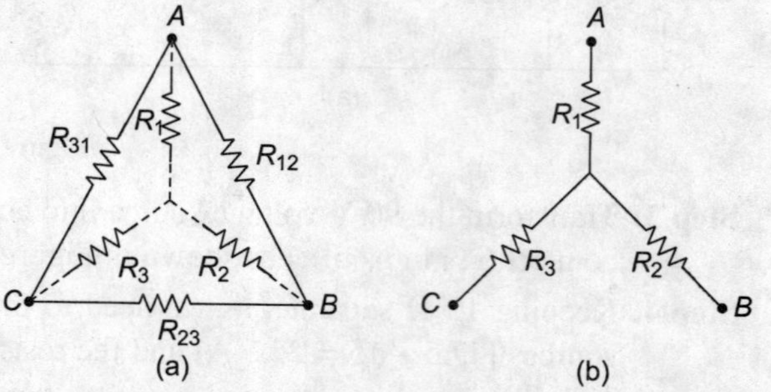

Figure 1.23

1.5.2 Star to Delta Transformation

Consider three resistances R_1, R_2 and R_3 connected in star between terminals A, B and C as shown in Figure 1.24 (a) and it is desired to convert it into delta formation as shown by dotted lines. The equivalent star formation between the same terminals is shown in Figure 1.24(b).

The formulae for converting star to delta are as follows.

$$R_{12} = \frac{R_1 \times R_2 + R_2 \times R_3 + R_3 \times R_1}{R_3}$$

$$R_{23} = \frac{R_1 \times R_2 + R_2 \times R_3 + R_3 \times R_1}{R_1}$$

$$R_{31} = \frac{R_1 \times R_2 + R_2 \times R_3 + R_3 \times R_1}{R_2}$$

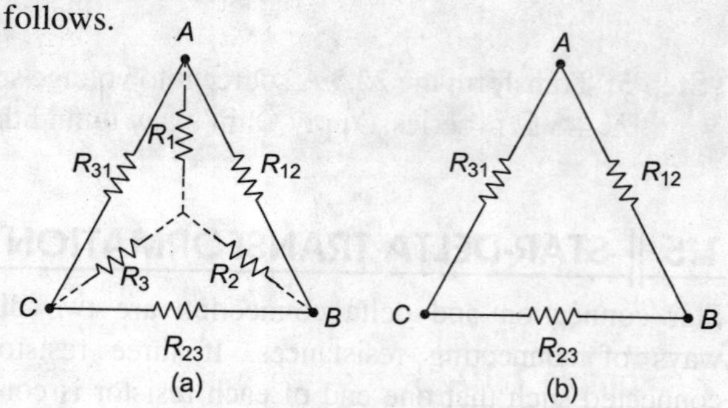

Figure 1.24

Example 1.9

Find the equivalent resistance between A and B as shown in Figure 1.25. **[AU, 2013]** ○○●

Solution

Step 1: Convert the two deltas formed by 4.5 Ω, 3 Ω and 7.5 Ω into equivalent star formations. The transformed circuit will look like Figure 1.26(a).

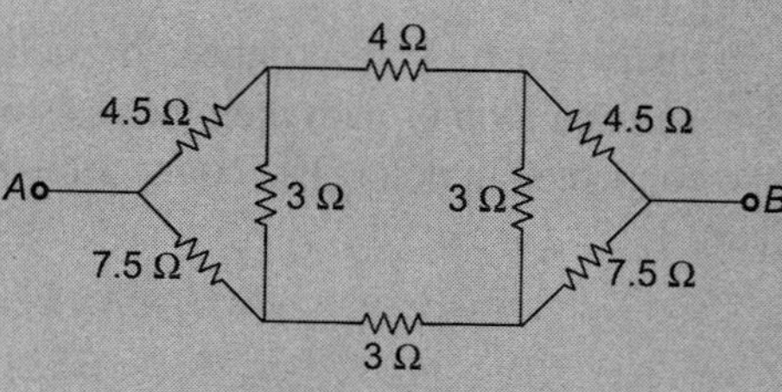

Figure 1.25

The values will be

$$R_1 = R_6 = \frac{4.5 \times 7.5}{4.5 + 7.5 + 3} = 2.25\,\Omega$$

$$R_2 = R_5 = \frac{7.5 \times 3}{4.5 + 7.5 + 3} = 1.5\,\Omega$$

$$R_3 = R_4 = \frac{4.5 \times 3}{4.5 + 7.5 + 3} = 0.9\,\Omega$$

as shown in Figure 1.26 (b).

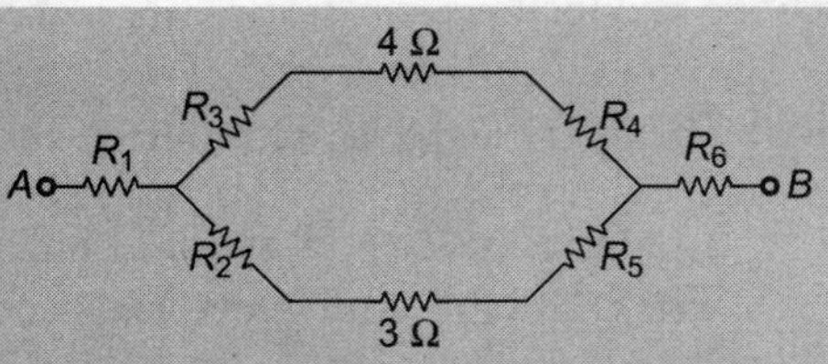

Figure 1.26(a)

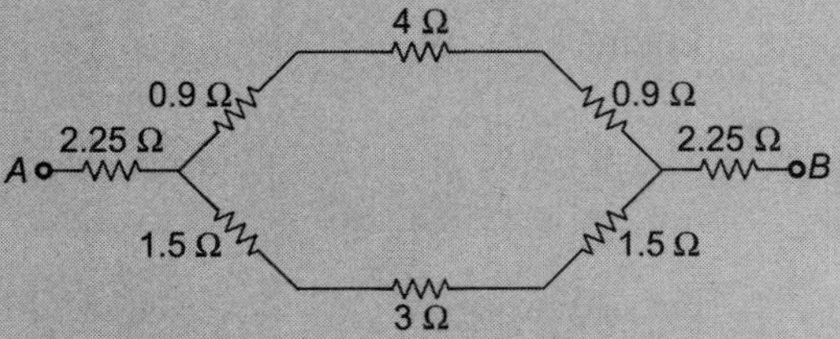

Figure 1.26(b)

Step 2: The 0.9 Ω, 4 Ω and 0.9 Ω are in series so the equivalent resistance is 0.9 + 4 + 0.9 = 5.8 Ω

Similarly the 1.5 Ω, 3 Ω and 1.5 Ω are in series. So the equivalent resistance is 1.5 + 3 + 1.5 = 6 Ω. The network becomes as shown in Figure 1.26 (c).

Step 3: The 5.8 Ω and 6 Ω are in parallel. So the equivalent resistance is $\frac{5.8 \times 6}{5.8 + 6}$ = 2.95 Ω. The network becomes as shown in Figure 1.26 (d).

Step 4: This 2.95 Ω, 2.25 Ω and 2.25 Ω are in series. So the total equivalent resistance of the network is 2.25 + 2.95 +2.25 = 7.45 Ω as shown in Figure 1.26 (e).

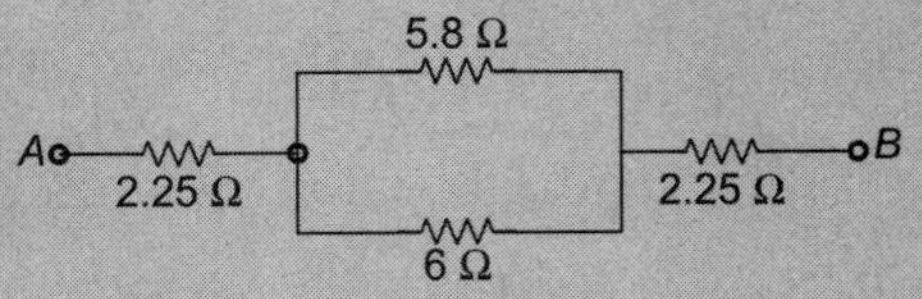

Figure 1.26(c)

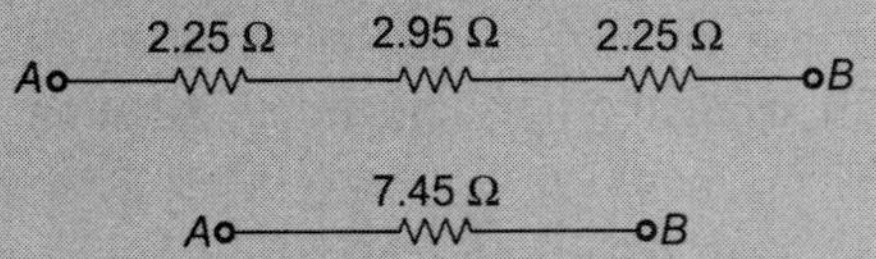

Figure 1.26 (d) and (e)

Example 1.10

Calculate the total current supplied by the battery in the network shown in Figure 1.27. **(JNTU, 2013)** ○●●

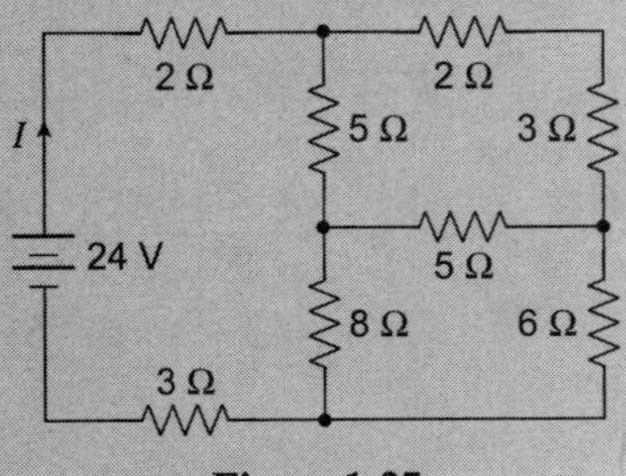

Figure 1.27

Solution

Step 1: The 3 Ω and 2 Ω are in series. So the equivalent resistance is 3 + 2 = 5 Ω. as shown in Figure 1.28 (a)

Step 2: Transform the delta of the three 5 Ω resistances into star.

The value of each transformed resistance is $\frac{5 \times 5}{5 + 5 + 5} = \frac{5}{3}$ Ω. as shown in Figure 1.28 (b)

Step 3: The 5/3 Ω and 8 Ω are in series. So the equivalent resistance is $8+\frac{5}{3}=9.67\ \Omega$

Similarly, the 5/3 Ω and 6 Ω are in series. So the equivalent resistance is $6+\frac{5}{3}=7.67\ \Omega$ as shown in Figure 1.28 (d)

Step 4: The 9.67 Ω and 7.67 Ω resistances are in parallel. So the equivalent resistance is $\frac{9.67\times 7.67}{9.67+7.67}=4.28\ \Omega$ as shown in Figure 1.28 (d)

Step 5: All the resistances are in series. So the total equivalent resistance is 2 + 1.67 + 4.28 + 3 = 10.95 Ω.

Step 6: The total current supplied by the 24 V battery as calculated using Ohm's law is $I = 24/10.95 = 2.2$ A.

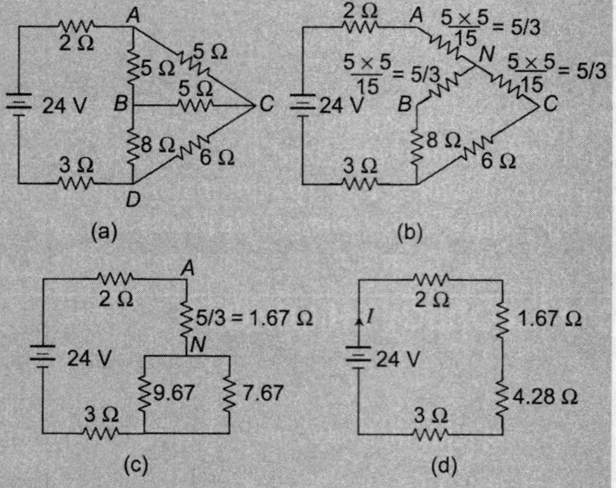

Figure 1.28

Example 1.11

Determine the equivalent resistance of the circuit shown in Figure 1.29, using the star-delta transformation.

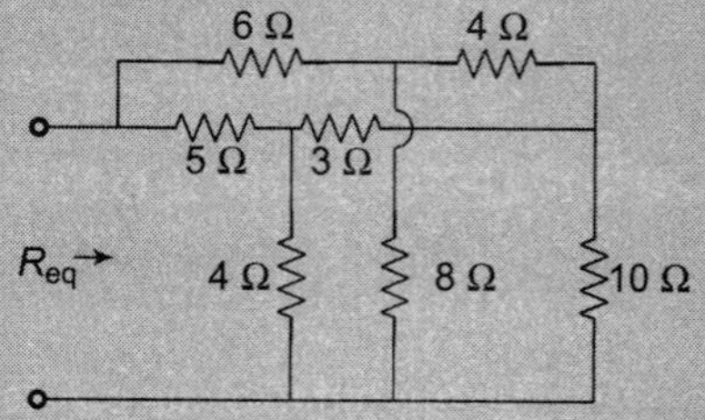

Figure 1.29

Solution

Step 1: There are two star connections – one consisting of the 5 Ω, 4 Ω and 3 Ω resistors and another of 6 Ω, 4 Ω and 8 Ω resistors. Transform both the connections into delta form as shown in Figure 1.30 (a) and (b).

The values are

$$R_1=\frac{5\times3+4\times3+5\times4}{4}=11.75\ \Omega$$

$$R_2=\frac{5\times3+4\times3+5\times4}{3}=15.67\ \Omega$$

$$R_3=\frac{5\times3+4\times3+5\times4}{5}=9.4\ \Omega$$

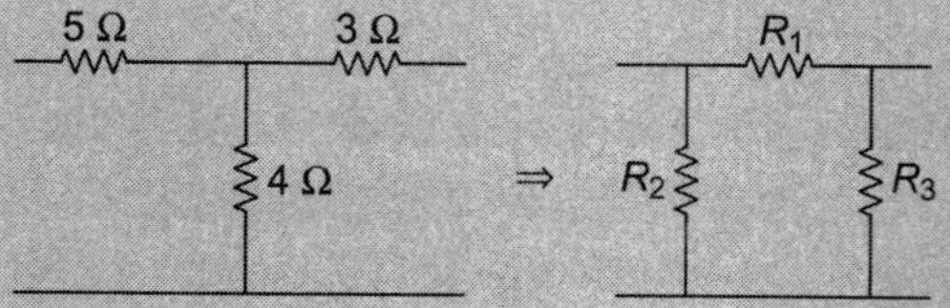

Figure 1.30(a)

Similarly,
The values are

$$R_1 = \frac{6\times4+4\times8+8\times6}{8} = 13\ \Omega$$

$$R_2 = \frac{6\times4+4\times8+8\times6}{4} = 26\ \Omega$$

$$R_3 = \frac{6\times4+4\times8+8\times6}{6} = 17.3\ \Omega$$

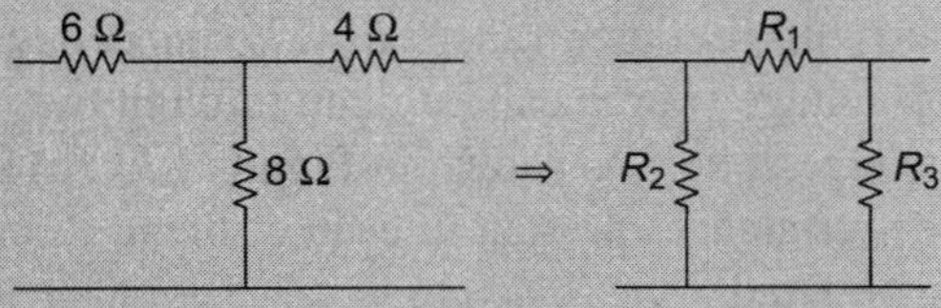

Figure 1.30(b)

The circuit becomes as shown in Figure 1.30 (c)

Step 2: The three resistors 9.4 Ω, 17.3 Ω and 10 Ω are in parallel. So the equivalent resistance is

$$\frac{1}{R_{eq}} = \frac{1}{9.4} + \frac{1}{17.3} + \frac{1}{10} \quad \text{or} \quad R_{eq} = 3.78\ \Omega$$

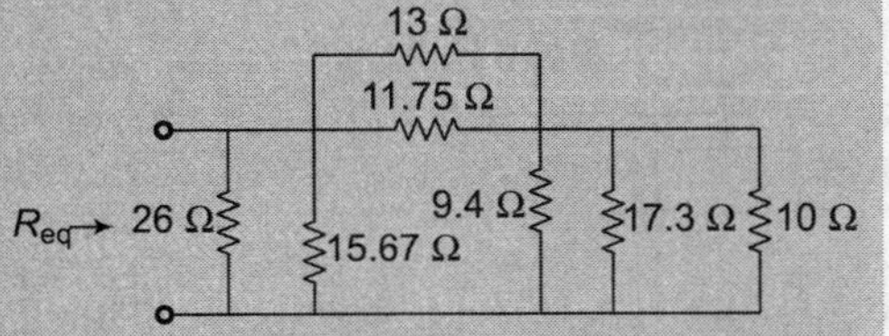

Figure 1.30(c)

Step 3: The resistances 13 Ω and 11.75 Ω are in parallel.

So the equivalent resistance is $\frac{13\times11.75}{13+11.75} =$ 6.17 Ω

Step 4: The resistances 26 Ω and 15.67 Ω are in parallel.

So the equivalent resistance is $\frac{26\times15.67}{26+15.67} =$ 9.78 Ω. The final transformed network is as shown in Figure 1.30 (d)

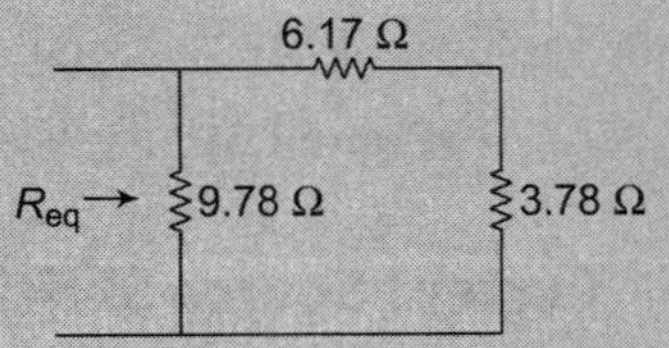

Figure 1.30(d)

Step 5: The resistances 6.17 Ω and 3.78 Ω are in series. So the equivalent resistance is 6.17 + 3.78 = 9.95 Ω

Step 6: The resistances 9.78 Ω and 9.95 Ω are in parallel.

So, the total equivalent resistance is $\frac{9.78\times9.95}{9.78+9.95} = 4.93\ \Omega$

1.6 || SOURCE SHIFTING

In a network, if there is no resistance in series with a voltage source or if there is no resistance in parallel with a current source, then before applying source transformation it may be required to carry out "shifting of source" first. The shifting of voltage source is known as 'V shift method' while the shifting of current source is known as 'I shift method'. Remember that the voltage and current configurations of the given network should not change while doing the source shifting.

1.6.1 Voltage Source Shifting

Consider the case where at a node in a network, a voltage source is connected to a couple of resistances and voltage source transformation cannot be carried out as shown in Figure 1.31 (a). In that case "pushing" of voltage source can be done through the node towards the individual branches of the network. The voltage source as shown in Figure 1.31 (b) now appears at every branch of the network in series with the resistances present in each of them. Remember the current distribution through the circuit remains unaffected.

Consider another case where there are a couple of resistances joined at either ends of the voltage source as shown in Figure 1.32 (b). In this case, the voltage source may be either pulled or pushed while maintaining the same current distribution through the network as shown in Figure 1.32 (b).

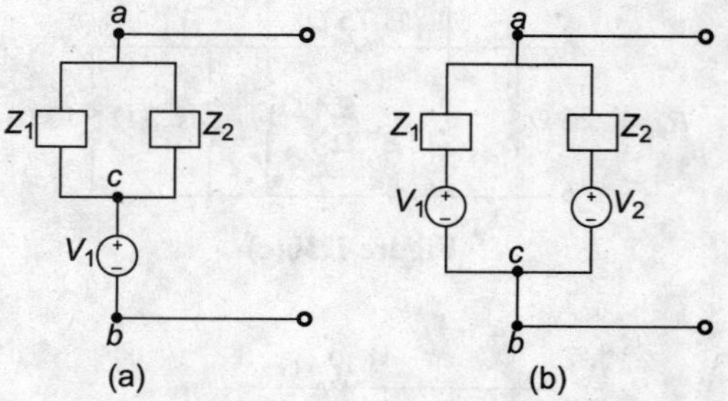

Figure 1.31

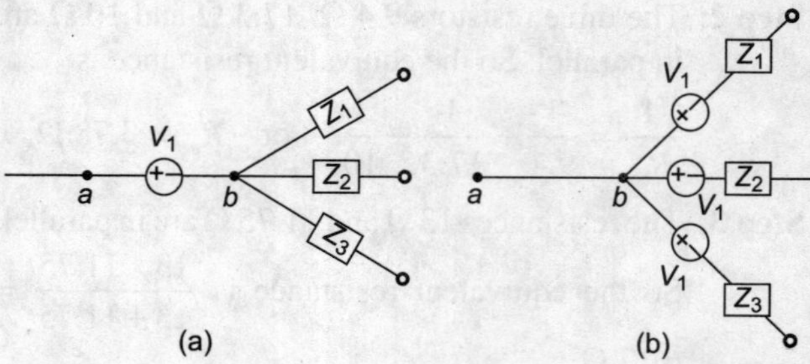

Figure 1.32

1.6.2 Current Source Shifting

Consider the case in which there is a current source connected between two nodes as shown in Figure 1.33 (a). The source can be shifted to facilitate current source transformation while maintaining the same current at all the nodes of the network as shown in Figure 1.33 (b).

Consider another case where the current source is connected between two nodes as shown in Figure 1.34 (a). In this case, though there is a parallel resistance with the current source, the current source can be shifted as shown without affecting the original current distribution at the nodes of the network as shown in Figure 1.34 (b).

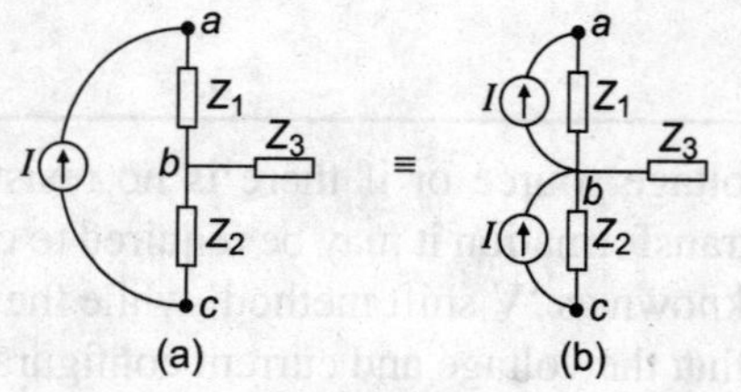

Figure 1.33

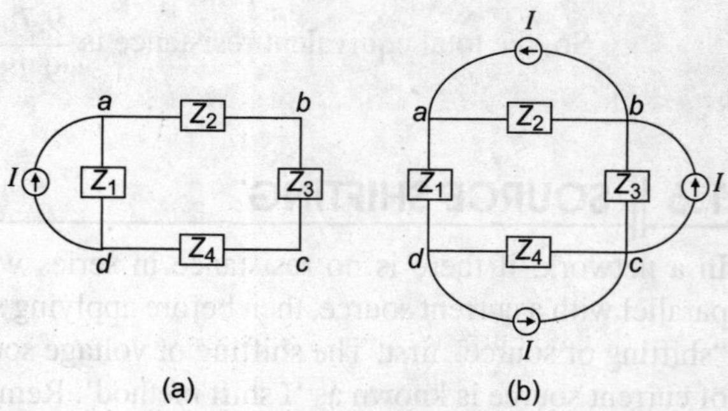

Figure 1.34

Example 1.12

Using source shifting and source transformation find out the voltage V_x across the circuit shown in Figure 1.35. ●●●

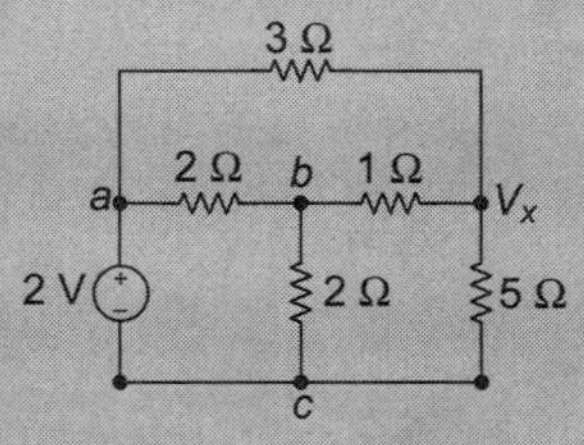

Figure 1.35

Solution

Step 1: Shift the voltage source through node while keeping in mind the polarities as shown in Figure 1.36 (a).

Step 2: Convert both the voltage sources into current sources as shown in Figure 1.36 (b).

Step 3: Both the 2 Ω resistances are in parallel. So the equivalent resistance is $\frac{2\times 2}{2+2}=1\ \Omega$ as shown in Figure 1.36 (c).

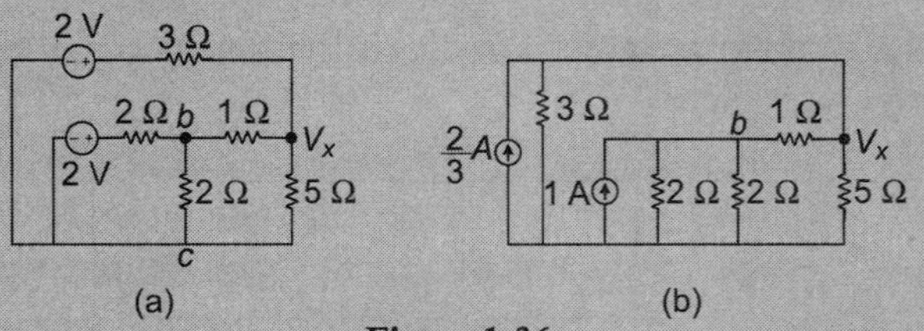

Figure 1.36

Step 4: Convert the 1 A current source to voltage source as shown in Figure 1.36 (d).

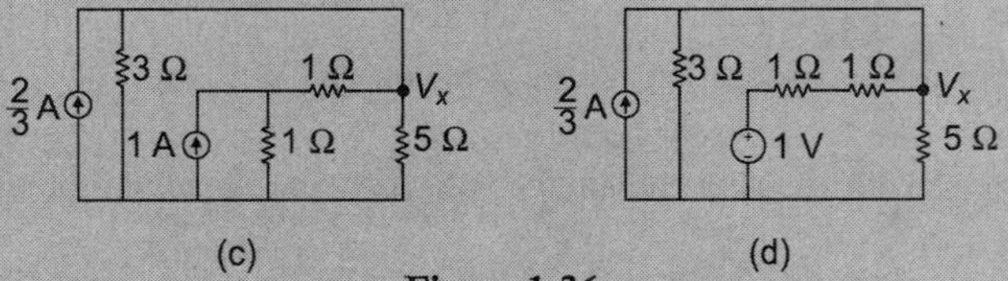

Figure 1.36

Step 5: Both the 1 Ω resistances are in series. So the equivalent resistance is 1 + 1 = 2 Ω as shown in Figure 1.36 (e).

Step 6: Convert the 1 V into current source of value 1/2 A and the same resistance in parallel as shown in Figure 1.36 (f).

Step 7: Combine the two current sources (2/3 + 1/2 = 7/6 A). Also combine the 3 Ω and 2 Ω in parallel. So the equivalent resistance is $\frac{3\times 2}{3+2}=1.2\ \Omega$ as shown in Figure 1.36 (g).

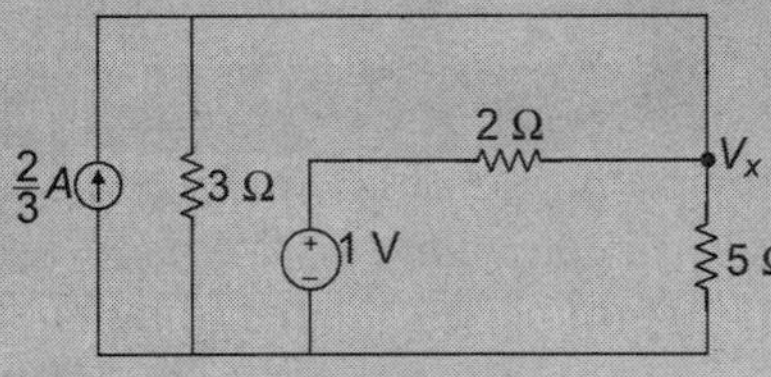

Figure 1.36(e)

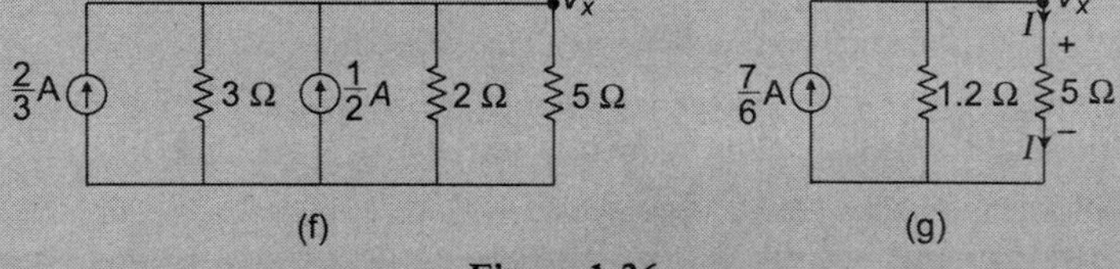

Figure 1.36

Step 8: The current flowing through the 5 Ω resistance is given by

$$I=\frac{7}{6}\times\frac{1.2}{1.2+5}=0.2258\ \text{A}$$

So the voltage $V_x = 0.2258 \times 5 = 1.129$ V

POINTS TO REMEMBER

☞ Electrical energy is measured in terms of watt-hour or kilowatt-hour given by the product of power in watts and time in hours.

☞ Resistance, inductance and capacitance are known as passive elements.

☞ The summary of three basic network elements is

Element	Voltage Across Element	Current Through Element
R	$v = iR$	$i = v/R$
L	$v = L\dfrac{di}{dt}$	$i = \dfrac{1}{L}\int v\,dt$
C	$v = \dfrac{1}{C}\int i\,dt$	$i = C\dfrac{dv}{dt}$

☞ Ohm's Law is given by $V = IR$ where V is the applied voltage in the circuit, I is the total current and R is the total resistance of the circuit.

☞ Ohm's law is not applicable for nonlinear devices such as diodes and non-metallic conductors.

☞ Since source transformation cannot be applied to ideal sources, it is essential to shift the source within the network.

☞ Currents through the elements of a network and the voltages across them must not be affected by the shifting operation.

☞ Shifting of current source is called I-shift and shifting of voltage source is called V-shift.

☞ Summary of the equivalent of basic elements in series

Element	Equivalent
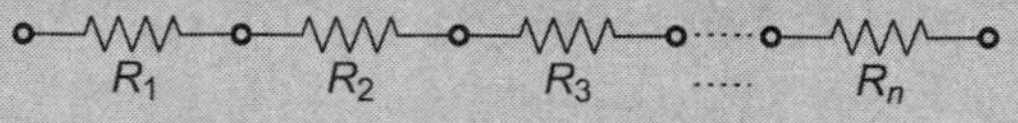	$R_{eq} = R_1 + R_2 + R_3 + \cdots + R_n$
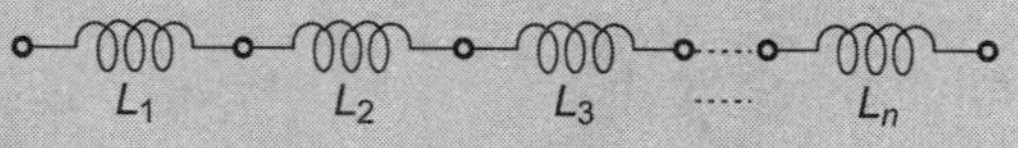	$\dfrac{1}{L_{eq}} = \dfrac{1}{L_1} + \dfrac{1}{L_2} + \cdots + \dfrac{1}{L_n}$
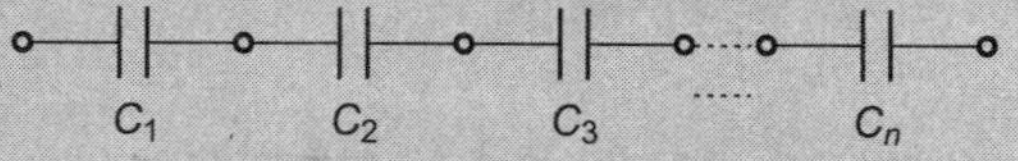	$C_{eq} = C_1 + C_2 + C_3 + \cdots + C_n$

☞ In a series resistive circuit, the same current flows in all the resistances.

☞ According to the voltage divider rule, voltage drop across any resistor in a series circuit is equal to the ratio of that resistance to the total resistance multiplied by the source voltage.

☞ Summary of the equivalent of basic elements in parallel is:

Element	Equivalent
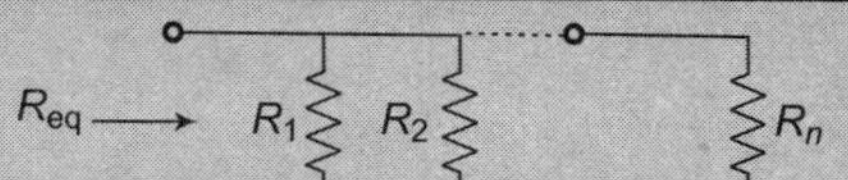	$\dfrac{1}{R_{eq}} = \dfrac{1}{R_1} + \dfrac{1}{R_2} + \dfrac{1}{R_3} + \cdots + \dfrac{1}{R_n}$

Element	Equivalent
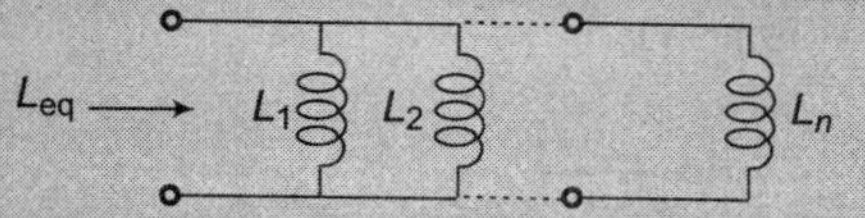	$L_{eq} = L_1 + L_2 + L_3 + \cdots + L_n$
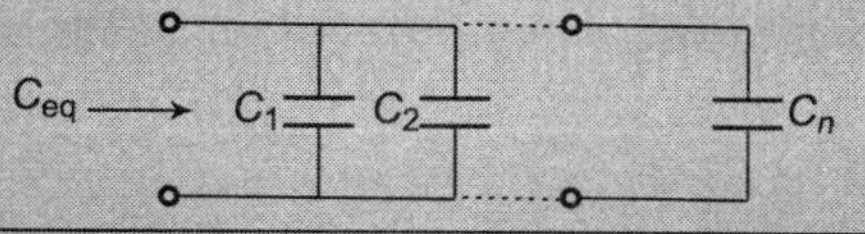	$\frac{1}{C_{eq}} = \frac{1}{C_1} + \frac{1}{C_2} + \cdots + \frac{1}{C_n}$

- In a parallel circuit the voltage is same across all the resistances.
- According to the current divider rule, the current in any branch resistor of a parallel circuit is equal to the ratio of the value of resistance in the opposite branch to the total resistance of the two branches multiplied by the total current in the network.
- An independent ideal voltage source with constant magnitude has zero internal resistance whereas an ideal current source has infinite internal resistance.
- If a voltage source has internal resistance it is represented as a resistor in series with the source whereas, if a current source has internal resistance it is represented as a resistor in parallel with the source.
- Source transformation is the method of replacing a voltage source in series with a resistor anywhere in the network by an equivalent current source in parallel with the same resistance value or vice versa to simplify networks and facilitate combination.
- Source transformation is not applicable for ideal sources.
- In source transformation the head of the current source arrow corresponds to the positive terminal of the voltage source.
- To convert a star network to a delta network, the new resistor values are calculated using

$$R_{12} = \frac{R_1 \times R_2 + R_2 \times R_3 + R_3 \times R_1}{R_3} \qquad R_{23} = \frac{R_1 \times R_2 + R_2 \times R_3 + R_3 \times R_1}{R_1}$$

$$R_{31} = \frac{R_1 \times R_2 + R_2 \times R_3 + R_3 \times R_1}{R_2}$$

- To convert a delta network to a star network, the new resistor values are calculated using

$$R_1 = \frac{R_{12}R_{31}}{R_{12} + R_{23} + R_{31}} \qquad R_2 = \frac{R_{12}R_{23}}{R_{12} + R_{23} + R_{31}} \qquad R_3 = \frac{R_{23}R_{31}}{R_{12} + R_{23} + R_{31}}$$

PRACTICE PROBLEM

1. A heater is operated at 220 V and has an efficient of 99%. The energy consumed is 1.5 kWhr in one hour. If it is required to boil a liquid that requires 100 kJ of energy, find the time needed to boil it. What is the resistance of the heater?

2. A circuit consists of two parallel resistors having resistances of 20 Ω and 30 Ω respectively, connected in series with a 15 Ω resistor. If the current through 30 Ω resistor is 1.2 A, find (i) currents in 20 Ω and 15 Ω (ii) the voltage across the whole circuit (iii) voltage across 15 Ω and 20 Ω resistor (iv) total power consumed in the circuit.

3. Find the equivalent resistance between A and B.

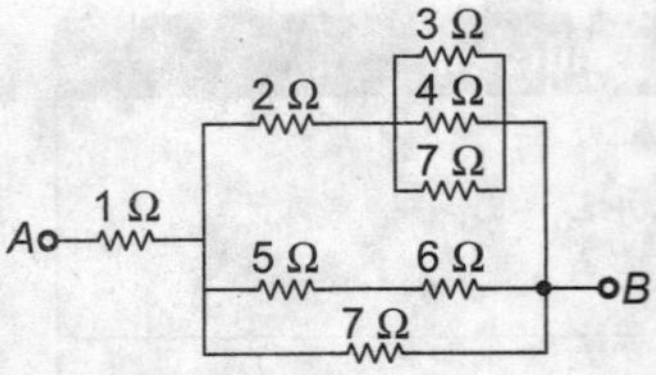

Figure 1.37

4. Replace the given circuit between A and B to a single voltage source and a resistor. ○○●

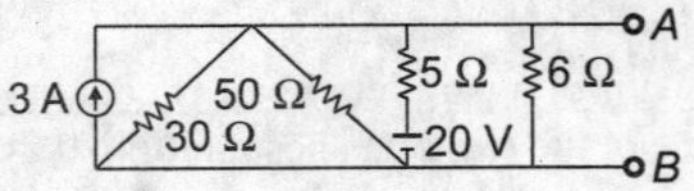

Figure 1.38

5. Find the equivalent resistance between A and B using star delta transformation technique. ○●●

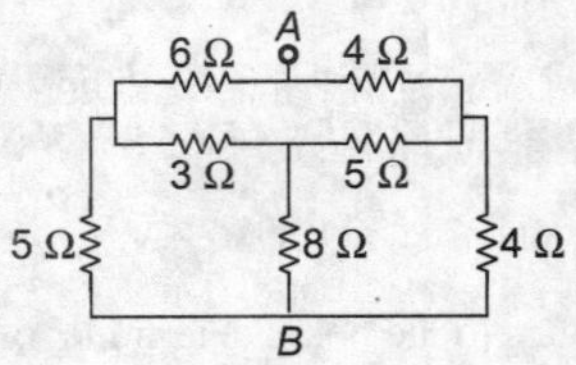

Figure 1.39

6. Find the equivalent resistance between A and B using star delta transformation technique. ●●●

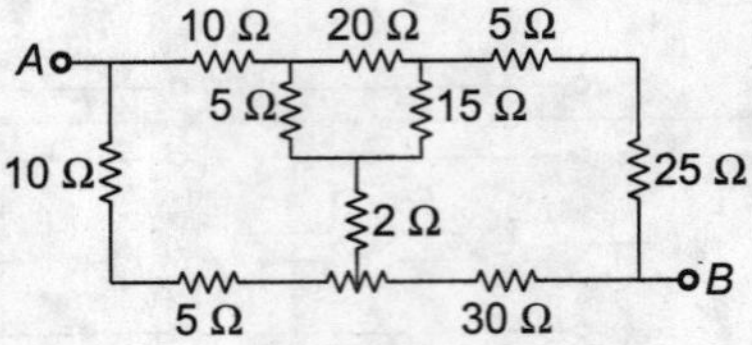

Figure 1.40

7. Calculate the voltage across the 6 Ω resistance using source–shifting and source transformation technique. ●●●

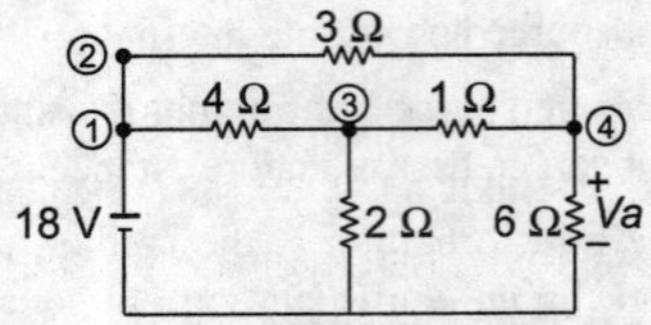

Figure 1.41

MULTIPLE CHOICE QUESTIONS

1. An electric heater is rated to 2 kW, 200 V. The resistance of the heater coil is ○●●
   (a) 10 Ω (b) 0.1 Ω (c) 20 Ω (d) 200 Ω
2. The condition for the validity under Ohm's Law is that the ○○●
   (a) temperature should remain constant
   (b) current should be proportional to voltage
   (c) resistance should be wire wound type
   (d) all of the above
3. Three resistors of 4 Ω, 6 Ω and 9 Ω are connected in parallel in a network. Maximum power will be consumed by ○●●
   (a) 4 Ω (b) 6 Ω (c) 9 Ω (d) All resistors
4. Three resistances each of equal value *R* are connected in star formation. The equivalent delta will have three resistances of equal value which is ○●●
   (a) *R*/3 (b) 3*R* (c) 2/3*R* (d) *R*/2
5. Three resistances each of equal value *R* are connected in delta formation. The equivalent star will have three resistances of equal value which is ○●●
   (a) *R*/3 (b) 3*R* (c) 2/3*R* (d) *R*/2

ANSWERS TO MULTIPLE CHOICE QUESTIONS

1. (c) 2. (a) 3. (b) 4. (c) and (d) 5. (c)

Methods of Analysing Circuits

2

CHAPTER OUTLINE

- Network topology
- Planar and non-planar graphs
- Incidence matrix (A), and its properties
- Link currents: Tie-set matrix
- Cut set and tree branch voltage
- Kirchoff's current law (KCL)
- Kirchoff's voltage law (KVL)
- Mesh analysis
- Mesh equations by inspection method
- Supermesh analysis
- Nodal analysis
- Nodal equations by inspection method
- Supernode analysis
- Network equilibrium equations
- Duality

2.1 INTRODUCTION

University Question

1. Explain the formulation of graph, tree, and incidence matrix using suitable examples. [GTU, 2012]

2.1.1 Application of Graph Theory in Electrical Circuit Analysis

Topology or Graph Theory is a branch of Mathematics which can be utilised to study an electrical network. Certain aspects of electrical network behaviour can be easily analysed by converting it into a graph. For example, network equations based on Kirchhoff's law can be formulated with relative ease and therefore can be visualised better from a graph of an electrical network.

2.1.2 Some Definitions Relating to Graph Theory

a. Graph

A graph of an electrical network consists of *nodes and branches* in which each branch represents the corresponding element in the electrical circuit such as resistor, capacitor or inductor, while nodes relate to similar terminals of the electrical circuit.

A branch is represented by a line segment, which connects a pair of nodes in the graph. Nodes are end points of a branch.

b. Directed Graph

Every branch of a directed graph is indicated with direction corresponding to the assumed direction of current in the electrical network.

c. Degree of Node

It is the number of branches which are incident or connected to a node.

d. Planar and Non-Planar Graphs

Planar graph can be drawn on a plane surface with no two branches intersecting each other. But there are some pairs of branches in a Non-Planar graph which are not in a same plane.

2.1.3 Conversion of an Electrical Network to a Graph

Figure 2.1 presents an equivalent graph of the electrical network. It can be noted from the figure that each circuit element of electrical network is represented as a line segment in the associated graph. Additionally, there are 5 nodes and the directions of branches corresponding to voltage and current sources are similar to those indicated in the electrical circuit. On the other hand, the directions of branches corresponding to resistances are indicated arbitrarily.

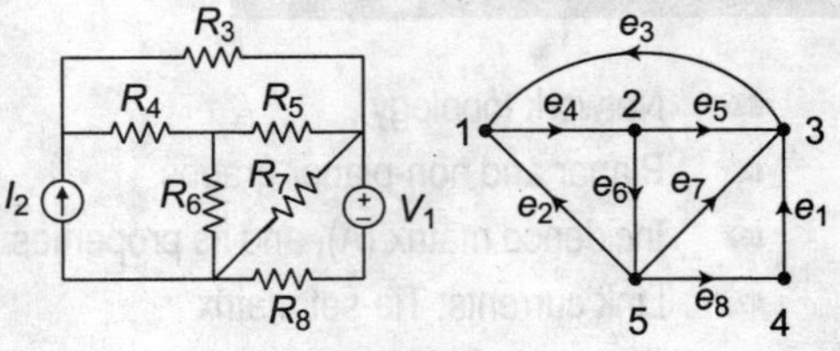

Figure 2.1

2.2 || NETWORK TOPOLOGY

University Questions

1. Define tree and co-tree. **[PTU, 2011-12]**
2. Define tree, co-tree, twig, and link. **[PTU, 2009-10]**

2.2.1 Tree and Twigs

A tree is a connected subgraph of a network, which consists of *all the nodes* of the original graph but *no closed paths.* Following points can be noted in this respect:

- A graph of an electrical network may have *a number of trees*.
- The number of nodes in a tree *is equal to* the number nodes in the corresponding graph.
- The number of branches in a tree *is less than* the number of branches in a graph.
- Branches of a tree are called **Twig**.

2.2.2 Co-Tree and Links

A co-tree is the remaining branches of a graph which are not utilised in a particular tree.

- Every tree has a corresponding co-tree.
- Branches of tree are called as *Links.*

It is clear from above that every pair of tree and co-tree when combined re-constructs the original graph.

- Graph = Tree + Co-Tree
- Number of branches of a Graph = Twigs + Links

For a graph of an electrical network, if b = *number of branches* and n = *number of nodes,* then for a particular set of tree and co-Tree,

- Number of Twigs (also known as *Rank of a Tree*) = $n - 1$
- Number of links $l = b - n + 1$
- If a link is added to a tree, then that tree subsequently contains one closed path. This closed path is called a loop.

For example, the following graph (Figure 2.2) has one possible combination of a tree and co-tree.

Graph = Tree + Co-tree

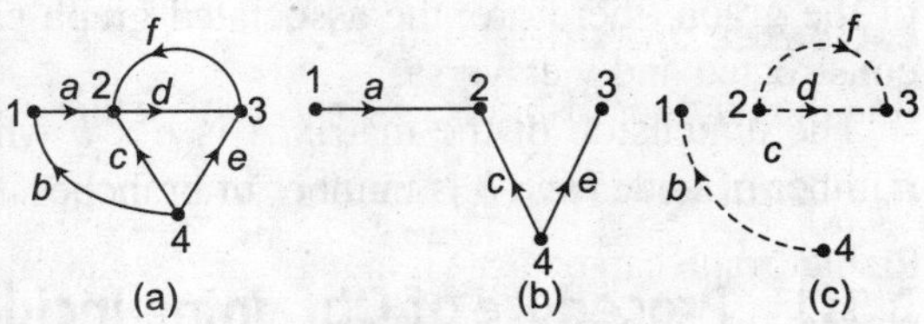

Figure 2.2

Example 2.1

Draw the graph, one tree and co-tree of the network shown in Figure 2.3. ○●●

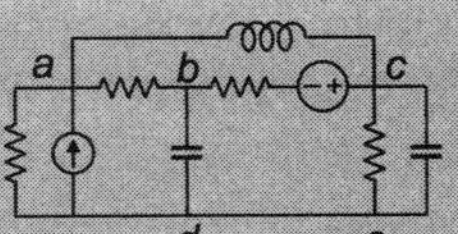

Figure 2.3

Solution We find that there are four nodes (N = 4) and seven branches (B = 7). Figure 2.4(a) represents the graph of the given network. It may be noted that node d, represented in the graph, represents both the nodes d and e of the network.

The tree is made up of branches 2, 5 and 6. The co-tree for this tree is obtained by considering the branches other than the tree branches. The co-tree has $L = B - N + 1$ $= 7 - 4 + 1 = 4$ links as shown in Figure 2.4(b).

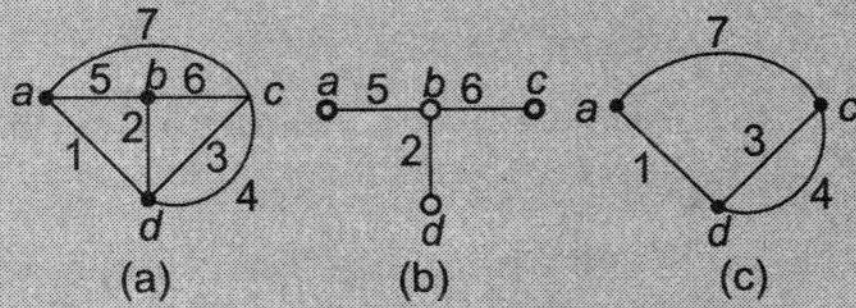

Figure 2.4

Example 2.2

Draw a tree of the network shown in Figure 2.5 taking the branches denoted by (b2), (b4), and (b5) as tree branches. **[GTU, 2011]** ○●●

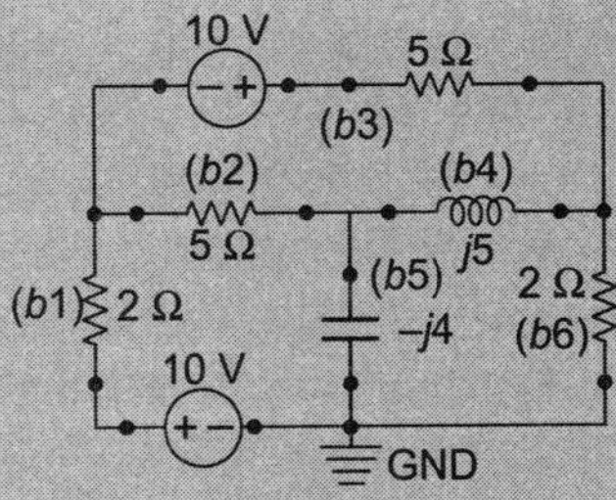

Figure 2.5

Solution The associated graph network can be obtained as shown in Figure 2.6(a).

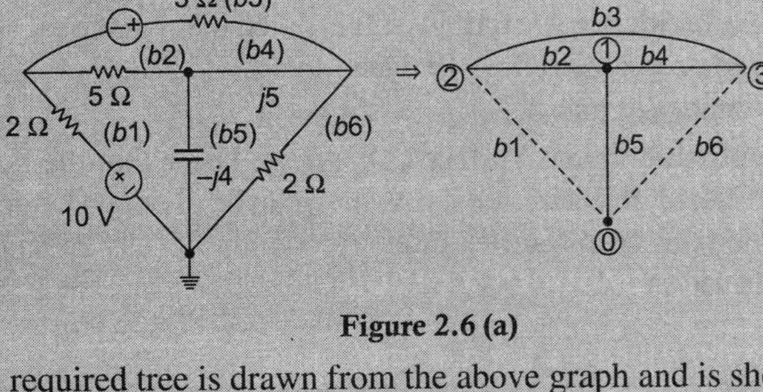

Figure 2.6 (a)

The required tree is drawn from the above graph and is shown in Figure 2.6(b).

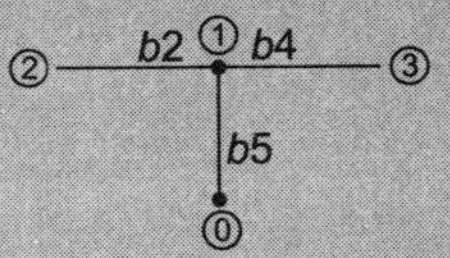

Figure 2.6 (b)

Note: Difficulty Level ⟶ ○○● — Easy; ○●● — Medium; ●●● — Difficult

2.3 || INCIDENCE MATRIX (*A*)

Incidence Matrix (*A*) shows an **incidence of elements to nodes** in a connected graph. It is a mathematical replica of the graph, therefore, the associated graph can be easily constructed and vice versa.

The dimension of the matrix *A* is $n \times b$ where n is the number of nodes and b is number of branches.

University Questions

1. Define incidence matrix. **[PTU, 2009-10]**
2. Discuss the procedure of forming reduced incidence matrix and its advantages. **[GTU, 2012]**
3. Explain about linear oriented graph, incidence matrix and circuit matrix. Show Kirchhoff's laws in incidence-matrix formulation and circuit-matrix formulation. **[GTU, 2010]**
4. Discuss the procedure of forming tie-set matrix and its advantages.
5. Define basic cut-sets and procedure for formulation of cut-set matrix.
6. Define basic cut-set. **[PTU, 2011–12]**
7. Explain the fundamental cut-set matrix taking a suitable example. **[PTU, 2009–10]**

2.3.1 Procedure of Obtaining Incidence Matrix (*A*)

Rows of Incidence Matrix refer to nodes while columns refer to branches of the connected graph. Each entry in Matrix *A* could be either 0, 1 or –1 depending upon the relation between the node and branch under consideration. It obeys the following rules:

- 0 = If a branch is not connected with the node under consideration.
- 1 = If a branch is connected with the node under consideration but its direction is away from the node.
- –1 = If a branch is not connected with the node under consideration but its direction is towards the node.

2.3.2 Reduced Incidence Matrix (A_l)

All rows of an Incidence Matrix are *not* linearly independent, i.e., any one row of an Incidence Matrix can be expressed in a linear combination of all remaining rows. This gives rise to a concept of a Reduced Incidence Matrix (A_l) wherein all rows are linearly independent and number of rows are one-less than from an Incidence Matrix.

For a graph having n nodes and b branches, the dimension of a complete Incidence Matrix A is $n \times b$, while the dimension of Reduced Incidence Matrix is $(n-1) \times b$.

- **Incidence Matrix (*A*) to Reduced Incidence Matrix (A_l):** It is noted that numerical sum of all entries of a column of Incidence Matrix is ZERO. A Reduced Incidence Matrix A_l is obtained by removing any one row of the incidence matrix.
- **Reduced Incidence Matrix (A_l) to Incidence Matrix (*A*):** As we know that the number of rows in A is one-more than A_l, therefore, this additional row in A_l can be obtained by generating additional entries such that a total sum of all entries in every column of *A* is ZERO. This is explained in the following two matrices:

$$[A_1]=\begin{vmatrix} -1 & 1 & 0 & 0 & 0 & 0 & 0 \\ 0 & -1 & 1 & 1 & 0 & 0 & 0 \\ 0 & 0 & 0 & -1 & 1 & 0 & 0 \\ 0 & 0 & 0 & 0 & -1 & 1 & 0 \\ 0 & 0 & -1 & 0 & 0 & -1 & 1 \end{vmatrix} \qquad [A]=\begin{array}{c|ccccccc|} a & -1 & 1 & 0 & 0 & 0 & 0 & 0 \\ b & 0 & -1 & 1 & 1 & 0 & 0 & 0 \\ c & 0 & 0 & 0 & -1 & 1 & 0 & 0 \\ d & 0 & 0 & 0 & 0 & -1 & 1 & 0 \\ e & 0 & 0 & -1 & 0 & 0 & -1 & 1 \\ f & 1 & 0 & 0 & 0 & 0 & 0 & -1 \end{array}$$

It can be noted from above that the order of A_I is 5 × 7 while the order of A is 6 × 7. The additional 6th row of A is obtained by ensuring that a total sum of all entries in every column is zero.

Example 2.3

Refer the network shown in Figure 2.7, obtain the corresponding incidence matrix. ○●●

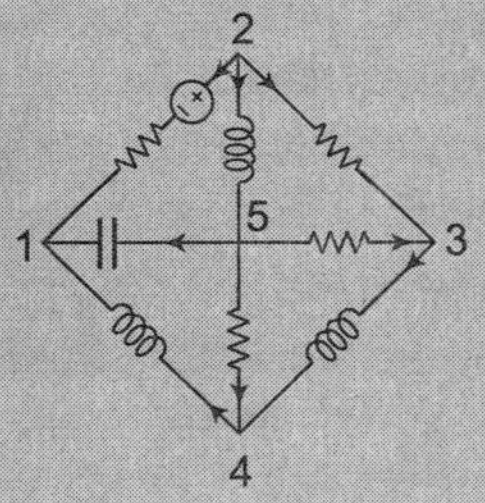

Figure 2.7

Solution The given network has five nodes and eight branches. The corresponding graph is drawn as in Figure 2.8.

Utilising the methodology given in relevant section of this chapter for obtaining Incidence matrix:

$[A] =$

Node	a	b	c	d	e	f	g	h
	Branches							
1	–1	0	0	1	0	1	0	0
2	1	–1	0	0	0	0	1	0
3	0	1	–1	0	1	0	0	0
4	0	0	1	–1	0	0	0	1
5	0	0	0	0	–1	–1	–1	–1

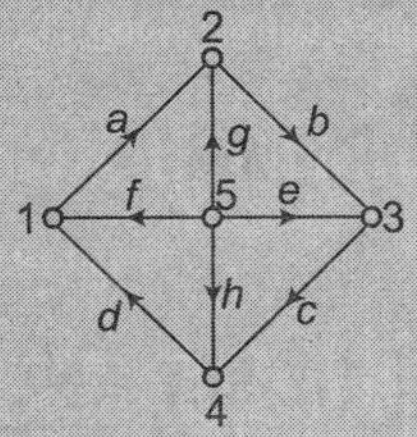

Figure 2.8

Example 2.4

For the network shown in Figure 2.9, draw the oriented graph and all possible trees and also prepare incidence matrix. **[GTU Dec. 2012]** ○●●

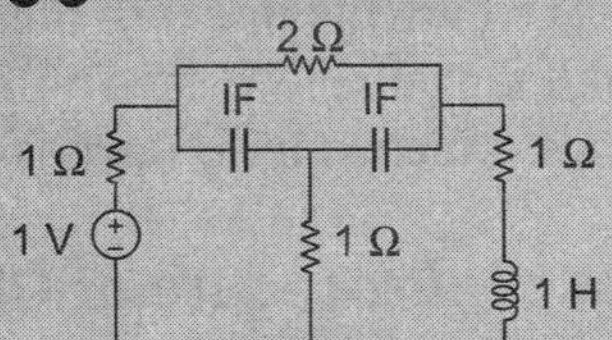

Figure 2.9

Solution The oriented graph is (Figure 2.10a)

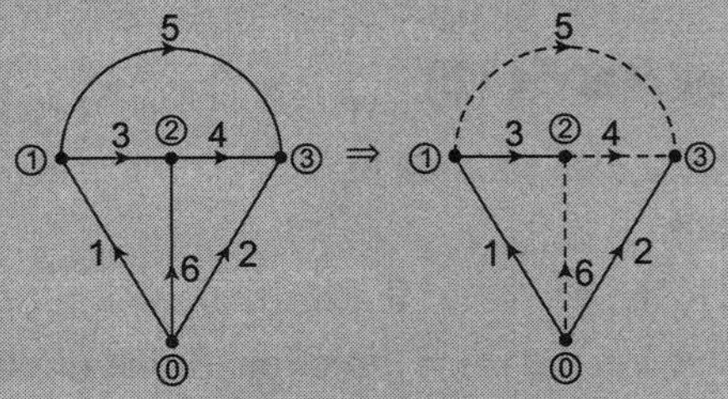

Figure 2.10 (a)

The possible trees are (Figure 2.10b)

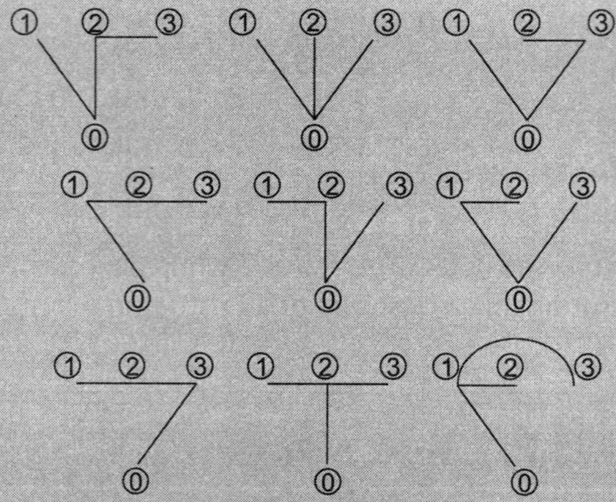

Figure 2.10 (b)

The incidence matrix is

Nodes	Elements 1	2	3	4	5	6
0	1	–1	0	0	0	1
1	–1	0	1	0	1	0
2	0	0	–1	1	0	–1
3	0	1	0	–1	–1	0

2.4 || TIE-SET AND TIE-SET MATRIX (*B*)

A tree of a graph does not contain any closed path or loop, while if a link (i.e. a branch of associated co-tree) is added to this tree then a loop will be formed. This loop is called Fundamental Loop or Tie-Set. It can be easily deduced that the number of fundamental loops for a tree will be equal to number of links (i.e. $l = b - n + 1$) of the associated co-tree.

The currents in every fundamental loop associated with every link are called link currents. These link/loop currents can be utilised to write Kirchhoff's voltage equations for the associated fundamental loops, which in turn, can be solved to obtain branch currents of a graph.

2.4.1 Procedure of Obtaining Tie-Set Matrix (*B*)

The dimension of a tie-set matrix is $l \times b$. Following procedure is utilised to construct a tie-set matrix:

- Arbitrarily select a tree in the graph.
- Form fundamental loops with each link in the graph for the entire tree.
- Assume directions of loop currents oriented in the same direction as that of the link.

- Rows of tie-set matrix refer to loop currents while columns refer to branch currents of the connected graph. Each entry in Matrix B could be either 0, 1 or –1 depending upon the relation between the loop currents and branch current under consideration. It obeys the following rules:
  - 0 = If a branch current is not the part of fundamental loop under consideration
  - 1 = If a branch current is in same direction to that of loop current under consideration
  - –1= If a branch current is in opposite direction to that of loop current under consideration

Example 2.5

Formulate the tie-set matrix for the graph shown in Figure 2.11.

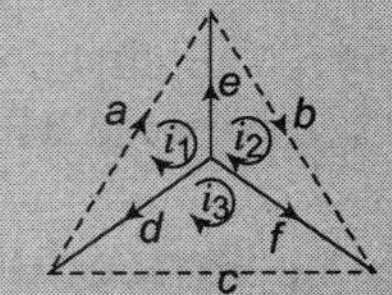

Figure 2.11

Solution Tree branches: *d*, *e*, *f*

Links: *a*, *b*, *c*

Link current directions will be similar to loop currents. Following is the procedure for constructing the tie-set matrix as outlined in relevant section:

Link **Branches**

$[B] =$

	a	b	c	d	e	f
a	1	0	0	1	–1	0
b	0	1	0	0	1	–1
c	0	0	1	–1	0	1

Example 2.6

Draw a tree of the electrical circuit and tie-set matrix as shown in Figure 2.12.

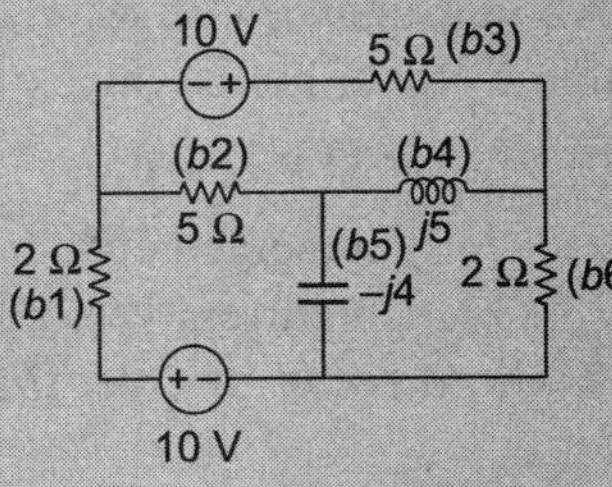

Figure 2.12

Solution The following tree [Figure 2.13(a)] is considered for the given problem:

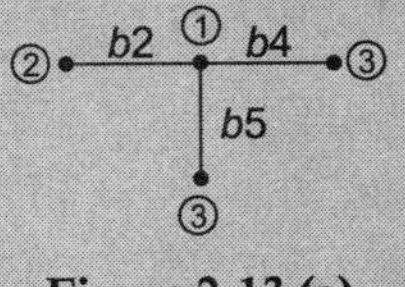

Figure 2.13 (a)

Arbitrary directions are assumed for each branch of the graph, therefore direction graph is obtained as given in Figure 2.13(b).

Let l_1, l_3, l_6 be the links with loop currents I_1, I_3, I_6 respectively.

The tie-set matrix is

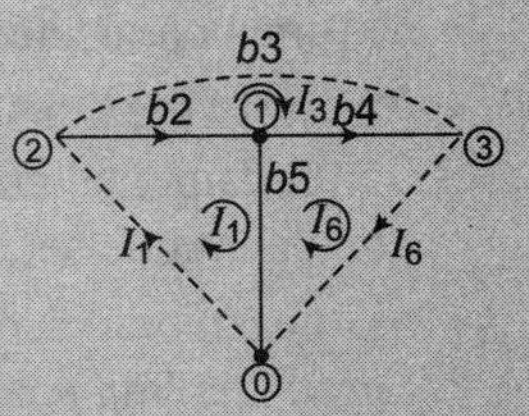

Figure 2.13 (b)

Link **Branches + Links**

$[B] =$

	b_1	b_2	b_3	b_4	b_5	b_6
l_1	1	1	0	0	1	0
l_3	0	–1	1	–1	0	0
l_6	0	0	0	1	–1	1

2.5 CUT-SETS

A cut-set is *a minimal set of branches* of a connected graph such that the removal of these branches causes the graph to be cut into exactly two parts. A cut-set is defined using the expression $\{x, y, z\}$, wherein x, y, and z represent the graph branches/links which cut the graph into two equal parts.

Following points can be noted in this respect:

- A cut-set consists of one and only one twig and links.
- The important property of a cut-set is that by restoring any one of the branches of the cut-set, the graph should become connected.
- The direction for cut-set is selected arbitrarily. The directions of some graph branches may coincide with the cut-set direction while other branches may have opposite direction.

2.5.1 Procedure of Obtaining Cut-Sets Matrix (Q)

Based on the direction of graph branches with respect to cut-set direction, Cut-Set Matrix (Q) is formulated. Rows of Cut-Set Matrix Q refer to cut-sets, which are identified for a graph while columns refer to branch currents of the connected graph. Each entry in Matrix Q could be either 0, 1 or –1 depending upon whether direction of a branch coincides with the cut-set direction or not. It obeys following rule:

- 0 = If a branch does not form the part of cut-set under consideration
- 1 = If a branch current is in same direction to that of cut-set direction under consideration
- –1= If a branch current is in opposite direction to that of cut-set direction under consideration

An **augmented cut-set matrix** is formed by utilising all possible number of cut-sets (q) associated with the graph. Following expression is utilised to form augmented cut-set matrix.

$$\mathbf{Q} \times \boldsymbol{I_b} = \mathbf{0}$$

where Q is augmented cut-set matrix of order $(q \times b)$,

I_b is branch-current vector of order $(b \times 1)$

0 is zero vector of order $(b \times 1)$

2.5.2 Fundamental Cut-Sets

The concept of fundamental cut-set (f-cut-set) can be used to obtain a set of linearly independent equations in branch current variables. The f-cut-sets are defined for a given tree of the graph.

Following procedure is utilised to obtain f-cut-sets

- From a connected graph, first select a tree and then select a twig.
- Identify the links which are required along with this twig to form the other part of the tree. Thus, a fundamental cut-set of a graph, with respect to a tree, is a cut-set that is formed by one twig and a unique set of links.
- For each branch of the tree, i.e. for each twig, there will be a f-cut-set. Therefore, for a connected graph having n nodes, there will be $(n - 1)$ twigs in a tree, and the number of f-cut-sets will also be equal to $(n - 1)$.

The fundamental cut-set matrix (Q_f) is one in which each row represents a cut-set associated with a twig of the selected tree. The rows of Q_f correspond to the fundamental cut-sets and the columns correspond to the branches of the graph.

The only difference between augmented cut-set matrix and fundamental cut-set matrix is that the latter represents a set of *t (number of twigs in a tree under consideration)* linearly independent equations which can be solved to obtain actual branch current values.

Example 2.7

Explain the fundamental cut-set matrix taking a suitable example. **[PTU 2009–10]** ○●●

Solution The fundamental cut-set matrix (Q_f) is one in which each row represents a cut-set associated with a twig of the selected tree. The rows of Q_f correspond to the fundamental cut-sets and the columns correspond to the branches of the graph.

Consider the electrical network shown in Figure 2.14(a).

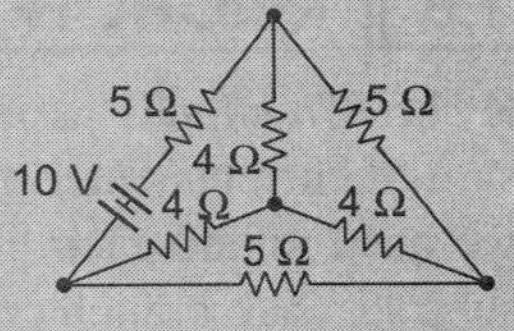

Figure 2.14 (a)

Fundamental cut-set C_1, C_2 and C_3 can be drawn for the network given in Figure 2.14(b):

The fundamental cut-sets are identified as,

f-cut-set-1: [1, 4, 6]
f-cut-set-2: [3, 5, 6]
f-cut-set-3: [1, 2, 3]

The fundamental cut-set matrix is given as:

$Q_f =$

	1	2	3	4	5	6
C_1	–1	0	0	1	0	1
C_2	0	0	–1	0	–1	–1
C_3	–1	–1	1	0	0	0

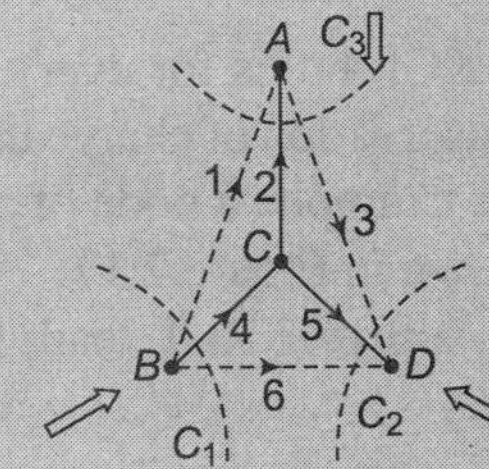

Figure 2.14 (b)

Example 2.8

For the network shown in Figure 2.15, obtain (a) Fundamental tie-set matrix (b) Fundamental cut-set matrix. **[GTU, 2012]** ○●●

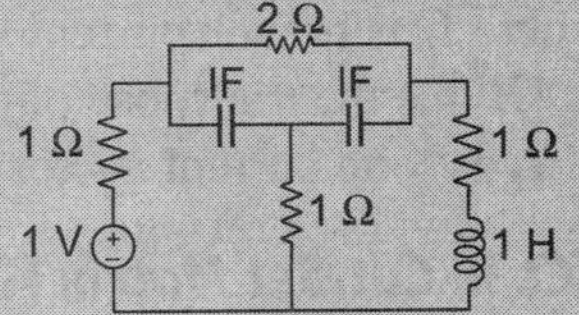

Figure 2.15

Solution The fundamental tie-set matrix is [Figure 2.16(a)]

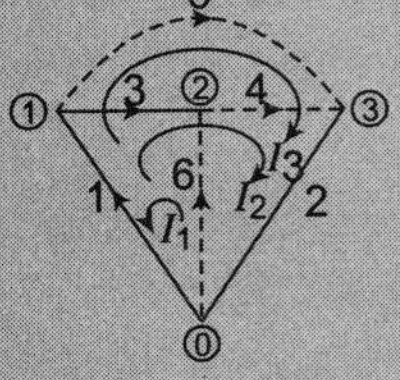

Figure 2.16 (a)

$$\text{Basic loop currents}\;\begin{matrix} \\ I_1 \\ I_2 \\ I_3 \end{matrix}\begin{matrix} 1 & 2 & 3 & 4 & 5 & 6 \\ \hline -1 & 0 & -1 & 0 & 0 & +1 \\ 1 & 1 & 1 & 1 & 0 & 0 \\ 1 & 1 & 0 & 0 & 1 & 0 \end{matrix}\;\text{elements}$$

The fundamental cut-set matrix is [Figure 2.16(b)]

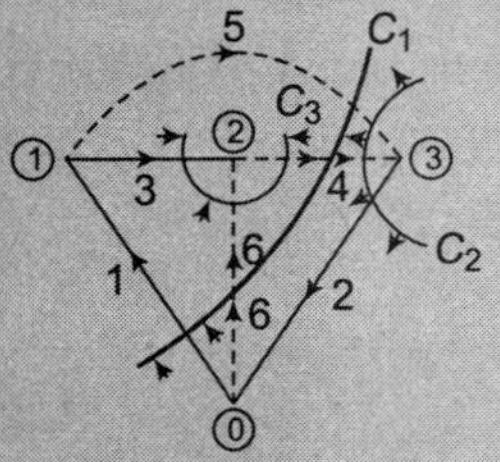

Figure 2.16 (b)

$$\text{Cut-sets}\quad \begin{matrix} & \begin{matrix}1 & 2 & 3 & 4 & 5 & 6\end{matrix} \\ \begin{matrix}C_1\\C_2\\C_3\end{matrix} & \begin{bmatrix}1 & 0 & 0 & -1 & -1 & 1\\ 0 & 1 & 0 & -1 & -1 & 0\\ 0 & 0 & 1 & -1 & -1 & 1\end{bmatrix}\end{matrix}\ \text{elements}$$

2.6 || KIRCHOFF'S CURRENT LAW (KCL)

University Question

1. Show Kirchhoff's current law in incidence-matrix and tie-set matrix formulation. **[GTU, 2010]**

KCL (*Kirchhoff's current law*) law states that the algebraic sum of currents entering a node is zero. For applying KCL, we need to add each branch current entering the node and subtract each branch current leaving the node.

$$\Sigma \text{ Current entering at the node} - \Sigma \text{ Current leaving at the node} = 0$$

KCL holds for every node in a network and it works at every point in time. KCL is essentially the conservation of charge that charge can neither be created nor be destroyed. For example, a node of an electrical network has current configuration as shown in Figure 2.17.

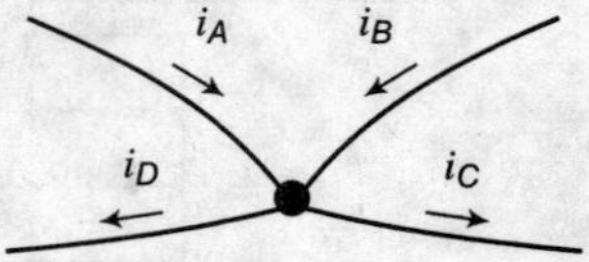

Figure 2.17

Applying KCL leads to the following equation:

$$i_A + i_B - i_C - i_D = 0$$

KCL in Tie-Set Matrix (B)

Tie-set matrix results in linear independent equation in terms of branch and link currents.

$$[I_b] = [B^T]\,[I_L]$$

where I_b is branch current vector of order $(b \times 1)$

$[B^T]$ is the transpose of the Tie-Set Matrix of order $(b \times l)$

I_L is loop current vector of order $(l \times 1)$

KCL in Cut-Set Matrix (Q)

Cut-set matrix results in linearly independent equations in terms of branch currents.

$$[Q_f][I_b] = 0$$

where I_b is branch current vector of order $(b \times 1)$

$[Q_f]$ is the augmented Cut-Set Matrix of order $(b \times t)$

Example 2.9

Find the current in 20 Ω resistance by applying KCL (Figure 2.18). **[PTU, 2011-12]** ○●●

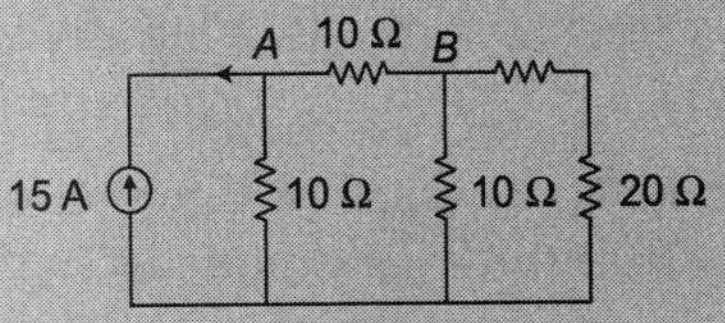

Figure 2.18

Solution Applying KCL for Node A:

$$-15+\frac{V_A-0}{10}+\frac{V_A-V_B}{10}=0$$

$$\Rightarrow \quad 2V_A - V_B = 150 \qquad (2.1)$$

Applying KCL for Node B:

$$\frac{V_B-V_A}{10}+\frac{V_B-0}{10}+\frac{V_B-0}{20}=0$$

$$\Rightarrow \quad V_A = 5V_B \qquad (2.2)$$

Solving Eqs (2.1) and (2.2) gives $V_B = 83.33$ V

Current in 20 Ω resistance = $V_B/20 = 83.33/20 = 4.165$ A

Example 2.10

Use KCL to find the current delivered by the 24V source (Figure 2.19). ○●●

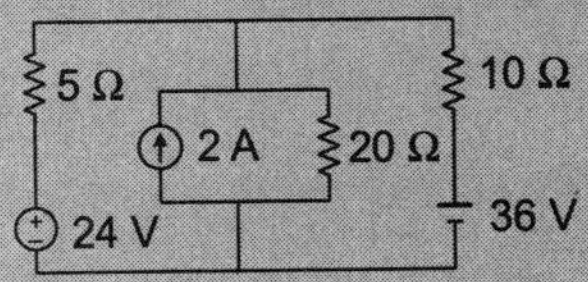

Figure 2.19

Solution Applying Kirchhoff's current law at the node assuming that voltage of this node is V_1, we have

$$\frac{V_1-24}{5}+\frac{V_1}{20}+\frac{V_1-36}{10}-2=0$$

Solving above equation, we get, $V_1 = 29.7$ V

Current delivered by the 24V source is:

$$I=\frac{V_1-24}{5}=1.14\text{ A}$$

2.7 || KIRCHOFF'S VOLTAGE LAW (KVL)

This law states that the algebraic sum of voltages around any closed path (loop) is zero. For applying KVL, beginning with one node, add voltages across each branch in the loop (if you encounter a + sign first, i.e. a voltage drop) and subtract voltages (if you encounter a – sign first, i.e. a voltage rise).

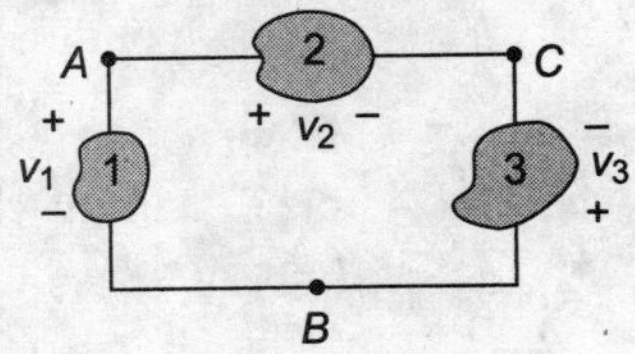

Figure 2.20

Σ voltage drops across the loop – Σ voltage rises across the loop = 0

Applying KVL in the electrical network shown in Figure 2.20.

$$v_1 + (-v_2) + (-v_3) = 0$$

KVL in Tie-Set Matrix (B)

Tie-set matrix results in linearly independent equations for branch voltages.

$$[B^T][V_b] = 0$$

where V_b is branch voltage vector of order $(b \times 1)$
$[B]$ is the transpose of the Tie-Set Matrix of order $(l \times b)$,

KVL in Fundamental Cut-Sets Matrix (Q_f)

Cut-set matrix results in linearly independent equations in terms of branch and twig voltages.

$$[V_b] = [Q_f^T][V_t]$$

where V_b is branch-voltage vector of order $(b \times 1)$
$[Q_f^T]$ is the transpose of the Fundamental Cut-Set Matrix of order $(b \times t)$
V_t is twig-voltage vector of order $(t \times 1)$.

Example 2.11

Determine the current I_L in the electrical circuit shown in Figure 2.21 using KVL. **[AU, 2012]** ○●●

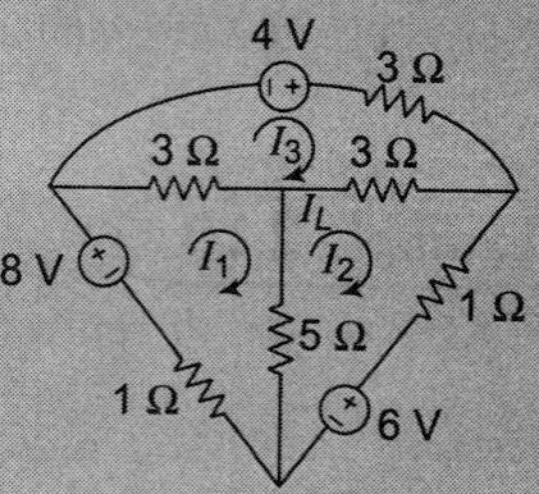

Figure 2.21

Solution Applying mesh analysis for Mesh 1,

$$-3(I_1 - I_3) - 5(I_1 - I_2) - I_1 + 8 = 0$$

$$3(I_1 - I_3) + 5(I_1 - I_2) + I_1 = 8$$

$$9I_1 - 5I_2 - 3I_3 = 8 \tag{2.3}$$

Applying mesh analysis for Mesh 2,

$$-3(I_2 - I_3) - I_2 - 6 - 5(I_2 - I_1) = 0$$

$$3(I_2 - I_3) + I_2 + 6 + 5(I_2 - I_1) = 0$$

$$-5I_1 + 9I_2 - 3I_3 = -6 \tag{2.4}$$

Applying mesh analysis for Mesh 3,

$$4 - 3I_3 - 3(I_3 - I_2) - 3(I_3 - I_1) = 0$$

$$3I_1 + 3I_2 - 9I_3 = -4 \tag{2.5}$$

Solving Eqs (2.3), (2.4), and (2.5), we get,

$$I_1 = 1.67 \text{ A}$$

$$I_2 = 0.67 \text{ A}$$

$$I_3 = 1.22 \text{ A}$$

$$I_L = I_1 - I_2 = 1.67 - 0.67 = 1 \text{ A}$$

2.8 MESH ANALYSIS

University Question

1. Distinguish between mesh and loop of an electric circuit. [AU, 2013]

Mesh Analysis is a useful technique for solving electrical circuits, which involves a number of voltage sources. The technique involves writing KVL equations for each identified mesh or closed circuit paths. In general, if we have B branches and N nodes, including the reference node, then the number of linearly independent mesh equations $M = B - (N - 1)$.

A mesh is a loop which does not contain any other loop within it. Following procedure is adopted for performing Mesh Analysis:

- Identify all possible meshes or closed paths in the given circuit.
- Assume current I_1, I_2, ...etc. for each identified mesh.
- Voltage drops for each impedance element should be indicated along the direction of current (i.e. + sign for current entering position and – sign for current leaving position).
- Write KVL equations for each mesh.
- Solve these KVL equations for unknowns.

Example 2.12

Using mesh analysis, determine the current through the 1 Ω resistor in the circuit shown in Figure 2.22. [AU, 2013] ○●●

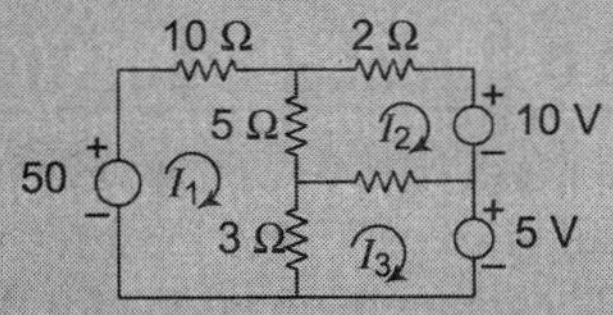

Figure 2.22

Solution Applying KVL

For the loop 1: $18I_1 - 5I_2 - 3I_3 = 50$ (2.6)

For the loop 2: $8I_2 - 5I_1 - I_3 = -10$ (2.7)

For the loop 3: $4I_3 - 3I_1 - I_2 = -5$ (2.8)

By solving Eqs (2.6), (2.7), and (2.8), we can get

$$I_1 = 3.30\text{ A},$$
$$I_2 = 0.9972\text{ A},$$
$$I_3 = 1.4747\text{ A}$$

Current through the 1 Ω resistor is $(I_3 - I_2) = (1.4747 - 0.9972) = 0.4775$ A

2.9 SUPERMESH ANALYSIS

Supermesh Analysis technique is suitable for electrical circuits involving current sources where it is tedious to write mesh analysis equations because the voltage drop across a current source is unknown.

For Supermesh analysis, we consider a Supermesh for those two meshes, which contain a common current source, and write KVL equations bypassing the current source instead of writing KVL equations separately for both meshes. Additionally, we write a current equation (current source constraint equation) involving both mesh current and current source.

Example 2.13

Find currents in various branches of the circuit shown in Figure 2.23.

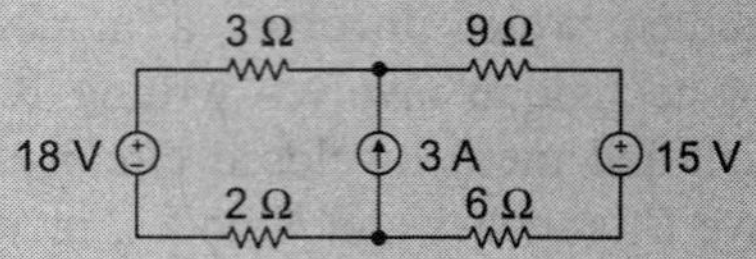

Figure 2.23

Solution The given circuit can be re-drawn as shown in Figure 2.24 by considering two meshes.

As we cannot write KVL for meshes *a* and *b* because there is no way to express the voltage drop across the current source in terms of the mesh currents.

Therefore, we define a "Supermesh" – a mesh which does not involve a branch containing the current source. Apply KVL for this Supermesh.

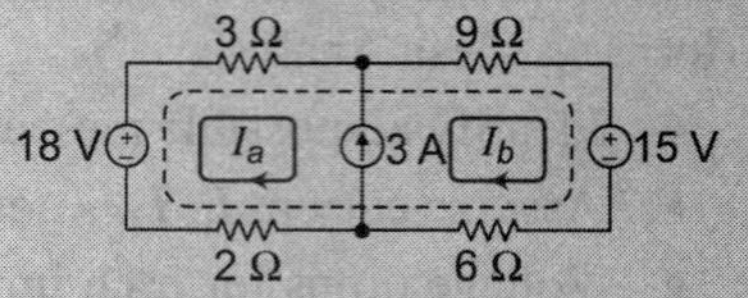

Figure 2.24

$$18 - 3I_a - 9I_b + 15 = 0 \quad (2.9)$$

Constraint due to current source:

$$I_b - I_a = 3 \quad (2.10)$$

Substituting Eq. (2.9) in Eq. (2.10)

$$I_a = 0.5 \text{ A}, \quad I_b = 3.5 \text{ A}$$

2.10 || MESH EQUATIONS BY INSPECTION METHOD

The mesh equations for a general planar network can be written by inspection without going through the detailed steps. Consider three mesh networks as shown in Figure 2.25.

The general equations for the three-mesh network are:

$$\pm R_1 1 I_1 \pm R_1 2 I_2 \pm R_1 3 I_3 = V_a$$

$$\pm R_2 1 I_1 \pm R_2 2 I_2 \pm R_2 3 I_3 = V_b$$

$$\pm R_3 1 I_1 \pm R_3 2 I_2 \pm R_3 3 I_3 = V_c$$

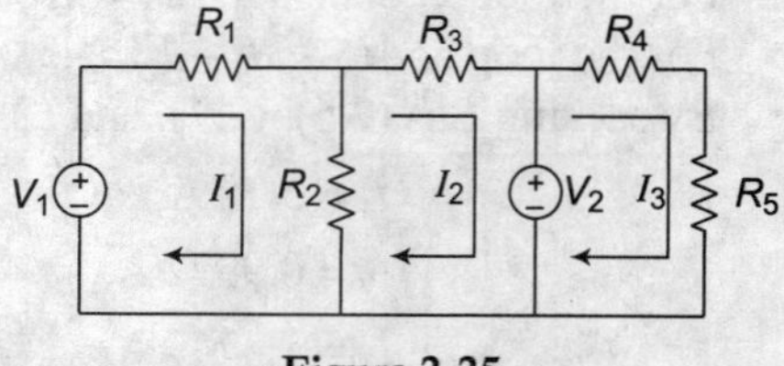

Figure 2.25

where,

R_{ii} = Self-resistance in mesh *i*

R_{ij} = Mutual resistance between mesh *i* and *j*

V_i = Sum of driving voltage in mesh *i*

Example 2.14

Formulate the mesh equation matrix through inspection method for the electrical circuit in Figure 2.26.

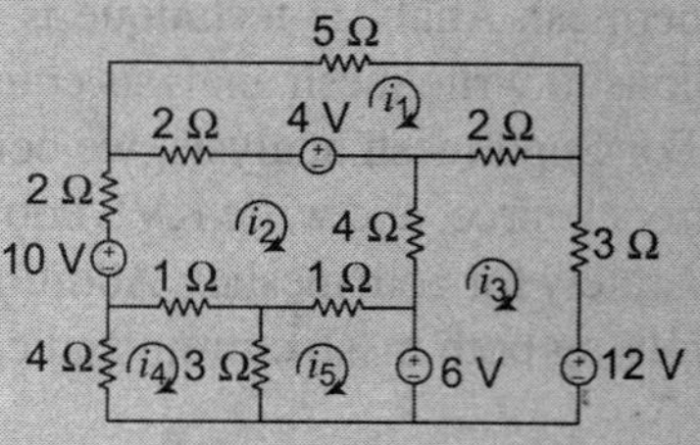

Figure 2.26

Solution Applying direct inspection method described in the relevant section of this chapter. The input voltage vector *v* in volts:

$$v_1 = 4, \quad v_2 = 10 - 4 = 6,$$

$$v_3 = -12 + 6 = -6, \quad v_4 = 0, \quad v_5 = -6$$

The mesh-current equations are:

$$\begin{bmatrix} 9 & -2 & -2 & 0 & 0 \\ -2 & 10 & -4 & -1 & -1 \\ -2 & -4 & 9 & 0 & 0 \\ 0 & -1 & 0 & 8 & -3 \\ 0 & -1 & 0 & -3 & 4 \end{bmatrix} \begin{bmatrix} i_1 \\ i_2 \\ i_3 \\ i_4 \\ i_5 \end{bmatrix} = \begin{bmatrix} 4 \\ 6 \\ -6 \\ 0 \\ -6 \end{bmatrix}$$

2.11 || NODE ANALYSIS

Node Analysis is a useful technique for solving electrical circuits, which involves a number of current sources. The technique involves writing KCL equations for each identified node except reference node or ground node. In general, if we have B branches and N nodes, including the reference node, then the number of *linearly independent* mesh equation is $M = B - (N - 1)$.

The following procedure is adopted for performing Mesh Analysis:

- Identify all possible nodes in the given circuit.
- Assume voltages V_1, V_2, ….etc. for each identified node and zero voltage for reference node.
- Expression for current in each circuit element can be obtained using Ohm's law, i.e. current will be voltage difference (across the element) divided by the impedance.
- Write KCL equations for each node.
- Solve these KCL equations for unknowns.

Example 2.15

Using nodal analysis techniques, determine the current 'i' in the network shown in Figure 2.27. **[JNTU, 2012]** ○●●

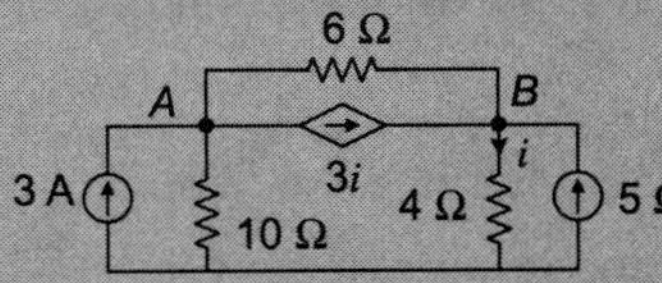

Figure 2.27

Solution

Applying KCL for node A: $\dfrac{V_A - 0}{10} + 3 + 3i + \dfrac{V_A - V_B}{10} = 0$ (2.11)

Applying KCL for node B: $\dfrac{V_B - V_A}{6} + i - 5 - 3i = 0$ (2.12)

Solving Eqs (2.11) and (2.12); $V_A = -226.74$ V, $V_B = 98.69$ V

Current 'i' can be obtained using Ohm's law:

$$\Rightarrow \qquad i = \frac{V_B}{4} = \frac{98.69}{4} = 24.67 \text{ A}$$

2.12 || NODAL EQUATIONS BY INSPECTION METHOD

The nodal equations for a general planar network can also be written by inspection, without going through the detailed steps. The general equations for the two-node network are:

$$G_{aa}V_a + G_{ab}V_b = I_1$$

$$G_{ba}V_a + G_{bb}V_b = I_2$$

where, G_{ii} = Self-conductance at node i

G_{ij} = Mutual conductance between node i and j

I_i = Sum of driving current node i

Example 2.16

Write the node equations by the inspection method shown in Figure 2.28.

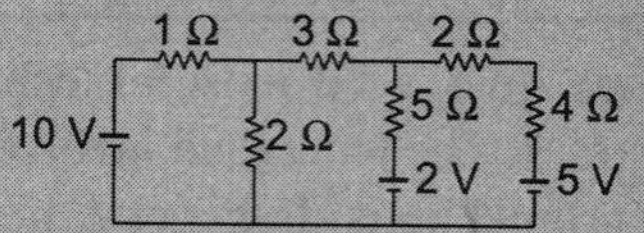

Figure 2.28

Solution Self-inductances at various nodes can be determined as follows.

- The self-conductance at the node a is the sum of the conductances connected to the node a.

$$G_{aa} = (1 + 1/2 + 1/3) \text{ mho}$$

- The self-conductance at the node b is the sum of the conductances connected to the node b.

$$G_{bb} = (1/6 + 1/5 + 1/3) \text{ mho}$$

- The mutual conductance between nodes a and b is the sum of the conductances connected between nodes a and b.

$$G_{ab} = (1/3) \text{ mho}$$

The sum of the mutual conductances between nodes b and a.

$$G_{ba} = -(1/3)$$

Source current at node a: $I_1 = 10/1 = 10\text{A}$

Source current at node b: $I_2 = (2/5 + 5/6) = 1.23\text{A}$

Therefore, nodal equations can be written as follows:

$$1.83V_a - 0.33V_b = 10$$

$$-0.33V_a + 0.7V_b = 1.23$$

2.13 || SUPERNODE ANALYSIS

Supernode Analysis technique is suitable for electrical circuits involving voltage sources connected between adjacent nodes.

In this method, the two adjacent nodes that are connected by a voltage source are reduced to a single node and then the equations are formed by applying KCL as usual.

Example 2.17

What is the current through a voltage source connected between nodes shown in Figure 2.29? ○●●

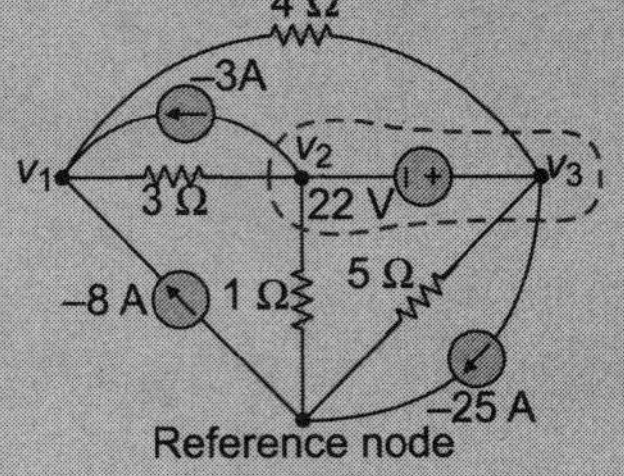

Figure 2.29

Solution The given problem can be solved using nodal analysis as there is no resistance in branch containing 22 V source. However, we can eliminate the need for introducing a current variable in this branch by applying KCL to the Supernode consisting of node 2 and node 3 (Figure 2.30).

Applying KCL at Node 1 and the Supernode (node 2 and node 3) and writing constraint equation for Supernode.

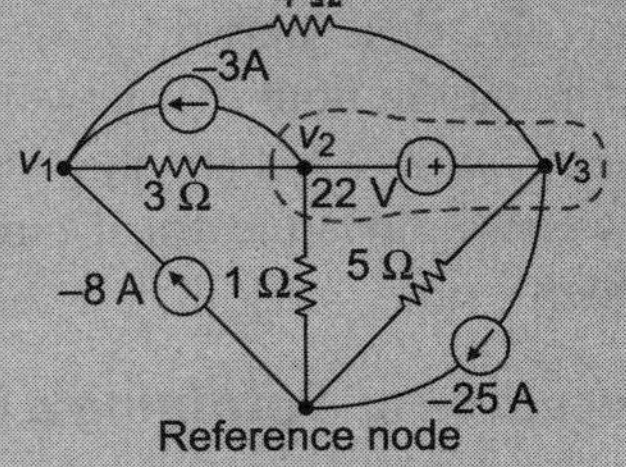

Figure 2.30

Applying KCL at Node 1:

$$\frac{V_1 - V_2}{3} + \frac{V_1 - V_3}{4} = -3 - 8 \tag{2.13}$$

Applying KCL for Supernode consisting of Node 2 and 3:

$$\frac{V_2}{1} + \frac{V_2 - V_1}{3} + \frac{V_3}{5} + \frac{V_3 - V_1}{4} = -(-25) - (-3) \tag{2.14}$$

Equation for Supernode:

$$v_3 - v_2 = 22 \tag{2.15}$$

Solving Eqs (2.13), (2.14) and (2.15);

$$v_1 = 1.071 \text{ V}$$

2.14 || NETWORK EQUILIBRIUM EQUATIONS

The Network Equilibrium Equations are a set of equations that completely and uniquely determine the state of a network at any instant of time. These equations are written in terms of suitably chosen current variables or voltage variables.

These equations will be unique if the number of independent variables chosen for the given network are equal to the number of independent equations.

Example 2.18

For the network shown in Figure 2.31, draw the graph and write down the tie-set matrix. Obtain network equilibrium equations for this network. **[RGTU, 2013]** ○●●

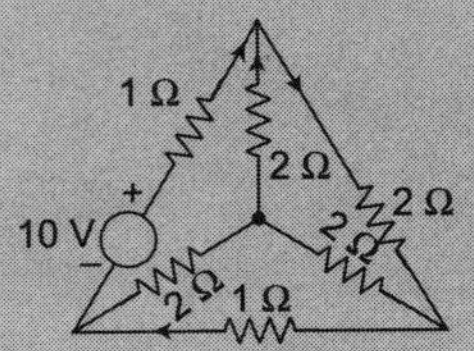

Figure 2.31

Solution The graph of given network can be drawn as shown in Figure 2.32. Tie-set Matrix of above graph is

$$\text{Tie-set matrix} = \begin{array}{c} \\ i_1 \\ i_2 \\ i_3 \end{array} \begin{array}{c} \begin{array}{cccccc} a & b & c & d & e & f \end{array} \\ \begin{bmatrix} 1 & -1 & 0 & 0 & 1 & 0 \\ 0 & 1 & 1 & 0 & 0 & -1 \\ 0 & 0 & 0 & 1 & -1 & 1 \end{bmatrix} \end{array}$$

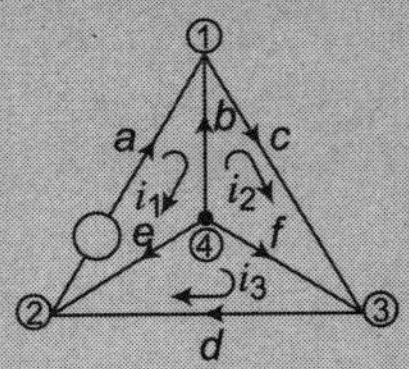

Figure 2.32

Network Equilibrium Equations involving branch voltage can be obtained from the rows of above tie-set matrix:

$$V_1 - V_2 + V_5 = 0$$
$$V_2 + V_3 - V_6 = 0$$
$$V_4 - V_5 + V_6 = 0$$

V_1 V_2 V_3 V_4 V_5 and V_6 are branch voltages.

2.15 || DUALITY

Two electrical networks are dual if electrical parameters in both the networks are dual to each other. Table 2.1 lists the duality which exists between various electrical circuit parameters and properties:

Table 2.1 Duality Between Electrical Quantities

Duality between		
Voltage (V)	⟷	Current (I)
Series	⟷	Parallel
Resistance (R)	⟷	Conductance (G)
Capacitance (C)	⟷	Inductance (L)
Reactance (X)	⟷	Susceptance (B)
Short circuit	⟷	Open circuit
KCL	⟷	KVL

Procedure of Obtaining a Dual Network

- Place a node at the center of each mesh of the circuit.
- Place a reference node (ground) outside the circuit.
- Draw lines between nodes such that each line crosses an element.
- Replace the element by its dual pair.
- Determine the polarity of the voltage source and direction of the current source. The underlying principle is: A voltage source that produces a positive mesh current has as its dual a current source that forces current to flow from the reference ground to the node associated with that mesh.

Example 2.19

Find the dual of the electrical circuit shown in Figure 2.33?

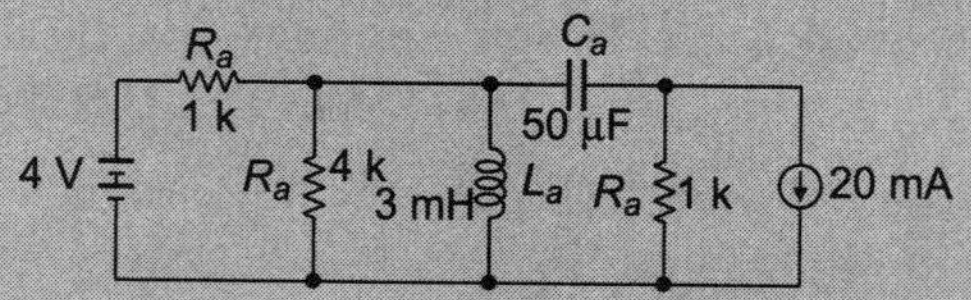

Figure 2.33

Solution The dual circuit for the given network can be found by following the steps listed above.

Step 1:

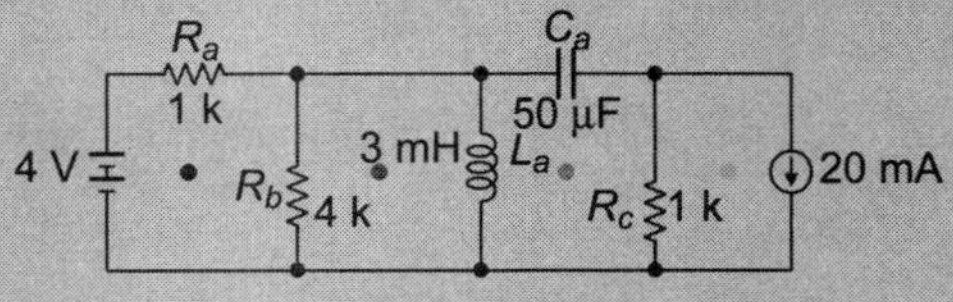

Figure 2.34 (a)

Step 2:

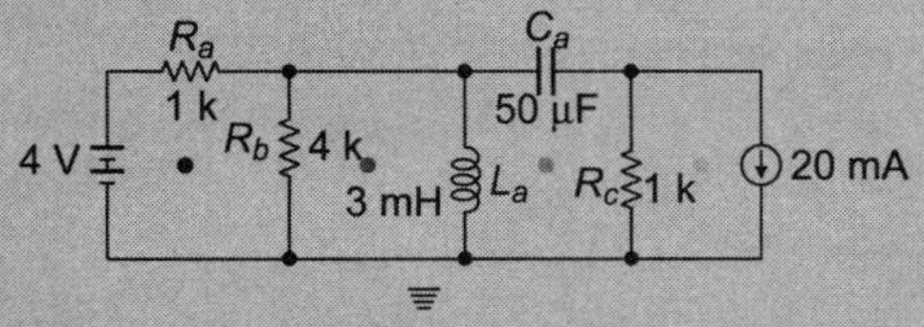

Figure 2.34 (b)

Step 3:

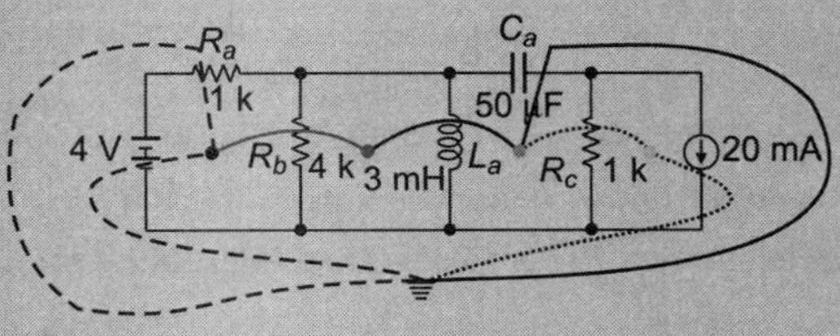

Figure 2.34 (c)

Step 4:

Component in Original circuit	Its Dual
Voltage source (4 V)	Current source (4 (A)
Resistor R_a (1 KΩ)	Conductor R_1 (1/1 kΩ = 1 mΩ)
Resistor R_b (4 kΩ)	Conductor R_2 (1/4 kΩ = 0.25 mΩ)
Resistor R_c (4 kΩ)	Conductor R_3 (1/1 kΩ = 1 mΩ)
Inductor L_a (3 mH)	Capacitor C_1 (3 mF)
Capacitor C_a (50 µF)	Inductor L_1 (50 µH)
Current Source (20 mA)	Voltage source (20 mV)

Step 5:

- The voltage source forces current to flow towards R_a. Its dual force current flows from the reference ground to the node that is shared by the current source and R_1, the dual of R_a.

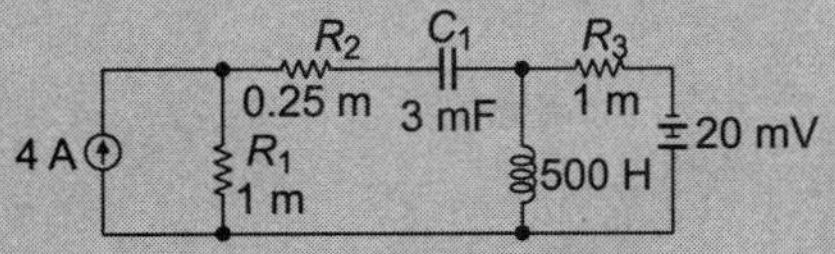

Figure 2.34 (d)

- The current source causes current to flow from the node where R_c is connected towards the other meshes. Its dual should cause current to flow from the node between it and R_3 to distributed node (reference) of the rest of the circuit.

Example 2.20

Find the dual of the electrical circuit shown in Figure 2.35? ○●●

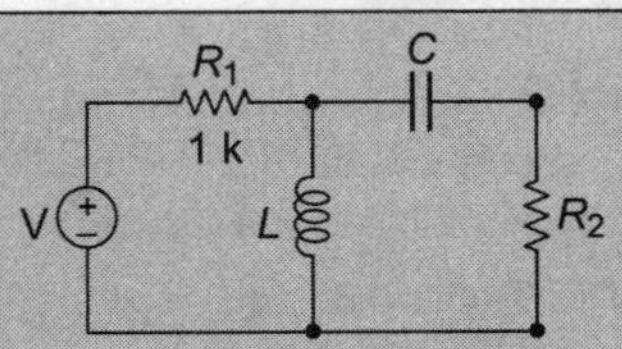

Figure 2.35

Solution The dual circuit for the given network can be found by the steps listed above (Figure 2.36(a)).

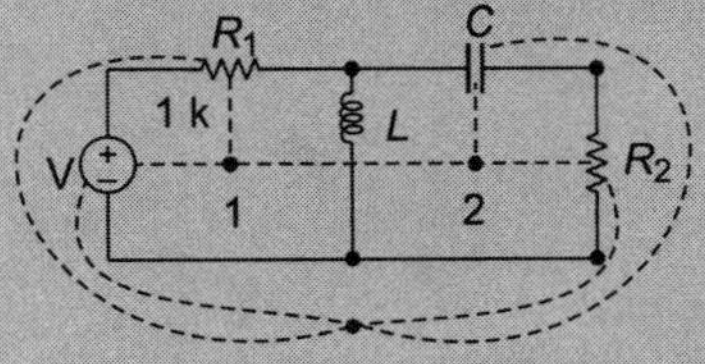

Figure 2.36

POINTS TO REMEMBER

☞ A graph of an electrical network consists of nodes and branches wherein each branch represents corresponding element in the electrical circuit.

☞ A tree is a connected subgraph of a network, which consists of all the nodes of the original graph but no closed paths.

☞ Graph = Tree + Co-Tree

☞ Number of branches of a Graph = Twigs + Links

☞ Number of Twigs (also known as Rank of a Tree) = $n - 1$

☞ Number of links $l = b - n + 1$

☞ Incidence Matrix (A) shows an incidence of elements to nodes in a connected graph. It is a mathematical replica of the graph; therefore, the associated graph can be easily constructed and vice versa.

☞ The dimension of the matrix A is $n \times b$ where n is the number of nodes and b is number of branches.

☞ A Reduced Incidence Matrix A_l is obtained by removing any one row of the incidence matrix.

☞ The number of fundamental loops for a tree will be equal to number of links (i.e. $l = b - n + 1$) of the associated co-tree.

☞ A cut-set is a minimal set of branches of a connected graph such that the removal of these branches causes the graph to be cut into exactly two parts. A cut-set is defined using the expression $\{x, y, z\}$, wherein x, y, and z represent the graph branches/links which cut the graph into two equal parts.

☞ KCL states that the algebraic sum of currents entering a node is zero.

☞ For applying KCL, add each branch current entering the node and subtract each branch current leaving the node.

☞ KCL is essentially the conservation of charge that charge can neither be created nor be destroyed.

☞ KCL holds for every node in a network and it works at every point in time.

☞ KVL states that the algebraic sum of voltages around any closed path (loop) is zero. For applying KVL, beginning with one node, add voltages across each branch in the loop.

☞ A mesh is a loop which doesn't contain any other loops within it.

☞ Mesh Analysis is a useful technique for solving electrical circuits, which involves a number of voltage sources.

☞ Mesh Analysis technique involves writing KVL equations for each identified mesh or closed circuit paths.

☞ Supermesh Analysis technique is suitable for electrical circuits involving current sources wherein two meshes contain a common current source.

☞ Supermesh Analysis technique involves writing combined KVL equation for both the meshes bypassing the current source. Additionally, writing a current equation (current source constraint equation) involving both mesh current and current source.

☞ The general equations for the three-mesh network are:

$$\pm R_1 1I_1 \pm R_1 2I_2 \pm R_1 3I_3 = V_a$$

$$\pm R_2 1I_1 \pm R_2 2I_2 \pm R_2 3I_3 = V_b$$

$$\pm R_3 1I_1 \pm R_3 2I_2 \pm R_3 3I_3 = V_c$$

where, R_{ij} is resistance between mesh i and j.

☞ Node Analysis is a useful technique for solving electrical circuits, which involves a number of current sources.

- The technique involves writing KCL equations for each identified node except reference node or ground node.
- Supernode Analysis technique is suitable for electrical circuits involving voltage sources connected between adjacent nodes.
- These two nodes are reduced to a single node and under this technique a common KCL is written.
- A dual of a relationship is formed by interchanging voltage and current in an expression. Duality means that the current or voltage in one circuit behaves in a similar manner as the voltage or current, respectively, in another circuit.
- Two circuits are said to be duals of one another if they are described by the same characterising equations with the dual pairs interchanged.

PRACTICE PROBLEMS

1. Determine the current I_1 in the following electrical circuit using KCL. ○●●

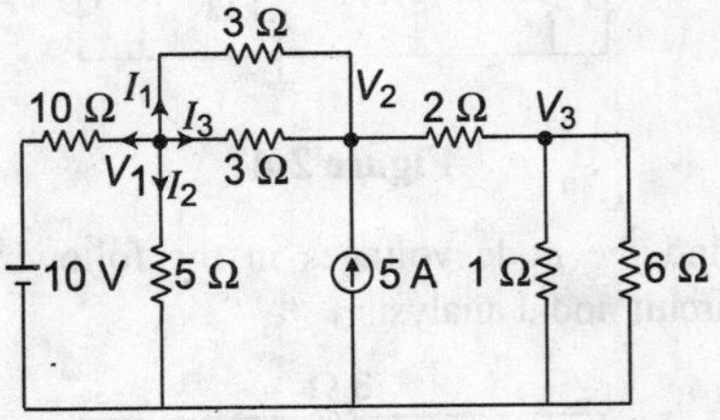

Figure 2.37

2. Write KVL equations for each of the indicated loops in the following circuit. ○●●

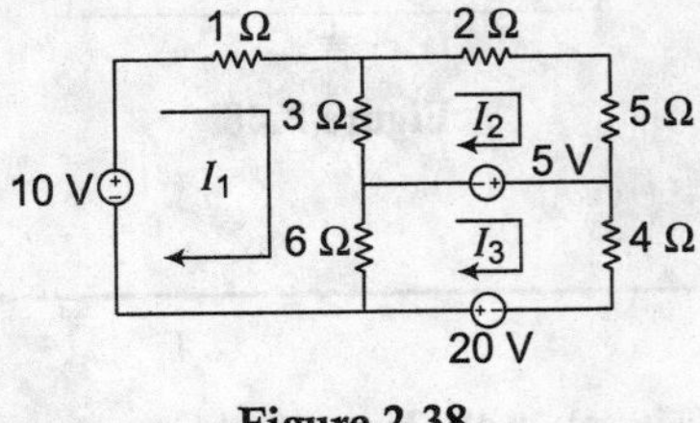

Figure 2.38

3. Write KCL equations for nodes *a* and *b*. ○●●

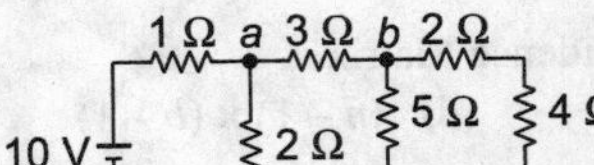

Figure 2.39

4. Find the value of *K* in the circuit shown in Figure 2.40 such that the power dissipated in the 2Ω resistor does not exceed 50 watts. ●●●
[PU 2012]

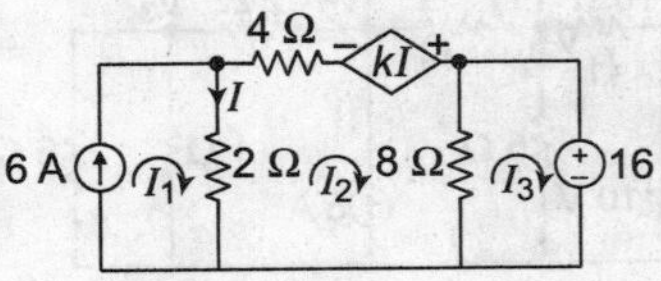

Figure 2.40

5. For the following circuit, find I_1, I_2, I_3 and I_4 using mesh analysis. ○●●

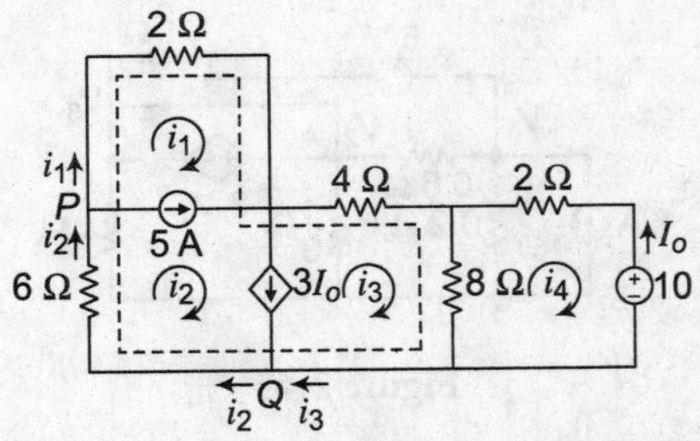

Figure 2.41

6. Find the current through the 10 V resistor by using mesh analysis. ○●●

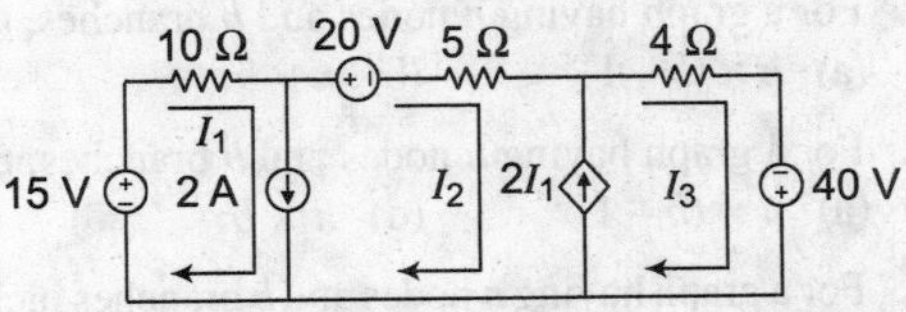

Figure 2.42

7. Find the mesh equations through inspection of the following network. ○●●

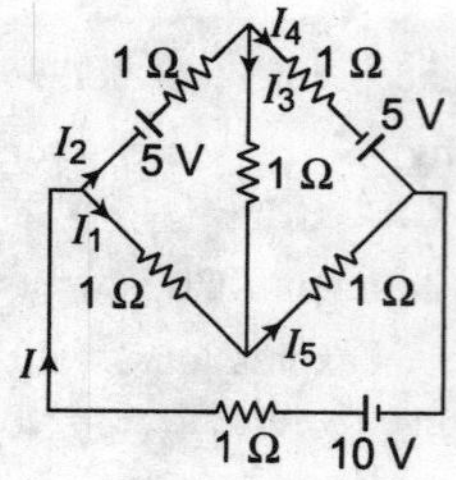

Figure 2.43

8. Find the power delivered by the current source in the following circuit. ●●●

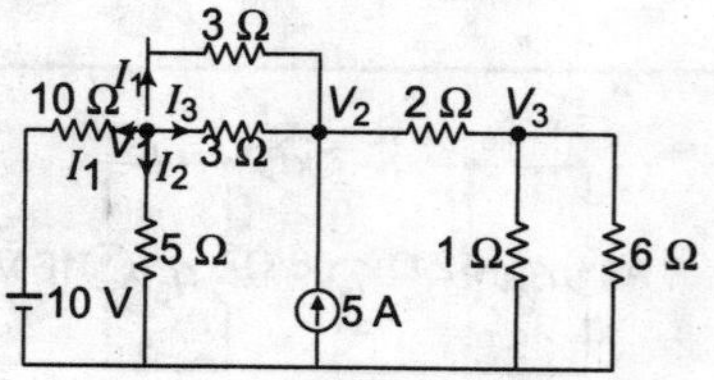

Figure 2.44

9. Write nodal equations for the following network and obtain node voltages. ●●●

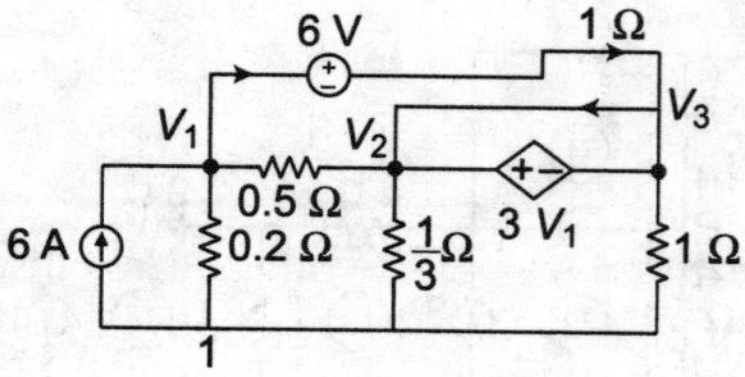

Figure 2.45

10. Find current I using nodal analysis. ○●●

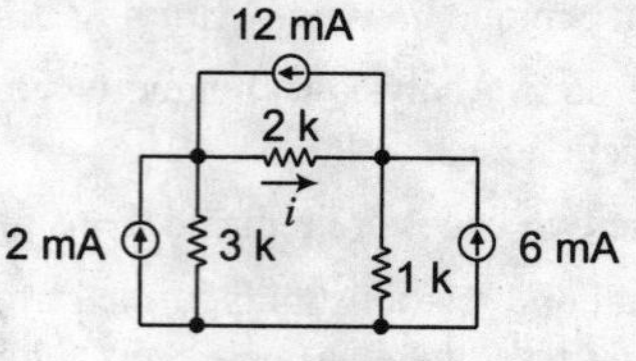

Figure 2.46

11. Formulate the nodal mesh equation matrix through inspection method for the following electrical circuit. ○●●

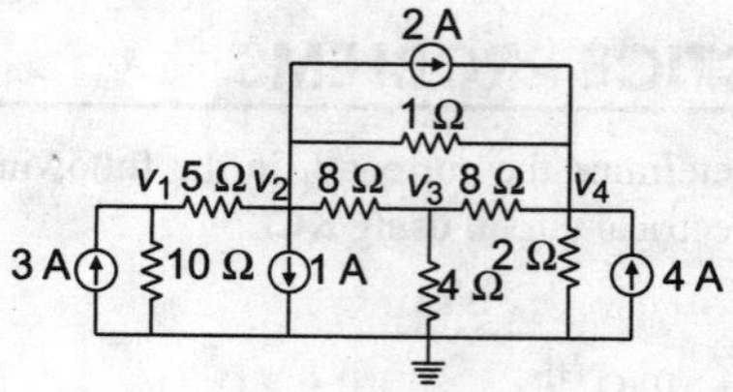

Figure 2.47

12. Find the node voltages in the following circuit nodal analysis. ○●●

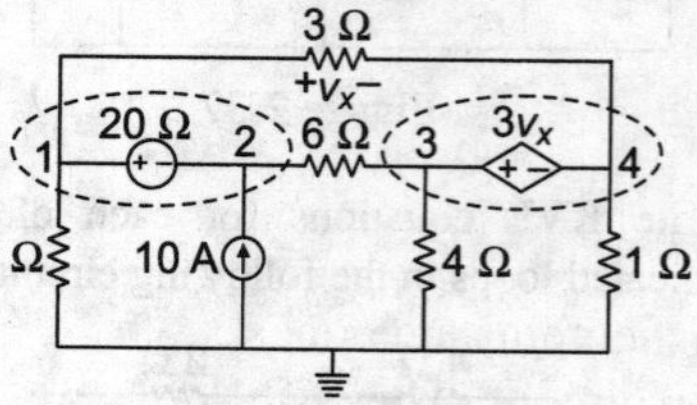

Figure 2.48

MULTIPLE CHOICE QUESTIONS

1. A branch of a tree and co-tree are respectively called ○●●

(a) Link and Twig (b) Twig and Link (c) Cut-set and Tie-set (d) Tie-set and Cut-set

2. For a graph having n nodes and b branches, the order of Reduced Incidence Matrix is ○○●

(a) $n \times (b-1)$ (b) $n \times b$ (c) $(n-1) \times b$ (d) $(n-1) \times (b-1)$

3. For a graph having n nodes and b branches, the order of Reduced Incidence Matrix is ○●●

(a) $n \times (b-1)$ (d) $n \times b$ (c) $(n-1) \times b$ (d) $(n-1) \times (b-1)$

4. For a graph having n nodes and b branches including the reference node, the number of linearly independent mesh equations which can be written are ○●●

(a) $b-n+1$ (b) $b-n-1$ (c) $b+n-1$ (d) $b+n+1$

5. Which of the following is not a dual pair (where symbols have usual meanings)? ○○●

(a) $R-Z$ (b) $L-C$ (c) $V-I$ (d) $X-B$

ANSWERS TO MULTIPLE CHOICE QUESTIONS

1. (b) 2. (c) 3. (c) 4. (a) 5. (a)

Network Theorem

3

Chapter Outline

- ☞ Superposition theorem
- ☞ Thevenin's theorem
- ☞ Norton's theorem
- ☞ Maximum power transfer theorem
- ☞ Reciprocity theorem
- ☞ Millman's theorem
- ☞ Tellegen's theorem
- ☞ Substitution theorem
- ☞ Compensation theorem

3.1 || INTRODUCTION

Network theorems are beneficial for the analysis and determination of various voltages and currents in multi loop circuits. These theorems use the fundamental laws of electrical and electronics and the basic equations of mathematics to analyse the parameters such as voltage, current, resistance, and so on in a circuit.

The network theorems discussed in this chapter include the Superposition theorem, Thevenin's theorem, Norton's theorem, Reciprocity theorem, Maximum Power Transfer theorem, Millman's theorem, Tellegan's theorem, and Compensation theorem.

3.2 || SUPERPOSITION THEOREM

University Questions

1. State Superposition theorem. Explain with an example. **[PTU, 2011-2012]**
2. Explain the use of network theorem in various circuit analyses.

- Superposition theorem states that in any linear circuit, the total current in the circuit is equal to the algebraic sum of the currents produced by each source acting alone, while the other sources are non-operative.
- While considering the individual sources to evaluate the current through the source, the other current sources are replaced by an open circuit and the voltage sources are replaced by a short circuit across their terminals.

- The superposition theorem can be applied only for linear networks.

Steps to Solve Problems

- Consider a single source. The other voltage sources have to be shorted while opening the current sources, if internal impedances are not known. If known, replace them with their internal impedances.
- Determine the voltage across or current through the required element, depending on the source under consideration.
- Repeat the above steps for all the sources.
- Sum the individual effects produced by the individual sources. This results in determining the total current or voltage across the required element.

Example 3.1

Using the superposition theorem, calculate the current in the 4 Ω resistor given in Figure 3.1. **[AU, 2014]** ○○●

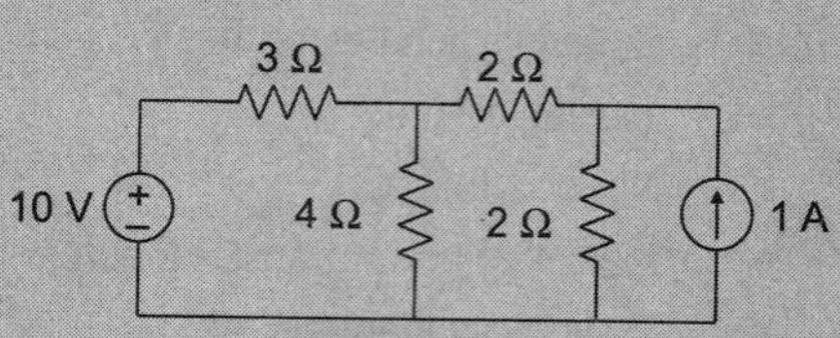

Figure 3.1

Solution Replace the 1 A current source with open circuit (Figure 3.2(a)).

By 10 V source,

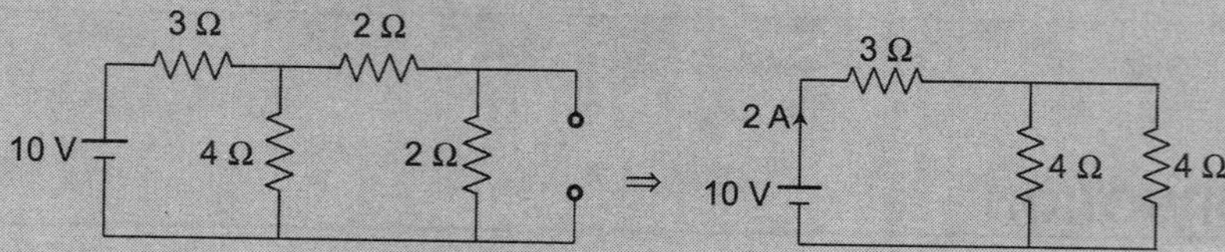

Figure 3.2 (a)

By 1 A source (Figure 3.2(b)),

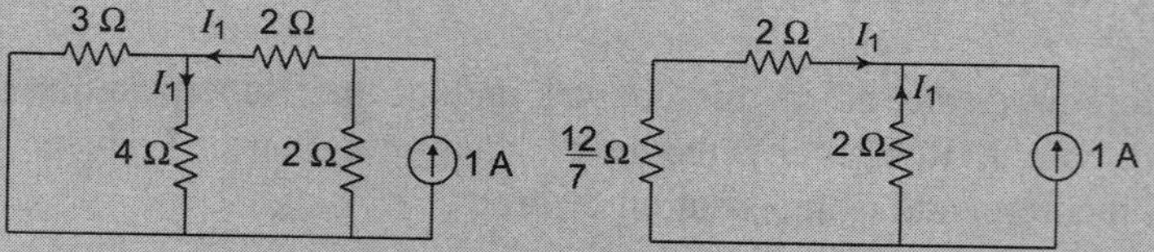

Figure 3.2 (b)

$$i_1 = \frac{2}{2+\frac{26}{7}} \times 1 = \frac{14}{40} = \frac{7}{20}$$

$$i_1^1 = \frac{3}{20} = 0.15A$$

So, the total current through the 4 Ohm resistor = 0.15 + 1 = 1.15 A

Note: Difficulty Level ⟶ ○○● — Easy; ○●● — Medium; ●●● — Difficult

Example 3.2

Find the current through the various branches of the circuits as shown in Figure 3.3 by using superposition theorem. **[AU, 2012]** ○○●

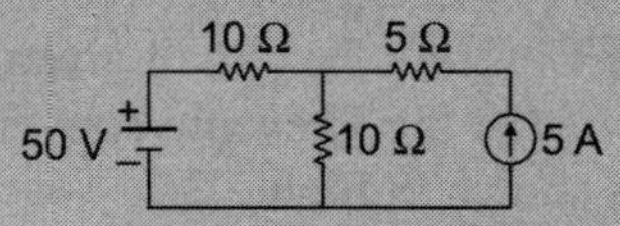

Figure 3.3

Solution Replace the 5 A source with an open circuit.

By 50 V supply, we get (Figure 3.4(a))

Since the 5 Ω is in series with an infinite resistance, it can be neglected. The current i_1 is found to be 2.5 A.

By 5 A source, we get (Figure 3.4(b))

The current splits equally in both the 10 Ω resistors to give 2.5 A each.

The total current through the 10 Ω branch is 2.5A + 2.5A = 5 A.

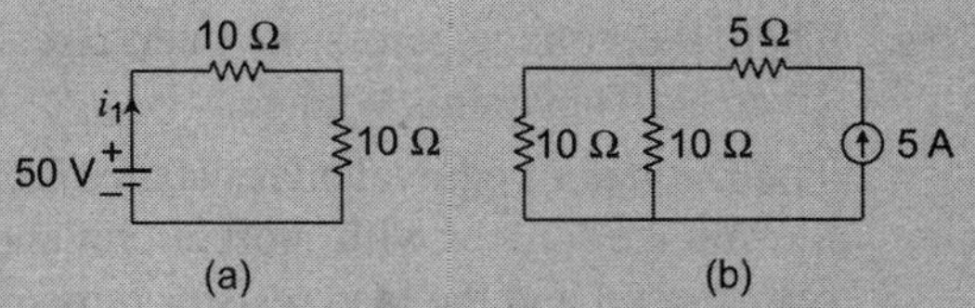

Figure 3.4

Example 3.3

Find the voltage across 1 kΩ resistor in the circuit shown in Figure 3.5. **[GTU, 2010]** ○○●

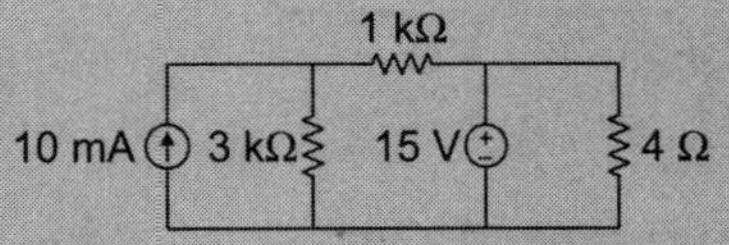

Figure 3.5

Solution Short the 15 V supply. A short circuit is present across the 4 kΩ resistor and therefore, it can be ignored.

The current flowing in the 1 kΩ is given as

$$I_1 = 10\text{m} \times \frac{3\text{k}}{1\text{k} + 3\text{k}} = 7.5\text{mA}$$

Open the 10 mA current source. The voltage applied is 15 V.

The current is given as

$$I_2 = \frac{15}{4\text{k}} = 3.75\text{mA}$$

The total current is 7.5 mA + 3.75 mA = 11.25 mA

3.3 THEVENIN'S THEOREM

- Thevenin's theorem states that any two terminal network having number of voltage and current sources and resistances can be replaced by a single equivalent voltage source with a single resistance in series with it.
- The voltage at the voltage source is equal to the open circuit voltage across the two terminals of the network.

University Question

1. Why do you short circuit the voltage source and open the current source when you find Thevenin's voltage of a network? **[AU, 2014]**

- The resistance is equal to the equivalent resistance measured between the terminals with all the energy sources replaced by their internal resistances.

Consider the circuit given below in Figure 3.6.

After the Thevenin conversion, the Thevenin's equivalent circuit is as shown in Figure 3.7.

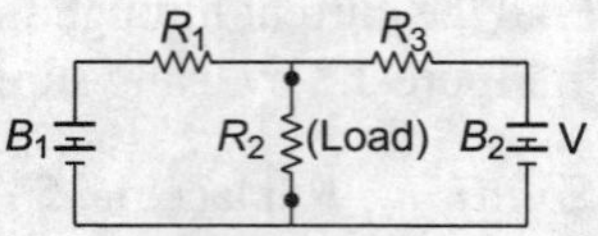

Figure 3.6

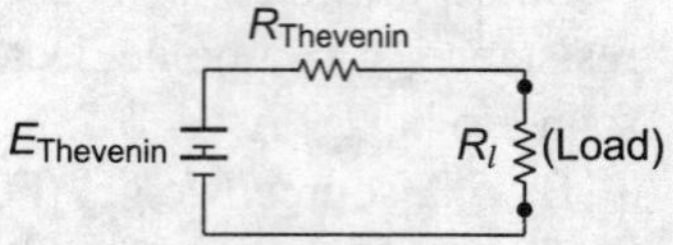

Figure 3.7

- The load resistor is removed and is replaced with an open circuit.
- Then, the voltage across the open circuit is determined. This gives the Thevenin's voltage.
- The Thevenin's equivalent resistance is calculated by replacing the voltage sources with short circuit and current sources with open circuit and the load resistor remaining open.
- Required current through the branch is given by $I = \dfrac{V_{th}}{R_l + R_{eq}}$

Example 3.4

Obtain the Thevenin's equivalent circuit for the network shown in Figure 3.8. **[PTU, 2009-10]** ○●●

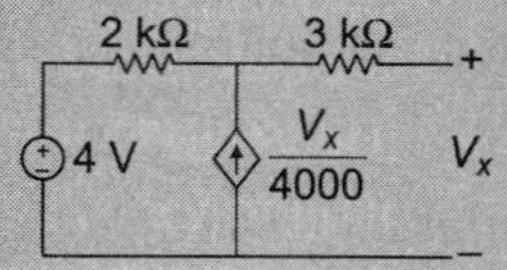

Figure 3.8

Solution To find R_{th},

Step 1: Making the output port open circuited and finding $V_{O.C}$

$$V_x = 4 - 2\times 10^3 \frac{V_x}{4000} = 4 - \frac{2}{4}V_x$$

$$V_x = 4 - \frac{V_x}{2} = \frac{8 - V_x}{2}$$

$$2V_x = 8 - V_x$$

$$V_x = \frac{8}{3} = V_{O.C}$$

Step 2: Finding the short circuit current, $I_{S.C}$ (Figure 3.8(a))

$$I_{S.C} = \frac{4}{5\times 10^3} A$$

$$R_{th} = \frac{V_{O.C}}{I_{S.C}} = \frac{\frac{8}{3}\times 10^3}{\frac{4}{5}} = \frac{40\times 10^3}{12} = \frac{10}{3} \text{ Kohm}$$

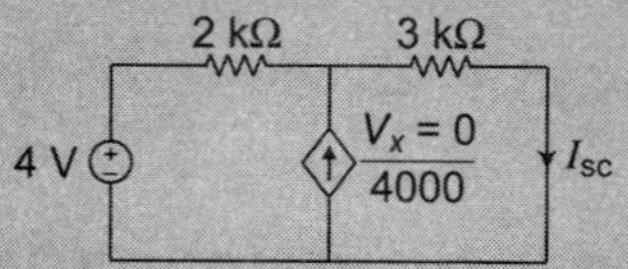

Figure 3.8 (a)

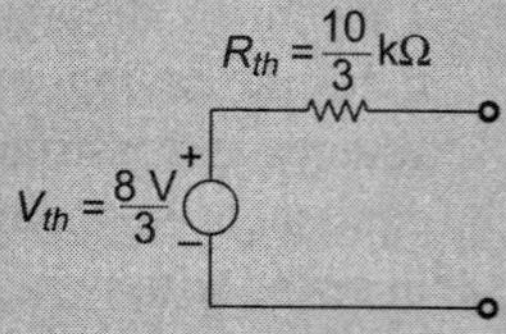

Figure 3.8 (b)

Therefore, the Thevenin's equivalent circuit is as shown in Figure 3.8(b).

Example 3.5

Find the current through the 4 Ω resistor using Thevenin's theorem for the circuit shown in Figure 3.9. **[PU, 2010]** ○○●

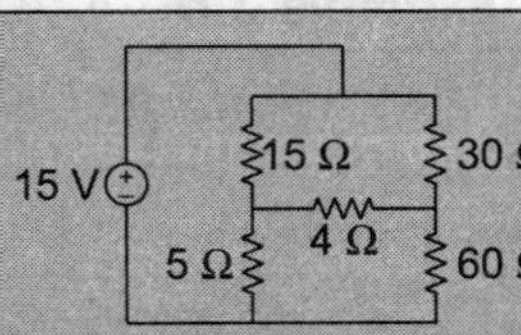

Figure 3.9

Solution According to Thevenin's theorem, we first need to open the 4 Ω resistor (Figure 3.10).

The 15 Ω and the 5 Ω resistors are in series. The 30 Ω and the 60 Ω resistors are also in series.

Therefore, the equivalent Thevenin resistance is

$$R_{th} = (15+5)//(30+60) = 20//90 = 16.363\ \Omega$$

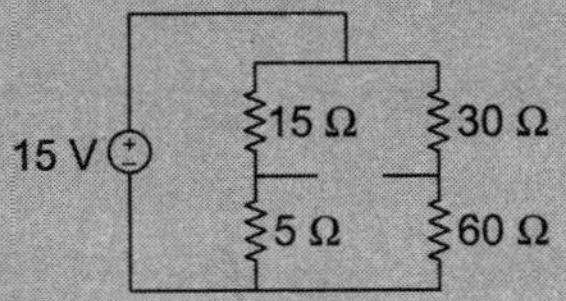

Figure 3.10

By applying nodal analysis, we get

$$V_{th} = \frac{15}{15+5} - \frac{15}{30+60} = \frac{15}{20} - \frac{15}{90} = 0.5834\text{ V}$$

Therefore, the current across the 4Ω resistor is

$$I = \frac{0.583}{16.363} = 35.63\text{ mA}$$

3.4 || NORTON'S THEOREM

Probe

1. How can you relate Thevenin's and Norton's theorems?

- Norton's theorem states that any two terminal networks having number of voltage and current sources and resistances can be replaced by a single equivalent current source with a single resistance in parallel with it.
- The current across the current source is equal to the short circuit current between the two terminals.
- The resistance is equal to the equivalent resistance between the specified terminals of the network with all the voltage sources replaced by short circuit and current sources replaced by open circuit.

Consider the circuit given in Figure 3.11.

After the Norton's conversion, the Norton's equivalent circuit is as shown in Figure 3.12.

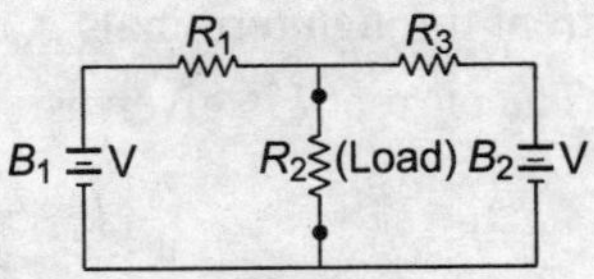

Figure 3.11

- The load resistor is replaced by short circuit. The current through the load resistor is then determined which in the given circuit is the sum of currents through the resistors R_1 and R_3.
- The obtained current is the Norton's current.
- The Norton's equivalent resistance is calculated by replacing the voltage sources with short circuit and current sources with open circuit and the load resistor being open.

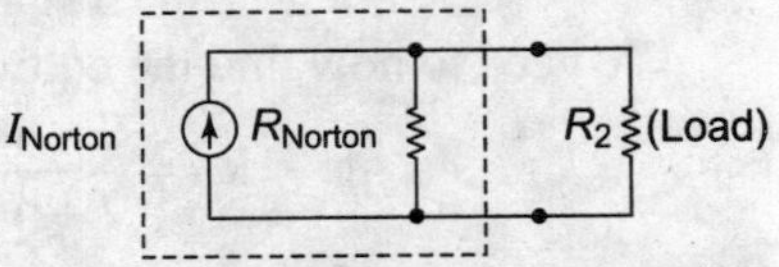

Figure 3.12

Example 3.6

Find the Norton's equivalent circuit for the network shown in Figure 3.13 and obtain the current in the 10 Ω resistor. **[GTU, 2010]** ○○●

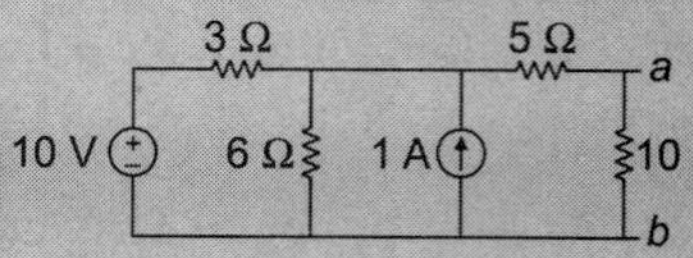

Figure 3.13

Solution By source transformation (Figures 3.14 (a), (b) and (c)),

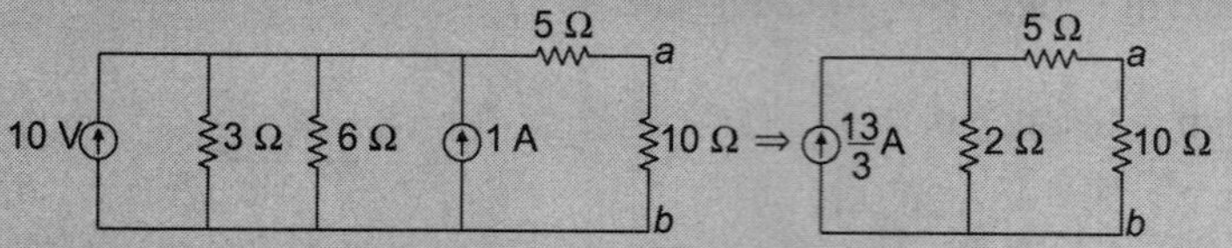

Figure 3.14 (a)

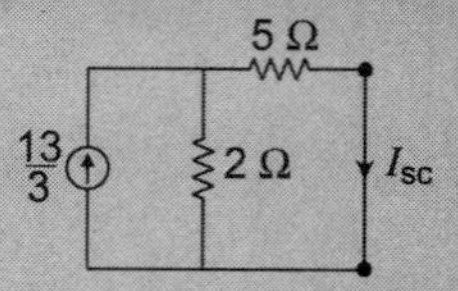

Figure 3.14 (b)

$$I_{S.C} = \frac{13}{3} \times \frac{2}{2+5} = 1.238 \text{ A}$$

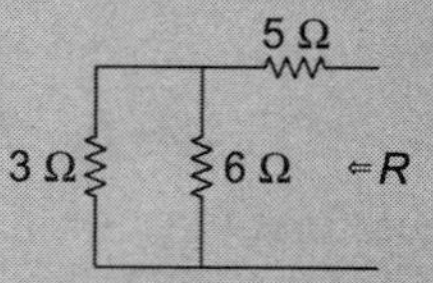

Figure 3.14 (c)

The Norton's resistance, *R*, is

$$R = \frac{6 \times 3}{6+3} + 5 = 7 \text{ ohm}$$

The total equivalent circuit is as shown in Figure 3.14 (d).
Current through the 10 ohm resistor is

$$I_{10} = 1.238 \times \frac{7}{7+10} = 0.5098 \text{ A}$$

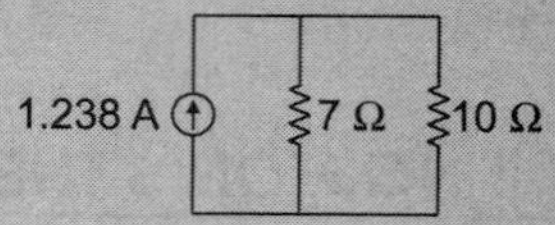

Figure 3.14 (d)

Example 3.7

Obtain the Norton's equivalent circuit for the circuit shown in Figure 3.15. **[PU, 2012]** ○●●

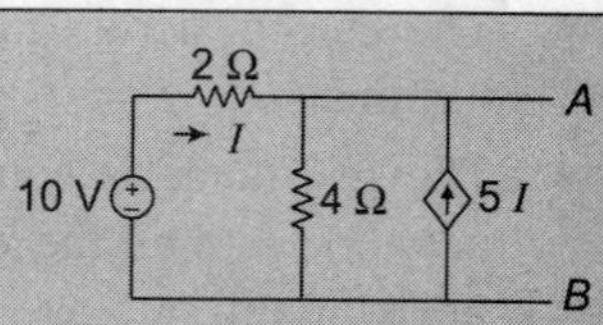

Figure 3.15

Solution By Norton's theorem, we need to find the short-circuit current through terminals A and B.

The current *I* is given as

$$I = \frac{10}{2} = 5 \text{ A}$$

Since both the currents flowing into terminal *A* are in the same direction, we have to add them

$$I_N = 5 \text{ A} + 5 \times 5 \text{ A} = 30 \text{ A}$$

We need to now find the equivalent Norton resistance.

$$R_N = \frac{2 \times 4}{2+4} = 1.33\Omega$$

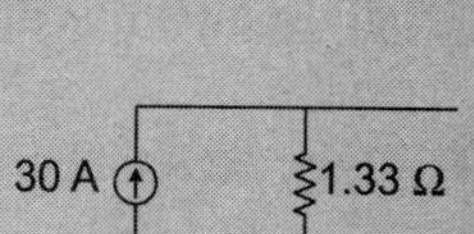

The equivalent Norton circuit is shown in Figure 3.16(a).

Figure 3.16 (a)

3.5 MAXIMUM POWER TRANSFER THEOREM

Probe

1. Why should maximum power be transferred to the load in any circuit?

- Maximum power transfer theorem states that maximum power is transferred from a source to a load when the load resistance is equal to the source resistance.
- If the resistance across the load is lower or higher than the source resistance of the network, the power dissipated will be less than the maximum.

Consider the circuit given in Figure 3.17.

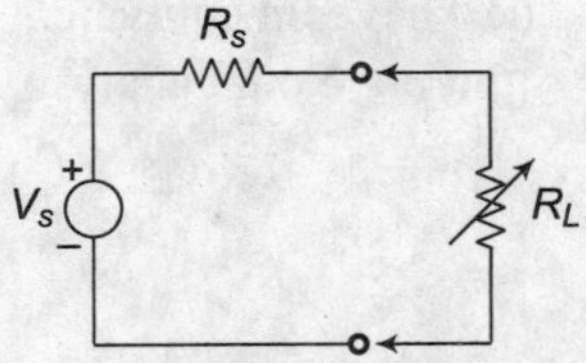

Figure 3.17

- Current in the circuit is $I = \dfrac{V_S}{R_S + R_L}$
- Power delivered to the load is $P = I^2 R_L = \dfrac{V_S^2 R_L}{(R_S + R_L)^2}$
- Maximum power is transferred when $\dfrac{dP}{dR_L} = 0$
- Solving this gives $R_S = R_L$.
- Therefore, maximum power is transferred from source to load when $R_S = R_L$.

Example 3.8

In the circuit shown in Figure 3.18, find the value of R for maximum power transfer. Also, calculate the maximum power.

[AU, 2014] ○○●

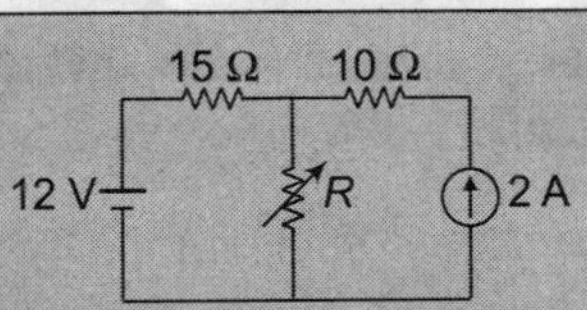

Figure 3.18

Solution To find the Thevenin's voltage, the load is open circuited as shown in Figure 3.19(a).

$$\frac{V_a - 12}{15} = 2$$

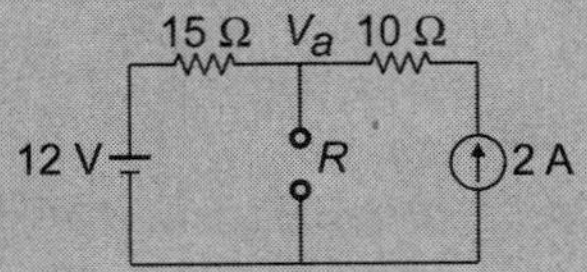

Figure 3.19 (a)

Therefore,

$$V_a = V_{th} = 42 \text{ V}$$

The Thevenin's resistance is as shown in Figure 3.19 (b).

Therefore,

$$R_{th} = R = 15\ \Omega$$

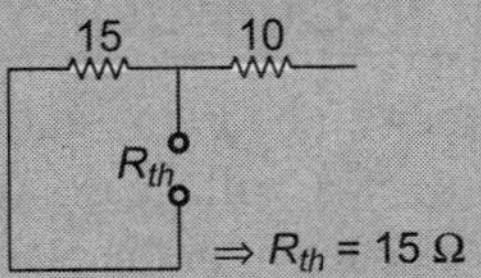

Figure 3.19 (b)

$$\text{Maximum power} = \frac{V_{th}^2}{4R_{th}} = \frac{42^2}{4 \times 15} = 29.4 \text{ watts}$$

Example 3.9

Obtain the Thevenin's equivalent circuit for the network shown in Figure 3.20, where $R_L = 5\ \Omega$. Find R_L for maximum power transfer.

[GTU, 2010] ○●●

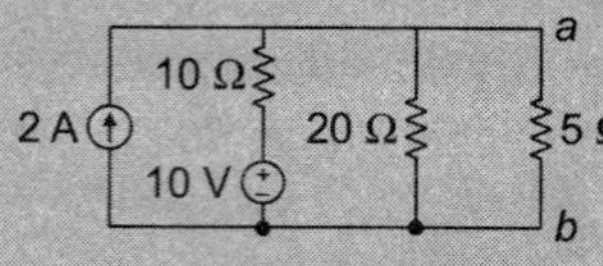

Figure 3.20

Solution The Thevenin resistance is given by removing all the sources. Therefore, the equivalent resistance is given as

$$R_{th} = 10 / /20 = 6.667\Omega$$

The Thevenin equivalent voltage for the circuit shown in Figure 3.21 is given by Applying Nodal analysis,

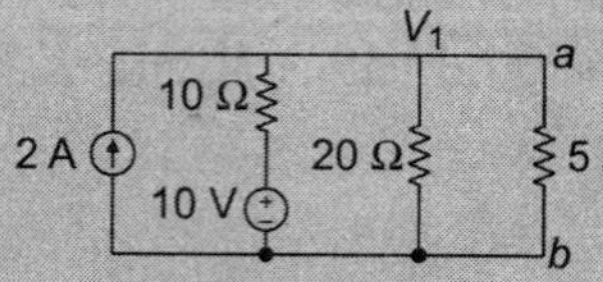

Figure 3.21

$$\frac{V_1}{20} + \frac{V_1 - 10}{10} = -2$$

$$V_{th} = V_1 = -\frac{20}{3} = -6.667 \text{ V}$$

The maximum power transferred is given as

$$P_{max} = \frac{1}{4}\frac{V_{th}^2}{R_{th}} = 1.667 \text{ W}$$

Example 3.10

Find the value of R that will receive maximum power transfer (Figure 3.22). ●●●

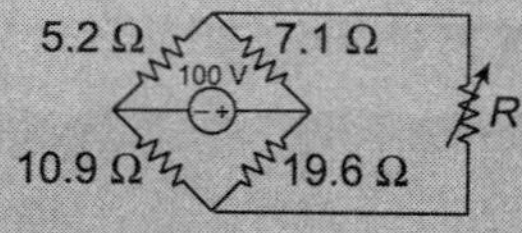

Figure 3.22

Solution Short the 100 V voltage source and find the equivalent resistance. The equivalent resistance is given as

$$R = \frac{R_2 R_4}{R_2 + R_4} + \frac{R_1 R_3}{R_1 + R_3} = 10\ \Omega$$

where,

$R_1 = 5.2\ \Omega$; $R_2 = 10.9\ \Omega$; $R_3 = 7.1\ \Omega$; $R_4 = 19.6\ \Omega$

3.6 || RECIPROCITY THEOREM

Reciprocity theorem states that in any bilateral linear network, if a voltage source of one branch of the circuit produces current in the other branch, then when the voltage and current sources are interchanged, the current produced in the first branch will be the same current the second branch has produced as shown in Figure 3.23.

Probe

1. Can a voltage source be interchanged with a current source producing the same current?

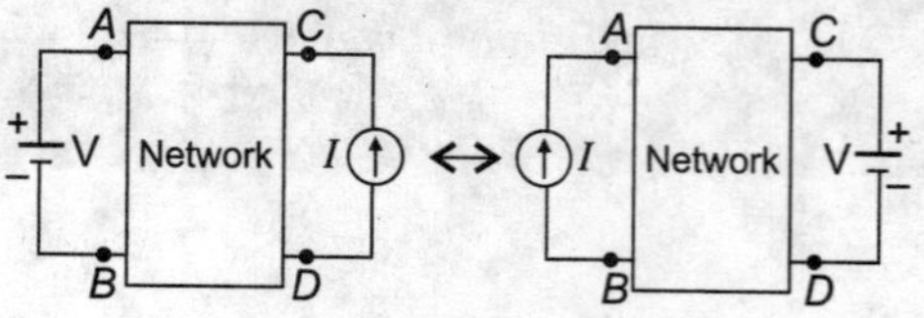

Figure 3.23

Example 3.11

Verify the reciprocity theorem for the circuit shown in Figure 3.24.

[AU, 2012] ○●●

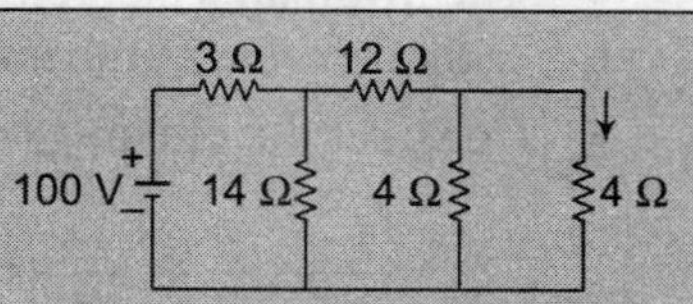

Figure 3.24

Solution Applying KCL at node 1 (Figure 3.25(a)):

$$\frac{V_1 - 100}{3} + \frac{V_1}{14} + \frac{V_1 - V_2}{12} = 0 \qquad (3.1)$$

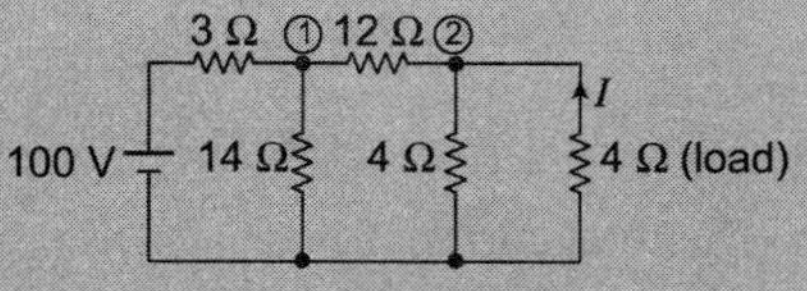

Figure 3.25 (a)

Applying KCL at node 2:

$$\frac{V_2 - V_1}{12} + \frac{V_2}{4} + \frac{V_2}{4} = 0 \qquad (3.2)$$

Solving Eqs (3.1) and (3.2), we get $V_1 = 69.87$ V, $V_2 = 9.968$ V

$$I = \frac{V_2}{4} = \frac{9.968}{4} = 2.497 \text{ A}$$

Using reciprocity (Figure 3.25(b)),

Applying KCL at node 1:

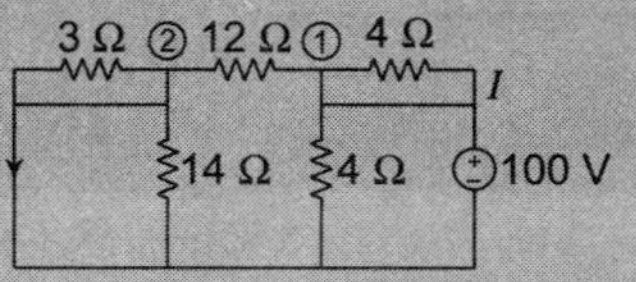

Figure 3.25 (b)

$$\frac{V_1 - 100}{4} + \frac{V_1}{4} + \frac{V_1 - V_2}{12} = 0 \qquad (3.3)$$

Applying KCL at node 2:

$$\frac{V_2}{3} + \frac{V_2}{14} + \frac{V_2 - V_1}{12} = 0 \qquad (3.4)$$

Solving Eqs (3.3) and (3.4), we get $V_1 = 41.86$ V and $V_2 = 7.22$ V

$$I = \frac{V_2}{3} = \frac{7.22}{3} = 2.407 \text{ A}$$

Therefore, the given circuit verifies reciprocity theorem.

3.7 || MILLMAN'S THEOREM

Probe

1. Can Millman's theorem be applicable for both voltage and current sources?

- Millman's theorem states that in any network, if a number of voltage sources, $V_1, V_2, ..., V_n$, in series with their respective internal resistances, $R_1, R_2, ...,$ R_n, are connected in parallel then these voltage sources can be replaced by a single voltage source, V, in series with resistance, R, where $R = \frac{1}{G_1 + G_2 + \cdots + G_n}$ and $V = \frac{V_1G_1 + V_2G_2 + \cdots + V_nG_n}{G_1 + G_2 + \cdots + G_n}$, G_n is the conductance of the nth branch.
- Figure 3.26 shows a circuit with several voltage sources in parallel and its Millman's circuit with a single voltage source and equivalent resistance.

- The Millman's theorem is also applicable in circuits with a number of current sources in parallel with their respective internal conductances and the combination in series.
- Consider the circuit given in Figure 3.27 and its Millman's equivalence.

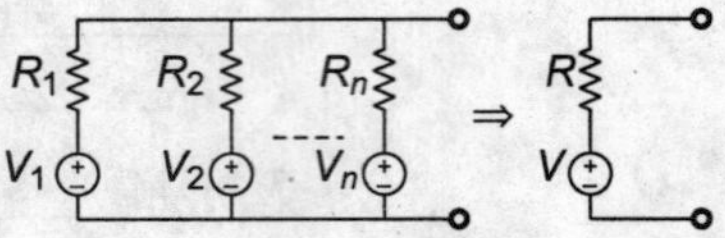

Figure 3.26

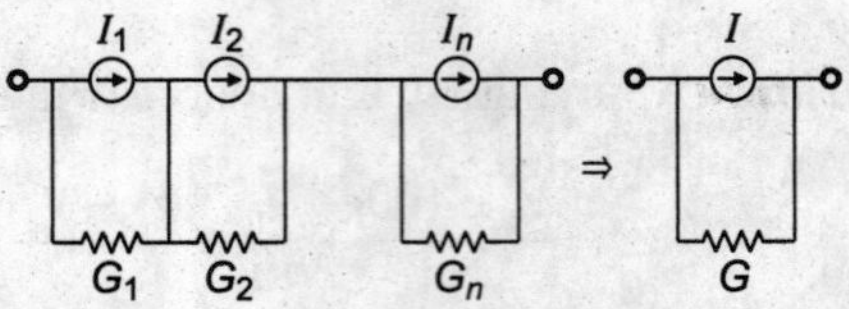

Figure 3.27

The total current I is

$$I = \frac{I_1R_1 + I_2R_2 + \cdots + I_nR_n}{R_1 + R_2 + \cdots + R_n} \quad \text{and} \quad G = \frac{1}{R_1 + R_2 + \cdots + R_n}$$

Example 3.12

Obtain the equivalent of a parallel connection of three branches each with a voltage source and a series resistance (2 V, 1 Ω), (3 V, 2 Ω), (5 V, 2 Ω). **[GTU, 2011]** ○●●

Solution The Millman's equivalent voltage can be found by

$$V_{eq} = \frac{2\times1+3\times2+5\times2}{1+2+2} = 3.6 \text{ V}$$

The Millman's equivalent resistance can be found by

$$\frac{1}{R_{eq}} = \frac{1}{1+2+2}$$

Therefore,

$$R_{eq} = 5\ \Omega$$

3.8 TELLEGEN'S THEOREM

Probe

1. What laws must the circuit obey for Tellegen's theorem to be applied?

- Tellegen's theorem states that in any lumped network, the algebraic sum of powers in all the branches at any instant is zero.
- Tellegen's theorem is applicable for any lumped network and is based on the Kirchhoff's laws.
- Suppose there are n number of branches in a network having instantaneous currents, $i_1, i_2, \ldots i_n$, and satisfying the Kirchhoff's current law and the instantaneous voltages across them, $v_1, v_2, \ldots v_n$, satisfying the Kirchhoff's voltage law, then $\sum_{k=1}^{n} v_k . i_k = 0$, where v_k is the instantaneous voltage across the kth branch and i_k is the instantaneous current flowing through that branch.

Example 3.13

Verify Tellegen's theorem for the network shown in the Figure 3.28. **[PTU, 2009-10]** ●●●

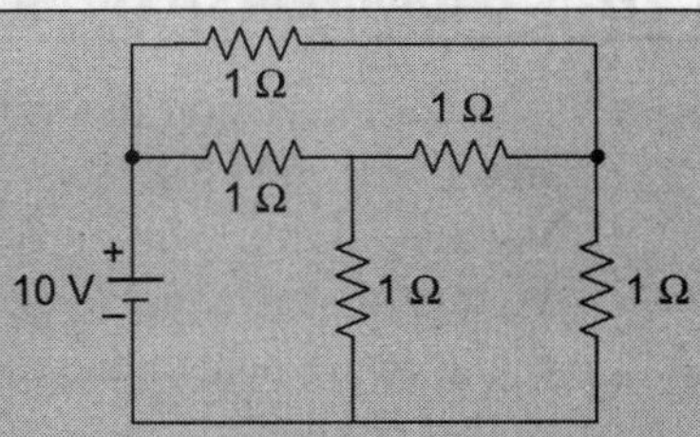

Figure 3.28

Solution Consider the given circuit with loop currents as shown in Figure 3.29.

Applying KVL in three loops, we get

$$2I_1 - I_2 - I_3 = 10 \quad (3.5)$$

$$-I_1 + 3I_2 - I_3 = 0 \quad (3.6)$$

$$-I_1 + 3I_2 - I_3 = 0 \quad (3.7)$$

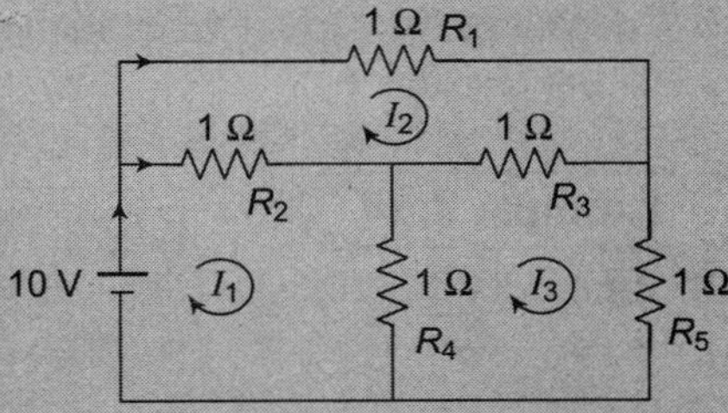

Figure 3.29

Solving the Eqs (3.5), (3.6), and (3.6), we get $I_1 = 10$ A, $I_2 = 5$ A, and $I_3 = 5$ A.

Power delivered by the source,

$$P = V_1 \times I_1 = 10 \times 10 = 100 \text{ W}$$

Power dissipated by each resistor

$$P_1 + P_2 + P_3 + P_4 + P_5 = 100 \text{ W}$$

Therefore, the Tellegen's theorem is verified.

3.9 SUBSTITUTION THEOREM

Probe

1. What will be the effect of replacing a 5 Ω resistance having a drop of 1 V across it with a 1 V voltage source?

- Substitution theorem states that if an element in a network is replaced by a voltage source, where the voltage at any time is equal to the voltage across the element before being replaced by source then the initial condition in the rest of the network will be unaltered.
- This also applies for a current source whose current at any instant of time is equal to the current through the element before being replaced by the source with the initial condition in the rest of the network being unaltered.

Consider the given circuit:

- First determine the respective branch voltage and current flowing through the branch given by V_{xy} and I_{xy}.
- The branch may be substituted by an independent voltage source as shown in Figure 3.30.
- The branch can also be substituted by an independent current source as shown in Figure 3.31.
- Therefore, it may be seen that the voltage drop and the current flowing through the circuit is the same even after being replaced by an independent voltage or current source.

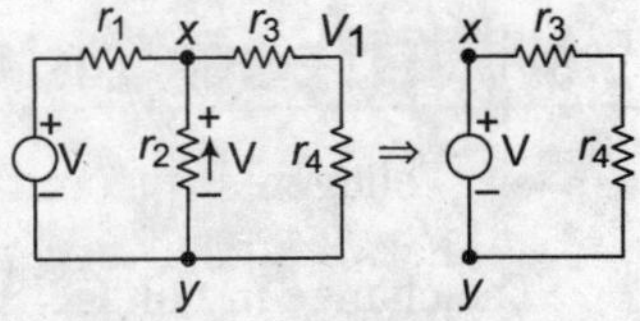

Figure 3.30

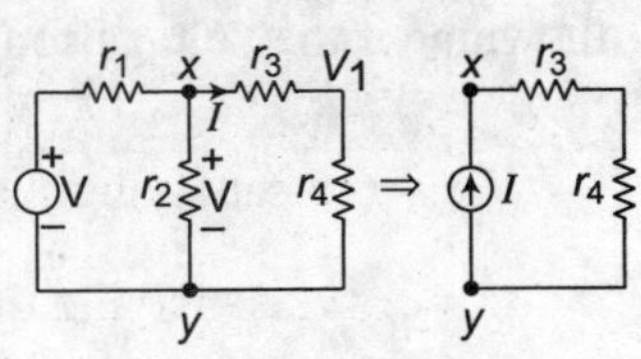

Figure 3.31

3.10 COMPENSATION THEOREM

- The compensation theorem states that any element in a linear, bilateral network may be replaced by a voltage source with zero internal resistance and a voltage that is equal to the voltage drop across the replaced element due to the current which was flowing in that element.
- This theorem is useful to determine the change in the voltage or current when there is a change in the value of resistance.

Probe

1. How can the change in voltage or current be determined if a new resistance is added to the circuit?

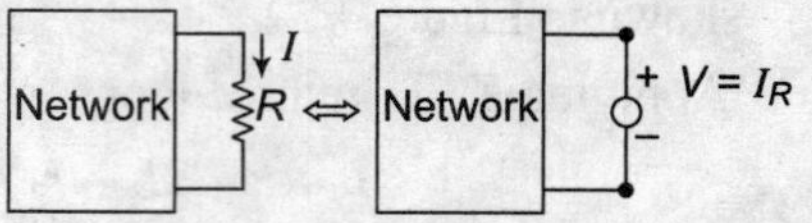

Figure 3.32

Example 3.14

In Figure 3.33, if the 1 Ω resistance is changed to 1.4 Ω then determine the source-voltage to compensate for the change. [GTU, 2014] ○●●

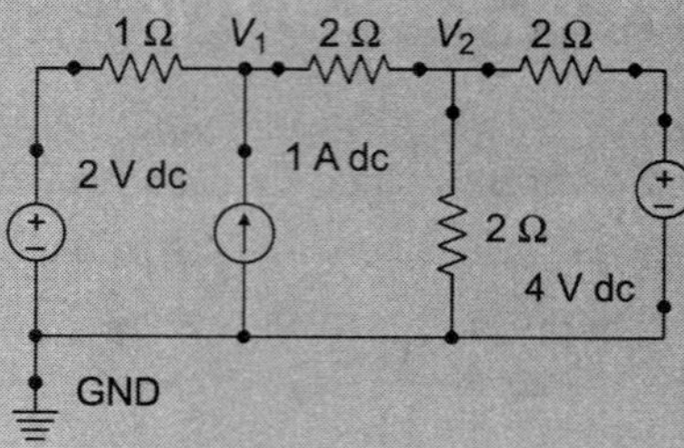

Figure 3.33

Solution Consider the circuit given with the 1 Ω resistance.

Let I_1 be the current through the 1 Ω resistance.

Applying nodal and current analysis, the value of I_1 is $\frac{-3}{4}A$.

The voltage, $V_1 = 2.25$ V

Now, replacing the 1 Ω resistance with 1.4 Ω resistance, the circuit is redrawn as shown in Figure 3.34.

The current through the 1.4 Ω resistance should be $\frac{-3}{4}$A. The voltage source will have a voltage equal to the voltage drop across the 1.4 Ω resistance.

$$\frac{V_1 - V}{1.4} = \frac{3}{4}$$

$$\frac{2.25 - V}{1.4} = \frac{3}{4}$$

$$V = 1.2 \text{ V}$$

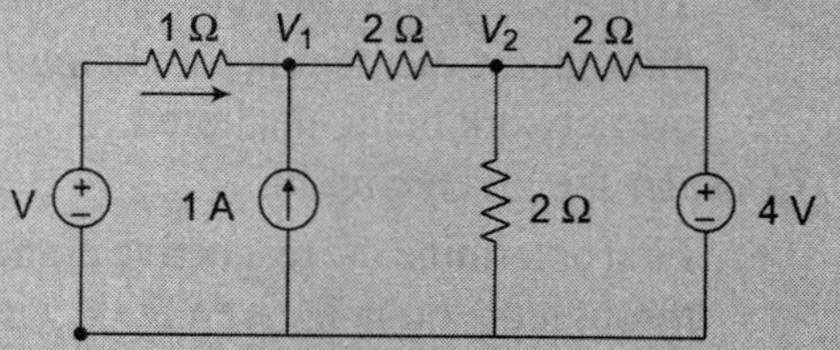

Figure 3.34

The change in voltage is 2 – 1.2 = 0.8 V

The source must therefore be reduced by 0.8 V and the value if the voltage source is 1.2 V.

POINTS TO REMEMBER

- ☞ When two or more sources are present in the circuit, keep one source while shorting or opening the others.
- ☞ Superposition can only be applied for linear circuits.
- ☞ The superposition voltage sources are to be shorted and current sources are to be opened.
- ☞ The Thevenin open-circuit voltage between its two terminals is equal to the voltage source.
- ☞ The Thevenin equivalent resistance is the resistance seen across the two terminals with the sources replaced by its internal resistances.
- ☞ The Norton equivalent short-circuit current between its two terminals is equal to the current source.
- ☞ The Norton equivalent resistance is the resistance seen across the two terminals with the sources replaced by its internal resistances.
- ☞ For the reciprocity theorem to be applicable, the ratio of response to the excitation must be the same.
- ☞ Millman's theorem can also be applicable to a number of current sources in parallel to their respective internal conductances.
- ☞ Kirchhoff's laws have to be satisfied before applying Tellegen's theorem.
- ☞ If Substitution theorem is satisfied, initial conditions will remain the same.
- ☞ Compensation theorem is used to determine the change in resistance of a circuit.

PRACTICE PROBLEMS

1. Using the Superposition theorem, determine the voltage drop and current across the resistor 3.3 K as shown in Figure 3.35. ○●●

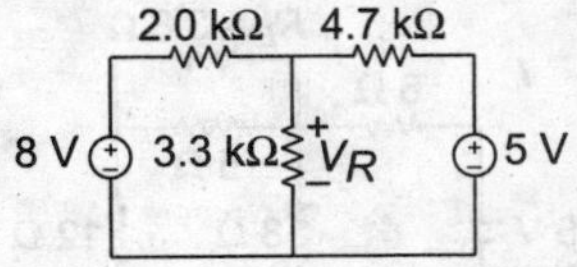

Figure 3.35

2. Using the superposition theorem, find the voltage, V_x, for the circuit shown in Figure 3.36. ○●●

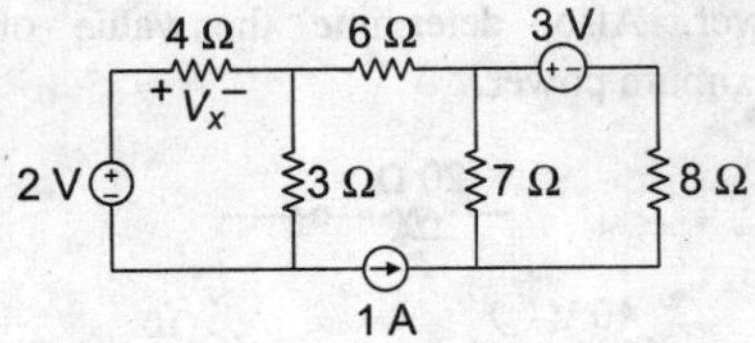

Figure 3.36

3. Determine the current, I_L, through $R_L = 6\Omega$ for the circuit shown in Figure 3.37, using the Thevenin's theorem. ○○●

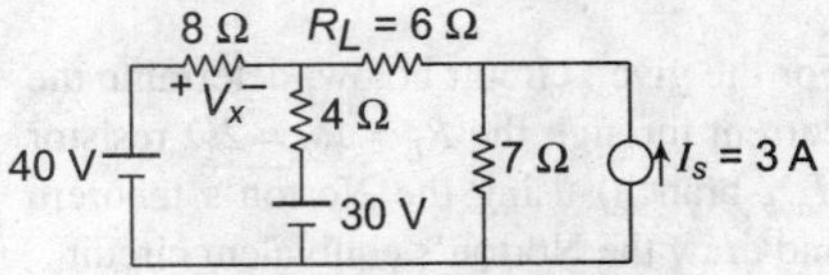

Figure 3.37

4. Determine the Thevenin's voltage and equivalent resistance across the 40 ohm load resistor for the circuit shown in the figure below and draw the Thevenin's equivalent circuit. ○○●

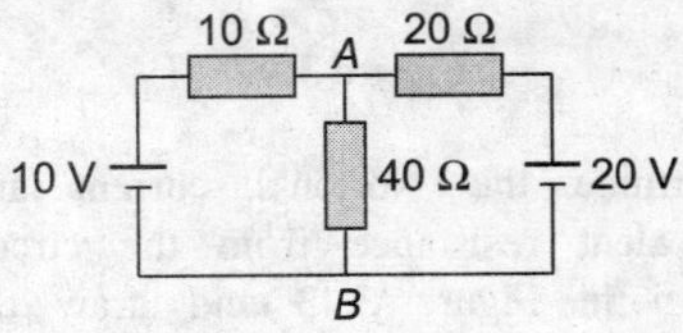

Figure 3.38

5. What is the Thevenin's equivalent across AB which has V_{oc} = V and R_{eq} respectively? ○●●

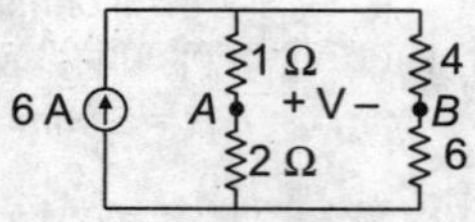

Figure 3.39

6. What is the Thevenin's equivalent R_{eq} to the left of AB? ○○●

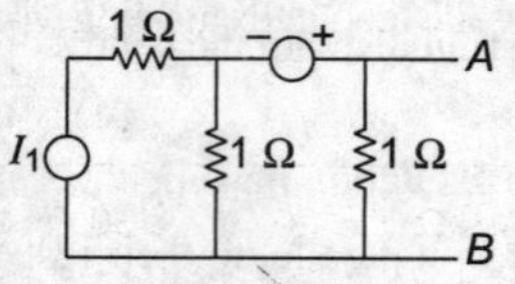

Figure 3.40

7. The Thevenin's and Norton's equivalent circuit of a DC network are shown in Figure 3.41. Find the values of current I and R in the Norton's equivalent. ○○●

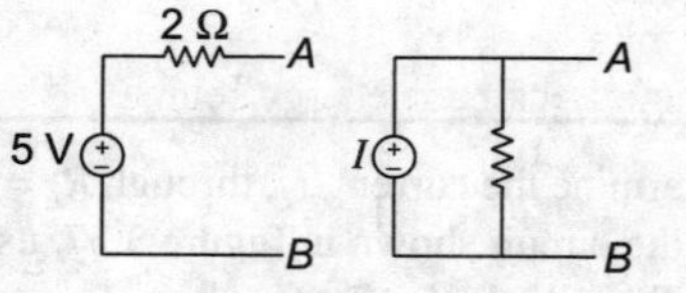

Figure 3.41

8. For the given circuit below, determine the current through the $R_L = R_2 = 2\Omega$ resistor (I_{a-b} branch) using the Norton's theorem and draw the Norton's equivalent circuit. ○●●

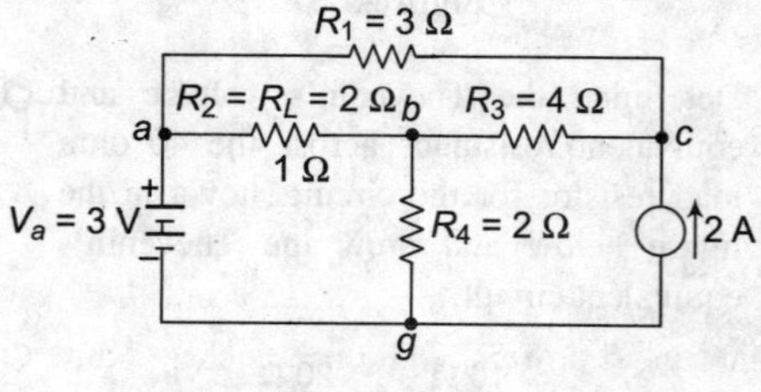

Figure 3.42

9. Determine the Norton's current and equivalent resistance from the circuit shown in Figure 3.43 and draw the Norton's equivalent circuit. ○○●

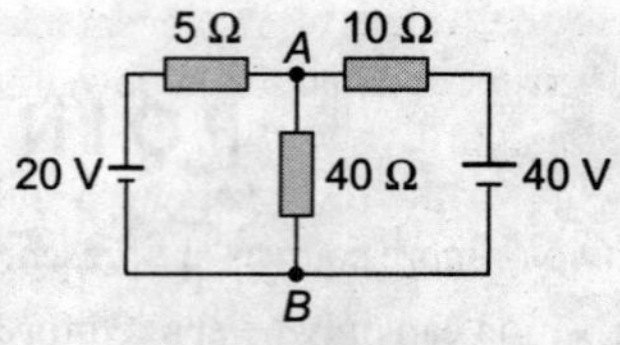

Figure 3.43

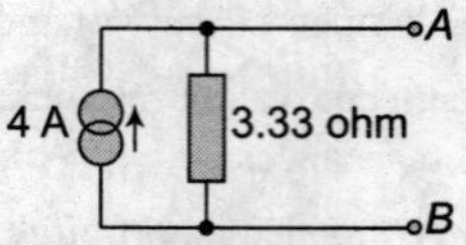

Figure 3.44

10. Determine the voltages and currents of the resistances in the circuit shown in Figure 3.45 using source transformation technique. ○○●

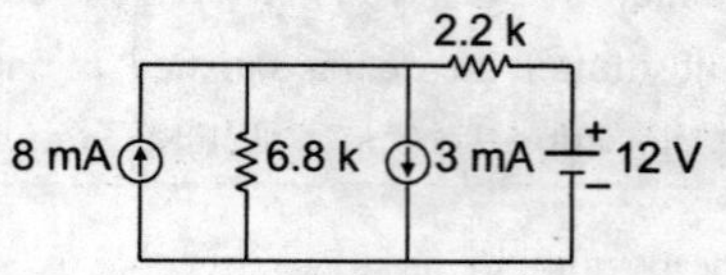

Figure 3.45

11. For the given network below, find the maximum power through R_L by using maximum power transfer theorem. ○○●

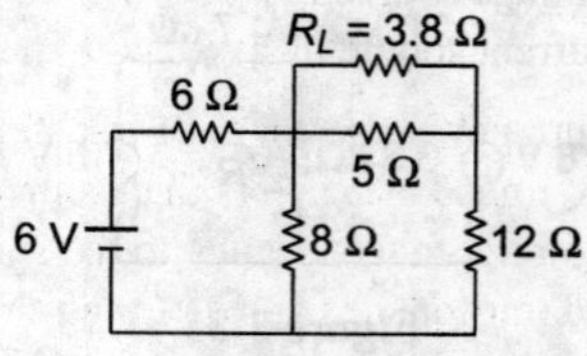

Figure 3.46

12. For the circuit shown in Figure 3.47, determine the value of load resistance when the load resistance draws maximum power. Also, determine the value of maximum power. ○○●

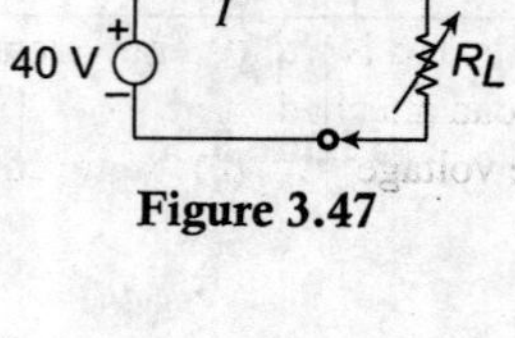

Figure 3.47

13. What is the value of R_L for maximum power transfer and maximum power in the given circuit?

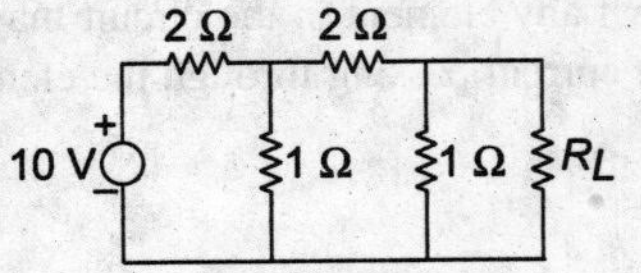

Figure 3.48

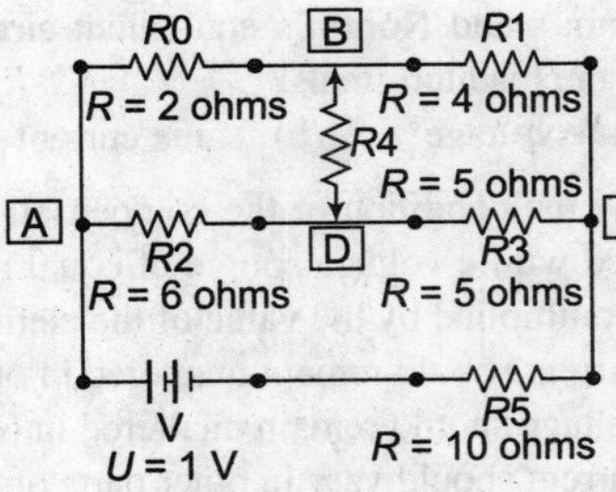

Figure 3.49

14. Calculate the current for the various branches of the network shown in Figure 3.49. Also, determine the current flowing through the one volt battery (V) when an extra e.m.f of 1 volt is added to branch BD opposing the flow of original current for that branch.

15. For the circuit shown in Figure 3.50, determine the load current using Millman's theorem.

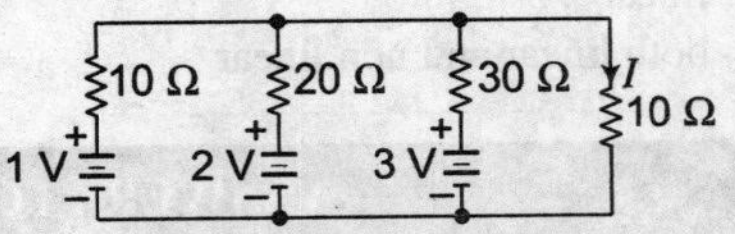

Figure 3.50

MULTIPLE CHOICE QUESTIONS

1. Superposition theorem is applicable in
   (a) linear circuits
   (b) nonlinear circuits
   (c) both linear and nonlinear circuits
   (d) circuits with more than one energy source

2. Thevenin's equivalent circuit consists of
   (a) a voltage source in parallel with the impedance
   (b) a current source in parallel with the impedance
   (c) a voltage source in series with the impedance
   (d) a current source in series with the impedance

3. Maximum power is said to be transferred when the
   (a) load impedance is less than source impedance
   (b) load impedance is equal to the source impedance
   (c) load impedance is greater than source impedance
   (d) load impedance is zero

4. Nortons's equivalent circuit consists of
   (a) a voltage source in parallel with the impedance
   (b) a current source in parallel with the impedance
   (c) a voltage source in series with the impedance
   (d) a current source in series with the impedance

5. _____ theorem states that in any lumped network, the algebraic sum of powers in all the branches at any instant is zero.
   (a) Thevenin's
   (b) Millman's
   (c) Tellegan's
   (d) Norton's

6. Thevenin's and Norton's equivalent circuits should ideally produce the _____ across the load terminals with no load attached.
   (a) same voltage
   (b) same current
   (c) different current
   (d) different voltage

7. Thevenin's and Norton's equivalent circuits should ideally produce the _____ through a short circuit across the load terminals. ○○●
(a) same voltage (b) same current (c) different current (d) different voltage

8. Identify the condition of the compensation theorem which states that any element in the circuit may be replaced with a voltage source of equal magnitude and equal to the current passing through the element that is multiplied by the value of the element. ○●●
(a) Current should remain unaltered in other parts of the circuit.
(b) Voltage should remain unaltered in other parts of the circuit.
(c) Current should vary in other parts of the circuit.
(d) Both current and voltage should remain unaltered in other parts of the circuit.

9. The dual component of an inductor is ○○●
(a) capacitor (b) resistor (c) voltage source (d) current source

10. Tellegen's theorem is valid for _____ networks. ○●●
(a) linear (b) nonlinear
(c) both linear and non linear (d) distributed

ANSWERS TO MULTIPLE CHOICE QUESTIONS

1. (a)	2. (c)	3. (b)	4. (b)	5. (c)
6. (a)	7. (b)	8. (d)	9. (a)	10. (c)

Steady State AC Analysis and Transient Response

4

Chapter Outline

- Phasors and Sinusoids
- Steady state analysis of R, L, C in series, parallel and series-parallel combinations
- Impedance, Reactance, Admittance
- Mesh and node analysis
- Superposition theorem
- Thevenin's theorem
- Norton's theorem
- Maximum power transfer theorem
- Reciprocity theorem
- Millman's theorem
- Tellegen's theorem
- Substitution theorem
- Compensation theorem
- DC transient of RL, RC, RLC circuit
- Sinusoidal transient of RL, RC, RLC circuit

4.1 || INTRODUCTION

A network having constant energy sources is said to be in DC steady state if the input voltage and all current variables are constant. Sinusoidal steady state refers to the networks with currents and voltages having constant amplitude and frequency sinusoidal functions. The condition existing in an electric circuit between two steady state conditions is known as the transient state. It may occur due to sudden disconnection or connection or short circuit. A transient response is the electrical response of a system to a change in equilibrium. The analysis of behaviour of network elements to sinusoidal varying alternating excitations is called steady state AC analysis.

The methods of solving networks that have been discussed in earlier chapters with reference to resistive load and DC sources are also valid for a network consisting of AC sources, resistors, inductors and capacitors. All network theorems except Maximum Power Transfer are applicable to phasor equivalent circuits used to solve for sinusoidal steady state variables in a linear dynamic circuit excited by sinusoidal sources with a common frequency. The maximum power transfer theorem needs some modification.

4.2 || PHASORS AND SINUSOIDS

University Question

1. Define the following.
   (a) Time period (b) Frequency (c) RMS value (d) Average value **[JNTU, 2012]**

A sinusoid, or simply a sine wave, is a mathematical curve that corresponds to the sine function. An alternating quantity is that which acts in alternate directions and whose magnitude undergoes a definite cycle of change in definite intervals of time. The wave's magnitude and direction varies with time. The wave starts at a reference point $t = 0$ seconds with a value of zero. It reaches the positive peak (V_m) and returns to its original value zero. It further decreases in the negative direction until it reaches the negative peak ($-V_m$).

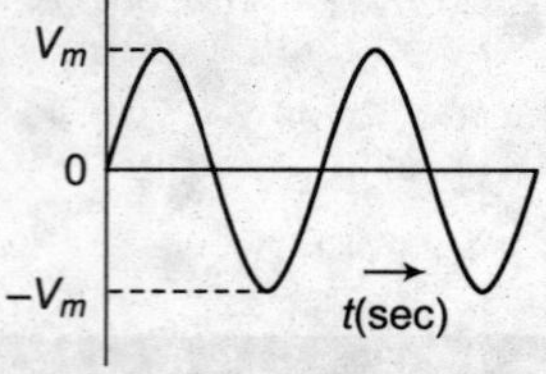

Figure 4.1

When the voltage applied is positive, the flow of current is in a certain direction; when the voltage applied is negative, the flow of current is in the opposite direction (Figure 4.1). Both the positive and negative voltages constitute to one cycle in the sine wave. The general expression of an alternating quantity is

$$x(t) = A \sin (\omega t + \phi)$$

where, A = Peak value or amplitude, ϕ = Phase angle in radians, ω = Angular frequency in radians per second.

Before proceeding, there are different terms we need to define when dealing with waves. They are as follows.

- **Cycle**: A cycle may be defined as one complete set of positive and negative values of an alternating quantity repeating at equal intervals.
- **Period**: The time taken by an alternating quantity in seconds to trace one complete cycle is called periodic time or time-period. It is usually denoted by symbol T.
- **Frequency**: The number of cycles per second is called frequency and is denoted by symbol f Frequency is generally measured in Hertz.

  $$f = \frac{1}{T}$$

  If the angular velocity ω is expressed in radians per second, then $\omega = 2\pi f$.
- **Instantaneous value**: It is given by the value of the sine wave at any given point of time. It is denoted by small letter.
- **Peak value**: The maximum value during the positive cycle or the maximum value during the negative cycle is known as the peak value of the sine wave. It is denoted by V_m or I_m.
- **Peak-to-peak value**: For a sine wave, the peak-to-peak value is calculated from the positive peak to the negative peak.
- **Average value**: The average value of the wave corresponds to the total area covered divided by the distance measured by the curve. It is given by

  $$V_{av} = 0.637 V_m$$

- **Root mean square (RMS) value**: It is that value of an alternating voltage or current which produces the same amount of heat in a resistor connected to AC as the amount of heat produced when the resistor is connected to DC. It is denoted by capital letter. It is given by

$$V_{rms} = \frac{V_m}{\sqrt{2}}$$

- **Peak factor:** The peak factor is known as the ratio of peak value to the RMS value of the wave.

$$\text{Peak factor} = \frac{V_m}{V_{rms}}$$

- **Form factor:** The form factor is known as the ratio of the RMS value of the average value of the wave.

$$\text{Form factor} = \frac{V_{rms}}{V_{av}}$$

A sine wave can be expressed with its magnitude and its associated angular position using a phasor diagram as shown in Figure 4.2.

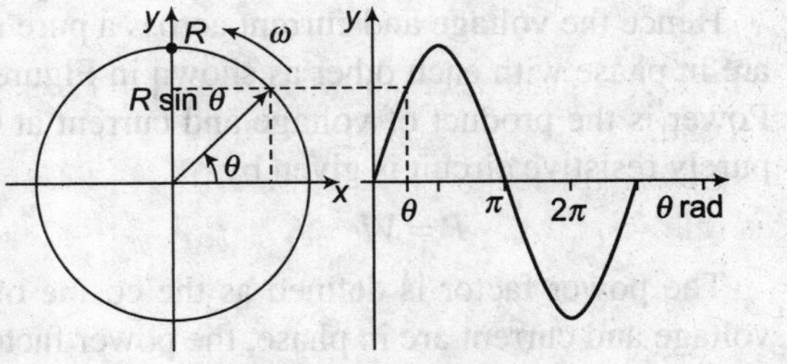

Figure 4.2

For example, consider a wave defined by $R \sin \theta$. Here the amplitude of the wave is R and the angle created is θ. In the phasor diagram, the length of the line drawn is equal to the amplitude of the wave, which is R, with the subtended angle of the wave, which is θ. The 'phase' of an AC wave may be defined as its position with respect to a reference axis or reference wave. Phase angle is the angle of lead or lag with respect to reference axis or with respect to another wave. Signals with the same frequency that begin with different references can incur a phase difference (Figure 4.3).

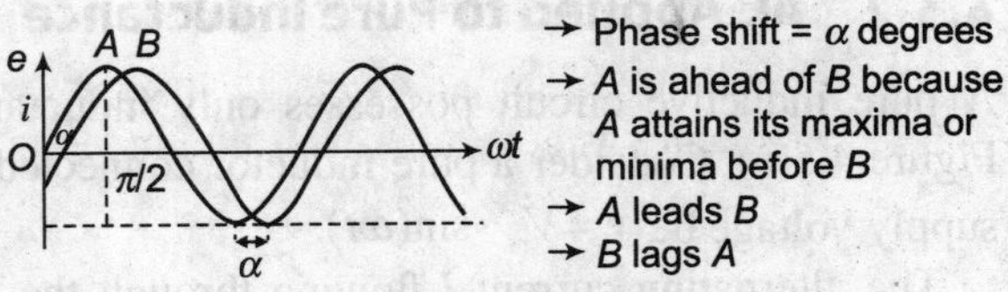

Figure 4.3

An alternating voltage or current is a phasor quantity, but since the instantaneous values are changing continuously, it must be represented by a rotating vector phasor j.

4.3 STEADY STATE ANALYSIS OF R, L, C IN SERIES, PARALLEL AND SERIES-PARALLEL COMBINATIONS

University Question

1. Draw the Phasor diagram for a series RL circuit. **[AU, 2012]**

Firstly let us understand the behaviour of the elements – resistance, inductance and capacitance when excited by sinusoidal varying excitations. Then we shall study the various series and parallel combinations of R, L and C.

4.3.1 AC Applied to Pure Resistance

Consider a resistor R connected across an AC supply as shown in Figure 4.4(a). Let the supply voltage be

$$v = V_m \cdot \sin(\omega t)$$

From Ohm's Law $i = \frac{v}{R} = \frac{V_m \cdot \sin(\omega t)}{R} = \frac{V_m}{R} \sin(\omega t)$

or $\quad i = I_m \cdot \sin(\omega t)$

where $I_m = \frac{V_m}{R} \Rightarrow I = \frac{V}{R}$ in rms values.

The rms value of current is given by $I = \frac{I_m}{\sqrt{2}}$

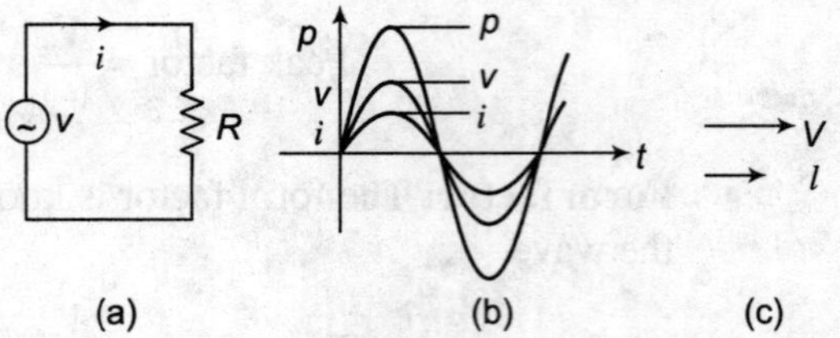

Figure 4.4

Hence the voltage and current across a pure resistor are in phase with each other as shown in Figure 4.4(b). The phasor diagram is shown in Figure 4.4(c). Power is the product of voltage and current at every instant of time. The average value of power in a purely resistive circuit is given by

$$P = VI$$

The power factor is defined as the cosine of the angle between the voltage and current. Since the voltage and current are in phase, the power factor angle ϕ is zero and power factor ($\cos\phi$) is unity.

4.3.2 AC Applied to Pure Inductance

A pure inductive circuit possesses only inductance and no resistance or capacitance as shown in Figure 4.5(a). Consider a pure inductor connected across an ac supply as shown in the figure. Let the supply voltage be $v = V_m \cdot \sin(\omega t)$.

The alternating current I flowing through the inductor will produce an alternating magnetic field which in turn will induce an emf given by

$$e = L\frac{di}{dt}$$

where L is the self-inductance of the coil. As there is no ohmic resistance drop, the applied voltage has to oppose the self-induced emf only. So the applied voltage is equal and opposite to the back emf at all instants.

$$v = e \Rightarrow V_m \cdot \sin(\omega t) = L\frac{di}{dt} \cdot di = \frac{V_m}{L} \sin(\omega t)$$

The expression for current obtained after integration is

$$i = \frac{V_m}{\omega L} \sin\left(\omega t - \frac{\pi}{2}\right) = I_m \sin\left(\omega t - \frac{\pi}{2}\right), \text{ where } I_m = \frac{V_m}{\omega L} \Rightarrow I = \frac{V}{\omega L} \text{ in rms values}$$

The voltage, current and instantaneous power wave shapes are shown in Figure 4.5(b) and the phasor diagram in Figure 4.5(c). The current lags the voltage by 90° in a purely inductive circuit. The average power in a purely inductive circuit is zero and the power factor is cos 90° = 0.

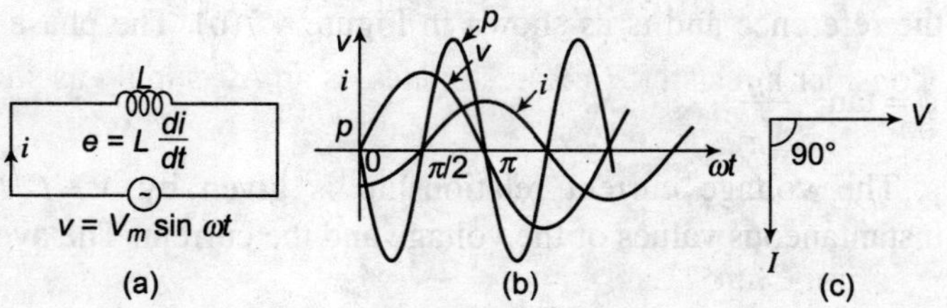

Figure 4.5

4.3.3 AC Applied to Pure Capacitance

Consider a pure capacitor connected across an AC supply as shown in Figure 4.6(a). Let the supply voltage be $v = V_m \cdot \sin(\omega t)$.

When the current starts to flow, the capacitor starts getting charged. The charge in the capacitor is given by $q = Cv$ where C is the capacitance of the capacitor.

Current is given by

$$i = \frac{dq}{dt} = C\frac{dv}{dt} = C\frac{d}{dt}(V_m \cdot \sin(\omega t))$$

The expression for current obtained is

$$i = \omega C V_m \sin\left(\omega t + \frac{\pi}{2}\right) = I_m \sin\left(\omega t + \frac{\pi}{2}\right), \text{ where } I_m = \omega C V_m \Rightarrow I = \omega C V \text{ in rms values}$$

The voltage, current and instantaneous power wave shapes are shown in Figure 4.6(b) and the phasor diagram in Figure 4.6(c). The current leads the voltage by 90°in a pure capacitive circuit. The average power in a purely capacitive circuit is zero and the power factor is cos 90°= 0.

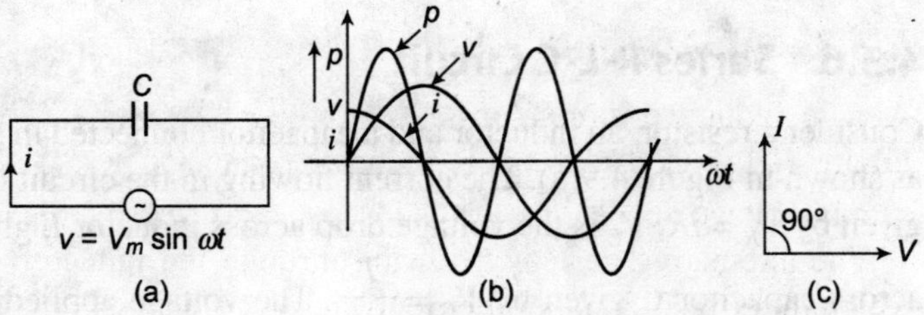

Figure 4.6

4.3.4 Series R-L Circuit

Consider a resistor and an inductor connected in series across an ac voltage V of frequency f as shown in Figure 4.7(a). The current flowing in the circuit is I. V_R is the voltage drop across resistor R given by $V_R = IR$ and V_L is the voltage drop across inductor L given by $V_L = \omega L.I$. The voltage applied is given by $V^2 = V_R{}^2 + V_L{}^2$. The phasor diagram is drawn with current as

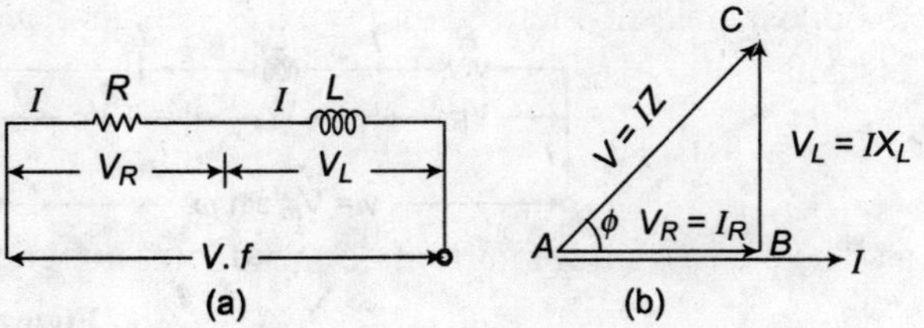

Figure 4.7

the reference and is as shown in Figure 4.7(b). The phase angle for the given circuit can be given as $\phi = \tan^{-1}\frac{V_L}{V_R}$.

The voltage current relationship is given by $V = I\sqrt{R^2 + (\omega L)^2}$. The power is the product of instantaneous values of the voltage and the current. The average power is given by $P = VI\cos\phi$.

4.3.5 Series R-C Circuit

Consider a resistor and a capacitor connected in series across an ac voltage V of frequency f as shown in Figure 4.8(a). The current flowing in the circuit is I. V_R is the voltage drop across resistor R given by $V_R = I_R$ and V_C is the voltage drop across capacitor C given by $V_C = \frac{I}{\omega C}$. The voltage applied is given by $V^2 = {V_R}^2 + {V_C}^2$. The phasor diagram is drawn with current as the reference and is as shown in Figure 4.8(b). The phase angle for the given circuit can be given as $\phi = \tan^{-1}\frac{V_C}{V_R}$.

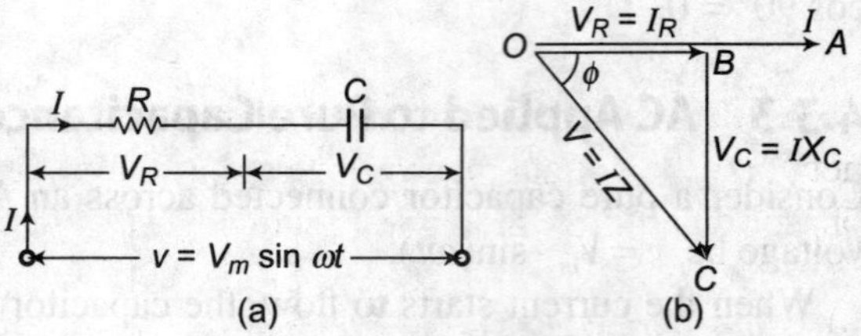

Figure 4.8

The voltage current relationship is given by $V = I\sqrt{R^2 + \left(\frac{1}{\omega C}\right)^2}$. The power is the product of instantaneous values of the voltage and the current. The average power is given by $P = VI\cos\phi$.

4.3.6 Series R-L-C Circuit

Consider a resistor, an inductor and a capacitor connected in series across an ac voltage V of frequency f as shown in Figure 4.9(a). The current flowing in the circuit is I. V_R is the voltage drop across resistor R given by $V_R = IR$, V_L is the voltage drop across inductor L given by $V_L = \omega L$ and V_C is the voltage drop across capacitor C given by $V_C = \frac{I}{\omega C}$. The voltage applied is given by $V^2 = {V_R}^2 + (V_L - V_C)^2$. The phasor diagram is drawn with current as the reference and is as shown in Figure 4.9 (b). The phase angle for the given circuit can be given as $\phi = \tan^{-1}\frac{(V_L - V_C)}{V_R}$.

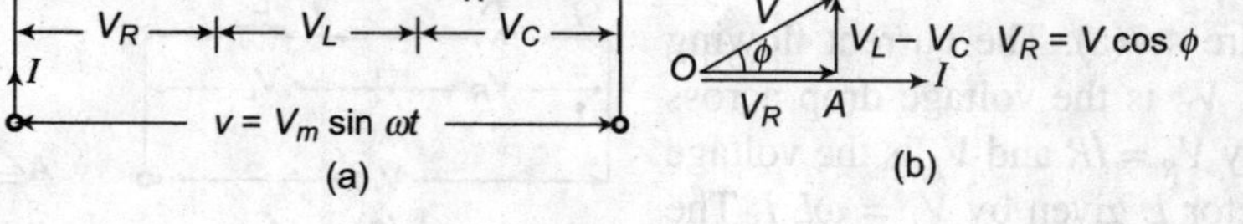

Figure 4.9

The voltage current relationship is given by $V = I\sqrt{R^2 + \left(\omega L - \frac{1}{\omega C}\right)^2}$. The power is the product of instantaneous values of the voltage and the current. The average power is given by $P = VI\cos\phi$.

4.3.7 Parallel R-L Circuit

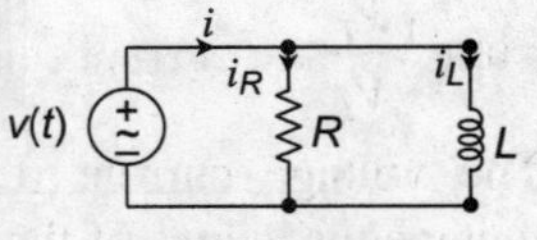

Figure 4.10

Consider a resistor and an inductor connected in parallel across an AC voltage V of frequency f as shown in Figure 4.10.

Let the supply voltage be $v = V_m \cdot \sin(\omega t)$

The total current is the phasor summation of all the branch currents. It is given by

$$i = i_R + i_L = \frac{v}{R} + \frac{v}{\omega L}$$

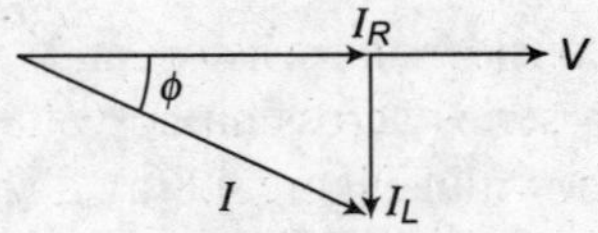

Figure 4.11

As the voltage across each element is the same for a parallel network, the voltage phasor is taken as the reference for drawing the phasor diagram as shown in Figure 4.11.

4.3.8 Parallel R-C Circuit

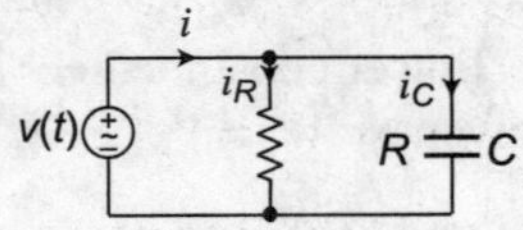

Figure 4.12

Consider a resistor and a capacitor connected in parallel across an AC voltage V of frequency f as shown in Figure 4.12.

Let the supply voltage be $v = V_m \cdot \sin(\omega t)$

The total current is the phasor summation of all the branch currents. It is given as

$$i = i_R + i_C = \frac{v}{R} + \omega v C$$

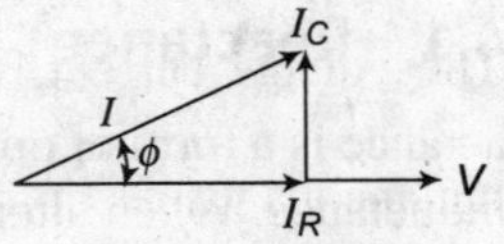

Figure 4.13

The phasor diagram is as shown in Figure 4.13.

4.3.9 Parallel R-L-C Circuit

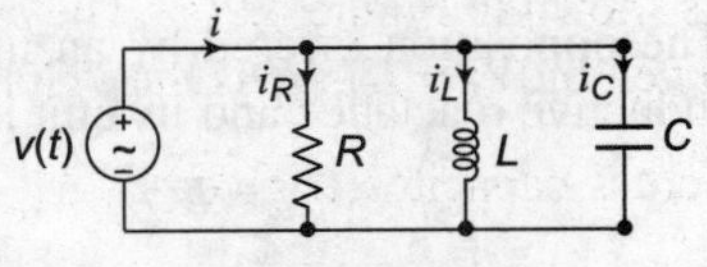

Figure 4.14

Consider a resistor, an inductor and a capacitor connected in parallel across an ac voltage V of frequency f as shown in Figure 4.14.

Let the supply voltage be $v = V_m \cdot \sin(\omega t)$

The total current is the phasor summation of all the branch currents. It is given by

$$i = i_R + i_L + i_C = \frac{v}{R} + \frac{v}{\omega L} + \omega v C$$

Example 4.1

A 230 V, 50 Hz ac supply is applied to a coil of 0.06 H inductance and 2.5 Ω resistance connected in series with a 6.8 μF capacitor. Calculate (i) current (ii) phase angle between current and voltage (iii) power factor (iv) power consumed. ○○●

Solution It is a series RLC circuit where R = 2.5 Ω, L = 0.06 H, C = 6.8 μF, V = 230 V, $\omega = 2 \times 3.14 \times 50 = 314$

Note: Difficulty Level ⟶ ○○● — Easy; ○●● — Medium; ●●● — Difficult

The voltage current relationship is given by $V = I\sqrt{R^2 + \left(\omega L - \frac{1}{\omega C}\right)^2}$

$$\sqrt{R^2 + \left(\omega L - \frac{1}{\omega C}\right)^2} = \sqrt{2.5^2 + \left((314 \times 0.06) - \frac{1}{(314 \times 6.8 \times 10^{-6})}\right)^2} = 449.2\,\Omega$$

$$I = \frac{V}{449.2} = \frac{230}{449.2} = 0.512\,\text{A}$$

$$\phi = \tan^{-1}\frac{(V_L - V_C)}{V_R} = \tan^{-1}\left(\frac{(314 \times 0.06) - (1/314 \times 6.8 \times 10^{-6}}{2.5}\right) = -89.7°$$

Power factor cos (–89.7°) = 0.0056

Power consumed = $VI \cos\phi = 230 \times 0.512 \times 0.0056 = 0.66$ W

4.4 || IMPEDANCE, REACTANCE, ADMITTANCE

4.4.1 Reactance

Reactance is a form of opposition exhibited to the passage of alternating current because of capacitance or inductance. When alternating current passes through a component that contains reactance, energy is alternately stored in, and released from, a magnetic field or an electric field. In the case of a magnetic field, the reactance is inductive. In the case of an electric field, the reactance is capacitive.

Inductive Reactance

The opposition offered by an inductor to the flow of current is X_L given by $X_L = \omega L$. This is called inductive reactance and its unit is ohms. So for a pure inductor

$$V = IX_L$$

Capacitive Reactance

The opposition offered by an capacitor to the flow of current is X_c given by $X_c = \frac{1}{\omega C}$. This is called capacitive reactance and its unit is Ohms. So for a pure capacitor

$$V = IX_C$$

4.4.2 Impedance

The impedance of a circuit element is defined as the ratio of the phasor voltage across the element to the phasor current through the element. It is represented by Z and measured in Ohms.

$$Z = \frac{V}{I}$$

When resistors, capacitors, and inductors are combined in an AC circuit, the impedances of the individual components can be combined in the same way that the resistances are combined in a DC circuit. The resulting equivalent impedance is in general, a complex quantity. That is, the equivalent impedance has a real part and an imaginary part. The real part is denoted with an R and the imaginary part is denoted with an X.

$$Z = R + jX$$

R is termed the resistive part of the impedance while X is termed the reactive part of the impedance.

For an RL series circuit $V = I\sqrt{R^2 + X_L{}^2} \Rightarrow Z = \sqrt{R^2 + X_L{}^2}$ or $Z = R + jX_L$.

So if ϕ is the phase angle, $R = Z\cos\phi$ and $X_L = Z\sin\phi$.

For an RC series circuit $V = I\sqrt{R^2 + X_C{}^2} \Rightarrow Z = \sqrt{R^2 + X_C{}^2}$ or $Z = R - jX_C$.

So if ϕ is the phase angle, $R = Z\cos\phi$ and $X_C = Z\sin\phi$.

For an RLC series circuit $V = I\sqrt{R^2 + (X_L - X_C)^2} \Rightarrow Z = \sqrt{R^2 + (X_L - X_C)^2}$ or $Z = R + j(X_L - X_C)$.

Combining impedances in series, parallel, or in delta-wye configurations, is the same as for resistors. The difference is that combining impedances involves manipulation of complex numbers.

Combining impedances in series is simple:

$$Z_{eq} = Z_1 + Z_2 = (R_1 + R_2) + j(X_1 + X_2)$$

Combining impedances in parallel is much more difficult than combining simple properties like resistance or capacitance, due to a multiplication term.

$$Z_{eq} = Z_1 \parallel Z_2 = \frac{Z_1 Z_2}{Z_1 + Z_2}$$

4.4.3 Admittance

It is the reciprocal of impedance and is denoted by Y. Admittance is measured in mhos or Siemens. It is given by $I = VY$. The impedance Z has two components resistance R and reactance X. Admittance has also two components, the conductance 'G' and susceptance 'B'.

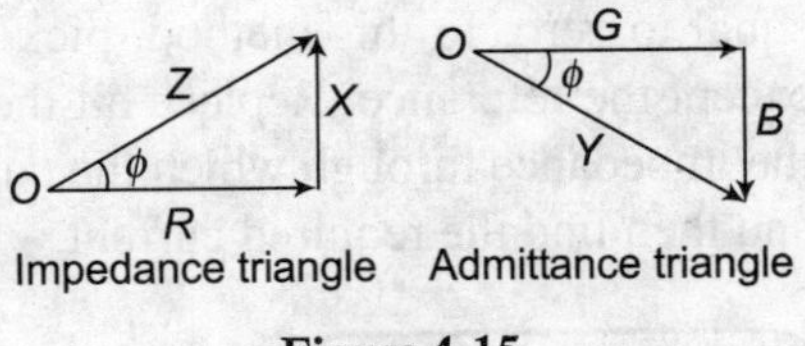

Figure 4.15

$$Y = G \pm jX$$

The value of B is negative if the circuit is inductive and the value of B is positive if the circuit is capacitive. The impedance and admittance triangles are similar as shown in Figure 4.15.

Example 4.2

For the circuit shown in Figure 4.16, find the current and power drawn from the source.

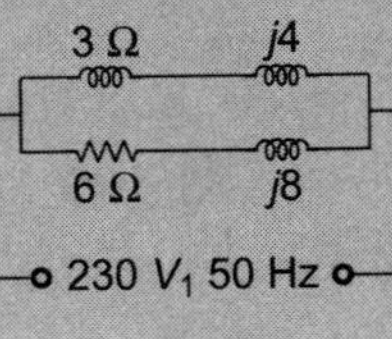

Figure 4.16

Solution Let

$$Z_1 = 3 + j4 = 5\angle 53.13°\Omega$$

$$Z_2 = 6 + j8 = 10\angle 53.13°\Omega$$

Both impedances are in parallel. So the equivalent impedance is

$$Z_{eq} = \frac{Z_1 Z_2}{Z_1 + Z_2} = \frac{5\angle 53.13 \times 10\angle 53.13}{3 + j4 + 6 + j8} = \frac{50\angle 106.26}{15\angle 53.13} = 3.33\angle 53.13\Omega$$

Current drawn

$$I = \frac{V}{Z_{eq}} = \frac{230}{3.33\angle 53.13} = 69\angle -53.13 \text{ A}$$

Power drawn from source

$$P = VI\cos\phi = 230 \times 69 \times \cos 53.13 = 9.522 \text{ kW}$$

4.5 MESH AND NODE ANALYSIS

University Question

1. Define 'mesh analysis' of a circuit. [AU, 2011]

4.5.1 Mesh Analysis

Mesh analysis is useful if a network has a large number of voltage sources. In this method, currents are assigned in each mesh. When mesh equations, based on Kirchhoff's voltage law, are written in terms of unknown mesh currents and solved to obtain the required quantity, the thumb rule is that the number of equations should be equal to the number of unknown currents.

4.5.2 Nodal Analysis

Nodal analysis is based on Kirchhoff's current law and is used to find currents and voltages in a network. For AC networks Kirchhoff's current law states that the phasor sum of currents meeting at a point is equal to zero. In this method, pick a reference node and apply Kirchhoff's current law at each node except the reference. Replace all the unknown currents in terms of the potential difference divided by the impedance through which the current is flowing. Solve the resulting equation for the nodal voltages and then find the required current.

Example 4.3

Find the mesh currents I_1, I_2 and I_3 in the network shown in Figure 4.17.

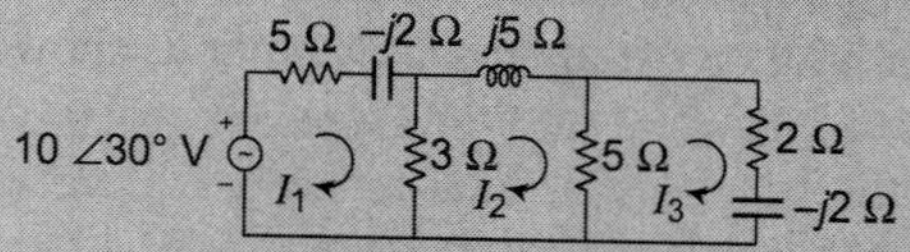

Figure 4.17

Solution Applying KVL to mesh 1

$$10\angle 30° - (5 - j2)I_1 - 3(I_1 - I_2) = 0 \Rightarrow (8 - j2)I_1 - 3I_2 = 10\angle 30°$$

Applying KVL to mesh 2

$$-3\,(I_2 - I_1) - j5I_2 - 5(I_2 - I_3) = 0 \Rightarrow -3I_1 + (8 + j5)I_2 - 5I_3 = 0$$

Applying KVL to mesh 3

$$-5(I_3 - I_2) - (2 - j2)I_3 = 0 \Rightarrow -5I_2 + (7 - j2)I_3 = 0$$

Writing these equations in matrix form

$$\begin{bmatrix} 8-j2 & -3 & 0 \\ -3 & 8+j5 & -5 \\ 0 & -5 & 7-j2 \end{bmatrix}\begin{bmatrix} I_1 \\ I_2 \\ I_3 \end{bmatrix} = \begin{bmatrix} 10\angle 30^\circ \\ 0 \\ 0 \end{bmatrix}$$

Solving using Cramer's rule

$$I_1 = \frac{\begin{bmatrix} 10\angle 30^\circ & -3 & 0 \\ 0 & 8+j5 & -5 \\ 0 & -5 & 7-j2 \end{bmatrix}}{\begin{bmatrix} 8-j2 & -3 & 0 \\ -3 & 8+j5 & -5 \\ 0 & -5 & 7-j2 \end{bmatrix}} = 1.43\angle 38.7^\circ\ \text{A}$$

$$I_2 = \frac{\begin{bmatrix} 8-j2 & 10\angle 30^\circ & 0 \\ -3 & 0 & -5 \\ 0 & 0 & 7-j2 \end{bmatrix}}{\begin{bmatrix} 8-j2 & -3 & 0 \\ -3 & 8+j5 & -5 \\ 0 & -5 & 7-j2 \end{bmatrix}} = 0.693\angle -2.2^\circ\ \text{A}$$

$$I_3 = \frac{\begin{bmatrix} 8-j2 & -3 & 10\angle 30^\circ \\ -3 & 8+j5 & 0 \\ 0 & -5 & 0 \end{bmatrix}}{\begin{bmatrix} 8-j2 & -3 & 0 \\ -3 & 8+j5 & -5 \\ 0 & -5 & 7-j2 \end{bmatrix}} = 0.476\angle 13.8^\circ\ \text{A}$$

4.6 || SUPERPOSITION THEOREM

The superposition theorem can be used to analyse an ac network containing more than one source. The theorem for ac sources states that in a network containing more than

University Question

1. State and illustrate superposition theorem. **[VTU, 2016]**

one voltage source or current source, the total current or voltage in any branch of the network is the phasor sum of currents or voltages produced in that branch by each source acting separately while all other sources have been replaced by their internal impedances. This theorem is valid only for linear networks.

Example 4.4

Find the current through the $3 + j4\ \Omega$ impedance (Figure 4.18).

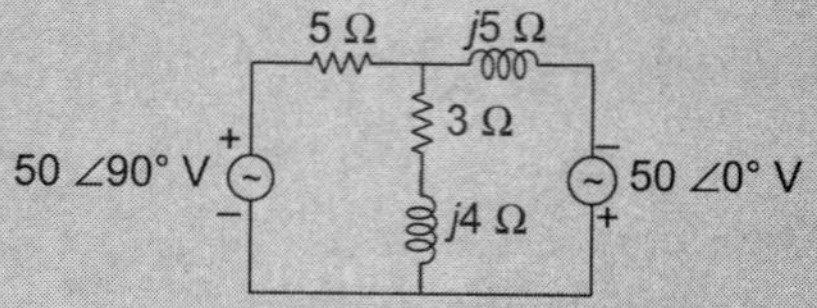

Figure 4.18

Solution **Step 1:** When the $50\angle 90°$V source is acting alone (Figure 4.19(a)).

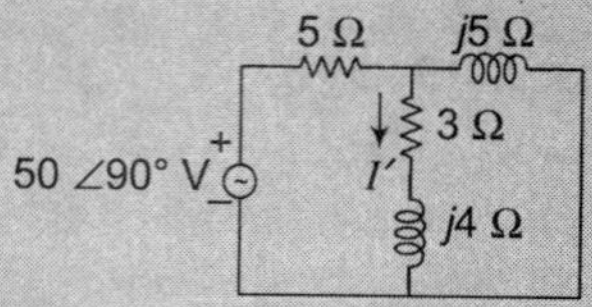

Figure 4.19(a)

$$Z_T = 5 + \frac{(3 + j4)j5}{3 + j9} = 5.83 + j2.5 = 6.35\angle 23.2°$$

$$I_T = \frac{50\angle 90}{6.35\angle 23.2} = 7.87\angle 66.8°\ \text{A}$$

$$I' = 7.87\angle 66.8°\left(\frac{j5}{3 + j9}\right) = 4.15\angle 85.3°\ \text{A}\downarrow$$

Step 2: When the $50\angle 0°$V source is acting alone (Figure 4.19(b)).

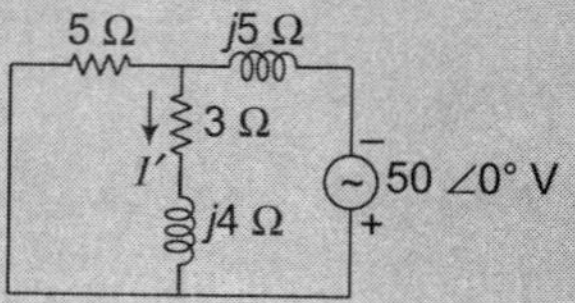

Figure 4.19 (b)

$$Z_T = j5 + \frac{(3 + j4)5}{8 + j4} = 2.5 + j6.25 = 6.74\angle 68.2°$$

$$I_T = \frac{50\angle 0}{6.74\angle 68.2} = 7.42\angle -68.2°\ \text{A}$$

$$I'' = 7.42\angle -68.2°\left(\frac{5}{8 + j4}\right) = 4.15\angle -94.77°\ \text{A}\uparrow = 4.15\angle 85.3°\downarrow$$

Step 3: By Superposition theorem

$$I = I' + I'' = 4.15\angle 85.3° + 4.15\angle 85.3° = 8.31\angle 85.3°\text{A}$$

Example 4.5

Determine the voltage across the $2 + j5\ \Omega$ impedance for the network shown in Figure 4.20.

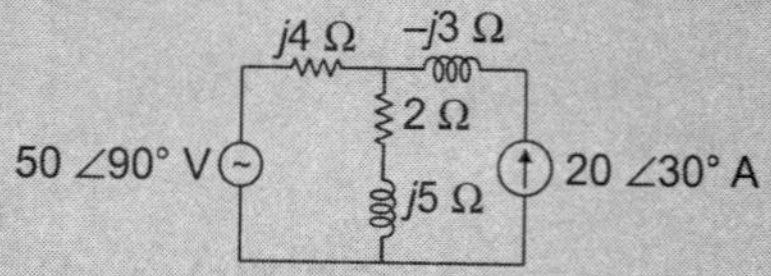

Figure 4.20

Solution **Step 1:** When the $50\angle 0°$V source is acting alone (Figure 4.21(a)).

$$I = \frac{50\angle 0°}{2 + j4 + j5} = \frac{50\angle 0°}{2 + j9} = \frac{50\angle 0°}{9.22\angle 77.47°}$$

$$= 5.42\angle -77.47°\ A$$

Voltage across $2 + j5\ \Omega$ $V' = 5.42\angle -77.47°(2 + j5) = 29.16\angle -9.28°$ V

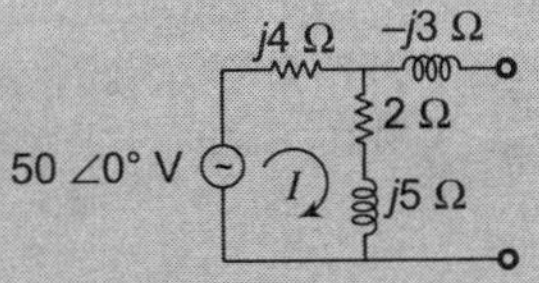

Figure 4.21 (a)

Step 2: When the $20\angle 30° V$ source is acting alone (Figure 4.21(b)

$$I = 20\angle 30°\left(\frac{j4}{2 + j9}\right) = \frac{20\angle 30° \times 4\angle 90°}{9.22\angle 77.47°} = 8.68\angle 42.53°\ \text{A}$$

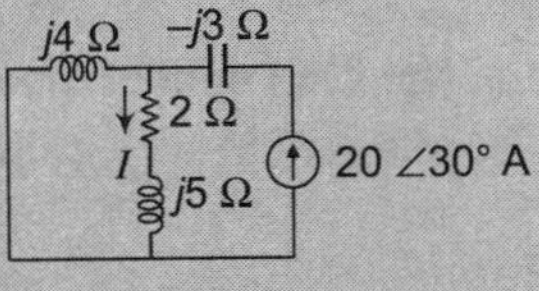

Figure 4.21 (b)

Voltage across $(2 + j5)\ \Omega$ impedance

$$V'' = (8.68\angle 42.53°)(2 + j5) = 46.69\angle 110.72°\ \text{V}$$

Step 3: By Superposition theorem

$$V = V' + V'' = 29.16\angle -9.28 + 46.69\angle 110.72$$

$$V = 28.78 - j4.7 - 16.52 + j43.67 = 12.26 + j38.97 = 40.85\angle 72.53°\ \text{V}$$

4.7 THEVENIN'S THEOREM

University Question

1. State and prove Thevenin's theorem. Show that Thevenin's equivalent circuit is the dual of Norton's equivalent circuit. **[VTU, 2009]**

According to Thevenin's theorem, any linear network connected to a load impedance Z_L may be replaced by a simple two terminal network consisting of a single voltage source V_{th} and single impedance Z_{eq} in series with the voltage source, across the load terminals. V_{th} is the open circuit voltage measured at the two terminals after removing Z_L and Z_{eq} is the equivalent impedance of the given network as viewed through the terminals where Z_L is connected, with all the sources replaced by their internal impedances. When the network is replaced by Thevenin's equivalent across the load terminals, then the load current can be obtained as

$$I = \frac{V_{th}}{Z_L + Z_{eq}}$$

Example 4.6

Obtain Thevenin's equivalent network for the terminals A and B as shown in Figure 4.22.

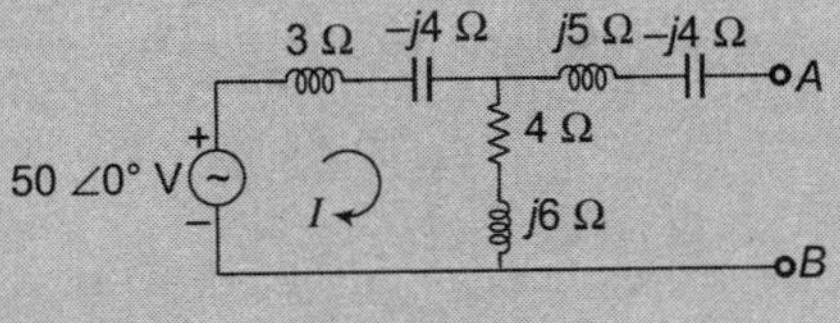

Figure 4.22

Solution **Step 1:** Calculation of V_{th}

Applying KVL to the mesh

$$50\angle 0° - (3 - j4)I - (4 + j6)I = 0$$

$$I = \frac{50\angle 0°}{(3 - j4) + (4 + j6)} = \frac{50\angle 0°}{7 + j2}$$

$$= \frac{50\angle 0°}{7.28\angle 15.95°} = 6.87\angle -15.95°\ \text{A}$$

$$V_{th} = (4 + j6)I = (4 + j6)6.87\angle -15.95° = (7.21\angle 56.3)6.87\angle -15.95° = 49.5\angle 40.35°\text{ V}$$

Step 2: Calculation of Z_{th} (Figure 4.23(a)).

$$Z_{th} = (j5 - j4) + \frac{(3 - j4)(4 + j6)}{(3 - j4) + (4 + j6)} = j1 + \frac{5\angle -53.13 \times 7.21\angle 56.3}{7.28\angle 15.95} = j1 + 4.95\angle -12.78$$

$$Z_{th} = j1 + 4.83 - j1.095 = 4.83 - j0.095 = 4.83\angle -1.13°\Omega$$

The Thevenin equivalent network is shown in Figure 4.23(b).

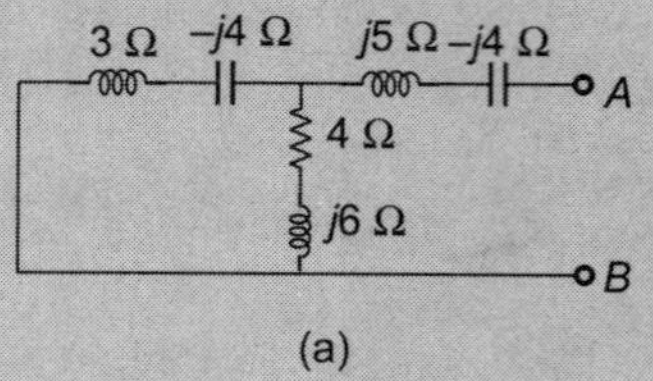

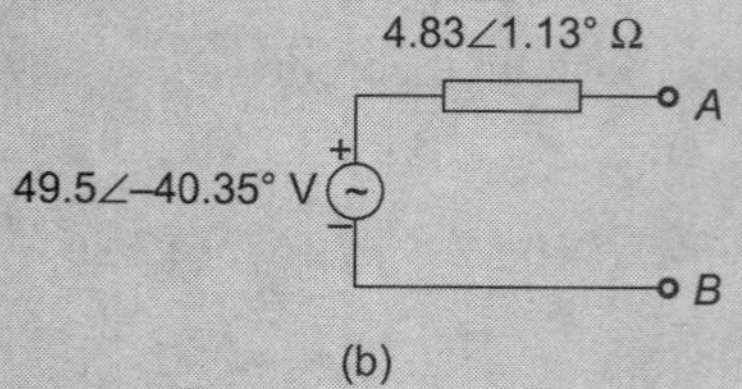

Figure 4.23

Example 4.7

Obtain Thevenin's equivalent network for the network shown in Figure 4.24.

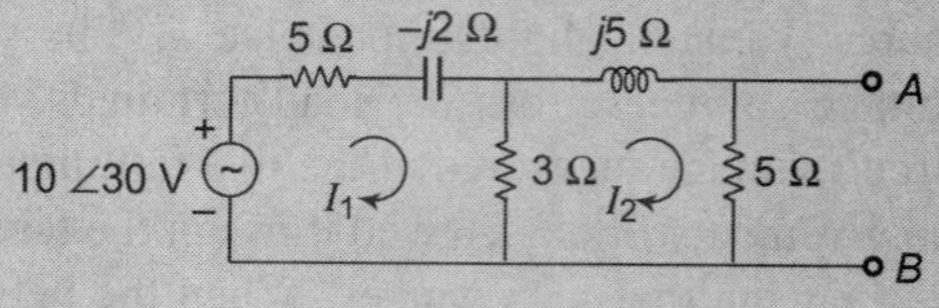

Figure 4.24

Solution **Step 1:** Calculation of V_{th}

Applying KVL to mesh 1

$$10\angle 30° - (5 - j2)I_1 - 3(I_1 - I_2) = 0$$

$$(8 - j2)I_1 - 3I_2 = 10\angle 30$$

Applying KVL to mesh 2

$$-3(I_2 - I_1) - j5I_2 - 5I_2 = 0$$

$$-3I_1 + (8 + j5)I_2 = 0$$

Solving equations by Cramer's rule

$$I_2 = \frac{\begin{vmatrix} 8 - j2 & 10\angle 30 \\ -3 & 0 \end{vmatrix}}{\begin{vmatrix} 8 - j2 & -3 \\ -3 & 8 + j5 \end{vmatrix}} = \frac{30\angle 30}{69.25\angle 20.3} = 0.433\angle 9.7°\text{ A}$$

$$V_{th} = V_{AB} = 5I_2 = 5(0.433\angle 9.7°) = 2.16\angle 9.7°\text{ V}$$

Step 2: Calculation of Z_{th} (Figure 4.25(a)).

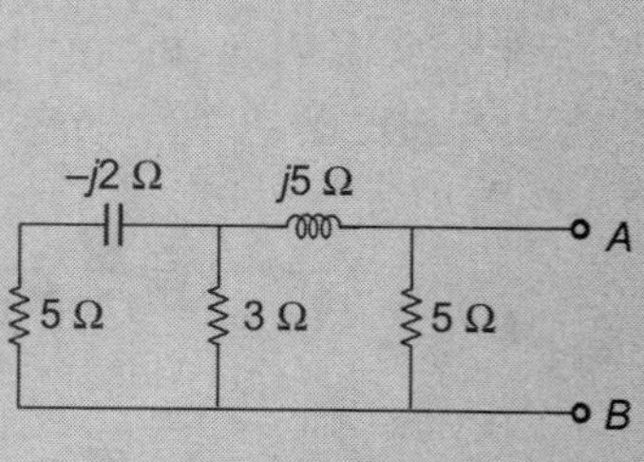

Figure 4.25 (a)

$$Z_{th} = \left[\left(\frac{(5 - j2)3}{5 - j2 + 3}\right) + j5\right] \| 5$$

$$= (1.94 - j0.265 + j5) \| 5 = (1.94 + j4.735) \| 5$$

$$Z_{th} = \frac{(1.94 + j4.735)5}{6.94 + j4.735} = 3.04\angle 33.4°\Omega$$

The Thevenin equivalent network is shown in Figure 4.25(b).

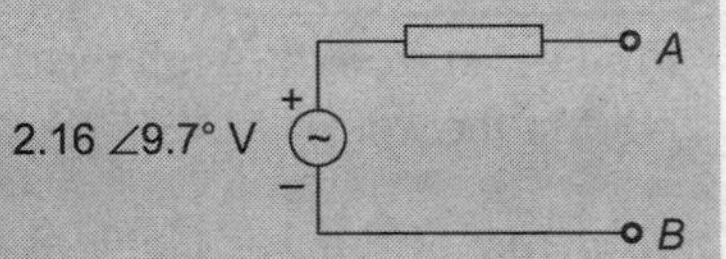

Figure 4.25 (b)

4.8 NORTON'S THEOREM

University Question

1. Draw the general form of Norton equivalent circuit. [AU, 2008]

According to Norton's theorem, any linear network connected to a load impedance Z_L may be replaced by a simple two terminal network consisting of a single current source I_N or I_{SC} and single impedance Z_{eq} in parallel with it, across the load terminals. I_N is the short circuit current measured at the two terminals after removing Z_L and Z_{eq} is the equivalent impedance of the given network as viewed through the terminals where Z_L is connected, with all the sources replaced by their internal impedances. When the network is replaced by Norton's equivalent across the load terminals, then the load current can be obtained as

$$I_L = I_N \frac{Z_{eq}}{Z_L + Z_{eq}}$$

Example 4.8

Obtain the Norton's equivalent network between the terminals A and B as shown in Figure 4.26.

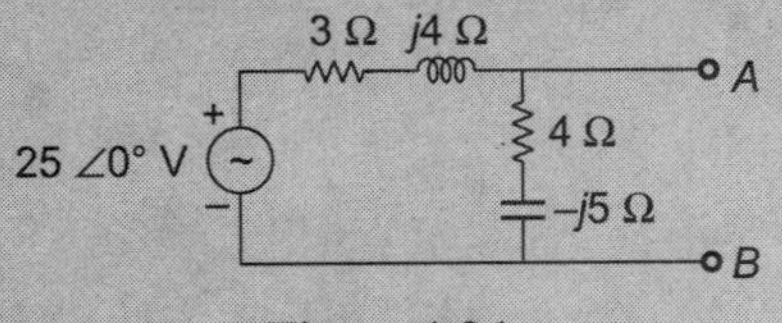

Figure 4.26

Solution **Step 1:** Calculation of I_{SC} (Figure 4.27(a))

$$I_{SC} = \frac{25\angle 0}{3 + j4} = \frac{25\angle 0}{5\angle 53.13°} = 5\angle -53.13° A$$

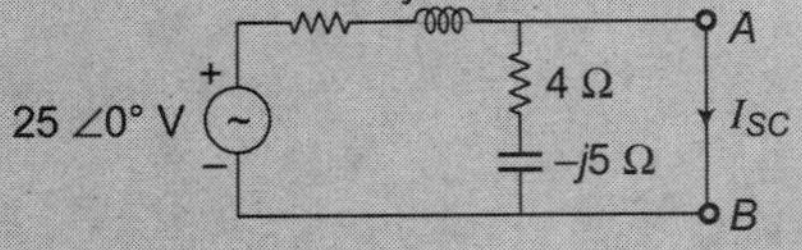

Figure 4.27 (a)

Step 2: Calculation of Z_{eq}

$$Z_{eq} = \frac{(3 + j4)(4 - j5)}{3 + j4 + 4 - j5} = \frac{5\angle 53.13° \times 6.4\angle -51.34}{7.07\angle -8.13} = 4.53\angle 9.92°\Omega$$

The Norton's equivalent network is shown in Figure 4.27(b).

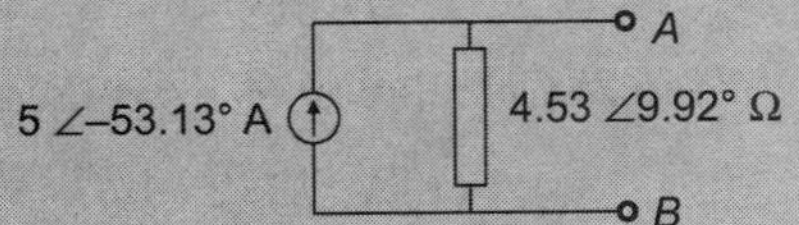

Figure 4.27 (b)

Example 4.9

Find the current through the $2 + j5\ \Omega$ impedance in the network shown in Figure 4.28 using Norton theorem.

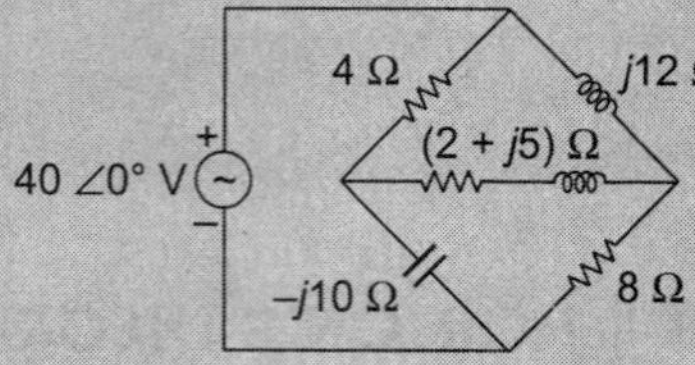

Figure 4.28

Solution **Step 1:** Calculation of I_N (Figure 4.29(a))

Writing the KVL equations for the three meshes

$$40\angle 0 - 4(I_1 - I_2) + j10(I_1 - I_3) = 0 \Rightarrow (4 - j10)I_1 - 4I_2 + j10I_3 = 40\angle 0$$

$$-4(I_2 - I_1) - j12I_2 = 0 \Rightarrow -4I_1 + (4 + j12)I_2 = 0$$

$$-8I_3 + j10(I_3 - I_1) = 0 \Rightarrow j10I_1 + (8 - j10)I_3 = 0$$

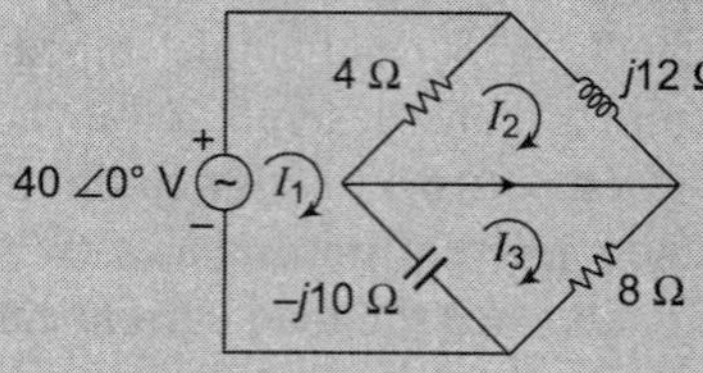

Figure 4.29(a)

Writing in matrix form

$$\begin{bmatrix} 4 - j10 & -4 & j10 \\ -4 & 4 + j12 & 0 \\ j10 & 0 & 8 - j10 \end{bmatrix} \begin{bmatrix} I_1 \\ I_2 \\ I_3 \end{bmatrix} = \begin{bmatrix} 40\angle 0 \\ 0 \\ 0 \end{bmatrix}$$

Using Cramer's Rule

$$I_2 = \frac{\begin{vmatrix} 4 - j10 & 40\angle 0 & j10 \\ -4 & 0 & 0 \\ j10 & 0 & 8 - j10 \end{vmatrix}}{\begin{vmatrix} 4 - j10 & -4 & j10 \\ -4 & 4 + j12 & 0 \\ j10 & 0 & 8 - j10 \end{vmatrix}} = \frac{1280 - j1600}{1440 + j64} = (0.8379 - j1.1483)\text{A}$$

$$I_3 = \frac{\begin{vmatrix} 4 - j10 & -4 & 40\angle 0 \\ -4 & 4 + j12 & 0 \\ j10 & 0 & 0 \end{vmatrix}}{\begin{vmatrix} 4 - j10 & -4 & j10 \\ -4 & 4 + j12 & 0 \\ j10 & 0 & 8 - j10 \end{vmatrix}} = \frac{4800 - j1600}{1440 + j64} = (3.2775 - j1.2568)\text{A}$$

$$I_N = I_3 - I_2 = 2.44\angle -2.55^\circ\ \text{A}$$

Step 2: Calculation of Z_{eq} (Figure 4.29(b))

$$Z_{eq} = [4 \parallel (-j10)] + [(j12) \parallel 8]$$

$$= (3.4483 - j1.3793) + (5.5385 + j3.6923)$$

$$= 8.9868 + j2.313\ \Omega$$

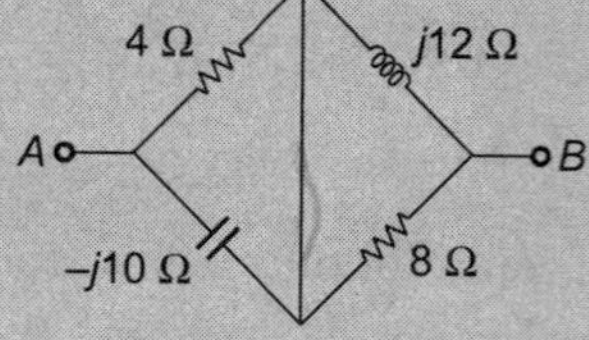

Figure 4.29 (b)

The Norton's equivalent network is shown in Figure 4.29(c).
Current through 2 + $j5$ impedance

$$= 2.44\angle{-2.55^\circ} \times \frac{8.9868 + j2.313}{8.9868 + j2.313 + 2 + j5}$$

$$= 1.72\angle{-21.8^\circ}\text{ A}$$

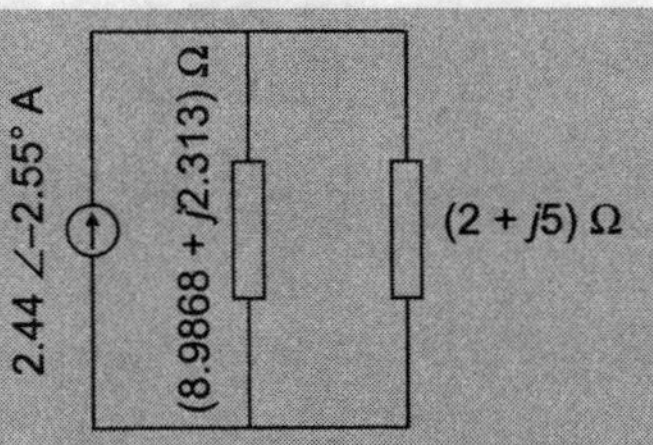

Figure 4.29 (c)

4.9 MAXIMUM POWER TRANSFER THEOREM

University Question

1. State and prove maximum power transfer theorem for AC circuits. **[VTU, 2016]**

The maximum power transfer theorem states that the maximum power is delivered from a source to the load when the load resistance is equal to the source resistance in case of resistive loads. In case of complex impedance networks, maximum power transfer to the load takes place when the load impedance is the complex conjugate of an equivalent impedance of the network as viewed from the terminals of the load. The resistance of load and resistance of Z_{eq} must be same while the reactances of load and Z_{eq} must also be same in magnitude but opposite in sign, So if Z_{eq} reactance is inductive, Z_L must be capacitive and vice versa (Figure 4.30).

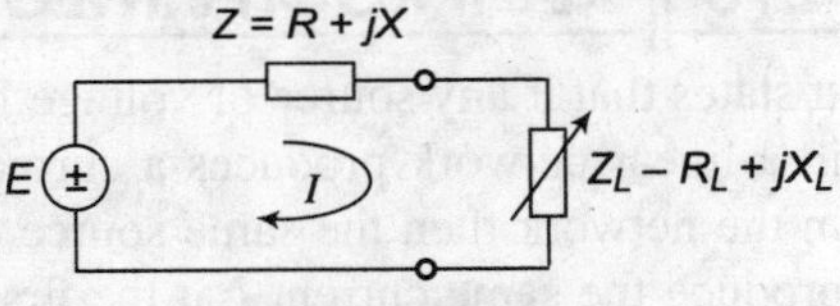

Figure 4.30

Example 4.10

Calculate the value of Z_L to be connected across terminals AB for maximum power transfer and also find power absorbed by Z_L for the circuit shown in Figure 4.31.

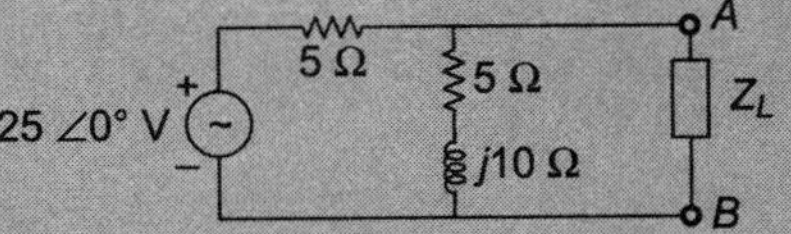

Figure 4.31

Solution **Step 1:** Calculation of Z_{eq} or Z_{th}

$$Z_{eq} = 5 \times \frac{(5 + j10)}{5 + 5 + j10} = \frac{5 + j10}{2 + j2}$$

$$= \frac{(5 + j10)(2 - j2)}{(2 + j2)(2 - j2)} = \frac{30 + j10}{8} = 3.75 + j1.25\ \Omega$$

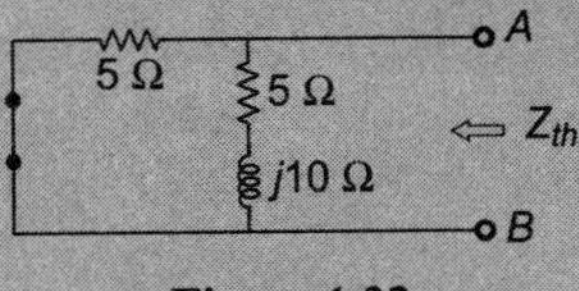

Figure 4.32

For maximum power transfer the load impedance is the complex conjugate of Z_{eq}

$$Z_L = 3.75 - j12.5\ \Omega$$

Step 2: Calculate the equivalent voltage across the terminals *AB*
Assuming current I in the mesh and writing KVL

$$25\angle 0 - 5I - 5I - j10I = 0 \Rightarrow I = \frac{25\angle 0}{10 + j10}\text{ A}$$

The equivalent voltage across the terminals is

$$V_{AB} = (5 + j10)I = 5 + j10 \times \frac{25\angle 0}{10 + j10} = \frac{125 + j250}{10 + j10} = \frac{279\angle 63.43°}{14.14\angle 45°} = 19.77\angle 18.43° \text{ V}$$

Step 3: Calculate the load current I_L in the equivalent circuit.

$$I_L = \frac{V_{AB}}{Z_{eq} + Z_L} = \frac{19.77\angle 18.43°}{3.75 + j1.25 + 3.75 - j12.5} = \frac{19.77\angle 18.43°}{7.5} = 2.636\angle 18.43$$

Step 4: Calculate the power absorbed

$$P_{max} = (I_L)^2 R_L = 2.636^2 \times 3.75 = 26.06 \text{ W}$$

4.10 RECIPROCITY THEOREM

University Question

1. What is reciprocity theorem? **[AU, 2014]**

It states that if any source of voltage V, located at one point in a linear network produces a current I at a second point in the network then the same source of voltage V acting at the second point of the same network will produce the same current I at the first point. In other words the ratio of the excitation to the response remains same even if their positions are interchanged.

Example 4.11

Verify Reciprocity theorem for the network given in Figure 4.33.

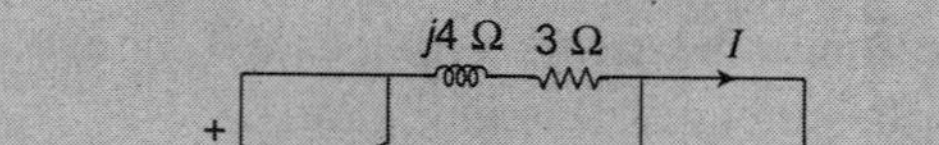

Figure 4.33

Solution **Step 1:** Find the current I and the ratio V/I

Writing KVL equations for the three meshes

$$100\angle 0 - 5(I_1 - I_2) = 0 \Rightarrow I_1 - I_2 = 20\angle 0$$

$$-j4I_2 - 3I_2 + j5(I_2 - I_3) - 5(I_2 - I_1) = 0 \Rightarrow 5I_1 - (8 - j1)I_2 - j5I_3 = 0$$

$$-10I_3 + j5(I_3 - I_2) = 0 \Rightarrow -j5I_2 + (-10 + j5)I_3 = 0$$

Writing in matrix form

$$\begin{bmatrix} 1 & -1 & 0 \\ 5 & -8 + j & -j5 \\ 0 & -j5 & -10 + j5 \end{bmatrix} \begin{bmatrix} I_1 \\ I_2 \\ I_3 \end{bmatrix} = \begin{bmatrix} 20\angle 0 \\ 0 \\ 0 \end{bmatrix}$$

Using Cramer's Rule

$$I_3 = I = \frac{\begin{vmatrix} 1 & -1 & 20\angle 0 \\ 5 & -8+j & 0 \\ 0 & -j5 & 0 \end{vmatrix}}{\begin{vmatrix} 1 & -1 & 0 \\ 5 & -8+j & -j5 \\ 0 & -j5 & -10+j5 \end{vmatrix}} = \frac{500\angle 90}{55.901\angle -26.65} = 8.9443\angle -63.44°\text{A}$$

$$\frac{V}{I} = \frac{100\angle 0}{8.9443\angle -63.44} = 11.1803\angle 63.43°$$

Step 2: Interchange the positions of V and I and calculate V/I (Figure 4.34)

$$Z_T = \frac{(3+j4)\times(-j5)}{(3+j4)+(-j5)} + 10$$

$$= \frac{5\angle 53.13 \times 55\angle -90}{3.1622\angle -18.434} + 10$$

$$= 7.5 - j2.5 + 10 = 17.5 - j2.5\Omega$$

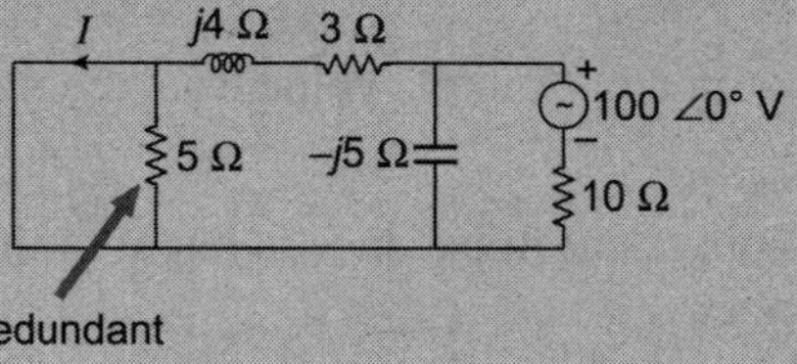

Figure 4.34

$$I_T = \frac{100\angle 0}{17.5 - j2.5} = \frac{100\angle 0}{17.677\angle -8.13} = 5.6568\angle 8.13°\text{ A}$$

Using current division

$$I = I_T \times \frac{-j5}{j4+3-j5} = 8.944\angle -63.43°\text{ A}$$

$$\frac{V}{I} = \frac{100\angle 0}{8.944\angle -63.44} = 11.1803\angle 63.43°$$

The ratio V/I are same in both cases. Hence reciprocity theorem is verified.

4.11 || MILLMAN'S THEOREM

University Question

1. State and explain Millman's theorem. **[GTU, 2011]**

Using this theorem, number of parallel voltage sources can be replaced by a single equivalent voltage source.

Theorem Statement

Arrangement of voltage sources ($V_1, V_2 ..., V_n$) with internal/series impedances ($Z_1, Z_2 ..., Z_n$) respectively, connected in parallel, can be replaced by an equivalent voltage source (V) with an equivalent series impedance (Z) (Figure 4.35).

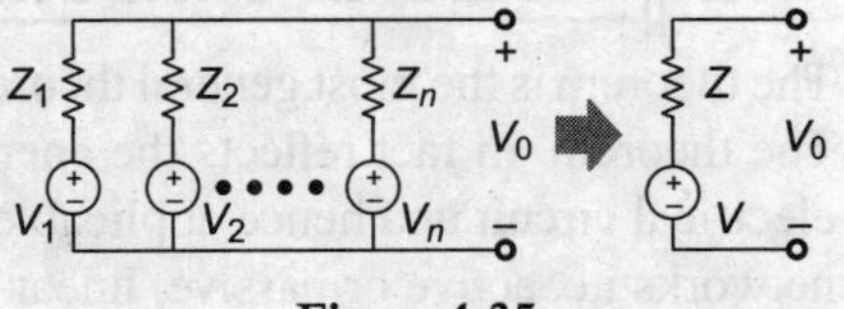

Figure 4.35

$$V = \sum (V_k Y_k) / Y_k \; Z = \sum \frac{1}{Y_k}$$

Explanation: If all the voltage sources are converted into current sources then,

$$I_1 = \frac{V_1}{Z_1}; I_2 = \frac{V_2}{Z_2} \cdots I_n = \frac{V_n}{Z_n}$$

Since all current sources are in parallel, equivalent current source

$$I = I_1 + I_2 + \cdots I_n = \frac{V_1}{Z_1} + \frac{V_2}{Z_2} + \cdots \frac{V_n}{Z_n}$$

And since all resistances are in parallel, equivalent resistance, $= \frac{1}{Y} = \sum \frac{1}{Y_k}$. If this current source is converted back into a voltage source then, $V = I \times R = \left(\frac{V_1}{Z_1} + \frac{V_2}{Z_2} + \cdots \frac{V_n}{Z_n} \right) x \left(\sum \frac{1}{Y_k} \right)$ and $R = \sum \frac{1}{Y_k}$.

Equivalent impedance is equal to the net impedance taken all series impedances ($Z_1, Z_2 ..., Z_n$) in parallel.

Example 4.12

Obtain the equivalent of a parallel connection of three branches each with a voltage source and a series resistance (2 V, 1Ω); (3 V, 2 Ω); (5 V, 2 Ω) as shown in Figure 4.36. **[GTU, 2011]**

Solution Given $V_1 = 2$ V, $V_2 = 3$ V, $V_3 = 5$ V and $R_1 = 1\ \Omega \Rightarrow G_1 = 1/R_1 = 1\text{S}$, $R_2 = 2\ \Omega \Rightarrow G_2 = 1/R_2 = 0.5\text{S}$, $R_3 = 2\ \Omega \Rightarrow G_3 = 1/R_3 = 0.5\text{S}$

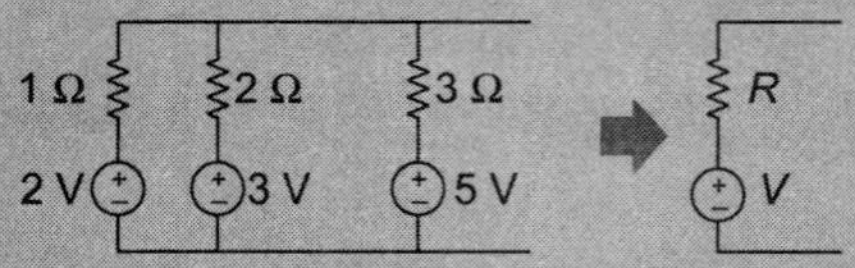

Figure 4.36

Step 1: Find equivalent voltage-

$$V = \frac{V_1 G_1 + V_2 G_2 + V_3 G_3}{G_1 + G_2 + G_3} = \frac{2 \times 1 + 3 \times 0.5 + 5 \times 0.5}{1 + 0.5 + 0.5} \Rightarrow V = 3 \text{ Volt}.$$

Step 2: Find equivalent resistance:

$$G_{eq} = G_1 + G_2 + G_3 = 1 + 0.5 + 0.5 = 2\text{S}, \; R_{eq} = \frac{1}{G_{eq}} = \frac{1}{2} = 0.5\ \Omega$$

4.12 TELLEGAN'S THEOREM

The theorem is the most general theorem for circuit analysis. The theorem, in fact reflects the energy conservation in an electrical circuit and hence applicable to all kind of electric networks i.e. active or passive, linear or non-linear.

University Questions

1. Explain Tellegan's theorem. **[DU, 2011]**
2. Draw the variation of circuit parameters with frequency in a series resonance circuit. **[AU, 2011]**

Statement: For any instant of time, algebraic sum of power delivered to each branch is zero.

$$\sum P_k = \sum (V_k I_k) = 0$$

Example 4.13

For Verify Tellegen's theorem for the network shown in Figure 4.37. **[PTU, 2011-12]**

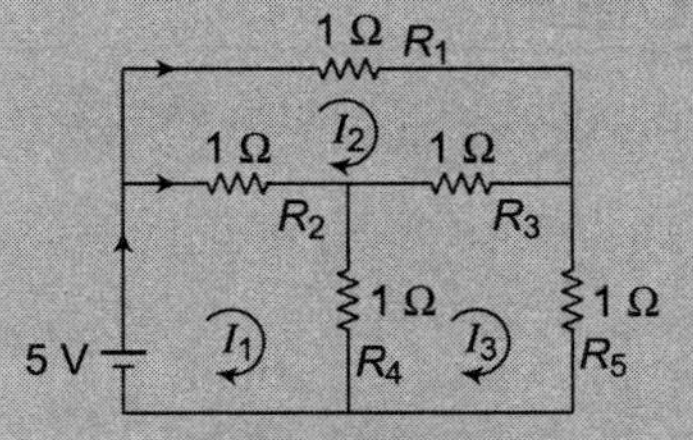

Figure 4.37

Solution Step 1 to 3: Find currents though each resistor by finding their current by applying KVL in each loop.

Step 1: By KVL to Loop 1:

$$5-(I_1-I_2)-(I_1-I_3)=0 \qquad P_1=6.25$$
$$5-I_1+I_2-I_1+I_3=0 \qquad P_2=6.25$$
$$5-2I_1+I_2+I_3=0 \qquad P_3=0$$
$$2I_1-I_2-I_3=5 \quad (4.1) \qquad P_4=6.25$$

Step 2: By KVL to Loop 3: $\qquad P_5=6.25$

$$(I_3-I_2)+I_3-(I_1-I_3)=0 \qquad P=25$$
$$I_2-I_3+I_3-I_1+I_3=0 \qquad P=5\times I_1$$
$$-I_2-I_1+2I_3=0 \quad (4.2) \qquad P=25$$

Step 3: By KVL to Loop 2:

$$I_2+(I_2-I_3)+(I_2-I_1)=0$$
$$I_2+I_3-I_2-I_2+I_1=0$$
$$I_3-I_2+I_1=0 \quad (4.3)$$

By Eqs (4.1), (4.2), (4.3), we get

$$2I_1-I_2-I_3=5 \qquad I_1=5$$
$$-I_1+3I_2-I_3=0 \qquad I_2=2.5$$
$$-I_1-I_2+3I_3=0 \qquad I_3=2.5$$

Step 4: Find Power delivered by the source: $P = V_1 \times I_1 = 5 \times I_1 = 25$

Step 5: Total power dissipated by resistors:

$$= P_1+P_2+P_3+P_4+P_5$$

$$= I_2^2R_1 + (V_1 - V_2)^2R_2 + (I_2 - I_3)^2R_3 + (I_1 - I_3)^2R_4 + (I_3)^2R_5$$

$$= 6.25 + 6.25 + 0 + 6.25 + 6.25 = 25$$

Tellegen's theorem is verified.

4.13 SUBSTITUTION THEOREM

With the help of this theorem, any element in a branch can be replaced with another one leaving the circuit parameters un-affected.

Statement

The voltage across any branch or the current through that branch of a network being known, the branch can be replaced by the combination of various elements that will make the same voltage and current through that branch.

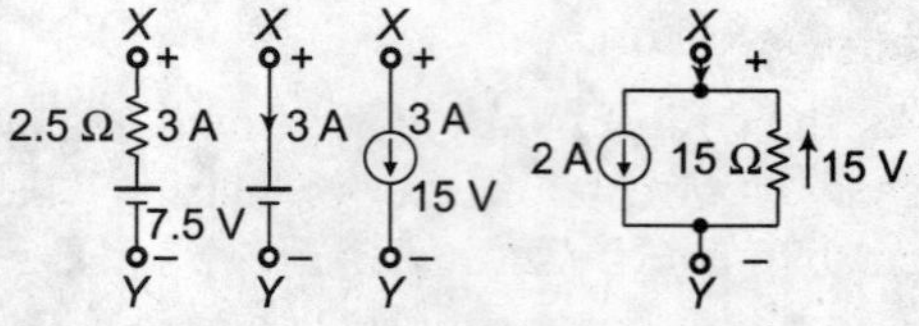

Figure 4.38

Explanation

A branch with 2.5 Ω resistance and 7.5 V voltage source can be replaced with 3 other branches. For each of these 3 combinations, voltage drop between X and Y is 15 V and current from X to Y is 3 A. Hence circuit does not get affected if any of these 4 is replaced by other one

Example 4.14

In the circuit shown in Figure 4.39, if the 40 Ω resistance is replaced by a voltage source V, find the value of V.

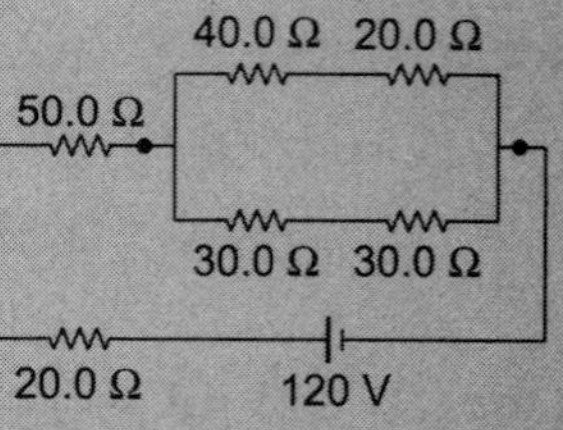

Figure 4.39

Solution 40 Ω resistance can be replaced by a voltage source whose voltage is equal to the voltage drop across the 40 Ω resistance.

Find voltage across 40 Ω resistance:

Circuit resistance, $R = 20 + 50 + (40 + 20)||(30 + 30) = 70 + 30 = 100\ \Omega$

Circuit current, $I = V/R = 120/100 = 1.2$ A

Since this current gets divided in 2 branches, current through 40 Ohm resistance,

By applying current division: $I' = 1.2\,(40 + 20)/((30 + 30) + (30 + 30)) = 1.2/2 = 0.6$ A

Voltage drop across 40 Ohm $= 0.6 \times 40 = 2.4$ V

Hence 40 Ohm resistance can be replaced by a voltage source of value 2.4 volt. V = 2.4 Volt (Figure 4.40).

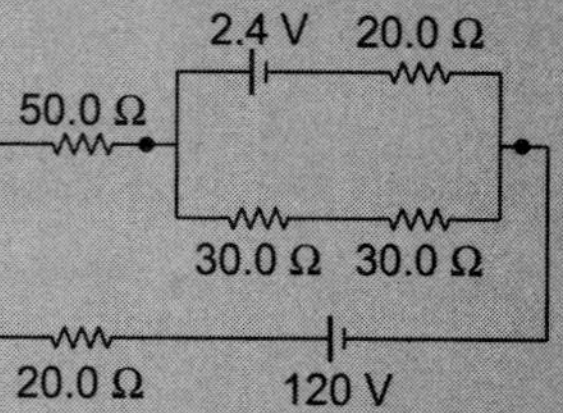

Figure 4.40

4.14 || COMPENSATION THEOREM

Change in resistance in one branch will affect the currents of other branches too. The theorem relates the change in current of one branch with the other one due to variation in resistance of that branch.

Statement

In a linear time invariant network when the resistance (R) of an uncoupled branch, carrying a current (I), is changed by (ΔR). The currents in all the branches would change and can be obtained by assuming that an ideal voltage source of (V_C) has been connected such that $V_C = I(\Delta R)$ in series with ($R + \Delta R$) when all other sources in the network are replaced by their internal resistances.

Explanation

As shown in Figure 4.41, a small change in R, ΔR will change currents of other branches of the network. This can be found by setting all active sources of the circuit to zero and by connecting a voltage source of $\Delta V = I\Delta R$ and a resistance ΔR in series with R, where I is the current through R before change.

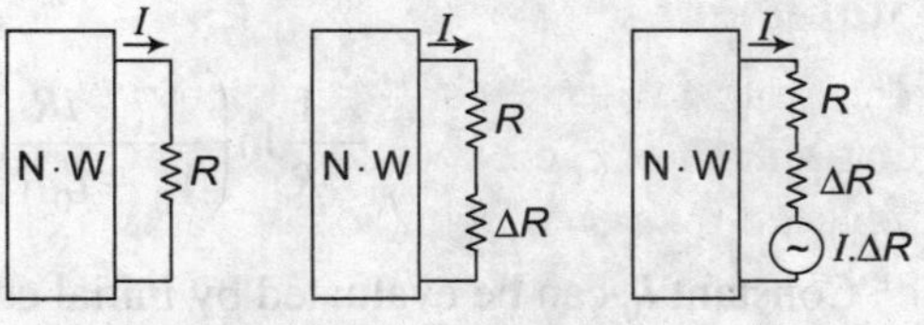

Figure 4.41

Example 4.15

In Figure 4.42, if the 1 ohm resistance is changed to 1.2 ohms then determine the source voltage for compensating for the change. **[GTU, 2014]** ○●●

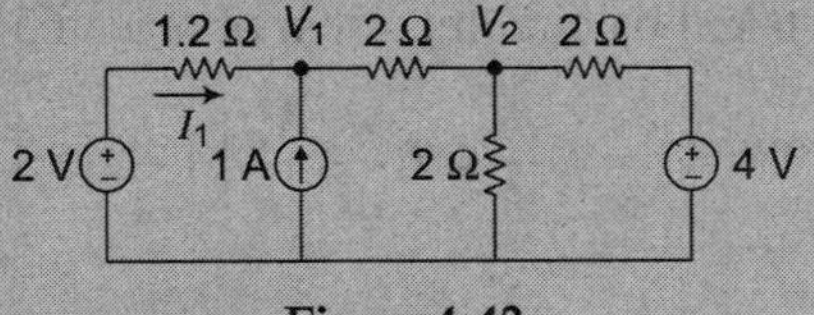

Figure 4.42

Solution Since I_1 should not change,

$$I_1 = -3/4 \text{ A}$$

$$\frac{V_1 - V}{1.2} = \frac{3}{4}$$

$$\Rightarrow \quad V = 1.85 \text{ V}$$

Change in voltage, $\Delta V = 2 - 1.85 = 0.15$ V. Therefore, source voltage must be reduced by 0.15 V.

4.15 || DC-TRANSIENT OF RL, RC, RLC CIRCUIT

University Question

1. Obtain the response $V_C(t)$ and $I_L(t)$ for the source free RC and RL circuits respectively. Assume initial voltage V_0 and initial current I_0 respectively. **[GTU, 2010]**

4.15.1 DC-transient of RL Circuit

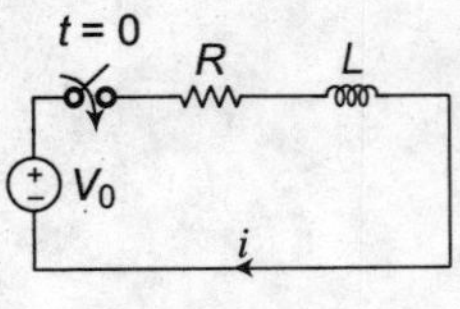

Figure 4.43

Charging

A voltage source of V_0 volt is connected in series with an inductor of L henry and resistance R ohm as shown in Figure 4.43. At time, $t = 0$, switch S is closed. Now circuit current (i) and voltage across each resistor (V_R) and inductor (V_L) is to be evaluated.

Applying KVL in the circuit,

$$V_0 = V_L + V_R \tag{4.4}$$

Since, $V_L = L\dfrac{di}{dt}$ and $V_R = iR$, Eq. (4.4) becomes,

$$V_0 = L\frac{di}{dt} + iR \Rightarrow \frac{di}{V_0 - iR} = \frac{dt}{L} \tag{4.5}$$

Integrating the equation both sides,

$$\int_{I_0}^{i} \frac{di}{V_0 - iR} = -\int_0^t \frac{dt}{L}$$

$$-\frac{1}{R}\ln\left(\frac{V_0 - iR}{V_0 - I_0R}\right) = \frac{t}{L} \Rightarrow i = \frac{V_0}{R}\left(1 - e^{-\frac{t}{L/R}}\right) + I_0 e^{-\frac{t}{L/R}} \tag{4.6}$$

Constant I_0 can be evaluated by initial condition,

Since $i = 0$ for $t < 0$, and inductor current cannot be instantly changed, I_0 for an initially relaxed inductor is zero. Substituting value of $I_0 = 0$ in Eq. (4.6).

$$i = \frac{V_0}{R}\left(1 - e^{-\frac{t}{L/R}}\right) \Rightarrow i = \frac{V_0}{R}(1 - e^{-\frac{t}{\tau}})$$

Here, L/R is called time constant of an RL (Unit- second) circuit and denoted as τ. It is defined as time taken by circuit current of reach 63% $(1 - 1/e)$ of its final value.

Now, $V_L = L\dfrac{di}{dt} = L\dfrac{d}{dt}\left[\dfrac{V_0}{R}\left(1 - e^{-\frac{t}{\tau}}\right)\right]$

$\Rightarrow \quad V_L = V_0 e^{-\frac{t}{\tau}}$ and $V_R = iR = V_0(1 - e^{-\frac{t}{\tau}})$

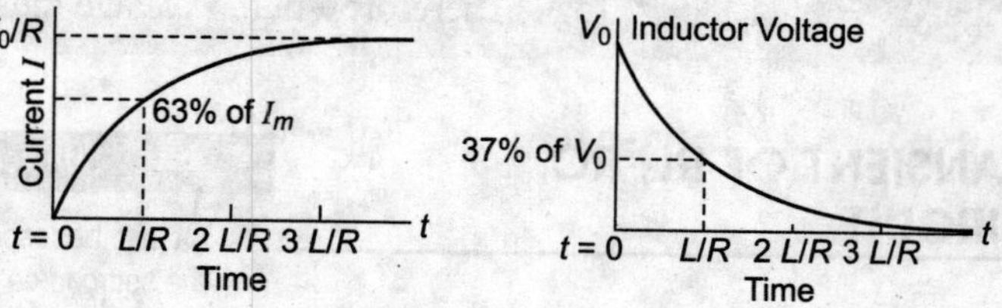

Figure 4.44

Discharging

Now, if voltage source is replaced with a short circuit shunt, Eq. (4.4) becomes

$$L\frac{di}{dt} + iR = 0 \Rightarrow \int_{I_0}^{i} \frac{di}{i} = -\int_0^t \frac{R}{L}dt \Rightarrow i = I_0 e^{-\frac{t}{L/R}} = I_0 e^{-\frac{t}{\tau}}$$

$$V_L = L\frac{di}{dt} = L\,(RI_0 / L)e^{-\frac{t}{\tau}} = RI_0 e^{-\frac{t}{\tau}} \quad \text{and} \quad V_R = iR = RI_0 e^{-\frac{t}{\tau}}$$

4.15.2 DC-transient of RC Circuit

Charging

A voltage source of V_0 volt is connected in series with a capacitor of C farad and resistance R ohm as shown in Figure 4.45. At time, $t = 0$, switch S is closed. Now circuit current (i) and voltage across each resistor (V_R) and capacitor (V_C) is to be evaluated.

Applying KVL in the circuit,

$$V_0 = V_C + V_R \tag{4.7}$$

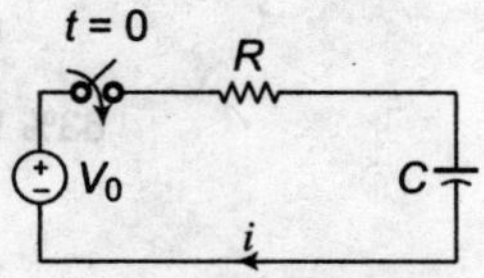

Figure 4.45

Since,

$$V_C = \frac{1}{C}\int i dt \quad \text{and} \quad V_R = iR$$

Equation (4.7) becomes, $V_0 = \frac{1}{C}\int i dt + iR$ (4.8)

Differentiating the equation both sides,

$$0 = \frac{i}{C} + R\frac{di}{dt}$$

$$\int_{I_0}^{i} \frac{di}{i} = -\int_{0}^{t} \frac{dt}{RC}$$

$$\ln\left(\frac{i}{I_0}\right) = -\frac{t}{RC} \Rightarrow i = I_0 e^{-\frac{t}{RC}} \tag{4.9}$$

Constant I_0 can be evaluated by initial condition,

Since $i = 0$ for $t < 0$, at $t = 0$, $\frac{1}{C}\int i dt = 0$ or $V_C\,(t = 0) = 0$. (This can also be understood as: Since capacitor is initially discharged, capacitor voltage (V_C) at $t = 0$ is zero)

Substituting initial conditions in Eq. (4.7)

$$V_0 = V_C + V_R \Rightarrow V_0 = 0 + V_R \Rightarrow V_0 = 0 + I_0 R$$

So,

$$I_0 = \frac{V_0}{R} \tag{4.10}$$

Substituting value of I_0 in Eq. (4.9),

$$i = \frac{V_0}{R} e^{-\frac{t}{RC}} \Rightarrow i = \frac{V_0}{R} e^{-\frac{t}{\tau}}$$

Here, RC is called time constant of an RC (Unit- second) circuit and denoted as τ. It is defined as time taken by capacitor voltage to reach its 63% $(1 - 1/e)$ of final value.

$$\Rightarrow \quad \text{Now, } V_C = \frac{1}{C}\int idt = \frac{1}{C}\int \frac{V_0}{R} e^{-\frac{t}{RC}} dt$$

$$\Rightarrow \quad V_C = V_0\left(1 - e^{-\frac{t}{\tau}}\right) \text{ and } V_R = iR = V_0 e^{-\frac{t}{\tau}}$$

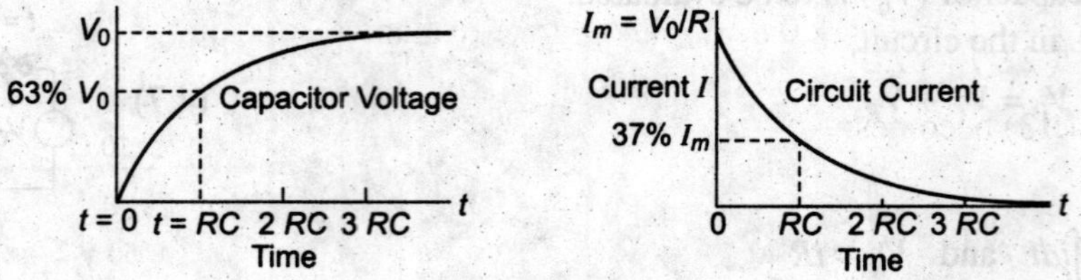

Figure 4.46

Discharging

Now, if voltage source is replaced with a short circuit shunt,

$$\text{Current } \frac{1}{C}\int idt + iR = 0 \Rightarrow \int_{I_0}^{i}\frac{di}{i} = -\int_0^t \frac{dt}{RC} \Rightarrow \ln\left(\frac{i}{I_0}\right) = -\frac{t}{RC} \Rightarrow i = I_0 e^{-\frac{t}{RC}} = I_0 e^{-\frac{t}{\tau}}$$

$$\text{Resitor Voltage: } V_R = iR = V_0 e^{-\frac{t}{\tau}}; \text{ Capacitor Voltage: } V_C = V_R = V_0 e^{-\frac{t}{\tau}}$$

4.15.3 DC-transient of RLC Circuit

Now, if both inductor and capacitor are connected in series with a resistance and a voltage source of V_0 as shown in Figure 4.47 and the circuit is switched on by closing S at time, $t = 0$. Let us see, how circuit current (i), voltage across each resistor (V_R), capacitor (V_C) and inductor (V_L) are going to vary.

Applying KVL in the circuit,

$$V_0 = V_L = V_C + V_R \tag{4.11}$$

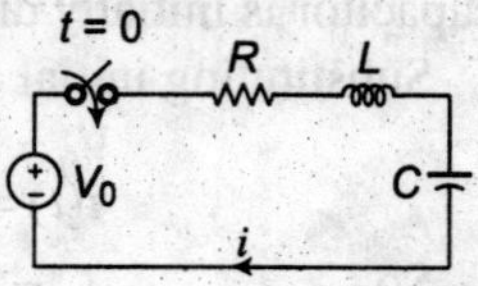

Figure 4.47

$$\text{Since, } V_C = \frac{1}{C}\int idt, \; V_R = iR \text{ and } V_L = L\frac{di}{dt}$$

Equation (4.11) becomes,

$$V_0 = L\frac{di}{dt} + \frac{1}{C}\int idt + iR \tag{4.12}$$

Differentiating the equation both sides,

$$0 = L\frac{d^2i}{dt^2} + R\frac{di}{dt} + \frac{i}{C} \Rightarrow LC\frac{d^2i}{dt^2} + RC\frac{di}{dt} + i = 0$$

It is a second order homogeneous differential equation and when solved for *i (t);mm*

$$i(t) = Ae^{m_1 t} + Be^{m_2 t} \tag{4.13}$$

where, $m_1 = -\dfrac{R}{2L} + \sqrt{\left(\dfrac{R}{2L}\right)^2 - \dfrac{1}{LC}}$ and $m_2 = -\dfrac{R}{2L} - \sqrt{\left(\dfrac{R}{2L}\right)^2 - \dfrac{1}{LC}}$

Values of m_1 and m_2 may be real or imaginary depending upon value of $\sqrt{\left(\dfrac{R}{2L}\right)^2 - \dfrac{1}{LC}}$.

Case 1: When $\left(\dfrac{R}{2L}\right)^2 - \dfrac{1}{LC} > 0$ *i.e.* m_1 and m_2 are real and distinct.

Solution Eq. (4.13) becomes:

$$i(t) = e^{-\frac{R}{2L}t}\left(Ae^{\left(\sqrt{\left(\frac{R}{2L}\right)^2 - \frac{1}{LC}}\right)t} + Be^{\left(\sqrt{\left(\frac{R}{2L}\right)^2 - \frac{1}{LC}}\right)t}\right)$$

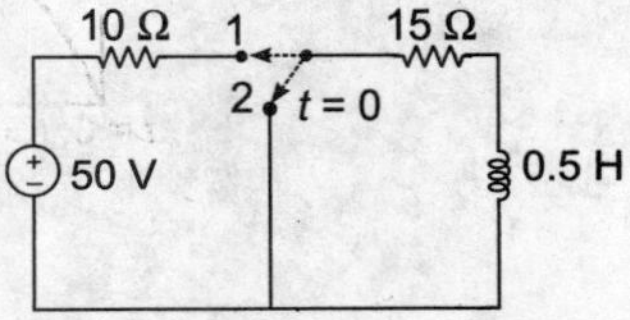

Figure 4.48

The response is shown in Figure 4.48.
Response is overamped.

Case 2: When $\left(\dfrac{R}{2L}\right)^2 - \dfrac{1}{LC} = 0$ *i.e.* m_1 and m_2 are real and distinct.

Solution Eq. (4.13) becomes:

$$i(t) = Ae^{-\frac{R}{2L}t} + Bte^{-\frac{R}{2L}t}$$

The response is critically damped.

Case 3: When $\left(\dfrac{R}{2L}\right)^2 - \dfrac{1}{LC} < 0$ *i.e.* m_1 and m_2 are imaginary and conjugate.

Solution Eq. (4.13) becomes:

$$i(t) = e^{-\frac{R}{2L}t}\left(Ae^{\left(\sqrt{\left(\frac{R}{2L}\right)^2 - \frac{1}{LC}}\right)t} + Be^{\left(\sqrt{\left(\frac{R}{2L}\right)^2 - \frac{1}{LC}}\right)t}\right)$$

Here, the solution posses two patterns in the response

- Exponential decreasing
- Periodic because of complex power of *e*

Expansion of the solution further with using Euler identity results:

$$i(t) = e^{-\frac{R}{2L}t}\left((A+B)\cos\left(\left(\sqrt{\left(\frac{R}{2L}\right)^2 - \frac{1}{LC}}\right)t\right) + j(A-B)\cos\left(\left(\sqrt{\left(\frac{R}{2L}\right)^2 - \frac{1}{LC}}\right)t\right)\right)$$

$$i(t) = e^{-\alpha}t((A+B)\cos(\omega t) + j\,(A-B)\cos(\omega t))$$

Response is periodic with frequency equal to ω rad/s enveloped by $e^{-\frac{R}{2L}t}$.
Response is under damped response is shown in Figure 4.49

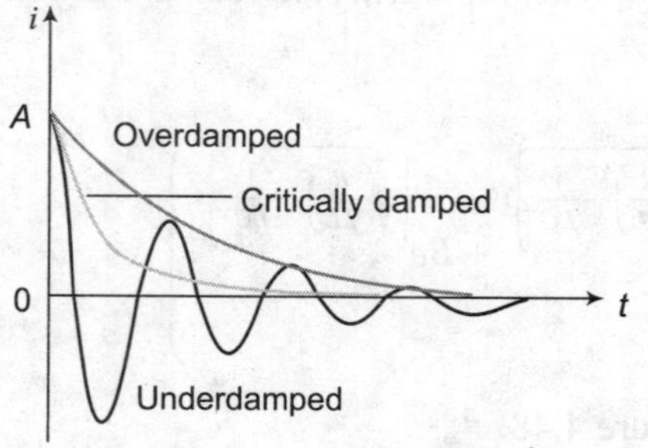

Figure 4.49

Example 4.16

For the circuit shown in Figure 4.50, the switch 'S' is at position '1' and the steady-state condition is reached. The switch is moved to a position '2' at $t = 0$. Find the current $i(t)$ in both the cases, i.e., with the switch at positions 1 and 2. **[AU, 2011]** ○●●

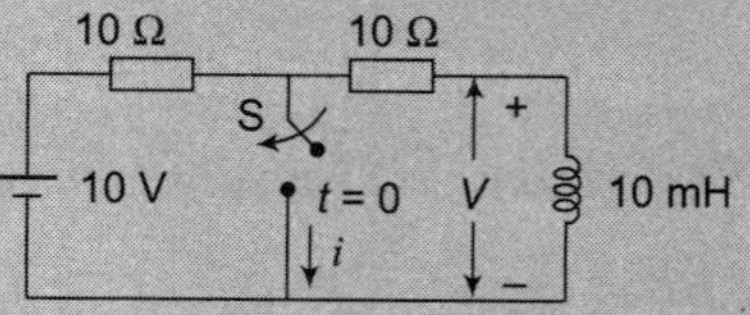

Figure 4.50

Solution **Case 1:** When the switch is in the position 1 and steady state is not reached, $50 = 0.5\frac{di}{dt} + 25i = Ce^{-50t} + 2$

Current i passes through the inductor and must be zero at $t = 0$.

$\Rightarrow \quad C = -2$ at $t = 0 \quad \therefore\; i = -2e^{-50t} + 2 = 2(1 - e^{-50t})$ A

Case 2: When the switch is in the position 1, steady state is reached [inductor acts as short-circuit].

$-50 + 25i = 0$ (steady-state) $\Rightarrow i = 2$A

Case 3: When the switch is moved to the position 2,

$$0 = 0.5\frac{di}{dt} + 15i \Rightarrow i = Ce^{-30t}$$

At $t = 0$, $\quad i(0) = i(0^-) = 2$A (Case 1)

$= i = C = 2$ at $t = 0$

$\therefore \quad i = 2e^{-30t}$A

Example 4.17

For the network shown in Figure 4.51, the switch k is closed at $t = 0$, with the capacitor uncharged. Find the values of i, $\frac{d^2i}{dt^2}$, $\frac{di}{dt}$ at $t = 0+$. **[PU, 2012]** ○●●

Solution When the switch is closed; KVL in the loop

$V_0 = \frac{1}{C}\int idt + i.$

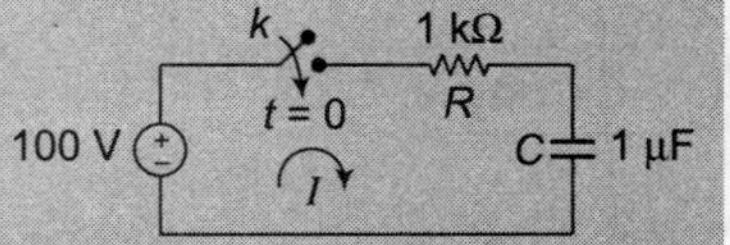

Figure 4.51

Differentiating the equation both sides,

$$0 = \frac{i}{C} + R\frac{di}{dt} \Rightarrow \int_{I_0}^{i}\frac{di}{i} = -\int_{0}^{t}\frac{dt}{RC} \Rightarrow \ln\left(\frac{i}{I_0}\right) = -\frac{t}{RC} \Rightarrow i = I_0 e^{-\frac{t}{RC}}$$

At $t = 0$, $i = V/R = 100/1000 = 0.1$ A

$$\text{so,}\quad i = I_0 e^{-\frac{t}{RC}} \Rightarrow i = 0.1 e^{-\frac{t}{0.001}}$$

$$\text{Now,}\quad \frac{di}{dt} = \frac{d}{dt}\left(I_0 e^{-\frac{t}{RC}}\right) = -\frac{I_0}{RC}e^{-\frac{t}{RC}};$$

$$\left(\frac{di}{dt}\right)_{t=0} = -\frac{I_0}{RC}e^0 = -\frac{I_0}{RC} = -\frac{0.1}{1000\times 10^{-6}} = -100 \text{ A/s}.$$

$$\text{Similarly,}\quad \frac{d^2i}{dt^2} = \frac{d}{dt}\left(-\frac{I_0}{RC}e^{-\frac{t}{RC}}\right) = \frac{I_0}{(RC)^2}e^{-\frac{t}{RC}};$$

$$\left(\frac{d^2i}{dt^2}\right)_{t=0} = \frac{I_0}{(RC)^2}e^0 = \frac{0.1}{10^6\times 10^{-12}} = 10^5 \text{ A/s}^2$$

Example 4.18

Solve for i and V as functions of time in the circuit shown in Figure 4.52, when the switch is closed at time $t = 0$. **[AU, 2012]** ○●●

Solution **Step 1:** Find I_0: For $t < 0$; switch S is open and circuit was in steady state. Since at steady state inductor acts as short-circuit with DC current. So circuit current at $t < 0$; $i = 10/(10 + 10) = 0.5$ A;

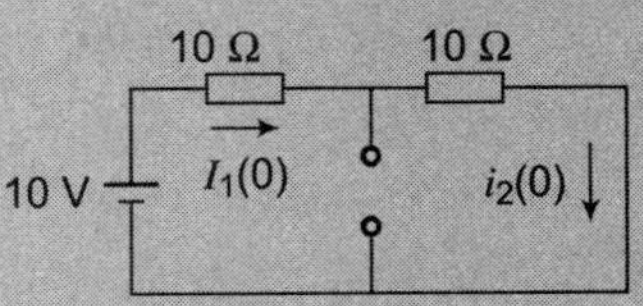

Figure 4.52

Step 2: Switch is closed at $t = 0$, so $I_0 = i(t < 0) = 0.5\ A$

Applying KVL in loop-2 after S is closed; Inductor –Resistor Pair (10 Ohm and 10 mH) is short circuited.

$$0 = (10\times 10^{-3})\frac{di}{dt} + 10i \Rightarrow i = I_0 e^{-\frac{10}{10\times 10^{-3}}t} = i = 0.5e^{-1000t}$$

V is the voltage across inductor, $V = L\dfrac{di}{dt} = 10 \times 10^{-3}\dfrac{d}{dt}(0.5e^{-1000t}) = -5e^{-1000t}$ Volt

Example 4.19

The circuit shown in Figure 4.53 consists of resistance, inductance, and capacitance in series with 100 V dc, when the switch is closed at $t = 0$. Find the current transient. ●●●

[AU, 2013; BPUT, 2008]

Solution **Step 1:** *Apply KVL and find the current expression:*

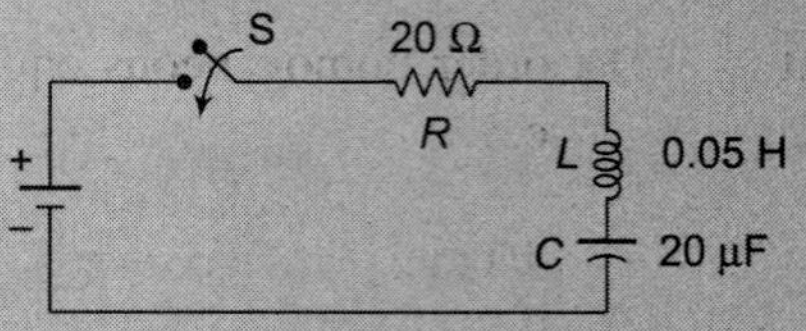

Figure 4.53

At $t = 0$, Applying KVL,

$$100 = 0.5\frac{di}{dt} + \frac{1}{20 \times 10^{-6}}\int i dt + 20i$$

Differentiating both sides of equation-

$$\frac{d^2i}{dt^2} + 400\frac{di}{dt} + 10^6 i = 0$$

$$\therefore \quad (D^2 + 400\,D + 10^6)i = 0$$

$$D_1, D_2 = -200 \pm j979.8$$

Therefore, the current,

$$i = e^{+K1} + [C_1 \cos K_2 t + C_2 \sin K_2 t] = e^{-200t}[C_1 \cos 979.8t + C_2 \sin 979.8t] \text{ A}$$

Step 2: Apply initial condition and find value of constants in solution.

At $t = 0$, the current flowing through the circuit is zero.

$$i = 0 = (1)\,[C_1 \cos 0 + C_2 \sin 0];\ C_1 = 0 \quad \therefore \quad i = e^{-200t} C_2 \sin 979.8\,t \text{ A}$$

Differentiating, we have

$$di/dt = C_2\,[e^{-200t}\,979.8 \cos 979.8t + e^{-200t}\,(-200) \sin 979.8t]\,dt$$

At $t = 0$, the voltage across the inductor is 100 V; $L\dfrac{di}{dt} = 100$

$$L\frac{di}{dt} = 100 \Rightarrow \frac{di}{dt} = 2000$$

$C_2\,979.8 \cos 0 = 2000;\ C_2 = 2000/979.8 = 2.04$

The current equation is: $i = e^{-200t}[2.04 \sin 979.8t]$ A

4.15.4 Sinusoidal Response of RC

A resistance (R) and a capacitor (C) are excited by a sinusoidal voltage source at $t = 0$ as shown in Figure 4.54. To determine the circuit current,

We apply KVL in the circuit of single loop:

$$V_S = V_C + V_R \tag{4.14}$$

Since, $V_C = \frac{1}{C}\int i\,dt,\ V_R = iR$ and $V_s = V_m\ \sin(\omega t + \alpha)$

Equation (4.14) becomes, $\frac{1}{C}\int i\,dt + iR = V_m\ \sin(\omega t + \alpha)$.

It is a first order homogeneous equation whose response is given as sum of natural response and forced response.

I. Natural/Transient response: $\frac{1}{C}\int i\,dt + iR = 0 \Rightarrow i = Xe^{-\frac{t}{RC}}$ (4.15)

II. Forced/Steady state response:

$$\frac{1}{C}\int i\,dt + iR = V_m\ \sin(\omega t + \alpha) \Rightarrow RC\frac{di}{dt} + i = \omega C\ V_m\ \sin(\omega t + \alpha) \tag{4.16}$$

$$i = Y\sin(\omega t + \alpha) + Z\cos(\omega t + \alpha) \tag{4.17}$$

$$\frac{di}{dt} = Y\omega\cos(\omega t + \alpha) - Z\,\omega\sin(\omega t + \alpha)$$

Similar analysis to the RL circuit yields,

$$i = \frac{V_0}{\sqrt{\left[R^2 + \left(\frac{1}{\omega C}\right)^2\right]}}\sin(\omega t + \alpha + \phi),\ \text{where}\ \phi = \tan^{-1}\left(\frac{1}{R\omega C}\right)$$

Complete solution will be the sum of these two currents,

$$i = Xe^{-\frac{t}{RC}} + \frac{V_0}{\sqrt{\left[R^2 + \left(\frac{1}{\omega C}\right)^2\right]}}\sin(\omega t + \alpha + \phi)$$

To find X, we apply initial condition, at $t = 0$, $I = 0$.

$$i(0) = Xe^0 + \frac{V_0}{\sqrt{\left[R^2 + \left(\frac{1}{\omega C}\right)^2\right]}}\sin(0 + \alpha + \phi) = 0;\ X = \frac{V_0}{\sqrt{\left[R^2 + \left(\frac{1}{\omega C}\right)^2\right]}}\sin(\alpha - \phi)$$

$$i = \left[\frac{V_0}{\sqrt{\left\{R^2 + \left(\frac{1}{\omega C}\right)^2\right\}}}\sin(\alpha - \phi)e^{-\frac{t}{RC}t}\right] + \left[\frac{V_0}{\sqrt{\left\{R^2 + \left(\frac{1}{\omega C}\right)^2\right\}}}\sin(\omega t + \alpha + \phi)\right]$$

Transient response — Steady-state response

4.15.5 Sinusoidal Response of RLC

For a series RLC circuit with sinusoidal voltage source, KVL equation will be

$$V_0 \sin(\omega t + \alpha) = L\frac{di}{dt} + \frac{1}{C}\int idt + iR$$

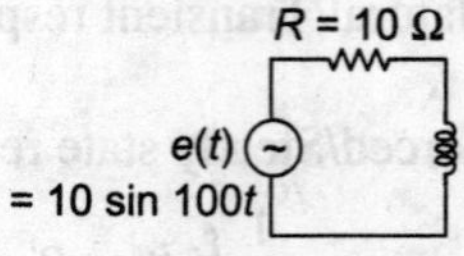

Figure 4.54

Differentiating the equation both sides,

$$V_0\omega \cos(\omega t + \alpha) = L\frac{d^2i}{dt^2} + R\frac{di}{dt} + \frac{i}{C}$$

$$\Rightarrow \qquad LC\frac{d^2i}{dt^2} + RC\frac{di}{dt} + i = V_0\omega\cos(\omega t + \alpha)$$

I. Its Transient response (Complementary Function) is found by equating source voltage to zero,

or $LC\frac{d^2i}{dt^2} + RC\frac{di}{dt} + i = 0$, Solution as per Eq. (4.12) and (4.13) is: $i(t) = Ae^{m_1 t} + Be^{m_2 t}$

II. Now, find its steady state response, *i.e.* find its particular solution

$$LC\frac{d^2i}{dt^2} + RC\frac{di}{dt} + i = V_0\omega\cos(\omega t + \alpha) \tag{4.18}$$

Assuming $i = E\sin(\omega t + \alpha) + D\cos(\omega t + \alpha)$

$$\frac{di}{dt} = E\omega\cos(\omega t + \alpha) - D\,\omega\sin(\omega t + \alpha) \text{ and}$$

$$\frac{d^2i}{dt^2} = -E\omega^2\sin(\omega t + \alpha) - D\,\omega^2\cos(\omega t + \alpha)$$

Substituting these values in Eq. (4.18) and finding out values of E, D results: (As done previously for RL circuit)

$$i = \frac{V_0}{\sqrt{\left(R^2 + \left(\omega L - \frac{1}{\omega C}\right)^2\right)}}\sin(\omega t + \alpha - \phi), \text{ where } \phi = \tan^{-1}\left(\frac{R}{\left(\omega L - \frac{1}{\omega C}\right)}\right) = \tan^{-1}\left(\frac{R}{X}\right)$$

$$i = \frac{V_0}{Z}\sin(\omega t + \alpha - \phi), \text{ where } \phi = \tan^{-1}\left(\frac{R}{X}\right)$$

Now, depending upon values of m_1 and m_2 in C.F. (Transient response); response can be classified in three categories (This is similar to the RLC response with a DC source discussed earlier)

Case I: When $\left(\frac{R}{2L}\right)^2 - \frac{1}{LC} > 0$ i.e. m_1 and m_2 are real and distinct. (*Response is underdamped*)

$$i(t) = e^{-\frac{R}{2L}t}\left(Ae^{\left(\sqrt{\left(\frac{R}{2L}\right)^2 - \frac{1}{LC}}\right)t} + Be^{\left(\sqrt{\left(\frac{R}{2L}\right)^2 - \frac{1}{LC}}\right)t}\right) + i = \frac{V_0}{Z}\sin(\omega t + \alpha - \phi), \text{ where} \phi = \tan^{-1}\left(\frac{R}{X}\right)$$

Case II: When $\left(\frac{R}{2L}\right)^2 = \frac{1}{LC}$ i.e. m_1 and m_2 equal. (*Response is critically damped*)

$$i(t) = Ae^{-\frac{R}{2L}t} + Bte^{-\frac{R}{2L}t} + \frac{V_0}{Z}\sin(\omega t + \alpha - \phi), \text{ where} \phi = \tan^{-1}\left(\frac{R}{X}\right)$$

Case III: When $\left(\frac{R}{2L}\right)^2 - \frac{1}{LC} < 0$ i.e. m_1 and m_2 are imaginary conjugates. (*Response is underdamped*)

$$i(t) = e^{-\alpha}t((A+B)\cos(\omega t) + j(A-B)\cos(\omega t)) + \frac{V_0}{Z}\sin(\omega t + \alpha - \phi), \text{ where } \phi = \tan^{-1}\left(\frac{R}{X}\right)$$

Example 4.20

Obtain the current at $t > 0$, if ac voltage V is applied when the switch k is moved to 2 from 1 at $t = 0$. Assume a steady-state current of 1A in LR circuit when switch was at position 1 (Figure 4.55). **[RTU, 2011]** ○●●

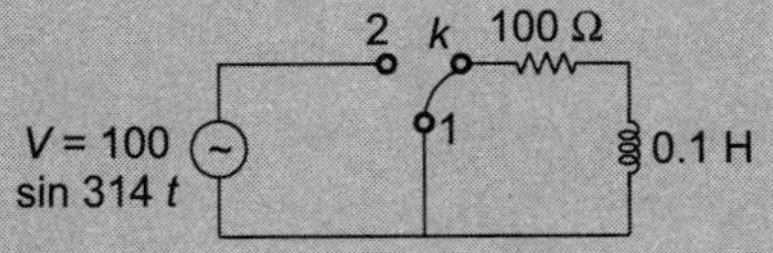

Figure 4.55

Solution At the position 1 of the switch k, the steady-state current in the circuit is 1 A, i.e., $I(0^-) = 1$ A. If the switch is moved to the position 2 at $t = 0$, the ac voltage appears

$$\therefore \quad i(0^-) = i(0^+) = 1 \text{ A}, Z = R + jX_L = 100 + j2\pi \times 50 \times 0.1 = 104.8 \angle 17.47°$$

Step 1: Apply KVL in the loop:

$$0.1\frac{di}{dt} + 100i = 100 \sin 314\, t;$$

Step 2: Find transient and steady state solutions:

Solution of the equations will be: Transient response: $ic = ce^{-1000t}$ Steady state response:

$$ip = \frac{V}{Z} = \frac{100}{104.8}\sin(314t - 17.47°)$$

$$\therefore \quad i = ic + ip = ce^{-1000t} + 0.954\sin(314t - 0.304)$$

Step 3: Apply initial condition and find exact current:

But $i(0^+) = 1\text{A}$ $\quad \therefore\ 1 = c + 0.945\sin(-0.304) = c - 0.28 \Rightarrow c = 1 + 0.28 = 1.28$

$$\therefore \quad i = 1.28e^{-1000t} + 0.945\sin(314t - 0.304)$$

Example 4.21

An RC series circuit is excited by a sinusoidal source $e(t) = 1000\sin 100t$ volts, by closing the switch at $t = 0$. Take $R = 10\ \Omega$ and $C = 10\ \mu\text{F}$. Determine the current $i(t)$ flowing through the RC circuit.

○●●

Solution Given: $R = 10$ Ohm, $C = 10\ \mu\text{F}$ and $\omega = 100$ rad/s. $V_0 = 1000$ V

Step 1: KVL Equation in the loop:

$$\frac{1}{C}\int i\,dt + iR = V_m\sin(\omega t + \alpha)$$

I. Natural/Transient response: $\frac{1}{C}\int i\,dt + iR = 0 \Rightarrow i_{tr} = Xe^{-\frac{t}{RC}} = Xe^{-\frac{t}{10\times 10\times 10^{-6}}} = Xe^{-10^4 t}$

II. Forced/Steady state response: $\frac{1}{C}\int i\,dt + iR = V_m\sin(\omega t) \Rightarrow RC\frac{di}{dt} + i = \omega C\,V_m\sin(\omega t)$

Step 2: Find steady state and transient response:

$$i_{ss} = \frac{V_0}{\sqrt{\left(R^2 + \left(\frac{1}{\omega C}\right)^2\right)}}\sin(\omega t + \phi),\ \text{where}\ \phi = \tan^{-1}\left(\frac{1}{R\omega C}\right)$$

$$i_{ss} = \frac{1000}{\sqrt{\left(10^2 + \left(\frac{1}{100\times 10\times 10^{-6}}\right)^2\right)}}\sin\left(100t + \tan^{-1}\left(\frac{1}{10\times 100\times 10\times 10^{-6}}\right)\right) = 1\sin(100t + 1.56)$$

$$i = i_{ss} + i_{tr}$$

Step 3: Apply initial condition to find outvalue of X in X *in* i_{tr}:

Since $i(t = 0) = 0$; $i(0) = i_{ss}(0) + i_{tr}(0) = 0$

$$Xe^{-10^4 t} + 1\sin(100(0) + 1.56) = 0 \Rightarrow X = 1\sin(1.56) = 1A$$

$$i = 1\ e^{-10^4 t} + 1\sin(100t + 1.56)\ \text{A}$$

Example 4.22

In the network shown in Figure 4.56, the switch K is closed at $t = 0$ with zero capacitor voltage and zero inductor current. Solve for (a) v_1 and v_2 at $t = 0$, (b) v_1 and v_2 at $t = \infty$, and (c) $\frac{dV_1}{dt}$ and $\frac{dV_2}{dt}$ at $t = 0$. **[JNTU, 2012]** ○●●

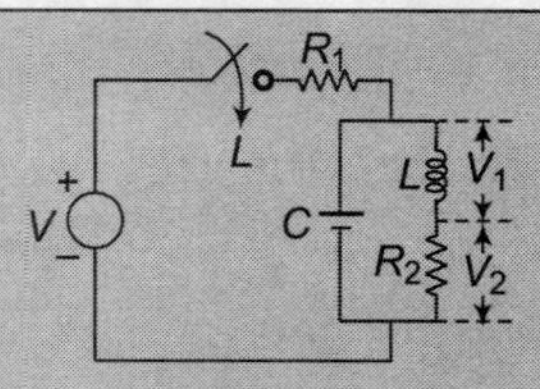

Figure 4.56

Solution Before the switch is closed, no current flows through the circuit so

$V_1 = 0$ and $V_2 = 0$

When the switch is closed, and $t = 0^+$, the circuit will be as follows.

L = open circuit C = short circuit

So, $V_1 = V_2 = 0$ V at $t = 0^+$

(i) At $t = 0$ (Figure 4.57 (a))

$V_1 = 0$; $V_2 = 0$

At $t = 0+$ $V_1 = 0$; $V_2 = 0$

$$\text{So } \frac{dV_1}{dt} = 0, \quad \frac{dV_2}{dt} = 0 \text{ at } t = 0_+$$

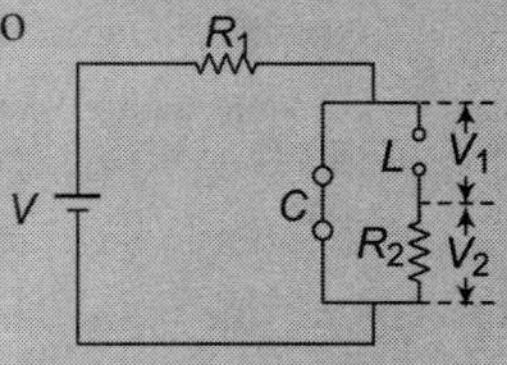

Figure 4.57 (a)

(ii) At $t = \infty$, there is nothing but steady state. Circuit will be

C = open circuit L = short circuit (Figure 4.57 (b))

So, $V_1 = 0$ V; $V_2 = (R_2V)/(R_1 + R_2)$

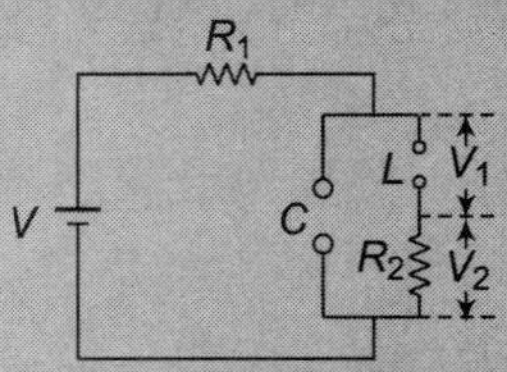

Figure 4.57 (b)

Example 4.23

An RL series circuit is excited by a sinusoidal source $e(t) = 10 \sin 100t$ volts, by closing the switch at $t = 0$. Take $R = 10\ \Omega$ and $L = 0.1$ H. Determine the current $i(t)$ flowing through the RL circuit. **[AU, 2014]** ○●●

Solution

$$I(s) = \frac{10(100/S^2 + 100^2)}{0.15 + 10} = \frac{(100)10}{(S^2 + 100^2)(0.15 + 10)} = \frac{100^2}{(S^2 + 100^2)(S + 100)}$$

By partial fractions.

$$I(s)=\frac{100^2}{(S^2+100^2)(S+100)}=\frac{-\frac{1}{2}S+50}{S^2+100^2}+\frac{\frac{1}{2}}{S+100}$$

$$I(s)=+\frac{1}{2}\frac{-5}{S^2+100^2}+\frac{50}{S^2+100^2}+\frac{1}{2}\frac{1}{S+100}$$

$$I(t)=\frac{1}{2}-\cos 100t+\frac{1}{2}\sin 100t+\frac{1}{2}e^{-100t}$$

POINTS TO REMEMBER

- The resultant of two or more quantities varying sinusoidally at the same frequency is another sinusoidal quantity of same frequency.
- j is defined as an operator which turns a phasor by 90° counter-clockwise without changing the magnitude of phasor and $j^2=-1$.
- Peak factor of the sine wave is 1.414
- For the sine wave, the form factor is 1.11
- In parallel circuits the phase angles must be considered in calculations.
- The voltage current relationship is given by $V=I\sqrt{R^2+(\omega L)^2}$ in a series RL circuit.
- The voltage current relationship is given by $V=I\sqrt{R^2+\left(\frac{1}{\omega C}\right)^2}$ in a series RC circuit.
- The voltage current relationship is given by $V=I\sqrt{R^2+\left(\omega L-\frac{1}{\omega C}\right)^2}$ in a series RLC circuit.
- The total current is the phasor summation of all the branch currents in a parallel circuit.
- An inductor acts as a short circuit to DC voltage or current at steady state.
- A capacitor acts as an open circuit to DC voltage or current at steady state.
- A capacitive reactance refers to a negative reactance while an inductive reactance refers to a positive reactance.
- While solving complex numbers multiplication and division are done in polar form while addition and subtraction are done in rectangular form.
- The power indicated by the product of the applied voltage and the total current is known as apparent power S and measured in volt-ampere.
- Power that is returned to the source by the reactive components in the circuit is called reactive power Q and is measured in VAR.
- Power that actually used in the circuit (dissipated in resistance) is true or active power P and is measured in watts or kW.

- Active (Real) Power = Voltage magnitude × Current magnitude × cos θ

  $$S = \sqrt{P^2 + Q^2}$$

- The power factor of an alternating-current device or circuit or electric power system is defined as the ratio of real or true power to the apparent power (VA) and is between 0 to 1.
- In a single-phase circuit the power factor is also a measure of the phase angle - between the phase voltage (V_{ph}) and phase current (I_{ph})
- Mesh analysis is based on KVL whereas nodal analysis is based on KCL.
- These methods are not useful for complex networks with too many unknown variables.
- Superposition theorem is not applicable to networks containing only dependent sources.
- Superposition theorem is not applicable for calculation of power.
- Superposition theorem is not applicable to networks containing unilateral and non-linear elements.
- Thevenin theorem is not applicable for networks containing unilateral, non-linear elements.
- Thevenin theorem is not applicable for networks containing magnetic coupling between the load and any other circuit element.
- If internal impedances of sources are not given then voltage sources are replaced by short circuit and current sources by open circuit for calculating Thevenin equivalent impedance.
- Norton's theorem is the dual of Thevenin's theorem.
- The Thevenin equivalent voltage source can be transformed into an equivalent current source and vice versa.

  $$I_N = \frac{V_{TH}}{Z_{TH}}.$$

- The Norton equivalent impedance is the same as Thevenin equivalent impedance.
- Maximum power will be transferred from a network to load if the load impedance is the complex conjugate of the Thevenin equivalent impedance of the network.
- When any network delivers maximum power to the load, then corresponding efficiency of the network will be 50%.
- The condition for maximum power to the load is not same as the condition for maximum power delivered by the source.
- Reciprocity theorem allows interchange of position of excitation and response in a network.
- Reciprocity theorem is not applicable for networks containing multiple energy sources.
- Reciprocity theorem is not applicable for networks containing dependent sources.

PRACTICE PROBLEMS

1. A circuit having a resistance of 20 Ω and inductance of 0.07 H is connected in parallel with a series combination of 50 Ω resistance and 60 μF capacitance. Calculate the total current, when the parallel combination is connected across 230V, 50Hz supply. ○○●

2. Two coils of 5 Ω and 10 Ω and inductances 0.04 H and 0.05 H respectively are connecting in parallel across a 200 V, 50 Hz supply. Calculate: (i) Conductance, susceptance and admittance of each coil. (ii) Total current drawn by the circuit and its power factor. (iii) Power absorbed by the circuit. ●●●

3. In the network shown determine V_a and V_b. ○●●

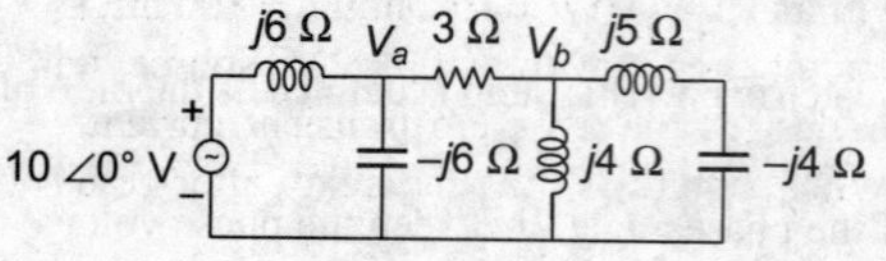

Figure 4.58

4. Find the current I in the network. ●●●

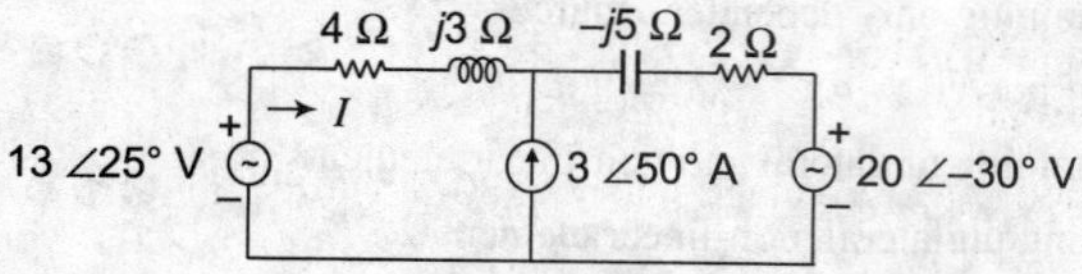

Figure 4.59

5. Obtain Thevenin's equivalent network for the shown network. ○●●

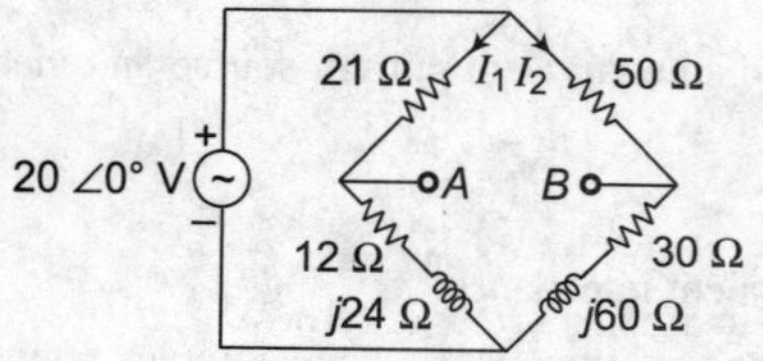

Figure 4.60

6. Determine the load current I_L by using Norton's theorem. ○●●

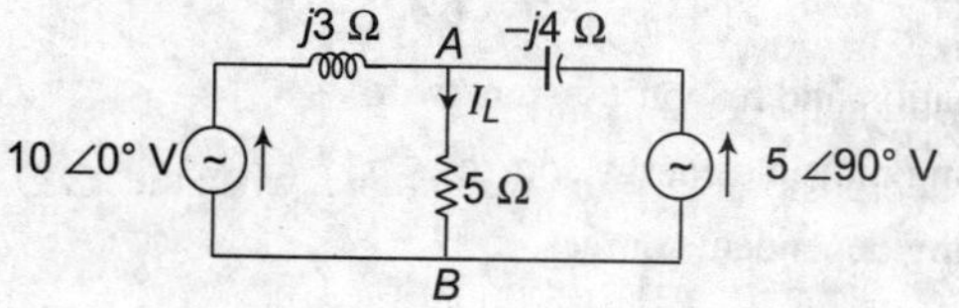

Figure 4.61

7. Find the impedance Z_L so that maximum power can be transferred to it in the shown network. Find maximum power. ●●●

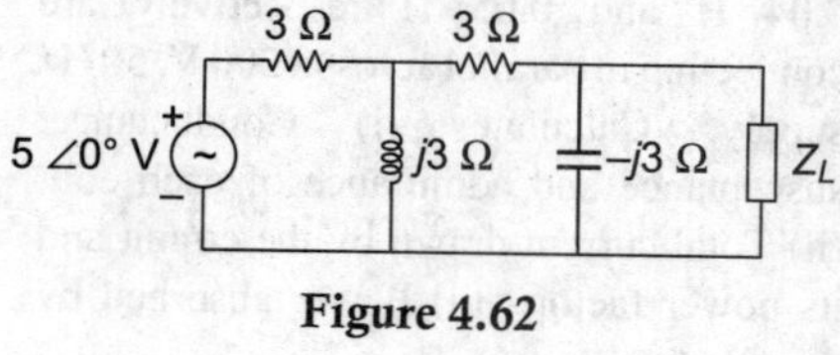

Figure 4.62

8. Verify Reciprocity theorem for the given network. ○●●

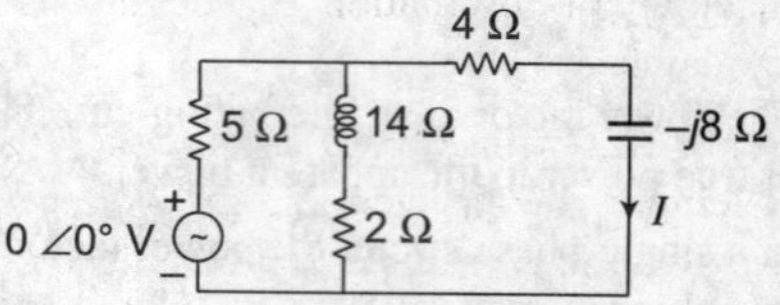

Figure 4.63

9. Find the current in 12 Ω resistor using Millman's theorem.

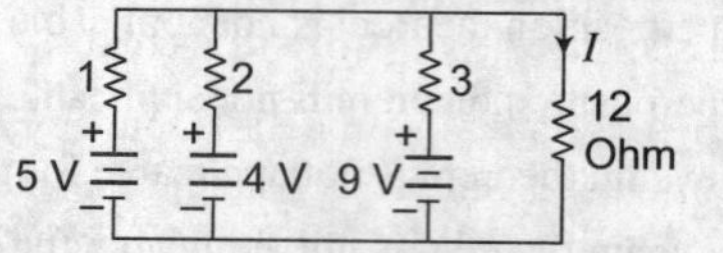

Figure 4.64

10. For the circuit shown below, if the current source is to be substituted with a resistance of 1 Ω and a voltage source, find the value of voltage source.

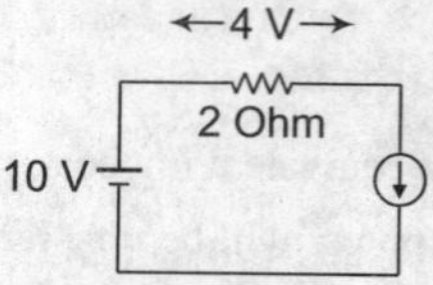

Figure 4.65

11. If the resistance 6 Ω is changed by 15%. Find the change in current in 2 Ω resistance using compensation theorem.

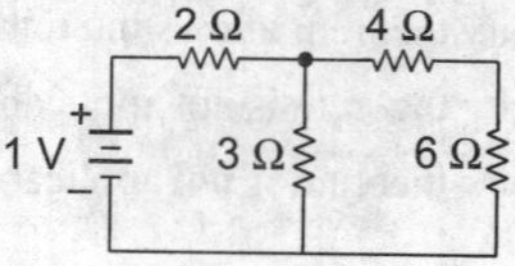

Figure 4.66

12. For the circuit shown below, find output voltage at $t = 5^-$ second.

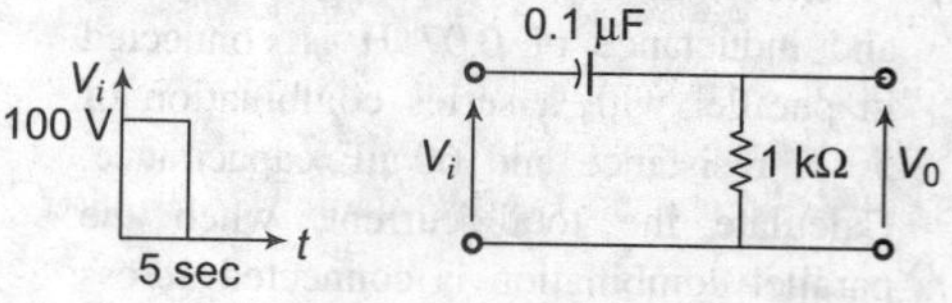

Figure 4.67

13. For a series RLC circuit with $R = 2$ Ohm, $L = 2.5$H, $C = 2$F and $V = 50$V, find the frequency of oscillation if circuit is underdamped.

14. A series *RL* (with $R = 10$ Ohm, $L = 100$ mH) circuit is connected to a DC voltage source of 100 V at time $t = 0$. Find the circuit current expression if current through the circuit for $t < 0$ was 5 A.

15. For an RL (with $R = 10$ Ohm, $L = 100$ mH) circuit excited with a 50 Hz AC source, it is desired to have zero transient current. What should be the time delay after zero crossing of the voltage waveform?

MULTIPLE CHOICE QUESTIONS

1. For a RC circuit, with $R = 10$ Ohm and $C = 0.1$ F time constant will be:
(a) 1 second (b) 10 second (c) 0.1 second (d) 2 second

2. A series RC circuit with $R = 10$ Ohm and $C = 0.1$ is connected to a DC voltage source of 20 V. Current in the circuit at the moment just after the circuit is completed is:
(a) 2 A (b) 200 A (c) 0 A (d) 20 A

3. For a critically damped series RLC circuit with $R = 2$ Ohm and $L = 1$ H, value of C will be:
(a) 0.5 F (b) 2 F (c) 1 F 9 (d) 4 F

4. For an RL ($R = 10$ Ohm, $L = \sqrt{3}$ H) circuit excited with AC source of 10 rad/s; transient current will be zero for delay angle equal to:
(a) 45 degree (b) 30 degree (c) 60 degree (d) 0 degree

5. Read following statements regarding DC transient:
I. Time constant of R-L circuit is L/R.
II. Inductor acts as open circuit at $t = 0$ on closing the switch if its initial current is zero.
III. Capacitor acts as open circuit at $t = 0$ on closing the switch if its initial current is zero.
IV. With DC supply to an RLC circuit, circuit cannot have a sinusoidal current.

Which one of above is correct?
(a) I only (b) I, II (c) I, II and III (d) All

6. In balanced bridge, if the positions of detector and source are interchanged, the bridge will still remain balanced. This can be explained from which theorem
(a) Reciprocity theorem (b) Thevinin's theorem
(c) Norton's theorem (d) Compensation theorem

7. If all the elements in a particular network are linear, then the superposition theorem would hold, when the excitation is
(a) DC only (b) AC only (c) Either AC or DC (d) An Impulse

8. In a series R, L circuit, voltage across resistor and inductor are 3 V and 4 V respectively, then what is the applied voltage?
(a) 7V (b) 5V (c) 4V (d) 3V

9. Form factor is equal to Peak factor in case of
(a) Square wave (b) Triangle wave (c) Saw tooth wave (d) All of the above

10. In RLC series circuit, if the voltage across capacitor is greater than voltage across inductor, then power factor of the network is
(a) lagging (b) leading (c) unity (d) zero

ANSWERS TO MULTIPLE CHOICE QUESTIONS

1. (a)	2. (a)	3. (c)	4. (b)	5. (b)
6. (a)	7. (c)	8. (b)	9. (a)	10. (b)

Resonance

5

CHAPTER OUTLINE

- Exploration of frequency response of RLC series and parallel circuits/Variation of magnitude and phase angle of resonant circuit impedance with frequency
- Evaluation of resonant frequency for series and parallel resonance
- Determination of half power frequency, band width
- Determination of quality factor for each type of resonance

5.1 || INTRODUCTION

Resonance is an important phenomenon in electric circuits, which occurs when two energy storing elements viz. capacitor and inductor are present in an AC circuit. At a certain frequency of power supply i.e. resonant frequency, energy stored in capacitor is supplied by inductor and vice versa. Hence, the circuit draws power, if any, from the source at unity power factor.

5.2 || SERIES RESONANCE

University Questions

1. Define resonance and write its properties of series RLC circuit. **[JNTU, 2015]**
2. Discuss resonance in R-L-C series circuit. **[GTU, 2009]**

In series RLC circuit, resonance is a condition at which capacitive reactance and inductive reactance are equal in magnitude. Voltage across inductor and capacitor are equal in magnitude but 180° phase shifts and cancel out each other (Figure 5.1).

At resonance, $|X_L| = |X_C|$ i.e. $2\pi fL = 1/2\pi fC$

This yields resonant frequency, $f_0 = 1/2\pi\sqrt{LC}$

Input impedance of circuit at resonance, $Z = R + j\,(X_L - X_C) = R$

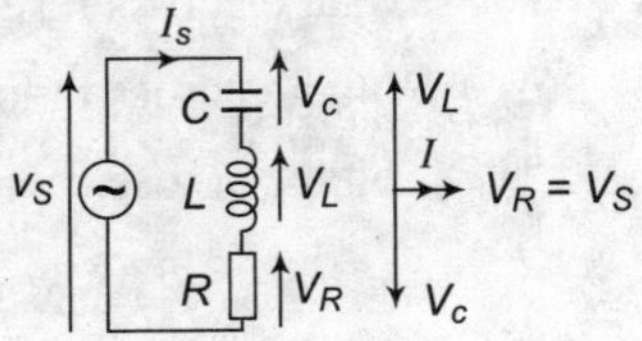

Figure 5.1

Example 5.1

For a series RLC circuit, if voltage measured across induction and capacitor are equal in magnitude, what will be the power factor of circuit? ○○●

Solution Here, $|V_L| = |V_C| \Rightarrow |IX_L| = |IX_C|$.

Since it is a series RLC circuit, so $|X_L| = |X_C| \Rightarrow Z = R$

Which means circuit is at resonance and power factor is unity.

Example 5.2

If phase plane scope is connected to observe V_R and V_{Supply}. Discuss the shape of the curve in scope at resonance. ○●●

Solution Assuming, $V_{\text{Supply}} = V_S = V \sin \omega t$.

Voltage across resistance will be $V_R = IR = \dfrac{RV}{\sqrt{R^2 + (X_L - X_C)^2}} \sin\left(\omega t - \tan^{-1}\dfrac{(X_L - X_C)}{R}\right)$

And at resonance, $X_L - X_C = 0$, so $V_R = V \sin \omega t = V_S$

So, if V_R is presented on Y axis and V_S at X axis of the scope, than $\dfrac{V_Y}{V_X} = \dfrac{V_R}{V_S} = 1$ or $V_Y = V_X$ which is a straight line.

Example 5.3

A series RLC circuit has the following parameters: $R = 15\ \Omega$, $L = 2$ H, $C = 100$ µf. Calculate the resonant frequency. Under resonant condition, calculate the current, power and voltage drops across various elements if the applied voltage is 100 V. **[JNTU, 2012]** ○●●

Solution

(a) Resonant frequency, $f_0 = 1/2\pi\sqrt{LC} = 1/2\pi\sqrt{2 \times 100 \times 10^{-6}} = 11.25$ Hz
At resonance, circuit impedance, $Z = R = 15\Omega$

(b) Circuit current, $I = V/Z = V/R = 100/15 = 6.67$ Amp.

(c) Power dissipated, $P = I^2R = 6.67^2 \times 15 = 666.67$ W

(d) Voltage across resistance, $V_R = IR = 6.67 \times 15 = 100$ V

(e) Voltage across inductor, $V_L = jIX_L = jI(2\pi fL) = j6.67 \times (2\pi \times 11.25 \times 2) = j943$ V

(f) Voltage across capacitor, $V_C = -jIX_C = -jI(1/2\pi fC) = -j6.67 \times (1/(2\pi \times 11.25 \times 100 \times 10^{-6}))$
$= -j943$ V

Note: Difficulty Level ⟶ ○○● — Easy; ○●● — Medium; ●●● — Difficult

5.3 IMPEDANCE AND PHASE ANGLE OF A SERIES RESONANT CIRCUIT

University Question

1. Draw the variation of circuit parameters with frequency in a series resonance circuit. **[AU, 2011]**

5.3.1 Variations of Individual Element's Impedance with Frequency

(a) Resistance: Ideally constant for all frequencies.

(b) Inductive Reactance: $jX_L = jI(2\pi fL)$ varies linearly with frequency.

(c) Capacitive Reactance: $-jIX_C = -jI(1/2\pi f C)$ inversely proportional to frequency.

5.3.2 Impedance of Series RLC Circuit

$$Z = \sqrt{R^2 + (X_L - X_C)^2}$$

Z is infinite for both $f = 0$ and $f = \infty$ and finds its minimum value ($Z = R$) at $f = f_0$, i.e. at resonance, where $X_L = X_C$ (Figure 5.2(a)).

5.3.3 Phase Angle of Series RLC Circuit Impedance

$$\tan\phi = (X_L - X_C)/R$$

ϕ is zero at resonance, negative (I leads V) for $f < f_0$ and positive (I lags V) for $f > f_0$ (Figure 5.2(b)).

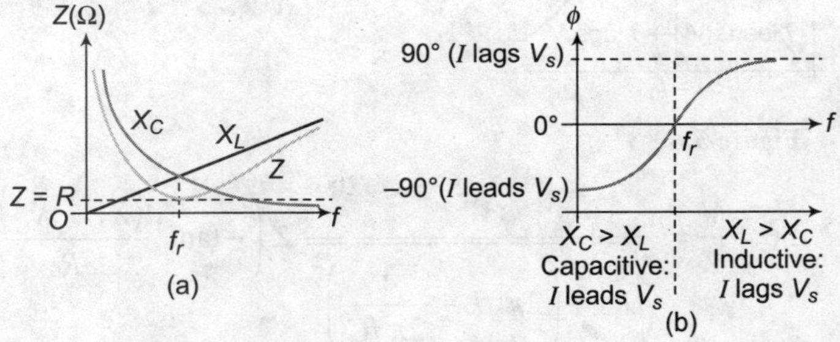

Figure 5.2 *Variation of magnitude and phase angle of input impedance for series RLC*

Example 5.4

For the circuit shown in Figure 5.3, determine the impedance at resonant frequency, 10 Hz above resonant frequency and 10 Hz below resonant frequency. ○○●

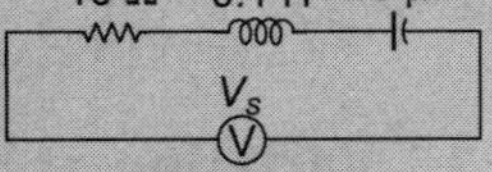

Figure 5.3

Solution Resonant frequency,

$$f_0 = 1/2\pi\sqrt{LC} = 1/2\pi\sqrt{(0.1 \times 10 \times 10^{-6})} = 159.2 \text{ Hz}$$

At 10 Hz below f_0 = 159.2 – 10 = 149.2 Hz
At 10 Hz above f_0 = 159.2 + 10 = 169.2 Hz

For series RLC circuit, $Z = \sqrt{R^2 + \left(2\pi fL - \frac{1}{2\pi fC}\right)^2}$

$$Z\Big|_{f=149.2} = \sqrt{10^2 + \left(2\pi \times 149.2 \times 0.1 - \frac{1}{2\pi \times 149.2 \times 10 \times 10^{-6}}\right)^2} = 16.28\ \Omega$$

$$Z\Big|_{f=169.2} = \sqrt{10^2 + \left(2\pi \times 169.2 \times 0.1 - \frac{1}{2\pi \times 169.2 \times 10 \times 10^{-6}}\right)^2} = 15.81\ \Omega$$

5.4 VOLTAGE AND CURRENT IN SERIES RLC CIRCUIT

University Questions

1. Draw frequency response curve for series RLC circuit with equations. **[AU, 2013]**
2. Explain the variation of current with frequency in a RLC series circuit and also the resonance condition. **[AU, 2013]**

5.4.1 Variation of Current

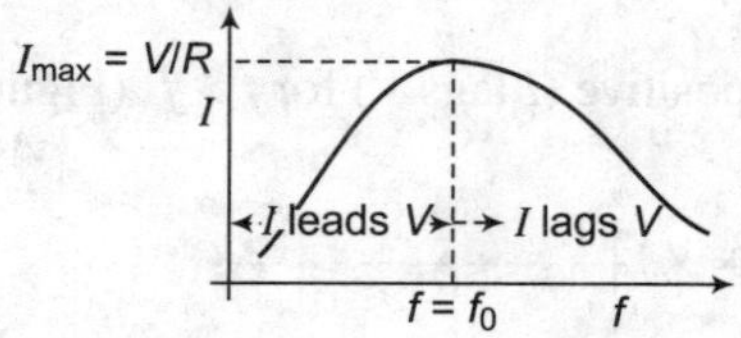

Figure 5.4

$$I\angle\theta = \frac{V}{Z} = \frac{V}{\sqrt{R^2 + \left(2\pi fL - \frac{1}{2\pi fC}\right)^2}} \angle\left(-\tan^{-1}\frac{(X_L - X_C)}{R}\right)$$

For:

(a) $f = 0$ and ∞, Z = ∞. So $I = 0$.
(b) At $f = f_0$, Z is minimum and equal to R. So $I = I_{max} = V/R$.
(c) For $f < f_0$, $X_L < X_C$, so current leads supply voltage.
(d) For $f < f_0$, $X_L > X_C$, so current lags supply voltage.

5.4.2 Variation of Voltages

1. Voltage Across Resistance

Voltage across resistance is directly proportional to current (even when frequency varies). It follows same pattern/characteristics of current as shown in Figure 5.4.

2. Voltage Across Inductor

$$V_L = \frac{V}{Z} X_L = \frac{V}{\sqrt{R^2 + \left(\omega L - \frac{1}{\omega C}\right)^2}} \omega L$$

(a) At $f = 0$, $V_L = 0$.

(b) At $f = \infty$, $V_L = V$ i.e. supply voltage.

(c) Maximum value of V_L occurs when $\frac{dV_L}{d\omega} = 0$ which yields, $\omega_L = \frac{1}{\sqrt{LC}} \sqrt{\frac{1}{1 - \frac{R^2 C}{2L}}}$. ω_L is higher than resonant frequency.

3. Voltage Across Capacitor

$$V_C = \frac{V}{Z} X_C = \frac{V}{\sqrt{R^2 + \left(\omega L - \frac{1}{\omega C}\right)^2}} \frac{1}{\omega C}$$

(a) At $f = 0$, $V_C = V$ i.e. supply voltage.

(b) At $f = \infty$, $V_C = 0$.

(c) Maximum value of V_C occurs when $\frac{dV_C}{d\omega} = 0$ which yields, $\omega_C = \sqrt{\frac{1}{LC} - \frac{R_L^2}{2L}}$. ω_C is lower than resonant frequency.

Example 5.5

For RLC circuit with $R = 10$ Ohm, $L = 0.1$ H and $C = 50$ microfarad, find out the frequency at which voltage is: (a) maximum across capacitor (b) Maximum across inductor. ○●●

Solution **Step 1:** Find out the frequency for maximum voltage:

(a) Voltage across capacitor is maximum at

$$f_C = \frac{1}{2\pi} \sqrt{\frac{1}{LC} - \frac{R_L^2}{2L}} = \frac{1}{2\pi} \sqrt{\frac{1}{0.1 \times 50 \times 10^{-6}} - \frac{10^2}{2 \times 0.1}} = 72.076 \text{ Hz}$$

(b) Voltage across inductor is maximum at

$$f_L = \frac{1}{2\pi} \frac{1}{\sqrt{LC}} \sqrt{\frac{1}{1 - \frac{R^2 C}{2L}}} = \frac{1}{2\pi} \frac{1}{\sqrt{0.1 \times 50 \times 10^{-6}}} \sqrt{\frac{1}{1 - \frac{10^2 \times 50 \times 10^{-6}}{2 \times 0.1}}} = 71.08 \text{Hz}$$

Example 5.6

For RLC circuit with $R = 10$ Ohm, $L = 0.1$ H and C = 10 micro-farad, find out the frequency at which voltage is maximum across the capacitor. What is maximum value (rms) of voltage across capacitor? Also, find out voltage across inductor at that frequency. Supply voltage is 100V.

[AU, 2013]

Solution **Step 1:** Find out the frequency for maximum voltage:

Voltage across capacitor is maximum at

$$\omega_C = \sqrt{\frac{1}{LC} - \frac{R_L^2}{2L}} = \sqrt{\frac{1}{0.1 \times 10 \times 10^{-6}} - \frac{10^2}{2 \times 0.1}} = 1000 \text{ rad/sec.}$$

Step 2: Find out the impedance at that frequency:

$$\text{Impedance at 1000 rad/sec} = \sqrt{R^2 + \left(\omega L - \frac{1}{\omega C}\right)^2}$$

$$= \sqrt{10^2 + \left(1000 \times 0.1 - \frac{1}{1000 \times 10 \times 10^{-6}}\right)^2} = 10 \text{ Ohm}$$

Step 3: Calculate current and hence voltage:

$$I = V/Z = 100/10 = 10 \text{ Amp.}$$

$$\text{Voltage across capacitor} = I \times X_c = 10 \times \frac{1}{1000 \times 10 \times 10^{-6}} = 1000\text{V}$$

Voltage across resistance = $IR = 10 \times 10 = 100$ V

Since $V_R = V_S$, applying KVL in the loop results, $V_L = -V_C = -1000$V.

5.5 BANDWIDTH OF AN RLC CIRCUIT

University Question

1. Define bandwidth and quality factor and derive relation between them. **[JNTU, 2015]**

Bandwidth (BW) of a circuit is the frequency span for which the response of the circuit is higher than $\mathbf{1/\sqrt{2}}$ **times (70.7%) of the maximum** value (Figure 5.5).

Frequency at which response is exactly $1/\sqrt{2}$ times of the maximum value is called **cut-off frequency**.

For a series RLC circuit, current is maximum at resonant frequency with **two cut-off frequencies.** Since power at cut-off frequencies is half of the maximum power (or power at resonance), they are also called **half power frequencies**.

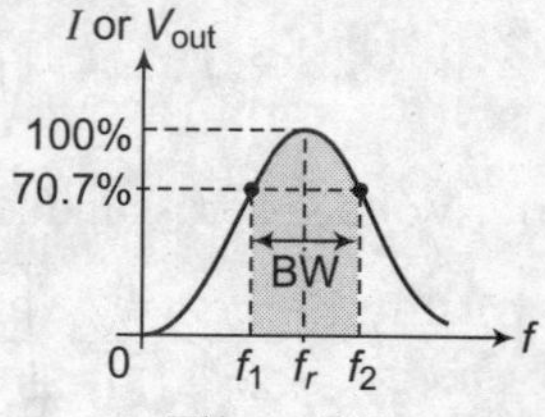

Figure 5.5

Lower cut-off frequency f_1: lower than resonance frequency, circuit impedance is capacitive in nature i.e. I leads V.

Higher cut-off frequency f_2: higher than resonance frequency, circuit impedance is inductive in nature i.e. I lags V.

$$\text{BW} = f_2 - f_1 \ \textbf{Hz}$$

Derivation of bandwidth in terms of circuit parameters:

Magnitude of current at cut-off frequencies $= \dfrac{V}{Z_{\text{cut-off}}} = \dfrac{Im}{\sqrt{2}} = \dfrac{V}{\sqrt{2}R}$

So, $\quad Z_{\text{cut-off}} = \sqrt{2}\,R$

$\Rightarrow \quad 2R^2 = R^2 + (2\pi f L - 1/2\pi f C)^2$

Solving this expression gives two different values of frequencies (corresponding to lower and higher cut-off frequencies).

$$f_1 = f_r - \frac{R}{4\pi L} \text{ and } f_2 = f_r + \frac{R}{4\pi L} \text{ where } f_r \text{ is resonant frequency.}$$

$$\text{BW} = f_2 - f_1 = \frac{R}{4\pi L} \text{ Hz}$$

Example 5.7

Calculate the half-power frequencies of a series resonant circuit where the resonance frequency is 250×10^3 Hz and the bandwidth is 150 kHz. **[BPUT, 2007]** ○●●

Solution **Step 1:** Find out first relation between cut-off frequencies from bandwidth:

Let f_1 and f_2 be the lower and higher cut-off frequencies respectively.

Now, Bandwidth $= f_2 - f_1 = 150$ kHz (5.1)

Step 2: Find out second relation between cut-off frequencies from resonance frequency:

Also, $\quad f_1 f_2 = f_r^2 = (250)^2 = 62500 \text{ (kHz)}^2$

$\therefore \quad (f_2 + f_1)^2 = (f_2 - f_1)^2 + 4f_1 f_2$

$\Rightarrow \quad f_2 + f_1 = 522.0153$ kHz (5.2)

Step 3: Solving relations: (5.1) and (5.2)

$f_2 = 336$ kHz and $f_1 = 186$ kHz

5.6 || THE QUALITY FACTOR (Q) AND ITS EFFECT ON BANDWIDTH

Because of coil resistance, a fraction of energy supplied to an inductor is dissipated in form of heat and hence, stored energy is less than the energy supplied by the source. Same is true for a capacitor.

Quality factor is a parameter, which represents how efficiently an inductor or a capacitor, can store the energy.

$$\text{Quality factor } (Q) = 2\pi \frac{\text{maximum energy stored}}{\text{energy dissipated per cycle}} \tag{5.3}$$

(a) For an inductor: $Q = \dfrac{X_L}{R} = \dfrac{\omega L}{R}$

(b) For a capacitor: $Q = \frac{X_C}{R} = \frac{1}{\omega CR}$

$$Q = \frac{f_r}{\text{Bandwidth}} \tag{5.4}$$

Example 5.8

An *RLC* series circuit consists of $R = 16\ \Omega$, $L = 5$ mH and $C = 2\ \mu$F. Calculate the quality factor at resonance, bandwidth. If it is desired to increase the bandwidth by 20% keeping the central frequency fixed, find out circuit current, quality factor. **[AU, 2014]** ○●●

Solution Given that, $R = 16\ \Omega$, $L = 5$mH and $C = 2\ \mu$F

Resonant frequency, $f_0 = 1/2\pi\sqrt{LC} = 1/(2\pi\sqrt{5\times10^{-3}\times2\times10^{-6}}) = 1591.5$ Hz

Quality factor, $Q = \frac{\omega L}{R} = 2\pi(1591.5)(5\times10^{-3})/16 = 3.125$

Bandwidth = $\frac{f_r}{Q}$ = 1591.5/3.125 = 509.28 Hz

Now, it is desired to increase the band width by 20% with constant f_r:

$$\frac{BW'}{BW} = \frac{Q}{Q'} \Rightarrow Q' = \frac{BW}{BW'}Q = \frac{1}{1.2}\times3.125 = 2.604$$

Since, selectivity or bandwidth is controlled by resistance only, the new value of resistance, $R' = 1.2$ R

So new current, $I' = I/1.2 = 83.33\%$ of I.

5.7 || PARALLEL RESONANCE

University Question

1. Explain the phenomena of resonance in AC parallel circuit. Derive the mathematical expression of resonant frequency. **[GTU, 2011]**

A circuit having a real inductor and capacitor connected in parallel is at resonance if imaginary parts of their currents (in phase or representation) are equal in magnitude (Figure 5.6). This results in net current or source current in phase with source voltage and circuit which does not draw any reactive power from source.

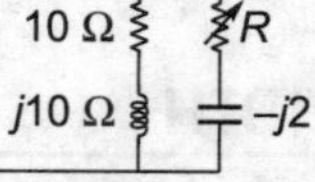

Figure 5.6

5.7.1 Determination of Resonant Frequency, f_0

In the circuit shown in Figure 5.7, non-ideal inductor and capacitor are realised by addition of series resistances with an ideal inductor or a capacitor.

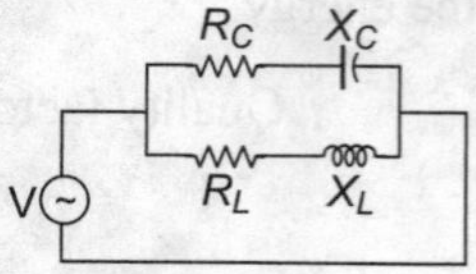

Figure 5.7

Since at resonance, circuit does not draw reactive power, **imaginary part of input admittance (susceptance) is equal to zero.**

i.e. $$I_m(Y)\Big|_{f=f_0} = I_m\left[\frac{1}{R_L + j2\pi f_0 L} + \frac{1}{R_C + \dfrac{1}{j2\pi f_0 C}}\right] = 0 \quad (5.5)$$

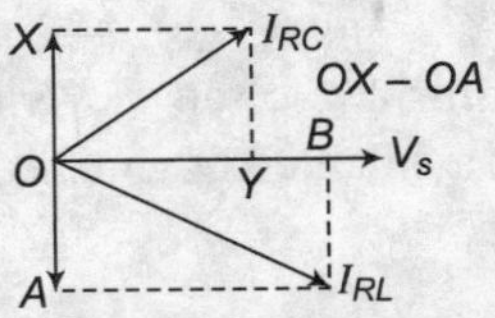

Figure 5.8 *Phasor diagram: Parallel resonance*

Solving it for f_0 gives,

$$f_0 = \frac{1}{2\pi\sqrt{LC}} \frac{\sqrt{\left(R_L^2 - \dfrac{L}{C}\right)}}{\sqrt{\left(R_C^2 - \dfrac{L}{C}\right)}} \quad (5.6)$$

Special Cases

(a) If $R_L = 0$; $R_C = 0$. $f_0 = \dfrac{1}{2\pi\sqrt{LC}}$, it is equal to the resonant frequency of a series RLC circuit.

(b) If $R_L = R_C$. $f_0 = \dfrac{1}{2\pi\sqrt{LC}}$

(c) If $R_C = 0$; $f_0 = \dfrac{1}{2\pi}\sqrt{\dfrac{1}{LC} - \dfrac{R_L^2}{L^2}}$

Example 5.9

Calculate the value of R in the circuit shown in Figure 5.9 for resonance. **[BPUT, 2007]** ○○●

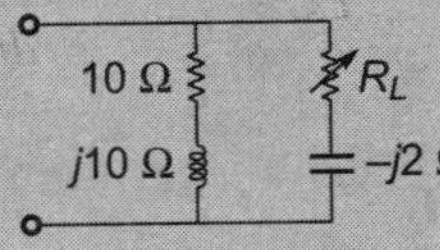

Figure 5.9

Solution **Step 1:** Calculation of admittance, as we know its imaginary part is 0 at resonance.

Admittance, $$Y = \frac{1}{10+10j} + \frac{1}{R-2j}$$

$$Y = \frac{10-10j}{100+100} + \frac{R+2j}{R^2+4}$$

Step 2: Equating imaginary part of $Y = 0$.

$$\frac{-10j}{100+100} + \frac{2j}{R^2+4} = 0,\ R = +6 \text{ Ohm}$$

Example 5.10

Find the value of L for which the circuit shown in Figure 5.10 is resonant at frequency of $\omega_0 = 1000$ rad/s. **[PU, 2010]** ○●●

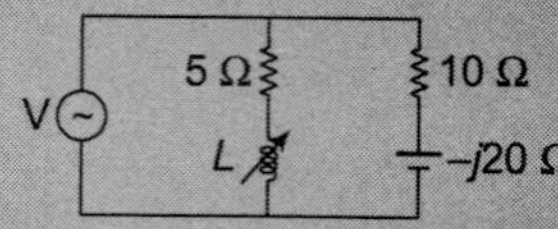

Figure 5.10

Solution **Step 1:** Writing expression for resonant frequency in terms of available known and unknown parameters

Frequency of resonance for a parallel RLC circuit, $$\omega_0 = \frac{1}{\sqrt{LC}}\frac{\sqrt{\left(R_L^2 - \frac{L}{C}\right)}}{\sqrt{\left(R_C^2 - \frac{L}{C}\right)}}$$

$$1000 = \frac{1}{\sqrt{LC}}\frac{\sqrt{\left(R_L^2 - \frac{L}{C}\right)}}{\sqrt{\left(R_C^2 - \frac{L}{C}\right)}}, \text{ here } C = 1/\omega X_C = 1/(1000 \times 20) = 50\ \mu\text{F}$$

Putting the value of R and C in the expression of resonant frequency,

Step 2: Equating frequency expression to given frequency:

$$\Rightarrow \quad 1000 = \frac{1}{\sqrt{(50 \times 10^{-6}\, L)}}\frac{\sqrt{\left(5^2 - \frac{L}{50 \times 10^{-6}}\right)}}{\sqrt{\left(10^2 - \frac{L}{50 \times 10^{-6}}\right)}}$$

$$\Rightarrow (1000)^2 \times 50 \times 10^{-6} \times L^2 + [(1000)^2 (50 \times 10^{-6})^2 (10^2) + 1]\, L - 5^2 \times 50 \times 10^{-6}$$

$$= 50L^2 + [50 \times 10^{-6} \times 10^2 + 1]\, L - [25 \times 5 \times 10^{-5}] = 0$$

$$\Rightarrow \quad 50\, L^2 + 1.005\, L - 0.00125 = 0$$

$L = 1.175$ mH (or) -0.0212 H. Taking positive value, $L = 1.175$ mH

5.8 RESONANT FREQUENCY FOR A TANK CIRCUIT

Parallel LC combination is also known as tank circuit. In its simplest form of realisation, it is represented as shown in Figures 5.11 and 5.12.

Resonant frequency for a tank circuit is determined by putting $R_C = 0$ in Eq. (5.6),

$$f_0 = \frac{1}{2\pi}\sqrt{\frac{1}{LC} - \frac{R_L^2}{L^2}} \tag{5.7}$$

University Question

1. An inductive coil of resistance R and inductance L is connected in parallel with capacitor of C. Derive an expression for the resonant frequency. **[GTU, 2011]**

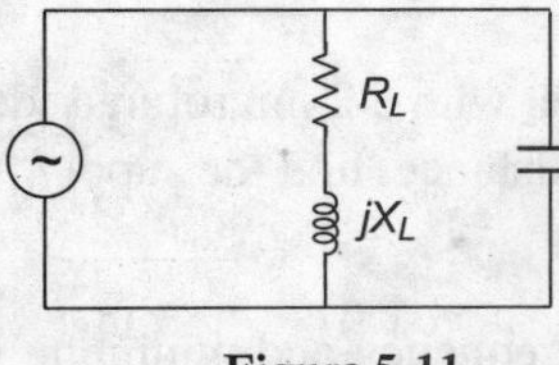

Figure 5.11

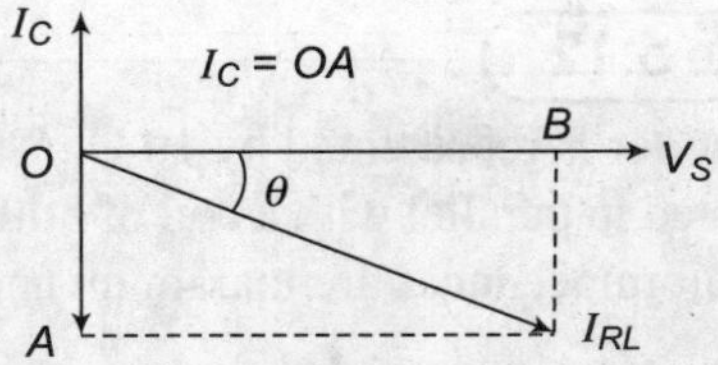

Figure 5.12 *Phasor diagram: Tank circuit*

Example 5.11

A coil of 10 Ohm resistance and 5 mH inductance is connected in parallel with a capacitor of 2 microfarad, find the supply frequency at which circuit draws only active power from voltage source.

Solution At resonant frequency, power factor is unity and circuit does not draw reactive power from the source.

Resonant frequency for a tank circuit, $f_0 = \dfrac{1}{2\pi}\sqrt{\dfrac{1}{LC} - \dfrac{R_L^2}{L^2}}$

$$f_0 = \frac{1}{2\pi}\sqrt{\frac{1}{5\times 10^{-3}\times 2\times 10^{-6}} - \frac{100}{25\times 10^{-6}}} = 1559.39 \text{ Hz}$$

5.9 || VARIATION OF IMPEDANCE WITH FREQUENCY

For an ideal parallel RLC circuit as shown in Figure 5.13, expression of admittance (Y) is written as:

$$Y = G - jB_L + jB_C = \frac{1}{R} + \frac{1}{j\omega L} + j\omega C \text{ mho} \tag{5.8}$$

Source current, $I_S = YV_S$

From the above expressions, it can be concluded that:

1. Y is minimum (or Z is maximum) at resonance frequency, where $B_L = B_C$.
2. At higher frequencies, I_C dominates and hence overall Z is capacitive in nature.
3. At lower frequencies, I_L dominates and hence overall Z is inductive in nature.
4. At resonance, both I_C and I_L are equal but 180° phase shifted and hence $Z = R$.

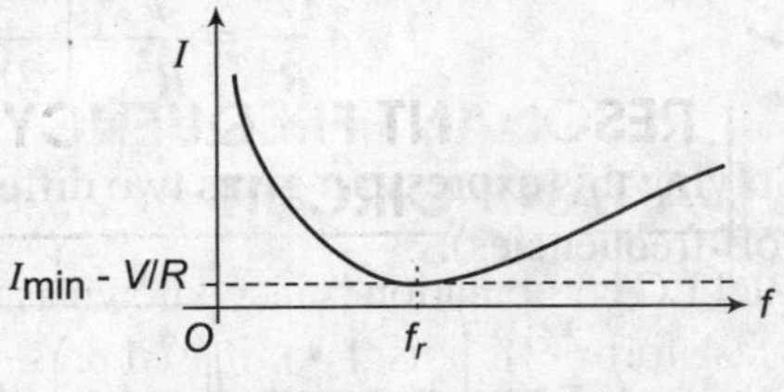

Figure 5.13 *Source current: Parallel resonance*

Example 5.12

A real capacitor is represented by 10 Ohm resistance in parallel with a 2 microfarad ideal capacitor. It is connected in parallel with a coil of 5mH and negligible resistance; find the supply frequencies at which circuit impedances are maximum and minimum.

Solution Here, circuit impedance is maximum at resonant frequency and minimum i.e. 0 at $f = 0$ and $f = \infty$

$$f_0 = \frac{1}{2\pi}\sqrt{\frac{1}{LC}} = \frac{1}{2\pi}\sqrt{\frac{1}{5\times10^{-3}\times2\times10^{-6}}} = 1591.55 \text{ Hz}$$

5.10 Q-FACTOR OF PARALLEL RESONANCE

University Question

1. Derive expression for *Q*-factor of parallel resonance. [GTU, 2011]

5.10.1 Cut-off Frequencies for a Parallel RLC Circuit

For the circuit shown here (Figure 5.14),

$$V_0 = ZI_S$$

Z is maximum at resonance and $Z_{max} = R$, so $V_{omax} = RI_S$

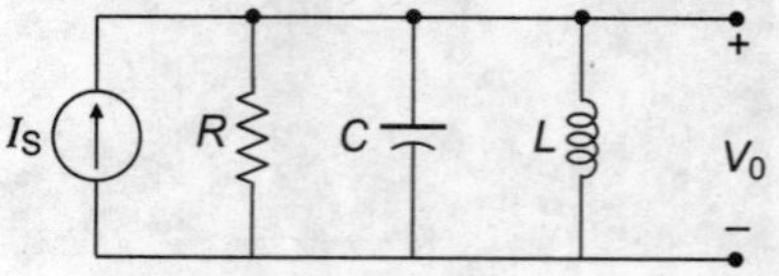

Figure 5.14

At cut-off frequencies, $V_0 = Z_{\text{cut-off}}\, I_s = \frac{V_{omax}}{\sqrt{2}} = R\frac{I_S}{\sqrt{2}}$

So, $$Z_{\text{cut-off}} = \frac{R}{\sqrt{2}} \quad \text{or} \quad Y_{\text{cut-off}} = \frac{\sqrt{2}}{R} \tag{5.9}$$

Using Eqs (5.8) and (5.9);

$$\frac{2}{R^2} = \frac{1}{R^2} + \left(\frac{1}{2\pi fL} - 2\pi fC\right)^2$$

Solving this expression gives two different values of frequencies (corresponding to lower and higher cut-off frequencies).

$$f_1 = \frac{1}{2\pi}\left(-\frac{1}{2RC} + \sqrt{\left(\frac{1}{2RC}\right)^2 + \frac{1}{LC}}\right) \text{ and } f_2 = \frac{1}{2\pi}\left(\frac{1}{2RC} + \sqrt{\left(\frac{1}{2RC}\right)^2 + \frac{1}{LC}}\right) \tag{5.10}$$

5.10.2 Bandwidth of a Parallel RLC Circuit

Using of Eq. (5.10),

$$BW = f_2 - f_1 = \frac{1}{2\pi RC} \text{ Hz}$$

5.10.3 *Q*-Factor

Defined as Eq. (5.3), for a parallel RLC circuit also it can be found using Eq. (5.4).

$$Q = \frac{f_r}{\text{Bandwidth}} = \frac{\frac{1}{2\pi\sqrt{LC}}}{\frac{1}{2\pi RC}} = R\sqrt{\frac{C}{L}} = \frac{R}{2\pi f_r L} = 2\pi RCf_r$$

Example 5.13

A parallel resonant circuit has a coil of 100 mH with a *Q*-factor of 50. The coil is resonant with a frequency of 900 kHz. Find (a) value of the capacitor, (b) resistance in series with the coil, (c) circuit impedance at resonance. **[PU, 2012]** ○●●

Solution

(a) $f_0 = \frac{1}{2\pi}\sqrt{\frac{1}{LC}} \Rightarrow \frac{1}{2\pi}\sqrt{\frac{1}{xC}} = 900 \times 10^3 \Rightarrow C = 4.86 \times 10^{12}$ F

(b) $Q = \frac{\omega L}{R} \Rightarrow R = \frac{\omega L}{Q} = \frac{2\pi \times 900 \times 10^3 \times 100 \times 10^{-3}}{50} = 11309.73\ \Omega$

(c) At resonance, $Z = R = 11309.73\ \Omega$

Example 5.14

A parallel resonant circuit has a bandwidth of 200 Hz and a quality factor of 10. The inductor value is 100 mH. Find the value of *R* of this circuit. ○●●

Solution Bandwidth $BW = 20$ kHz; $Q = 40$; $R = 10$ kΩ; $L = ?$

$$Q = \frac{f_r}{BW} \Rightarrow f_r = Q\ BW \Rightarrow f_r = 10 \times 200 = 2000 \text{ Hz}$$

$$Q = \frac{R}{2\pi f_r L} \Rightarrow L = \frac{2\pi f_r Q}{R} \Rightarrow R = \frac{2\pi \times 2000 \times 10}{0.1} = 1.25 \times 10^7 \Omega$$

POINTS TO REMEMBER

☞ At resonance:

Supply frequency, $f = 1/2\pi\sqrt{LC}$.

Input impedance of a RLC circuit is purely resistive which means power factor is unity.

Inductor-Capacitor pair can be replaced by short circuit.

☞ At resonance (Series RLC):

Impedance is minimum.

For $f < f_0$, Z is capacitive in nature. For $f > f_0$, Z is inductive in nature.

☞ At resonance:

$V_C = V_s$ at $f = 0$, $V_L = V_s$ at $f = \infty$ and $V_R = V_s$ at $f = f_0$

V_C becomes maximum before f_0 while V_L becomes maximum after f_0

I leads V before resonance, I lags V after resonance

☞ At cut-off frequencies: Current becomes $1/\sqrt{2}$ times of maximum value, power is halved.

$$\text{BW} = f_2 - f_1 = \frac{R}{4\pi L} \text{ Hz}$$

Increasing the bandwidth will reduce selectivity

☞ For a coil: higher the frequency, higher will be the Q-factor.

At resonance, $|V_L| = |V_C| = Q\,|V_S|$

Coil made of high resistance will have poor selectivity or higher bandwidth.

☞ Supply frequency, $f_0 = \dfrac{1}{2\pi\sqrt{LC}} \dfrac{\sqrt{\left(R_L^2 - \dfrac{L}{C}\right)}}{\sqrt{\left(R_C^2 - \dfrac{L}{C}\right)}}$.

Input impedance is purely resistive which means power factor is unity.

Imaginary components of I_{RL} and I_{RC} become equal.

☞ At resonant frequency,

Z is maximum.

Parallel LC branches can be replaced with an open circuit.

☞ For a coil, if connected in parallel with resistance, higher the frequency, lower will be the Q-factor.

At resonance, $|I_L| = |I_C| = Q\,|I_S|$

A capacitor with higher dielectric loss will have a smaller resistance in parallel and hence poor Q-factor.

PRACTICE PROBLEMS

1. For a series RLC circuit with $R = 10$ Ohm, $L = 10$ mH and supply voltage $V = 100$ V, if voltage across capacitor at resonance is 1000 V, find out resonant frequency.

2. Two inductors of 1000 mH and 500 mH are connected in series with a resistance and capacitor of 10 micro farad. If mutual inductance between inductors is 250 mH and inductors are connected in series additive pattern.

3. A 1000 V, 50 Hz transmission line represented as a T-network is having series impedance of $1 + 3j$. Impedance of shunt branch is $-2.5j$. If line is open-circuited at load end i.e. receiving end, find the receiving end voltage. If receiving end voltage is required to maintain at 1000 V by series compensation i.e. by connecting a series inductance in series with series branch inductance, find out value of additional inductance connected.

4. For a series RLC circuit with $R = 15\ \Omega$, $L = 2$H, $C = 100\ \mu f$, V =150V. Find out: (a) Half-power frequencies. (b) Capacitive reactive power (c) Inductive reactive power.

5. With a series RLC circuit having $R = 10$ kΩ, $L = ?$ H, it is intended to design a band pass filter with bandwidth of 20 kHz and central frequency 800 kHz. Find out: (a) Quality factor. (b) Value of inductor.

6. For a real tank circuit (A series RL branch in parallel with C), if $R = 20$ Ohm and Q-factor of RL branch = 40, find out effective input impedance at resonant frequency?

7. An electric circuit has two parallel branches. Branch X–Y consists of a 10 Ω resistance connected in series with a capacitor of 50 μF and branch AB has a 5Ω resistance connected in series with an inductor of 1.175 mH. Find out equivalent impedance of the circuit at resonance.

8. For the circuit shown below, what find the value of capacitance such that overall power factor is unity at 1000 rad/s ?

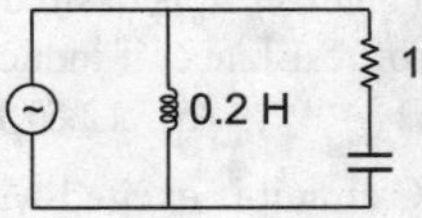

Figure 5.15

9. Two impedances $Z_1 = 5\ \Omega$ and $Z_2 = 5 - jX_c\ \Omega$ are connected in parallel and this combination is connected in series with $Z_3 = 6.25 + j1.25\ \Omega$. Determine the value of capacitance in X_c to achieve resonance if supply is 100 V, 50 Hz.
(Civil Services Exam, UPSC-2016)

10. For a circuit having R, L and connected C in parallel, resonant frequency and bandwidth are 500 Hz and 50 Hz. Find out inductor and capacitor current at resonance if circuit is excited with a variable frequency current source of 50 Amp.

11. For a magnetically coupled circuit shown below, find the frequency of supply voltage for which circuit operates at unity power factor. Given that: $R_1 = 10\ \Omega$, $L_1 = 0.4$ H, $L_2 = 0.25$ H, M = 0.25 H. Secondary side resistance and inductance are 20 Ω and 5 μF.

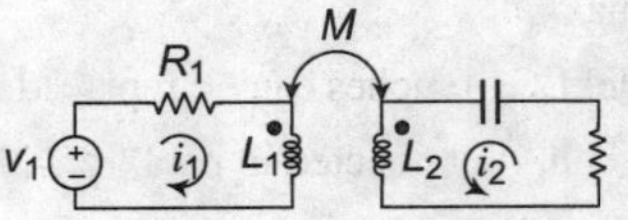

Figure 5.16

MULTIPLE CHOICE QUESTIONS

1. If value of capacitance and inductance are increased to four times with keeping resistance constant for a series RLC circuit: current at resonance and resonant frequency will become respectively: ○○●
   (a) Resonant current remains same, resonant frequency becomes one fourth.
   (b) Resonant frequency remains same, resonant current becomes one fourth.
   (c) Both resonant current and resonant frequency remain same.
   (d) Resonant current remains same, resonant frequency is halved.

2. For an audio receiver, it is desired to receive signals of frequency band 500 kHz – 600 kHz. What should be the value of resistance, if inductance of tuning circuit is 20 mH. ○●●
   (a) 25.13 kΩ (b) 12.57 kΩ (c) 4.00 kΩ (d) 2.00 kΩ

3. A series RLC circuit is excited with a variable frequency voltage source of 20V. Find voltage across the capacitor if resonant frequency is 300Hz and bandwidth is 20Hz. ○●●
   (a) 10 V (b) 20 V (c) 300 V (d) 1.33 V

4. At resonance, a series and parallel LC circuit can be replaced by respectively: ○●●
   (a) Open circuit and Short circuit (b) Short circuit and Open circuit
   (c) Short circuit (Both) (d) Open circuit (Both)

5. Read following statements regarding resonance in an electric circuit: ○●●
   i. At resonance, power factor of the circuit is unity.
   ii. Impedance for series RLC circuit is minimum.
   iii. Impedance for parallel RLC circuit is maximum.
   iv. Reactive power becomes equal to active power.

   Which one of above is correct?
   (a) i only (b) i, ii (c) i, ii and iii (d) All

ANSWERS TO MULTIPLE CHOICE QUESTIONS

1. (a) 2. (a) 3. (c) 4. (b) 5. (c)

Coupled Circuits

6

Chapter Outline

- ☞ Conductively coupled circuit and mutual impedance
- ☞ Self-inductance and mutual inductance
- ☞ Dot convention
- ☞ Coefficient of coupling
- ☞ Series connection of coupled inductors
- ☞ Parallel connection of coupled coils
- ☞ Tuned circuits
- ☞ Analysis of coupled circuits
- ☞ Conductively coupled equivalent circuit (series and parallel magnetic circuits)
- ☞ Analysis of magnetic circuits
- ☞ Magnetic leakage and fringing
- ☞ Comparison of electric and magnetic circuits
- ☞ Time domain and frequency domain analysis of network equations
- ☞ Application of an ideal transformer

6.1 || INTRODUCTION

Two circuits are said to be 'coupled' when energy transfer takes place from one circuit to the other when one of the circuits is energised.

The following types of coupling are possible between electrical circuits:

(a) Conductive coupling (e.g. in potential divider circuit)

(b) Inductive (Magnetic) coupling (e.g. in two winding transformer)

(c) Conductive and Inductive coupling (e.g. in auto-transformer)

Transistors and electronic pots are other examples of coupled circuits which are represented as two-port network.

6.2 CONDUCTIVELY COUPLED CIRCUIT AND MUTUAL IMPEDANCE

A conductively coupled circuit is electrically connected and does not involve inductive coupling. A two-port network is an example of such circuit which consists of an input port corresponding to input loop circuit and an output port corresponding to output loop circuit. Impedance, which is common to both the loops, is known as mutual impedance. The mutual impedance could be resistive, inductive, capacitive or any combination of these type of impedances.

Probe

1. What do you understand by conductively and inductively coupling? Explain with examples.

6.3 SELF-INDUCTANCE AND MUTUAL INDUCTANCE

University Questions

1. Define mutual inductance. [AU, 2012]
2. Write voltage expressions which relates to self and mutual inductance. [AU, 2014]

6.3.1 Self-Inductance

An inductor is a circuit element that stores magnetic field. If the magnetic field is changing, i.e. if the current is changing, it will have an induced EMF across it with a magnitude proportional to the rate of change of current:

$$\varepsilon = \Delta V = V_b - V_a = -L\frac{di}{dt} \tag{6.1}$$

The proportionality constant L is called the *inductance* of the device. It is a property of the device (geometry, windings) and does not depend on the current. Inductance is measured in units of 'henrys', where 1 henry = 1 volt-second/ampere.

6.3.2 Mutual Inductance

A mutual inductance is a property associated with two or more coils / inductors which are in close proximity and the presence of the common magnetic flux which links these coils. A transformer is such a device whose operation is based on mutual inductance.

When two or more inductors are in close proximity in a medium of constant permittivity, a change in a common magnetic flux among them with respect to time also induces an additional voltage across those inductors. The magnitude of this voltage depends upon the mutual inductance between those inductors and the time rate of change of current in other inductors.

The mutually induced voltage across the coupled inductors can be determined using the following formula.

$$v_{12}(t) = v_{21}\ (t) = \pm M\frac{di(t)}{dt} \tag{6.2}$$

where $v_{12}(t)$ is voltage induced in inductor 1 due to change in current of inductor 2, while $v_{21}(t)$ is the voltage induced in inductor 2 due to change in current of inductor 1.

Mutual Inductance can be explained through the following example.

Consider coil 1 and coil 2 are placed in close proximity. Coil 1 is carrying current I_1 and has N_1 turns while Coil 2 is carrying current I_2 and has N_2 turns. Coil 1 and Coil 2 produces magnetic flux ϕ_1 and ϕ_2 respectively due to associated currents such that:

Magnetic flux produced by Coil 1: $\phi_1 = \phi_{11} + \phi_{12}$

Magnetic flux produced by Coil 2: $\phi_2 = \phi_{22} + \phi_{12}$

where ϕ_{12} is a portion of magnetic fluxes ϕ_1 and ϕ_2 which links both the coils. The mutual inductance between two coils can be determined using following formula:

$$M = \frac{N_2\phi_{12}}{I_1} = \frac{N_1\phi_{12}}{I_2}$$

Voltage expressions for coupled inductors:

Consider the following electrical circuit consists of two coupled inductors with self-inductance L_1 and L_2 and are carrying currents $i_1(t)$ and $i_2(t)$ respectively, are placed in close proximity in a medium of constant permittivity (Figure 6.1).

The mutual inductance between these inductors is M. The voltages $v_1(t)$ and $v_2(t)$ across the inductors can be calculated using the following formulae:

$$v_1(t) = L_1\frac{di_1(t)}{dt} \pm M\frac{di_2(t)}{dt} \text{ volts} \quad (6.3)$$

$$v_2(t) = L_2\frac{di_2(t)}{dt} \pm M\frac{di_1(t)}{dt} \text{ volts} \quad (6.4)$$

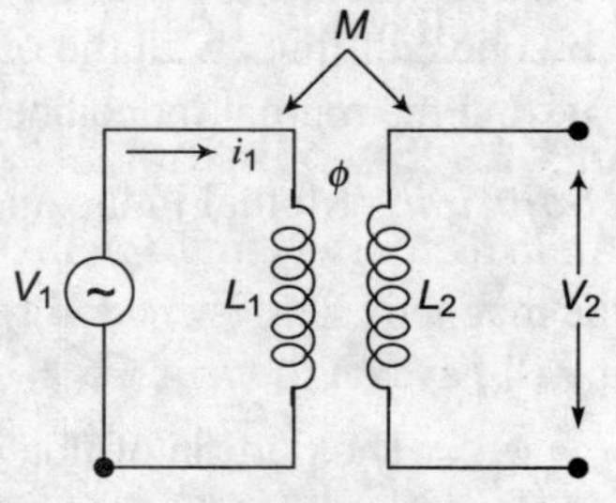

Figure 6.1

The mutual inductance could be positive or negative between the coils in above formulae depending upon the physical constructions of the coils and reference directions. To determine the polarity of the mutually inducted voltage (i.e. the sign to be used for the mutual inductance), the dot convention is used.

Example 6.1

A large research solenoid has a self-inductance of 25H. What induced emf opposes shutting it off when 100 A of current through it is switched off in 80 ms? ○●●

Solution Induced emf in solenoid due to self-inductance can be calculated using the following formula.

$$E = L\frac{\Delta I}{\Delta t} = 25 \times \frac{100}{0.08} = 31.3 \text{ kV}$$

Example 6.2

The current in a 2.0-H inductor is decreased linearly from 5.0 A to zero over 10 ms.

(a) What is the average rate at which energy is being extracted from the inductor during this time?

(b) Is the instantaneous rate constant? ○○●

Note: Difficulty Level ⟶ ○○● — Easy; ○●● — Medium; ●●● — Difficult

Solution

(a) The energy falls from $Ui = 25$ J to $U f = 0$ in D$t = 10$ ms,
So the rate of decrease is $dU/dt = -25$ J/10 ms $= -2.5$ kW.

(b) The instantaneous power, i.e. $LI\frac{dI}{dt}$ rate of changed of instantaneous energy in an inductor is not constant as even through rate of decrease of current is constant but current itself is not constant.

Example 6.3

Two identical coils *X* and *Y* of 1000 turns each lie in parallel planes such that 80% of flux produced by one coil links with the other coil. If a current of 5 A flowing in *X* produces a flux of 0.5 mWb in it, find the mutual inductance between *X* and *Y*. ○●●

Solution Mutual inductance can be found using the following formula:

$$M = \frac{N_2 \phi_{12}}{I_1}$$

ϕ_{12} = The portion of flux produced by Coil 1 which links coil 2 = 0.8 ϕ_1 = 0.4 mWb
N_2 = Number of turns of Coil 2 = 1000 turns
I_1 = Current in Coil 1 = 5 A
Substituting above values in formula, we get $M = 80$ mH

Example 6.4

Two identical coils *X* and *Y* of 100 turns are perfectly coupled. If a current of 10A flowing in *X* produces a flux of 5 mWb in it, find the mutual inductance between *X* and *Y*. ○○●

Solution Mutual inductance can be found using the following formula:

$$M = \frac{N_2 \phi_{12}}{I_1} = \frac{100 \times 5}{10} = 50 \text{ mH}$$

6.4 DOT CONVENTION

University Question

1. What is dot convention in coupled circuits? Explain. **[BPUT, 2007]**

Dot convention is utilised to indicate sign for the mutually induced voltages across coupled circuits. Circular dot marks and/or special symbols can be utilised for this purpose.

These symbols implicitly represent orientation of the windings around its core of an inductor which in turn affect the polarity of inducted voltage.

Consider following electrical circuit consisting of coupled inductors with self-inductance L_1 and L_2 and a mutual inductance M. It is to be noted that the *dots* are kept at same terminals of both the inductors and current is entering the *dots* from both the inductors. The polarity of mutually induced voltages in inductors is determined by considering these two aspects only while writing voltage drop equations (Figure 6.2).

Sign of M for mutually induced voltage will be determined by

+ if currents are either entering or leaving in the *dots* of both the inductors under consideration

– if current is entering in one *dot* and is leaving in another *dot* of inductors under consideration

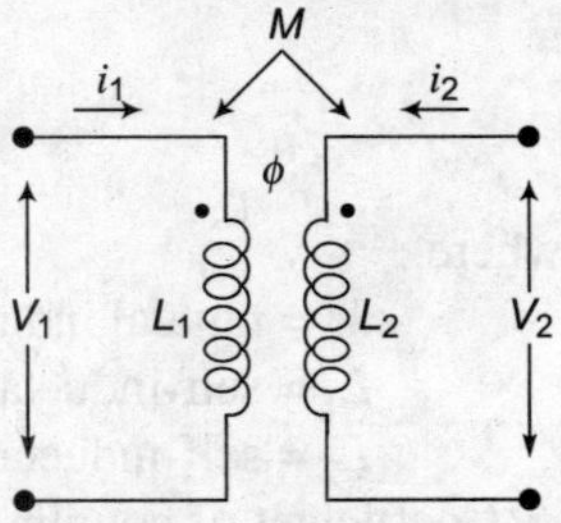

Figure 6.2

Considering above principles, following induced voltage equations can be written:

$$v_1(t) = L_1 \frac{di_1(t)}{dt} + M \frac{di_2(t)}{dt} \text{ volts}$$

$$v_2(t) = L_2 \frac{di_2(t)}{dt} + M \frac{di_1(t)}{dt} \text{ volts}$$

The physical interpretation of putting the dots in electrical circuit is to indicate that the *dotted* terminals attains similar voltage polarity simultaneously.

Example 6.5

Find the equivalent electrical network of the following magnetic circuit using dot convention (Figure 6.3). **[GTU, 2012]** ○○●

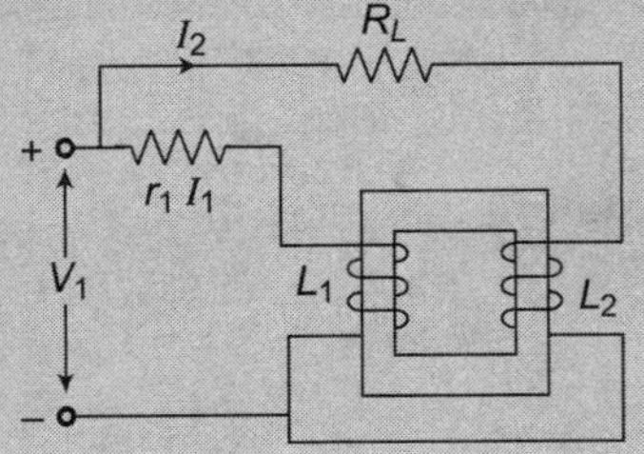

Figure 6.3

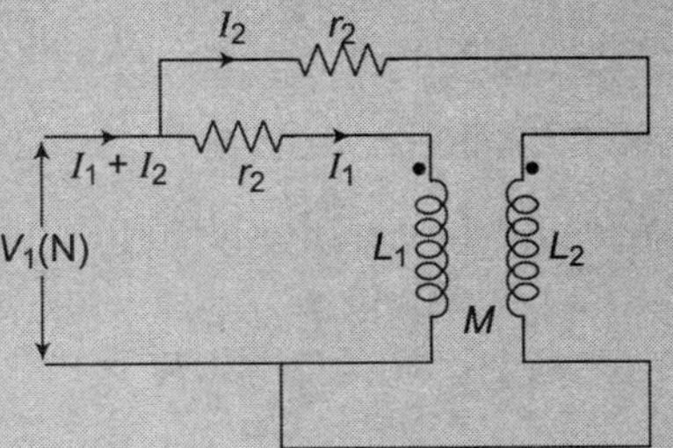

Figure 6.4

Solution Finding the direction of fluxes produced by both the winding in the core, it is evident that first winding produces flux in upward direction while the second winding produces flux in downward direction. This in turn leads to conclusion that at any point both these fluxes are adding to each other. Therefore, the sign of mutually inducted emf will be positive. This gives following equivalent circuit (Figure 6.4).

6.5 COEFFICIENT OF COUPLING

> **Probe**
>
> 1. What do you understand by coefficient of coupling?

The amount of coupling between the inductively coupled coils is expressed in terms of the coefficient of coupling, which is defined by the following formula:

$$K = \frac{M}{\sqrt{L_1 L_2}}$$

where,

M = mutual inductance between the coils.

L_1 = self-inductance of the first coil.

L_2 = self-inductance of the second coil.

Coefficient of coupling is always less than unity and has a maximum value of 1 (or 100%). For the case in which $K = 1$, is called perfect coupling, when the entire flux of one coil links the other. The greater the coefficient of coupling between the two coils, the greater the mutual inductance between them and vice versa.

It can also be expressed as the fraction of the magnetic flux produced by the current in one coil that links the other coil. For example, current $i(t)$ produces total flux ϕ, out of which only flux ϕ_1 links with other coil, then the coefficient of coupling between these coils can be calculated by evaluating $\frac{\phi_1}{\phi}$.

Example 6.6

Two coupled coils have self-inductances of $L_1 = 100$ mH and $L_2 = 400$ mH. The coupling coefficient is 0.8. Find M. If N_1 is 1000 turns, what is the value N_2? ○●●

Solution Mutual inductance of coupled coil is given by:

$$M = K\sqrt{L_1 L_2} = 0.16\text{ H}$$

Inductance of coil is proportional to square of number of turns present in the coil.

$$\frac{L_2}{L_1} = \frac{N_2^2}{N_1^2} \Rightarrow \frac{N_2^2}{N_1^2} = \frac{L_2}{L_1} \Rightarrow N_2 = N_1\sqrt{\frac{L_2}{L_1}} \Rightarrow N_2 = 1000 \times 2 = 2000\text{ turns.}$$

Example 6.7

Two inductively coupled coils have self-inductances $L_1 = 50$ mH and $L_2 = 200$ mH. If the coefficient of coupling is 0.5, compute the value of mutual inductance between the coils?

[AU, 2011] ○●●

Solution Mutual inductance of coupled coil is given by:

$$M = K\sqrt{L_1 L_2} = 0.5\sqrt{50 \times 200} = 0.05\text{ H}$$

6.6 SERIES CONNECTION OF COUPLED INDUCTORS

Inductors can be connected in series with two configurations—one is series aiding and the other is series opposition. Two inductors with self-inductance are connected in both configurations.

University Question

1. Find the equivalent inductance for the series and parallel connections of L_1 and L_2 and if their mutual inductance is M. **[GTU, 2011]**

6.6.1 Series-Aiding Connection

In the following electrical circuit, inductors are connected in series-aiding connection, wherein the currents in both inductors at any instant of time are in the same direction relative to like terminals (Figure 6.5).

Because of this, the magnetic fluxes of self-induction and of mutual induction linking with each element add together. The total inductance in series-aiding connection is calculated using the following formula:

$$L = L_1 + L_2 + 2M$$

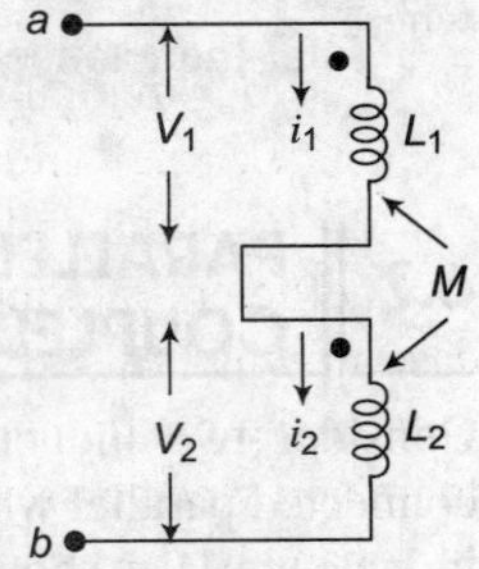

Figure 6.5

6.6.2 Series-Opposition Connection

In the case of series-opposition connection, the currents in the two inductors at any instant of time are in opposite direction relative to like terminals as shown in following electrical circuit (Figure 6.6).

Because of this, the magnetic fluxes of self-induction and of mutual induction linking with each element oppose each other. The total inductance in series-opposition connection is calculated using following formula:

$$L = L_1 + L_2 - 2M$$

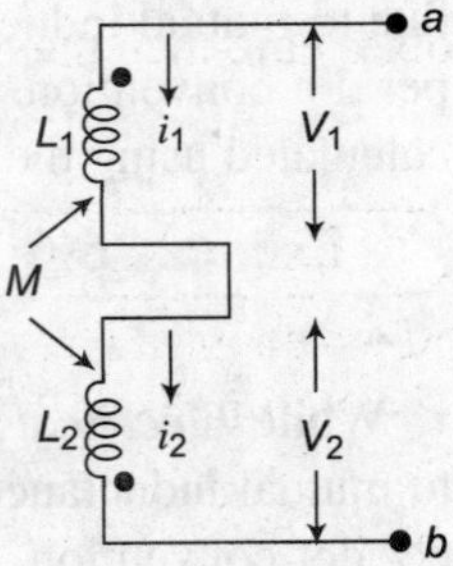

Figure 6.6

Example 6.8

What is the expression for total inductance of the three series-connected coupled coils shown in Figure 6.7. **[BPUT, 2007]** ○○●

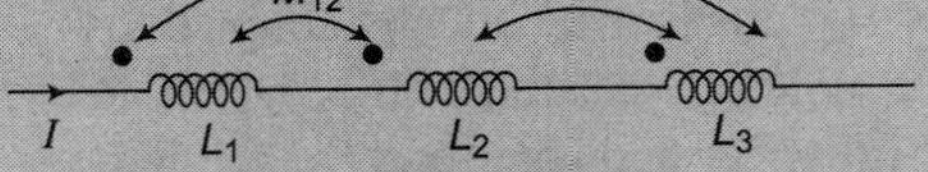

Figure 6.7

Solution

$$L_{eq} = (L_1 + M_{12} + M_{13}) + (L_2 + M_{12} + M_{23}) + (L_3 + M_{23} + M_{13})$$

$$\therefore \quad L_{eq} = (L_1 + L_2 + L_3) + 2(M_{12} + M_{23} + M_{13})$$

Example 6.9

For the three coupled inductors (Figure 6.8), calculate the total inductances.

Solution

For Coil 1, $L_1 = L_{11} - M_{12} + M_{13} = 4$ H

For Coil 2, $L_2 = L_{22} - M_{21} - M_{23} = -1$ H

For Coil 3, $L_3 = L_{33} - M_{32} - M_{31} = 7$ H

Total Inductance = $L_{eq} = L_1 + L_2 + L_3 = 10$ H

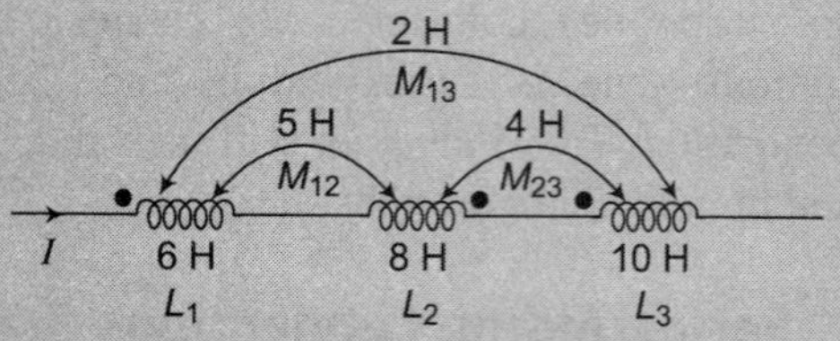

Figure 6.8

6.7 PARALLEL CONNECTION OF COUPLED COILS

Probe

1. Explain parallel connection of coupled inductors and write an expression for total inductances for such configuration?

Consider two inductors with self-inductances L_1 and L_2 connected parallel which are mutually coupled with mutual inductance M as shown in following electrical circuits.

In *Electrical Network*-1 (Figure 6.9), the voltage induced due to mutual inductance aids the self-induced voltage in each coil as per dot convention. The equivalent inductance in this network can be calculated using the following formula:

$$L_{eq} = \frac{L_1 L_2 - M^2}{L_1 + L_2 - 2M}$$

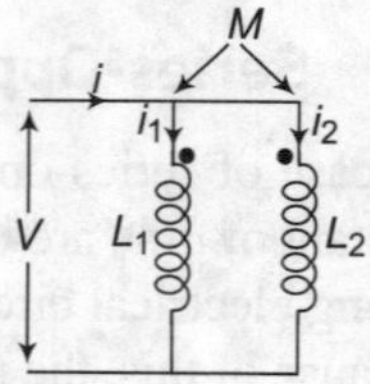

Figure 6.9 *Electrical Network-1*

While *Electrical Network-2* (Figure 6.10), the voltage induced due to mutual inductance opposes the self-induced voltage in each coil as per dot convention. The equivalent inductance in this network can be calculated using the following formula:

$$L_{eq} = \frac{L_1 L_2 - M^2}{L_1 + L_2 + 2M}$$

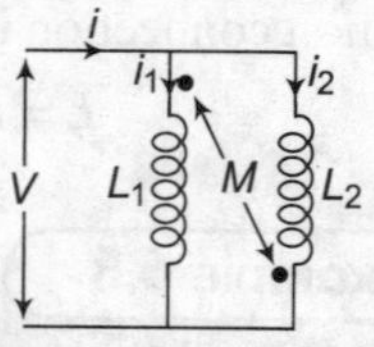

Figure 6.10 *Electrical Network-2*

Example 6.10

A coil having an inductance of 100 mH is magnetically coupled to another coil having an inductance of 900 mH. The coefficient of couple between the coils is 0.45. Calculate the equivalent inductance if the two coils are connected in (a) series opposing, and (b) parallel opposing. **[AU, 2014]**

Solution Given that $L_1 = 100$ mH $L_2 = 900$ mH and $K = 0.45$

$$M = K\sqrt{L_1 L_2} = 0.45\sqrt{100 \times 900} = 135 \text{ mH}$$

Applying formulae for series opposing and parallel opposing connections:

(a) Series opposing $L_{eq} = L_1 + L_2 - 2\,M = 730$ mH

(b) Parallel opposing $L_{eq} = \dfrac{L_1 L_2 - M^2}{L_1 + L_2 + 2M} = 56.51$ mH

Example 6.11

Find equivalent T and π circuit of the network shown in Figure 6.11.

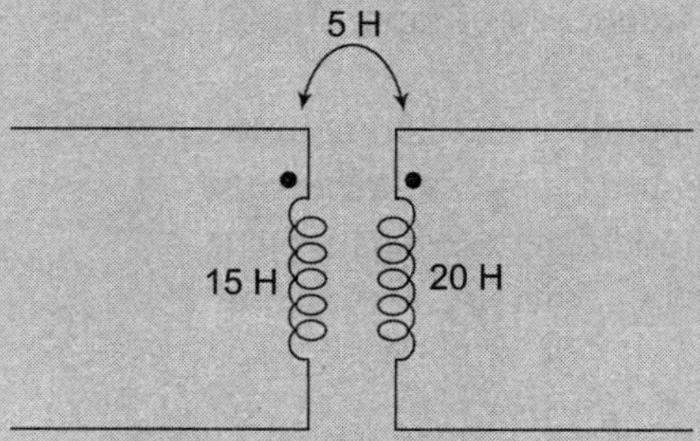

Figure 6.11

Solution Given, $L_1 = 15$ H, $L_2 = 20$ H and $M = 5$ H.

Equivalent T network (Figure 6.12 (a))

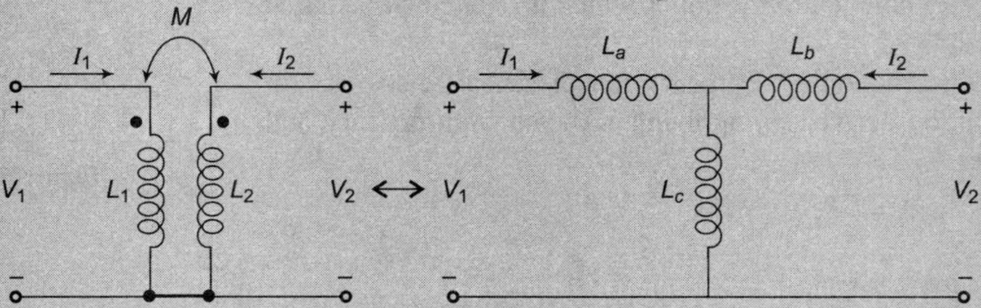

Figure 6.12(a)

Inductances for Equivalent T network are calculated as below:

$L_a = L_1 - M = 10$ H $\quad L_b = L_2 - M = 15$ H $\quad L_c = M = 5$ H

Equivalent π network (Figure 6.12 (b))

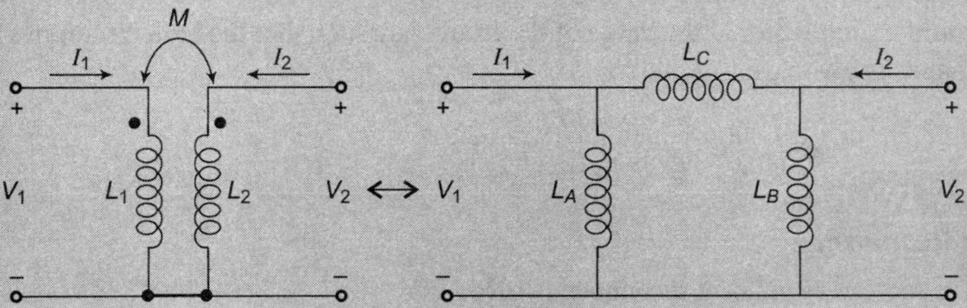

Figure 6.12(b)

Inductances for Equivalent π network are calculated as below:

$$L_A = \frac{L_1L_2 - M^2}{L_2 - M} = 18.33 \text{ H}; \quad L_B = \frac{L_1L_2 - M^2}{L_1 - M} = 27.5 \text{ H}; \quad L_C = \frac{L_1L_2 - M^2}{M} = 55 \text{ H}$$

6.8 || TUNED CIRCUITS

University Questions

1. Derive the expressions for maximum output voltage and maximum amplification of a single-tuned circuit. **[AU, 2011]**
2. Give the applications of tuned circuits. **[AU, 2013]**
3. Derive the expressions for maximum output voltage and maximum amplification of a single-tuned and a double-tuned circuit.

Electrical circuits can be made selective to respond to a particular frequency or a band of frequency of input signal. These circuits are called tuned circuits.

Tuned circuits are, in general, single-tuned and double-tuned. Double-tuned circuits are used in radio receivers to produce uniform response to modulated signals over a specified bandwidth; double-tuned circuits are very useful in a communication system.

6.8.1 Single Tuned Circuit

A tank circuit (i.e. a parallel resonant circuit) consisting of inductor and capacitor is an example of single tuned circuit.

Following electrical circuit wherein a tank circuit on the secondary side is inductively coupled to the coil 1 which is excited by a source at the primary side.

Following expressions pertinent to electrical network in Figure 6.13 can be derived by applying KVL on both primary and secondary sides.

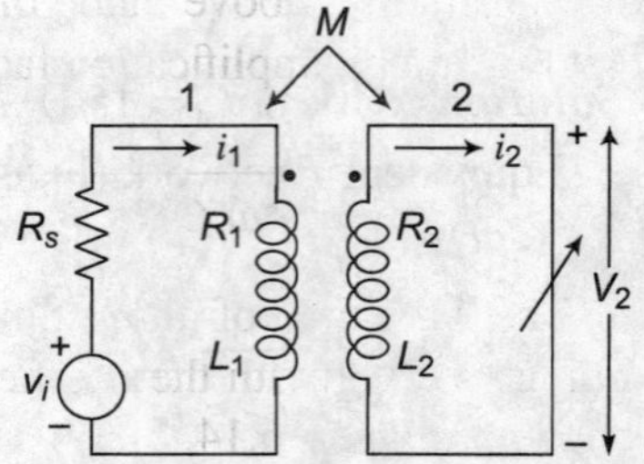

Figure 6.13

$$v_i = i_1 R_s - j\omega M i_2$$

Output Voltage

$$v_o = \frac{j v_i \omega M}{j\omega C\left\{R_s\left[R_2 + \left(j\omega L_2 - \frac{1}{\omega C}\right)\right] + \omega^2 M^2\right\}} \tag{6.5}$$

Voltage Amplification Factor

The voltage amplification factor at the value of the frequency such that the tank circuit in secondary side is under resonances is given as:

$$A = \frac{v_o}{v_i} = \frac{M}{C(R_s R_2 + \omega_r^2 M^2)} \tag{6.6}$$

Current i_2 at Resonance

The current i_2 in secondary sides at resonance is given as:

$$i_2 = \frac{j v_i \omega_r M}{R_s R_2 + \omega_r^2 M^2} \tag{6.7}$$

Thus, it can be observed that the output voltage, current, and amplification depend on the mutual inductance M at resonance frequency. The value of mutual inductance at resonance frequency is given as $M = K\sqrt{L_1 L_2}$.

Maximum Output Voltage and Maximum Amplification Factor

The maximum output voltage v_{0M} and amplification factor A_m at resonance frequency can be obtained by varying the value of mutual inductance M.

Utilising Eqs (6.5) and (6.6) for getting the value of M at which v_{0M} and A_m are obtained:

$$M = \frac{\sqrt{R_s R_2}}{\omega_r} \tag{6.8}$$

Substituting above value of M in Eq. (6.5) to get maximum output voltage:

$$v_{oM} = \frac{v_i}{2\omega_r C\sqrt{R_s R_2}} \tag{6.9}$$

Substituting above value of M in Eq. (6.6) to get maximum amplification factor:

$$A_m = \frac{1}{2\omega_r C\sqrt{R_s R_2}} \tag{6.10}$$

The variation of the amplification factor or output voltage with the coefficient of coupling is shown in Figure 6.14.

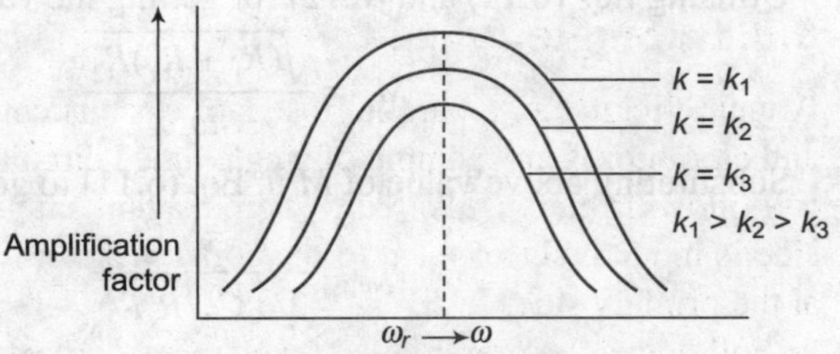

Figure 6.14

6.8.2 Double Tuned Circuit

A double-tuned transformer circuit consists of two series resonant circuit. This circuit is a particular frequency at which both circuits are under resonance condition.

An example of a double tuned circuit is provided in Figure 6.15.

The frequency ω_r at which both tuned circuits are under resonance condition is:

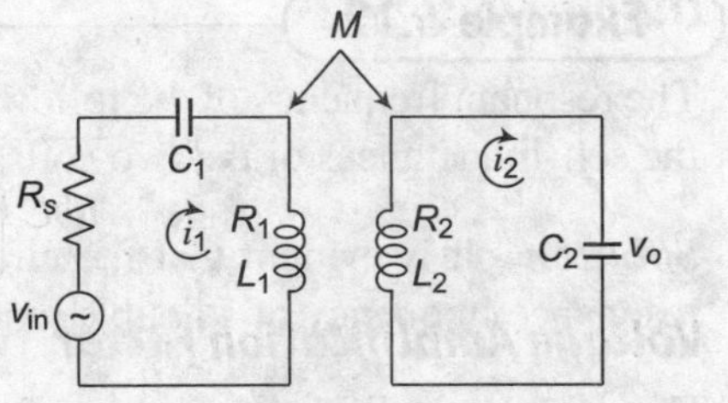

Figure 6.15

$$\omega_r^2 = \frac{1}{L_1 C_1} = \frac{1}{L_2 C_2}$$

Following expressions pertinent to the electrical network in Figure 6.15 can be derived by applying KVL on both primary and secondary sides.

$$v_{in} = i_1\left(R_s + R_1 + j\omega L_1 - \frac{j}{wC_1}\right) - i_2 j\omega M$$

Output Voltage

$$v_o = \frac{v_{in} M}{C_2\left[(R_s + R_1)R_2 + \omega_r^2 M^2\right]} \tag{6.11}$$

Voltage Amplification Factor

The voltage amplification factor at the value of the frequency such that the tank circuit in secondary side is under resonances is given as:

$$A = \frac{M}{C_2\left[(R_1 + R_s) R_2 + \omega_r^2 M^2\right]} \tag{6.12}$$

Maximum Output Voltage and Maximum Amplification Factor

The maximum output voltage v_{OM} and amplification factor A_m at resonance frequency can be obtained by varying the value of mutual inductance M.

Utilising Eqs (6.11) and (6.12) for getting the value of M at which v_{OM} and A_m are obtained:

$$M_c = \frac{\sqrt{(R_1 + R_s)R_2}}{\omega_r} \tag{6.13}$$

Substituting above value of M in Eq. (6.11) to get maximum output voltage:

$$v_{om} = \frac{v_i}{2\omega_r C\sqrt{R_s R_2}} \tag{6.14}$$

Substituting above value of M in Eq. (6.12) to get maximum amplification factor:

$$A_m = \frac{1}{2\omega_r C\sqrt{R_s R_2}} \tag{6.15}$$

Example 6.12

The resonant frequency of the following tuned circuit shown in Figure 6.16 is 1000 rad/sec. Calculate the self-inductances of the two coils and the optimum value of the mutual inductance. ○○●

Solution It is evident that the circuit in Figure 6.16 is an example of double tuned circuit. The resonance frequency of a double tuned circuit is given as:

$$\omega_r^2 = \frac{1}{L_1 C_1} = \frac{1}{L_2 C_2}$$

Given that ω_r = 1000 rad/s, substituting values of C_1 and C_2 in separate equations of above expression, values of L_1 and L_2 can be obtained.

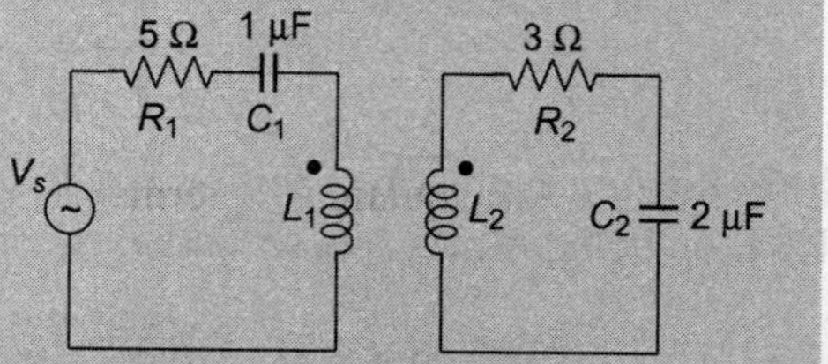

Figure 6.16

$$L_1 = \frac{1}{C_1 \times \omega_r \times \omega_r} = 1 \text{ H}$$

$$L_2 = \frac{1}{C_2 \times \omega_r \times \omega_r} = 0.5 \text{ H}$$

The optimum value of mutual inductance can be calculated

$$M_c = \frac{\sqrt{(R_1 + R_s)R_2}}{\omega_r} \tag{6.16}$$

Substituting $R_s = 0\ \Omega$, $R_1 = 5\ \Omega$, $R_2 = 3\ \Omega$ and $\omega_r = 1000\frac{\text{rad}}{s}$ in Eq. (6.16), we get

$$M_c = 3.87\ \text{mH}$$

6.9 ANALYSIS OF COUPLED CIRCUITS

Probe

1. Write network equations for coupled inductors circuits in the time domain and frequency domain.

A magnetically coupled electrical network can be analysed in either time domain or frequency domain. Frequency domain network equations for a particular network can be obtained by substituting $j\omega$ in the time domain equations.

Time Domain Network Equations

Time Domain (Figure 6.17)

$$v_1 = i_1 R_1 + L_1\frac{di_1}{dt} + M\frac{di_2}{dt}$$

$$v_2 = i_2 R_2 + L_2\frac{di_2}{dt} + M\frac{di_1}{dt}$$

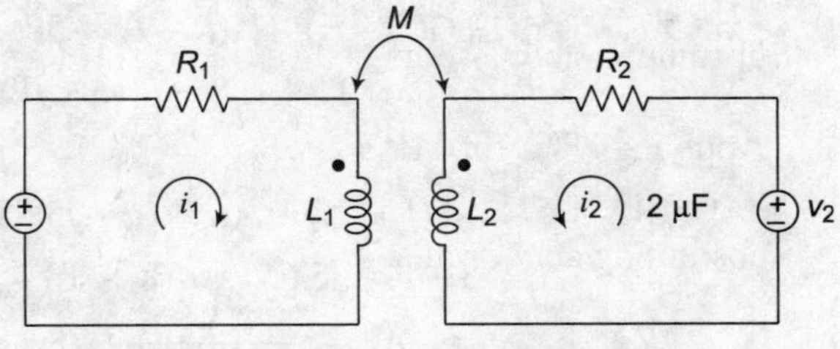

Figure 6.17 *Time-domain circuit*

Frequency Domain Network Equations

Frequency Domain (Figure 6.18)

$$V_1 = (R_1 + j\omega L_1)I_1 + j\omega M I_2$$

$$V_2 = j\omega M I_2 + (R_2 + j\omega L_2)I_2$$

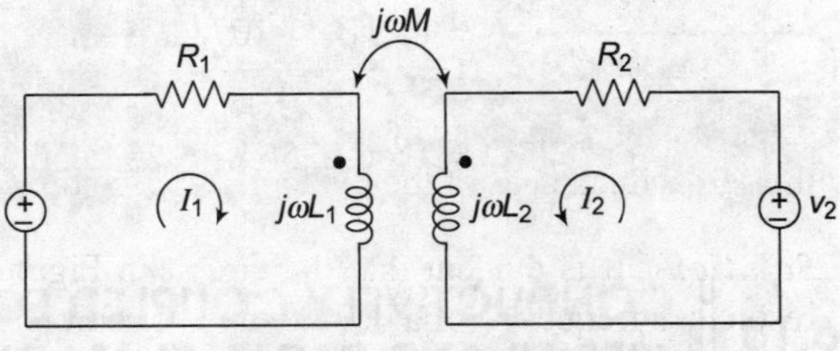

Figure 6.18 *Frequency-domain circuit*

Example 6.13

Write the mesh equations in terms of the phasor currents I_1 and I_2 for the circuit shown in Figure 6.19.

Solution Applying KVL in mesh-1 and mesh-2 while considering the mutually induced voltage in inductors.

For mesh-1,

$$-12 + (-j4 + j5)I_1 - j3I_2 = 0$$

$$\Rightarrow \quad jI_1 - j3I_2 = 12 \qquad (6.17)$$

For mesh-2 $\quad -j3I_1 + (12 + j6)I_2 = 0 \qquad (6.18)$

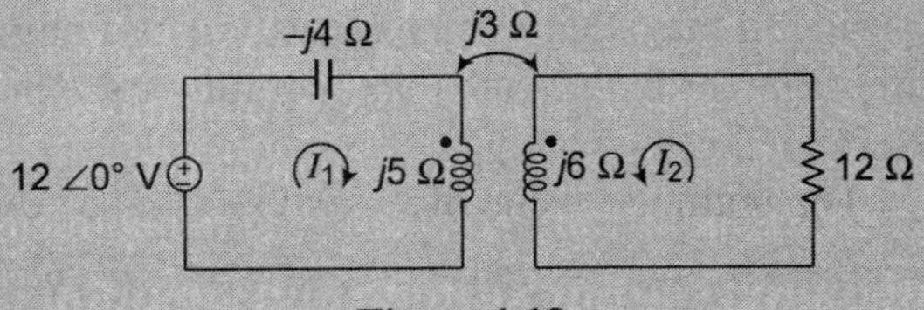

Figure 6.19

Example 6.14

Find the voltage across 5 Ω resistance in circuit shown in Figure 6.20. **[AU, 2011]** ○●●

Solution Given data: $K = 0.8$, $j\omega L_1 = j5\Omega$, $j\omega L_2 = j10\ \Omega$

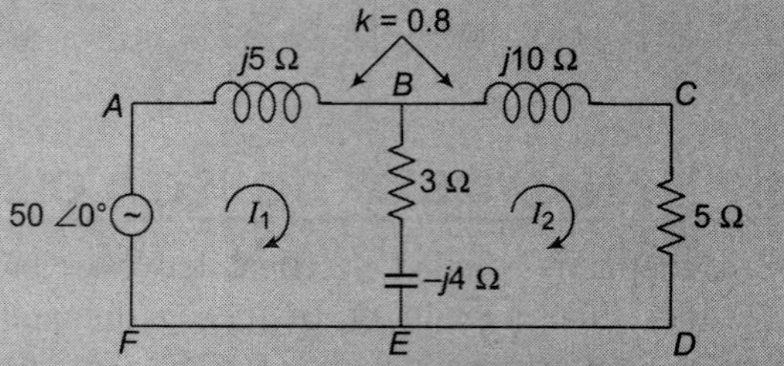

Figure 6.20

Mutual Inductance $j\omega M = K\sqrt{L_1 L_2}$

$\Rightarrow \quad j\omega M = 0.8\ (j5)\ (j10)$

$\Rightarrow \quad j\omega M = j0.8\ 50 = j5.65$

$\Rightarrow \quad j\omega M = j5.65$

Voltage across the '5 Ω' resistor $V5\Omega = 5 \times I_2$

Applying KVL for Mesh 1,

$$-j5.65\ I_2 + (j5)I_1 + 3(I_1 - I_2) - j4(I_1 - I_2) - 50 \angle 0^\circ = 0$$

$$(3 + j)\ I_1 - I_2\ (3 + j1.65) = 50 \angle 0^\circ \qquad (6.19)$$

Applying KVL for Mesh 2,

$$j10\ I_2 + 5I_2 - j4(I_2 - I_1) + 3(I_2 - I_1) - j5.65\ I_1 = 0$$

$$I_1\ (-3 + j4 - j5.65) + I_2(8 + j10 - j4) = 0$$

$$I_1\ (-3 - j1.65) + I_2\ (8 + j6) = 0 \qquad (6.20)$$

Solving Eqs (6.19) and (6.20) simultaneously, we get;

$$I_1 = 11.31 \angle -107.09^\circ\ (A)$$

$$I_2 = 5 \angle 56.81^\circ$$

$$V5\,\Omega = 5 \times 5 \angle 56.81 = 25 \angle 56.81 \text{ volts}$$

6.10 CONDUCTIVELY COUPLED EQUIVALENT CIRCUITS (SERIES AND PARALLEL MAGNETIC CIRCUIT)

An analogy between an electrical quantity and the corresponding magnetic quantity allow us to apply Kirchhoff's laws for magnetic circuits also.

Kirchhoff's Voltage Law (KVL) can be applied to series magnetic circuit while Kirchhoff's Current Law (KCL) can be utilised for parallel magnetic circuit. The application of these laws permits to determine equivalent reluctance of the magnetic circuit having series and parallel elements.

6.10.1 Series Connection

Consider a magnetic circuit consisting of a number of different magnetic connected in series material with different length, area and permittivity. The equivalent reluctance of this magnetic circuit can be determined using following formula:

$$R = \frac{l_1}{\mu_1 A_1} + \frac{l_2}{\mu_2 A_2} + \frac{l_3}{\mu_3 A_3} + \cdots$$

The above formula can be derived by applying KVL for various mmfs in the magnetic circuit.

6.10.2 Parallel Connection

Consider a magnetic circuit consisting of a number of different magnetic materials connected in parallel with different length, area and permittivity. The equivalent reluctance of this magnetic circuit can be determined using the following formula:

$$R = \frac{1}{l_1 / \mu_1 A_1} + \frac{1}{l_2 / \mu_2 A_2} + \frac{1}{l_3 / \mu_3 A_3} + \cdots$$

The above formula can be derived by applying KCL for various mmfs in the magmatic circuit.

Example 6.15

For the parallel magnetic circuit of Figure 6.21, assume that the core material is infinitely permeable. Let $\delta_1 = 3$ mm and $\delta_2 = 2$ mm. The thickness of all core members is $l = 50$ mm. The core has a uniform depth into the page of 75 mm. $N_1 = 2N_2 = 100$ turns. Neglect air gap fringing.

(a) If $I_2 = 0$ and $\phi_1 = 15$ mWb, find the value of I_1.

(b) If $I_1 = 10$ A and $I_2 = 20$ A, determine ϕ_1 and ϕ_2.

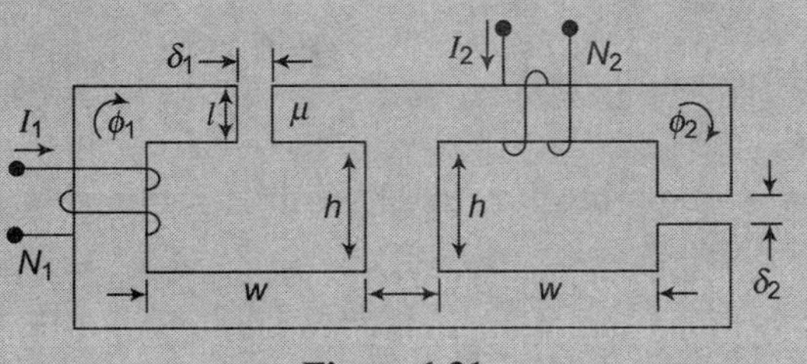

Figure 6.21

Solution Given that the core material is infinitely permeable and the equivalent electrical network can be drawn as in Figure 6.22:

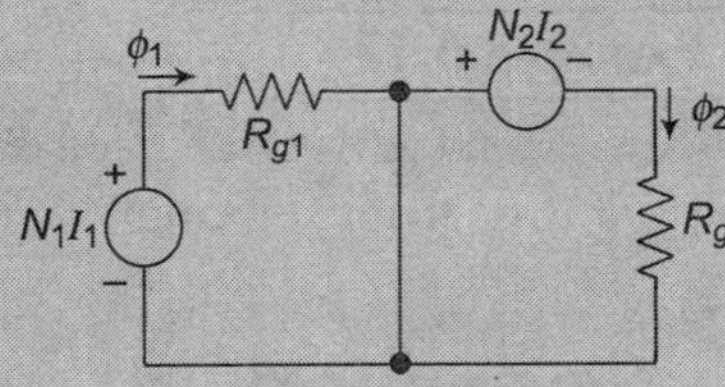

Figure 6.22

$$R_{g1} = \frac{\delta_1}{\mu_0 A_1} = \frac{0.003}{4\pi \times 10^{-7}(0.050)(0.075)} = 6.366 \times 10^5 \text{ H}^{-1}$$

$$R_{g2} = \frac{\delta_2}{\mu_o A_2} = \frac{0.002}{4\pi \times 10^{-7}(0.050)(0.075)} = 4.244 \times 10^5 \text{ H}^{-1}$$

(a) Summation of mmf's around the decoupled left-hand branch gives

$$N_1 I_1 = \phi_1 R_{g1} = (0.015)(6.366 \times 10^5) = 9549 \text{ A}-t$$

$$I_1 = \frac{9549}{N_1} = \frac{9549}{100} = 95.49 \text{ A}$$

(b) Since the two branches are decoupled,

$$\phi_1 = \frac{N_1 I_1}{R_{g1}} = \frac{(100)(10)}{6.366 \times 10^5} = 1.57 \text{ mWb}$$

$$\phi_2 = \frac{N_2 I_2}{R_{g2}} = \frac{(50)(20)}{4.244 \times 10^5} = 2.36 \text{ mWb}$$

Example 6.16

Obtain a conductively coupled equivalent circuit for the following magnetically coupled circuit (Figure 6.23) and then find the Z parameters of the electrical network. ○●●

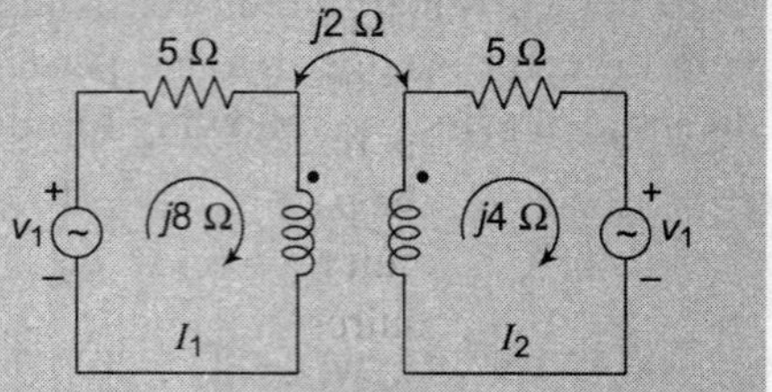

Figure 6.23

Solution Applying KVL in loop-1

$$(5 + j8)\, I_1 - j2I_2 = V_1 \qquad (6.21)$$

Applying KVL in loop-2

$$-j2I_1 + (5 + j4)\, I_2 = -V_2 \qquad (6.22)$$

Writing Eqs (6.21) and (6.22) in matrix form:

$$\begin{bmatrix} 5 + j8 & -j2 \\ -j2 & 5 + j4 \end{bmatrix} \begin{bmatrix} I_1 \\ I_2 \end{bmatrix} = \begin{bmatrix} V_1 \\ V_2 \end{bmatrix} \qquad (6.23)$$

Comparing Eq. (6.23) with Z-parameters equation form (i.e. $[V] = [I][Z]$) gives, Z matrix as follows:

$$[Z] = \begin{bmatrix} 5 + j8 & -j2 \\ -j2 & 5 + j4 \end{bmatrix}$$

Example 6.17

Obtain a conductively coupled equivalent circuit for the following magnetically coupled circuit (Figure 6.24).

[AU, 2012] ○●●

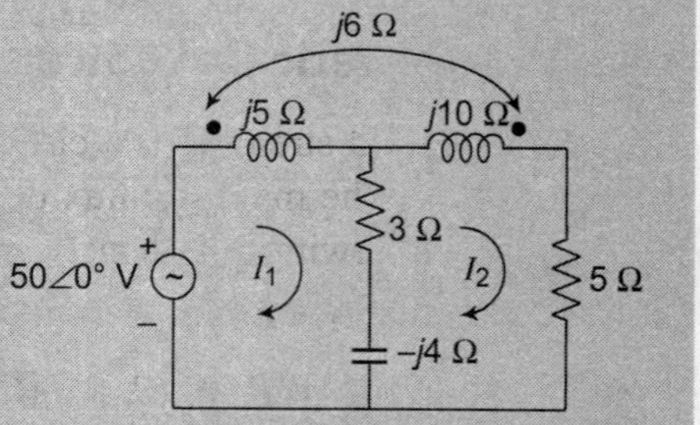

Figure 6.24

Solution M is negative as I_1 enters the $j5\ \Omega$ coil through the dot end, I_2 enters the $j10\ \Omega$ coil through the indented end. In the common branch, I_1 and I_2 are directed opposite (Figure 6.25).

Conductively Coupled Equivalent Circuit:

Thus, from the theory of conductivity coupled circuits,

$$Z_A = L_1 - M;\ Z_B = L_2 - M;\ Z_C = M$$

Here,

$$Z_A = j5 - j6\ \Omega = -j1\ \Omega$$

$$Z_B = j10\ \Omega - j6\ \Omega = j4\ \Omega$$

$$Z_C = j6$$

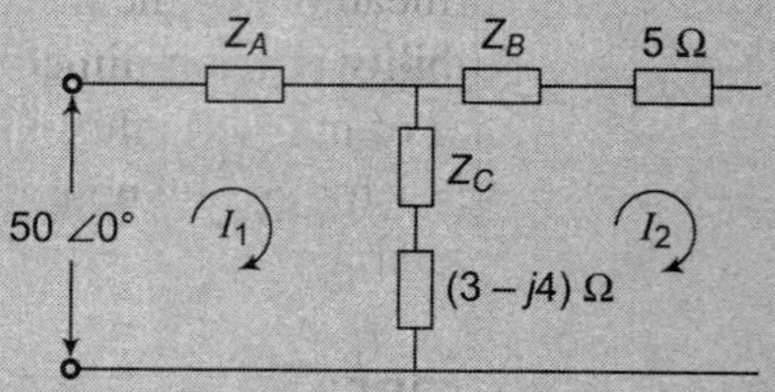

Figure 6.25

6.11 ANALYSIS OF MAGNETIC CIRCUITS

The presence of charges in space or in a medium creates an electric field; similarly, the flow of current in a conductor sets up a magnetic field.

Electric field is represented by electric flux lines, and magnetic flux lines are used to describe the magnetic field. The path of the magnetic flux lines is called the magnetic circuit. Just as a flow of current in the electric circuit requires the presence of an electromotive force, in the same way, the production of magnetic flux requires the presence of magneto-motive force (mmf).

This section discusses some properties related to magnetic flux.

6.11.1 Flux Density (B)

The magnetic flux lines start and end in such a way that they form closed loops. Weber (Wb) is the unit of magnetic flux (ϕ). Flux density (B) is the flux per unit area. Tesla (T) or Wb/m^2 is the unit of flux density.

$$B = \frac{\phi}{A} \text{ Wb/m}^2 \text{ or Tesla}$$

6.11.2 Magneto-motive Force (MMF)

A measure of the ability of a coil to produce a flux is called the magneto-motive force. A coil with N turns, carrying a current of I amperes constitutes a magnetic circuit and produces an mmf of NI ampere turns. The source of flux (ϕ) in the magnetic circuit is the mmf. The flux produced in the circuit depends on mmf and the length of the circuit.

6.11.3 Magnetic Field Strength (*H*)

The magnetic field strength of a circuit is given by the mmf per unit length. Ampere turns per meter is the unit of H. The magnetic flux density (B) and its intensity (field strength H) in a medium can be related by the following equation:

$$H = B/\mu.$$

where,

μ is the permeability of the medium in Henrys/metre (H/m),

μ_0 is absolute permeability of free space and is equal to 4p 3 10^{-7} H/m, and

μ_r is relative permeability of the medium.

Relative permeability is a non-dimensional numeric which indicates the degree to which the medium is a better conductor of magnetic flux as compared to free space.

The value of $\mu_r = 1$ for air and nonmagnetic materials. It varies from 1,000 to 10,000 for some types of ferromagnetic materials.

6.11.4 Reluctance (*R*)

Reluctance is the property of the medium which opposes the passage of magnetic flux. Its unit is AT/Wb. The reciprocal of reluctance is known as *permeance*.

$$R = \frac{mmf(F)}{\text{flux}(\phi)}$$

Air has a much higher reluctance than does iron or steel. For this reason, magnetic circuits used in electrical machines are designed with very small air gaps.

Example 6.18

In the magnetic circuit shown in Figure 6.26, the relative permeability of iron is 10^5. The length of the airgap is $g = 3$ mm and the total length of the iron is 0.4 m. For the magnet $B_r = 1.07$ T, $H_c = 800$ kA/m and the length of the magnet l_m is 5 cm. Assuming the cross section is uniform, what is the flux density in the air gap? ○●●

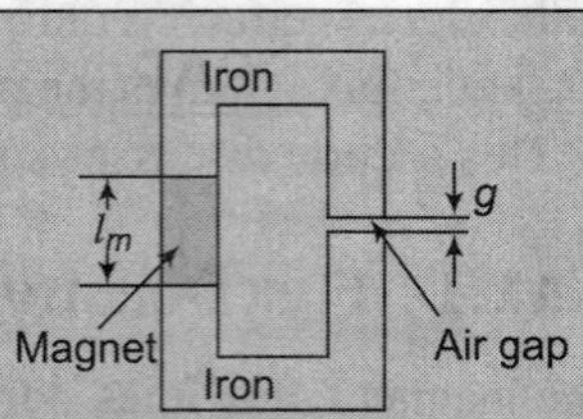

Figure 6.26

Solution Since the cross section is uniform, B is the same everywhere and there is no current. Applying KVL for magnetic circuit involving magnetic field intensity,

$$H_{\text{iron}} \cdot l_{\text{iron}} + H_m \cdot l_m + H_g \cdot l_g = 0$$

$$B_i = B_m = B_g = B$$

$$\frac{B}{\mu_0 \mu_{ri}} \cdot l_{\text{iron}} + B\frac{H_c l_m}{B_r} - H_c l_m + \frac{B}{\mu_0} g = 0$$

$$B\left(\frac{0.4}{4\pi \times 10^{-7} \times 10^5}\right) + B\left(\frac{800 \times 10^3}{1.07}\right) \times 5 \times 10^{-2} - (800 \times 10^3) \times 5 \times 10^{-2} + B\left(\frac{3 \times 10^{-3}}{4\pi \times 10^{-7}}\right) = 0$$

Solving for B, $\quad B = 1.005$ Tesla

6.12 || MAGNETIC LEAKAGE AND FRINGING

A part of magnetic flux produced by a magnetised iron specimen that does not confine to the specimen is regarded as leakage flux. This flux while crossing the air gap bulges outwards due to variation in reluctance. This is known as fringing. This is because the lines of force repel each other when passing through the air as a result the flux density in the air gap decreases.

The ratio of total flux to useful flux is called the *leakage coefficient* or leakage factor.

Example 6.19

The following data refers to two coupled coils – 1 and 2, as shown in the electrical network of Figure 6.27. $\phi_{11} = 0.5 \times 10^{-3}$ Wb; $\phi_{12} = 0.3 \times 10^{-3}$ Wb; $N_1 = 100$ turns; $N_2 = 500$ turns; $i_1 = 1$ A. Find k, the coefficient of coupling, the inductances L_1 and L_2 and M, the mutual inductance. ○●●

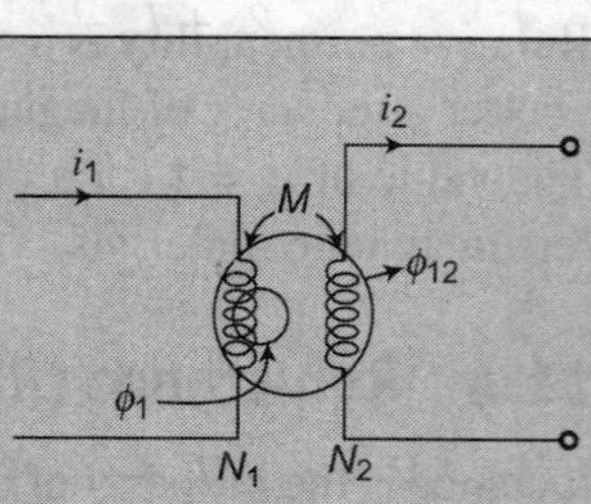

Figure 6.27

Solution $\quad k$ = Leakage factor = $\phi_{12}/\phi_{11} = 0.6$

$$L_1 = N_1\, \phi_{11}/i_1 = 0.05 \text{ H}$$

$$M = N_2\, \phi_{12}/i_1 = 0.15 \text{ H}$$

$$L_2 = \frac{M^2}{L_1 k^2} = 1.25 \text{ H}$$

6.13 COMPARISON OF ELECTRIC AND MAGNETIC CIRCUITS

Table 6.1 presents analogy between an electrical circuit and a magnetic circuit. These analogies allow us to apply Kirchhoff's laws for magnetic circuits also.

Table 6.1 Analogy between magnetic and electric circuits

Analogues Quantity	Electrical Circuit	Magnetic Circuit
Exciting force	emf in Volts	mmf in Ampere-Turns
Response	Current in Ampere	Flux in Weber
Opposition to response	Resistance, $R = \dfrac{\rho l}{A}$	Reluctance, $R = \dfrac{l}{\mu A}$
Quantity drop	Voltage drop (Current × Resistance)	mmf drop (Flux × Reluctance)

6.14 TIME DOMAIN AND FREQUENCY DOMAIN ANALYSIS NETWORK EQUATIONS

Probe

1. Write network equations for coupled inductors circuits in the time domain and frequency domain.

A magnetic coupled electrical network can be solved in either time domain or frequency domain. This section presents time domain and frequency domain network equations for a particular coupled circuit.

Time Domain Network Equations

Time Domain (Figure 6.28)

$$v_1 = i_1 R_1 + L_1 \frac{di_1}{dt} + M \frac{di_2}{dt}$$

$$v_2 = i_2 R_2 + L_2 \frac{di_2}{dt} + M \frac{di_1}{dt}$$

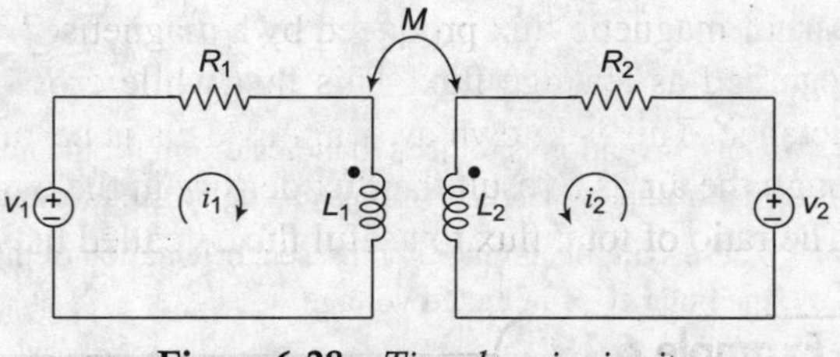

Figure 6.28 *Time-domain circuit*

Frequency Domain Network Equations

Frequency Domain (Figure 6.29)

$$V_1 = (R_1 + j\omega L_1)I_1 + j\omega M I_2$$

$$V_2 = j\omega M I_2 + (R_2 + j\omega L_2)I_2$$

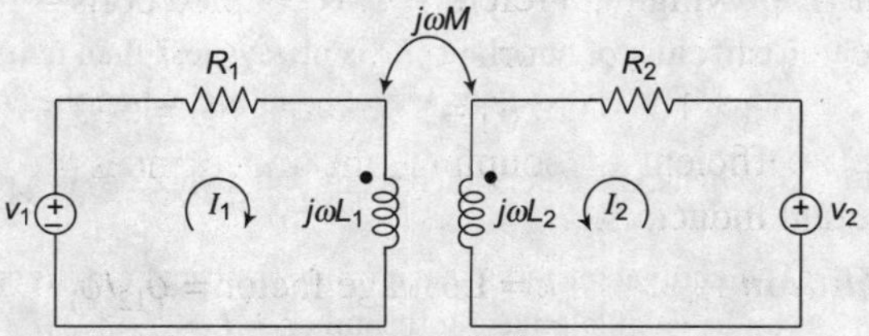

Figure 6.29 *Frequency-domain circuit*

6.15 APPLICATION OF AN IDEAL TRANSFORMER

Probe

1. Explain the application of coupled inductors for transferring the maximum power?

According to Maximum Power Transfer Theorem, the power supplied from a source to the associated load will be maximum when the load impedance becomes equal to the source impedance.

An ideal transformer with primary and secondary winding turns N_1 and N_2 respectively is utilised for delivering the maximum power from an amplifier (source) to a loudspeaker (load). The amplifier output is connected to primary winding of the ideal transformer while the loudspeaker is connected to secondary winding.

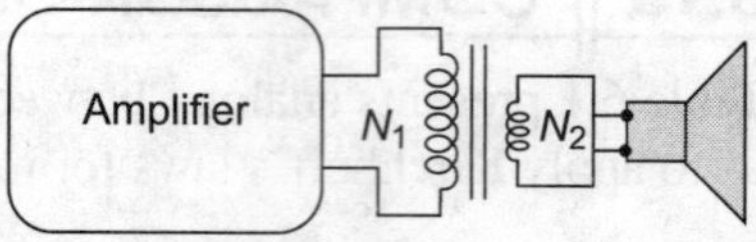

Figure 6.30

N_1 and N_2 are selected such that the loudspeaker impedance, when referred to primary winding, becomes equal to the output impedance of the amplifier. This is called load matching as the load impedance, when transformed, becomes equal to the source impedance and thus maximum power transfer occurs to the loudspeaker.

POINTS TO REMEMBER

☞ A two-winding transformer is an example of inductive coupling, while an auto transformer demonstrates conductive and inductive coupling.

☞ The mutual inductance between two coils can be determined using following formula:

$$M = \frac{N_2\phi_{12}}{I_1} = \frac{N_1\phi_{12}}{I_2}$$

☞ The voltages $v_1(t)$ and $v_2(t)$ across the coupled inductors can be calculated using following formulae

$$v_1(t) = L_1\frac{di_1(t)}{dt} \pm M\frac{di_2(t)}{dt},\ v_2(t) = L_2\frac{di_2(t)}{dt} \pm M\frac{di_1(t)}{dt}$$

☞ Dot convention is utilised to indicate sign for the mutually induced voltages across coupled circuits. Circular dot marks and/or special symbols can be utilised for this purpose.

☞ These symbols implicitly represent orientation of the windings around its core of an inductor which in turn affect the polarity of inducted voltage.

☞ Two coils are said to be mutually coupled if the magnetic flux emanating from one passes through the other. The mutual inductance between the two coils is given as $M = K\sqrt{L_1L_2}$

☞ Coefficient of coupling (K) is always less than unity, and has a maximum value of 1 (or 100%). For the case in which $K = 1$, is called perfect coupling, when the entire flux of one coil links the other.

☞ K can also be determined using $\frac{\phi_1}{\phi}$, where ϕ_1 is a portion of flux ϕ which links with other coil.

☞ The equivalent inductance of an electrical circuit consisting of inductors connected in series-aiding connection can be calculated using formula $L = L_1 + L_2 + 2M$

☞ The equivalent inductance of an electrical circuit consisting of inductors connected in series-opposition connection can be calculated using formula $L = L_1 + L_2 - 2M$

☞ The equivalent inductance of an electrical circuit consisting of inductors connected in parallel-aiding connection can be calculated using formula:

$$L_{eq} = \frac{L_1L_2 - M^2}{L_2 + L_2 - 2M}$$

☞ The equivalent inductance of an electrical circuit consisting of inductors connected in parallel-opposition connection can be calculated using formula:

$$L_{eq} = \frac{L_1L_2 - M^2}{L_2 + L_2 + 2M}$$

☞ Double-tuned circuits are used in radio receivers to produce uniform response to modulated signals over a specified bandwidth; double-tuned circuits are very useful in a communication system.

☞ The value of M at which maximum output voltage and maximum amplification is obtained for a single and double tuned electrical circuit are

- Single tuned circuit – $M = \dfrac{\sqrt{R_sR_2}}{\omega_r}$
- Double tuned circuit – $M_c = \dfrac{\sqrt{(R_1 + R_s)R_2}}{\omega_r}$

☞ The expressions for the maximum output voltage and maximum amplification for a single and double tuned electrical circuit are:

- Single tuned circuit $v_{om} = \dfrac{v_i}{2\omega_r C\sqrt{R_sR_2}}$ $\qquad A_m = \dfrac{1}{2\omega_r C\sqrt{R_sR_2}}$
- Double tuned circuit $v_{om} = \dfrac{v_i}{2\omega_r C\sqrt{R_sR_2}}$ $\qquad A_m = \dfrac{1}{2\omega_r C\sqrt{R_sR_2}}$

☞ Equivalent Reluctance for Series Connection of a number of magnetic paths

$$R = \frac{l_1}{\mu_1A_1} + \frac{l_2}{\mu_2A_2} + \frac{l_3}{\mu_3A_3} + \cdots$$

☞ Equivalent Reluctance for Parallel Connection of inductors

$$R = \frac{1}{l_1/\mu_1A_1} + \frac{1}{l_2/\mu_2A_2} + \frac{1}{l_3/\mu_3A_3} + \cdots$$

☞ Flux Density $B = \phi/A$

☞ Magneto-Motive Force $F = NI = H/l$

☞ Magnetic Field Strength $H = B/\mu$

☞ Reluctance $R = \dfrac{\text{mmf }(F)}{\text{flux }(\varphi)}$

☞ An analogy between an electrical quantity and the corresponding magnetic quantity allow us to apply Kirchhoff's laws for magnetic circuits also.

☞ A transformer is a four-terminal device containing two or more magnetically coupled coils. It is used in changing the current, voltage, or impedance level in a circuit. Important uses of transformers in electronics applications are as electrical isolation devices and impedance-matching devices.

☞ An ideal transformer with primary and secondary winding turns N_1 and N_2 respectively is utilised for delivering the maximum power from an amplifier (source) to a loudspeaker (load). N_1 and N_2 are selected such that the loudspeaker impedance, when referred to primary winding, becomes equal to the output impedance of the amplifier. This is called load matching as the load impedance, when transformed, becomes equal to the source impedance and thus maximum power transfer occurs to the loudspeaker.

PRACTICE PROBLEMS

1. A 25 H inductor has 100A of current turned off in 1ms. ○●●

(a) What voltage is induced to oppose this?

(b) What is unreasonable about this result?

(c) Which assumption or premise is responsible?

2. What is the mutual inductance of a pair of coils if a current change of 6 A in one coil causes the flux in the second coil of 2000 turns to change by 12×10^{-4} Wb per turn? ○●●

3. Explain how the dot convention is utilised to determine the sign of mutually induced voltage in coils. ○●●

4. The following data refers to two coupled coils 1 and 2, as shown in following electrical network. $\phi_{11} = 0.5 \times 10^{-3}$ Wb; $\phi_{12} = 0.3 \times 10^{-3}$ Wb; $N_1 = 100$ turns; $N_2 = 500$ turns; $i_1 = 1$A. Find k, the coefficient of coupling, the inductances L_1 and L_2 and M, the mutual inductance. ○●●

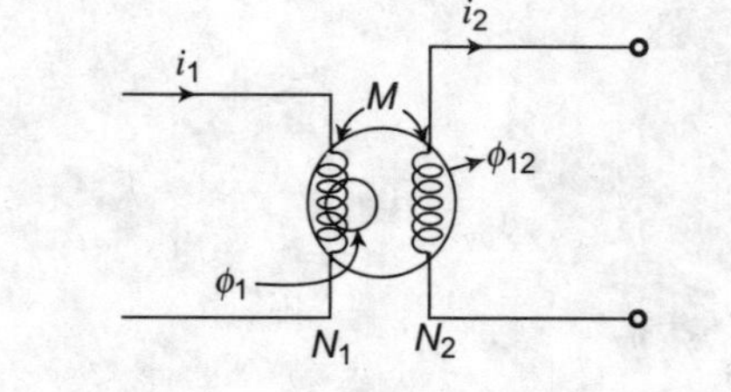

Figure 6.31

5. Two inductively coupled coils have self-inductances $L_1 = 20$ mH and $L_2 = 80$ mH. If the coefficient of coupling is 0.6.

(a) find the value of mutual inductance between the coils, and

(b) the maximum possible mutual inductance.

6. Two coils connected in series have an equivalent inductance of 0.8 H when connected in aiding, and an equivalent inductance of 0.5 H when the connection is opposing. Calculate the mutual inductance of the coils.

7. For the following circuit, determine the voltage ratio V_1/V_2. Which will make the current I_1 equal to zero? ○●●

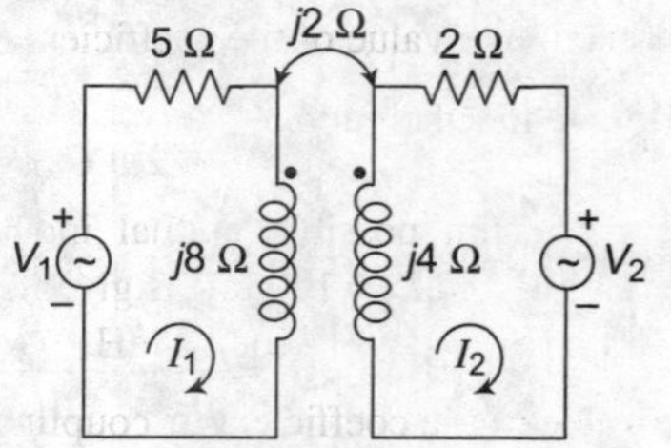

Figure 6.32

8. Find the impedance matrix for the following network. ○●●

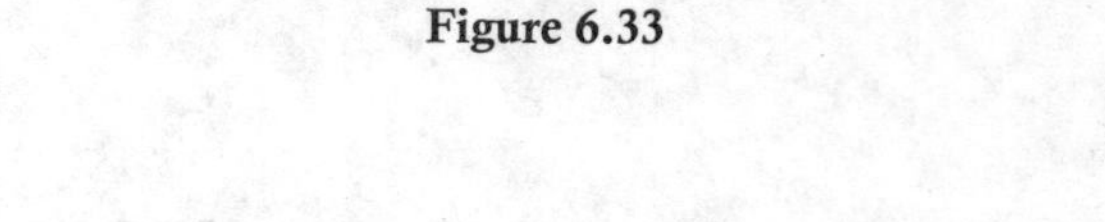

Figure 6.33

9. Draw the equivalent electrical network of the following circuit involving inductive coupling between the coils. Given that $M = 1$, find values of I_1 and I_2.

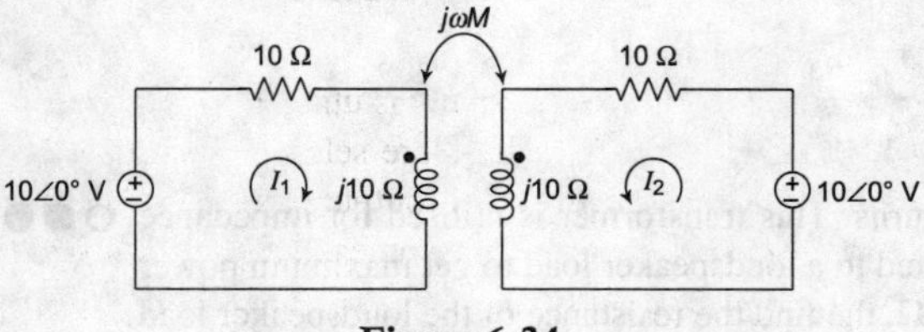

Figure 6.34

10. The following circuit has $L_1 = 4$ H, $L_2 = 9$ H, $K = 0.5$, $i_1 = 5\cos(50t - 30°)$ A and $i_2 = 2\cos(50t - 30°)$ A. Obtain the conductively coupled equivalent and then find the values of (a) v_1 (b) v_2 (c) the total energy in the system at $t = 0$.

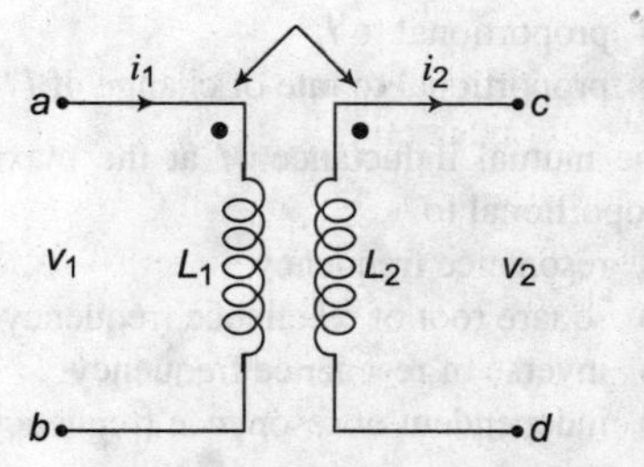

Figure 6.35

11. Draw an analog electric schematic for the parallel magnetic circuit of the following figure for both cases of $\mu = \infty$ and $\mu \neq \infty$.

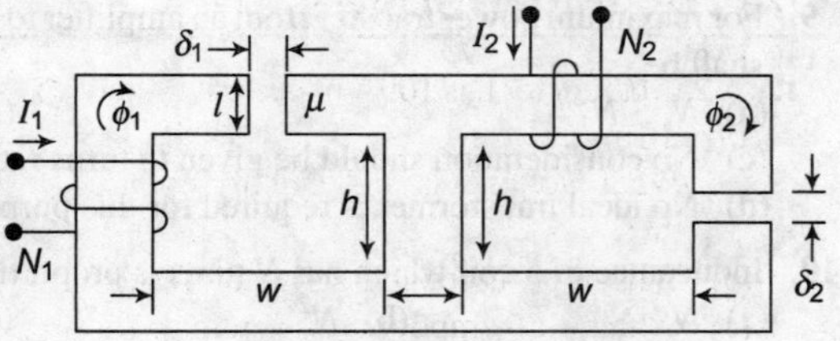

Figure 6.36

MULTIPLE CHOICE QUESTIONS

1. Mutual inductance is a property associated with
   (a) only one coil (b) two or more coils
   (c) two or more coils with magnetic coupling (d) only for conductively coupled inductors

2. The maximum value of the coefficient of coupling is
   (a) 100% (b) more than 100%
   (c) 90% (d) 50%

3. The maximum possible mutual inductance of two inductively coupled coils with self-inductances $L_1 = 64$ mH and $L_2 = 100$ mH is given by
   (a) 80 mH (b) 40 mH (c) 100 mH (d) 64 mH

4. The value of the coefficient of coupling is more for air-cored coupled circuits compared to the iron core coupled circuits.
   (a) true (b) false
   (c) depending upon the rate of change of current
   (d) depending upon the rate of change of voltage

5. Dot convention in coupled circuits is used
   (a) to measure the mutual inductance
   (b) to determine the polarity of the mutually induced voltage in coils
   (c) to determine the polarity of the self-induced voltage in coils
   (d) to determine energy stored in a coil

6. The current is entering in the dot of a coil which is mutually coupled with another coil for which current is leaving the its dot, the mutually induced voltage in first coil is

(a) proportional to I_1
(b) proportional to I_2
(c) proportional to rate of change of I_2
(d) proportional to negative rate of change of I_2

7. The mutual inductance M at the maximum output voltage is obtained from a single tuned circuit is proportional to ○●●
(a) resonance frequency
(b) square root of resonance frequency
(c) inverse of resonance frequency
(d) independent of resonance frequency

8. An ideal transformer has $N_1 = 100$ turns, and $N_2 = 10$ turns. This transformer is utilised for impedance matching purpose for an amplifier required to be connected to a loudspeaker load to get maximum power output. If the output impedance of the amplifier is 2500 Ω, the find the resistance of the loudspeaker load will be ○●●
(a) 100 Ω
(b) 25 Ω
(c) 10 Ω
(d) 2500 Ω

9. For maximum power transfer from an amplifier to a loudspeaker load, the turns ratio of an ideal transformer shall be ○●●
(a) $N_1 > N_2$
(b) $N_1 < N_2$
(c) No consideration should be given to turns ratio an ideal transformer
(d) No ideal transformer is required for this purpose

10. Inductance of a coil which has N turns is proportional to ○○●
(a) N
(b) N^2
(c) N^3
(d) $N^{1/2}$

ANSWERS TO MULTIPLE CHOICE QUESTIONS

1. (c)	2. (a)	3. (a)	4. (b)	5. (b)
6. (d)	7. (c)	8. (b)	9. (a)	10. (b)

Polyphase Circuits

7

Chapter Outline

- Voltage, current and power relations for star and delta configurations
- Analysis of three-phase 3-wire and 4-wire circuits with star and delta connected loads
- Phasor diagram
- Star-Delta conversion
- Relation between power in delta and star system
- Measurement of three-phase power
- Advantages of 3-ϕ system
- Interconnection of three phases

7.1 INTRODUCTION

A three-phase system is a multi-phase system in which electric power is generated, transmitted and consumed by using three phases simultaneously. Voltages of these three phases are equal in magnitude but 120° phase shifted for a balanced 3-ϕ system. It is the most common method of electric power generation and transmission worldwide.

7.2 THREE-PHASE STAR (*Y*), THREE-PHASE DELTA (Δ)

For a balanced system, instantaneous voltages across three phases are expressed as:

$E_R = E_m \cos\omega t$; $E_Y = E_m \cos(\omega t - 2\pi/3)$; $E_B = E_m \cos(\omega t + 2\pi/3)$ for R-Y-B phase sequence.

$E_R = E_m \cos\omega t$; $E_Y = E_m \cos(\omega t + 2\pi/3)$; $E_B = E_m \cos(\omega t - 2\pi/3)$ for R-B-Y phase sequence.

There are two patterns in which the three phases of a 3-phase equipment (load or source) are connected. These are discussed as follows:

7.2.1 Three-phase Star

In this pattern, three phases are connected in such a way that they have one common terminal. The common terminal is called ***star or neutral*** terminal. There are total 4 terminals: One ***star or neutral*** and three terminals of each phase.

There are two possible configurations of connection for a star connected device: (i) 3-Phase, 4 wire (with star terminal connected), (ii) 3-Phase, 3 wire (with star terminal isolated) is shown in Figure 7.1.

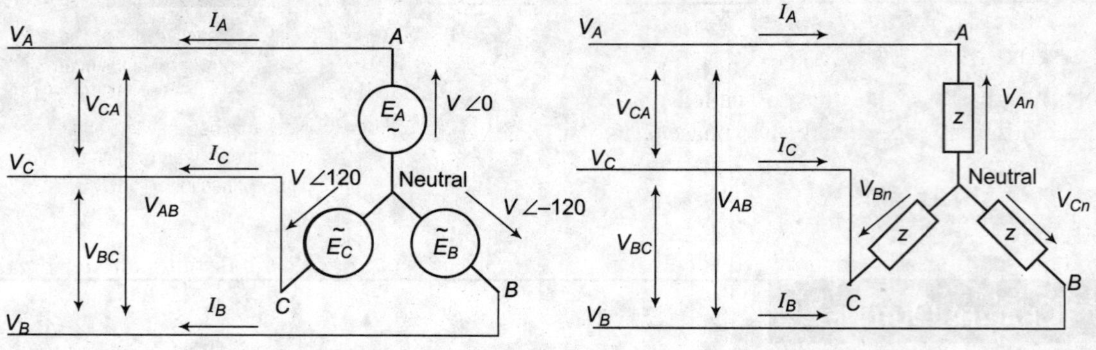

Figure 7.1 *Star connected source and load*

7.2.2 Three-phase Delta

In this pattern, three phases are connected together forming a closed loop with three junctions as shown in Figure 7.2.

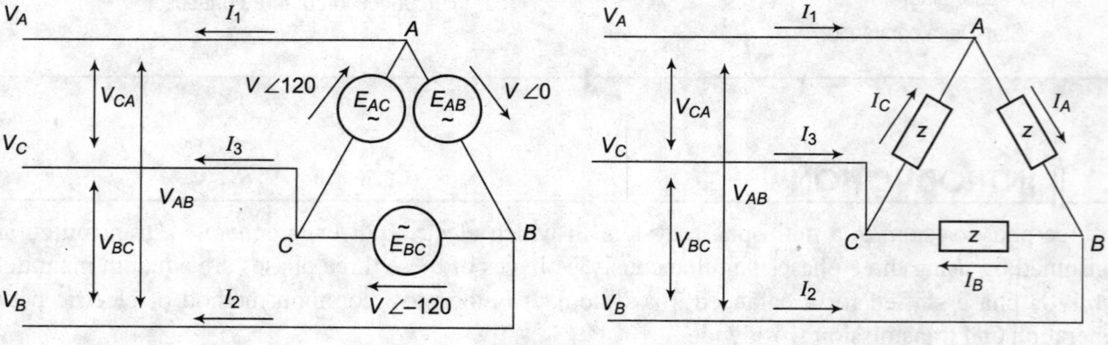

Figure 7.2 *Delta connected source and load*

These three junctions form three terminals of a delta connected device. *There is no star or neutral terminal.*

Example 7.1

In a three-phase balanced delta system, the voltage across *R* and *Y* is 400 ∠ 0° V. What will be the voltage across *Y* and *B*? Assume *RYB* phase sequence. ○○●

Solution Given: Delta-connected system $V_{RY} = 400 \angle 0°$ V.

Since it is a balanced 3-phase system, magnitude of voltage differences between any two of three terminals will be equal. So, V_{YB} is either 400 ∠ 120° V or 400 ∠ –120° V. With RYB phase sequence, V_{YB} lags behind V_R. So, $V_{RY} = 400 \angle -120°$ V.

Note: Difficulty Level → ○○● — Easy; ○●● — Medium; ●●● — Difficult

7.3 VOLTAGE, CURRENT AND POWER IN STAR AND DELTA CONNECTIONS

University Questions

1. Describe volt-amp reactive in 3-phase ac circuit and derive power relations in ac circuit. **[RTU, 2015]**
2. Derive relationship between line and phase current and voltage relation in 3-phase delta connection. **[GTU, 2016]**

Line and Phase Voltages

Voltage across a single phase is called phase voltage and voltage difference between the two phase terminals is called line voltage.

Line and Phase Current

Similarly, current of a single phase is called phase current and current passing through any terminal is called line current.

7.3.1 Star Connection

A star connected balance load is shown in Figure 7.3.

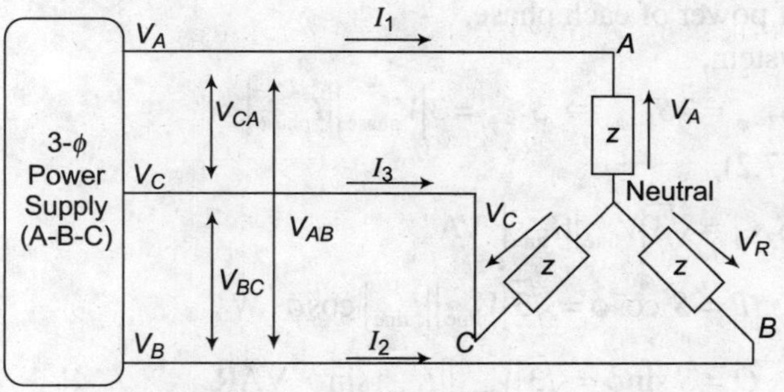

Figure 7.3 *Star connected balanced load*

Voltage

Since each phase is connected between a line terminal and a neutral, line voltage and phase voltage are not same.

For a balanced power supply, with V_{An} as reference and A-B-C phase sequence (Figure 7.4),

$$V_{An} = |V_{\text{phase}}| \angle 0$$

$$V_{Bn} = |V_{\text{phase}}| \angle \left(-\frac{2\pi}{3}\right)$$

$$V_{Cn} = |V_{\text{phase}}| \angle \left(+\frac{2\pi}{3}\right)$$

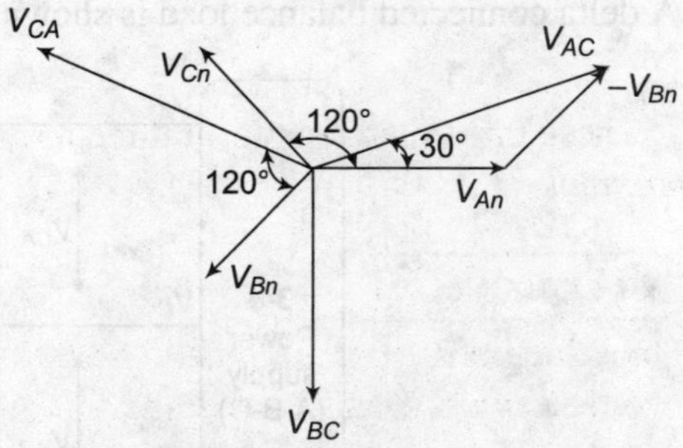

Figure 7.4 *Phase and line voltage for star connection*

and
$$V_{AB} = |V_{\text{line}}| \angle \left(\frac{\pi}{6}\right);\ V_{BC} = |V_{\text{line}}| \angle \left(-\frac{\pi}{2}\right);\ V_{CA} = |V_{\text{line}}| \angle \left(+\frac{5\pi}{6}\right)$$

$$V_{AB} = V_{An} - V_{Bn}$$

Since, phase voltages are 120° phase shifted,

$$\Rightarrow \quad |V_{AB}| = \sqrt{(|V_{An}|^2 + |V_{Bn}|^2 + 2|V_{An}||V_{Bn}|\cos(180-120)}$$

$$\Rightarrow \quad |V_{AB}| = \sqrt{(|V_{An}|^2 + |V_{An}|^2 + 2|V_{An}||V_{An}|\cos(60)} = |V_{An}|\sqrt{(1+1+2\cos 60)}$$

$$|V_{AB}| = \sqrt{3}|V_{An}|$$

So, $$|V_{\text{line}}| = \sqrt{3}|V_{\text{phase}}| \tag{7.1}$$

Current

Since there is no current division at terminals,

$$|I_{\text{line}}| = |I_{\text{phase}}| \tag{7.2}$$

Power

Total power = sum of power of each phase,
For a balanced 3-ϕ system,

Total power, $S_{3-\phi} = 3S_{1-\phi} \Rightarrow S_{3-\phi} = 3|V_{\text{phase}}||I_{\text{phase}}|$

Using Eqs (7.1) and (7.2),

$$S_{3-\phi} = \sqrt{3}|V_{\text{line}}||I_{\text{line}}| \text{ VA}$$

Active power: $$P = S\cos\phi = \sqrt{3}|V_{\text{line}}||I_{\text{line}}|\cos\phi \text{ W}$$

Reactive power: $$Q = S\sin\phi = \sqrt{3}|V_{\text{line}}||I_{\text{line}}|\sin\phi \text{ VAR}$$

7.3.2 Delta Connection

A delta connected balance load is shown in Figure 7.5.

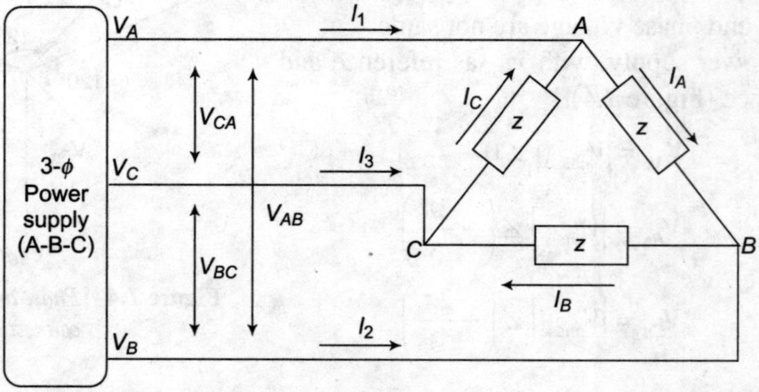

Figure 7.5 *Delta connected balanced load*

Voltage

Since each phase is connected between a line terminal and neutral, line voltage and phase voltage are not same.

For a balanced power supply, $|V_{AB}| = |V_{BC}| = |V_{CA}| = |V_{\text{line}}|$

Since voltage across a phase equals to the voltage difference between the two phase terminals,

$$|V_{\text{line}}| = |V_{\text{Phase}}| \tag{7.3}$$

Current

Line current gets divided (load)/added (source) at each terminal, hence, phase and line current are not same here.

$$I_1 = I_A - I_C$$

Since phase currents are 120° phase shifted,

$$\Rightarrow \quad |I_1| = \sqrt{(|I_A|^2 + |I_C|^2 + 2|I_A||I_C|\cos(180-120)}$$

$$\Rightarrow \quad |I_1| = \sqrt{(|I_A|^2 + |I_A|^2 + 2|I_A|^2\cos(60)}$$

$$= |I_A|\sqrt{(1+1+2\cos 60)}$$

$$|I_1| = \sqrt{3}\,|I_A|$$

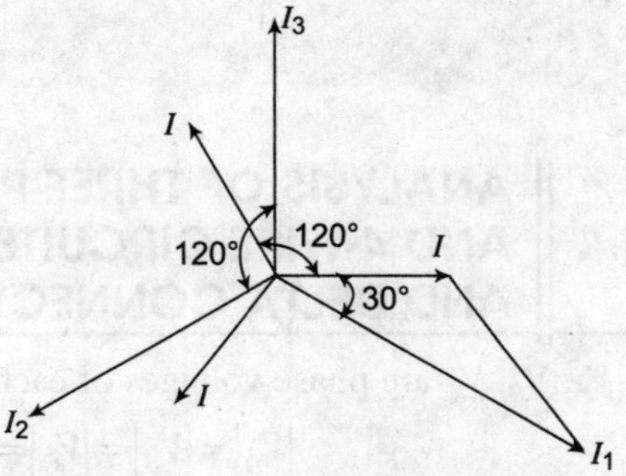

Figure 7.6 *Phase and line voltage for delta connection*

So, $$|I_{\text{line}}| = \sqrt{3}\,|I_{\text{phase}}| \tag{7.4}$$

Power

Total power = sum of power of each phase,

For a balanced 3-ϕ system,

Total power, $S_{3-\phi} = 3S_{1-\phi} \Rightarrow S_{3-\phi} = 3V_{\text{phase}}\,I_{\text{phase}}$

Using Eqs (7.3) and (7.4),

$$S_{3-\phi} = \sqrt{3}\,V_{\text{line}} I_{\text{line}} \mid \text{VA}$$

Active power: $P = S\cos\phi = \sqrt{3}\,V_{\text{line}}\,I_{\text{line}}\cos\phi$ W

Reactive power: $Q = S\sin\phi = \sqrt{3}\,V_{\text{line}} I_{\text{line}}\sin\phi$ VAR

Example 7.2

Three inductive coils having resistance of 16 Ω and reactance of $j12$ Ω are connected in star across a 400V, 3ϕ, 50 Hz supply. Calculate phase voltage. ○○●

Solution Here, line voltage is given 400V.

For a star connected load, $|V_{\text{line}}| = \sqrt{3}\,|V_{\text{phase}}| \Rightarrow |V_{\text{Phase}}| = \dfrac{400}{\sqrt{3}} = 230.94$ V

Example 7.3

A star-connected balanced load draws a current of 35 A per phase when connected to a 440 V supply. Determine the apparent power.

Solution Apparent power, $S = \sqrt{3}\,|V_{\text{line}}||I_{\text{line}}|$

For a star connection, $|I_{\text{line}}| = |I_{\text{phase}}| = 35$ A Here, $V_{\text{line}} = 440$ V

$$S = \sqrt{3}\,|V_{\text{line}}||I_{\text{line}}| = \sqrt{3}\,|440 \times 35| = 26.67 \text{ kVA}$$

7.4 ANALYSIS OF THREE-PHASE 3-WIRE AND 4-WIRE CIRCUITS WITH STAR AND DELTA CONNECTED LOADS

University Question

1. Derive an expression for the total power for a balanced three-phase star connected load in terms of line voltage, line current and power factor. **[GTU, 2013]**

If V_A, V_B, V_C are phase voltages of each phase, than;

$$|V_A| = |V_B| = |V_C| = |V_{Ph}|$$

$$V_A = |V_{Ph}| \angle 0;\ V_B = |V_{Ph}| \angle \left(-\frac{2\pi}{3}\right);\ V_C = |V_{Ph}| \angle \left(-\frac{4\pi}{3}\right)$$

7.4.1 Star Connected Load

For a star connected load shown in Eq. (7.5),

$$I_A = \frac{V_{An}}{Z_A \angle \phi_A},\ I_B = \frac{V_{Bn}}{Z_B \angle \phi_B},\ I_C = \frac{V_{Cn}}{Z_C \angle \phi_C} \tag{7.5}$$

For a balanced 3-ϕ circuit, $Z_A = Z_A = Z_C$ and hence, $|I_A| = |I_B| = |I_C| = \dfrac{|V_{Ph}|}{Z \angle \phi}$

1. 3-wire Circuits

A. Balanced load For a balanced load: Voltage of neutral is zero (given that supply voltages equal in magnitude and 120° shifted).

$$|V_{An}| = |V_{Bn}| = |V_{Cn}| = |V_{Ph}|$$

$$V_{\text{phase}} = \frac{V_{\text{line}}}{\sqrt{3}};\ I_{Ph} = \frac{V_{Ph}}{Z \angle \phi}$$

$$I_A = |I_{Ph}| \angle -\phi;\ I_B = |I_{Ph}| \angle \left(-\phi - \frac{2\pi}{3}\right);\ I_C = |I_{Ph}| \angle \left(-\phi - \frac{4\pi}{3}\right)$$

B. Unbalanced load ($Z_A \neq Z_B \neq Z_C$) If load is not a balanced one, $|V_{An}| \neq |V_{Bn}| \neq |V_{Cn}|$ and also, voltage of neutral point is **not zero**.
Using Eq. (7.5),

$$I_A = \frac{V_A - V_n}{Z_A}, I_B = \frac{V_B - V_n}{Z_B}, I_C = \frac{V_C - V_n}{Z_C} \tag{7.6}$$

Since neutral is isolated, applying KCL at neutral:

$$I_A + I_B + I_C = 0$$

Using Eq. (7.6),

$$\frac{V_A - V_n}{Z_A} + \frac{V_B - V_n}{Z_B} + \frac{V_C - V_n}{Z_C} = 0$$

Here $V_{A/B/C}$ are phase voltages which yields,

$$V_n = \frac{\frac{V_A}{Z_A} + \frac{V_B}{Z_B} + \frac{V_C}{Z_C}}{\frac{1}{Z_A} + \frac{1}{Z_B} + \frac{1}{Z_C}} = \frac{V_A Y_A + V_B Y_B + Y_C V_C}{Y_A + Y_B + Y_C}$$

I_A, I_B, I_C can be determined substituting V_n in Eq. (7.6).
Power:

$$P = V_{An} I_A \cos\phi_A + V_{Bn} I_B \cos\phi_B + V_{Cn} I_C \cos\phi_C$$

ϕ_A is phase difference between V_{An} and I_A.

2. 4-wire Circuits

For a 4-wire circuit as shown in Figure 7.7, voltage of neutral is always equal to zero.
Hence, $V_{An} = V_A$, $V_{Bn} = V_B$, $V_{Cn} = V_C$ (7.7)

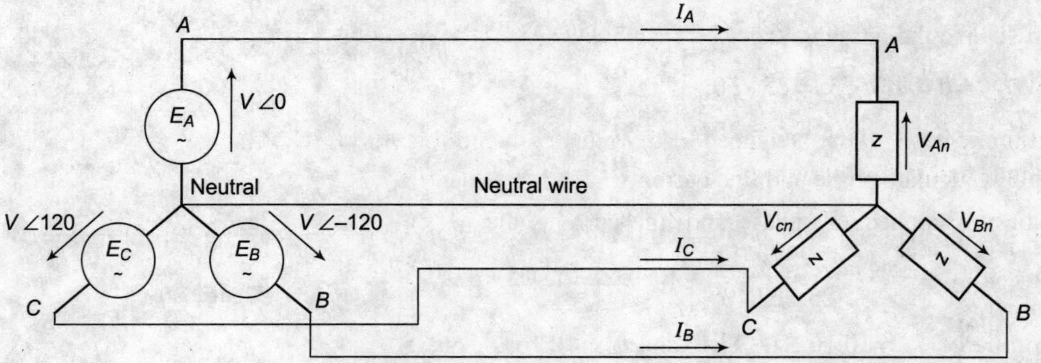

Figure 7.7 *4-wire star connected load*

A. Balanced load Same analysis as of 3-wire connection.

B. Unbalanced load ($Z_A \neq Z_A \neq Z_C$) Since voltage of neutral is kept 0 with 4th *or neutral wire*, even if *f* load is not a balanced one.

Using Eqs (7.5) and (7.7),

$$I_A = \frac{V_A}{Z_A}, I_B = \frac{V_B}{Z_B}, I_C = \frac{V_C}{Z_C}$$

Power:

$$P = V_A I_A \cos\phi_A + V_B I_B \cos\phi_B + V_C I_C \cos\phi_C$$

ϕ_A is phase difference between V_A and I_A.

7.4.2 Delta Connected Load

Since load with delta connection has only three terminals, it can be supplied voltage with 3-wire only.

If I_A, I_B, I_C are phase currents,

$$I_A = \frac{V_{AB}}{Z_{AB}\angle\phi_A}, I_B = \frac{V_{BC}}{Z_{BC}\angle\phi_B}, I_C = \frac{V_{CA}}{Z_{CA}\angle\phi_C}$$

Line currents I_1, I_2, I_3 can be found as:

$$I_1 = I_A - I_C; I_2 = I_B - I_A; I_3 = I_C - I_B$$

Example 7.4

A balanced star-connected load having an impedance of (15 + 20*j*) Ω per phase is connected to 3ϕ, 440 V, 50 Hz as shown in Figure 7.8. Find the line current and power absorbed by the load.

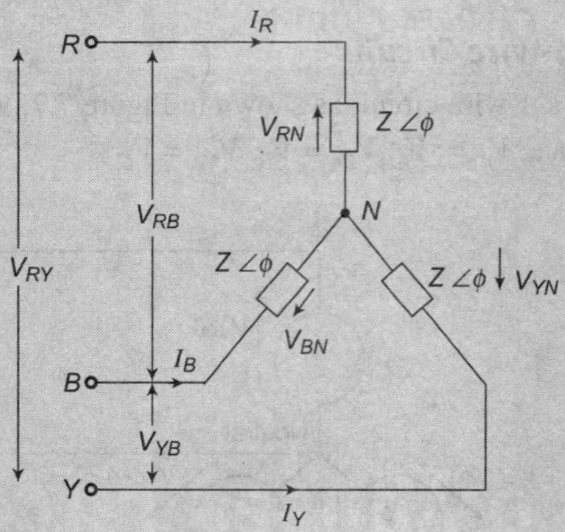

Figure 7.8

Solution Given: $Z = (15 + 20j)\ \Omega = 25\angle 53.13°\ \Omega$.

Assuming *RYB* phase sequence and then taking V_{RN} as the reference voltage, we have:

Step 1: Find the phase voltages:

$$V_{RN} = 440\angle 0/\sqrt{3} = 254\angle 0;$$

$$V_{YN} = 254\angle -120;\ V_{BN} = 254\angle +120$$

Step 2: Calculate phase and line currents:

For star connection, phase and line currents are same, so $I_R = \frac{V_{RN}}{Z} = \frac{254\angle 0}{25\angle 53.13°} = 10.16\angle -53.15$

Similarly, $I_Y = 10.16\angle -173.13$ and $I_B = 10.16\angle -66.85$

Step 3: Power calculation:

It is a balanced 3-phase star connected system with $\phi = -53.13°$, $V_{line} = 440$ V and $I_{line} = 10.16$ A

$$P = \sqrt{3}|V_{line}||I_{line}|\cos\phi = \sqrt{3} \times 440 \times 10.16\cos(-53.13) = 4645.78\text{W}$$

Example 7.5

A delta-connected load has $(30 - j40)\ \Omega$ impedance per phase as shown in Figure 7.9. Determine the phase current if it is connected to a 415 V 3-phase, 50 Hz supply. ○●●

Solution In a delta-connected system,

Phase voltage = line voltage = 415 V.

$$Z = 50\angle -53.13^\circ$$

Taking, V_{RY} as reference,

$$I_{RY} = \frac{V_{RY}}{Z} = \frac{415\angle 0}{50\angle -53.130} = 8.3\angle 53.13^\circ \text{ Amp}$$

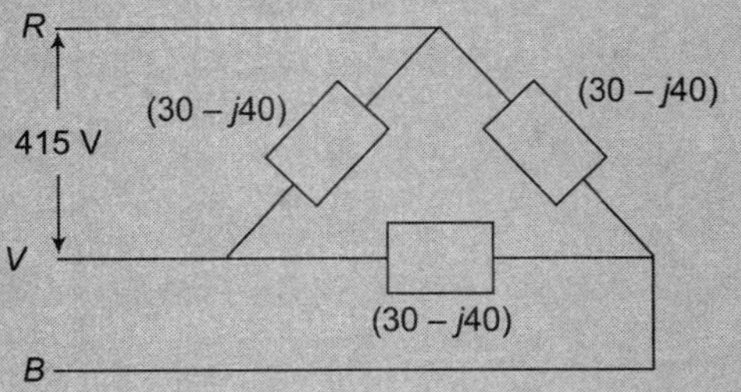

Figure 7.9

In a balanced load, the phase shift of the current is 120° apart.

$$I_{YB} = 8.3\angle -66.87^\circ \text{ Amp. and } I_{BR} = 8.3\angle 186.87^\circ \text{ Amp}$$

Example 7.6

Three impedances $Z_1 = (17.32 + j10)\ \Omega$, $Z_2 = (20 + j34.64)\ \Omega$, and $Z_3 = (0 - j10)\ \Omega$ are delta-connected to a 400 V three-phase system as shown in Figure 7.10. Determine the phase currents, line current, and total power consumed by the load. ●●●

Solution **Step 1:** Find out phase voltages:

$Z_1 = (17.32 + j10)\ \Omega = 20\angle 30^\circ\ \Omega.$

$Z_2 = (20 + j34.64)\ \Omega = 40\angle 60^\circ\ \Omega.$

$Z_3 = (0 - j10)\ \Omega = 10\angle -90^\circ\ \Omega.$

The three-phase currents are I_R, I_Y, and I_B, and the three line currents are I_1, I_2, I_3.

Taking $V_{RY} = 400\angle 0^\circ$ V as reference phasor, and assuming *RYB* phase sequence, we have $V_{RY} = 400\angle 0^\circ$; $V_{YB} = 400\angle -120^\circ$ V; $V_{BR} = 400\angle -240^\circ$ V

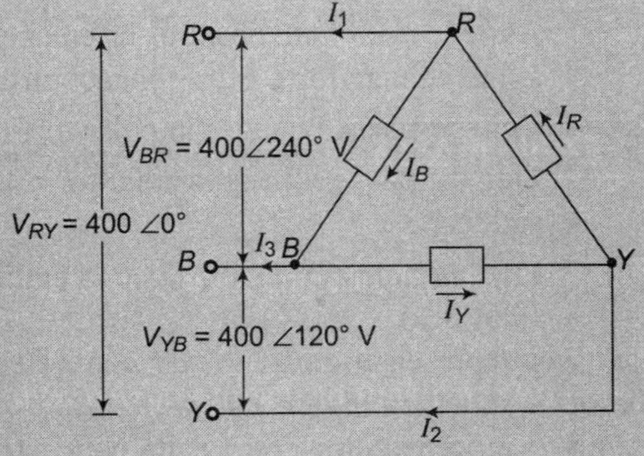

Figure 7.10

Step 2: Calculate phase current:

$$I_R = \frac{V_{RY}}{Z_1\angle\phi_1} = \frac{400\angle 0^\circ}{20\angle 30^\circ} = 20\angle -30^\circ \text{ A} = (17.32 - j10) \text{ A}$$

$$I_Y = \frac{V_{YB}}{Z_2\angle\phi_2} = \frac{400\angle -120^\circ}{40\angle 60^\circ} = 10\angle -180^\circ = (-10 + j10)\text{A}$$

$$I_B = \frac{V_{BR}}{Z_3\angle\phi_3} = \frac{400\angle 120^\circ}{10\angle -90^\circ} = 40\angle -150^\circ = (-34.64 - j20)\text{A}$$

Step 3: Determine line currents (Figure 7.11):

$$I_1 = I_R - I_B = 52.91 \angle 10.89° \text{ A}$$

$$I_2 = I_Y - I_R = 29.09 \angle 159.89° \text{ A}$$

$$I_3 = I_B - I_Y = 31.75 \angle -140.94° \text{ A}$$

To calculate the total power, first the powers in the individual phasors are to be calculated and then they are added to get the total power in the unbalanced load.

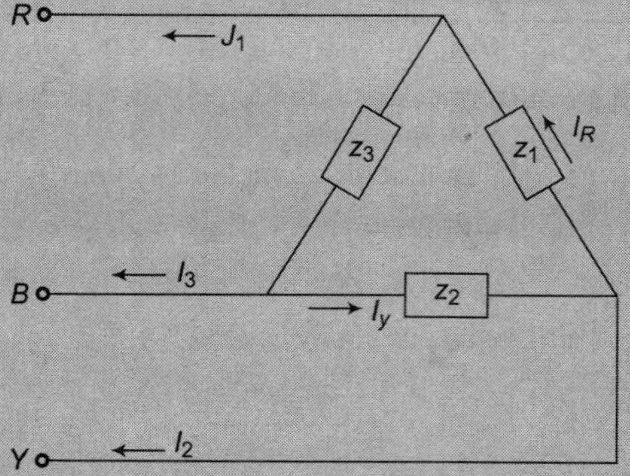

Figure 7.11

Power in R-phase $= I_R^2 \times R_R = (20)^2 \times 17.32 = 6928$ watts

Power in Y-phase $= I_Y^2 \times R_Y = (10)^2 \times 20 = 2000$ watts

Power in B-phase $= I_B^2 \times R_B = (40)^2 \times 0 = 0$

$\therefore$ Total power in the load = 6928 + 2000 = 8928 watts

7.5 || PHASOR DIAGRAM

A Phasor represents a sinusoidal varying quantity with a constant magnitude and phase angle. Quantity with phase angle zero is considered as a reference phasor.

How to draw a reference phasor ?

- Assume one of the phase as reference phasor (generally a phase voltage for star connection and a line voltage for a delta connection).
- Convert phase voltages in polar form and draw all phase voltages (displace by 120°).
- Find the phase current in polar form and draw them in phase plane according to their magnitude and angle.
- Find the line currents (if load is delta) using method of parallelogram (as it is done for vector additions).

Phasor representation for a star connected balanced 3-ϕ system's voltages (with V_a as reference Phasor) is shown in Figure 7.4.

Phasor representation for a delta connected balanced 3-ϕ system's voltages (with V_a as reference Phasor) is shown in Figure 7.6

7.6 || STAR-DELTA AND DELTA-STAR CONVERSION

University Question

1. Derive the equation of Star to Delta and Delta to Star transformation. **[GTU, 2017]**

Conversion Strategy

Impedance measured between two terminals (with third terminal open circuited) should match with impedance measured between same two terminals of other circuit, if the two 3-ϕ circuits are equivalent.

i.e.

$$(Z_{AB}\big|_{C\text{ open}})_{\text{Star}} = (Z_{AB}\big|_{C\text{ open}})_{\text{Delta}} \tag{7.8}$$

$$(Z_{AC}\big|_{B\text{ open}})_{\text{Star}} = (Z_{AC}\big|_{B\text{ open}})_{\text{Delta}} \tag{7.9}$$

$$(Z_{BC}\big|_{A\text{ open}})_{\text{Star}} = (Z_{BC}\big|_{A\text{ open}})_{\text{Delta}} \tag{7.10}$$

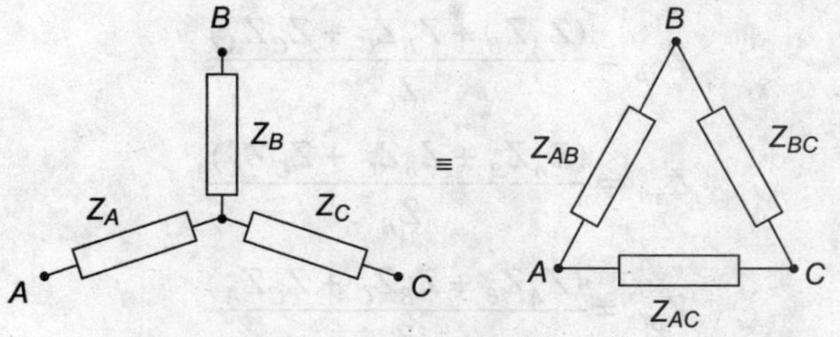

Figure 7.12 *Star-Delta transformation*

For the circuit shown in Figure 7.12;

$$(Z_{AB}\big|_{C\text{ open}})_{\text{Star}} = (Z_{AB}\big|_{C\text{ open}})_{\text{Delta}}$$

$$Z_A + Z_B = \frac{(Z_{AC} + Z_{BC})Z_{AB}}{(Z_{AC} + Z_{BC} + Z_{AB})} \tag{7.11}$$

$$(Z_{AC}\big|_{B\text{ open}})_{\text{Star}} = (Z_{AC}\big|_{B\text{ open}})_{\text{Delta}}$$

$$Z_A + Z_C = \frac{(Z_{AB} + Z_{BC})Z_{AC}}{(Z_{AC} + Z_{BC} + Z_{AB})} \tag{7.12}$$

$$(Z_{BC}\big|_{A\text{ open}})_{\text{Star}} = (Z_{BC}\big|_{A\text{ open}})_{\text{Delta}}$$

$$Z_B + Z_C = \frac{(Z_{AB} + Z_{AC})Z_{BC}}{(Z_{AC} + Z_{BC} + Z_{AB})} \tag{7.13}$$

7.6.1 Delta-Star Conversion

Eq. (7.12) – Eq. (7.13) + Eq. (7.11): $$Z_A = \frac{(Z_{AB}Z_{AC})}{(Z_{AC} + Z_{BC} + Z_{AB})} \tag{7.14}$$

Eq. (7.11) + Eq. (7.13) – Eq. (7.12): $$Z_B = \frac{(Z_{AB}Z_{BC})}{(Z_{AC} + Z_{BC} + Z_{AB})} \tag{7.15}$$

Eq. (7.12) + Eq. (7.13) – Eq. (7.11): $$Z_C = \frac{(Z_{AC}Z_{BC})}{(Z_{AC} + Z_{BC} + Z_{AB})} \tag{7.16}$$

7.6.2 Star-Delta Conversion

Using Eqs (7.14), (7.15), (7.16),

$$Z_A Z_B + Z_B Z_C + Z_C Z_A = \frac{(Z_{AB} Z_{AC} Z_{BC})}{(Z_{AC} + Z_{BC} + Z_{AB})}$$

$$\Rightarrow \quad Z_A Z_B + Z_B Z_C + Z_C Z_A = Z_A Z_{BC} = Z_B Z_{AC} = Z_C Z_{AB}$$

$$\Rightarrow \quad Z_{AB} = \frac{(Z_A Z_B + Z_B Z_C + Z_C Z_A)}{Z_C}$$

$$\Rightarrow \quad Z_{AC} = \frac{(Z_A Z_B + Z_B Z_C + Z_C Z_A)}{Z_B}$$

$$\Rightarrow \quad Z_{BC} = \frac{(Z_A Z_B + Z_B Z_C + Z_C Z_A)}{Z_A}$$

For a balanced 3-ϕ system: $(Z_{AB} = Z_{BC} = Z_{AC} = Z_{\text{delta}}$ and $Z_A = Z_B = Z_C = Z_{\text{star}})$

$$Z_{\text{delta}} = 3.Z_{\text{star}}$$

Example 7.7

If a star connected balanced load with impedance $Z = (10 + j15)\ \Omega$ is to be represented by delta configuration, what will be the value of impedance? ○○●

Solution For a balanced load, if a delta connected system is equivalent to a star connected system, then

$$Z_{\text{Delta}} = 3 \times Z_{\text{Star}} \Rightarrow Z_{\text{Delta}} = 3 \times (10 + j15)\ \Omega = (30 + j45)\Omega$$

Example 7.8

A symmetrical three-phase, three-wire 440 V supply goes to a star-connected load. The impedances in each branch are $Z_A = (2 + j3)\ \Omega$, $Z_B = (1 - j2)\ \Omega$, and $Z_C = (3 + j4)\ \Omega$. Find its equivalent delta-connected load. ○●●

Solution

$$(Z_A Z_B + Z_B Z_C + Z_C Z_A) = 19.10\ \angle 47.3^\circ$$

$$Z_{AB} = \frac{(Z_A Z_B + Z_B Z_C + Z_C Z_A)}{Z_C} = \frac{19.10\ \angle 47.3^\circ}{(3 + j4)} = 3.82\angle -5.83^\circ = (3.8 - j0.38)\ \Omega$$

$$Z_{AC} = \frac{(Z_A Z_B + Z_B Z_C + Z_C Z_A)}{Z_B} = \frac{19.10\angle 47.3^\circ}{(2 + j3)} = 5.29\angle -9^\circ = (5.22 - j0.82)\ \Omega$$

$$Z_{BC} = \frac{(Z_A Z_B + Z_B Z_C + Z_C Z_A)}{Z_A} = \frac{19.10\ \angle 47.3^\circ}{(1 - j2)} = (-3.02 - j8)\ \Omega$$

Example 7.9

Symmetrical three-phase, three-wire 400 V supply is connected to a delta-connected load. Impedances in each branch are $Z_{RY} = 10 \angle 30^\circ\ \Omega$, $Z_{YB} = 10 \angle 45^\circ\ \Omega$, and $Z_{BR} = 2.5 \angle 60^\circ\ \Omega$. Find its equivalent star-connected load.

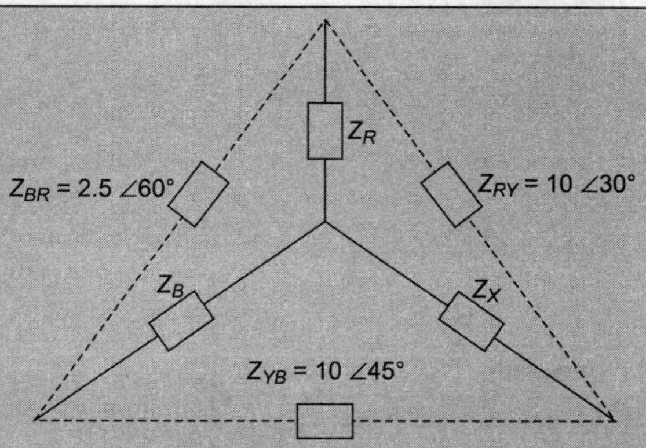

Figure 7.13

Solution

$$Z_{AC} + Z_{BC} + Z_{AB} = 10 \angle 30^\circ + 10 \angle 45^\circ + 2.5 \angle 60^\circ$$
$$= (22.159 \angle 39.97)\ \Omega$$
$$= (16.98 + j\,14.24)\ \Omega$$

$$Z_R = \frac{(Z_{RY} Z_{BR})}{(Z_{RY} + Z_{YB} + Z_{BR})} = \frac{10 \angle 30^\circ \times 2.5 \angle 60^\circ}{22.159 \angle 39.97}, \quad Z_R = 1.13 \angle 50.03\ \Omega$$

$$Z_X = \frac{(Z_{RY} Z_{YB})}{(Z_{RY} + Z_{YB} + Z_{BR})} = \frac{10 \angle 30^\circ \times 10 \angle 45^\circ}{22.159 \angle 39.97}, \quad Z_X = 4.51 \angle 35.03\ \Omega$$

$$Z_B = \frac{(Z_{BR} Z_{YB})}{(Z_{RY} + Z_{YB} + Z_{BR})} = \frac{2.5 \angle 60^\circ \times 10 \angle 45^\circ}{22.159 \angle 39.97}, \quad Z_B = 1.128 \angle 65.03\ \Omega$$

7.7 RELATION BETWEEN POWER IN DELTA AND STAR SYSTEMS

Three equal impedances $Z = |Z| \angle \phi$ are connected in star,

$$V_{\text{phase}} = \frac{V_{\text{line}}}{\sqrt{3}};\ I_{Ph} = \frac{V_{\text{Phase}}}{Z\angle\phi};\ |I_{Ph}| = \frac{|V_{\text{Phase}}|}{|Z|}$$

$$P_{\text{Star}} = 3|V_{\text{phase}}||I_{Ph}|\cos\phi = 3\frac{|V_{\text{Phase}}|^2}{|Z|}\cos\phi = \frac{|V_{\text{line}}|^2}{|Z|}\cos\phi$$

Now, if the same impedances are connected in delta fashion,

$$V_{\text{phase}} = V_{\text{line}};\ I_{Ph} = \frac{V_{\text{Phase}}}{Z\angle\phi};\ |I_{Ph}| = \frac{|V_{\text{Phase}}|}{|Z|}$$

$$P_{\text{Delta}} = 3|V_{\text{phase}}||I_{Ph}|\cos\phi = 3\frac{|V_{\text{Phase}}|^2}{|Z|}\cos\phi = 3\frac{|V_{\text{line}}|^2}{|Z|}\cos\phi$$

$$P_{\text{Star}} = \frac{P_{\text{Delta}}}{3}$$

Example 7.10

A delta connected balanced load consumes 3 kW power. If the same device is reconnected in star, find the power consumption?

Solution With the same phase impedance, power consumed in star is 1/3rd of power consumed in delta.

So, $P_{star} = 3000/3 = 1000 \text{ W} = 1 \text{ kW}$

Example 7.11

A star connected three-phase purely capacitive load (C) is connected in parallel with a delta connected resistive load (R). A connected purely inductive load (L) draws power at unity power factor when supplied with 400 V, 50Hz, 3-phase supply source. Find the value of capacitance and power consumed if $R = 100\ \Omega$, $X_L = 200\ \Omega$.

Solution Given: $R = 100\ \Omega$, $X_L = 200\ \Omega$, line voltage = 400 V, $f = 50$ Hz

Step 1: Simplify the circuit by converting star-connected capacitors in delta:

Since it is a balanced star, equivalent delta will have impedance 3-times.

Now, capacitor of each phase is in parallel with inductor.

Step 2: Find impedance (X) of capacitor-inductor pair:

$$X = (jX_L) \,||\, (-jX_C)$$

$$\Rightarrow \quad X = (jX_L)(-jX_C)/(jX_L - jX_C)$$

Step 3: Evaluate condition for unity power factor:

Here, resistances are connected in parallel with X. So, unity power factor is only possible if current through X i.e. capacitor inductor pair is zero.

Which is true for, $X = \infty$.

$$jX_L - jX_C = 0;$$

$$|X_L| = |X_C| \Rightarrow \frac{1}{2\pi fC} = X_L \Rightarrow C = \frac{1}{2\pi f X_L} = \frac{1}{2\pi \times 50 \times 100} = 31.83\ \mu\text{F}$$

Step 4: Power consumed by resistors:

Each resistance is connected between the line conductors.

$$V_R = 400 \text{ V}$$

$$P = 2(V_R^2/R) = 2 \times 1600 \text{ W} = 3200\text{W}$$

7.8 MEASUREMENT OF THREE-PHASE POWER

University Questions

1. Explain two wattmeter methods of three-phase power measurement. **[AU, 2013]**
2. Explain two wattmeter methods for 3-phase power measurement. **[GTU, 2017]**

Average power of a three-phase system can be measured by two methods:

1. Three-Wattmeter Method

Total three numbers of watt-meters are connected (one watt-meter across each phase). Reading of each watt-meter indicates the power consumed by that phase.

Net power is the sum of readings of three watt-meters.

2. Two-Wattmeter Method

In this method, two watt-meters are connected as shown in Figure 7.14.

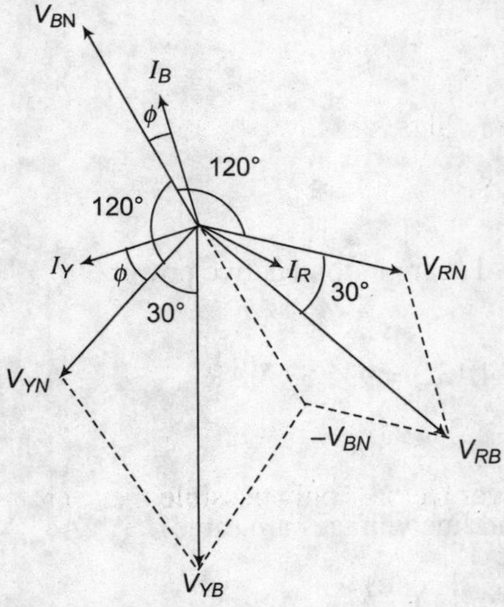

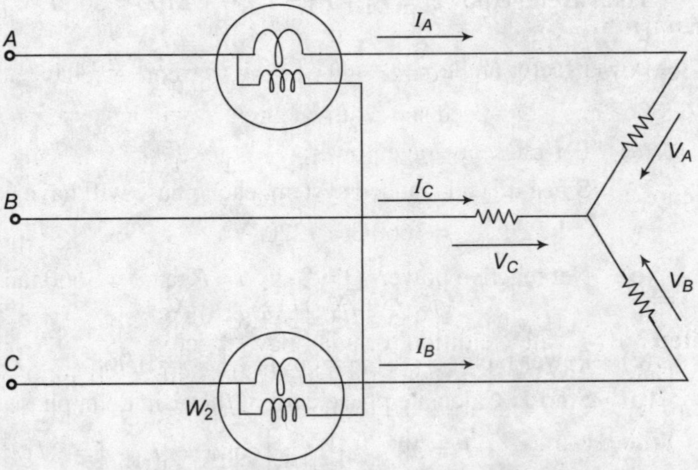

Figure 7.14 *Power measurement with 2-Wattmeter method*

Figure 7.15 *Phasor diagram for 2-Wattmeter method*

Reading of wattmeter-1, $W_1 = |V_{AB}||I_A|\cos\theta_1$ *here* θ_1 is the angle between V_{AB} and I_A.

Reading of wattmeter-2, $W_2 = |V_{CB}||I_C|\cos\theta_2$ *here* θ_2 is the angle between V_{CB} and I_C.

Net power, $W = W_1 + W_2 = |V_{AB}||I_A|\cos\theta_1 + |V_{CB}||I_C|\cos\theta_2$

From the Figure 7.15, it can be observed that, $\theta_1 = 30 + \phi$ and $\theta_2 = 30 - \phi$.

$$\Rightarrow \quad W = |V_{AB}||I_A|\cos(30+\phi) + |V_{CB}||I_C||\cos(30-\phi)$$

$$\Rightarrow \text{ Since } \quad |V_{AB}| = |V_{CB}| = |V_{AC}| = |V_{\text{line}}| \text{ and } |I_A| = |I_B| = |I_C| = |I_{\text{line}}|$$

$$\Rightarrow \qquad W = |V_{\text{line}}||I_{\text{line}}|\cos(30+\phi) + |V_{\text{line}}||I_{\text{line}}|\cos(30-\phi)$$

Solving above expression gives: $W = \sqrt{3}\,|V_{\text{line}}||I_{\text{line}}|\cos\phi$

It shows that sum of reading of two watt meters is the total active power consumed by a 3-phase circuit.

Also, power factor angle for a 3-phase circuit: $\tan\phi = \sqrt{3}\dfrac{W_1 - W_2}{W_1 + W_2}$

Example 7.12

The two-wattmeter method produces wattmeter readings P_1 = 1560 W and P_2 = 2100 W when concerted to a delta-concerted load. If the line voltage is 220 V, calculate (a) the per-phase average power, (b) the per-phase reactive power, (c) the power factor, (d) phase impedance. ●●●

Solution Given: $P_1 = 1560$ W, $P_2 = 2100$ W

Total average power = $P_1 + P_2 = 1560 + 2100 = 3660$ W

$$\text{Power factor angle} = \phi = \tan^{-1}\left(\sqrt{3}\frac{W_1 - W_2}{W_1 + W_2}\right) = 14.13^\circ$$

(a) Per-phase average power:

Since it is a balanced system, each phase will have equal share in total active power,

$$P_{\text{per-phase}} = 3660/3 = 1220 \text{ W.}$$

(b) Net reactive power, $Q = S\sin\phi = P\tan\phi = 3660\tan(14.13^\circ) = 935.57$ VAR

$$Q_{\text{per-phase}} = 935.57/3 = 311.85 \text{ VAR}$$

(c) Power factor = $\cos(\phi) = \cos(14.13^\circ) = 0.968$

(d) **Step 1:** Calculate phase current (here, in delta phase and line voltages are same)

$$P = 3|V_{\text{phase}}||I_{\text{phase}}|\cos\phi \Rightarrow |I_{\text{phase}}| = P/(3|V_{\text{phase}}|\cos\phi)$$

$$\Rightarrow \qquad |I_{\text{Phase}}| = 3660/(3\times 220\times 0.968) = 5.73 \text{ Amp}$$

Step 2: Calculate phase voltage to phase current ratio.

$$\Rightarrow \qquad Z_{Ph} = \frac{|V_{\text{Phase}}|}{|I_{\text{Phase}}|} = \frac{220}{\frac{220}{5.73}} = 38.42\ \Omega.$$

7.9 ADVANTAGES OF 3-ϕ SYSTEM

University Question

1. Mention the advantages of three-phase system. **[AU, 2014]**

1. **Small size and cost:** For the same amount of power generation, a three-phase device is smaller in size as compare to single phase device. Hence higher power to weight ratio.

2. **Power transmission:** A three-phase system requires 3 wires of transmission for each phase, while a system of three single phases require 6 wires, which reduces transmission cost. Also, the same voltage level and current ratings, a three-phase system transmits $|\sqrt{3}|$ times power.
3. **Constant power and torque:** Instantaneous power for a balanced 3-phase system is constant, which ensures constant torque requirement/generation for a three-phase generator/motor.
4. Electric motors with three-phase power supply are **self-starting** in nature, while an alternate winding arrangement is required for a single phase motors for self-starting.
5. A **single phase power supply can be derived from** three-phase supply while reverse is not possible.
6. Rectifier with 3-phase power supply **has very less ripple** in comparison with 1-phase power supply.

7.10 || SOME DEFINITIONS

1. **Line voltage:** Voltage difference between two line conductors of a three-phase system is called line voltage.
2. **Phase voltage:** Voltage across the impedance of one phase of a 3-phase equipment is called phase voltage.
3. **Phase current:** Current passing through the impedance of one phase of a 3-phase equipment is called phase current.
4. **Phase sequence:** Sequence in which, voltages of the three phases of a three-phase system attain their peak value is called phase sequence. Phase sequence R-Y-B is called positive phase sequence.
5. **Balanced load:** If impedances of all phases of a 3-phase device are equal in magnitude and phase angle, load is called balanced load.

7.11 || INTERCONNECTION OF THREE PHASES

Figures 7.16 and 7.17 are the various configurations of interconnection of three-phase connections.

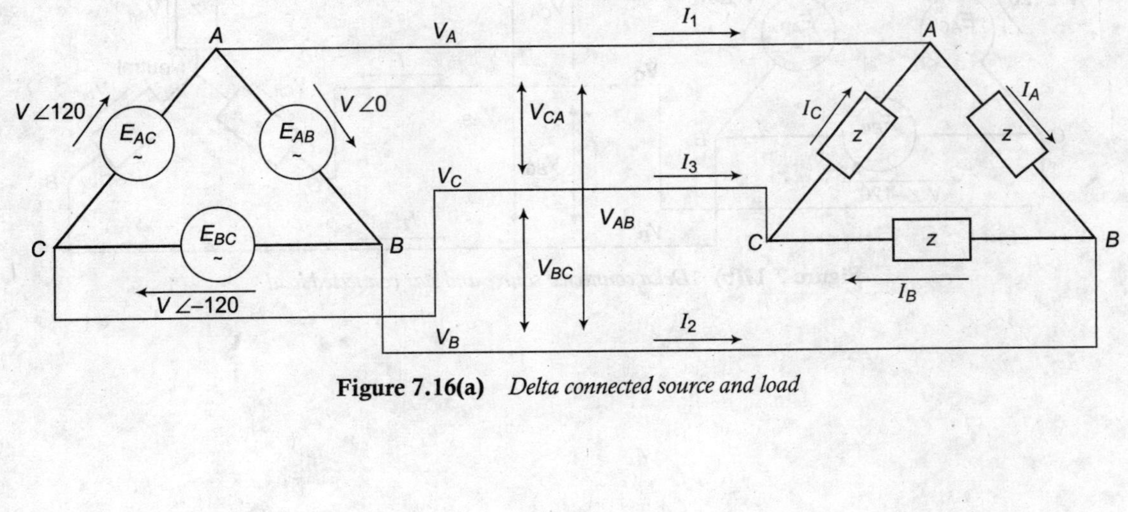

Figure 7.16(a) *Delta connected source and load*

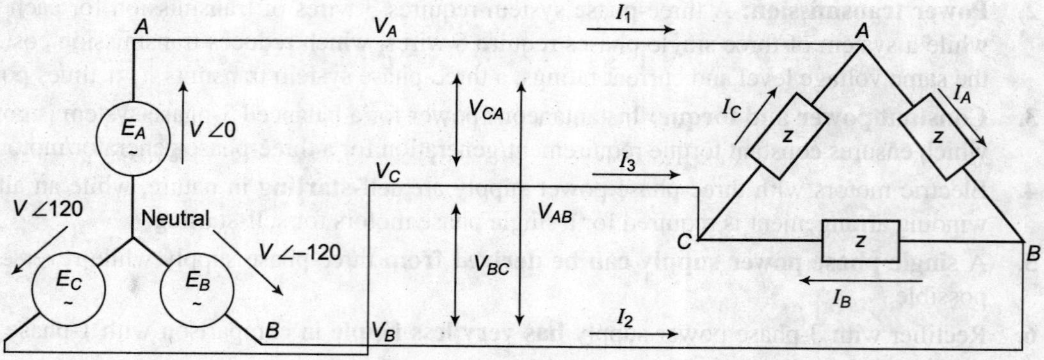

Figure 7.16(b) *Star connected source and delta connected load*

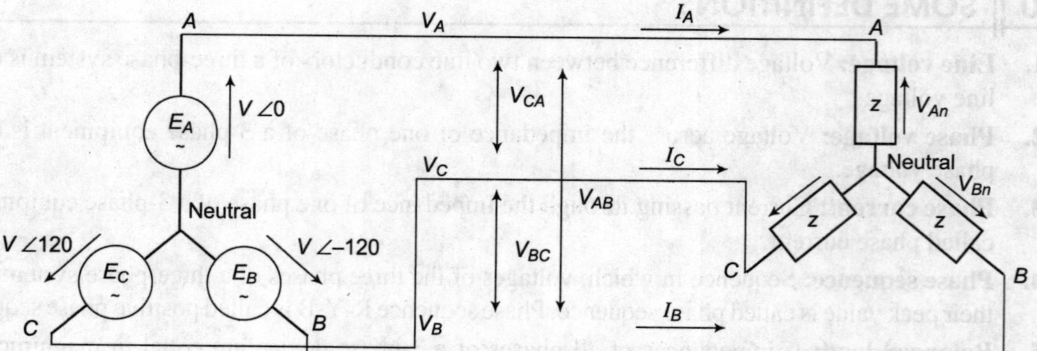

Figure 7.17(a) *Star connected source and load*

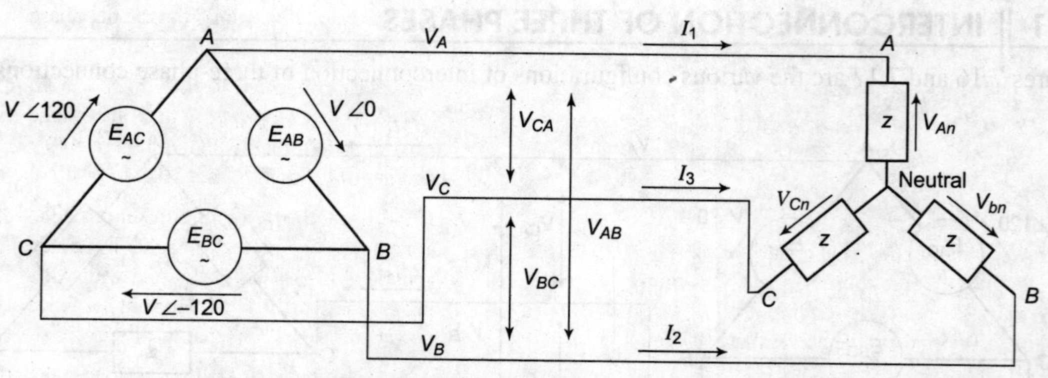

Figure 7.17(b) *Delta connected source and star connected load*

POINTS TO REMEMBER

- For Delta connection: Voltage across each phase is the voltage across the two line terminals.
- For Star connection: Phasor sum of voltages across two phases is the voltage across the two line terminals.
- In a balanced 3-ϕ system,
- For Delta: $|V_{\text{line}}| = |V_{\text{phase}}|$ and $|I_{\text{line}}| = \sqrt{3}|I_{\text{phase}}|$
- For Star: $|V_{\text{line}}| = \sqrt{3}|V_{\text{phase}}|$ and $|I_{\text{line}}| = |I_{\text{phase}}|$ and V_{line} leads V_{phase} by 30°
- Power: $S_{3-\phi} = 3V_{\text{phase}}I_{\text{phase}}$ and $S_{3-\phi} = \sqrt{3}\,V_{\text{line}}I_{\text{line}}$.
- Voltage of neutral for an unbalanced 3-wire star load: $V_n = \dfrac{V_AY_A + V_BY_B + Y_CV_C}{Y_A + Y_B + Y_C}$
- For all types of configuration: $I_{\text{Phase}} = \dfrac{V_{\text{Phase}}}{Z_{\text{Phase}}}$
- Voltage of neutral is zero for a balanced star load and for a 4-wire star load.
- Value of impedance for a delta configuration are higher than that of star.
- If reading of both watt-meter is equal, load is purely resistive in nature.
- If $W_1 > W_2$, load is capacitive and $W_1 < W_2$, load is inductive in nature.

PRACTICE PROBLEMS

1. For a balanced three-phase star connected load, if active and reactive power consumptions at 200V are found to be 4000 W and 3000 VAR respectively, find out value of resistance and reactance per phase. ●●●

2. For a star connected balanced three-phase system, if line voltages are given as: ●●●
$V_{AB} = 200\angle 20°$; $V_{BC} = 200\angle -100°$; $V_{CA} = 200\angle 140°$
Find out phase voltages and phase sequence.

3. An induction machine connected in star is fed by a voltage source of 3.3 kV. If motor draws 2 Amp current while driving a load of 8 kW. Find out the power factor is motor efficiency is 92%. ○●●

4. A balanced delta-connected load with $Z = 6 + j8\ \Omega$ is connected across a 400 V, 3ϕ balanced supply, Find-out the phase currents and line current (phase sequence is RYB). ○●●

5. A 400 V, 40 KVA star connected 3-phase generator is running at rated power with 0.8 lagging power factor. A star connected capacitor bank is connected in parallel with the generator to raise its power factor to 0.9 at rated KVA. Find out the per phase reactance of the capacitor bank. ○●●

6. For a star connected load with $Z_R = 5\ \Omega$, $Z_Y = j2\ \Omega$ and $Z_B = -j4\ \Omega$, find out voltage of neutral terminal if line voltage is 440V and neutral is not grounded. ○●●

7. If the line currents of an unbalanced delta connected system are $I_1 = 5\angle 0$, $I_2 = 5\angle 20$ and $I_3 = 5\angle -30$ (wrt to V_{AB} and with ABC phase sequence) at 440V. Find out net active power consumed/delivered by the circuit. ●●●

8. A delta connected, balanced load with $Z = 6 + j12\ \Omega$ is connected in parallel with a balanced star load with $Z = 2 + j4\ \Omega$. Find per phase impedance seen as connected in star. ○○●

9. Readings of two watt-meters (W_r/W_1 and W_y/W_2) are 300 W and 400 W respectively. ○●●

Does load consume or supply reactive power? Also determine the reactive power supplied or consumed by the load.

10. Star connected imbalanced load with $Z_R = 5\,\Omega, Z_Y = 10\angle 30°\,\Omega$ and $Z_B = 20\angle -20°\,\Omega$ derives power from a 440 V balanced source. If power is measured following the 2 watt-meter method, what would be the readings of watt meters if neutral terminal of load is grounded? ●●●

MULTIPLE CHOICE QUESTIONS

1. If two terminals of a balanced three-phase system are interchanged, phase sequence: ○○●
   (a) Remains same (b) Gets changed (c) Depends upon load (d) Cannot be determined
2. Magnitude of phase voltages for delta and star connected load connected to 300V, 50 Hz 3-phase source are respectively: ○○●
   (a) 300 V, 300V (b) 173.21V, 173.21V (c) 300V, 173.21V (d) 173.21V, 300V
3. A three-phase current source supplies 20A line current to balanced 3-phase load. Phase current for star and delta configuration of load will be respectively: ○○●
   (a) 10 A, 10 A (b) 5.77 A, 5.77 A (c) 5.77 A, 10 A (d) 10 A, 5.77 A
4. Voltage of neutral for a star connected load is not zero in case: ○●●
   (a) Neutral is not grounded and load is imbalanced
   (b) Neutral is not grounded
   (c) Load is imbalanced (d) Load is balanced and neutral is not grounded
5. A purely resistive 3 phase load is deriving power from a balanced supply source. What can be possible readings of 2 wattmeters: ●●●
   (a) 200W, 200W (b) 100W, 200W (c) –100W, –100W (d) 200W, 100W
6. A 3-phase load connected to 400V, 50Hz supply draws 2.5A line current, reactive power consumed by load for 0.8 lag power factor: ○●●
   (a) 1039.2 VAR (b) 1385.6 VAR (c) 1732 VAR (d) 600 VAR
7. Read following statements regarding 3-phase electric circuit with R-Y-B phase sequence: ○●●
   I. V_{RY} leads V_R with 30° for a star connection.
   II. Line current pertaining to R phase lags its phase current by 30° for a delta connection.
   III. Angle between V_R and V_{YB} is – 90°.
   IV. Line current pertaining to R phase leads its phase current by 30° for a delta connection.
   Which one of above is correct:
   (a) I, II (b) I, III (c) I, II, III (d) I, III, IV
8. A three-phase star load is rearranged as delta and connected to same power supply source, power consumed will be: ○●●
   (a) Doubled (b) Three times (c) Same (d) One third
9. For an unbalanced star connected load (4-wire), three line currents are 10 A, $2 + 3j$ A and $-8 - 2j$, neutral current will be: ○●●
   (a) 0 (b) $4 + 1j$ (c) $\sqrt{3}\,(4 + 1j)$ (d) $(4 + 1j)/\sqrt{3}$
10. A three-phase star connected motor is connected to a balanced delta connected generator. Ratio of phase current of motor to generator is: ○●●
   (a) $\sqrt{3}$ (b) 1 (c) $1/\sqrt{3}$ (d) $2/\pi$

ANSWERS TO MULTIPLE CHOICE QUESTIONS

1. (b)	2. (c)	3. (d)	4. (a)	5. (a)
6. (a)	7. (c)	8. (b)	9. (b)	10. (c)

Network Functions

8

CHAPTER OUTLINE

- Transfer functions and driving-point functions
- Analysis of ladder and non-ladder networks
- Minimise power transfer
- Poles and zeros of network functions
- Time domain response from pole-zero behaviour
- Graphical method for determination of residue

8.1 INTRODUCTION

It is known that, a circuit with capacitance and inductance needs differential equations to be solved in order to get the time response. With the help of Laplace transform, these equations can be solved in s-domain (frequency domain). Network function relates voltages or currents of different segments of the network. Network functions are defined in s-domain only. Sometimes, voltages of every node (or current of every branch) are not matter of concern. In such cases, entire network can be replaced with desired number of ports and their transfer functions.

This chapter explains the various types of network functions, their properties and time domain solutions for a network function.

8.2 TRANSFER FUNCTIONS AND DRIVING-POINT FUNCTIONS

University Questions

1. Define open circuit driving point impedance. [AU, 2014]
2. Define transfer function. [PTU, 2014]

8.2.1 Transfer Functions

For a network with at least two ports, ratio of Laplace transform of voltage or current of one port to Laplace transform of voltage or current of another port is known as *transfer function*.

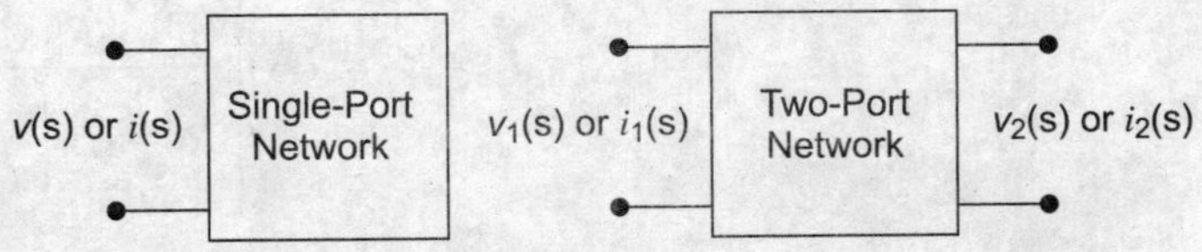

Figure 8.1

A network must be initially relaxed while finding this ratio, i.e. initial condition(s) must be set at zero. Since Laplace transform of a unit impulse is 1, transfer function is also defined as unit impulse response.

Hence, for a two port network, there exist four number of transfer functions:

Voltage transfer function: $G_{12}(s)=\dfrac{V_2(s)}{V_1(s)}$ and $G_{21}(s)=\dfrac{V_1(s)}{V_2(s)}$

Current transfer function: $\alpha_{12}(s)=\dfrac{I_2(s)}{I_1(s)}$ and $\alpha_{21}(s)=\dfrac{I_1(s)}{I_2(s)}$

Transfer impedance function: $Z_{12}(s)=\dfrac{V_2(s)}{I_1(s)}$ and $Z_{21}(s)=\dfrac{V_1(s)}{I_2(s)}$

Transfer admittance function: $Y_{12}(s)=\dfrac{I_2(s)}{V_1(s)}$ and $Y_{21}(s)=\dfrac{I_1(s)}{V_2(s)}$

8.2.2 Driving-point Function

For a network (for any number of ports), ratio of Laplace transform of voltage or current of a port to Laplace transform of voltage or current of same is known as *driving-point function*.

It can be classified as driving point impedance, $Z(s)=\dfrac{V(s)}{I(s)}$ and driving point admittance, $Y(s)=\dfrac{I(s)}{V(s)}$.

Hence, total number of driving point functions will be twice the number of ports.

Example 8.1

Determine the transfer function $V(s)/I(s)$ for the network shown in Figure 8.2. ○○●

Solution **Step 1:** Transform the circuit in *s* domain.

Step 2: Find out current through $V(s)$.

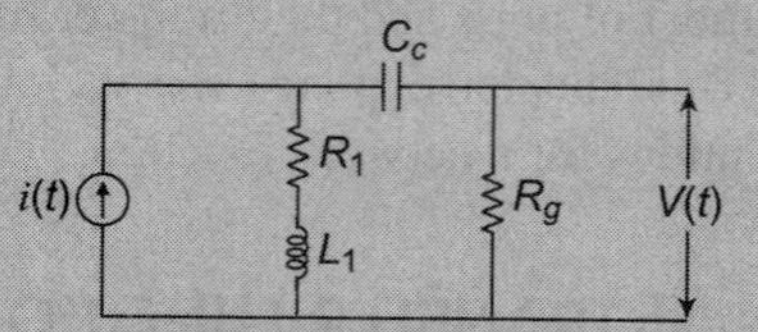

Figure 8.2

$$I_b = I(s)\times\left[\frac{R_1+sL_1}{R_1+sL_1\left(\dfrac{1}{C_c s}\right)+R_g}\right]$$

Also,

Step 3: Evaluate $V(s)$ in terms of $I(s)$ and the desired transfer function:

$$V(s)=I_b\times R_g = I(s)\left[\frac{R_1+sL_1}{R_1+sL_1\left(\dfrac{1}{C_c s}\right)+R_g}\right]R_g$$

Note: Difficulty Level ⟶ ○○● — Easy; ○●● — Medium; ●●● — Difficult

$$\Rightarrow \quad \frac{V(s)}{I(s)} = \frac{R_1 + sL_1}{R_1 + sL_1\left(\frac{1}{C_c s}\right) + R_g} R_g$$

Example 8.2

For the circuit shown in Figure 8.3, find the driving point impedance.

Solution

$$Z_{CD} = \frac{s \times \frac{1}{2s}}{s + \frac{1}{2s}} = \frac{s}{2s^2 + 1}$$

$$Z(s) = 3s + \frac{1}{5s} + \frac{s}{2s^2 + 1}$$

$$Z(s) = \frac{(2s^2+1)15s^2 + (2s^2+1) + 5s^2}{5s(2s^2+1)} = \frac{30s^4 + 22s^2 + 1}{10s^3 + 5s}$$

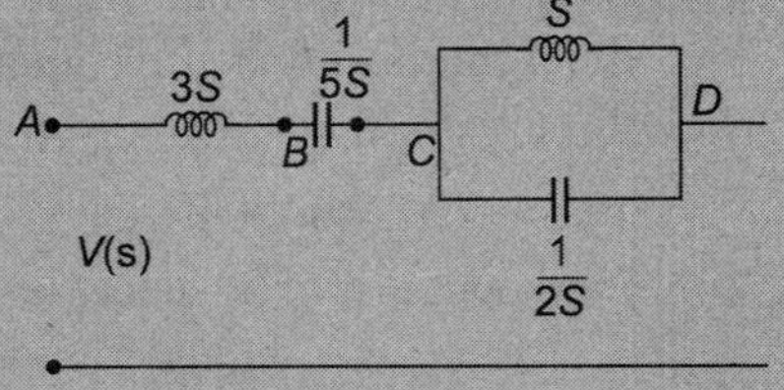

Figure 8.3

Example 8.3

Solve the circuit shown in Figure 8.4 for driving point impedance.

Solution Applying KCL at nodes A and B,

$$I_1(s) - 3I(s) = \frac{(V_A - V_B)}{2s} \tag{8.1}$$

$$\frac{(V_A - V_B)}{2s} = \frac{V_B}{\frac{2}{s}} + I(s) \tag{8.2}$$

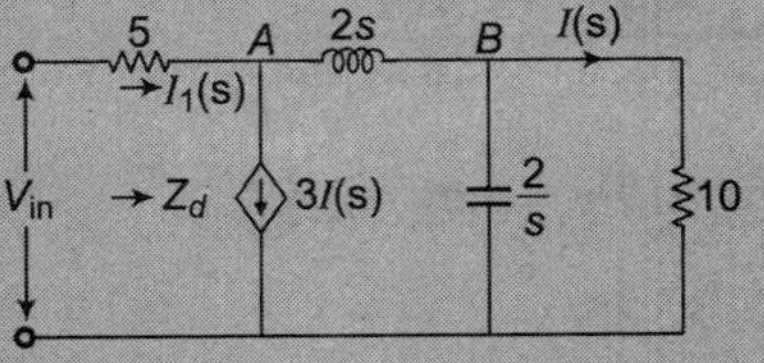

Figure 8.4

Replacing $V_B = 10I(s)$, and substituting Eq. (8.2) in Eq. (8.1):

$$I_1(s) = (3 + 5s + 1)\, I(s) = (5s + 4)\, I(s)$$

Now, applying KVL in outer loop:

$$V_{\text{in}} = 5I_1(s) + V_A \tag{8.3}$$

$$V_{\text{in}} = 5I_1(s) + V_A(s) \tag{8.4}$$

Using Eq. (8.1) to Eq. (8.4),

$$Z_d = \frac{V_{\text{in}}(s)}{I_1(s)} = \frac{10s^2 + 27s + 30}{5s + 4}$$

8.3 ANALYSIS OF LADDER AND NON-LADDER NETWORKS

University Question

1. Write short notes on analysis of ladder network **[RU, 2006]**

8.3.1 Analysis of Ladder Networks

A typical ladder network is shown in Figure 8.5 (a)

The circuit can be analysed in the following manner:

(a) Evaluate current of right most shunt branch:

$$I_X = V_X Y_4 = V_2 Y_4$$

(b) Find out current entering to successive node: (for the right most node it is equal to I_X)

(c) Find out voltage of successive node:

$$V_Y = V_X + Z_2 I_X$$

(d) Find out current of successive shunt branch and repeat step b, c and d up to left most terminals:

$$I_Y = V_Y Y_3 \text{ and } V_Z = V_Y + Z_1 I_Y$$

(e) Equate this voltage to the applied voltage of left most port terminal to solve unknown/transfer function: $V_Z = V_1$.

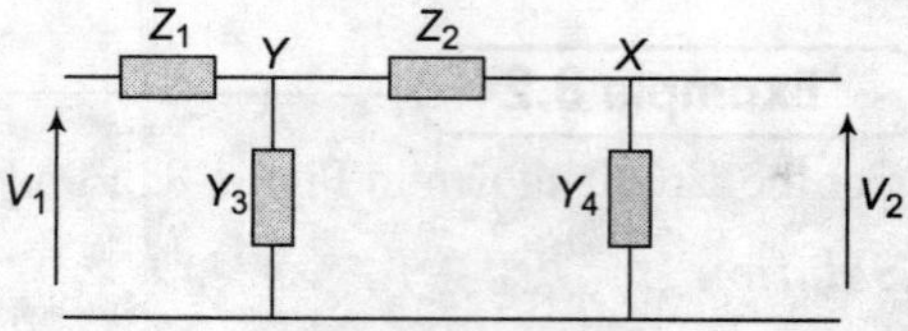

Figure 8.5 (a)

8.3.2 Analysis of Non-ladder Networks

Figure 8.5 (b) shows a non-ladder type of network.

Non-ladder networks are solved with using conventional KVL and KCL or any of circuit solving methods which suits the network for minimum complexity.

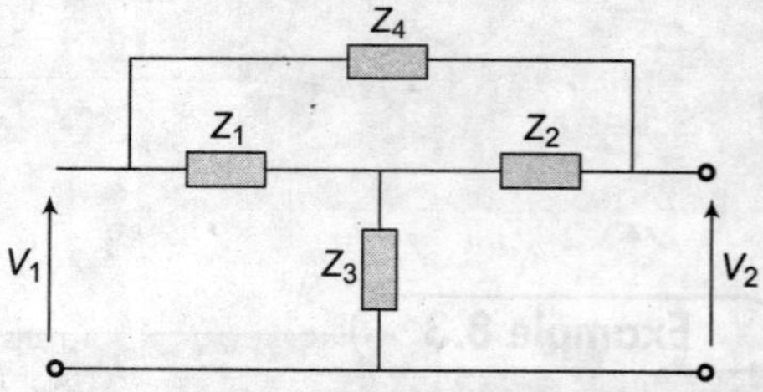

Figure 8.5 (b)

Example 8.4

For the network shown in Figure 8.6, determine voltage transfer function V_2/V_1.

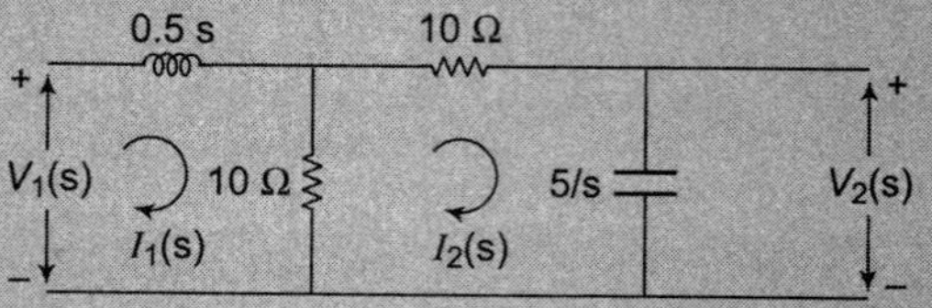

Figure 8.6

Solution Here, $V_X = V_2$

$$\Rightarrow \quad I_X = \frac{V_2}{\frac{5}{s}}$$

$$\Rightarrow \quad V_Y = V_X + Z_2 I_X = V_2 + 10\frac{V_2}{\frac{5}{s}} \Rightarrow I_Y = \frac{V_Y}{10}$$

$$\Rightarrow \quad I_1 = I_Y + I_X = V_2 + 10\frac{V_2}{\frac{5}{s}} + \frac{V_Y}{10} \Rightarrow V_1 = V_Y + Z_1 I_1 = \left(V_2 + 10\frac{V_2}{\frac{5}{s}}\right) + 0.5s\left(V_2 + 10\frac{V_2}{\frac{5}{s}} + \frac{V_Y}{10}\right)$$

$$\Rightarrow \quad V_1 = V_2\left(1+\frac{10}{\frac{5}{s}}+0.5s+0.5s\frac{10}{\frac{5}{s}}+0.5s\left(1+\frac{10}{\frac{5}{s}}\right)\right)$$

$$\Rightarrow \quad \frac{V_2(s)}{V_1(s)}=\left(\frac{1}{2s^2+3s+1}\right)$$

Example 8.5

Find V_2/V_1, V_2/I_1 and I_2/I_1 for the network shown in Figure 8.7.(1 2 3 5 $r_1 = 1$ $V_1 = 37$) ○○●

Solution **Step 1:** Assign mesh currents and apply KVL in each mesh

KVL in mesh-1: $3I_1 + 2I_2 - 5I_3 = 37$

KVL in mesh-2: $2I_1 + 6I_2 + 3I_3 = 0$

KVL in mesh-3: $-5I_1 + 3I_2 + 9I_3 = 0$

Solving above three equations:

$$I_1 = -15\text{ A}, I_2 = 11\text{ A}, I_3 = -12\text{ A}$$

Now, $\quad I_2 = 1 \times 11 = 11\text{ V}$

$$V_2/V_1 = 11/37,\ V_2/I_1 = -11/15\ \Omega,\ I_2/I_1 = -11/15$$

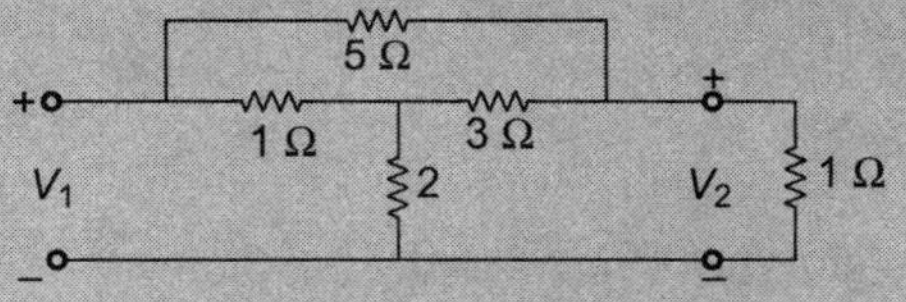

Figure 8.7

8.4 MINIMISE POWER TRANSFER

For a network (as a load or a receiver) connected to another network (operating as a source or transmitter), maximum power is transferred when impedances of both the network are matched.

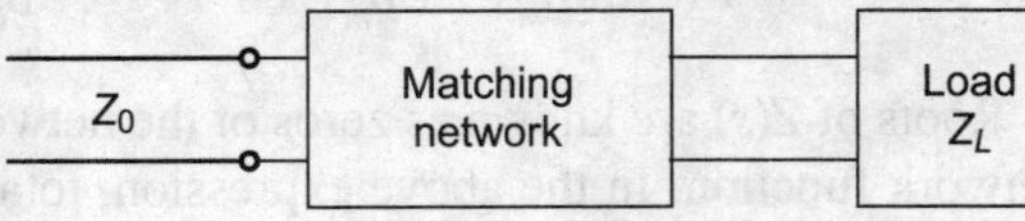

Figure 8.8

If impedances are not matched, a matching network (as shown in Figure 8.8) is connected between source and load, so that the impedance between the source and the load is matched. A matching network may be varying or fixed depending upon the application.

In order to match the impedance, Z_0 should be equal to the impedance of source.

Example 8.6

A typical matching network is shown in Figure 8.9. ○●●

$L = \dfrac{1}{10\pi}H$, Load impedance at 100 Hz = 50 Ohm and load impedance at 100 Hz = $j10$ Ohm. Find the value of B at 100 Hz for impedance matching.

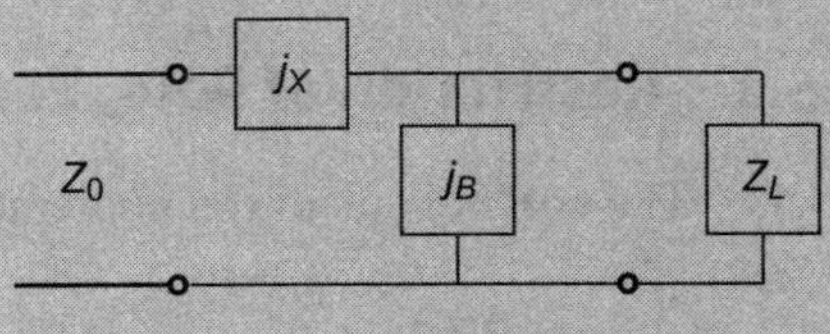

Figure 8.9

Solution For the given value of L, $X_L = 2\pi f L = 20$ Ohm.

Step 1: Now,

$$\Rightarrow \quad Z_0 = jX + Z_L \parallel \left(\frac{1}{jB}\right)$$

$$\Rightarrow \quad Z_0 = j20 + 50 \parallel \left(\frac{1}{jB}\right)$$

$$\Rightarrow \quad Z_0 = j20 + \frac{50}{jB+1}$$

Step 2: Equate the total impedance to the source impedance for maximum power transfer-

$$Z_0 = Z_s, \text{ here } Z_s = 10j$$

$$\Rightarrow \quad j20 + \frac{50}{jB+1} = j10$$

Solving this, $B = -0.07j$ *(–shown B is a capacitor)*

8.5 POLES AND ZEROS OF NETWORK FUNCTIONS

University Question

1. Explain poles and zeros of network function. Provide features of them.

[GTU, 2016]

A network function can be expressed in terms of two polynomials as:

$$T(s) = \frac{Z(s)}{P(s)} = \frac{a_n s^n + a_{n-1}s^{n-1} + \cdots + a_1 s + a_0}{b_m s^m + b_{m-1}s^{m-1} + \cdots + b_1 s + b_0}$$

Roots of $Z(s)$ are known as zeros of the network function and roots of $P(s)$ are known as poles of the network function. In the above expression, total number of poles will be m and total number of zeros will be n.

Since, a polynomial can be written in terms of its roots, the network function can be expressed in terms of their poles and zeros as:

$$T(s) = \frac{Z(s)}{P(s)} = H\frac{(s-z_n)(s-z_{n-1})\cdots(s-z_0)}{(s-p_m)(s-p_{m-1})\cdots(s-p_0)}$$

Since, z and p denotes complex frequencies only, poles and zeros are the frequencies at which network function is infinite and zero respectively.

8.5.1 Restriction of Pole, Zero for a Transfer Function

1. The coefficients of the numerator and denominator polynomials are real and positive.

2. The poles and zeros of $Y(s)$ have only negative real part (or zero), i.e., $Y(s)$ does not have poles or zeros in the right half s-plane.
3. A driving point function does not have multiple poles or zeros on the imaginary axis and at origin.
4. The degrees of the numerator and denominator polynomials in $Y(s)$ differ at the most by 1. Thus, the number of finite poles and finite zeros of $Y(s)$ would differ at most by 1.
5. The terms of lowest degree in the numerator and denominator polynomials of $Y(s)$ differ in degree at most by 1. So $Y(s)$ does not have multiple number of poles or zeros at the origin.
6. No missing terms in numerator and denominator polynomials unless all even or all odd terms are missing.

8.5.2 Restriction of Pole, Zero for a Network Function

1. The coefficients of the numerator and denominator polynomials are real but coefficients of the denominator polynomials are always positive.
2. The poles have only negative real part (or zero), i.e., a transfer function does not have poles in the right half s-plane.
3. A transfer function does not have multiple poles on the imaginary axis and at origin.
4. Numerator polynomial may have missing terms between highest and lowest degree.
5. No missing terms in denominator polynomials unless all even or all odd terms are missing.

Example 8.7

For the network shown in Figure 8.10, find the driving point function and plot its pole-zero locations in s-plane. ○●●

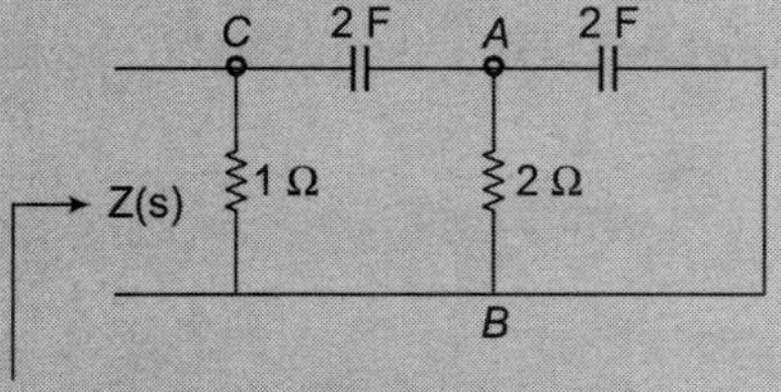

Figure 8.10

Solution **Step 1:** Solve the series and parallel branches to find total impedance in Laplace transformed form

$$Z(s) = 1 \parallel \left(\frac{1}{2s} + \left(2 \parallel \frac{1}{2s}\right)\right)$$

if Z_1 is the impedance of right most paralleled connected R-L, then,

$$Z_1 = \frac{2 \times \frac{1}{2s}}{2 + \frac{1}{2s}} = \frac{2}{4s+1}$$

$$Z(s) = 1 \parallel \left(\frac{1}{2s} + Z_1\right) = Z(s) = 1 \parallel \left(\frac{1}{2s} + \frac{2}{4s+1}\right)$$

$$Z(s) = 1 \parallel \left(\frac{8s+1}{8s^2+2s}\right)$$

$$Z(s)=\frac{\left(1\times\left(\frac{8s+1}{8s^2+2s}\right)\right)}{\left(1+\left(\frac{8s+1}{8s^2+2s}\right)\right)}=\frac{8s+1}{8s^2+10s+1}$$

Step 2: Find out location of pole and zero:

If $Z(s)=\frac{8s+1}{8s^2+10s}=\frac{Q(s)}{P(s)}$

Then, roots of $Q(s)$ are the zeros of $Z(s)$, $Q(s)=0\Rightarrow 8s+1=0\Rightarrow z_1=-\frac{1}{8}$ and;

Roots of $P(s)$ are the poles of $Z(s)$,

$$P(s)=0\Rightarrow 8s^2+10s+1=0\Rightarrow p_1=-\frac{10}{16}+\frac{\sqrt{68}}{16}=-0.11;\ p_2=-\frac{10}{16}-\frac{\sqrt{68}}{16}=-1.14$$

Here zeros will be: 8s + 1 = 0 or s = –1/8

Example 8.8

For a parallel RLC circuit, find out the poles and zero for driving point impedance. ○●●

Solution For a parallel RLC circuit, admittances of each branch: $Y_R=\frac{1}{R}, Y_C=\frac{1}{\frac{1}{sC}}=sC, Y_L=\frac{1}{sL}$

Net admittance, $Y=Y_R+Y_C+Y_L$

$$Y=\frac{1}{R}+sC+\frac{1}{sL}$$

$$Y=\frac{s^2RLC+sL+R}{sLR}$$

Impedance,

$$Z=\frac{1}{Y}=\frac{sLR}{s^2RLC+sL+R}$$

Poles; root of $s^2RLC+sL+R\Rightarrow p_1, p_2=-\frac{1}{2RC}\pm\sqrt{\left(\left(\frac{1}{2RC}\right)^2-\frac{1}{LC}\right)}$

Zeros: root of $sLR=0\Rightarrow$, $z_1=0$.

8.6 TIME DOMAIN RESPONSE FROM POLE-ZERO BEHAVIOUR

University Questions

1. Write a short note on time domain behaviour of poles and zeros. **[PTU, 2009]**
2. Summarise significance of pole-zero location in *s*-plane. **[GTU, 2016]**

From the location of poles and zeros in the *s*-plane, time response/behaviour of a system can be predicted. It is generally extracted by taking inverse Laplace of the transfer function.

Time response of a single pole (or 2 in case complex) system is given as:

$$r(t) = Ae^{-st}$$

(Response of multi-pole system can be found by superposition)

Here, *s* is the pole of system.

Time response of a system is easily determined by the following two steps:

1. Decompose the response using partial fraction. i.e.

$$R(s) = \frac{Z(s)}{P(s)} = \frac{a_n s^n + a_{n-1}s^{n-1} + \cdots + a_1 s + a_0}{b_m s^m + b_{m-1}s^{m-1} + \cdots + b_1 s + b_0} = \frac{A_m}{s - p_m} + \frac{A_{m-1}}{s - p_{m-1}} + \cdots \frac{A_0}{s - p_0}$$

2. Take inverse Laplace of the decomposed function.

$$r(t) = L^{-1}\left[\frac{A_m}{s - p_m} + \frac{A_{m-1}}{s - p_{m-1}} + \cdots \frac{A_0}{s - p_0}\right]$$

From the above expression, time response for different possible values of the pole is drawn in Figure 8.11. Also, location of pole is drawn in *s*-plan accordingly. For $s = 0$, response is constant with time. For a real value of s, response is exponential with time in nature.

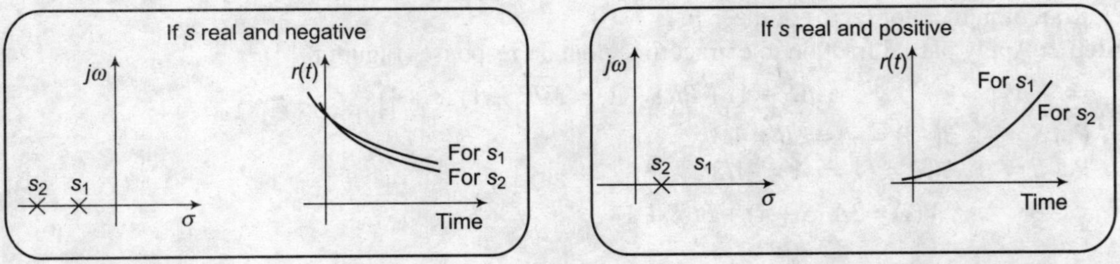

Figure 8.11

It can be noted that if *s* is imaginary (Figure 8.12), transfer function (using Euler identity), $r(t) = Ae^{-st} = A(\cos st + j\sin st)$ becomes sinusoidal. The response is oscillatory in nature with constant magnitude and frequency.

An increased value of *s* will result in increment in frequency of oscillation.

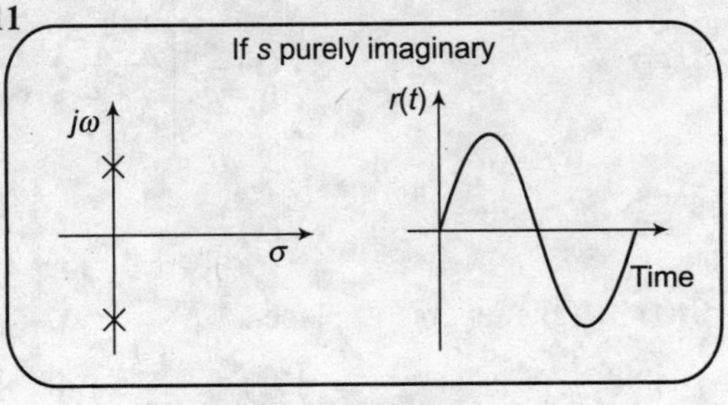

Figure 8.12

Now, if **s** is imaginary with a real part (Figure 8.13), response become

$$r(t) = Ae^{-st} = Ae^{-s_r t}(\cos s_i t + j\sin s_i t)$$

Here, s_r and s_i are the real and imaginary parts of **s** respectively.

This suggests that a complex **s** with real part will result in oscillations with time varying amplitude.

If real part is negative, oscillations get damped with time and if real part is positive, oscillations grow with time and the system is considered unstable.

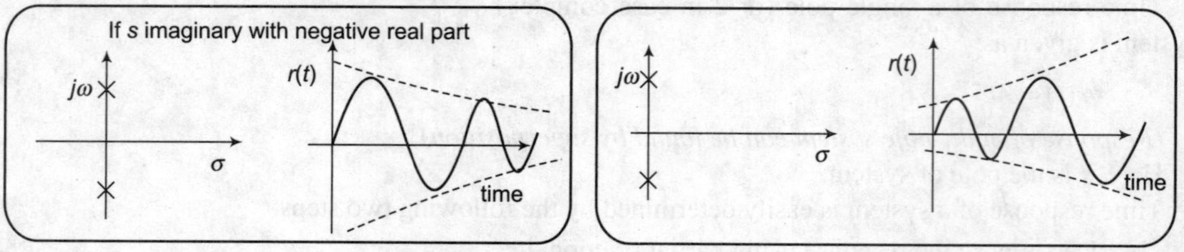

Figure 8.13

Example 8.9

A transform voltage is given by: $V(s) = 3s/(s + 1)(s + 4)$. Plot the pole-zero in the s-plane and obtain the time-domain response.

Solution Given transfer function is:

$$V(s) = 3s/(s + 1)(s + 4)$$

Step 1: Find the pole, zero locations;

Poles are the roots of denominator i.e. –1 and –4

Root of numerator (zero) of the T.F. is $s = 0$

Step 2: Apply partial fraction to extract time domain response (Figure 8.14):

$$\Rightarrow \quad A/(S + 4) + B/(S + 1) = 3s/(s + 1)(s + 4)$$

Put $S = -4$, $B(-3) = -4 \Rightarrow B = 4/3$

Put $S = -1$, $A(3) = -1 \Rightarrow A = -1/3$

$$\therefore\ V(s) = 3A/(S + 4) + B/(S + 1)$$

$$\Rightarrow \quad V(s) = 3\left[\frac{-\frac{1}{3}}{s+4} + \frac{\frac{4}{3}}{s+1}\right]$$

$$\Rightarrow \quad V(s) = \frac{-1}{s+4} + \frac{4}{s+1}$$

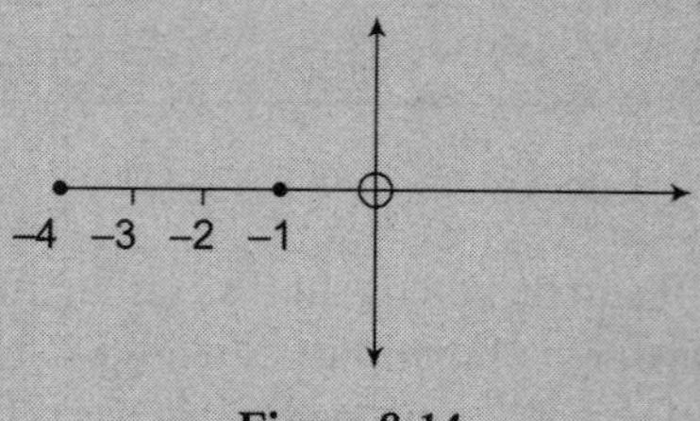

Figure 8.14

Step 3: Take inverse Laplace:

$$\Rightarrow \quad V(t) = -e^{-4t} + 4e^{-t}\,\text{V}$$

Example 8.10

Find the response of a network if,

$$H(s) = \frac{s^2 + 3s + 5}{(s+1)(s+2)}$$

And excitation is $x(t) = e^{-3t}$.

Solution

Step 1: Taking Laplace transform of excitation,

$$X(s) = \frac{1}{s+3}$$

Step 2: Find out Laplace of response *C(s)*

$$C(s) = X(s)\,H(s)$$

$$C(s) = \frac{1}{(s+3)}\,\frac{s^2 + 3s + 5}{(s+1)(s+2)}$$

$$C(s) = \frac{s^2 + 3s + 5}{(s+3)(s+1)(s+2)}$$

Step 3: Partial fraction:

$$C(s) = \frac{A}{(s+1)} + \frac{B}{(s+2)} + \frac{C}{(s+3)}$$

Solving it for *A*, *B* and *C* results:

$$C(s) = \frac{1.5}{(s+1)} - \frac{3}{(s+2)} + \frac{2.5}{(s+3)}$$

Step 4: Taking inverse Laplace:

$C(t) = 1.5e^{-t} - 3e^{-2t} + 2.5e^{-3t}$ as Laplace of unit impulse is 1., where $X = A + B$ and $Y = A–B$

8.7 || GRAPHICAL METHOD FOR DETERMINATION OF RESIDUE

As discussed, transfer function of a system is given as:

$$T(s) = \frac{Z(s)}{P(S)} = \frac{a_n s^n + a_{n-1}s^{n-1} + \cdots + a_1 s + a_0}{b_n s^n + b_{n-1}s^{n-1} + \cdots + b_1 s + b_0}$$

Which further had been re-written as:

$$T(s) = \frac{Z(s)}{P(S)} = H\frac{(s - z_n)(s - z_{n-1})\cdots(s - z_0)}{(s - p_m)(s - p_{m-1})\cdots(s - p_0)}$$

To determine the time response using superposition, this expression can be decoded as:

$$T(s) = \frac{K_m}{s - p_m} + \frac{K_{m-1}}{s - p_{m-1}} + \cdots + \frac{K_0}{s - p_0} \tag{8.5}$$

Coefficients K_m, K_{m-1}..., K_0 are known as residues.
From the partial fraction,

$$K_m = (s - p_m)T(s)|_{s=p_m} = H\frac{(p_m - z_n)(p_m - z_{n-1})\cdots(p_m - z_0)}{(p_m - p_{m-1})(p_m - p_{m-2})\cdots(p_m - p_0)} \tag{8.6}$$

It can be observed here that numerator is the multiplication of all displacement phasors between p_m and zeros (of s-plane). And, denominator is the multiplication of all displacement phasors between p_m and rest of poles.

$$K_i = \frac{\prod_{k=1}^{kn}(p_i - z_k)}{\prod_{k=1}^{km}(p_i - p_k),\, k \neq i}$$

Drawing all the poles and zeros in s-plane and finding out these phasors will yield desired residue with the help of Eq. 8.6.
Steps:

- Draw the location of all poles and zero in s-plane.
- Select a pole, corresponding to which residue is desired to find.
- Join the selected pole to all poles and zeros.
- Find out angles and distances for all joined segments and convert them in polar form.
- Put these phasors in Eq. 8.5 and calculate the residue.

Example 8.11

Transform current $I(s)$ of a network is given by:

$$I(s) = \frac{2s}{(s+1)(s+2)}$$

Determine residues using graphical method and determine time-response.

Solution **Step 1:** Determine pole and zero locations:

Poles are at $s = -1, -2$
Only one zero at $s = 0$.

Step 2: Write T.F. in form of residues:

$$I(s) = \frac{A}{(s+1)} + \frac{B}{(s+2)}$$

Step 3: Evaluate residue corresponding to pole $s = -1$ i.e. A:

$$A = \frac{2 \times 1e^{j180}}{1e^{j0}} = -2$$

Step 4: Evaluate residue corresponding to pole $s = -2$ i.e. B:

$$B = \frac{2 \times 2e^{j180}}{1e^{j0}} = 4$$

$$I(s) = \frac{-2}{(s+1)} + \frac{4}{(s+2)}$$

Step 5: Taking inverse Laplace:

$$I(t) = -2e^{-t} + 4e^{-2t} \quad A = \frac{(-6-(-4)) \times (-6-2) \times (-6-0)}{(-6-(-3) \times (-6-(-1))}$$

POINTS TO REMEMBER

- ☞ Network functions are defined in *s*-domain only.
- ☞ Transfer function is unit impulse response of the system.
- ☞ Driving point functions are input impedances or input admittances seen into the port.
- ☞ Power transfer is maximum, when load impedance = source impedance.*
- ☞ Poles of a T.F. are the frequencies at which, its value is infinite.
- ☞ Zeros of a T.F. are the frequencies at which, its value is zero.
- ☞ Complex conjugate of a pole/zero is also pole/zero.
- ☞ A system with one or more positive pole is unstable.
- ☞ Pattern of response is governed by the pole(s).
- ☞ An imaginary pole reflects oscillatory response.

PRACTICE PROBLEMS

1. Differential equation of a system is ○○● described as: $(t) = 4\frac{d^2y}{dt^2} + 5\frac{dy}{dt} + 3t$, find out its transfer function.

2. If voltage transfer function for the circuit ○●● shown in Figure 8.15 is expressed as:

$$\frac{v_0(s)}{v_i(s)} = \frac{50}{(s+2)(s+4)}$$

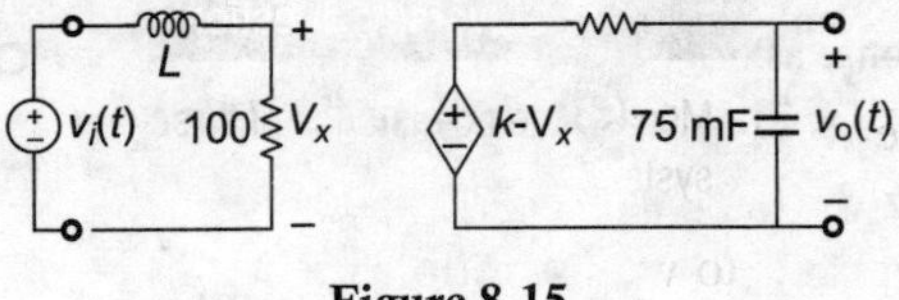

Figure 8.15

Find the value of L and DC gain K (take both R =100 Ohm).

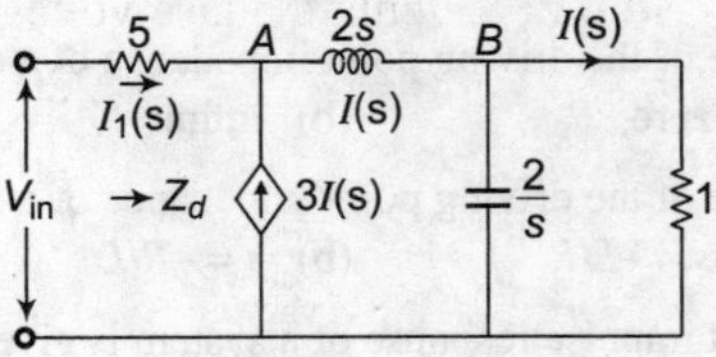

Figure 8.16

3. Find the transfer function I_3/V_1 for the ○●● ladder network shown in Figure 8.17.

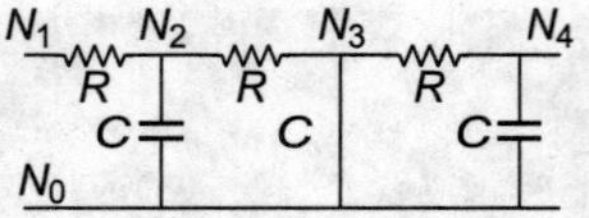

Figure 8.17

4. Find out voltage transfer function for the network shown in Figure 8.18. ○●●

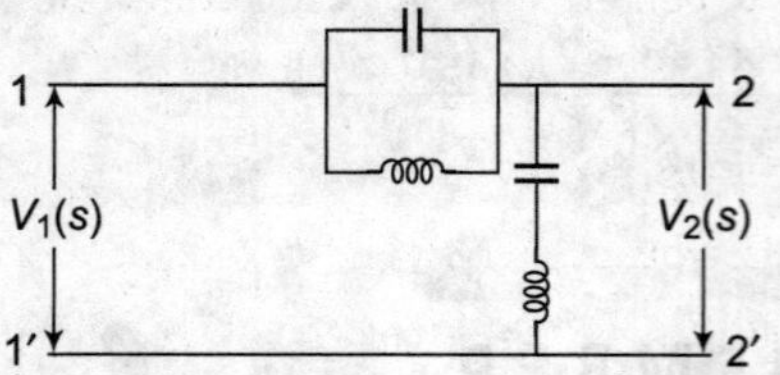

Figure 8.18

5. For the network shown in Figure 8.19, if R = 10 ohm, L = 0.2 H, find the value of C for which poles of the shown transfer function are real and coincident. ○●●

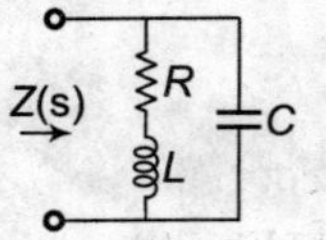

Figure 8.19

6. Pole zero location of a network function is shown in Figure 8.20. If $T(0) = 5$. Find the transfer function. ○○●

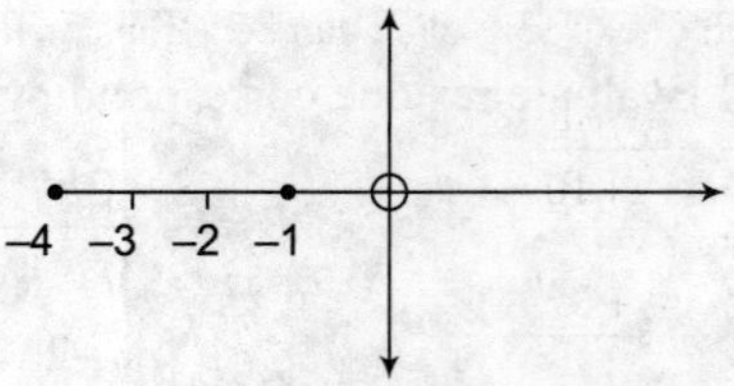

Figure 8.20

7. Driving point impedance of a single port network is given as $Z(s) = \dfrac{s+1}{(s+1)(s+4)}$, if the circuit is excited by a unit impulse signal; find the expression for its current. ○●●

8. Network function defined as $T(s) = \dfrac{2s}{s^2 + 5s + 6}$ is excited with unit step voltage, determine the time response and comment on system's stability. ●●●

9. A system with transfer function $T(s) = 50/(s^2 + 8s + 25)$ is excited with unit impulse voltage. Is response oscillatory? If yes, then find frequency of oscillation in Hz.

10. Time domain response of a transfer function is described as: $Ae^{-6t} + Be^{-3t} + Ce^{-t}$, if DC gain is 1, and location of poles and zeros are p = –6, –3, –1 and z = – 4, 2, 0. Evaluate A, B and C using method of residue. (A, B ,C are constants here) ○●●

MULTIPLE CHOICE QUESTIONS

1. Pole of the driving point impedance of a capacitor C is located at: ○○●
   (a) zero (b) infinity (c) $1/C$ (d) C
2. Pole of the driving point impedance of a series R-L circuit is located at: ○●●
   (a) $s = -L/R$ (b) $s = -R/L$ (c) $s = L/R$ (d) $s = -RL$
3. Unit impulse response of a system is given as $y(t) = e^{-5t}$. Its transfer function will be: ○●●
   (a) $1/(s - 5)$ (b) $1/(s + 5)$ (c) $1/5s$ (d) $5s + 1$
4. A system with poles at $s = -5$ and $s = -3$ will show time response as: ○●●
   (a) $y(t) = Ae^{-5t} + Be^{-3t}$ (b) $y(t) = Ae^{5t} + Be^{3t}$ (c) $y(t) = Ae^{-5t}e^{-3t}$ (d) $y(t) = Ae^{-2t}$

5. Which one of following can be a transfer function: ○●●

(I) $\dfrac{8s+1}{8s^2+10s}$ (II) $\dfrac{1}{s^3+8s^2+10s+1}$

(III) $\dfrac{s^2+3s+5}{(s-1)(s+2)}$ (IV) $\dfrac{1}{(s-1)(s+2)}$

(a) I only (b) II, IV (c) II, I (d) IV only

6. Two networks with poles at $s = -4, -2$ and $s = -3, -1$ are cascaded, poles of the cascaded network will be: ○●●

(a) $s = -7, -3$ (b) $s = -3.5, -1.5$
(c) $s = -4, -2, -3, -1$ (d) $s = -3.5, -1.5, -0.5, -0.5$

7. Time response of series RLC circuit initially excited with an impulse voltage will be: ○●●

(a) exponentially decaying with or without oscillations
(b) exponentially growing with or without oscillations
(c) oscillatory always
(d) exponential always

8. Transfer function of a RC circuit, $V_c(s)/V_{in}(s)$ is given by ○●●

(a) $sC/(R + sC)$ (b) $1/(sCR + 1)$ (c) $1/(sC + R)$ (d) $sC/(sC + R)$

9. DC gain of transfer function $\dfrac{20}{(s+1)(s+4)}$ is ○●●

(a) 20 (b) 10 (c) –20 (d) 5

10. A pole is moved in parallel with imaginary axis, it will ○●●

(a) not affect the system (b) decrease frequency of oscillation
(c) increase frequency of oscillation (d) increase the amplitude of response

ANSWERS TO MULTIPLE CHOICE QUESTIONS

1. (a)	2. (a)	3. (b)	4. (a)	5. (d)
6. (c)	7. (a)	8. (b)	9. (d)	10. (c)

Two-Port Networks

9

CHAPTER OUTLINE

- Open-circuit impedance parameters (Z)
- Short-circuit admittance parameters (Y)
- Transmission parameters (ABCD)
- Inverse transmission parameters (A′B′C′D′)
- Hybrid parameters (h)
- Inverse hybrid parameters (g)
- Relationship between parameters
- Interconnection of two port networks
- Terminated two port
- Image parameters
- Attenuation and phase shift in symmetrical T and π networks.

9.1 INTRODUCTION

A port is defined as any pair of terminals into which energy is supplied or from which energy is withdrawn or where the network variables may be measured. A linear time invariant two-port network is a linear network which has two pairs of terminals and the current entering one terminal of a pair exits the other terminal in the pair and which has no independent sources. A two port network is as shown in Figure 9.1.

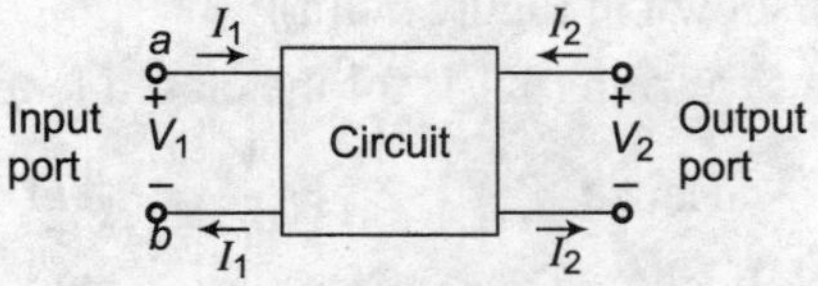

Figure 9.1

Input port and its variables are represented by 1 whereas output port and its variables are represented by 2. There are four variables in a two-port network namely V_1, I_1, and V_2, I_2. Only two of these variables are independent. The parameters of a two-port network represent the behaviour of network in terms of voltage and current at each port. Hence it is essential to study these parameters to be able to apply two port networks in applications such as transistors, op-amps, and transmission lines.

9.2 OPEN-CIRCUIT IMPEDANCE (Z) PARAMETERS

University Question

1. Explain the short-circuit admittance and the open-circuit impedance parameters for a two port network. **[GTU, 2011]**

These are also called Z parameters of a two port network and are obtained when the voltages at two ports are expressed in terms of currents at two ports. So, V_1, and V_2 are dependent variables whereas I, and, I_2 are independent variables.

The equations are $V_1 = Z_{11}I_1 + Z_{12}I_2$; $V_2 = Z_{21}I_1 + Z_{22}I_2$

The individual parameters are given by

$$Z_{11} = \left.\frac{V_1}{I_1}\right|_{I_2=0} \qquad Z_{12} = \left.\frac{V_1}{I_2}\right|_{I_1=0}$$

$$Z_{21} = \left.\frac{V_2}{I_1}\right|_{I_2=0} \qquad Z_{22} = \left.\frac{V_2}{I_2}\right|_{I_1=0}$$

Z_{11} is called the open-circuit input impedance, Z_{21} is called open-circuit forward transfer impedance, Z_{12} is called open-circuit reverse transfer impedance and Z_{22} is called the open circuit output impedance.

The equivalent circuit of a two port network in terms of Z parameters is as shown in Figure 9.2.

The network is said to be reciprocal if $Z_{21} = Z_{12}$ and symmetrical if $Z_{11} = Z_{22}$.

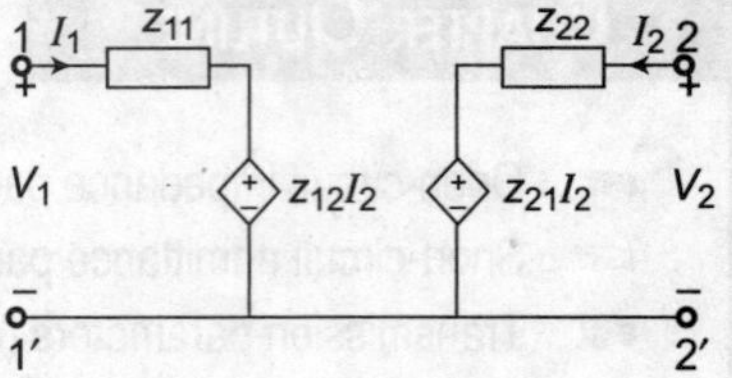

Figure 9.2

Example 9.1

Find the Z parameters of the circuit shown in Figure 9.3. ○○●

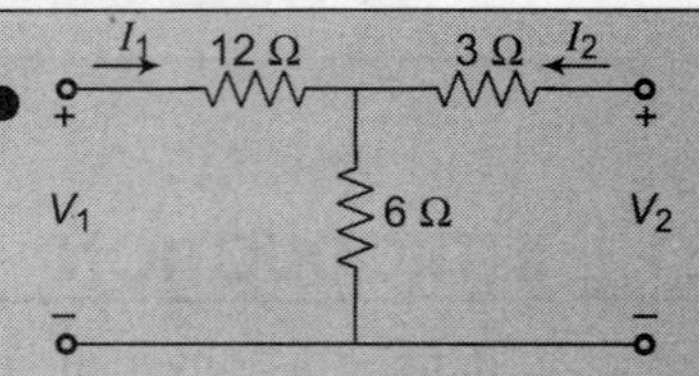

Figure 9.3

Solution **Step 1:** To find Z_{11} and Z_{21}, the output terminals are open circuited and a voltage source is connected to the input terminal as shown in Figure 9.4(a).

Writing KVL for the closed loop, $12I_1 + 6I_1 = V_1$ or $V_1 = 18I_1$

Hence $Z_{11} = \dfrac{V_1}{I_1} = 18\ \Omega$

Applying KVL to the other loop, $-V_2 + 3 \times 0 + 6I_1 = 0$ or $V_2 = 6I_1$

Hence $Z_{21} = \dfrac{V_2}{I_1} = 6\ \Omega$

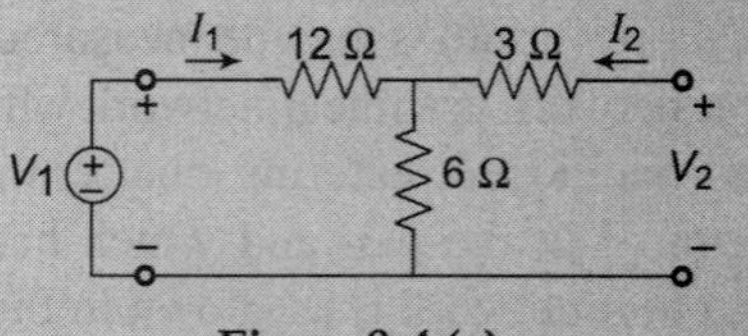

Figure 9.4 (a)

Step 2: To find Z_{12} and Z_{22}, the input terminals are open circuited and a voltage source is connected to the output terminal as shown in Figure 9.4(b).

Writing KVL for the closed loop, $3I_2 + 6I_2 = V_2$ or $V_2 = 9I_2$

Hence $Z_{22} = \dfrac{V_2}{I_2} = 9\ \Omega$

Applying KVL to the other loop, $V_1 = 12 \times 0 + 6I_2$ or $V_2 = 6I_2$

Hence $Z_{12} = \dfrac{V_1}{I_2} = 6\ \Omega$

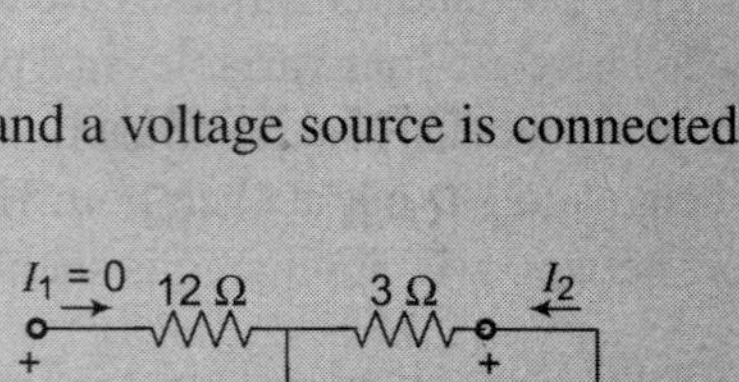

Figure 9.4 (b)

Note: Difficulty Level ➔ ○○● — Easy; ○●● — Medium; ●●● — Difficult

Example 9.2

Find the Z parameters for the network as shown in Figure 9.5.

[RTU, 2011] ○●●

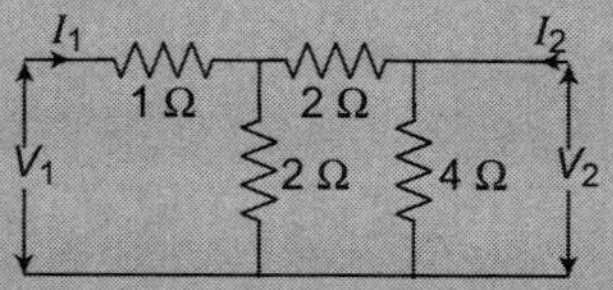

Figure 9.5

Solution To find Z_{11} and Z_{21}, as shown in Figure 9.6 (a) the output terminals are open circuited. The equivalent circuit is

$$Z_{eq} = 1 + \frac{2 \times 6}{2+6} = 2.5\ \Omega$$

$$V_1 = I_1 Z_{eq} = I_1 \times 2.5 \Rightarrow Z_{11} = \frac{V_1}{I_1} = 2.5\Omega$$

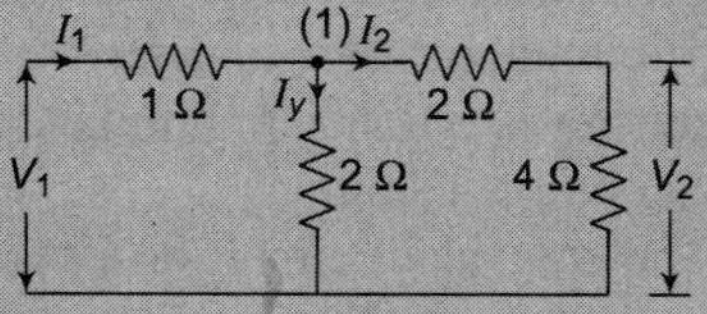

Figure 9.6 (a)

Applying current division, $I_x = I_1 \times \dfrac{2}{2+6} = \dfrac{I_1}{4}$

$$V_2 = I_x \times 4 \Rightarrow V_2 = \frac{I_1}{4} \times 4 \Rightarrow Z_{21} = \frac{V_2}{I_1} = 1\ \Omega$$

To find Z_{12} and Z_{22}, the input terminals are open circuited. The equivalent circuit is as shown in Figure 9.6 (b).

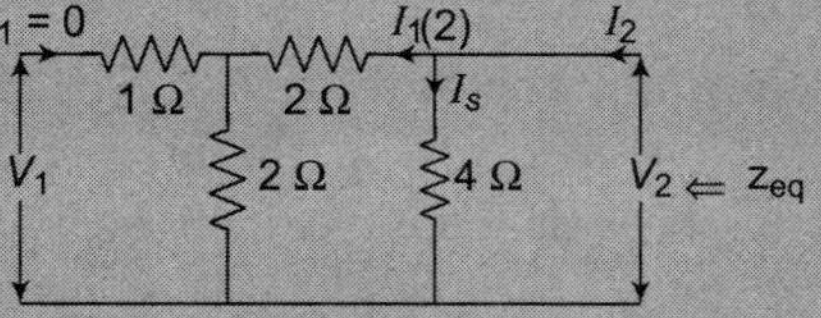

Figure 9.6 (b)

$$Z_{eq} = \frac{4 \times 4}{4+4} = 2\ \Omega$$

$$V_2 = I_2 Z_{eq} = I_2 \times 2 \Rightarrow Z_{22} = \frac{V_2}{I_2} = 2\ \Omega$$

Applying current division, $I_x = I_2 \times \dfrac{4}{4+4} = \dfrac{I_2}{2}$

$$V_1 = I_x \times 2 \Rightarrow V_1 = \frac{I_2}{2} \times 2 \Rightarrow Z_{12} = \frac{V_1}{I_2} = 1\ \Omega$$

9.3 SHORT-CIRCUIT ADMITTANCE (Y) PARAMETERS

These are also called Y parameters of a two port network and are obtained when the currents at two ports are expressed in terms of voltages at two ports. So, V_1, and V_2 are independent variables whereas I, and, I_2 are dependent variables. The equations are

$$I_1 = Y_{11}V_1 + Y_{12}V_2; \qquad I_2 = Y_{21}V_1 + Y_{22}V_2$$

University Question

1. Obtain the reciprocity and symmetry conditions for Z and Y parameters. **[PU, 2012]**

The individual parameters are given by

$$Y_{11} = \left.\frac{I_1}{V_1}\right|_{V_2=0} \qquad Y_{12} = \left.\frac{I_1}{V_2}\right|_{V_1=0}$$

$$Y_{21} = \left.\frac{I_2}{V_1}\right|_{V_2=0} \qquad Y_{22} = \left.\frac{I_2}{V_2}\right|_{V_1=0}$$

Y_{11} is called the short-circuit input admittance, Y_{21} is called short-circuit forward transfer admittance, Y_{12} is called short-circuit reverse transfer admittance and Y_{22} is called the short-circuit output admittance.

The equivalent circuit of a two port network in terms of Y parameters is as shown in Figure 9.7.

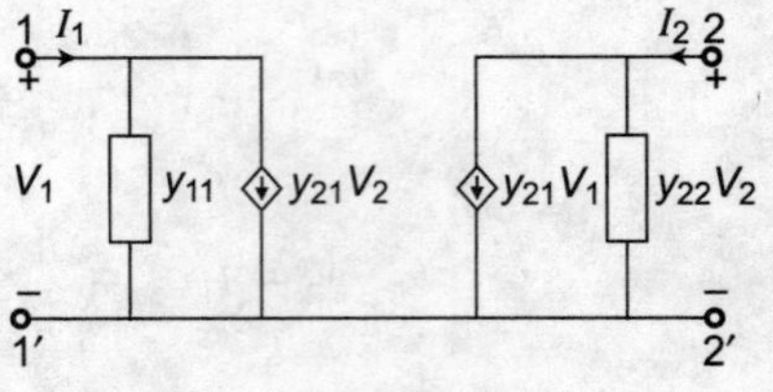

Figure 9.7

The network is said to be reciprocal if $Y_{21} = Y_{12}$ and symmetrical if $Y_{11} = Y_{22}$

Example 9.3

Determine the admittance parameters of the T network shown in Figure 9.8.

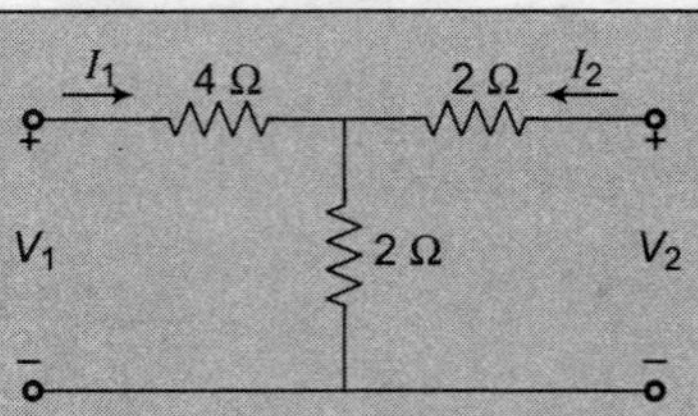

Figure 9.8

Solution **Step 1:** To find Y_{11} and Y_{21}, the output terminals are short circuited and a current source is connected to the input terminal as shown in Figure 9.9 (a).

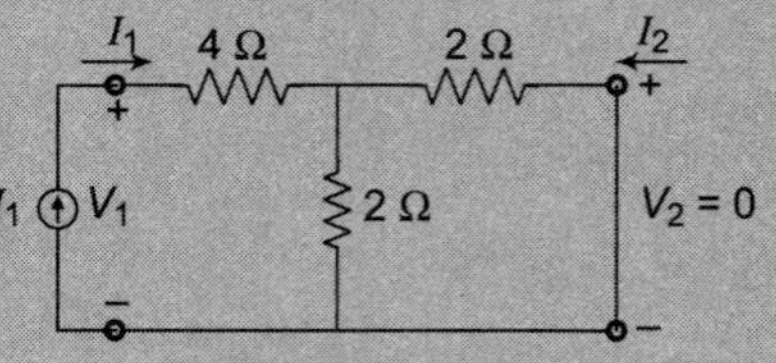

Figure 9.9 (a)

$$I_1 = \frac{V_1}{4 + \dfrac{2 \times 2}{2+2}} = \frac{V_1}{5}$$

$$Y_{11} = \left.\frac{I_1}{V_1}\right|_{V_2=0} = \frac{1}{5}\text{ S}$$

Using current division rule, $-I_2 = \dfrac{I_1 \times 2}{2+2} = \dfrac{I_1}{2} \Rightarrow -I_2 = \dfrac{1}{2}\left[\dfrac{V_1}{5}\right]$

Hence, $$Y_{21} = \left.\frac{I_2}{V_1}\right|_{V_2=0} = \frac{-1}{10}\text{S}$$

Step 2: To find Y_{12} and Y_{22}, the input terminals are short circuited and a current source is connected to the output terminal. as shown in Figure 9.9 (b)

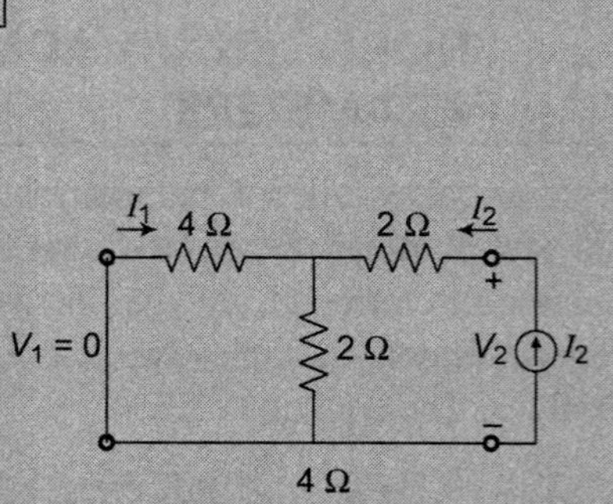

Figure 9.9 (b)

$$I_2 = \frac{V_2}{2 + \dfrac{4 \times 2}{4+2}} = \frac{3V_2}{10} \Rightarrow Y_{22} = \left.\frac{I_2}{V_2}\right|_{V_1=0} = \frac{3}{10}\text{S}$$

Using current division rule

$$-I_1 = \frac{I_2 \times 2}{2+4} = \frac{I_2}{3} \Rightarrow -I_1 = \frac{1}{3}\left[\frac{3V_2}{10}\right] \Rightarrow Y_{12} = \left.\frac{I_1}{V_2}\right|_{V_1=0} = \frac{-1}{10}\text{S}$$

Example 9.4

Find Y parameters for the network shown in Figure 9.10.

[RTU, 2011] ○●●

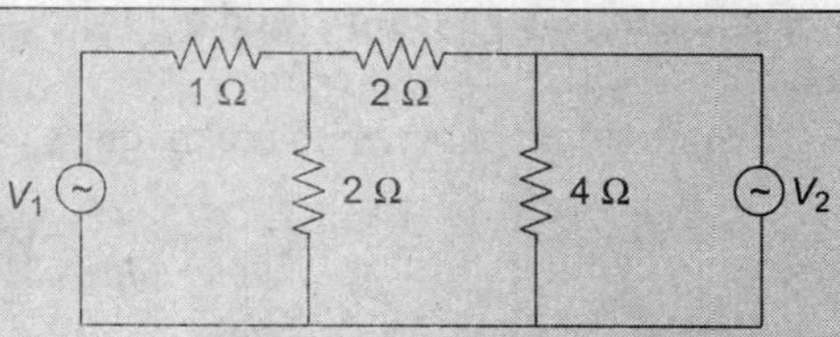

Figure 9.10

Solution When $V_2 = 0$, the equivalent circuit for the given network in Figure 9.11 (a) is

$$Z_{eq} = 1 + \frac{2 \times 2}{2+2} = 2\ \Omega$$

$$V_1 = I_1 Z_{eq} = 2I_1;\ Y_{11} = \left.\frac{I_1}{V_1}\right|_{V_2=0} = \frac{I_1}{2I_1} = 0.5\text{ S}$$

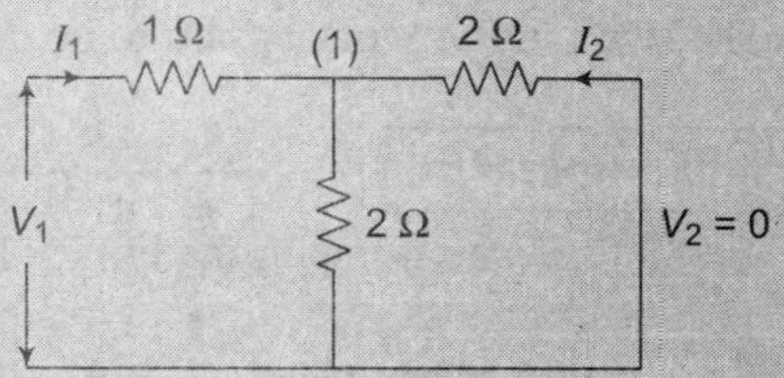

Figure 9.11 (a)

Using current division rule

$$-I_2 = \frac{I_1 \times 2}{2+2} = \frac{I_1}{2} \Rightarrow -I_2 = \frac{1}{2}\left[\frac{V_1}{2}\right] = \frac{V_1}{4}$$

Hence, $$Y_{21} = \left.\frac{I_2}{V_1}\right|_{V_2=0} = -0.25\text{ S}$$

When $V_1 = 0$, the equivalent circuit for the given network in Figure 9.11 (b) is

$$Z_{eq} = 1.6\ \Omega$$

$$V_2 = I_2 Z_{eq} = I_2 \times 1.6$$

$$\Rightarrow Y_{22} = \left.\frac{I_2}{V_2}\right|_{V_1=0} = 0.625\text{ S}$$

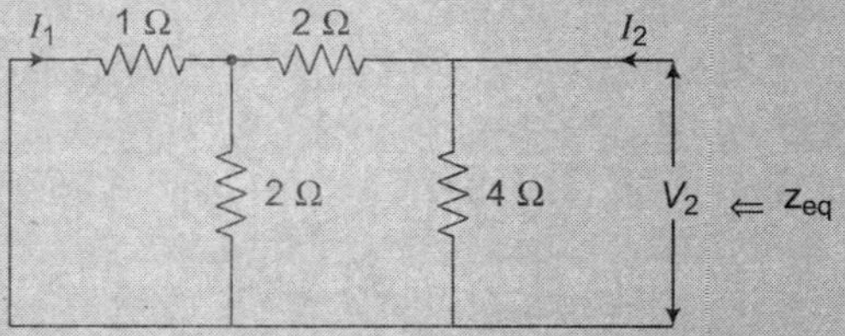

Figure 9.11 (b)

Using current division rule

$$-I_1 = \frac{I_2 \times 2}{5}\ \text{But}\ I_2 = \frac{5V_2}{8} \Rightarrow -I_1 = \frac{2}{5} \times \frac{5V_2}{8} = \frac{V_2}{4}$$

Hence, $$Y_{12} = \left.\frac{I_1}{V_2}\right|_{V_1=0} = -0.25\text{ S}$$

9.4 TRANSMISSION PARAMETERS (ABCD)

University Question

1. Define ABCD parameters for a two-port network. **[RGTU, 2014]**

These are also called ABCD parameters of a two-port network and are obtained when the voltage and current at the input port or the sending end are expressed in terms of voltage and current at the output port or receiving end. The equations are:

$$V_1 = AV_2 - BI_2; \qquad I_1 = CV_2 - DI_2$$

The negative sign is for I_2 and not for parameters, because the current is considered to be leaving the network.

The individual parameters are given as

$$A = \left.\frac{V_1}{V_2}\right|_{I_2=0} \quad B = \left.\frac{V_1}{-I_2}\right|_{V_2=0} \quad C = \left.\frac{I_1}{V_2}\right|_{I_2=0} \quad D = \left.\frac{I_1}{-I_2}\right|_{V_2=0}$$

A is called open circuit reverse voltage gain, *B* is called the short circuit transfer impedance, C is called the open circuit transfer admittance and *D* is called the short circuit reverse current gain.

The two port network is said to be reciprocal if $AD - BC = 1$ and symmetrical if $A = D$.

Example 9.5

Find the transmission parameters for the circuit shown in Figure 9.12. **[PU, 2010]**○○●

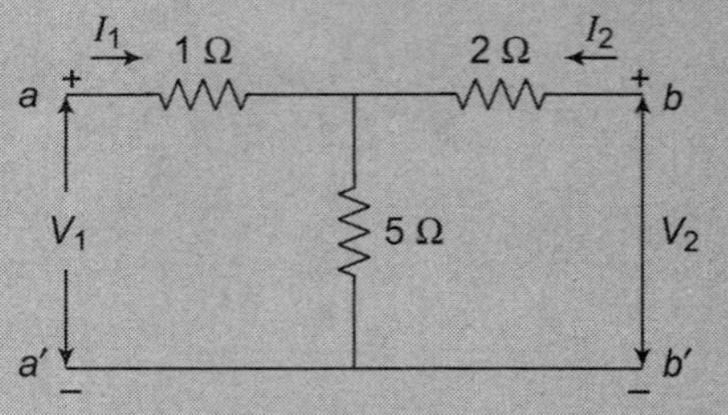

Figure 9.12

Solution When the output port *b–b′* is open i.e. $I_2 = 0$

$$V_1 = 6\,I_1 \text{ and } V_2 = 5\,I_1 = \frac{5}{6}V_1$$

we get $A = \left.\dfrac{V_1}{V_2}\right|_{I_2=0} = \dfrac{6}{5}$ and $C = \left.\dfrac{I_1}{V_2}\right|_{I_2=0} = \dfrac{1}{5}\text{ S}$

When the output port *b–b′* is shorted, i.e., $V_2 = 0$

In the circuit $V_1 = \left(1 + \dfrac{10}{7}\right)I_1$ and $I_2 = \dfrac{5}{7}I_1$

So

$$-B = \left.\frac{V_1}{-I_2}\right|_{V_2=0} = \frac{17}{5}\,\Omega$$

$$-D = \left.\frac{I_1}{-I_2}\right|_{V_2=0} = \frac{-I_1}{I_1\left(\frac{5}{7}\right)} = \frac{-7}{5}$$

$$D = \frac{7}{5}$$

Example 9.6

Obtain ABCD parameters for the network shown in Figure 9.13.

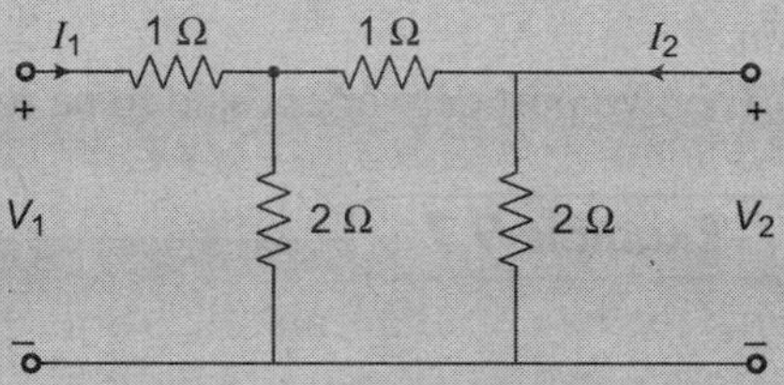

Figure 9.13

Solution Applying KVL to the three meshes shown in Figure 9.14.

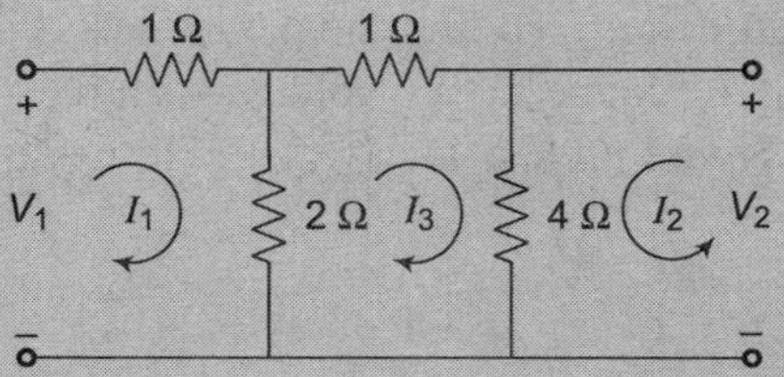

Figure 9.14

we get the following equations

$$V_1 = I_1 + 2(I_1 - I_3) = 3I_1 - 2I_3$$

$$V_2 = 2(I_2 + I_3) = 2I_2 + 2I_3$$

$$2(I_3 - I_1) + I_3 + 2(I_3 + I_2) = 0 \Rightarrow I_3 = \frac{2}{5}I_1 - \frac{2}{5}I_2$$

Substituting and eliminating I_3 we get

$$V_1 = \frac{11}{5}I_1 + \frac{4}{5}I_2$$

$$I_1 = \frac{5}{4}V_2 - \frac{3}{2}I_2$$

Substituting we get

$$V_1 = \frac{11}{4}V_2 - \frac{5}{2}I_2$$

Comparing with the standard ABCD equations

$$V_1 = AV_2 - BI_2$$

$$I_1 = CV_2 - DI_2$$

we get $A = \dfrac{11}{4}$, $B = \dfrac{5}{2}$, $C = \dfrac{5}{4}$ and $D = \dfrac{3}{2}$

9.5 || INVERSE TRANSMISSION PARAMETERS (A′B′C′D′)

These are dual of transmission parameters. These are also called $A'B'C'D'$ parameters of a two-port network and are obtained when the voltage and current at the output port or the receiving end are expressed in terms of voltage and current at the input port or sending end. The equations are

$$V_2 = A'V_1 - B'I_1; \quad I_2 = C'V_1 - D'I_1$$

The negative sign is for I_2 and not for parameters, because the current is considered to be leaving the network.

The individual parameters are given as

$$A' = \left.\frac{V_2}{V_1}\right|_{I_1=0} \quad B' = \left.\frac{-V_2}{I_1}\right|_{V_1=0} \quad C' = \left.\frac{I_2}{V_1}\right|_{I_1=0} \quad D' = \left.\frac{-I_2}{I_1}\right|_{V_1=0}$$

A' is called open circuit forward voltage gain, B' is called the short circuit forward transfer impedance, C' is called the open circuit forward transfer admittance and D' is called the short circuit forward current gain.

The two port network is said to be reciprocal if $A'D' - B'C' = 1$ and symmetrical if $A' = D'$.

Example 9.7

Find the inverse transmission parameters shown in Figure 9.15. ○●●

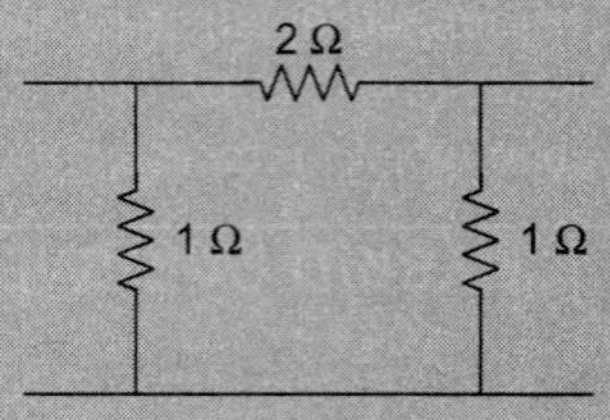

Figure 9.15

Solution To find the parameters A' and C', open the input port and connect a voltage source V_2 at the output port (Figure 9.16 (a)).

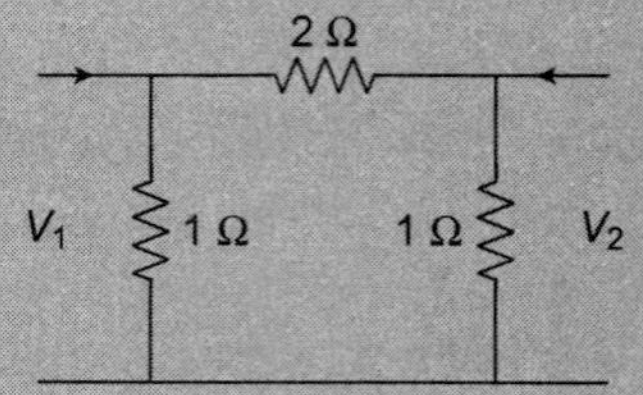

Figure 9.16 (a)

$$V_2 = \left(\frac{1\times 3}{1+3}\right) I_2 = \frac{3}{4} I_2 \text{ and } V_1 = 1\times I_2 = \frac{4}{3} V_2$$

$$A' = \left.\frac{V_2}{V_1}\right|_{I_1=0} = \frac{3}{4} \text{ and } C' = \left.\frac{I_2}{V_1}\right|_{I_1=0} = 1\,\text{S}$$

To find the parameters B' and D', short the input port and connect a voltage source V_2 at the output port (Figure 9.16 (b)).

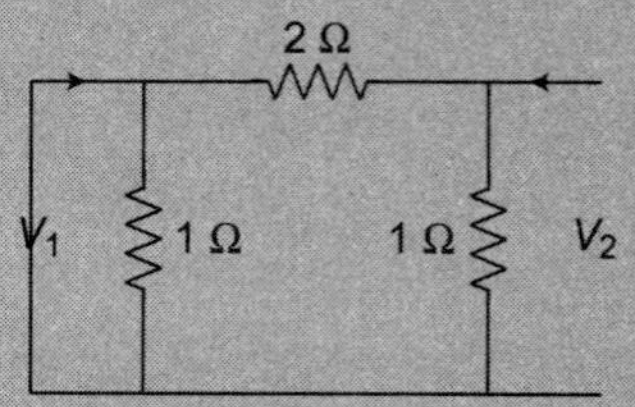

Figure 9.16 (b)

$$V_2 = \left(\frac{1\times 2}{1+2}\right) I_2 = \frac{2}{3} I_2 \Rightarrow I_2 = \frac{3}{2} V_2$$

$$I_1 = I_2 \times \frac{1}{1+2} = \frac{I_2}{3} = \frac{1}{3}\left[\frac{3}{2} V_2\right] = \frac{V_2}{2}$$

$$D' = \left.\frac{-I_2}{I_1}\right|_{V_1=0} = 3 \text{ and } B' = \left.\frac{-V_2}{I_1}\right|_{V_1=0} = 2\,\Omega$$

Example 9.8

Obtain the $A'B'C'D'$ parameters for the shown network as shown in Figure 9.17. ○●●

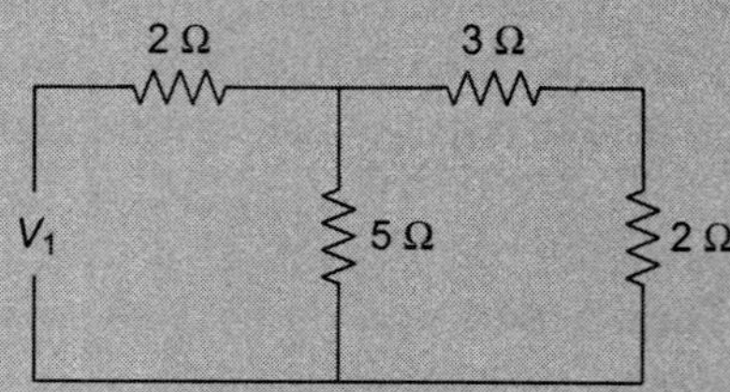

Figure 9.17

Solution From the Figure 9.18 (a)

$$V_2 = \frac{8}{5} I_2$$

$$\text{Current in } 5\,\Omega = I_2 \times \frac{2}{2+3+5}$$

$$V_1 = \frac{5\times 2}{10} I_2 = I_2$$

$$A' = \left.\frac{V_2}{V_1}\right|_{I_1=0} = \frac{8}{5} \text{ and } C' = \left.\frac{I_2}{V_1}\right|_{I_1=0} = 1\text{ S}$$

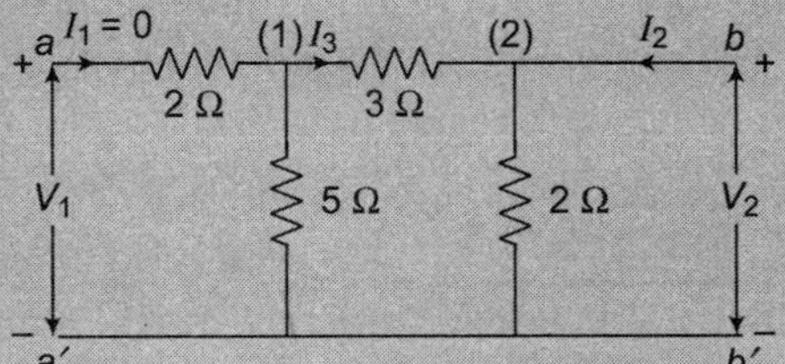

Figure 9.18 (a)

To find the parameters B' and D', short the input port and connect a voltage source V_2 at the output port (Figure 9.18 (b)).

$$V_2 = \frac{62}{45} I_2$$

$$\text{Current in } 3\ \Omega = I_2 \times \frac{2}{2+3+\frac{10}{7}}$$

$$I_1 = I_2 \times \frac{2}{2+3+\frac{10}{7}} \times \frac{5}{2+5} = \frac{2}{9} I_2$$

$$D' = \left.\frac{-I_2}{I_1}\right|_{V_1=0} = \frac{9}{2} \text{ and } B' = \left.\frac{-V_2}{I_1}\right|_{V_1=0} = \frac{31}{5}\Omega$$

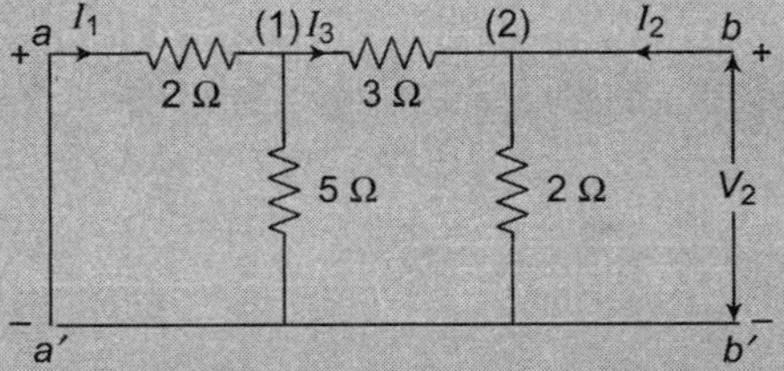

Figure 9.18 (b)

9.6 HYBRID PARAMETERS (h)

University Question

1. Explain hybrid parameters for two-port networks and state where one makes use of these parameters. **[GTU, 2010]**

This parameter representation is a mixture of some parameters obtained by open circuiting the input port and some parameters obtained by short circuiting the output port. Hence, they are called hybrid parameters or h parameters.

In this, the voltage of the input port and the current of the output port are expressed in terms of the current of the input port and the voltage of the output port.

The equations are

$$V_1 = h_{11} I_1 + h_{12} V_2$$

$$I_2 = h_{21} I_1 + h_{22} V_2$$

The individual parameters are given as

$$h_{11} = \left.\frac{V_1}{I_1}\right|_{V_2=0} \qquad h_{12} = \left.\frac{V_1}{V_2}\right|_{I_1=0}$$

$$h_{21} = \left.\frac{I_2}{I_1}\right|_{V_2=0} \qquad h_{22} = \left.\frac{I_2}{V_2}\right|_{I_1=0}$$

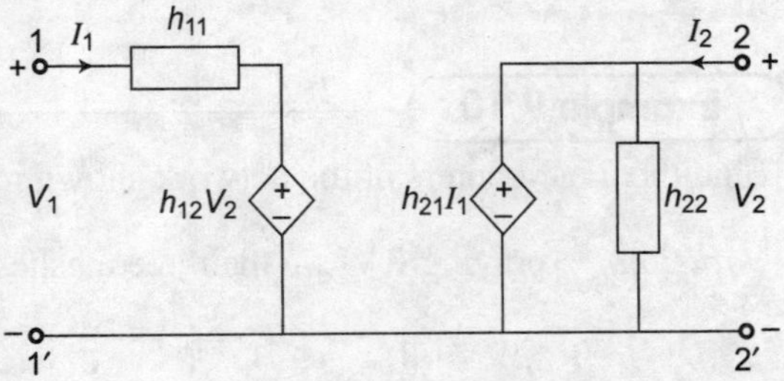

Figure 9.19

h_{11} is called the short-circuit input impedance, h_{21} is called short-circuit forward current gain, h_{12} is called open-circuit reverse voltage gain and h_{22} is called the open-circuit output admittance.

The equivalent circuit of a two-port network in terms of h parameters is as shown in Figure 9.19.

The network is said to be reciprocal if $h_{21} = h_{12}$ and symmetrical if $h_{11}h_{12} - h_{21}h_{12} = 1$.

Example 9.9

Find the hybrid parameters for the two-port network shown in Figure 9.20.

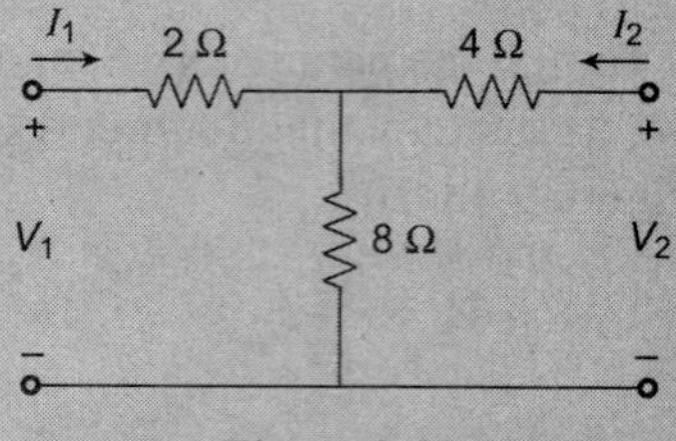

Figure 9.20

Solution To find h_{11} and h_{21}, short-circuit the output port and connect a current source I_1 to the input port as shown in Figure 9.21 (a).

$$V_1 = I_1\left[2 + \frac{8\times 4}{8+4}\right] = I_1 \times 4.67$$

$$h_{11} = \left.\frac{V_1}{I_1}\right|_{V_2=0} = 4.67\ \Omega$$

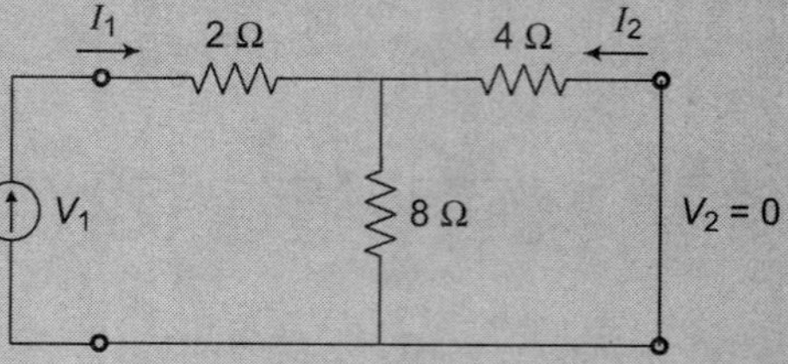

Figure 9.21 (a)

Applying current division

$$-I_2 = I_1 \times \frac{8}{8+4} = \frac{2}{3}I_1$$

$$h_{21} = \left.\frac{I_2}{I_1}\right|_{V_2=0} = \frac{-2}{3}$$

To obtain h_{12} and h_{22}, open-circuit the input port and connect a voltage source V_2 to the output port as shown in Figure 9.21 (b).

Applying voltage division

$$V_1 = V_2 \times \frac{8}{8+4} = \frac{2}{3}V_2 \Rightarrow h_{12} = \left.\frac{V_1}{V_2}\right|_{I_1=0} = \frac{2}{3}$$

$$V_2 = (8+4)I_2 = 12I_2 \Rightarrow h_{22} = \left.\frac{I_2}{V_2}\right|_{I_1=0} = \frac{1}{12}\ \text{S}$$

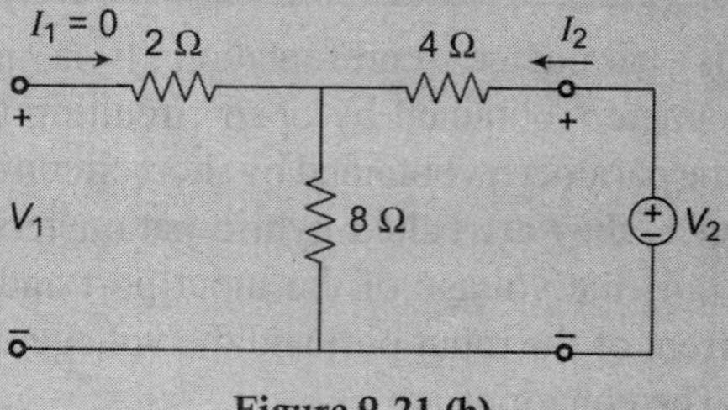

Figure 9.21 (b)

Example 9.10

Find the h parameters of the network shown in Figure 9.22.

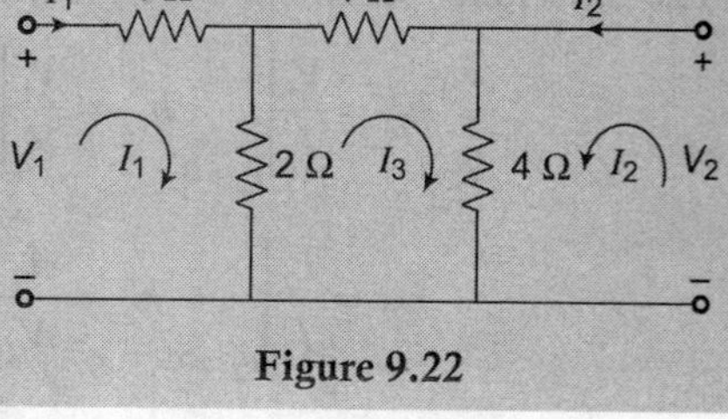

Figure 9.22

Solution Applying KVL in the three meshes

$$V_1 = I_1 + 2(I_1 - I_3)$$

$$0 = 2I_3 + 4(I_3 + I_2) + 2(I_3 - I_1)$$

$$V_2 = 4(I_2 + I_3)$$

To find h_{11} and h_{21}, short-circuit the output port i.e. $V_2 = 0$

So $-I_2 = I_3$ and $2I_2 = -I_1$

$$V_1 = 3I_1 - 2I_3 = 2I_1$$

$$h_{11} = \left.\frac{V_1}{I_1}\right|_{V_2=0} = 2\ \Omega$$

Also $$h_{21} = \left.\frac{I_2}{I_1}\right|_{V_2=0} = \frac{-1}{2}$$

To obtain h_{12} and h_{22}, open-circuit the input port i.e. $I_1 = 0$

$$h_{12} = \left.\frac{V_1}{V_2}\right|_{I_1=0} = \frac{3I_1 - 2I_3}{4(I_2 + I_3)} = \frac{-2I_3}{4(I_2 + I_3)} = \frac{-2I_3}{4(-2I_3 + I_3)} = \frac{1}{2}$$

$$4I_2 + 8I_3 = 0$$

$$I_2 = -2I_3$$

$$h_{22} = \left.\frac{I_2}{V_2}\right|_{I_1=0} = \frac{1}{2}\ \text{S}$$

Example 9.11

Find the h-parameters of the network shown in Figure 9.23. ●●●

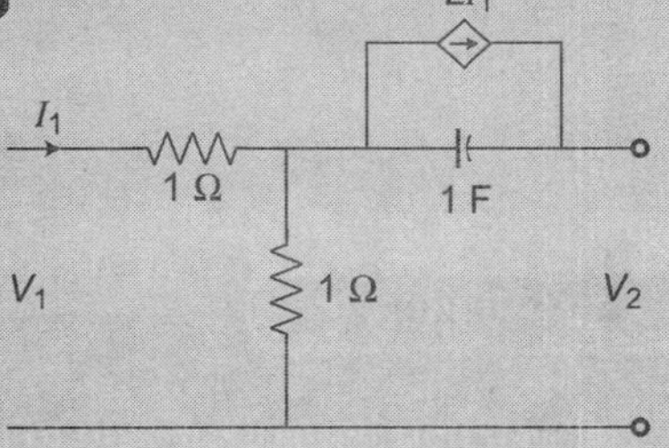

Figure 9.23

Solution To find h_{11} and h_{21}, short-circuit the output port i.e. $V_2 = 0$ as shown in Figure 9.24 (a)

By applying KCL, $-I_1 + \frac{V_x}{1} + 2I_1 + \frac{V_x - 0}{1/s} = 0$

$$I_1 + (1 + S)V_x = 0$$

and $$I_1 = \frac{V_x}{1} - I_2 \Rightarrow I_1 + I_2 = V_x$$

Substituting this, we get

$$I_1 + (1 + S)(I_1 + I_2) = 0 \Rightarrow h_{21} = \left.\frac{I_2}{I_1}\right|_{V_2=0} = \frac{s+2}{s+1}$$

$$I_1 = \frac{V_1 - V_x}{1} = V_1 - (I_1 + I_2) \Rightarrow V_1 = 2I_1 + I_2 = 2I_1 - \frac{s+2}{s+1} I_1$$

$$h_{11} = \left.\frac{V_1}{I_1}\right|_{V_2=0} = 2 - \frac{s+2}{s+1}$$

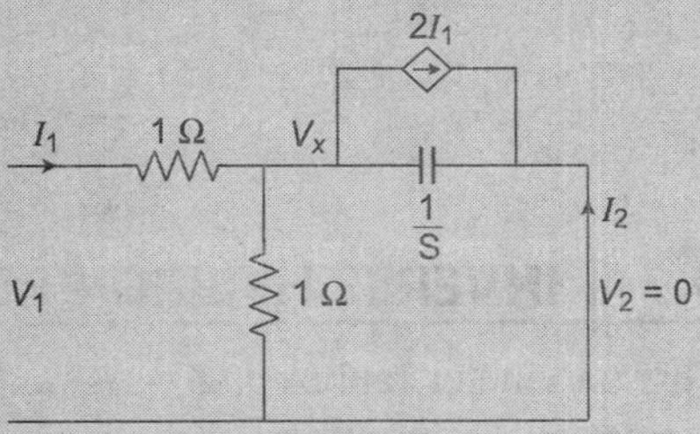

Figure 9.24 (a)

To obtain h_{12} and h_{22}, open-circuit the input port i.e. $I_1 = 0$ as shown in Figure 9.24 (b)

$$I_2 = \frac{V_2}{1+\frac{1}{s}} \Rightarrow h_{22} = \left.\frac{I_2}{V_2}\right|_{I_1=0} = \frac{s}{1+s}$$

$$V_1 = 1 \times I_2 = \frac{V_2}{1+\frac{1}{s}} \Rightarrow h_{12} = \left.\frac{V_1}{V_2}\right|_{I_1=0} = \frac{s}{1+s}$$

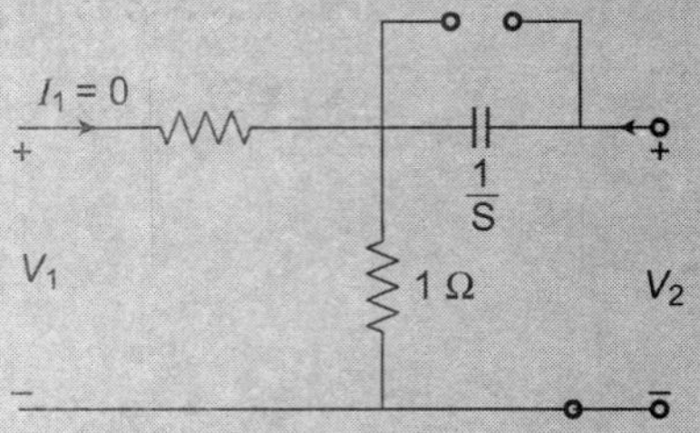

Figure 9.24 (b)

Example 9.12

Find the input impedance of the network shown in Figure 9.25.

Solution The equations are

$$V_1 = h_{11}I_1 + h_{12}V_2$$

$$I_2 = h_{21}I_1 + h_{22}V_2$$

But

$$V_2 = I_L Z_L = -I_2 Z_L$$

where, $Z_L = 75$ kΩ

Substituting the value of V_2

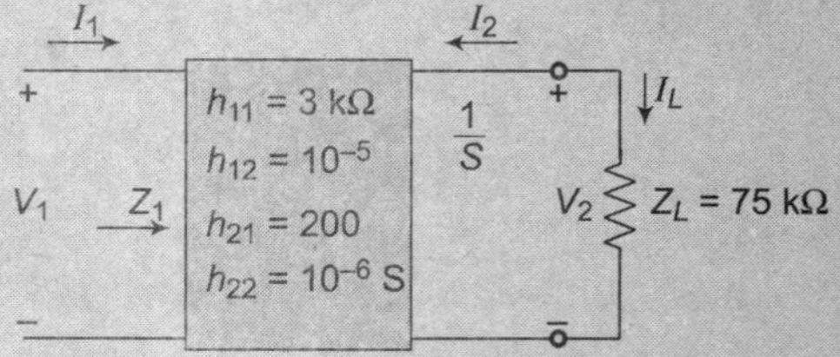

Figure 9.25

$$I_2 = h_{21}I_1 - h_{22}I_2Z_L \Rightarrow I_2 = \frac{h_{21}I_1}{1+Z_Lh_{22}}$$

$$V_2 = \frac{-Z_Lh_{21}I_1}{1+Z_Lh_{22}}$$

Substituting

$$V_1 = h_{11}I_1 - h_{12}\frac{Z_Lh_{21}I_1}{1+Z_Lh_{22}}$$

$$Z_{in} = \frac{V_1}{I_1} = h_{11} - h_{12}\frac{Z_Lh_{21}}{1+Z_Lh_{22}} = 3\times10^3 - \frac{75\times10^3\times10^{-5}\times200}{1+75\times10^3\times10^{-6}}$$

$$Z_{in} = 2.86 \text{ k}\Omega$$

9.7 INVERSE HYBRID PARAMETERS (*g*)

This parameter representation is dual of hybrid parameters. These are called *g* parameters. In this the current of the input port and the voltage of the output port are expressed in terms of the voltage of the input port and the current of the output port.

The equations are

$$I_1 = g_{11}V_1 + g_{12}I_2 ; \qquad V_2 = g_{21}V_1 + g_{22}I_2$$

The individual parameters are given as

$$g_{11} = \left.\frac{I_1}{V_1}\right|_{I_2=0} \qquad g_{12} = \left.\frac{I_1}{I_2}\right|_{V_1=0}$$

$$g_{21} = \left.\frac{V_2}{V_1}\right|_{I_2=0} \qquad g_{22} = \left.\frac{V_2}{I_2}\right|_{V_1=0}$$

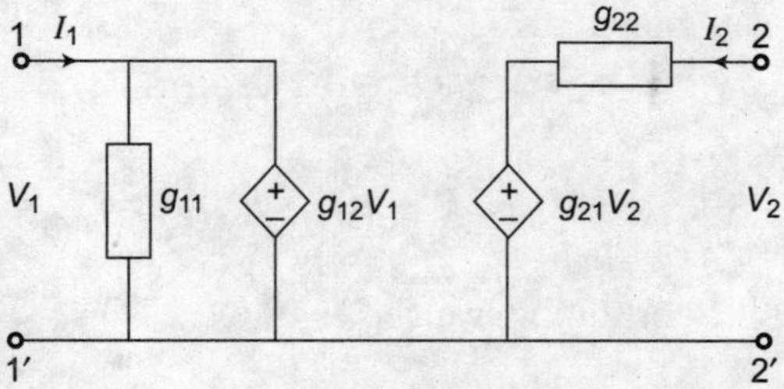

Figure 9.26

g_{11} is called the open-circuit input admittance, g_{21} is called open circuit voltage gain, g_{12} is called short-circuit reverse current gain and g_{22} is called the short-circuit output impedance.

The equivalent circuit of a two port network in terms of g parameters is as shown in Figure 9.26.

The network is said to be reciprocal if $g_{12} = -g_{21}$ and symmetrical if $g_{11}g_{22} - g_{21}g_{12} = 1$.

Example 9.13

Determine the g parameters of the network shown in Figure 9.27. ○○●

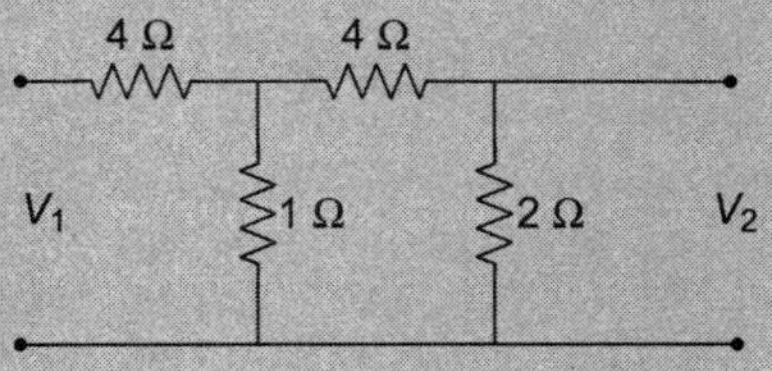

Figure 9.27

Solution To find g_{11} and g_{21}, open-circuit the output port i.e. $I_2 = 0$

$$V_1 = I_1\left[4 + \frac{1\times 6}{1+6}\right] = \frac{34}{7}I_1 \Rightarrow g_{11} = \left.\frac{I_1}{V_1}\right|_{I_2=0} = \frac{7}{34}\text{ S}$$

Applying current division the current in 2 Ω = $I_1 \times \dfrac{1}{1+4+2} = \dfrac{I_1}{7}$

$$V_2 = 2\times\frac{I_1}{7} \Rightarrow g_{21} = \left.\frac{V_2}{V_1}\right|_{I_2=0} = \frac{2/7}{34/7} = \frac{1}{17}$$

To obtain g_{12} and g_{22}, short-circuit the input port i.e. $V_1 = 0$

$$V_2 = I_2\frac{\left[4+\dfrac{1\times 4}{1+4}\right]\times 2}{\left[4+\dfrac{1\times 4}{1+4}\right]+2} = \frac{24}{17}I_2 \Rightarrow g_{22} = \left.\frac{V_2}{I_2}\right|_{V_1=0} = \frac{24}{17}\Omega$$

$$-I_1 = \left(I_2\times\frac{2}{2+4+\dfrac{4}{5}}\right)\times\frac{1}{1+4} = \frac{1}{17}I_2 \times g_{12} = \left.\frac{I_1}{I_2}\right|_{V_1=0} = \frac{-1}{17}$$

Example 9.14

Determine the g parameters of the network shown in Figure 9.28.

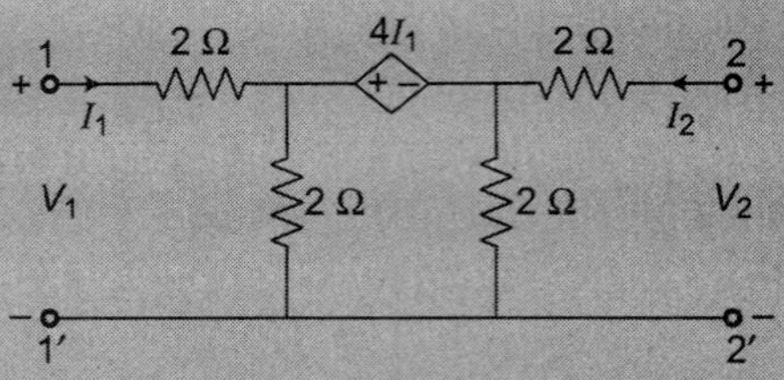

Figure 9.28

Solution To find g_{11} and g_{21}, open-circuit the output port i.e. $I_2 = 0$. Let the currents be shown as in Figure 9.29 (a).

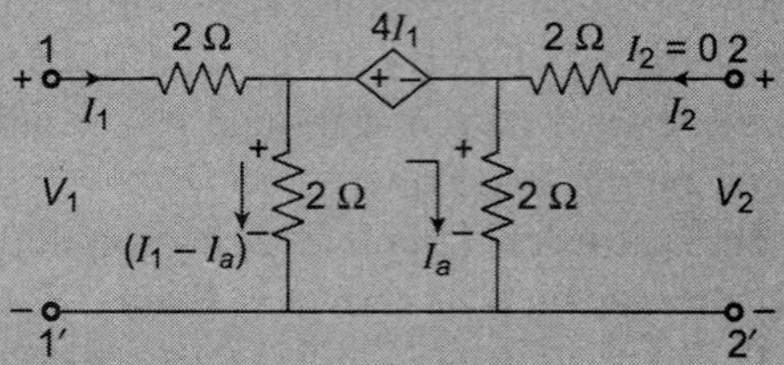

Figure 9.29 (a)

Applying KVL

$$-2I_1 - 2(I_1 - I_a) + V_1 = 0 \Rightarrow 4I_1 - 2I_a = V_1$$

$$-4I_1 - 2I_a + 2(I_1 - I_a) = 0 \Rightarrow I_a = -\frac{I_1}{2}$$

Substituting, we get

$$5I_1 = V_1 \Rightarrow g_{11} = \left.\frac{I_1}{V_1}\right|_{I_2=0} = \frac{1}{5}\text{ S}$$

$$V_2 = 2I_a = -I_1 = -\frac{V_1}{5} \Rightarrow g_{21} = \left.\frac{V_2}{V_1}\right|_{I_2=0} = -\frac{1}{5}$$

To obtain g_{12} and g_{22}, short-circuit the input port i.e. $V_1 = 0$. Let the currents be as shown in Figure 9.29 (b).

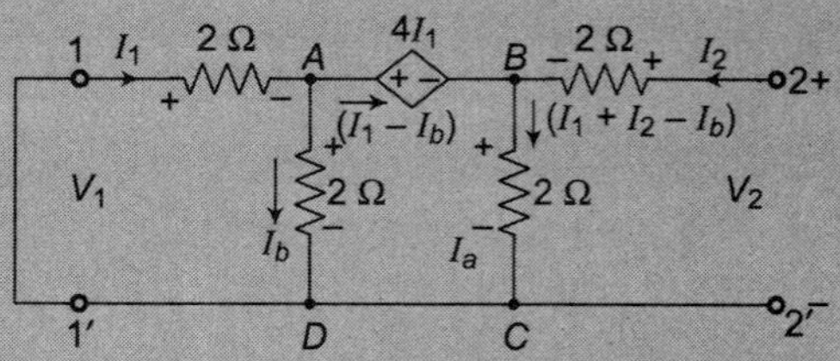

Figure 9.29 (b)

Applying KVL

$$-2I_2 - 2(I_1 + I_2 - I_b) + V_2 = 0$$

$$\Rightarrow \quad 2I_1 + 4I_2 - 2I_b = V_2$$

$$-2I_1 - 2I_b = 0 \Rightarrow I_b = -I_1$$

$$-4I_1 - 2(I_1 + I_2 - I_b) + 2I_b = 0 \Rightarrow -6I_1 - 2I_2 + 4I_b = 0$$

Substituting I_b in equations and solving we get

$$I_1 = -\frac{1}{5}I_2$$

$$g_{12} = \left.\frac{I_1}{I_2}\right|_{V_1=0} = \frac{-1}{5}$$

Also
$$4I_1 + 4I_2 = V_2 \Rightarrow -\frac{4}{5}I_2 + 4I_2 = V_2 \Rightarrow \frac{16}{5}I_2 = V_2$$

$$g_{22} = \left.\frac{V_2}{I_2}\right|_{V_1=0} = \frac{16}{5}\,\Omega$$

9.8 || RELATIONSHIP BETWEEN PARAMETERS

To make analysis of a two port network easier, any set of parameters can be expressed in any other set of parameters by appropriate algebraic manipulations and comparison of standard equations with the equations written. The summary of relationships between various parameters is given in Table 9.1.

University Questions

1. Explain *ABCD* parameters in terms of *Y* parameters. **[PTU, 2011-12]**
2. Derive transmission parameters in terms of hybrid parameters. **[PTU, 2011-12]**
3. Obtain hybrid parameters in terms of admittance parameters. **[PU, 2010]**

Table 9.1 Interrelationship between two port parameters.

	Z	*Y*	*h*	*ABCD*	*g*	*A′B′C′D′*
Z	$\begin{bmatrix} Z_{11} & Z_{12} \\ Z_{21} & Z_{22} \end{bmatrix}$	$\begin{bmatrix} \frac{Y_{22}}{\Delta Y} & \frac{-Y_{12}}{\Delta Y} \\ \frac{-Y_{21}}{\Delta Y} & \frac{-Y_{11}}{\Delta Y} \end{bmatrix}$	$\begin{bmatrix} \frac{\Delta h}{h_{33}} & \frac{h_{12}}{h_{33}} \\ -\frac{h_{21}}{h_{33}} & \frac{1}{h_{33}} \end{bmatrix}$	$\begin{bmatrix} \frac{A}{C} & \frac{\Delta T}{C} \\ \frac{1}{C} & \frac{D}{C} \end{bmatrix}$	$\begin{bmatrix} \frac{1}{g_{11}} & \frac{-g_{12}}{g_{11}} \\ \frac{g_{21}}{g_{11}} & \frac{\Delta g}{g_{11}} \end{bmatrix}$	$\begin{bmatrix} \frac{D'}{C'} & \frac{1}{C'} \\ \frac{\Delta T'}{C'} & \frac{A'}{C'} \end{bmatrix}$
Y	$\begin{bmatrix} \frac{Z_{22}}{\Delta Z} & \frac{-Z_{12}}{\Delta Z} \\ \frac{Z_{21}}{\Delta Z} & \frac{Z_{11}}{\Delta Z} \end{bmatrix}$	$\begin{bmatrix} Y_{11} & Y_{12} \\ Y_{21} & Y_{22} \end{bmatrix}$	$\begin{bmatrix} \frac{1}{h_{11}} & \frac{-h_{12}}{h_{11}} \\ \frac{h_{21}}{h_{11}} & \frac{\Delta h}{h_{11}} \end{bmatrix}$	$\begin{bmatrix} \frac{D}{B} & \frac{-\Delta T}{B} \\ \frac{-1}{B} & \frac{A}{B} \end{bmatrix}$	$\begin{bmatrix} \frac{\Delta g}{g_{22}} & \frac{g_{12}}{g_{22}} \\ \frac{-g_{21}}{g_{22}} & \frac{1}{g_{22}} \end{bmatrix}$	$\begin{bmatrix} \frac{A'}{B'} & \frac{1}{B'} \\ \frac{-\Delta T'}{B'} & \frac{D'}{B'} \end{bmatrix}$
h	$\begin{bmatrix} \frac{\Delta Z}{Z_{22}} & \frac{Z_{12}}{Z_{22}} \\ -\frac{Z_{21}}{Z_{22}} & \frac{1}{Z_{22}} \end{bmatrix}$	$\begin{bmatrix} \frac{1}{Y_{11}} & \frac{-Y_{12}}{Y_{11}} \\ \frac{Y_{21}}{Y_{11}} & \frac{\Delta Y}{Y_{11}} \end{bmatrix}$	$\begin{bmatrix} h_{11} & h_{12} \\ h_{21} & h_{22} \end{bmatrix}$	$\begin{bmatrix} \frac{B}{D} & \frac{\Delta T}{D} \\ \frac{-1}{D} & \frac{C}{D} \end{bmatrix}$	$\begin{bmatrix} \frac{g_{22}}{\Delta g} & \frac{-g_{12}}{\Delta g} \\ \frac{-g_{21}}{\Delta g} & \frac{g_{11}}{\Delta g} \end{bmatrix}$	$\begin{bmatrix} \frac{B'}{A'} & \frac{1}{A'} \\ \frac{-\Delta T'}{A'} & \frac{C'}{A'} \end{bmatrix}$
ABCD	$\begin{bmatrix} \frac{Z_{11}}{Z_{21}} & \frac{\Delta Z}{Z_{21}} \\ \frac{1}{Z_{21}} & \frac{Z_{22}}{Z_{21}} \end{bmatrix}$	$\begin{bmatrix} -\frac{Y_{22}}{Y_{21}} & -\frac{1}{Y_{21}} \\ -\frac{\Delta Y}{Y_{21}} & -\frac{Y_{11}}{Y_{21}} \end{bmatrix}$	$\begin{bmatrix} -\frac{\Delta h}{h_{21}} & -\frac{h_{11}}{h_{21}} \\ -\frac{h_{22}}{h_{21}} & -\frac{1}{h_{21}} \end{bmatrix}$	$\begin{bmatrix} A & B \\ C & D \end{bmatrix}$	$\begin{bmatrix} \frac{1}{g_{21}} & \frac{g_{22}}{g_{21}} \\ \frac{g_{11}}{g_{21}} & \frac{\Delta g}{g_{21}} \end{bmatrix}$	$\begin{bmatrix} \frac{D'}{\Delta T'} & \frac{B'}{\Delta T'} \\ \frac{C'}{\Delta T'} & \frac{A'}{\Delta T'} \end{bmatrix}$
g	$\begin{bmatrix} \frac{1}{Z_{11}} & \frac{-Z_{12}}{Z_{11}} \\ \frac{Z_{21}}{Z_{11}} & \frac{\Delta Z}{Z_{11}} \end{bmatrix}$	$\begin{bmatrix} \frac{\Delta Y}{Y_{22}} & \frac{Y_{12}}{Y_{22}} \\ \frac{-Y_{21}}{Y_{22}} & \frac{1}{Y_{22}} \end{bmatrix}$	$\begin{bmatrix} \frac{h_{22}}{\Delta h} & \frac{-h_{12}}{\Delta h} \\ \frac{-h_{21}}{\Delta h} & \frac{h_{11}}{\Delta h} \end{bmatrix}$	$\begin{bmatrix} \frac{C}{A} & \frac{-\Delta T}{A} \\ \frac{1}{A} & \frac{B}{A} \end{bmatrix}$	$\begin{bmatrix} g_{11} & g_{12} \\ g_{21} & g_{22} \end{bmatrix}$	$\begin{bmatrix} \frac{C'}{D'} & \frac{-1}{D'} \\ \frac{\Delta T'}{D'} & \frac{B'}{D'} \end{bmatrix}$
A′B′C′D′	$\begin{bmatrix} \frac{Z_{22}}{Z_{12}} & \frac{\Delta Z}{Z_{12}} \\ \frac{1}{Z_{12}} & \frac{Z_{11}}{Z_{12}} \end{bmatrix}$	$\begin{bmatrix} \frac{-Y_{11}}{Y_{12}} & \frac{-1}{Y_{12}} \\ \frac{-\Delta Y}{Y_{12}} & \frac{-Y_{22}}{Y_{12}} \end{bmatrix}$	$\begin{bmatrix} \frac{1}{h_{12}} & \frac{h_{11}}{h_{12}} \\ \frac{h_{22}}{h_{12}} & \frac{\Delta h}{h_{12}} \end{bmatrix}$	$\begin{bmatrix} \frac{D}{\Delta T} & \frac{B}{\Delta T} \\ \frac{C}{\Delta T} & \frac{A}{\Delta T} \end{bmatrix}$	$\begin{bmatrix} \frac{-\Delta g}{g_{12}} & \frac{-g_{22}}{g_{12}} \\ \frac{-g_{11}}{g_{12}} & \frac{1}{g_{12}} \end{bmatrix}$	$\begin{bmatrix} A' & B' \\ C' & D' \end{bmatrix}$

where $\Delta Z = Z_{11}Z_{22} - Z_{12}Z_{21}\Delta Y = Y_{11}Y_{22} - Y_{12}Y_{21}$

$$\Delta h = h_{11}h_{22} - h_{12}h_{21};\ \Delta g = g_{11}g_{22} - g_{12}g_{21};\ \Delta T = AD - BC;\ \Delta T' = A'D' - B'C'$$

Example 9.15

The Z-parameters of a two-port network are $Z_{11} = 10\ \Omega$, $Z_{22} = 20\ \Omega$, $Z_{12} = Z_{21} = 5\ \Omega$. Find the ABCD-parameters of this two-port network. ○○●

Solution

$$A = \frac{Z_{11}}{Z_{21}} \qquad B = \frac{Z_{11}Z_{22} - Z_{12}Z_{21}}{Z_{21}} \qquad C = \frac{1}{Z_{21}} \qquad D = \frac{Z_{22}}{Z_{21}}$$

$$A = \frac{10}{5} = 2 \qquad B = \frac{10\times 20 - 5\times 5}{5} = 35\Omega \qquad C = \frac{1}{5} = 0.2\ \text{S} \qquad D = \frac{20}{5} = 4$$

Example 9.16

Find the Y-parameters of the circuit shown in Figure 9.30. Then find the ABCD parameters. ○○○

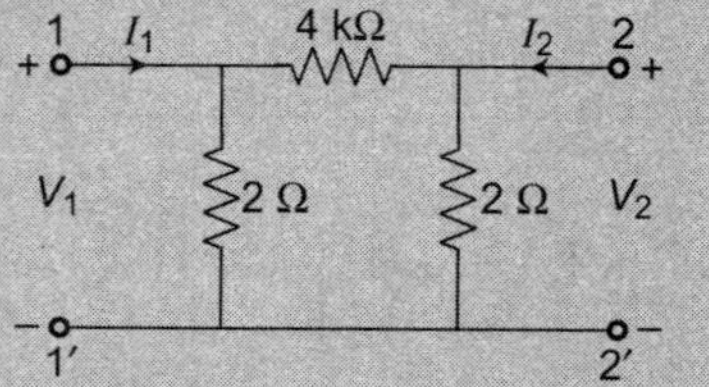

Figure 9.30

Solution When $V_2 = 0$, the equivalent circuit for the given network is as shown in Figure 9.31 (a).

$$V_1 = 4\times 10^3 (I_1 + I_2)$$

By current divider

$$I_2 = -I_1\left[\frac{4\times 10^3}{4\times 10^3 + 4\times 10^3}\right] = \frac{-1}{2} I_1$$

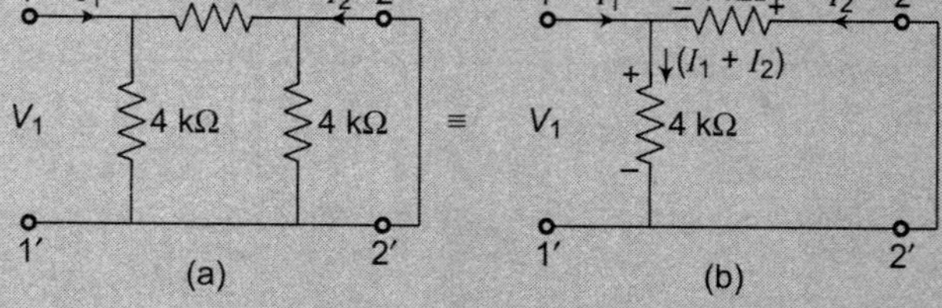

Figure 9.31 (a)

$$V_1 = 4\times 10^3\left(I_1 - \frac{1}{2} I_1\right) = 2\times 10^3 (I_1)$$

$$Y_{11} = \left.\frac{I_1}{V_1}\right|_{V_2 = 0} = 0.5\times 10^{-3}\ \text{S}$$

$$V_1 = 4 \times 10^3(-2I_2 + I_2) = -4 \times 10^3 (I_2)$$

$$Y_{21} = \left.\frac{I_2}{V_1}\right|_{V_2 = 0} = -0.25 \times 10^{-3}\ \text{S}$$

When $V_1 = 0$, the circuit becomes as shown in Figure 9.31 (b).

$$V_2 = 4 \times 10^3(I_1 + I_2)$$

By current divider

$$I_1 = -I_2\left[\frac{4 \times 10^3}{4 \times 10^3 + 4 \times 10^3}\right] = \frac{-1}{2} I_2$$

$$V_2 = 4 \times 10^3\left(-\frac{1}{2}I_2 + I_1\right) = 2 \times 10^3 (I_2)$$

$$Y_{22} = \left.\frac{I_2}{V_2}\right|_{V_1 = 0} = 0.5 \times 10^{-3}\ \text{S}$$

$$V_2 = 2 \times 10^3(-2I_1) = -4 \times 10^3 (I_1)$$

$$Y_{12} = \left.\frac{I_1}{V_2}\right|_{V_1 = 0} = -0.25 \times 10^{-3}\ \text{S}$$

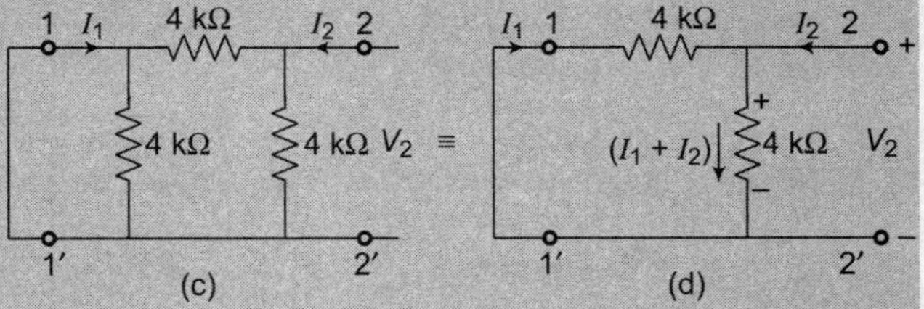

Figure 9.31 (b)

So the Y parameter matrix is $\begin{bmatrix} 0.5 \times 10^{-3} & -0.25 \times 10^{-3} \\ -0.25 \times 10^{-3} & 0.5 \times 10^{-3} \end{bmatrix}$

The *ABCD* parameters are

$$A = -\frac{Y_{22}}{Y_{21}} = -\frac{0.5 \times 10^{-3}}{0.25 \times 10^{-3}} = 2$$

$$B = -\frac{1}{Y_{21}} = -\frac{1}{-0.25 \times 10^{-3}} = 4000$$

$$C = -\frac{\Delta Y}{Y_{21}} = -\frac{Y_{11}Y_{22} - Y_{12}Y_{21}}{Y_{21}} = 0.75 \times 10^{-3}$$

$$D = -\frac{Y_{11}}{Y_{21}} = -\frac{0.5 \times 10^{-3}}{-0.25 \times 10^{-3}} = 2$$

Example 9.17

Find the Z and h parameters for the network shown in Figure 9.32.

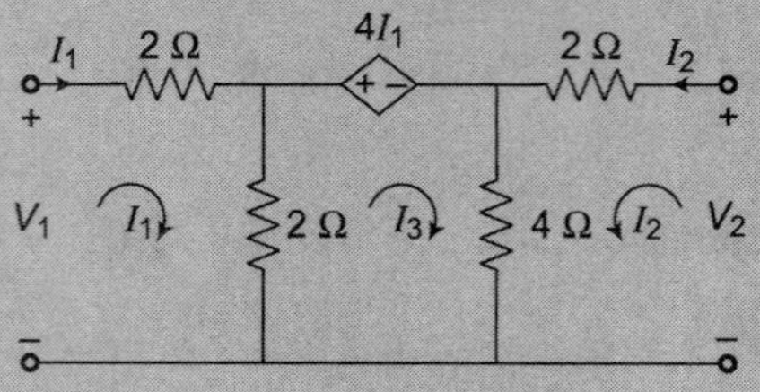

Figure 9.32

Solution

Applying KVL to mesh 1 $\quad V_1 = 2I_1 + 2(I_1 - I_3) = 4I_1 - 2I_3$

Applying KVL to mesh 2 $\quad V_2 = 2I_2 + 2(I_2 + I_3) = 4I_2 + 2I_3$

Applying KVL to mesh 3 $\quad 2(I_3 - I_1) + 4I_1 + 2(I_3 + I_2) = 0 \Rightarrow I_1 + I_2 = -2I_3$

Substituting and solving $\quad V_1 = 5I_1 + I_2 V_2 = -I_1 + 3I_2$

Comparing with standard equations for Z parameters

$$\begin{bmatrix} Z_{11} & Z_{12} \\ Z_{21} & Z_{22} \end{bmatrix} = \begin{bmatrix} 5 & 1 \\ -1 & 3 \end{bmatrix}$$

h parameters

$$h_{11} = \frac{\Delta Z}{Z_{22}} = \frac{Z_{11}Z_{22} - Z_{12}Z_{21}}{Z_{22}} = \frac{16}{3} \qquad h_{12} = \frac{Z_{12}}{Z_{22}} = \frac{1}{3}$$

$$h_{21} = -\frac{Z_{21}}{Z_{22}} = \frac{1}{3} \qquad h_{22} = \frac{1}{Z_{22}} = \frac{1}{3}$$

9.9 || INTERCONNECTION OF TWO PORT NETWORKS

Simple two-port networks can be interconnected to form an equivalent network. The parameters of this network are related to the parameters of the component networks. The various types of interconnections are given below:

9.9.1 Cascade Connection

The cascade connection is also called tandem connection. In this connection the output port of one network is the input port of the other. When two ports are connected in cascade, we can multiply their individual transmission parameters to get overall transmission parameters of the cascade connection. The cascade connection of two networks N_1 and N_2 is as shown in Figure 9.33.

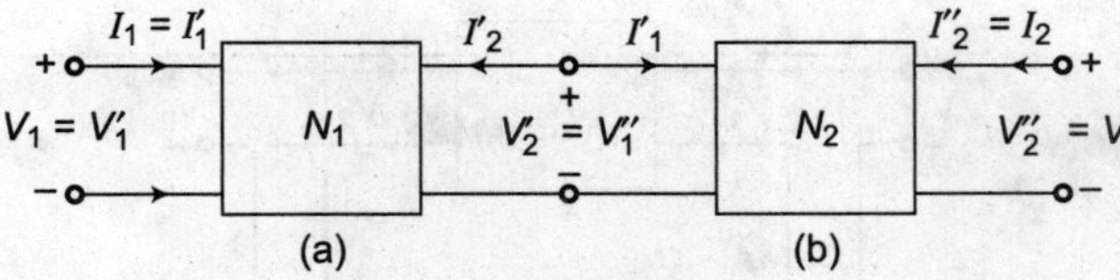

Figure 9.33

The equation is

$$\begin{bmatrix} V_1 \\ I_1 \end{bmatrix} = \begin{bmatrix} A_1 & B_1 \\ C_1 & D_1 \end{bmatrix} \begin{bmatrix} A_2 & B_2 \\ C_2 & D_2 \end{bmatrix} \begin{bmatrix} V_2 \\ I_2 \end{bmatrix}$$

9.9.2 Series Connection

Two two-port networks are said to be connected in series if the corresponding input and output ports are connected in series. The currents of the input ports are made equal as also those of the output ports. The open circuit impedance matrix of the equivalent two-port network is the sum of the open circuit impedance matrices of the individual networks. The series connection of two networks X and Y is as shown in Figure 9.34.

The describing equations are

$$\begin{bmatrix} V_1 \\ V_2 \end{bmatrix} = \begin{bmatrix} Z_{11X} + Z_{11Y} & Z_{12X} + Z_{12Y} \\ Z_{21X} + Z_{21Y} & Z_{22X} + Z_{22Y} \end{bmatrix} \begin{bmatrix} I_1 \\ I_2 \end{bmatrix}$$

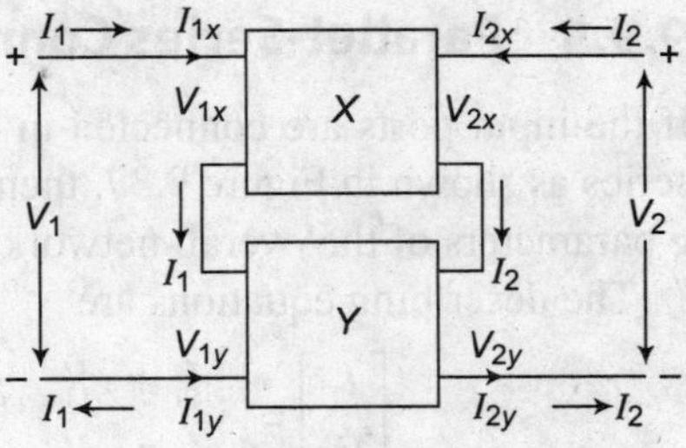

Figure 9.34

9.9.3 Parallel Connection

Two two-port networks are said to be connected in series if the corresponding input and output ports are connected in parallel. The currents of the input ports are made equal as also those of the output ports. The short circuit admittance matrix of the equivalent two-port network is the sum of the short-circuit admittance matrices of the individual networks. The parallel connection of two networks X and Y is as shown in Figure 9.35.

The describing equations are

$$\begin{bmatrix} I_1 \\ I_2 \end{bmatrix} = \begin{bmatrix} Y_{11X} + Y_{11Y} & Y_{12X} + Y_{12Y} \\ Y_{21X} + Y_{21Y} & Y_{22X} + Y_{22Y} \end{bmatrix} \begin{bmatrix} V_1 \\ V_2 \end{bmatrix}$$

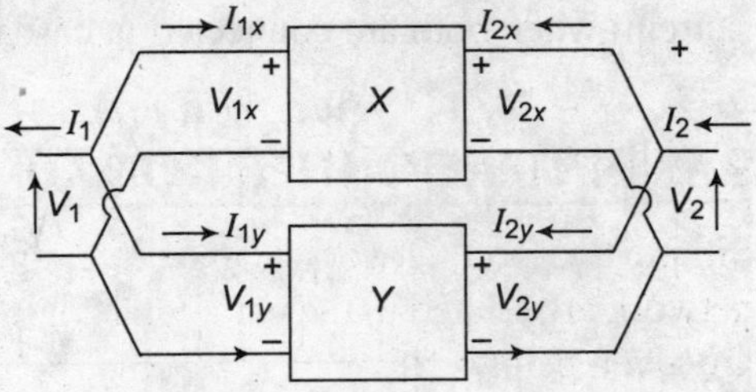

Figure 9.35

9.9.4 Series–Parallel Connection

If one port each of the two two-port networks is connected in series and the other in parallel it is convenient to find the overall parameters of the two networks using the h-parameters. Suppose the two networks, as shown in Figure 9.36, are connected in series-parallel.

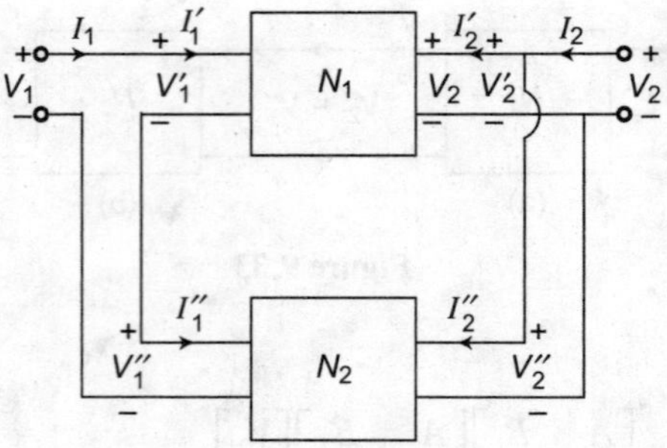

Figure 9.36

The describing equations are

$$\begin{bmatrix} V_1 \\ I_2 \end{bmatrix} = \begin{bmatrix} h'_{11} + h''_{11} & h'_{12} + h''_{12} \\ h'_{21} + h''_{21} & h''_{22} + h''_{22} \end{bmatrix} \begin{bmatrix} I_1 \\ V_2 \end{bmatrix}$$

9.9.5 Parallel-Series Connection

If the input ports are connected in parallel and the output in series as shown in Figure 9.37, then it is convenient to obtain g parameters of the overall networks.

The describing equations are

$$\begin{bmatrix} I_1 \\ V_2 \end{bmatrix} = \begin{bmatrix} g'_{11} + g''_{11} & g'_{12} + g''_{12} \\ g'_{21} + g''_{21} & g'_{22} + g''_{22} \end{bmatrix} \begin{bmatrix} V_1 \\ I_2 \end{bmatrix}$$

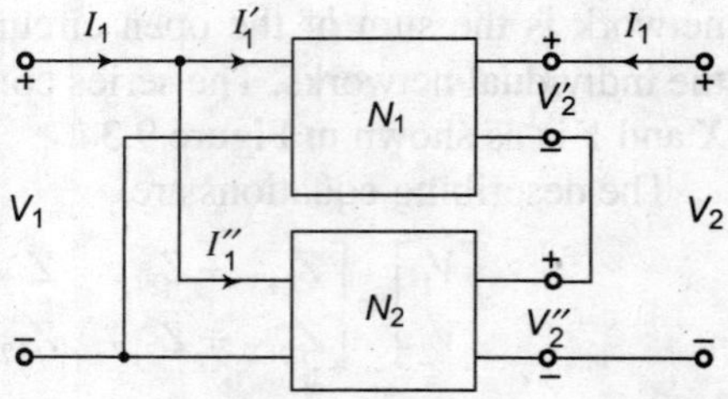

Figure 9.37

Example 9.18

Two networks have been shown in Figure 9.38. Obtain the transmission parameters of the resulting circuit when both are connected in cascade.

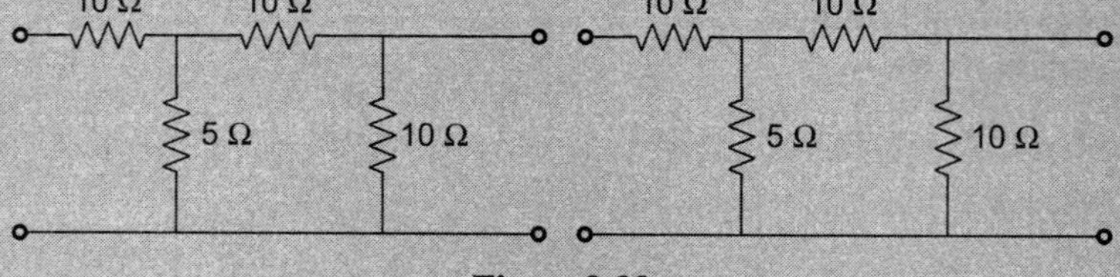

Figure 9.38

Solution Let us find the ABCD parameters of one network as shown in Figure 9.39.

The output port is open circuited i.e. $I_2 = 0$.

$$V_1 = \left(\frac{20 \times 5}{20 + 5} + 10 \right) I_1 = 14 I_1$$

Current in the 10 Ω resistor $= I_1\left(\dfrac{5}{5+10+10}\right) = \dfrac{I_1}{5}$

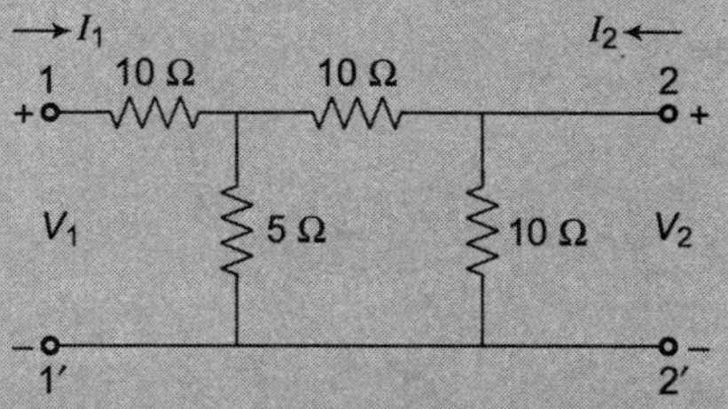

Figure 9.39

$$V_2 = 10\times\frac{I_1}{5} = 2I_1$$

$$C = \left.\frac{I_1}{V_2}\right|_{I_2=0} = 0.5\text{ S}$$

$$A = \left.\frac{V_1}{V_2}\right|_{I_2=0} = \frac{14I_1}{2I_1} = 7$$

The output port is short-circuited i.e. $V_2 = 0$

$$V_1 = \left(\frac{10\times 5}{10+5} + 10\right)I_1 = \frac{40}{3}I_1$$

Applying current division

$$-I_2 = I_1\left(\frac{5}{5+10}\right) = \frac{I_1}{3} \Rightarrow D = \left.\frac{I_1}{-I_2}\right|_{V_2=0} = 3$$

$$B = \left.\frac{V_1}{-I_2}\right|_{V_2=0} = 40\ \Omega$$

So the $ABCD$ parameters are $\begin{bmatrix} 7 & 40 \\ 0.5 & 3 \end{bmatrix}$. As the two networks are identical, the transmission parameters of the equivalent network in cascade is given as

$$\begin{bmatrix} 7 & 40 \\ 0.5 & 3 \end{bmatrix}\times\begin{bmatrix} 7 & 40 \\ 0.5 & 3 \end{bmatrix} = \begin{bmatrix} 69 & 400 \\ 5 & 29 \end{bmatrix}$$

Example 9.19

Determine Z parameters of the network shown in Figure 9.40. An identical network is connected in series with this network. Obtain the Z parameters of the overall network. Also verify by direct calculation

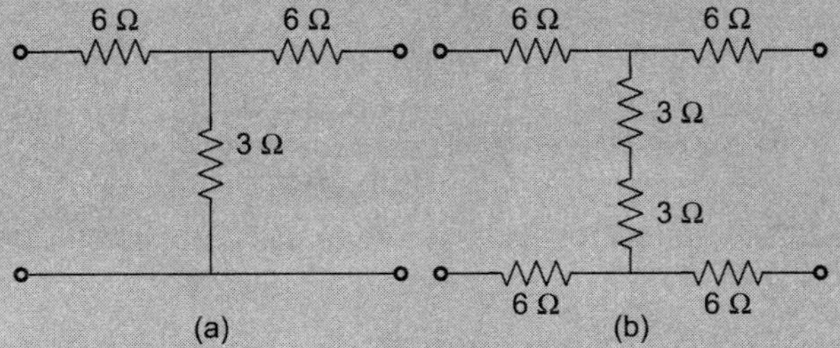

Figure 9.40

Solution To find Z_{11} and Z_{21}, the output terminals are open circuited.

$$V_1 = (6+3)I_1 = 9I_1$$

$$Z_{11} = \left.\frac{V_1}{I_1}\right|_{I_2=0} = 9\Omega$$

$$V_2 = 3I_1 \Rightarrow Z_{21} = \left.\frac{V_2}{I_1}\right|_{I_2=0} = 3\Omega$$

To find Z_{12} and Z_{22}, the input terminals are open circuited.

$$V_2 = (6+3)I_2 \Rightarrow Z_{22} = \left.\frac{V_2}{I_2}\right|_{I_1=0} = 9\Omega$$

$$V_1 = 3I_2 \Rightarrow Z_{12} = \left.\frac{V_1}{I_2}\right|_{I_1=0} = 3\Omega$$

So the overall Z parameters of the combination circuit is

$$\begin{bmatrix} 9 & 3 \\ 3 & 9 \end{bmatrix} + \begin{bmatrix} 9 & 3 \\ 3 & 9 \end{bmatrix} = \begin{bmatrix} 18 & 6 \\ 6 & 18 \end{bmatrix}$$

By direct calculation

$$V_1 = (6+3+3+6)I_1 = 18I_1$$

$$Z_{11} = \left.\frac{V_1}{I_1}\right|_{I_2=0} = 18\Omega$$

$$V_2 = (3+3)I_1 \Rightarrow Z_{21} = \left.\frac{V_2}{I_1}\right|_{I_2=0} = 6\Omega$$

To find Z_{12} and Z_{22}, the input terminals are open circuited.

$$V_2 = (6+3+3+6)I_2 \Rightarrow Z_{22} = \left.\frac{V_2}{I_2}\right|_{I_1=0} = 18\Omega$$

$$V_1 = (3+3)I_2 \Rightarrow Z_{12} = \left.\frac{V_1}{I_2}\right|_{I_1=0} = 6\Omega$$

Example 9.20

Determine Y parameters of the network shown in Figure 9.41. An identical network is connected in series with this network. Obtain the Y parameters of the overall network. ○●●

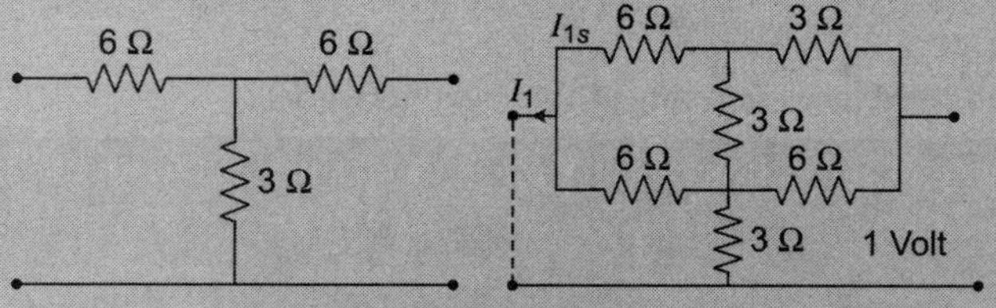

Figure 9.41

Solution To find Y_{11} and Y_{21}, the output terminals are short circuited.

$$V_1 = \left(6 + \frac{3 \times 6}{3+6}\right) I_1 = 8I_1 \Rightarrow Y_{11} = \left.\frac{I_1}{V_1}\right|_{I_2=0} = \frac{1}{8}\Omega$$

Using current division rule $-I_2 = \dfrac{I_1 \times 3}{3+6} = \dfrac{I_1}{3} \Rightarrow -I_2 = \dfrac{1}{3}\left[\dfrac{V_1}{8}\right]$

Hence, $$Y_{21} = \left.\frac{I_2}{V_1}\right|_{V_2=0} = \frac{-1}{24}\text{S}$$

To find Y_{12} and Y_{22}, the input terminals are short circuited

$$I_2 = \frac{V_2}{\left(6 + \dfrac{3 \times 6}{3+6}\right)} = \frac{V_2}{8} \times Y_{22} = \left.\frac{I_2}{V_2}\right|_{V_1=0} = \frac{1}{8}\text{S}$$

Using current division rule $-I_1 = \dfrac{I_2 \times 3}{3+6} = \dfrac{I_2}{3} \times -I_1 = \dfrac{1}{3}\left[\dfrac{V_2}{8}\right]$

Hence, $$Y_{12} = \left.\frac{I_1}{V_2}\right|_{V_1=0} = \frac{-1}{24}\text{S}$$

So the overall Y parameters of the combination circuit is

$$\begin{bmatrix} \frac{1}{8} & -\frac{1}{24} \\ -\frac{1}{24} & \frac{1}{8} \end{bmatrix} + \begin{bmatrix} \frac{1}{8} & -\frac{1}{24} \\ -\frac{1}{24} & \frac{1}{8} \end{bmatrix} = \begin{bmatrix} \frac{1}{4} & -\frac{1}{12} \\ -\frac{1}{12} & \frac{1}{4} \end{bmatrix}$$

9.10 TERMINATED TWO-PORT NETWORKS

If the two-port network is terminated into a load impedance at either output port or input port, then it is possible to express input impedance or output impedance in terms of the parameters of two-port network.

Table 9.2 Driving point impedances in terms of two port networks.

	In terms of Z parameters	In terms of Y parameters	In terms of ABCD parameters	In terms of A'B'C'D' parameters	In terms of h parameters	In terms of g parameters
Driving point impedance at input port V_1/I_1	$Z_{11}-\frac{Z_{12}Z_{21}}{Z_L+Z_{22}}$	$\frac{Y_{22}+Y_L}{Y_{11}(Y_L+Y_{22})-Y_{12}Y_{21}}$	$\frac{AZ_L+B}{CZ_L+D}$	$\frac{B'-D'Z_L}{C'Z_L-A'}$	$\frac{\Delta_h Z_L+h_{11}}{1+h_{22}Z_L}$	$\frac{1+g_{22}Y_L}{\Delta_g Y_L+g_{11}}$
Driving point impedance at input port V_2/I_2	$\frac{\Delta_z+Z_{22}Z_s}{Z_s+Z_{11}}$	$\frac{Y_{11}+Y_s}{\Delta_Y+Y_sY_{22}}$	$\frac{DZ_s+B}{CZ_s+A}$	$\frac{A'Z_s+B'}{C'Z_s+D'}$	$\frac{h_{11}+Z_s}{\Delta_h+h_{22}Z_s}$	$\frac{g_{22}+\Delta_g}{1+g_{11}Z_s}$

Note: The above relations are obtained when $V_s = 0$ and $I_s = 0$ at the input port.

Example 9.21

The currents I_1 and I_2 at input and output ports respectively of a two port network are expressed as

$$I_1 = 5V_1 - V_2$$
$$I_2 = -V_1 + V_2$$

Find the Y parameters. If a load impedance of $(3 + j5)\ \Omega$ is connected across the output port, find the input impedance. ○○●

Solution Comparing the equations with the standard Y parameter equations

$$Y_{11} = 5\ \Omega \quad Y_{12} = Y_{21} = -1\Omega \quad Y_{22} = 1\ \Omega$$

Here the load impedance is $Z_L = (3 + j5)\ \Omega$

$$\text{Load admittance } Y_L = \frac{1}{Z_L} = \frac{1}{3+j5} = \frac{3}{34} - j\frac{5}{34}$$

$$\text{The input impedance } Z_{in} = \frac{V_1}{I_1} = \frac{Y_{22}+Y_L}{Y_{11}(Y_L+Y_{22})-Y_{12}Y_{21}} = \frac{1+\frac{3}{34}-j\frac{5}{34}}{5\times 1-(-1)^2+5\times\frac{3}{34}-j\frac{5}{34}}$$

$$Z_{in} = 0.248\angle 1.89°\Omega$$

9.11 || IMAGE PARAMETERS

University Questions

1. What are image and iterative impedances? [BPUT, 2007]
2. Explain reciprocal and symmetrical networks. [PTU, 2011-12]

In a two-port network, if two impedances Z_{i1} and Z_{i2} are such that Z_{i2} is the driving point impedance at port 1 when the port 2 of the network terminates into Z_{i2} and Z_{i2} is the driving point impedance at port 2 when port 1 of the network terminates into Z_{i1}. Then the two impedances are called image impedances of the network and can be expressed in terms of two port parameters as shown in Figure 9.42.

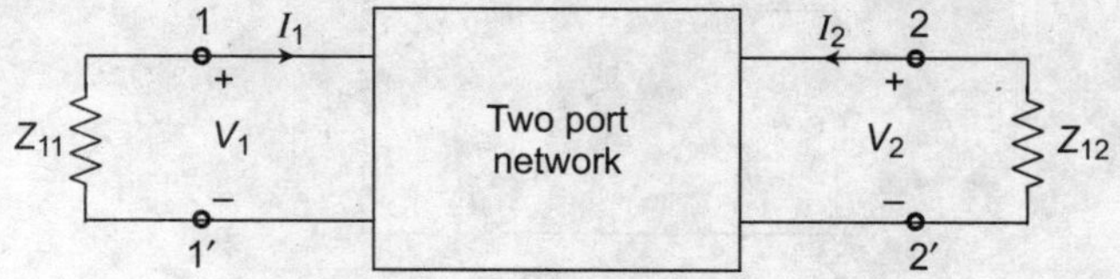

Figure 9.42

Z_{1o} is the input impedance measured from port 1 with port 2 kept open, Z_{1s} is the input impedance measured from port 1 with port 2 kept shorted, Z_{2o} is the input impedance measured from port-2 with port-1 kept open and Z_{2s} is the input impedance measured from port 2 with port 1 kept shorted.

$$v_1 = Av_2 - Bi_2$$

$$i_1 = Cv_2 - Di_2$$

When port 2 is open $\frac{v_1}{i_1} = \frac{A}{C}$ and when port 2 is shorted $\frac{v_1}{i_1} = \frac{B}{D}$

When port 1 is open $\frac{v_2}{i_2} = \frac{D}{C}$ and when port 1 is shorted $\frac{v_2}{i_2} = \frac{B}{A}$

Therefore, $Z_{1o} = \frac{A}{C}\ Z_{1s} = \frac{B}{D} Z_{2o} = \frac{D}{C} Z_{2s} = \frac{B}{A}$

The image impedances are given in terms of ABCD parameters as follows

$$Z_{i1} = \sqrt{Z_{1o}Z_{1s}} = \sqrt{\frac{AB}{CD}}$$

$$Z_{i2} = \sqrt{Z_{2o}Z_{2s}} = \sqrt{\frac{BD}{AC}}$$

A third parameter required to completely describe a reciprocal two port network is determined from the ratios $\frac{V_1}{V_2}$ and $\frac{i_1}{-i_2}$ when the second port is terminated in Z_{i2} and V_1 is applied at the first port. The geometric mean of these two ratios is expressed as the exponential of a number γ which is called the image transfer constant. The image transfer constant γ is given by

$$\gamma = \tanh^{-1}\sqrt{\frac{Z_{2s}}{Z_{2o}}} = \tanh^{-1}\sqrt{\frac{Z_{1s}}{Z_{1o}}} = \tanh^{-1}\sqrt{\frac{BC}{AD}}$$

Example 9.22

Find out the ABCD-parameters of the network as shown in Figure 9.43. Also find the image parameters for the network.

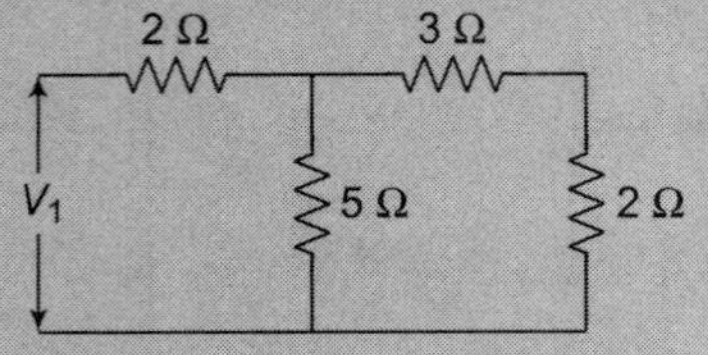

Figure 9.43

Solution To find A and C, open the output port as shown in Figure 9.44 (a).

$$V_1 = \left(\frac{5\times 5}{5+5}+2\right)I_1 = 4.5I_1$$

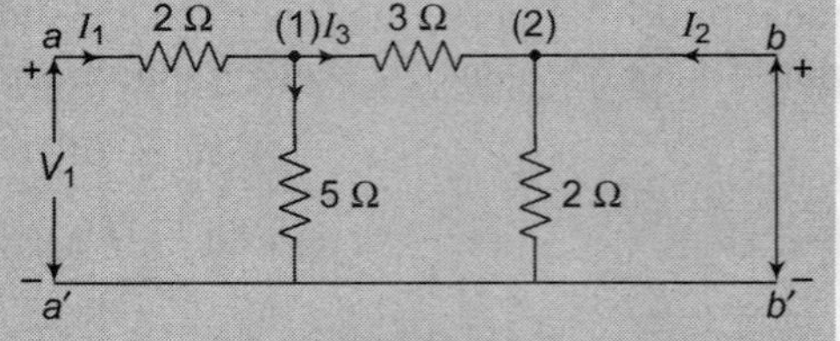

Figure 9.44 (a)

Current in 2 Ω $\quad I_3 = \left(\frac{5}{5+3+2}\right)I_1 = 0.5I_1$

$$V_2 = 2\times 0.5I_1 = 1\times I_1 \Rightarrow C = \left.\frac{I_1}{V_2}\right|_{I_2=0} = 1\text{S}$$

$$A = \left.\frac{V_1}{V_2}\right|_{I_2=0} = \frac{4.5I_1}{1I_1} = 4.5$$

To find B and D, short the output port as shown in Figure 9.44 (b).

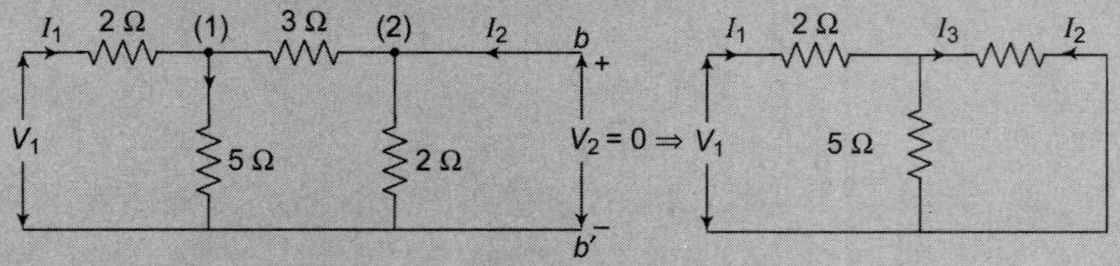

Figure 9.44 (b)

$$V_1 = \left(\frac{5\times 3}{5+3}+2\right)I_1 = \frac{31}{8}I_1$$

By current division, $-I_2 = \left(\frac{5}{5+3}\right)I_1 = \frac{5}{8}I_1 \Rightarrow D = \left.\frac{I_1}{-I_2}\right|_{V_2=0} = \frac{8}{5}$

$$B = \left.\frac{V_1}{-I_2}\right|_{V_2=0} = \frac{31}{5}$$

Image parameters are $Z_{i1} = \sqrt{\frac{AB}{CD}} = \sqrt{\frac{4.5 \times 6.2}{1 \times 1.6}} = 4.18\,\Omega$

$$Z_{i2} = \sqrt{\frac{BD}{AC}} = \sqrt{\frac{6.2 \times 1.6}{4.5 \times 1}} = 1.48\,\Omega$$

$$\gamma = \tanh^{-1}\sqrt{\frac{BC}{AD}} = 1.643$$

9.12 ATTENUATION AND PHASE SHIFT IN SYMMETRICAL *T* AND π NETWORKS

For a symmetrical reciprocal two-port network, the two image impedances Z_{i1} and Z_{i2} are equal and the image impedance is then called characteristic impedance or iterative impedance Z_0. It is given in terms of *ABCD* parameters as $Z_0 = \sqrt{\frac{B}{C}} = \sqrt{Z_{oc}Z_{sc}}$ where Z_{oc} and Z_{sc} are open and short-circuit impedances measured at any pair of terminals.

The two transfer ratios $\frac{V_1}{V_2}$ and $\frac{I_1}{-I_2}$, when the second port is terminated in Z_{i2} and V_1 is applied to port 1, will be equal for a symmetric network. So the image transfer constant e^{γ} can be considered as the ratio between input and output currents of the network when the network is terminated in its characteristic impedance. In such case, the number γ is called propagation constant and is given by $\gamma = \alpha + j\beta$ where α is the attenuation coefficient and β is the phase shift coefficient or phase constant. In such case γ is given by $\gamma = \log_e\left(\frac{I_1}{I_2}\right)$.

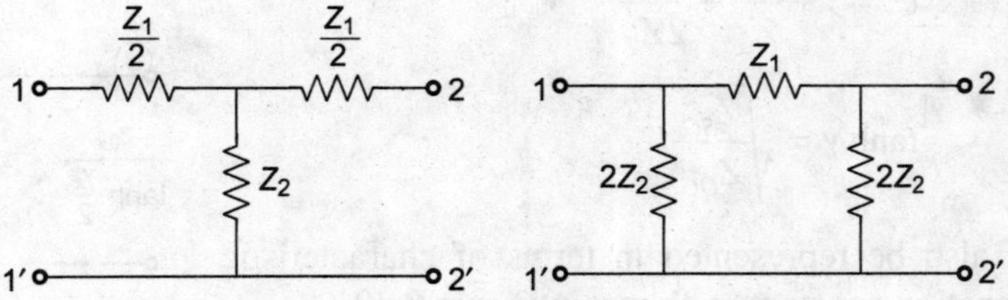

Figure 9.45

T and π type networks are two methods of network representation using two-port parameters as shown in Figure 9.45. All networks which satisfy the condition of reciprocity for Z parameters or Y parameters can be replaced by an equivalent T network or π network.

A filter is a reactive network which freely allows the desired bands of frequencies while blocking all other bands. Symmetrical T or π networks are used to design filters. For studying filters it is necessary to know the propagation constant γ, attenuation α, phase shift β and characteristic impedance Z_0 of symmetric T and π networks.

9.12.1 Symmetrical *T* Network

Consider a symmetrical T network terminated at its output terminal with its characteristic impedance as shown in Figure 9.46.

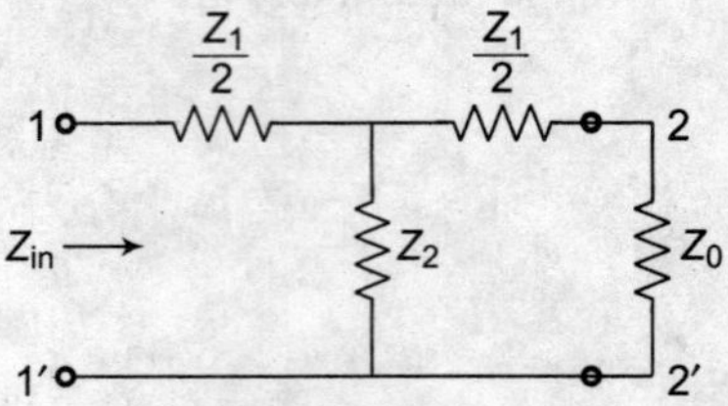

Figure 9.46

The characteristic impedance is given as $Z_0 = \sqrt{\frac{Z_1^2}{4} + Z_1Z_2}$

The propagation constant of T section is given as

$$\gamma = \ln\left[1 + \frac{Z_1}{2Z_2} + \frac{Z_0}{Z_2}\right]$$

$$e^{\gamma} = 1 + \frac{Z_1}{2Z_2} + \sqrt{\frac{Z_1^2}{4Z_2^2} + \frac{Z_1}{Z_2}} \Rightarrow \tanh\gamma = \sqrt{\frac{Z_{SC}}{Z_{OC}}}$$

The network can also be represented in terms of characteristic impedance and propagation constant as shown in Figure 9.47

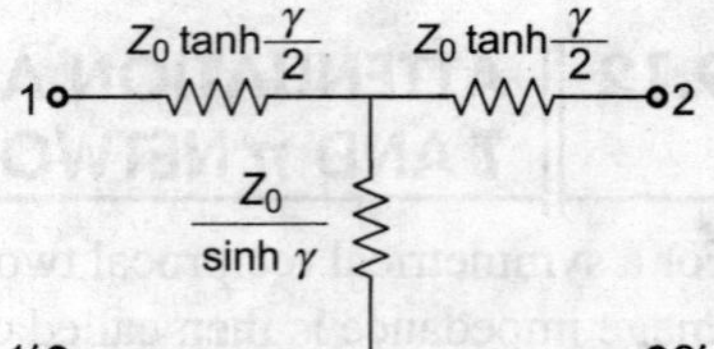

Figure 9.47

9.12.2 Symmetrical *π* Network

Consider a symmetrical π network terminated at its output terminal with its characteristic impedance as shown in Figure 9.48.

The characteristic impedance is given by

$$Z_0 = \frac{Z_1Z_2}{\sqrt{\frac{Z_1^2}{4} + Z_1Z_2}}$$

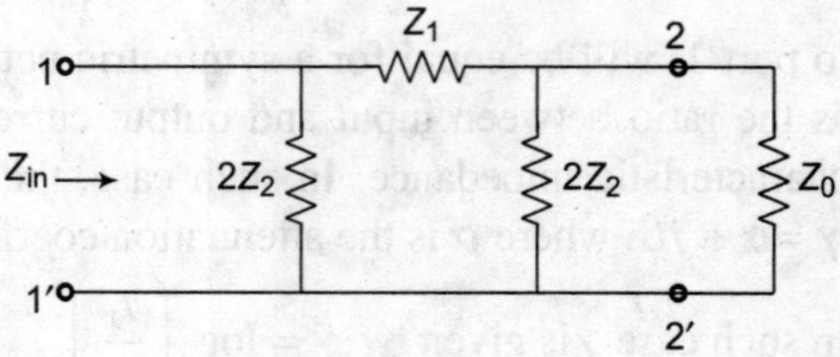

Figure 9.48

The propagation constant of π section is given by

$$e^{\gamma} = 1 + \frac{Z_1}{Z_0} + \frac{Z_1}{2Z_2}$$

$$\tanh\gamma = \sqrt{\frac{Z_{SC}}{Z_{OC}}}$$

The network can also be represented in terms of characteristic impedance and propagation constant as shown in Figure 9.49

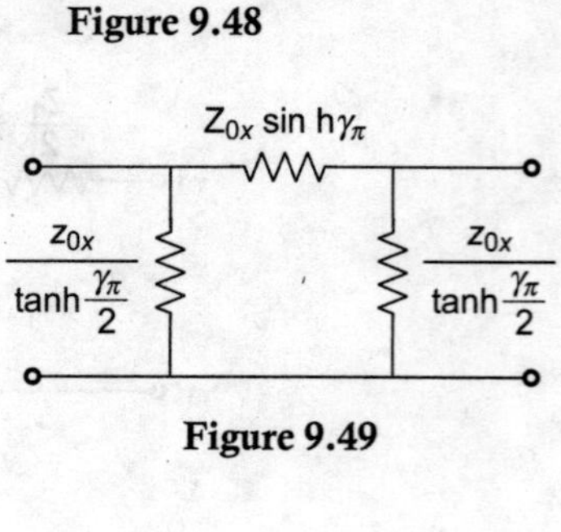

Figure 9.49

Example 9.23

Find the characteristic impedance and propagation constant of a T section as shown in Figure 9.50. Verify the value of impedance with the help of open and short circuit impedances. ○○●

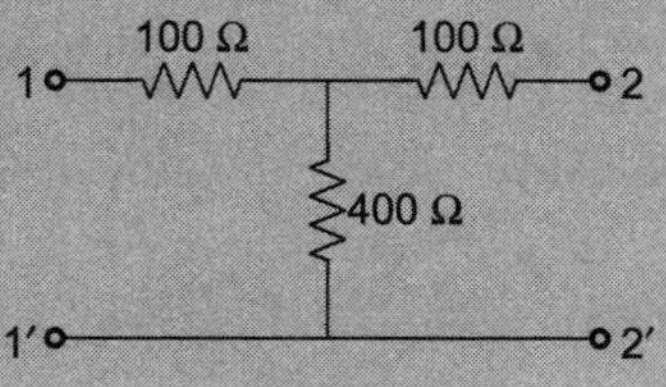

Figure 9.50

Solution From the network

$$\frac{Z_1}{2} = 100\ \Omega \Rightarrow Z_1 = 200\ \Omega\ Z_2 = 400\ \Omega$$

The characteristic impedance is given by

$$Z_0 = \sqrt{\frac{Z_1^2}{4} + Z_1 Z_2} = \sqrt{\frac{200^2}{4} + 200 \times 400} = 300\ \Omega$$

The propagation constant of T section is given by

$$\gamma = \ln\left[1 + \frac{Z_1}{2Z_2} + \frac{Z_0}{Z_2}\right] = \ln\left[1 + \frac{200}{2 \times 400} + \frac{300}{400}\right] = -0.2876$$

Verification: Open circuit impedance $Z_{oc} = (100 + 400) = 500\ \Omega$

Short circuit impedance $Z_{sc} = \left(100 + \left[\frac{100 \times 400}{100 + 400}\right]\right) = 180\ \Omega$

By property of symmetrical network $Z_0 = \sqrt{Z_{oc} Z_{sc}} = \sqrt{500 \times 180} = 300\ \Omega$

Example 9.24

Design a symmetrical T section to have $Z_0 = 600\ \Omega$ and $\gamma = 0 + j\frac{\pi}{4}$. ○○●

Solution The series arm impedance of symmetrical T network is given as

$$\frac{Z_1}{2} = Z_0 \tanh\left(\frac{\gamma}{2}\right) = 600 \tanh\left(\frac{0 + j\frac{\pi}{4}}{2}\right) = j248.528\Omega$$

The shunt arm impedance of symmetrical T network is given as

$$Z_2 = \frac{Z_0}{\sinh\gamma} = \frac{600}{\sinh j\frac{\pi}{4}} = -j848.528\Omega$$

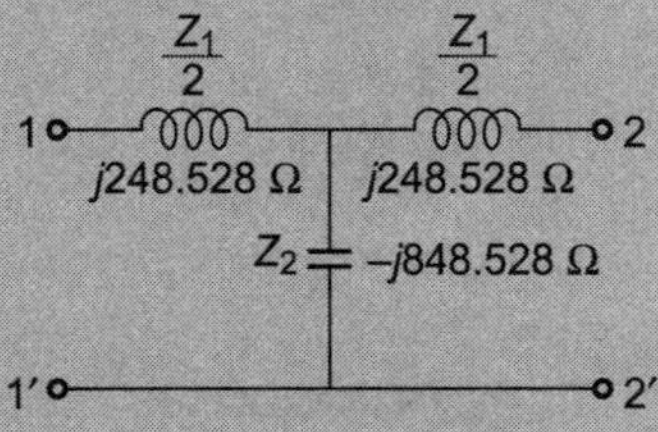

Hence the symmetrical T network is shown in Figure 9.51.

Figure 9.51

Example 9.25

For a symmetrical π network, $Z_1 = j\omega L Z_2 = \dfrac{1}{j\omega C}$. Calculate its characteristic impedance at 500 Hz and 1000 Hz if $L = 0.1$ H and $C = 2$ μF.

Solution The symmetrical π network is as shown in Figure 9.52.

The characteristic impedance is given by

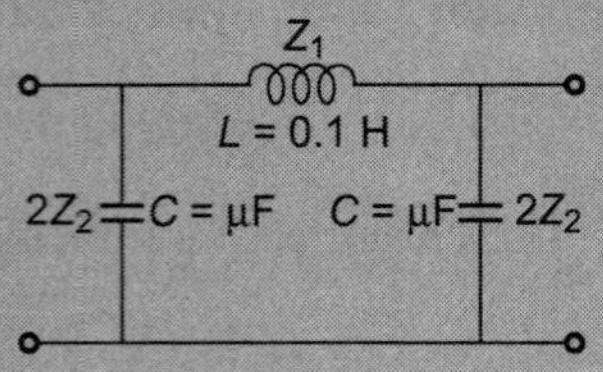

Figure 9.52

$$Z_0 = \frac{Z_1 Z_2}{\sqrt{\dfrac{Z_1^2}{4} + Z_1 Z_2}} = \frac{j\omega L\left(\dfrac{1}{j\omega C}\right)}{\sqrt{\dfrac{(j\omega L)^2}{4} + j\omega L\left(\dfrac{1}{j\omega C}\right)}}$$

$$Z_0 = \frac{\dfrac{L}{C}}{\sqrt{\dfrac{L}{C} - \dfrac{\omega^2 L^2}{4}}}$$

(i) At $f = 500$ Hz, $\omega = 2\pi f = 1000\pi$, $L = 0.1$ H and $C = 2$ μF

$$Z_0 = 314.18\ \Omega$$

(ii) At $f = 1000$ Hz, $\omega = 2\pi f = 2000\pi$, $L = 0.1$ H and $C = 2$ μF

$$Z_0 = -j226.58\,\Omega$$

is called propagation constant and is given by where is the attenuation coefficient and is the phase shift coefficient or phase constant.

POINTS TO REMEMBER

- Z_{11} and Z_{21} are obtained when the output terminals are open circuited and a voltage source is connected to the input terminal.
- Z_{12} and Z_{22} are obtained when the input terminals are open circuited and a voltage source is connected to the output terminal.
- The Z parameters are given by $Z_{11} = \left.\dfrac{V_1}{I_1}\right|_{I_2=0}$ $Z_{12} = \left.\dfrac{V_1}{I_2}\right|_{I_1=0}$ $Z_{21} = \left.\dfrac{V_2}{I_1}\right|_{I_2=0}$ $Z_{22} = \left.\dfrac{V_2}{I_2}\right|_{I_1=0}$
- Y_{11} and Y_{21} are obtained when the output terminals are short circuited and a current source is connected to the input terminal.
- Y_{12} and $Y_{22}$are obtained when the input terminals are short circuited and a current source is connected to the output terminal.

- The Y parameters are given by $Y_{11} = \left.\frac{I_1}{V_1}\right|_{V_2=0}$ $Y_{12} = \left.\frac{I_1}{V_2}\right|_{V_1=0}$ $Y_{21} = \left.\frac{I_2}{V_1}\right|_{V_2=0}$ $Y_{22} = \left.\frac{I_2}{V_2}\right|_{V_1=0}$
- To calculate A and C parameters open the output port and connect a voltage source at the input port.
- To find the parameters B and D, short the output port and connect a voltage source at the input port.
- The ABCD parameters are given by $A = \left.\frac{V_1}{V_2}\right|_{I_2=0}$ $B = \left.\frac{V_1}{-I_2}\right|_{V_2=0}$ $C = \left.\frac{I_1}{V_2}\right|_{I_2=0}$ $D = \left.\frac{I_1}{-I_2}\right|_{V_2=0}$
- To find the parameters A' and C', open the input port and connect a voltage source at the output port.
- To find the parameters B' and D', short the input port and connect a voltage source at the output port.
- The $A'B'C'D'$ parameters are given by $A' = \left.\frac{V_2}{V_1}\right|_{I_1=0}$ $B' = \left.\frac{-V_2}{I_1}\right|_{V_1=0}$ $C' = \left.\frac{I_2}{V_1}\right|_{I_1=0}$ $D' = \left.\frac{-I_2}{I_1}\right|_{V_1=0}$
- To find h_{11} and h_{21}, short-circuit the output port and connect a current source to the input port.
- To obtain h_{12} and h_{22}, open-circuit the input port and connect a voltage source to the output port.
- The h parameters are given by $h_{11} = \left.\frac{V_1}{I_1}\right|_{V_2=0}$ $h_{12} = \left.\frac{V_1}{V_2}\right|_{I_1=0}$ $h_{21} = \left.\frac{I_2}{I_1}\right|_{V_2=0}$ $h_{22} = \left.\frac{I_2}{V_2}\right|_{I_1=0}$
- To find g_{11} and g_{21}, open-circuit the output port and connect a voltage source to the input port.
- To obtain g_{12} and g_{22}, short-circuit the input port and connect a current source to the output port.
- The g parameters are given by $g_{11} = \left.\frac{I_1}{V_1}\right|_{I_2=0}$ $g_{12} = \left.\frac{I_1}{I_2}\right|_{V_1=0}$ $g_{21} = \left.\frac{V_2}{V_1}\right|_{I_2=0}$ $g_{22} = \left.\frac{V_2}{I_2}\right|_{V_1=0}$
- We can express any parameter in terms of other parameters in a two-port network.
- In order to obtain inter-relationships between the parameter steps to be followed as
  - o Write corresponding parameter equations for both
  - o By algebraic manipulation, rewrite that equation in terms in which we want to express the given parameters.
  - o Compare given parameter equations with manipulated equations, we get relationship between the parameters as desired.
- When two two-port networks are connected in cascade, we can multiply their individual transmission parameters to get overall transmission parameters of the cascade connection.
- In series connection of two port networks, the open circuit impedance matrix of the equivalent two port network is the sum of the open circuit impedance matrices of the individual networks.
- In parallel connection of two port networks, the short circuit admittance matrix of the equivalent two port network is the sum of the short circuit admittance matrices of the individual networks.
- The h parameters of the networks whose input ports are connected in series and output in parallel are the algebraic sum of the respective h parameters of the individual networks.
- In two port networks if the input ports are connected in parallel and output ports in series, the overall g parameters of the interconnected network is the sum of the corresponding g parameters of the individual networks.
- If the two port network is terminated into a load impedance at either output port or input port, then it is possible to express input impedance or output impedance in terms of the parameters of two port network.
- Analysis of transmission lines under transient conditions or with aperiodic inputs is done using an alternative way called the image parameter description.

☞ Two impedances called image impedances designated by Z_{i1} and Z_{i2} and a constant image transfer constant designated by γ are used to describe a reciprocal linear time-invariant two port network in image parameter description.

☞ The image impedances are given in terms of *ABCD* parameters as follows

$$Z_{i1} = \sqrt{Z_{1o}Z_{1s}} = \sqrt{\frac{AB}{CD}}$$

$$Z_{i2} = \sqrt{Z_{2o}Z_{2s}} = \sqrt{\frac{BD}{AC}}$$

☞ The image transfer constant γ is given as

$$\gamma = \tanh^{-1}\sqrt{\frac{Z_{2s}}{Z_{2o}}} = \tanh^{-1}\sqrt{\frac{Z_{1s}}{Z_{1o}}} = \tanh^{-1}\sqrt{\frac{BC}{AD}}$$

☞ If Z_{0T} is the characteristic impedance of a *T* section and $Z_{0\pi}$ is the characteristic impedance of a π section having the same series and shunt arm impedances, then $Z_{0\pi} = \frac{Z_1Z_2}{Z_{0T}}$.

☞ The propagation constant of symmetrical *T* and π networks are same.

☞ Attenuation constant is measured in nepers and phase constant is measured in radians.

☞ γ is called propagation constant and is given by $\gamma = \alpha + j\beta$ where α is the attenuation coefficient and β is the phase shift coefficient or phase constant.

☞ For a symmetrical network, characteristic impedance Z_0 is given as $Z_0 = \sqrt{\frac{B}{C}} = \sqrt{Z_{oc}Z_{sc}}$ where Z_{oc} and Z_{sc} are open and short-circuit impedances measured at any pair of terminals.

PRACTICE PROBLEMS

1. If $z = \begin{bmatrix} 40 & 10 \\ 20 & 30 \end{bmatrix}$ Ω for the two-port network, calculate the average power delivered to 50 Ω resistor.

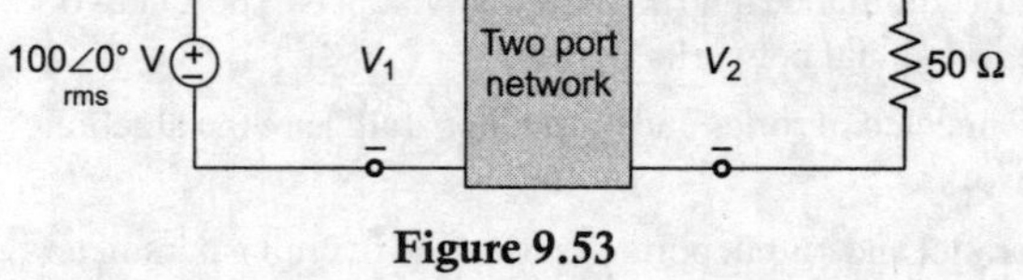

Figure 9.53

2. Find the *Y* parameters for the two-port network shown in Figure 9.54. ●●●

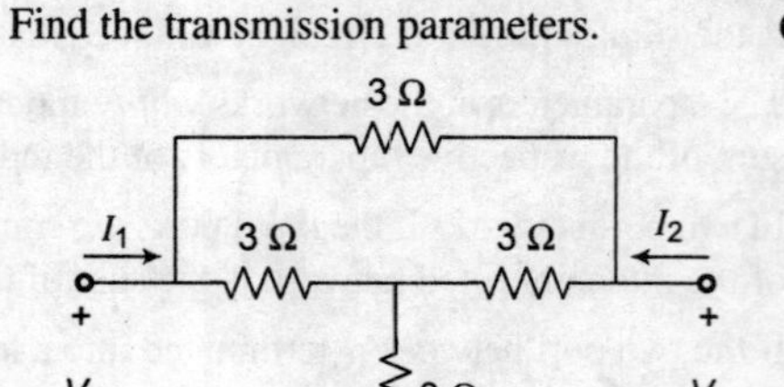

Figure 9.54

3. Find the transmission parameters. ●●●

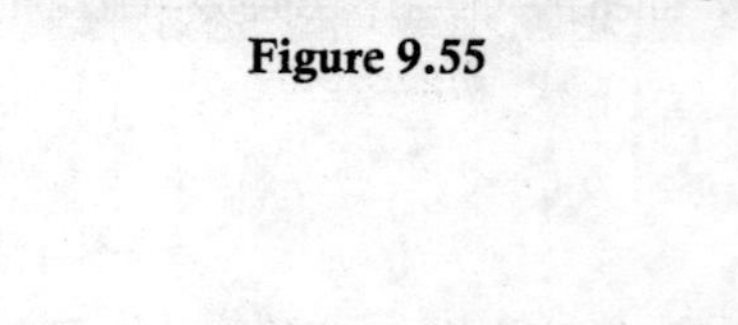

Figure 9.55

4. The following direct-current measurements were done on a two port network:

Port 1 open	Port 1 Short-circuited
$V_1 = 1$ mV	$I_1 = -0.5\ \mu$A
$V_2 = 10$ V	$I_2 = 80\ \mu A$
$I_2 = 200\ \mu$A	$V_2 = 5$ V

Calculate the inverse transmission parameters for the two port network.

5. Determine the h parameters of the circuit.

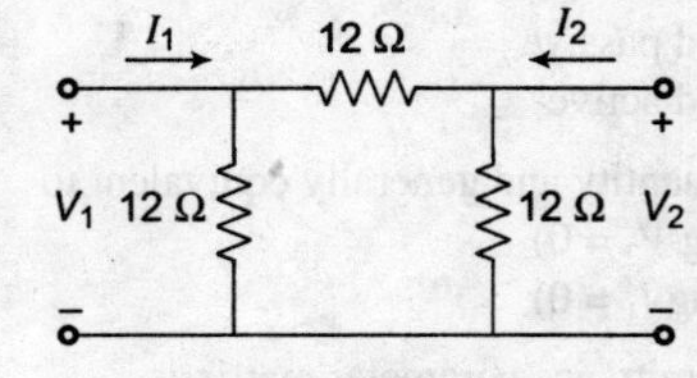

Figure 9.56

6. Determine the g parameters of the circuit.

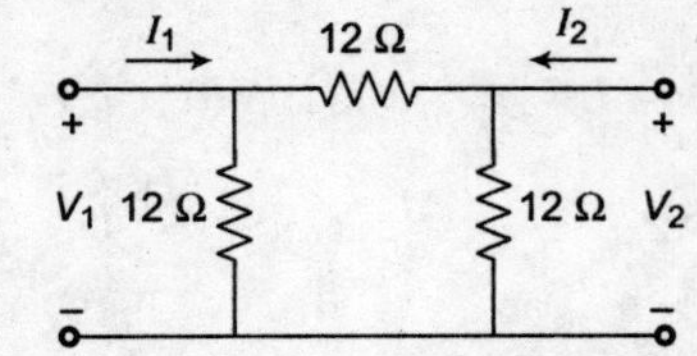

Figure 9.57

7. Determine the Z, Y and Transmission parameters of the network shown in Figure 9.62.

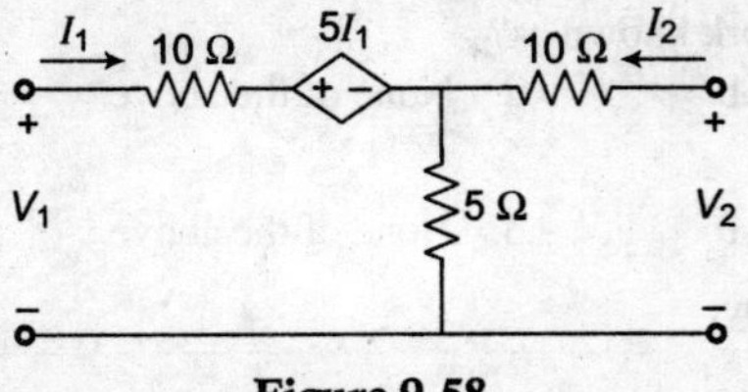

Figure 9.58

8. Two identical sections of the network shown in Figure 9.59 are connected in parallel. Obtain the Y parameters of the combination.

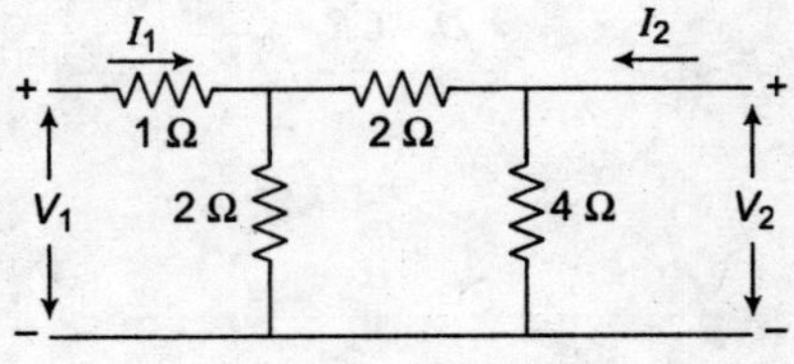

Figure 9.59

9. The Z parameters of two port network are
$Z_{11} = Z_{22} = 10\ \Omega$
$Z_{21} = Z_{12} = 4\ \Omega$
If the source voltage is 20 V, determine I_1, V_2, I_2 and input impedance.

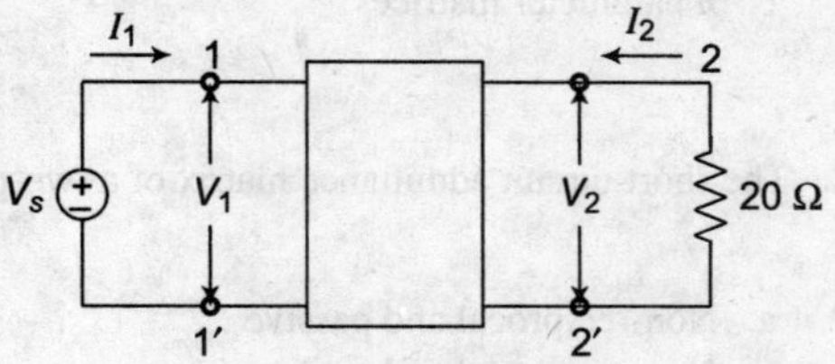

Figure 9.60

10. The h parameters of a two-port network shown are $h_{11} = 1\ \Omega$, $h_{12} = -h_{21} = 2$ and $h_{22} = 1$ S. The power absorbed by a load resistance of 1 Ω connected across port 2 is 100 W. The network is excited by a voltage source of generated voltage V_s and internal resistance 2 Ω. Calculate the value of V_s

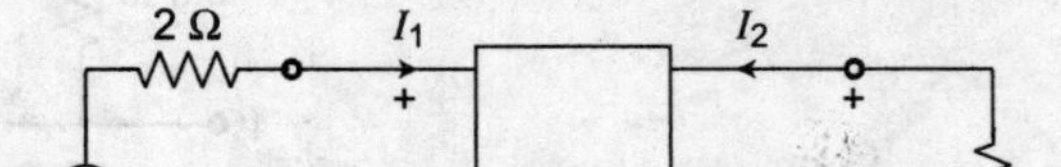

Figure 9.61

11. For the given two-port network in Figure 9.62, calculate the Z parameters and the image parameters.

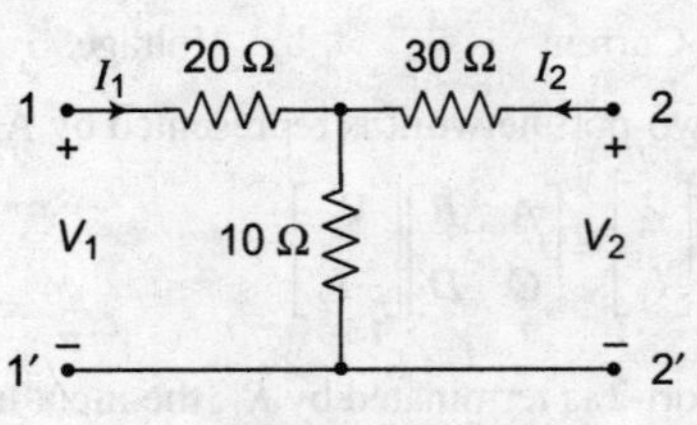

Figure 9.62

12. If the measurements made on a box enclosing a two-port network are $Z_{1OC} = 40\angle 0°\ \Omega$ and $Z_{1SC} = 20.3\angle 29.8°\ \Omega$. Find values of characteristic impedance and propagation constant along with attenuation constant and phase constant if the network is symmetrical.

MULTIPLE CHOICE QUESTIONS

1. Two two-port networks are connected in cascade. The combination is to be represented as a single two-port network, by multiplying the individual ○○●

a. Z parameter matrices b. Y parameter matrices
c. h parameter matrices d. ABCD parameter matrices

2. The short-circuit admittance matrix of a two-port network is $\begin{bmatrix} 0 & -\frac{1}{2} \\ \frac{1}{2} & 0 \end{bmatrix}$. The two port network is ○●●

a. Non-reciprocal and passive b. Reciprocal and passive
c. Non-reciprocal and active d. Reciprocal and active

3. An open circuit reverse voltage gain in h-parameters is a unitless quantity and generally equivalent to ○○●

a. V_1 / I_1 (keeping $V_2 = 0$) b. I_2 / I_1 (keeping $V_2 = 0$)
c. V_1 / V_2 (keeping $I_1 = 0$) d. I_2 / V_2 (keeping $I_1 = 0$)

4. For the two-port network shown in Figure 9.63, the short-circuit admittance parameter matrix is ○●●

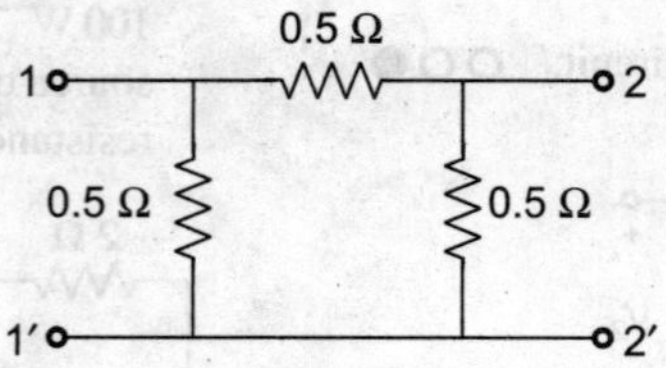

Figure 9.63

(a) $\begin{bmatrix} 4 & -2 \\ -2 & 4 \end{bmatrix}$ (b) $\begin{bmatrix} 1 & -0.5 \\ -0.5 & 1 \end{bmatrix}$ (c) $\begin{bmatrix} 1 & 0.5 \\ 0.5 & 1 \end{bmatrix}$ (d) $\begin{bmatrix} 4 & 2 \\ 2 & 4 \end{bmatrix}$

5. What does the connectivity of energy source at the port of network known as? ○○●

a. Driving Point b. Transfer Point c. Both a and b d. None of the above

6. Which elements act as independent variables in Y-parameters? ○○●

a. Current b. Voltage c. Both *a* and *b* d. None of the above

7. A two-port network is represented by ABCD parameters given by ○●●

$$\begin{bmatrix} V_1 \\ I_1 \end{bmatrix} = \begin{bmatrix} A & B \\ C & D \end{bmatrix} \begin{bmatrix} V_2 \\ -I_2 \end{bmatrix}$$

If port-2 is terminated by R_L, the input impedance seen at port-1 is given by

a. $\dfrac{A + BR_L}{C + DR_L}$ b. $\dfrac{AR_L + C}{BR_L + D}$ c. $\dfrac{DR_L + A}{BR_L + C}$ d. $\dfrac{B + AR_L}{D + CR_L}$

8. The *h* parameters of the circuit shown in the Figure 9.64 are bind ○●●

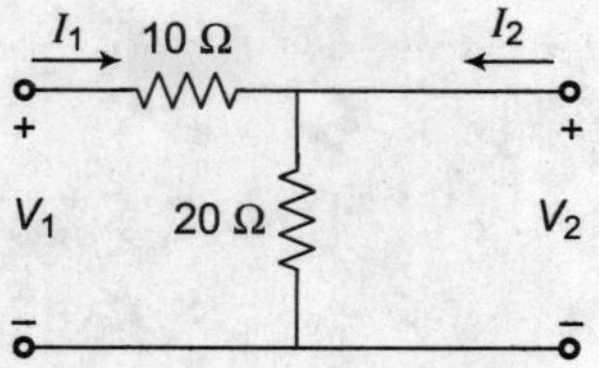

Figure 9.64

a. $\begin{bmatrix} 0.1 & 0.1 \\ -0.1 & 0.3 \end{bmatrix}$ b. $\begin{bmatrix} 10 & -1 \\ 1 & 0.05 \end{bmatrix}$ c. $\begin{bmatrix} 30 & 20 \\ 20 & 20 \end{bmatrix}$ d. $\begin{bmatrix} 10 & 1 \\ -1 & 0.05 \end{bmatrix}$

9. For a two port bilateral network, the three transmission parameters are given by $A = 6/5$; $B = 17/5$ and $C = 1/5$, what is the value of D? ○○●

a. 7/5 b. 12/5 c. 3/5 d. 9/5

10. Which parameters are widely used in transmission line theory? ○○●

a. Z parameters b. Y parameters c. h parameters d. ABCD parameters

ANSWERS TO MULTIPLE CHOICE QUESTIONS

1. (d)	2. (c)	3. (c)	4. (a)	5. (a)
6. (b)	7. (d)	8. (d)	9. (a)	10. (d)

Fourier Method of Waveform Analysis

10

CHAPTER OUTLINE

- Fourier method of waveform analysis
- Frequency spectrum of periodic signal
- Fourier series as trigonometric series
- Complex Fourier series and properties
- Fourier transform and inverse Fourier transform
- Fourier transform of periodic signals
- Fourier transform of some functions
- Properties of Fourier transform

10.1 INTRODUCTION

This chapter introduces Fourier series and Fourier transforms which are the basic frequency techniques for finding responses for periodic and non-periodic voltages and currents in networks. Fourier series describe periodic signals while Fourier transforms describe non-periodic signals. The introductory sections discuss the sinusoidal and exponential expansion of periodic waveforms in circuit analysis and the second part explain the expansion of aperiodic waveforms in terms of sinusoids.

10.2 FOURIER METHOD OF WAVEFORM ANALYSIS

A real-valued time function $x(t)$ is said to be periodic if there exists a positive time constant T such that $x(t + T) = x(t)$ for all time t. The Fourier theorem states that any arbitrary periodic function can be represented by an infinite series of sinusoids of harmonically related frequencies. This infinite series comprising of the sum of sinusoids at the fundamental and harmonic frequencies and representing a periodic function is called the Fourier series and the process of representing a periodic function by a Fourier series is called Fourier analysis. Fourier series can be represented either in the form of infinite trigonometric series or infinite exponential series. Fourier analysis is applied mainly to complex periodic signals and not those of sinusoidal shape. Fourier analysis consists of two operations – (a) determination of the coefficients and (b) decision on the number of terms to be included in a truncated series to represent a given function within permissible limits of error.

Probe

1. What do you understand by Fourier analysis?

10.3 FREQUENCY SPECTRUM OF PERIODIC SIGNAL

Probe

1. A periodic signal can be expanded into a number of discrete frequency components. Discuss.

A pure sine wave is completely specified by its frequency (or basic period), its amplitude, and its phase at time $t = 0$. But in case of more complex periodic signals, the frequency alone does not completely specify the signal; one has to specify the content of each cycle as well. Complex periodic signals have, in addition to their main frequency, many other component frequencies. Specification of the contributions of all these components determines the signal. This specification is called the signal's spectrum. Any periodic signal can be represented as the sum of a finite or infinite number of sinusoidal functions whose frequencies are harmonics or integer multiples of fundamental frequency. These sinusoidal functions, as a group, are called frequency spectrum of that periodic signal. Fourier series is a way to find spectrums for periodic signals by representing the signals in frequency domain. Line spectrum is the representation of the signal $f(t)$ in frequency domain. It indicates the amplitude and phase of various frequency components present in the given signal.

10.4 FOURIER SERIES AS TRIGONOMETRIC SERIES

University Questions

1. Explain Dirichlet conditions of Fourier analysis.
2. Discuss the effect of symmetry for a periodic function to determine the trigonometric Fourier series coefficients. **[RGTU, 2013]**
3. What is waveform symmetry? **[RGTU, 2014]**

The mathematical conditions under which a convergent Fourier series can be written for a periodic function are known as Dirichlet conditions and are given as

1. The function $f(t)$ is a single-valued function within the period T.
2. The function $f(t)$ must be continuous in the period T. If it is discontinuous, the function $f(t)$ must have finite number of discontinuities in the period T.
3. The function $f(t)$ has a finite number of maxima and minima within the period T.
4. The function $f(t)$ is absolutely integrable, that is, $\int_{t_0}^{t_0+T} |f(t)|\, dt < \infty$ for any t_0.

If a periodic non-sinusoidal function $f(t)$ of period T satisfies the above Dirichlet conditions, then the function can be expanded into an infinite trigonometric Fourier series as

$$f(t) = a_0 + a_1 \cos \omega_0 t + a_2 \cos 2\omega_0 t + \cdots + a_n \cos n\omega_0 t + \cdots + b_1 \sin \omega_0 t + b_2 \sin 2\omega_0 t + \cdots + b_n \sin n\omega_0 t + \cdots$$

$$f(t) = a_0 + \sum_{n=1}^{\infty} (a_n \cos n\omega_0 t + b_n \sin n\omega_0 t)$$

where ω_0 – the fundamental frequency $= \dfrac{2\pi}{T}$

$n\omega_0$ – the nth harmonic of fundamental frequency

a_0, a_n, b_n – the Fourier coefficients

The Fourier coefficients a_0, a_n and b_n can be evaluated using following expressions:

$$a_0 = \frac{1}{T}\int_{t_0}^{T+t_0} f(t)dt$$

$$a_n = \frac{2}{T}\int_{t_0}^{T+t_0} f(t)\cos n\omega_0 t dt \quad n > 0$$

$$b_n = \frac{2}{T}\int_{t_0}^{T+t_0} f(t)\sin n\omega_0 t\, dt \quad n > 0$$

10.4.1 Use of Symmetry in Evaluating Fourier Series

Waveforms may not have cosine terms or sine terms because of certain types of symmetry associated with them, which results in some Fourier coefficient being absent from the series. If such symmetries are recognized, it simplifies the task of calculating Fourier coefficients in the Fourier series analysis. The four types of waveform symmetry, which can be identified are:

- Even-function symmetry
- Odd-function symmetry
- Half-wave symmetry
- Quarter wave symmetry

1. Even Function Symmetry

For any function $f(t)$ if $f(t) = f(-t)$ it is called even function. The Fourier series of an even function consists of a constant term and cosine terms only.

2. Odd Function Symmetry

For any function $f(t)$ if $f(-t) = -f(t)$ it is called odd function. The Fourier series of an even function consists of sine terms only.

3. Half-wave Symmetry

A periodic function $f(t)$ is said to have half-wave symmetry if $f(t) = -f\left(t - \frac{T}{2}\right)$

If the waveform has half-wave symmetry, the second half of each period looks like the first half turned upside down. In a half-wave symmetric function, both a_n and b_n are zero for even values of n.

4. Quarter-wave Symmetry

A waveform is said to have quarter wave symmetry if it has both half wave symmetry and symmetry about the midpoint of the positive and negative half cycles.

The effect of symmetry for a periodic function to determine the trigonometric Fourier series coefficients is summarized as follows.

Symmetry	Fourier Coefficients
1. Odd function $f(t) = -f(-t)$	$a_n = 0$ for all n $b_n = \frac{4}{T}\int_0^{T/2} f(t)\sin n\omega_0 t\, dt$
2. Even function $f(t) = f(-t)$	$b_n = 0$ for all n $a_n = \frac{4}{T}\int_0^{T/2} f(t)\cos n\omega_0 t\, dt$
3. Half-wave symmetry $f(t) = f\left(t - \frac{T}{2}\right)$	$a_0 = 0$ $a_n = 0$ for even n $b_n = 0$ for even n $a_n = \frac{4}{T}\int_0^{T/2} f(t)\cos n\omega_0 t\, dt$ for odd n $b_n = \frac{4}{T}\int_0^{T/2} f(t)\sin n\omega_0 t\, dt$ for odd n
4. Quarter-wave symmetry Half-wave symmetric and symmetric about the midpoints of the positive and negative half-cycles	A. Odd function: $a_0 = 0, a_n = 0$ for all n $b_n = 0$ for even n $b_n = \frac{8}{T}\int_0^{T/4} f(t)\sin n\omega_0 t\, dt$ for odd n B. Even function: $a_0 = 0, b_n = 0$ for all n $a_n = 0$ for even n $a_n = \frac{8}{T}\int_0^{T/4} f(t)\cos n\omega_0 t\, dt$ for odd n

Example 10.1

Find the Fourier series expansion of following periodic function.

$$f(x) = \frac{1}{2}(\pi - x) \text{ in } -\pi < x < \pi$$ ○●●

Solution The coefficients of associated Fourier series can be determined as following:

$$a_0 = \frac{1}{\pi}\int_{-\pi}^{\pi} f(x)dx = \frac{1}{\pi}\int_{-\pi}^{\pi} \frac{1}{2}(\pi - x)dx = \frac{1}{2\pi}\left[\pi x - \frac{x^2}{2}\right]_{-\pi}^{\pi} = \pi$$

Note: Difficulty Level ⟶ ○○● — Easy; ○●● — Medium; ●●● — Difficult

$$a_n = \frac{1}{\pi}\int_{-\pi}^{\pi} f(x)\cos nx dx = \frac{1}{\pi}\int_{-\pi}^{\pi} \frac{1}{2}(\pi - x)\cos nx dx$$

$$a_n = \frac{1}{2\pi}\left[(\pi - x)\frac{\sin nx}{n} - (-1)\left(\frac{-\cos nx}{n^2}\right)\right]_{-\pi}^{\pi} = \frac{1}{2\pi}[0] = 0$$

$$b_n = \frac{1}{\pi}\int_{-\pi}^{\pi} \frac{1}{2}(\pi - x)\sin nx dx = \frac{1}{2\pi}\left[(\pi - x)\frac{-\cos nx}{n} - (-1)\left(\frac{-\sin nx}{n^2}\right)\right]_{-\pi}^{\pi} = \frac{(-1)^n}{n}$$

Using the values of a_0, a_n and b_n in the Fourier expansion

$$f(x) = \frac{a_0}{2} + \sum_{n=1}^{\infty} a_n \cos nx + \sum_{n=1}^{\infty} b_n \sin nx$$

we get,

$$f(x) = \frac{\pi}{2} + \sum_{n=1}^{\infty} \frac{(-1)^n}{n} \sin nx$$

This is the required Fourier expansion of the given function.

Example 10.2

Find the Fourier series of the following periodic function whose definitions on one period is

$$f(t) = \begin{cases} 0 & -\pi < t < 0 \\ t & 0 < t < \pi \end{cases}$$

Solution The coefficient of associated Fourier series can be determined as following.

The constant term of the Fourier series is given by

$$a_0 = \frac{1}{\pi}\int_{-x}^{x} t\,dt = \frac{1}{\pi}\int_{0}^{x} t\,dt = \frac{\pi}{2}$$

$$a_n = \frac{1}{\pi}\int_{-x}^{x} f(t)\cos nt\,dt = \frac{1}{\pi}\int_{0}^{x} t\cos nt\,dt$$

$$= \frac{1}{\pi}\left[\frac{t}{n}\sin nt + \frac{t}{n^2}\cos nt\right]_0^x = \frac{1}{\pi n^2}(\cos n\pi - 1)$$

$$= \frac{1}{\pi n^2}((-1)^n - 1) = \begin{cases} 0 & \text{if } n \text{ is even} \\ -\dfrac{2}{\pi n^2} & \text{if } n \text{ is odd} \end{cases}$$

$$b_n = \frac{1}{\pi}\int_{-\pi}^{\pi} f(t)\sin nt\,dt = \frac{1}{\pi}\int_0^{x} t\sin nt\,dt = \frac{1}{\pi}\left[-\frac{t}{n}\cos nt = \frac{t}{n^2}\sin nt\right]_0^{x} = \frac{1}{n}(-\cos n\pi) = \frac{(-1)^{n+1}}{n}$$

Thus the function can be represented as

$$f(t) = \frac{\pi}{4} - \frac{2}{\pi}\left(\frac{\cos t}{1^2} + \frac{\cos 3t}{3^2} + \frac{\cos 5t}{5^2} + \cdots\right) + \left(\frac{\sin t}{1} - \frac{\sin 2t}{2} + \frac{\sin 3t}{3} + \cdots\right)$$

Example 10.3

Find the Fourier series of the waveform shown in Figure 10.1.

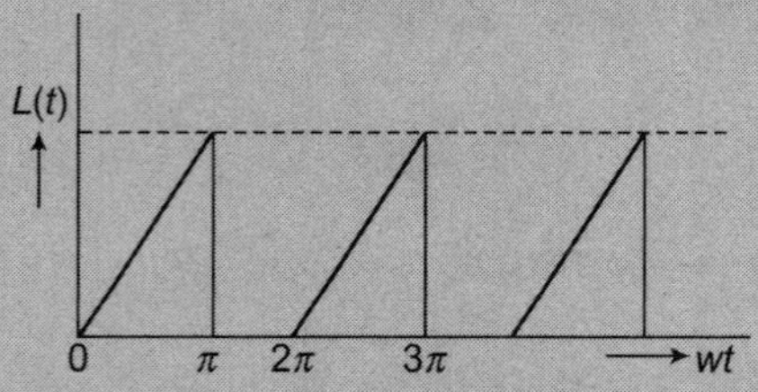

Figure 10.1

[RTU, 2011] ○●●

Solution

$$f(t) = \left(\frac{A}{\pi}\right)\omega_0 t \quad \text{for } 0 \le \omega_0 t \le \pi$$

$$= 0 \quad \text{for } \pi \le \omega_0 t \le 2\pi$$

$$a_0 = \frac{1}{2\pi}\int_0^{2\pi} f(t)\,dt = \frac{1}{2\pi}\left[\int_0^{\pi}\frac{A}{\pi}\omega_0 t\,d(\omega_0 t) + \int_{\pi}^{2\pi} 0.d(\omega_0 t)\right]$$

$$= \frac{1}{2\pi}\int_0^{\pi}\frac{A}{\pi}\omega_0 t\,d(\omega_0 t) = \frac{A}{2\pi^2}\cdot\left|\frac{(\omega_0 t)^2}{2}\right|_0^{\pi} = \frac{A}{4} \qquad (10.1)$$

$$a_n = \frac{2}{2\pi}\int_0^{2\pi} f(t)\cos n\omega_0 t\,d(\omega_0 t) = \frac{2}{2\pi}\left[\int_0^{\pi}\frac{A}{\pi}\omega_0 t\cos(n\omega_0 t)d(\omega_0 t) + \frac{2\pi}{\pi}0.\cos(n\omega_0 td(\omega_0 t)\right]$$

$$= \frac{1}{\pi}\int_0^{\pi}\frac{A}{\pi}(\omega_0 t)\cos(n\omega_0 t)d(\omega_0) = \frac{A}{\pi^2}\left|\frac{1}{n^2}\cos(n\omega_0 t) + \frac{\omega_0 t}{n}\sin(n\omega_0 t)\right|_0^{\pi} = \frac{A}{\pi^2 n^2}(\cos n\pi - 1) \qquad (10.2)$$

If n is even, $\cos(n\pi - 1) = 0$; therefore, a_2, a_4, a_6, ... terms are zero.

If n is odd, $a_n = -\frac{2A}{\pi^2 n^2} (\therefore \cos n\pi = -1)$

$$\therefore \quad a_1 = -\frac{2A}{\pi^2}; \; a_3 = -\frac{2A}{9\pi^2}; \; a_5 = -\frac{2A}{25\pi^2} \tag{10.3}$$

$$b_n = \frac{2}{2\pi}\int_0^{2\pi} f(t)\sin(n\omega_0 t)d(\omega_0 t)$$

$$= \frac{1}{\pi}\left[\int_0^{\pi} \frac{A}{\pi}(\omega_0 t)\sin(n\omega_0 t)d(\omega_0 t) + \int_{\pi}^{2\pi} 0.\sin(n\omega_0 t).d(\omega_0 t)\right]$$

$$= \frac{1}{\pi}\int_0^{\pi} \frac{A}{\pi}(\omega_0 t)\sin(n\omega_0 t)d(\omega_0 t)$$

$$= \frac{A}{\pi^2}\left[\frac{1}{\pi^2}\sin(n\omega_0 t) - \frac{\omega_0 t}{n}\cos n\omega_0 t\right]_0^{\pi} = \frac{-A}{n\pi}(\cos n\pi)$$

If n is odd, $\cos n\pi$ is –1, hence $b_n = \frac{A}{n\pi}$ (10.4)

If n is even, $\cos n\pi$ is –1, hence $b_n = \frac{-A}{n\pi}$ (10.5)

From Eqs (10.1) to (10.2), the desired Fourier series becomes

$$f(t) = \frac{A}{4} - \frac{2A}{\pi^2}\cos\omega_0 t - \frac{2A}{9\pi^2}\cos\omega_0 t - \frac{2A}{25\pi^2}\cos\omega_0 t \cdots + \frac{V}{\pi}\sin\omega_0 t$$
$$- \frac{V}{2\pi}\sin 2\omega_0 t + \frac{V}{3\pi}\sin 3\omega_0 t \cdots$$

10.5 COMPLEX FOURIER SERIES AND PROPERTIES

Probe

1. Write the Fourier Series in exponential form.

The exponential form or the complex form of the Fourier series is the form in which the sine and cosine terms of the trigonometric form are expressed as exponential functions with complex multiplying constants. The advantages of this form are:

- It gives the compact representation of the Fourier series.
- It generalises the concept of the Fourier transform.
- Only one integral has to be calculated, instead of three in the trigonometric form, for calculation of Fourier coefficients.

The trigonometric form of the Fourier series is given by

$$f(t) = a_0 + \sum_{n=1}^{\infty} (a_n \cos n\omega_0 t + b_n \sin n\omega_0 t)$$

The sine and cosine terms can be expressed in exponential form as

$$\cos n\omega_0 t = \frac{1}{2}\left[e^{jn\omega_0 t} + e^{-jn\omega_0 t}\right]$$

$$\sin n\omega_0 t = \frac{1}{j2}\left[e^{jn\omega_0 t} - e^{-jn\omega_0 t}\right]$$

So substituting these in the trigonometric form and after solving, the exponential form of the Fourier series is given by

$$f(t) = \sum_{n=-\infty}^{\infty} C_n e^{jn\omega_0 t}$$

The complex coefficients C_n of the exponential Fourier series can be calculated directly from $f(t)$ using

$$C_n = \frac{1}{T}\int_{t_0}^{t_0+T} f(t) e^{-jn\omega_0 t}\, dt$$

The effect of waveform symmetry is also present in the exponential form of Fourier series. For an even function, sine terms are absent and hence the complex coefficients are real. For an odd function, the cosine terms are zero and the complex coefficients are imaginary.

If C_n is plotted as a function of angular frequency ω, a Fourier spectrum is obtained. The Fourier spectrum is a graphical display of the amplitude and phase of the complex Fourier coefficients at the fundamental and harmonic frequencies and is also called a discrete or line spectrum.

Example 10.4

Find the complex exponential Fourier series of the following periodic function.

$$f(t) = e^{-t} \ (-1 < t < 1)$$

Solution The period of this function is 2

$$C_n = \frac{1}{2}\int_{-1}^{1} e^{-1} \exp\left(-\frac{ni\pi t}{p}\right) dt = \frac{1}{2}\left[\frac{\exp(-(1+ni\pi)t)}{-(1+ni\pi)}\right]_{-1}^{1}$$

$$= \frac{\exp(-(1+ni\pi)) - \exp(1+ni\pi)}{-2(1+ni\pi)} = \frac{e\exp(ni\pi) - e^{-1}\exp(-ni\pi)}{2(1+ni\pi)}$$

As we know that: $e^{i\pi} = \cos\pi + i\sin\pi = -1$

$$e^{in\pi} = e^{-in\pi} = (-1)^{\pi}$$

Therefore, Fourier coefficient becomes

$$C_n = \frac{(-1)^n}{(1+ni\pi)}\frac{e-e^{-1}}{2} = \frac{(-1)^n(1-ni\pi)}{1+n^2\pi^2}\sinh 1$$

The Fourier series of given function is therefore

$$f(t) = \sum_{n\to\infty}^{\infty}(-1)^n\frac{(1-ni\pi)\sinh 1}{1+n^2\pi^2}\exp(ni\pi t)$$

Example 10.5

Find the Complex Fourier series of the following function.

$$f(t) = t^2 \text{ if } 0 \le t < 2$$

○●●

Solution The Fourier coefficients may be calculated using the following integral:

$$C_n = \frac{1}{2}\int_0^2 f(t)e^{-2\pi int/2}dt = \frac{1}{2}\int_0^2 t^2e^{-i\pi nt}dt$$

$$= \frac{1}{2}\left\{\left[\frac{t^2e^{-i\pi nt}}{-i\pi n}\right]_0^2 + 2\int_0^2\frac{te^{-i\pi nt}}{i\pi n}dt\right\} \quad \text{(integration by parts)}$$

$$= \frac{1}{2}\left\{\frac{-4}{i\pi n} + \frac{2}{i\pi n}\int_0^2 te^{-i\pi nt}dt\right\} = \frac{2i}{\pi n} + \frac{1}{i\pi n}\int_0^2 te^{-i\pi nt}dt$$

$$= \frac{2i}{\pi n} + \frac{1}{i\pi n}\left(\frac{=-2}{\pi in}\right) \quad \text{(integration by parts again)}$$

$$= \frac{2(1+i\pi n)}{\pi^2n^2}, \quad n \ne 0$$

C_0 can be evaluated by finding average value of function over this period.

$$C_0 = \frac{1}{2}\int_0^2 f(t)dt = \frac{1}{2}\int_0^2 t^2dt = \frac{4}{3}$$

Example 10.6

Let $f(x) = x$ for $-\pi \le x \le \pi$. Evaluate confident of associated Fourier series and complex Fourier series of $f(x)$ on $[-\pi, \pi]$.

Solution The Fourier coefficients are

$$a_0 = \frac{1}{\pi}\int_{-\pi}^{\pi} x dx = 0.$$

$$a_n = \frac{1}{\pi}\int_{-\pi}^{\pi} x \cos x(nx)\, dx = \left[\frac{1}{n^2\pi}\cos(nx) + \frac{x}{n\pi}\sin(nx)\right]_{-\pi}^{\pi} = 0$$

and $$b_n = \frac{1}{\pi}\int_{-\pi}^{\pi} x \sin(nx)\, dx = \left[\frac{1}{n^2\pi}\sin(nx) - \frac{x}{n\pi}\cos(nx)\right]_{-\pi}^{\pi} = -\frac{2}{\pi}\cos(n\pi) = \frac{2}{n}(-1)^{n+1}$$

Since $\cos(n\pi) = (-1)^n$ if n is an integer.

The Fourier series of $f(x)$ on $[-\pi, \pi]$ is

$$\sum_{n=1}^{\infty} \frac{2}{n}(-1)^{n+1}\sin(nx) = 2\sin(x) - \sin(2x) + \frac{2}{3}\sin(3x) - \frac{1}{2}\sin(4x) + \frac{2}{5}\sin(5x) - \cdots$$

Coefficient of Complex Fourier Series is

$$C_n = \frac{1}{n}(-1)^{n+1}$$

Complex Fourier Series is

$$f(x) = \sum_{n=\infty}^{\infty} C_n[\exp(inx) - \exp(-inx)]$$

10.6 FOURIER TRANSFORM AND INVERSE FOURIER TRANSFORM

Probe

1. What do you understand by Fourier transform and what are the necessary conditions for its existence?

Fourier Transform

We can modify the Fourier series expansion for periodic functions such that it could represent non-periodic transient functions. The exponential Fourier series is given by

$$f(t) = \sum_{n=-\infty}^{\infty} C_n e^{nj\omega_0 t} \quad \text{where } C_n = \frac{1}{T}\int_{t_0}^{t_0+T} f(t)e^{-jn\omega_0 t}\, dt$$

When $f(t)$ is a non-periodic signal, as T approaches infinity the discrete line spectrum starts becoming a continuous spectrum, that is, the frequency components constituting a given signal $f(t)$ lie in a continuous range. As T approaches infinity, ω approaches zero and n becomes negligible. Fourier transform is an integral transformation of any non-periodic function $f(t)$ from time domain to frequency domain. The Fourier transform of any signal $f(t)$ is given by

$$F[\omega] = \int_{-\infty}^{\infty} f(t)e^{-j\omega t}\,dt$$

Inverse Fourier Transform

Consider a signal $f(t)$ with Fourier transform $F(\omega)$ such that $F(\omega) = F[f(t)]$, and $F(\omega)$ is evaluated using following expression:

$$F[\omega] = \int_{-\infty}^{\infty} f(t)e^{-j\omega t}\,dt$$

An Inverse Fourier transform of $F(\omega)$ is defined as $f(t) = F^{-1}[F(\omega)]$, and $f(t)$ is evaluated using following expression:

$$f(t) = \frac{1}{2\pi}\int_{-\infty}^{\infty} F(\omega)e^{j\omega t}\,d\omega$$

This pair of equations, known as Fourier transform pair, allow us to carry out the Fourier transformation to the frequency domain and the inverse process to the time domain.

A set of sufficient conditions, (also called Dirichlet conditions) for the existence of Fourier transform, are stated below:

- $f(t)$ is absolutely integrable i.e. $\int_{-\infty}^{\infty} f(t)dt < \infty$
- $f(t)$ is single valued and has only finite number of maxima and minima within any finite interval.
- $f(t)$ has a finite number of finite discontinuities within any finite interval.

Example 10.7

Find the Fourier transform of the signal $e^{3t}u(t)$.

Solution Given $x(t) = e^{3t}u(t)$

The given signal is not absolutely integrable as;

$$\int_{-\infty}^{\infty} e^{3t}u(t) = \infty$$

Therefore, Fourier transform of $x(t)$ does not exist.

Example 10.8

Obtain the Fourier transform of the function shown in shown in the Figure 10.2. ○○●

Solution The Fourier transform of the waveform shown in Figure 10.2.

$$V(\omega) = \int_{-\infty}^{\infty} v(t)e^{-j\omega t}\,dt = \int_{0}^{\infty} 100\,e^{-10t}e^{-j\omega t}\,dt = \int_{0}^{\infty} 100e^{-(10+j\omega)}\,dt$$

$$V(\omega) = \frac{-100}{10+j\omega}[e^{-(10+j\omega)t}]_0^{\infty} = \frac{100}{10+j\omega}$$

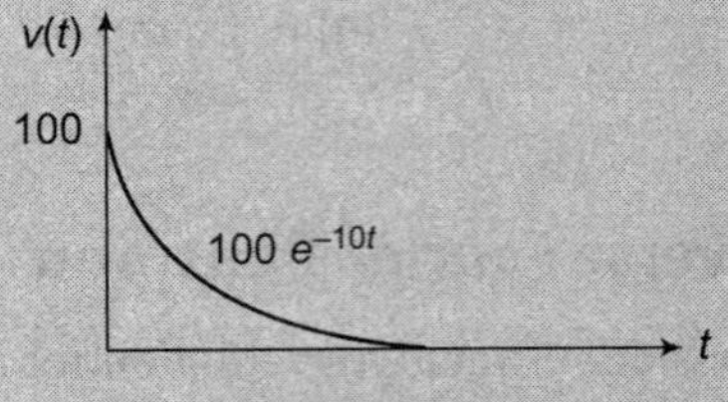

Figure 10.2

Example 10.9

Determine the Fourier transform of the signum function shown in Figure 10.3. ○●●

Solution The function is defined as

$$\begin{aligned} \operatorname{sign}(t) &= 1 && \text{for } t > 0 \\ &= 0 && \text{for } t = 0 \\ &= -1 && \text{for } t < 0 \end{aligned}$$

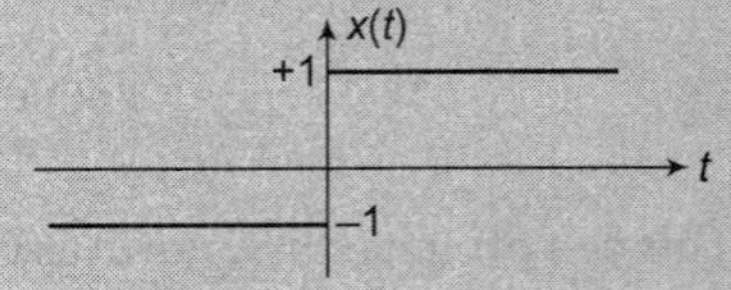

Figure 10.3

The Fourier transform of the function

$$X(\omega) = \int_{-\infty}^{\infty} x(t)e^{-j\omega t}\,dt = \int_{-\infty}^{0} (-1)e^{-j\omega t}\,dt + \int_{0}^{\infty} e^{-j\omega t}\,dt = \frac{+1}{J\omega} + \frac{1}{j\omega} = \frac{2}{j\omega}$$

Example 10.10

Find the inverse Fourier transform of $X(\omega) = j\omega/(2 + j\omega)^2$. ○●●

Solution We know that $F[te^{-at}u(t)] = \dfrac{1}{(a+j\omega)^2}$

$$\therefore \quad F[te^{-2t}u(t)] = \frac{1}{(2+j\omega)^2}$$

Let $\quad te^{-2t}u(t) = x_1(t)$

Then $\quad \dfrac{1}{(2+j\omega)^2} = X_1(\omega)$

Using differentiation in time domain property $\left[\text{i.e.}\ \dfrac{d}{dt}x(t) \xleftrightarrow{FT} j\omega X(\omega)\right]$, we have

$$F\left[\frac{d}{dt}x_1(t)\right] = j\omega X_1(\omega)$$

$$F^{-1}[j\omega X_1(\omega)] = \frac{d}{dt}[x_1(t)] = \frac{d}{dt}[te^{-2t}u(t)]$$

10.7 || FOURIER TRANSFORM OF PERIODIC SIGNALS

The periodic functions can be analysed using Fourier series and non-periodic function can be analysed using Fourier transform. But we can find the Fourier transform of a periodic function also. This means that the Fourier transform can be used as a universal mathematical tool in the analysis of both non-periodic and periodic waveforms over the entire interval. Fourier transform of periodic functions may be found using the concept of impulse function.

We know that using Fourier series, any periodic signal can be represented as a sum of complex exponentials. Fourier transform of periodic signals are not absolutely integrable and have infinite discontinuities. Therefore, we obtain the Fourier transform of a periodic signal by Fourier transforming its complex Fourier series term-by-term.

A Constant Function

$$f(t) = A \xleftrightarrow{F} F(j\omega) = A_2\pi\delta(\omega)$$

A unit Step Function

$$u(t) \xleftrightarrow{F} \pi\delta(\omega) + \frac{1}{j\omega}$$

An Exponential Function

$$f(t) = e^{j\omega_0 t} \xleftrightarrow{F} F(j\omega) = 2\pi\delta(\omega - \omega_0)$$

Sinusoidal Function

$$\cos\omega_0 t \xleftrightarrow{F} \pi\delta(\omega - \omega_0) + \pi\delta(\omega + \omega_0)$$

$$\sin\omega_0 t \xleftrightarrow{F} -j\pi\delta(\omega - \omega_0) + j\pi\delta(\omega + \omega_0)$$

Example 10.11

Find the Fourier transform of unit step function if the Fourier transform of a signum function is given as:

$$\text{sgn}(t) \longleftrightarrow \frac{2}{j\omega}$$

Solution A unit step function and signum function are related by the equation;

$$ut = \frac{1 + \text{sgn}(t)}{2}$$

Also, we know that Fourier transform of unity is $2\pi\delta\omega$.
Therefore, Fourier transform of a unit step function can be calculated as follows:

$$F(u(t)) = F\left(\frac{1}{2}(1+\text{sgn}(t))\right) = \frac{1}{2}F(1) + \frac{1}{2}F(\text{sgn}(t)) = \frac{1}{2}(\pi\delta(\omega)) + \frac{1}{2}\left(\frac{2}{j\omega}\right) = \pi\delta(\omega) + \frac{1}{j\omega}$$

Example 10.12

Find the Fourier transform of the following function.

$$f(t) = \begin{cases} e^{at}, & t \le 0 \\ & \quad a > 0 \\ e^{-at}, & t \ge 0 \end{cases}$$

Solution The Fourier Transform is evaluated as below:

$$F(\omega) = \int_{-\infty}^{\infty} f(t)\exp(-i\omega t)dt = \int_{0}^{\infty} e^{-at}\exp(-i\omega t)dt + \int_{-\infty}^{0} e^{at}\exp(-i\omega t)dt$$

$$= \left[\frac{\exp(-(a+i\omega)t)}{-(a+i\omega)}\right]_0^{\infty} + \left[\frac{\exp((a-i\omega)t)}{(a-i\omega)}\right]_0^{\infty} = \frac{1}{a+i\omega} + \frac{1}{a-i\omega} = \frac{2a}{a^2+\omega^2}$$

Example 10.13

Find the Fourier transform of the rectangular pulse (gate) shown in Figure 10.4. Find the magnitude and phase spectra.

Solution Fourier transform of the pulse can be calculated as following:

$$X(\omega) = \int_{-T}^{T} e^{-j\omega t}dt = 2\frac{\sin\omega T}{\omega} = 2T\frac{\sin\omega T}{\omega T} = 2T\,\text{sin}\,c\left(\frac{\omega T}{\pi}\right)$$

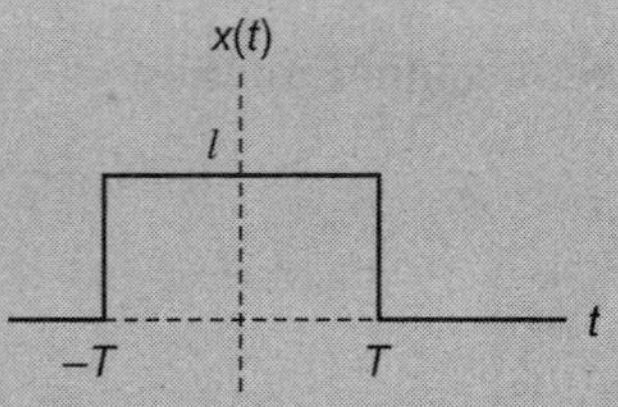

Figure 10.4

The magnitude spectrum is, $|X(\omega)| = 2\left|\frac{\sin\omega T}{\omega}\right|$,

the phase spectrum is, $\arg\{X(\omega)\} = \begin{cases} 0, & \frac{\sin(\omega T)}{\omega} > 0 \\ \pi, & \frac{\sin(\omega T)}{\omega} < 0 \end{cases}$

Example 10.14

Find the Fourier transform of the signal shown in Figure 10.5.

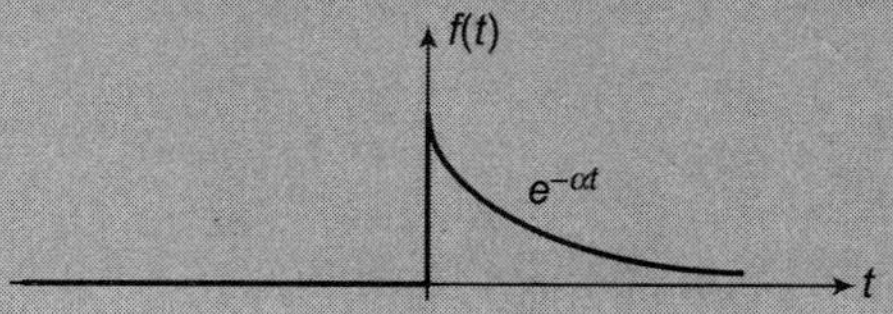

Figure 10.5

Solution

$$F(j\omega)=\int_{-\infty}^{\infty} f(t)e^{-j\omega t}\,dt=\int_{0}^{\infty} e^{-\alpha t}e^{-j\omega t}\,dt=\int_{0}^{\infty} e^{-(\alpha+j\omega)t}\,dt=\frac{1}{\alpha+j\omega}$$

10.8 FOURIER TRANSFORM OF SOME FUNCTIONS

This section presents Fourier transform of some important functions.

Function, $f(t)$	Function, $f(\omega)$
Definition of Inverse Fourier Transform $f(t)=\frac{1}{2\pi}\int_{-\infty}^{\infty} F(\omega)e^{j\omega t}\,d\omega$	Definition of Fourier Transform $F(\omega)=\int_{-\infty}^{\infty} f(t)e^{-j\omega t}\,dt$
$f(t-t_0)$	$F(\omega)e^{-j\omega_0}$
$f(t)e^{j\omega t}$	$F(\omega-\omega_0)$
$f(\alpha t)$	$\frac{1}{\lvert\alpha\rvert}F\left(\frac{\omega}{\alpha}\right)$
$F(t)$	$2\pi f(-\omega)$
$\frac{d^n f(t)}{dt^n}$	$(j\omega)^n F(\omega)$
$(-jt)^n f(t)$	$\frac{d^n F(\omega)}{d\omega^n}$
$\int_{-\infty}^{t} f(\tau)\,d\tau$	$\frac{F(\omega)}{j\omega}+\pi F(0)\delta(\omega)$
$\delta(t)$	1
$e^{j\omega_0 L}$	$2\pi\delta(\omega-\omega_0)$
sgn(t)	$\frac{2}{j\omega}$

Example 10.15

Find the inverse Fourier transform of the following Fourier transform.

$$F(\omega)=\frac{1}{(1+i\omega)(2+i\omega)}$$

Solution Carrying out partial fraction of given function

$$F(\omega)=\frac{1}{(1+i\omega)(2+i\omega)}=\frac{1}{1+i\omega}-\frac{1}{2+i\omega}$$

The inverse Fourier transform of the above function is

$$f(t)=F^{-1}[F(\omega)]=F^{-1}\left[\frac{1}{1+i\omega}-\frac{1}{2+i\omega}\right]=F^{-1}\left[\frac{1}{1+i\omega}\right]-F^{-1}\left[\frac{1}{2+i\omega}\right]$$

$$=\begin{cases}0 & t\le 0\\ e^{-t}-e^{-2t} & 0\le t\end{cases}$$

Example 10.16

Find the Fourier transform of the signals $e^{at}(t)\,u(-t)$.

Solution Given that $f(t) = e^{at}(t)\,u(-t)$

$u(-t)$ implies that signal will exist only for negative values of t.

$$\therefore \quad X(\omega)=F(e^{at}u(-t)]=\int_{-\infty}^{\infty} e^{at}u(-t)\,e^{-j\omega t}\,dt$$

$$=\int_{-\infty}^{0} e^{(a-j\omega)t}dt=\int_{0}^{\infty} e^{(a-j\omega)t}dt=\left[\frac{e^{-(a-j\omega)t}}{-(a-j\omega)}\right]_0^{\infty}=\frac{1}{a-j\omega}$$

10.9 PROPERTIES OF FOURIER TRANSFORM

Probe

1. List the properties of the Fourier Transform.

1. Linearity

The Fourier transform satisfies linearity and principle of superposition. Consider two signals $x_1(t)$ and $x_2(t)$.

If $\quad f_1(t) \longleftrightarrow F_1(\omega)$

And $\quad f_2(t) \longleftrightarrow F_2(\omega)$

Then $\quad [a*f_1(t)+b*f_1(t)] \longleftrightarrow [a*F_1(\omega)+b*F_2(\omega)]$

2. *Scaling*

If $\quad f(t) \longleftrightarrow F(\omega)$

Then for a real 'a'

$$f(a*t) \longleftrightarrow \frac{1}{|a|} F\left(\frac{\omega}{a}\right)$$

3. *Symmetry*

If $\quad f(t) \longleftrightarrow F(\omega)$

Then $\quad F(t) \longleftrightarrow 2\pi f(-\omega)$

4. *Time and Frequency Differentiation/Integration*

If $\quad f(t) \leftrightarrow F(\omega)$

Then, $\quad \frac{d}{dt}[f(t)] \leftrightarrow (j\omega)F(\omega)$

And $\quad \int_{-\infty}^{t} f(\tau)d\tau \leftrightarrow \frac{1}{j\omega}F(\omega)$

$$(-jt)^n f(t) \leftrightarrow \frac{d^n}{dt^n}F(\omega)$$

5. *Convolution*

The convolution of two functions $f_1(t)$ and $f_2(t)$ is defined as:

$$f_1(t) \otimes F_2(t) \equiv \int_{-\infty}^{\infty} f_1(\tau) * f_2(t-\tau)d\tau = \int_{-\infty}^{\infty} f_2(\tau) * f_1(t-\tau)d\tau$$

(a) Time Convolution

If $\quad f_1(t) \leftrightarrow F_1(\omega)$

And $\quad f_2(t) \leftrightarrow F_2(\omega)$

Then $\quad F\{f_1(t) \otimes f_2(t)\} \leftrightarrow F_1(\omega) * F_2(\omega)$

(b) Frequency Convolution

If $\quad f_1(t) \leftrightarrow F_1(\omega)$ and $f_2(t) \leftrightarrow F_2(\omega)$

Then $\quad f_1(t) * f_2(t) \leftrightarrow \frac{1}{2\pi} F_1(\omega) \otimes F_2(\omega)$

6. *Time Shifting*

If $\quad f(t) \leftrightarrow F(\omega)$

Then $\quad f(t-t_0) \leftrightarrow F(\omega_0) * \varepsilon^{-j\omega t_0}$

7. Frequency Shifting

If $f(t) \leftrightarrow F(\omega)$

Then $f(t) * \varepsilon^{j\omega_0 t} \leftrightarrow F(\omega - \omega_0)$

Example 10.17

Demonstrate the frequency differentiation property of Fourier transform.

Solution Let $f(t)$ and $F(\omega)$ are Fourier Transform pair. This implies that

$$f(t) \leftrightarrow F(\omega)$$

$$F(\omega) = \int_{-\infty}^{\infty} f(t) * \varepsilon^{-j\omega t} dt$$

Taking n^{th} differentiation of both sides.

$$\Rightarrow \quad \frac{d^n}{dt^n} F(\omega) = \frac{d^n}{dt^n}\left[\int_{-\infty}^{\infty} f(t) * \varepsilon^{-j\omega t} dt\right]$$

$$\Rightarrow \quad \frac{d^n}{dt^n} F(\omega) = \int_{-\infty}^{\infty} f(t) * \frac{d^n}{dt^n}\left[\varepsilon^{-j\omega t}\right] dt$$

$$\Rightarrow \quad \frac{d^n}{dt^n} F(\omega) = \int_{-\infty}^{\infty} f(t) * (-jt)^n \varepsilon^{-j\omega t} dt$$

$$\Rightarrow \quad \frac{d^n}{dt^n} F(\omega) = \int_{-\infty}^{\infty} \left[(-jt)^n * f(t)\right] * \varepsilon^{-j\omega t} dt$$

$$\Rightarrow \quad (-jt)^n f(t) \leftrightarrow \frac{d^n}{dt^n} F(\omega)$$

Example 10.18

Demonstrate the frequency shifting property of Fourier transform. What is the application of this property?

Solution Let $f(t)$ and $F(\omega)$ are Fourier Transform pair. This implies that

$$f(t) \leftrightarrow F(\omega)$$

$$\Rightarrow \quad F(\omega) = \int_{-\infty}^{\infty} f(t) * \varepsilon^{-j\omega t} dt$$

Shifting Fourier transform by constant frequency ω_0

$$\Rightarrow \quad F(\omega-\omega_0)=\int_{-\infty}^{\infty} f(t)*\varepsilon^{-j(\omega-\omega_0)t}\,dt$$

$$\Rightarrow \quad F(\omega-\omega_0)=\int_{-\infty}^{\infty} [f(t)*\varepsilon^{j\omega_0 t}]*\varepsilon^{-j\omega t}\,dt$$

$$\Rightarrow \quad F(\omega-\omega_0)=\Im\{f(t)*\varepsilon^{j\omega_0 t}\}$$

Frequency Modulation (FM) in communication utilises the shifting property of Fourier transform. The carrier signal is frequency modulated using the base signal and results in efficient transmission of signal.

Example 10.19

Find a particular solution of following differential equation using Fourier transform.

$$y''+3y'+2y=\begin{cases}0\,, & t\le 0\\ e^{-3t}, & t>0\end{cases}$$

○●●

Solution Writing the Fourier transforms of both members of the equation, we have

$$[(i\omega)^2+3i\omega+2]\,F(\omega)=F(\omega)$$

Solving for $Y(\omega)$, then using the partial fractions, we get

$$Y(\omega)=\left[\frac{1}{-\omega^2+3i\omega+2}\right]F(\omega)=\left[\frac{1}{1+i\omega}-\frac{1}{2+i\omega}\right]F(\omega)\equiv G(\omega)F(\omega)$$

Using convolution theorem of Fourier Transform

$$Y(t)=\int_{-\infty}^{\infty} g(t-\lambda)f(\lambda)\,d\lambda=\int_{0}^{\infty} g(t-\lambda)e^{-3\lambda}\,d\lambda$$

$$g(t)=\begin{cases}0 & , \quad t\le 0\\ e^{-t}-e^{-2t}, & 0\le t\end{cases} \text{ and } g(t-\lambda)=\begin{cases}0 & , \quad t\le\lambda\\ e^{-(t-\lambda)}-e^{-2(t-\lambda)}, & \lambda\le t\end{cases}$$

Depending on how t relates to the limits of integration, we have

$$y(t)=\begin{cases}0 & , \quad t\le 0\\ \int_0^t (e^{-t-2\lambda}-e^{-2t-\lambda})d\lambda, & 0\le t\end{cases}$$

Finally, performing the indicated integrations and simplifying, we obtain

$$y(t) = \begin{cases} 0 & t \le 0 \\ \frac{1}{2}e^{-t} - e^{-2t} + \frac{1}{2}e^{-3t} & 0 \le t \end{cases}$$

POINTS TO REMEMBER

- Even Function Symmetry – Fourier series contains only an average term and Cosine terms
- Odd Function Symmetry – Fourier series contains only Sine terms
- Half-wave Symmetry – Fourier series contains only both sine and cosine terms unless the function is also odd or even
- Complex Fourier Series provides an alternative representation of a Fourier Series by combining the sine and cosine terms.
- The exponential form of the Fourier series is given by

$$f(t) = \sum_{n=-\infty}^{\infty} C_n e^{jn\omega_0 t}$$

- The complex coefficients C_n of the exponential Fourier series can be calculated directly from $f(t)$ using

$$C_n = \frac{1}{T} \int_{t_0}^{t_0+T} f(t) e^{-jn\omega_0 t} dt$$

- The Fourier transform of any signal $f(t)$ is given by

$$F(\omega) = \int_{-\infty}^{\infty} f(t) e^{-j\omega t} dt$$

- The inverse Fourier transform of any signal $F[\omega]$ is given by

$$f(t) = \frac{1}{2\pi} \int_{-\infty}^{\infty} F(\omega) e^{j\omega t} d\omega$$

- Step function, sinusoidal function, etc. which do not satisfy the convergence condition (one of the Dirichlet conditions), however Fourier Transform can be evaluated for these functions using impulses.
- The Fourier transform of a periodic signal consists of a train of impulses in the frequency domain. The area of these impulses is directly proportional to the Fourier series coefficients.
- The unit impulse train in the time domain has a transform of an impulse train is the frequency domain.
- The properties of Fourier Transform are summarised in Table 10.1. These properties can be utilized to derive Fourier transform pairs.

Table 10.1

Name of Property	Function of Time	Fourier Transform
1. Definition	$f(t)$	$F(\omega)$
2. Multiplication by constant	$Af(t)$	$AF(\omega)$
3. Linearity	$af_1 + bf_2$	$aF_1(\omega) + bF_2(\omega)$
4. Time shift	$f(t - t_0)$	$e^{-j\omega t}F(\omega)$
5. Time scaline	$f(at),\ a > 0$	$\frac{1}{a}F\left(\frac{\omega}{a}\right)$
6. Modulation	$e^{j\omega_0 t}f(t)$	$F(\omega - \omega_0)$
7. Differentiation	$\frac{d^n f(t)}{dt^n}$	$(j\omega)^n F(\omega)$
8. Convolution	$\int_{-x}^{x} f_1(x) f_2(t - x)dx$	$F_1(\omega)F_2(\omega)$
9. Time multiplication	$t^n f(t)$	$(j)^n \frac{d^n F(\omega)}{d\omega^n}$
10. Time reversal	$f(-1)$	$F(-\omega)$
11. Integration	$\int_{-x}^{x} f(t)dt$	$\frac{F(\omega)}{j\omega} + \pi F(0)\delta(\omega)$

PRACTICE PROBLEMS

1. Find the Fourier series expansion for the standard square wave. ○●●

$$f(x) = \begin{cases} -1 & (-1 < x < 0) \\ +1 & (0 \le x < +1) \end{cases}$$

2. Obtain trigonometric Fourier series of the signal shown in Figure 10.6? ○●●

[RTU, 2011]

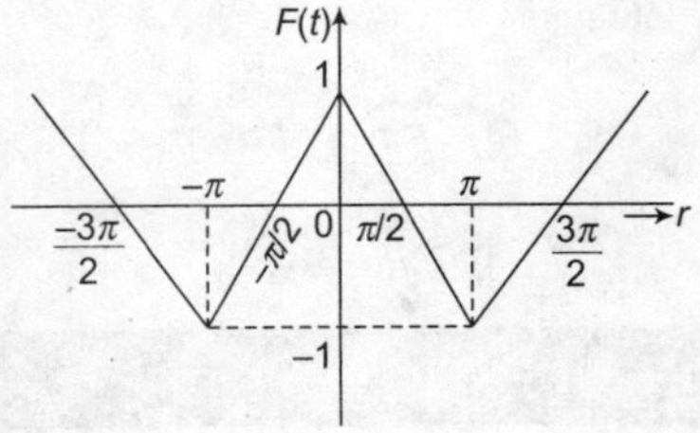

Figure 10.6

3. Find the Complex Fourier series for the square wave shown below. ○●●

$$f(x) = \begin{cases} 0 & \text{for } -3 \le x \le 0 \\ x & \text{for } 0 \le x \le 3 \end{cases}$$

4. Expand the square-wave voltage signal, as shown in the Figure 10.7 into a Fourier series. ○●●

[RGTU, 2014]

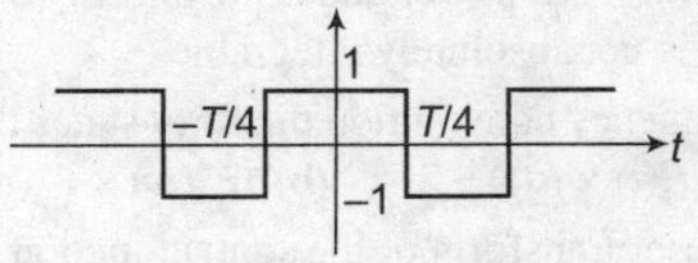

Figure 10.7

5. Find the Fourier transform of a rectangular pulse. Obtain the associated frequency spectrum and comment on it. ○●●

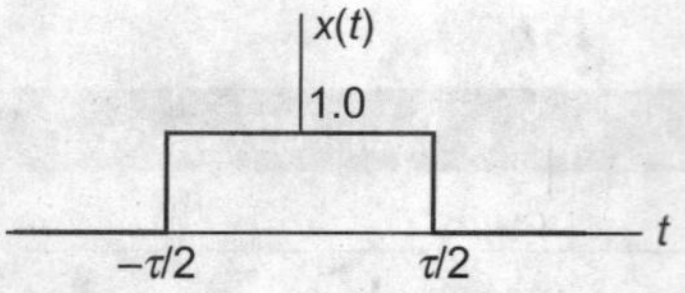

Figure 10.8

6. The output of a system in response to an input $x(t) = e^{-2t}u(t)$ is $y(t) = e^{-t}u(t)$. Find the frequency response and the impulse response of the system. ○●●
7. Consider a system with having impulse response $h(t) = 2e^{-2t}u(t)$ for an input $x(t) = 3e^{-t}u(t)$. Find the output of the system $y(t)$. ○●●
8. Evaluate Fourier Transform of Double sided real exponential function $e^{-a|t|}$ utilising the properties associated with the transform. ●●●
9. Find Fourier transform of triangular pulse shown in Figure 10.9. ●●●

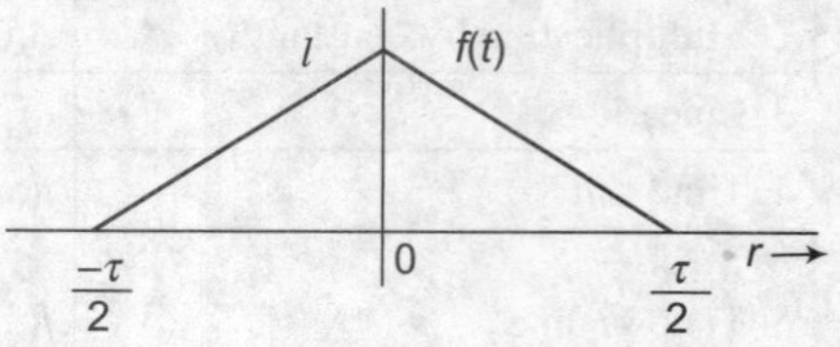

Figure 10.9

10. Evaluate Fourier Transform of Single sided real exponential function $e^{-at}u(t)$ utilising the properties associated with the transform. ●●●

MULTIPLE CHOICE QUESTIONS

1. Any periodic function can be expressed by a Fourier series when the function has ○○●
   (a) infinite number of finite discontinuities in a period
   (b) finite number of infinite discontinuities in a period
   (c) finite number of finite discontinuities in a period
   (d) infinite number of infinite discontinuities
2. Fourier transform for the signal $e^{-at}\,u(t)$ does not exist if ○●●
   (a) $a > 0$ (b) $a = 0$ (c) $a < 0$ (d) $a = 1$
3. In a periodic signal, the period T_0 is doubled, the fundamental frequency ω in the spectrum becomes ○○●
   (a) Doubled (b) Increased 4 times (c) Halved (d) No change
4. A periodic function $x(t)$, with a time period T, is said to have half-wave symmetry if $x(t)$ is: ○○●
   (a) $-x(t + T/2)$ (b) $x(t + T/2)$ (c) $x(t - T/2)$ (d) $-x(t - T/2)$
5. Time convolution of two signals is equal to ○●●
   (a) $f_1(t) \times f_2(t)$ (b) $F_1(\omega) \times F_2(\omega)$ (c) $f_1(t)/f_2(t)$ (d) $F_1(\omega) / F_2(\omega)$
6. Fourier transform of an impulse function of amplitude A? ●●●
   (a) $j\omega A$ (b) A (c) $2/j\omega A$ (d) None of these
7. A power signal ○○●
   (a) has infinite power and finite energy (b) has infinite energy and finite power
   (c) is not absolutely integrable (d) is absolutely integrable
8. An energy signal ○●●
   (a) has zero power and finite energy (b) has infinite energy and finite power
   (c) is not absolutely integrable (d) is absolutely integrable
9. Frequency convolution property states that ○○●
   (a) $f_1(t) \times f_2(t)$ (b) $F_1(\omega) \times F_2(\omega)$ (c) $f_1(t) / f_2(t)$ (d) $F_1(\omega) / F_2(\omega)$
10. Fourier transform of the sgn(t) function is ○○●
    (a) $2 / j\omega$ (b) $j\omega$ (c) $1 / j\omega$ (d) $2j\omega$

ANSWERS TO MULTIPLE CHOICE QUESTIONS

1. (c)	2. (c)	3. (c)	4. (a, d)	5. (b)
6. (b)	7. (b, c)	8. (a, d)	9. (a)	10. (a)

Introduction to Laplace Transform

11

Chapter Outline

- Definition of Laplace transform
- Laplace transform of some useful time functions
- Inverse transform techniques
- Properties of Laplace transform
- Initial and final value theorems
- Waveform synthesis
- Modelling of *R*, *L*, and *C*, in *s*-domain
- Nodal and mesh analysis in *s*-domain
- Additional circuit analysis techniques in *s*-domain
- RMS and average value of periodic waveform

11.1 INTRODUCTION

A Transform T can be regarded as a mathematical operator which operates on a function f to result in function Tf. Thus, Transform T maps function f into Tf. The Laplace transform is an integral transforms which that maps differential or integro-differential equations in the "time" domain into polynomial equations which is in the "complex frequency" domain.

11.2 DEFINITION OF LAPLACE TRANSFORM

University Questions

1. Why do we use Laplace transform in circuit analysis? **[RGTU, 2014]**
2. What is Laplace transform? Define its application. **[PTU, 2011-12]**

The Laplace transform is a powerful analytical technique that is widely used to study the behaviour of linear, lumped parameter circuits. Laplace transforms are useful in engineering, particularly when the driving function has discontinuities and appears for a short period only.

One significant advantage of the Laplace transform is that it includes both stead-state and initial conditions. The initial energy in L or C is taken into account by adding independent source in series or parallel with the element impedance in its s-domain equivalent. Therefore, allowing to obtain both the steady-state response as well as the transient response.

Laplace transform changes the time-domain function *f*(*t*) to the frequency-domain function *F*(*s*). Consider a function $f(t)$ which is to be continuous and defined for values of $t = 0$. The Laplace transform is then

$$\mathcal{L}[f(t)] = F(s) = \int_{-\infty}^{\infty} e^{-st} f(t)\, u(t)\, dt = \int_{0}^{\infty} f(t) e^{-st}\, dt$$

Laplace transform is a function of independent variable *s* corresponding to the complex variable in the exponent of e^{-st}. The complex variable *S* is, in general, of the form $s = \sigma + j\omega$, where σ and ω being the real and imaginary parts respectively.

Similarly, the inverse Laplace transformation converts frequency-domain function *F*(*s*) to the time-domain function $f(t)$ as follows:

$$\mathcal{L}^{-1}[F(s)] = f(t) = \frac{1}{2\pi j} \int_{-J}^{+J} F(s)\, e^{st}\, ds$$

An important condition for existence of Laplace Transform for a function $f(t)$ is

$$\int_{0}^{\infty} f(t) e^{-st}\, dt < \infty.$$

11.3 LAPLACE TRANSFORM OF SOME USEFUL TIME FUNCTIONS

University Question

1. What is the relation between unit step, unit ramp and unit impulse functions? **[PTU, 2011-12]**

1. Unit Step Function

In switching operations, abrupt changes may occur in current and voltages. This abrupt change is presented using a step function. A Unit Step Function *f*(*t*) = *u*(*t*) is defined as shown in Figure 11.1.

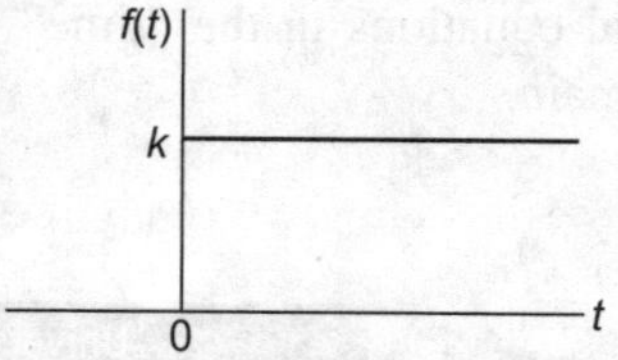

where $u(t) = 1$ for $t > 0$
$= 0$ for $t < 0$

Figure 11.1

If the amplitude is *K*, then function is written as *Ku*(*t*).

The Laplace transform of a step function can be evaluated as follows:

$$\mathcal{L}[f(t)] = \int_{0}^{\infty} f(t) e^{-st}\, dt = \int_{0}^{\infty} 1 e^{-st}\, dt = \left. \frac{e^{-st}}{-s} \right|_{0}^{\infty} = \frac{1}{s}$$

$$\mathcal{L}[u(t)] = \frac{1}{s}$$

This expression forms a Laplace Transform pair of a unit step function.

2. Unit Ramp Function

The function is defined as shown in Figure 11.2.

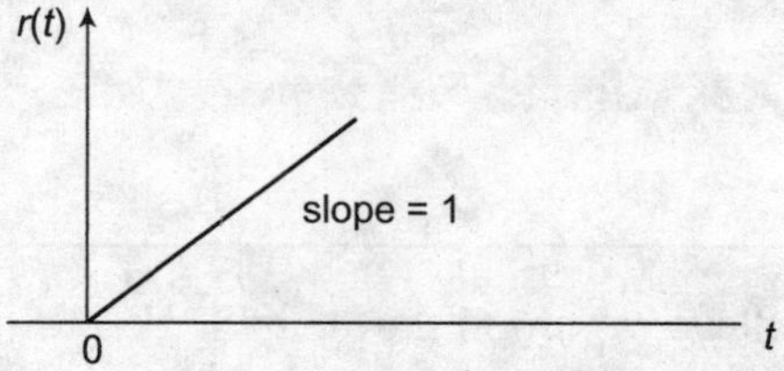

$$r(t) = \begin{cases} t & \text{for } t \geq 0 \\ 0 & \text{for } t < 0 \end{cases}$$

Figure 11.2

Laplace transform of unit ramp function is $\dfrac{1}{s^2}$.

3. Unit Impulse Function

An impulse function is represented by a vertical arrow and unbounded and discontinuous function. It is defined as shown in Figure 11.3.

Laplace transform of unit impulse function is 1.

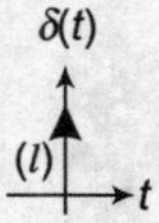

$$\delta[n] = \begin{cases} 0, & n = 0 \\ 1, & n \neq 0 \end{cases}$$

Figure 11.3

11.3.1 Relationship between Impulse, Step and Ramp Function

- Impulse function $\delta(t)$ is the derivative of step function $u(t)$
- Ramp function $r(t) = t\,u(t)$ or $\int_0^t u(t) = r(t) = t$

Example 11.1

Define 'unit impulse function' and derive its Laplace transform. **[RGTU, 2013]** ○○●

Solution An impulse is a signal of infinite amplitude and zero duration. In general, an impulse signal doesn't exist in nature, but some circuit signals come very close to approximating this definition. Due to switching operations, impulsive voltages and currents occur in circuit analysis. The impulse function enables us to define the derivative at a discontinuity, and thus to define the Laplace transform of that derivative.

An impulse function of magnitude K is represented as $f(t) = K\delta(t)$ is repressed using the expression as shown in Figure 11.4.

where $\delta(t) = 0,\ t \neq 0$

Laplace Transform of Unit Impulse Function is:

$$\mathcal{L}[\delta(t)] = \int_{0^-}^{\infty} \delta(t)e^{-st}\,dt = \int_{0^-}^{\infty} \delta(t)\,dt = 1$$

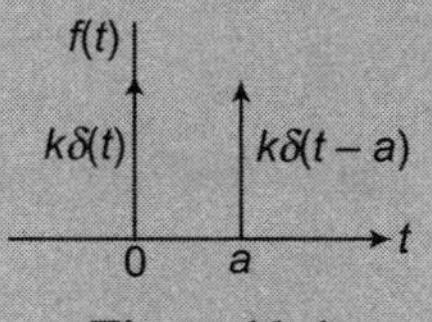

Figure 11.4

The magnitude of an impulse function represents area under the curve of the function. An important property of the impulse function is the shifting property, which is expressed as

Note: Difficulty Level ⟶ ○○● — Easy; ○●● — Medium; ●●● — Difficult

$$\int_{-\infty}^{\infty} f(t)\delta(t-a)\,dt = f(a)$$

Example 11.2

What are the Laplace transforms of the voltage waveform shown in Figure 11.5? **[BPTU, 2008]** ○○●

Solution

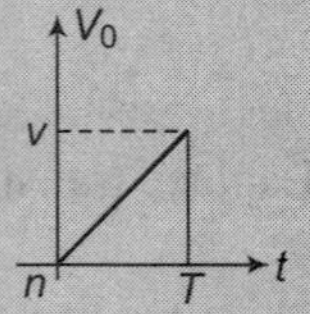

Figure 11.5

$$f(t) = V_o \begin{Bmatrix} 0; \ t \le 0 \\ \dfrac{V}{T}; t > 0 \ \& \ t \le T \end{Bmatrix}$$

$$V_o = \left(\frac{V-0}{T-0}\right)t = V_o = \frac{V}{T}t$$

$$\Rightarrow \qquad \frac{V_o(S)}{t(S)} = \frac{V}{T}\frac{1}{S} = F(S)$$

Example 11.3

Obtain the Laplace transforms for $f_1(t) = t$ and $f_2(t) = e^{-at}$. **[GTU, 2010]** ○○○

Solution

(a) Integration of unit step function gives the ramp function.

$$\int_0^t u(t) = r(t) = t$$

The Laplace transform of ramp function can be determined as following:

$$\mathcal{L}\left[\int_0^t u(t)dt\right] = \frac{1}{s}\mathcal{L}[u(t)] = \frac{1}{s^2}$$

$$\mathcal{L}[u(t)] = \frac{1}{s}$$

(b) The Laplace transform for function $f(t) = e^{-at}$ is evaluated as:

$$\mathcal{L}(e^{-st}) = \int_0^{\infty} e^{-st} \cdot e^{-st} dt = \int_0^{\infty} e^{-(s+s)t} = \frac{-1}{s+a}[e^{-(s+a)}]_0^{\infty} = \frac{1}{s+a}$$

$$\mathcal{L}[e^{-st}] = \frac{1}{s+a}$$

11.4 INVERSE TRANSFORM TECHNIQUES

Inverse Laplace transform can be determined using partial fraction method. This method is discussed for both proper and improper rational functions.

Probe

1. Explain use of Partial Fraction Method in determining the Inverse Laplace Transform.

11.4.1 Partial Fraction Expansion: Proper Rational Function

Let $F(s)$ is the Laplace transform of function $f(t)$ and is a proper rational function, then the Partial Fraction Method can be utilised to obtain Inverse Laplace transform $F^{-1}(s)$.

A proper rational function can be expressed in the form of a ratio of two polynomials in s such that no non-integral power of s appears in polynomials as given below.

$$F(s) = \frac{N(s)}{D(s)} = \frac{a_n s^n + a_{n-1}s^{n-1} + \cdots + a_1 s + a_0}{b_m s^m + b_{m-1}s^{m-1} + \cdots + b_1 s + b_0}$$

The coefficients a and b are real constants, and the exponents m and n are positive integers. The ratio $N(s)/D(s)$ is called a *proper rational function* if $m > n$, and an *improper rational function* if $m > n$.

Only a proper rational function can be expanded as a sum of partial fractions.

11.4.2 Partial Fraction Expansion: Improper Rational Function

An improper rational function can always be expanded into a polynomial plus a proper rational function. The polynomial is then inverse-transformed into impulse functions and derivatives of impulse functions.

Example 11.4

Solve the following differential equations using Laplace transform.

(a) $\frac{d^2i}{dt^2} + \frac{di}{dt} = t^2 + 2t, i(0^-) = 4, \frac{di}{dt}(0^-) = -2$ (b) $\frac{d^2i}{dt^2} + 4i = \sin t - \cos 2t, i(0^-) = 0, \frac{di}{dt}(0^-) = 0$

[PU, 2012] ○●●

Solution

(a) Taking Laplace transform of given equation:

$$[S^2 I(S) - Si(0) - i(0)] + [SI(S) - i(0)] = \frac{2}{S^3} + \frac{2}{S^2}$$

$$[S^2 I(S) - 4S + 2] + [SI(S) - 4] = \frac{2}{S^3} + \frac{2}{S^2}$$

$$I(S) = \frac{2}{S^3(S^2+S)} + \frac{2}{S^2(S^2+S)} + \frac{4S+2}{S^2+S} = \frac{2}{S^4(S+1)} + \frac{2}{S^3(S+1)} + \frac{4S+2}{S(S+1)}$$

$$= \left[\frac{-2}{S} + \frac{2}{S^2} - \frac{2}{S^3} + \frac{2}{S^4} + \frac{2}{S+1}\right] + \left[\frac{2}{S} - \frac{2}{S^2} + \frac{2}{S^3} - \frac{2}{S+1}\right] + \left[\frac{2}{S} - \frac{2}{S+1}\right]$$

Taking inverse Laplace transform of above expression

$$\Rightarrow \quad i = -2 + 2t - t^2 + \frac{t^3}{3} + 2e^{-t} + 2 - 2t + t^2 - 2e^{-t} + 2 - 2e^{-t} = \left(2 + \frac{t^3}{3} - 2e^{-t}\right)$$

(b) Taking Laplace transform of given equation

$$[S^2 I(S) - Si(0) - i^1(0)] + 4I(S) = \frac{1}{S^2+1} - \frac{S}{S^2+4}$$

$$\Rightarrow \quad [S^2 I(S) - 0 - 0] + 4I(S) = \frac{1}{S^2+1} - \frac{S}{S^2+4}$$

$$\Rightarrow \quad I(S) = \frac{1}{(S^2+1)(S^2+4)} - \frac{S}{(S^2+4)^2} = \frac{1}{3(S^2+1)} - \frac{1}{3(S^2+2^2)} - \frac{S}{(S^2+2^2)^2}$$

Taking inverse Laplace transform of above expression

$$\Rightarrow \quad t(t) = \frac{\sin t}{3} - \frac{\sin 2t}{6} - t\cos 2t$$

Example 11.5

Determine the partial fraction expansion for

$$Y(s) = \frac{10}{s^2 + 10s + 16}$$

○○●

Solution Using partial fraction method

$$Y(s) = \frac{10}{(s+8)(s+2)} = \frac{A}{s+8} + \frac{B}{s+2}$$

$$\frac{10}{(s+8)(s+2)} = \frac{A(s+2) + B(s+8)}{(s+8)(s+2)}$$

$$\Rightarrow \quad A(s+2) + B(s+8) = 10$$

$$\Rightarrow \quad \begin{cases} A + B = 0 \Rightarrow A = -B \\ 2A + 8B = 10 \Rightarrow -2B + 8B = 10 \end{cases}$$

$$\Rightarrow \quad B = 10/6 = 5/3; \; A = -5/3$$

Taking inverse Laplace transform of $Y(s)$

$$Y(s) = -\frac{5}{3}\cdot\frac{1}{s+8} + \frac{5}{3}\cdot\frac{1}{s+2}$$

$$\Rightarrow \quad y(t) = \left(-\frac{5}{3}e^{-8t} + \frac{5}{3}e^{-2t}\right)u(t)$$

Example 11.6

Determine the partial fraction expansion for

$$Y(s) = \frac{s^4 - 7s^3 + 13s^2 + 4s - 12}{s^2(s-1)(s-2)(s-3)}$$

Solution

$$Y(s) = \frac{s^4 - 7s^3 + 13s^2 + 4s - 12}{s^2(s-1)(s-2)(s-3)}$$

$$= \frac{C_2}{s^2} + \frac{C_1}{s} + \frac{A_1}{s-1} + \frac{A_2}{s-2} + \frac{A_3}{s-3}$$

Determining coefficients of partial fractions

$$C_2 = \lim_{s\to 0} \frac{s^4 - 7s^3 + 13s^2 + 4s - 12}{(s-1)(s-2)(s-3)} = \frac{-12}{-6} = 2$$

$$C_1 = \lim_{s\to 0} \frac{d}{ds}\left[\frac{s^4 - 7s^3 + 13s^2 + 4s - 12}{(s-1)(s-2)(s-3)}\right]$$

$$= \frac{4(-1)(-2)(-3) - (-12)[(-2)(-3) + (-1)(-3) + (-1)(-2)]}{[(-1)(-2)(-3)]^2}$$

$$= \frac{-24 + 12 \times 11}{6^2} = 3$$

$$A_1 = \lim_{s\to 1} \frac{s^4 - 7s^3 + 13s^2 + 4s - 12}{s^2(s-2)(s-3)} = \frac{-1}{2}$$

$$A_2 = \lim_{s\to 2} \frac{s^4 - 7s^3 + 13s^2 + 4s - 12}{s^2(s-1)(s-3)} = \frac{8}{-4} = -2$$

$$A_3 = \lim_{s\to 3} \frac{s^4 - 7s^3 + 13s^2 + 4s - 12}{s^2(s-1)(s-2)} = \frac{9}{18} = \frac{1}{2}$$

Taking inverse Laplace transform of $Y(s)$, we get

$$y(t) = 2t + 3 - \frac{1}{2}e^{t} - 2e^{2t} + \frac{1}{2}e^{3t}$$

11.5 || PROPERTIES OF LAPLACE TRANSFORM

Table 11.1 lists important properties of Laplace transform which allows to obtain transform and inverse-transform of complex functions.

Table 11.1 Properties of Laplace Transform

Description of Laplace Transform Property	Mathematical Formula
Linearity (Multiplication by a constant)	Consider a function $f(t)$ multiplied by a constant K. $\mathcal{L}\{Kf(t)\} = KF(s)$
Superposition (Addition / Subtraction) The Laplace transform of the sum of the two or more functions is equal to the sum of transforms of the individual function.	Consider two functions $f_1(t)$ and $f_2(t)$ $f_1(t) \xleftrightarrow{\mathcal{L}} F_1(s)$ and $f_2(t) \xleftrightarrow{\mathcal{L}} F_2(s)$, then $\mathcal{L}[f_1(t) \pm f_2(t)] = F_1(s) \pm F_2(s)$
Differentiation If a function $f(t)$ is piecewise continuous then the Laplace transform of its derivative $df(t)/dt$ is given by Similarly, Laplace transform of second derivative: Laplace transform of the nth derivative	$\mathcal{L}\left\|\frac{df(t)}{dt}\right\| = SF(s) - f(0)$ $\mathcal{L}[f''(t)] = \mathcal{L}\left\|\frac{d}{dt}(f'(t))\right\| = S^2F(s) - Sf(0) - f'(0)$ where $f'(0)$ is the initial value of the first derivative of $f(t)$. $\mathcal{L}\left\|\frac{d^n f(t)}{dt^n}\right\| = S^n F(s) - S^{n-1} f(0^-) - S^{n-2}\frac{dt(0)}{dt} - S^{n-3}\frac{d^2 f(0^-)}{dt^2} - K - \frac{d^{n-1}}{dt^{n-1}} f(0^-)$
Integration If a function $f(t)$ is continuous then the Laplace transform of its integral $\left\|\int f(t)dt\right\|$ is given by	$\mathcal{L}\left\|\int_0^t f(t)dt\right\| = \frac{1}{s}\mathcal{L}[f(t)] = \frac{F(s)}{s}$
Differentiation of Transforms If the Laplace transform of the function $f(t)$ exists then the derivative of the corresponding transform with respect to s in the frequency domain is equal to its multiplication by t in the time domain.	$\mathcal{L}[tf(t)] = \frac{-d}{ds}F(s)$
Integration of Transforms If the Laplace transform of the function $f(t)$ exists then the integral of corresponding transform with respect to s in the complex frequency domain is equal to its division by t in the time domain	$\int_0^\infty F(s)\,ds = \mathcal{L}\left\|\frac{f(t)}{t}\right\|$
Translation in the Time Domain If the function $f(t)$ has the transform $F(s)$ then the Laplace transform of $f(t-a)\,u(t-a)$ is $e^{at}F(s)$ (with $a > 0$).	$\mathcal{L}[f(t-a)\,u(t-a)] = e^{-as}F(s)$ Translation in the time domain corresponds to multiplication by an exponential in the frequency domain.

(Continued)

Table 11.1 *Continued*

Description of Laplace Transform Property	Mathematical Formula
Translation in the Frequency Domain If the function $f(t)$ has the transform $F(s)$ then the Laplace transform of $e^{-at}f(t)$ is $F(s+a)$. Similarly the Laplace transform of $e^{at}f(t)$ is $F(s-a)$.	$F(s+a) = \mathcal{L}(e^{-at} f(t)]$ $\mathcal{L}[e^{at} f(t) = F(s-a)$ Translation in the frequency domain corresponds to multiplication by an exponential in the time domain
Scale Changing The scale-change property gives the relationship between $f(t)$ and $F(s)$ when the time variable is multiplied by a positive constant.	$\mathcal{L}\{f(at)\} = \frac{1}{a} F\left(\frac{s}{a}\right), a > 0$
S - Derivative *S - Integral*	$t\,f(t) \quad -\frac{dF(s)}{ds}$ $t^n f(t) \quad (-1)^n \frac{d^n F(s)}{ds^n}$ $\frac{f(t)}{t} \quad \int_s^{\infty} F(u)\,du$

Example 11.7

Find the Laplace transforms of $t^2 \cos t$.

Solution We know that $L\{\cos t\} = \frac{s}{s^2+1}$

Therefore, we can work out from $L\{t^n f(t)\} = (-1)^n \frac{d^n}{ds^n}\{F(s)\}$

$$L\{t^2 \cos t\} = \frac{d^2}{ds^2}\left(\frac{s}{s^2+1}\right)$$

Find the first derivative

$$z = \frac{s}{s^2+1}$$

$$z = \frac{a}{b}, a = s, b = s^2+1, \frac{da}{ds} = 1, \frac{db}{ds} = 2s$$

$$\frac{dz}{ds} = \frac{b\frac{da}{ds} - a\frac{db}{ds}}{b^2} = \frac{(s^2+1)(1)-(s)(2s)}{(s^2+1)^2}$$

$$\Rightarrow \quad \frac{dz}{ds} = \frac{(s^2+1)-(2s^2)}{(s^2+1)^2} = \frac{1-s^2}{(s^2+1)^2}$$

Differentiate again.

$$z = \frac{1 - s^2}{(s^2+1)^2}$$

$$z = \frac{a}{b},\ a = 1 - s^2,\ b = (s^2+1)^2,$$

$$\frac{da}{ds} = -2s,\ \frac{db}{ds} = 4s^3 + 4s = 4s(s^2+1)$$

$$\frac{dz}{ds} = \frac{b\frac{da}{ds} - a\frac{db}{ds}}{b^2} = \frac{((s^2+1)^2)(-2s) - (1-s^2)(4s(s^2+1))}{((s^2+1)^2)^2}$$

$$\Rightarrow \quad \frac{dz}{ds} = \frac{-2s(s^2+1)^2 - 4s(1-s^2)(s^2+1)}{(s^2+1)^4} = \frac{-2s(s^2+1)^1 - 4s(1-s^2)}{(s^2+1)^3}$$

$$= \frac{-2s^3 - 2s - 4s + 4s^3}{(s^2+1)^3} = \frac{2s^3 - 6s}{(s^2+1)^3}$$

Example 11.8

Given that $L\{\sin 2t\} = \dfrac{2}{s^2+4}$, find the Laplace transform of $t \sin 2t$.

Solution Using Laplace transform property $L\{tf(t)\} = -F'(s)$

Therefore $\quad L\{t\sin 2t\} = -\dfrac{d}{ds}\left(\dfrac{2}{s^2+4}\right)$

Upon differentiating above expression

Therefore $\quad L\{t\sin 2t\} = -\dfrac{d}{ds}\left(\dfrac{2}{s^2+4}\right) = \dfrac{4s}{(s^2+4)^2}$

11.6 || INITIAL AND FINAL VALUE THEOREMS

University Question

1. State and explain the initial and final values theorems. **[GTU, 2012]**

The initial- and final-value theorems are useful because they enable us to determine from $F(s)$ the behaviour of $f(t)$ at $t = 0$ and $t = \infty$. Hence, we can check the initial and final values of $f(t)$ to see if they conform to known circuit behaviour, before actually finding the inverse transform of $F(s)$.

1. The initial-value theorem states that

$$\lim_{t\to 0} f(t) = \lim_{s\to\infty} SF(s)$$

The initial-value theorem is based on the assumption that $f(t)$ contains no impulse functions.

2. The final-value theorem states that

$$\lim_{t\to\infty} f(t) = \lim_{s\to 0} SF(s)$$

The final-value theorem is useful only if $f(\infty)$ exists.

11.7 WAVEFORM SYNTHESIS

Basic functions such as impulse, step and ramp functions can be utilised to synthesise any waveform. These signals may be combined by addition or subtraction to build a variety of general waveforms used in practice.

Example 11.9

Use ramp function to express the waveform shown in Figure 11.6.

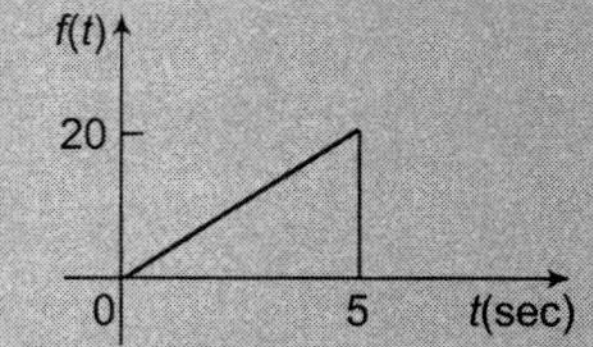

Figure 11.6

Solution The waveform shown in Figure 11.6 starts at $t = 0$ and ends at $t = 5$ seconds.

The waveform in Figure 11.6 is combination of a ramp function $r(t) = 4\,r(t)$ at $t = 0$ and another ramp function $r(t) = -4r(t-5)$ at $t = 5$.

Therefore, the waveform can be written as: $f(t) = 4\,[r(t) - r(t-5)]$

Example 11.10

Use step function to express the waveform shown in Figure 11.7.

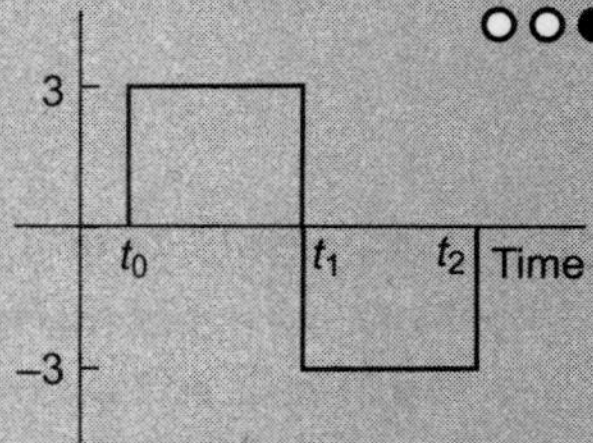

Figure 11.7

Solution The waveform shown in Figure 11.7 starts at $t = t_0$ and ends at $t = t_2$ seconds. The waveform is combination of the following step functions.

1. $3u(t)$ at $t = t_0$
2. $-6u(t)$ at $t = t_1$
3. $3u(t)$ at $t = t_2$

Above step functions can be added to get expression for the waveform

$$3[u(t-t_o) - 2u(t-t_1) + u(t-t_2)]$$

11.8 MODELLING OF *R, L,* AND *C,* IN *s*-DOMAIN

University Question

1. Obtain the domain (Laplace transform) equivalent circuit diagram of an inductor and capacitor with initial condition? **[MU, 2014]**

Electrical circuit elements *R*, *L* and *C* can be modelled in Laplace Transfer domain (i.e., *s*-domain). The initial energy in *L* or *C* is taken into account by adding independent source in series or parallel with the element impedance in its *s*-domain equivalent.

1. For a resistor, the voltage current relationship in the time domain is:

$$v(t) = Ri(t)$$

Taking the Laplace transform:

$$V(s) = RI(s)$$

2. Similarly, for an inductor, taking Laplace transform of voltage-current relationship

$$v(t) = L\frac{di(t)}{dt}; \qquad I(s) = \frac{1}{sL}V(s) + \frac{i(0^-)}{s}$$

Equivalent Circuit representation in *s*-domain is as shown in Figure 11.8.

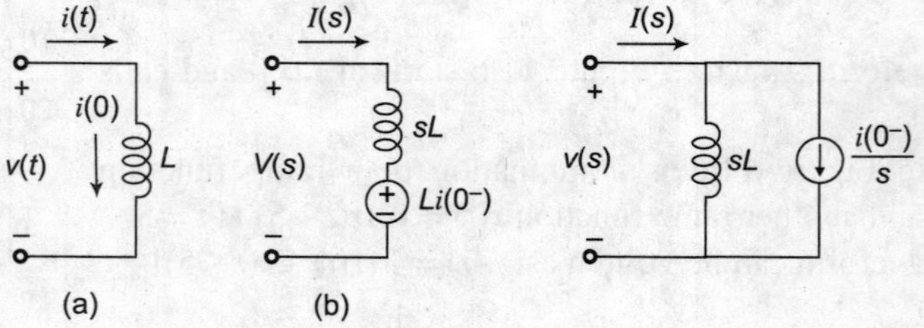

Figure 11.8

3. For a capacitor, taking Laplace transform of voltage-current relationship

$$i(t) = C\frac{dv(t)}{dt}; \qquad V(s) = \frac{1}{sC}I(s) + \frac{v(0^-)}{s}$$

Equivalent Circuit representation in *s*-domain is shown in Figure 11.9.

Note here that the initial conditions in case of a capacitor or an inductor can be represented either as a voltage or as a current source.

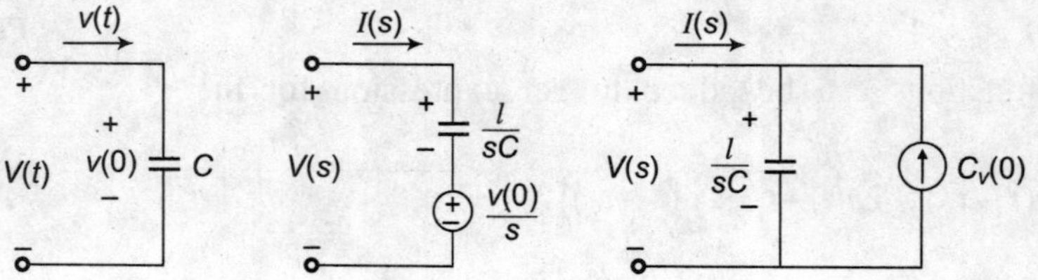

Figure 11.9

4. In many applications, we will assume the initial conditions are zero. In this condition, equivalent s-domain expression become simplified as below:

Resistor	$V(s) = RI(s)$
Inductor	$V(s) = sLI(s)$
Capacitor	$V(s) = \frac{1}{sC}I(s)$

Example 11.11

At $t = 0$, the switch is closed with a charged capacitor having voltage V_0. Find the equivalent s-domain of the circuit shown in Figure 11.10.

Solution The initial condition of capacitor can be represented using a voltage source. Utilising the s-domain equivalents, the circuit can be re-drawn as shown in Figure 11.11.

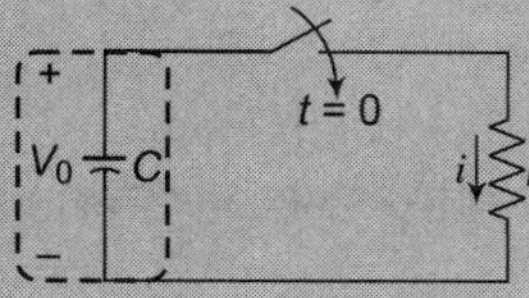

Figure 11.10

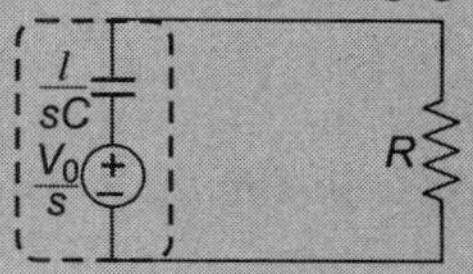

Figure 11.11

Example 11.12

Obtain frequency domain equivalent electrical circuit of the network shown in Figure 11.12.

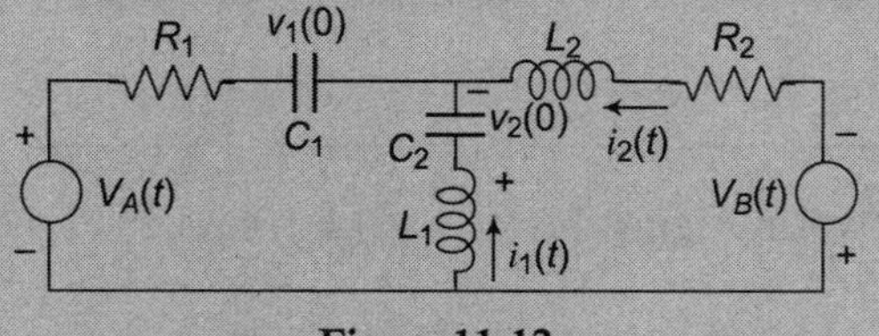

Figure 11.12

Solution Equivalent s-domain circuit can be obtained as shown in Figure 11.13.

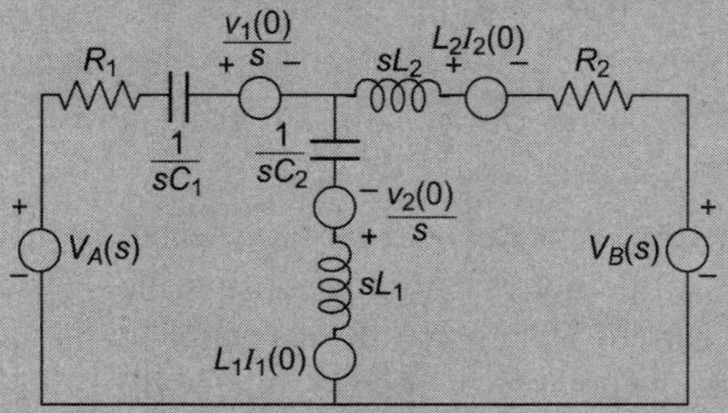

Figure 11.13

Example 11.13

At $t = 0$, the switch is opened as shown in Figure 11.14. Find the equivalent s-domain of the circuit.

●●●

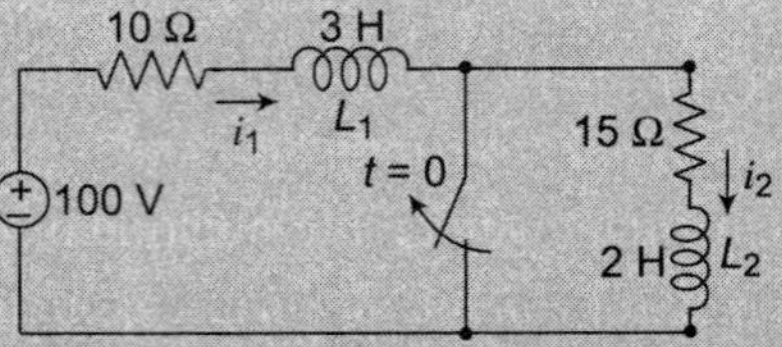

Figure 11.14

Solution The steady state current in inductor L_1 at $t = 0^-$ is 10A, while for inductor L_2 at $t = 0^-$ is 0A. Utilising the s-domain equivalents, the circuit can be re-drawn as shown in Figure 11.15.

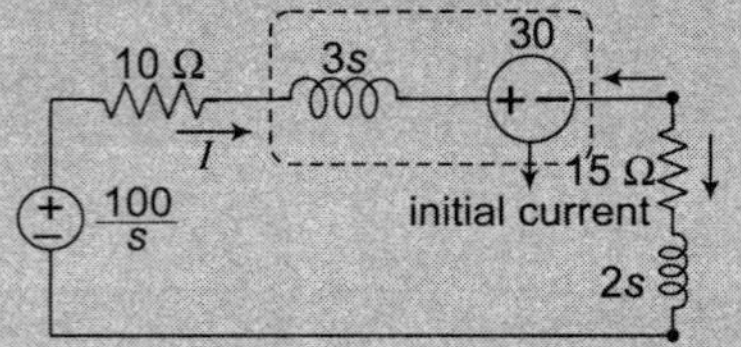

Figure 11.15

Example 11.14

Assume that for circuit shown in Figure 11.16, $v_c(0) = -4$ V. Find the s-domain equivalent of the circuit at $t = 0^+$.

○●●

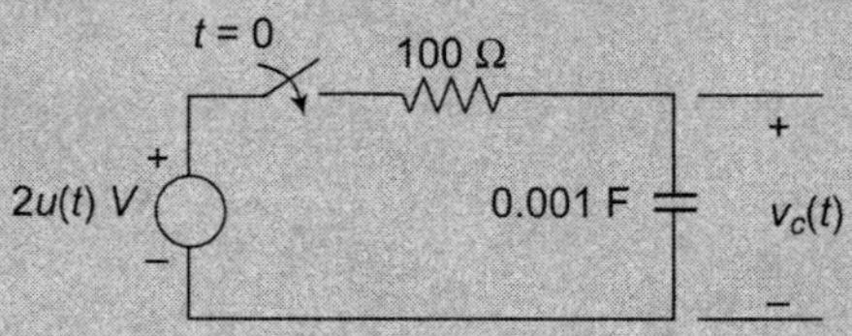

Figure 11.16

Solution Initial voltage across capacitor can be represented using a voltage source. It is to be noted that after closing the switch at $t = 0^+$, the circuit current will charge the capacitor in opposite direction. Therefore, the polarity of voltage source will be reversed to charging direction.

Utilising the s-domain equivalents, the circuit can be re-drawn as shown in Figure 11.17.

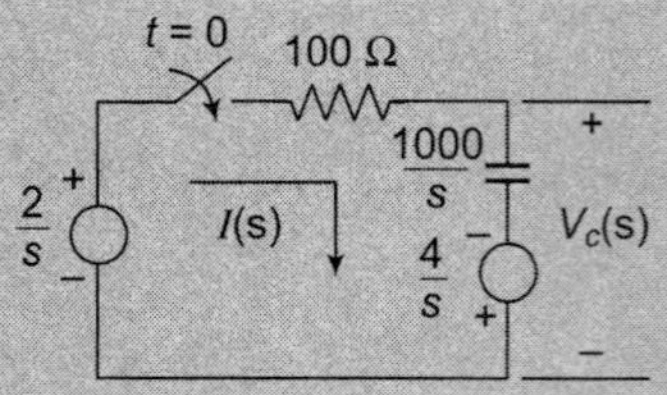

Figure 11.17

Example 11.15

Find the s-domain equivalent of the circuit shown in Figure 11.18.

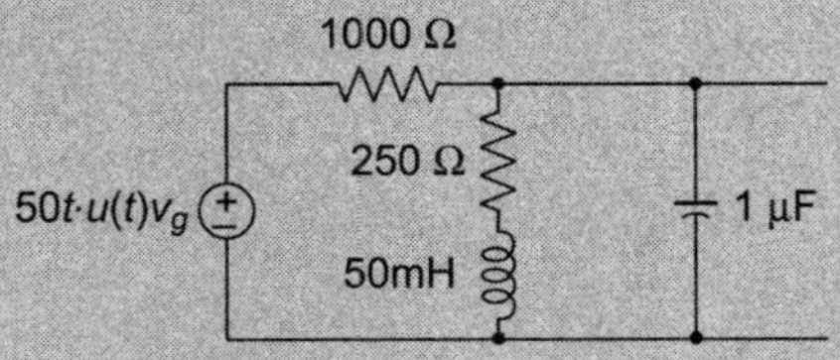

Figure 11.18

Solution The circuit is excited by a ramp source. Utilising the s-domain equivalents, the circuit can be re-drawn as shown in Figure 11.19.

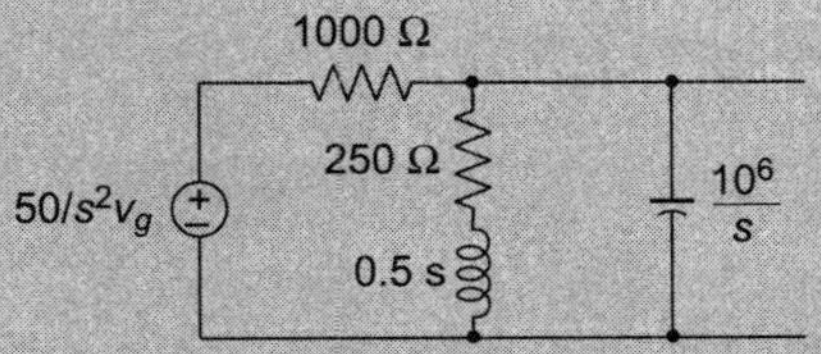

Figure 11.19

11.9 || NODAL AND MESH ANALYSIS IN *s*-DOMAIN

An electrical circuit in time domain can be converted into s-domain circuit by utilising above representation of circuit elements. The s-domain circuit, thus obtained, can be solved for any required quantity by using standard circuit analysis technique.

Following steps shall be undertaken for solving an electrical circuit in s-domain:

1. Re-draw the given electrical circuit using representation in s-domain.
2. Implement initial conditions, if any, of circuit elements
3. Use Kirchoff's current and voltage law to write nodal or mesh equations
4. Re-arrange the circuit equations to write in form of un-known variable
5. Take inverse Laplace transform of re-arranged equation and write un-known variable in time domain

Example 11.16

Find V_0 (t) of the circuit shown in Figure 11.20 using Laplace transform technique.

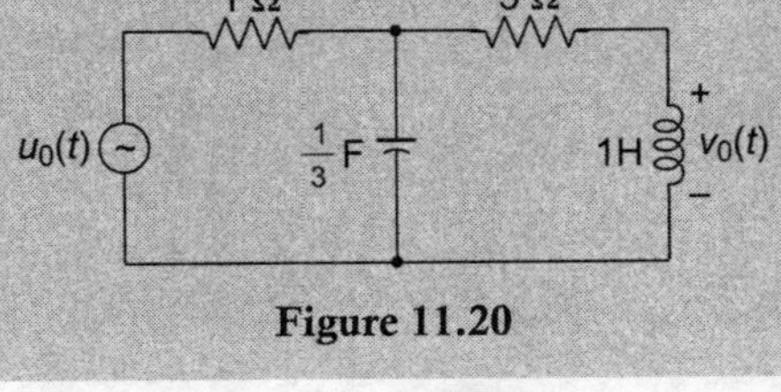

Figure 11.20

Solution Equivalent s-domain representation of the circuit elements are shown in Figure 11.21:

$$u(t) \to \frac{1}{s}$$

$$1H \to sL = s$$

$$\frac{1}{3}F \to \frac{1}{sC} = \frac{3}{s}$$

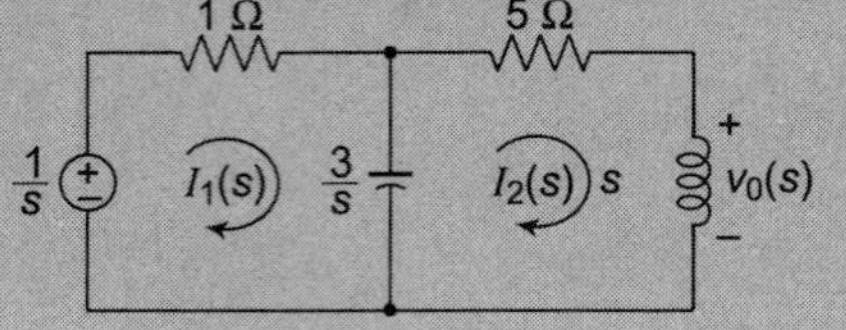

Figure 11.21

Following is the equivalent electrical circuit in s-domain.

Assuming currents in loop-1 and loop-2 are $I_1(s)$ and $I_2(s)$, writing mesh equations for both loops:

$$\frac{1}{s} = \left(1+\frac{3}{s}\right)I_1 - \frac{3}{s}I_2$$

$$0 = -\frac{3}{s}I_1 + \left(s+5+\frac{3}{s}\right)I_2$$

$$\therefore \qquad I_1 = \frac{1}{3}(s^2+5s+3)I_2$$

Solving equations (1) and (2) simultaneously:

$$\frac{1}{s} = \left(1+\frac{3}{5}\right)\frac{1}{3}(s^2+5s+3)I_2 - \left(\frac{3}{s}\right)I_2$$

$$3 = (s^3+8s^2+18s)I_2$$

$$\therefore \qquad I_2 = \frac{3}{s^3+8s^2+18s}$$

Voltage across inductor can be determined as following through use of Inverse Laplace transform:

$$V_0(s) = sI_2 = \frac{3}{s^2+8s+18} = \frac{3}{\sqrt{2}}\frac{\sqrt{2}}{(s+4)^2+(\sqrt{2})^2}$$

Example 11.17

Find V_0 (t) of the network shown in Figure 11.22 if in the initial voltage is given as $V_0(0^-) = 5$ V. ○●●

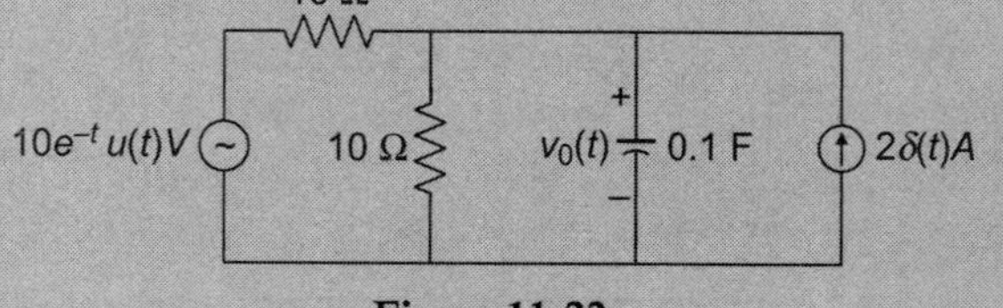

Figure 11.22

Solution Equivalent *s*-domain electrical circuit:

Applying nodal analysis in the circuit shown in Figure 11.23,

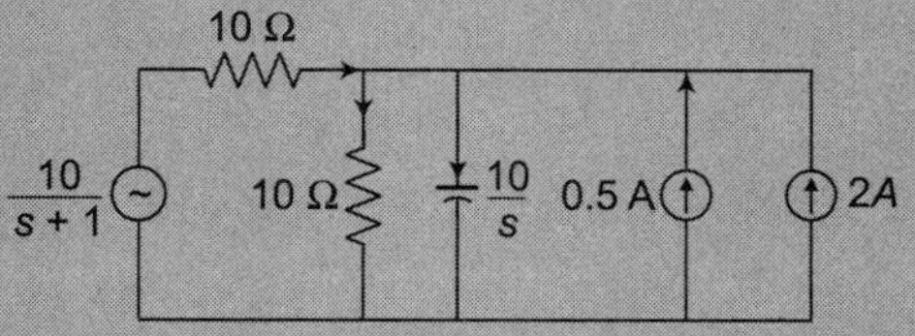

Figure 11.23

$$\frac{V_0 - \frac{10}{(s+1)}}{10} + \frac{V_0}{10} + \frac{V_0}{\frac{10}{s}} = 2 + 0.5$$

$$\Rightarrow \quad \frac{V_0}{10} - \frac{1}{s+1} + \frac{V_0}{10} + \frac{sV_0}{10} = 2.5$$

$$\Rightarrow \quad \frac{1}{10}V_0(s+2) = \frac{1}{s+1} + 2.5$$

Solving for $V_0\,(s)$ using partial fraction expansion:

$$V_0(s+2) = \frac{10}{s+1} + 25$$

$$\therefore \quad V_0 = \frac{25s+35}{(s+1)(s+2)}$$

$$V_0 = \frac{25s+35}{(s+1)(s+2)} = \frac{K_1}{s+1} + \frac{K_2}{s+2}$$

$$K_1 = 10;\; K_2 = 15$$

$$V_0(s) = \frac{10}{s+1} + \frac{15}{s+2}$$

Taking inverse Laplace transform of above expression:

$$v_0(t) = (10e^{-t} + 15e^{-2t})u(t)$$

11.10 || ADDITIONAL CIRCUIT ANALYSIS TECHNIQUES IN *s*-DOMAIN

The network analysis techniques and network theorems can also be applied to *s*-domain equivalent circuit of time-domain electrical network. This is illustrated using following examples.

Example 11.18

Determine $V_0(t)$ of the network shown in Figure 11.24, assuming zero initial conditions. ○●●

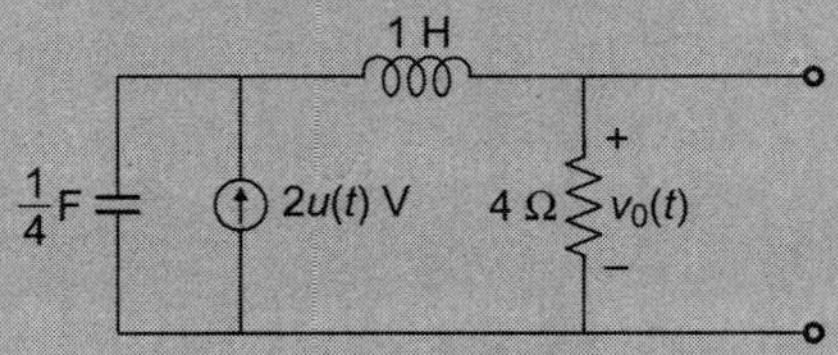

Figure 11.24

Solution Using current division (Figure 11.25),

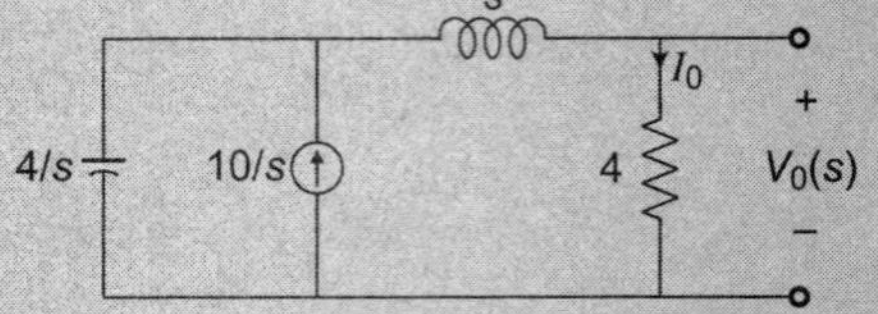

Figure 11.25

$$I_0 = \frac{\frac{4}{s}}{\frac{4}{s}+s+4}\cdot\frac{10}{s} = \frac{40}{s(s^2+4s+4)}$$

$$V_0(s) = 4I_0 = \frac{160}{s(s+2)^2}$$

$$\frac{160}{s(s+2)^2} = \frac{A}{s}+\frac{B}{s+2}+\frac{C}{(s+2)^2}$$

$$160 = A(s^2+4s+4)+B(s^2+2s)+Cs$$

Equating coefficients:

s^0 : $\quad 80 = 4A \longrightarrow A = 40$

s^1 : $\quad 0 = 4A+2B+C$

s^2 : $\quad 0 = A+B \longrightarrow B = -A = -40$

Hence, $0 = 4A+2B+C \longrightarrow C = -80$

$$V_0(s) = \frac{40}{s}-\frac{40}{s+2}-\frac{80}{(s+2)^2}$$

$$v_0(t) = 40(I - e^{-2t} - 2te^{-2t})u(t)V$$

Example 11.19

Consider the system shown in Figure 11.26 and obtain the equation of motion of mass using Laplace transform. Take m = 1 kg, c = 5 Ns/m, k = 4 N/m, and F = 2 N.

Solution Applying Newton's second law of motion $F = ma$, we get following equation

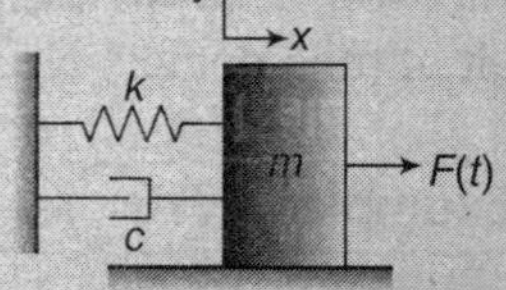

Figure 11.26

$$m\cdot\ddot{x}(t)+c\cdot\dot{x}(t)+k\cdot x(t) = F(t)$$

Taking the Laplace transform of both sides of the equation of motion gives

$$1\cdot s^2\cdot X(s)+5\cdot s\cdot X(s)+4\cdot X(s) = \frac{2}{s}$$

By rearranging this equation, we get

$$X(s) = \frac{2}{s\cdot(s^2+5\cdot s+4)}$$

Writing above equation as a sum of partial fractions

$$X(s) = \frac{2}{s \cdot (s+4) \cdot (s+1)}$$

Solving using Partial Fraction Method

$$\frac{2}{s \cdot (s+4) \cdot (s+1)} = \frac{A_1}{s} + \frac{A_2}{s+4} + \frac{A_3}{s+1}$$

$$X(s) = \frac{1}{2s} + \frac{1}{6 \cdot (s+4)} - \frac{2}{3 \cdot (s+1)}$$

and then taking Inverse Laplace Transform

$$x(t) = \mathcal{L}^{-1}\left[\frac{1}{2s} + \frac{1}{6 \cdot (s+4)} - \frac{2}{3 \cdot (s+1)}\right] = \frac{1}{2} + \frac{e^{-4 \cdot t}}{6} - \frac{2}{3} \cdot e^{-t}$$

Example 11.20

Consider the mixing system shown in Figure 11.27. Tank T_1 initially contains 100 liters of pure water. Tank T_2 initially contains 100 liters of water in which 150 kg of salt are dissolved. The inflow into T_1 is 3 kg/min from T_2 and 6 kg/min containing 6 kg of salt from the outside. The inflow into T_2 is 8 kg/min from T_1. The outflow from T_2 is 8 kg/min. The mixtures are kept uniform by stirring. Find the salt contents $y_1(t)$ and $y_2(t)$ in T_1 and T_2 respectively. ○●●

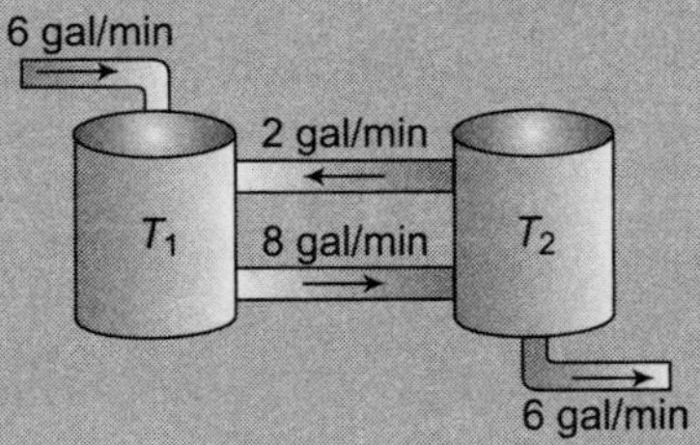

Figure 11.27

Solution Differential equation governing the salt concentration in both tanks can be obtained using the fact that

Time rate of change of salt concentration = Inflow rate – Outflow rate

$$y_1' = -\frac{8}{100}y_1 + \frac{2}{100}y_2 + 6.$$

$$y_2' = \frac{8}{100}y_1 - \frac{8}{100}y_2.$$

Taking Laplace transform for above equations

$$(-0.08 - s)Y_1 + 0.02Y_2 = -\frac{6}{s}$$

$$0.08Y_1 + (-0.08 - s)Y_2 = -150$$

Utilising Partial Fraction Method to solve above equations

$$Y_1 = \frac{9s+0.48}{s(s+0.12)(s+0.04)} = \frac{100}{s} - \frac{62.5}{s+0.12} - \frac{37.5}{s+0.04}$$

$$Y_2 = \frac{150s^2+12s+0.48}{s(s+0.12)(s+0.04)} = \frac{100}{s} + \frac{125}{s+0.12} - \frac{75}{s+0.04}.$$

and then taking Inverse Laplace Transform, we get

$$y_1 = 100 - 62.5e^{-0.12t} - 37.5e^{-0.04t}$$

$$y_2 = 100 + 125e^{-0.12t} - 75e^{-0.04t}$$

Example 11.21

Find $i_0(t)$ in the network shown in Figure 11.28 using Laplace transform.

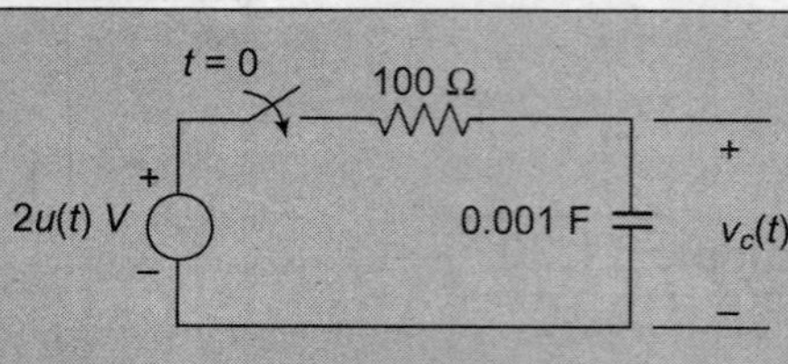

Figure 11.28

Solution Equivalent electrical circuit in *s*-domain can be obtained as shown in Figure 11.29,

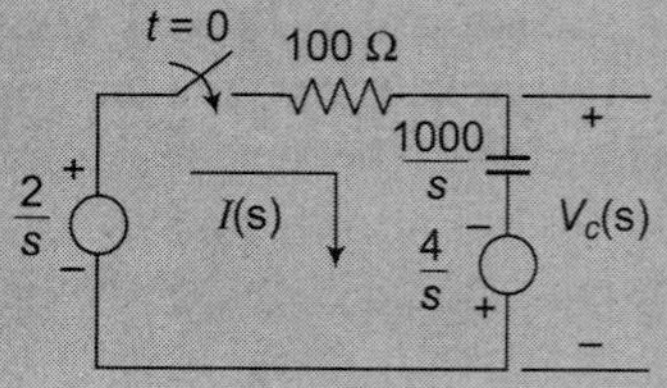

Figure 11.29

Writing KVL equation for above mesh:

$$\Rightarrow \quad \frac{2}{s} - 100I(s) - V_C(s) = 0$$

$$\Rightarrow \quad \frac{2}{s} - \frac{6}{s+10} = V_C(s)$$

$$\Rightarrow \quad V_C(s) = \frac{-4s+20}{s(s+10)} = \frac{A}{s} + \frac{B}{s+10}$$

$$\Rightarrow \quad V_C(s) = \frac{2}{s} - \frac{6}{s+10}$$

$$\Rightarrow \quad v(t) = \left[2 - 6e^{-10t}\right]u(t)$$

11.11 RMS AND AVERAGE VALUE OF PERIODIC WAVEFORM

The Root Mean Square (RMS) value of periodic waveform represented by continuous function $f(t)$ is defined over an interval $(T_1 \le t \le T_2)$ can evaluated using following formula:

$$f_{\text{rms}} = \sqrt{\frac{1}{T_2 - T_1}\int_{T_1}^{T_2} [f(t)]^2 dt}$$

The average value of any time-varying function over a time interval $\Delta t = T_2 - T_1$ is defined *as the integral of the function over this time interval, divided by* Δt.

The average value can be represented using following formula:

$$f_{avg} \equiv \frac{\int_{t_1}^{t_2} f(t)dt}{\Delta t} = \frac{1}{t_2 - t_1}\int_{t_1}^{t_2} f(t)dt$$

Example 11.22

Determine RMS values of the waveform shown in Figure 11.30. ○●●

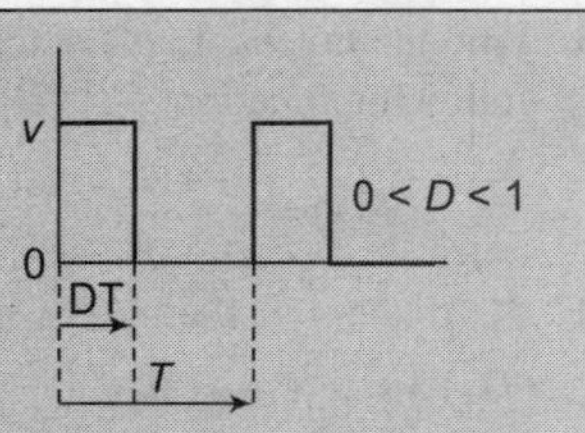

Figure 11.30

Solution Utilising formula for RMS value

$$V_{\text{rms}}^2 = \frac{1}{T}\int_0^T v^2(t)dt = \frac{1}{T}\int_0^{DT} V^2 dt = \frac{V^2}{T} \bullet DT = DV^2$$

$$V_{\text{rms}} = V\sqrt{D}$$

POINTS TO REMEMBER

☞ Laplace transform $F(s)$ of function $f(t)$ is evaluated using

$$\mathcal{L}[f(t)] = F(s) = \int_{-\infty}^{\infty} e^{-st} f(t)\, u(t)\, dt = \int_0^{\infty} f(t)e^{-st} dt$$

☞ Inverse Laplace transform $f(t)$ of function of $F(s)$ is evaluated using

$$\mathcal{L}^{-1}[F(s)] = f(t) = \frac{1}{2\pi j}\int_{-J}^{+J} F(s)e^{st} ds$$

☞ Function discontinuities are mathematically represented using step and impulse functions. A step function represents a function discontinuity while an impulse function enables us to define the derivative at a discontinuity.

☞ The magnitude of an impulse function represents area under the curve of the function. An important property of the impulse function is the shifting property, which is expressed as

$$\int_{-\infty}^{\infty} f(t)\, \delta(t-a)\, dt = f(a)$$

☞ A proper rational function is the one wherein the power of numerator in s is less than power of s in denominator. Only a proper rational function can be expanded as a sum of partial fractions.

☞ An improper rational function can always be expanded into a polynomial plus a proper rational function. The polynomial is then inverse-transformed into impulse functions and derivatives of impulse functions.

☞ Properties of Laplace transform allows to transform and inverse-transform the complex functions. These properties are listed in above section for reference.

PRACTICE PROBLEMS

1. Find the Laplace transform of the following functions. **[PTU, 2011-12]** ○●●
   a. $f(t) = \cos \omega t$ and $f(t) = \sin \omega t$
   b. $f(t) = \cosh at$ and $f(t) = \sinh at$

2. Determine the partial fraction expansion for ○●●

$$Y(s) = \frac{s^3 - 3s^2 + 6s - 4}{(s^2 - 2s + 2)^2}$$

3. Find the inverse Laplace transform for the following function. ○●●

$$F(s) = \frac{3s + 5}{s^2 + 7}$$

4. Find the Laplace transform of $f(t) = t^2 e^{-2x} \cos(3t)$ ○●●

5. Find the Laplace transform of $e^{3t}(t^2 + 4)$. ○●●

6. Find the Laplace transform of $e^{-3t} \sin 2t$. ○○●

7. Use ramp function to express the waveform shown in Figure 11.31, given that $t_1 - t_0 = t_2 - t_1$ ○○●

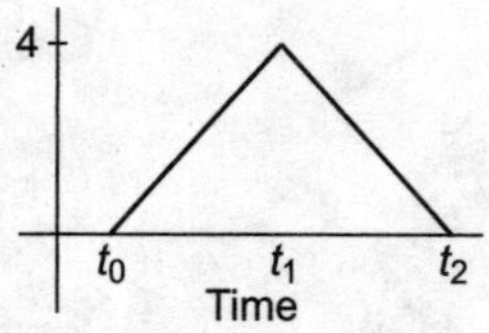

Figure 11.31

8. Consider the circuit shown in Figure 11.32. Find the value of the voltage across the capacitor assuming that the value of $v_s(t) = 10u(t)$ V and assume that at $t = 0$, -1A flows through the inductor and +5 is across the capacitor. ○●●

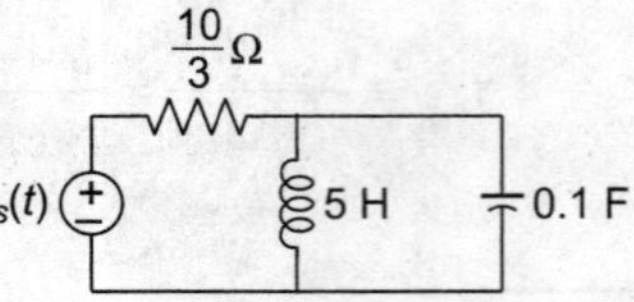

Figure 11.32

9. The switch shown in Figure 11.33 has been in position b for a long time. It is moved to position a at $t = 0$. Determine $v(t)$ for $t > 0$. ○●●

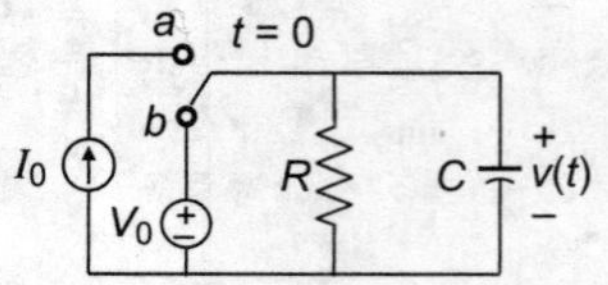

Figure 11.33

10. Find $i_0(t)$ of the network shown in Figure 11.34 using Laplace transform. ○●●

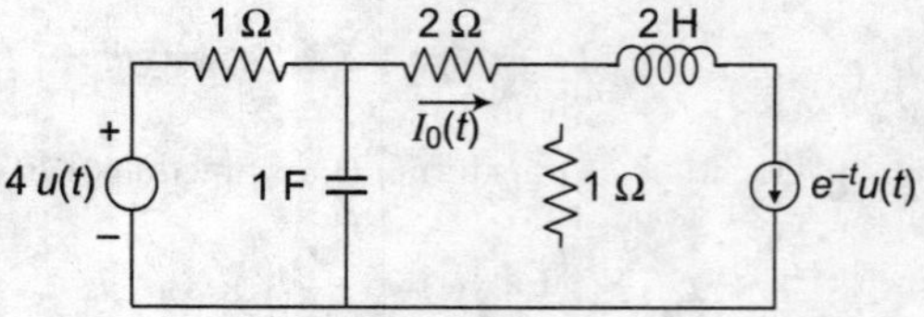

Figure 11.34

MULTIPLE CHOICE QUESTIONS

1. Laplace transform analysis gives ○○●
   (a) Time-domain response only
   (b) Frequency-domain response only
   (c) Both time- and frequency-domain
   (d) None

2. The final-value theorem is used to find the ○●●
   (a) steady-state value of the system output
   (b) initial value of the system output
   (c) transient behaviour of the system output
   (d) none of these

3. The average of a sinusoidal voltage wave over one half-cycle (with having maximum voltage V_p) ○●●
   (a) $0.637V_p$
   (b) $2V_p$
   (c) $0.577V_p$
   (d) $0.3V_p$

4. The RMS value of a triangular voltage waveform with 50% duty cycle and maximum and minimum amplitude V_p and $-V_p$ respectively is ○●●

(a) V_p (b) $2V_p$ (c) $0.577V_p$ (d) $0.3V_p$

5. The RMS value of a rectangular voltage waveform with 50% duty cycle and maximum and minimum amplitude V_p and $-V_p$ respectively is ○●●

(a) V_p (b) $2V_p$ (c) $0.5V_p$ (d) $0.3V_p$

ANSWERS TO MULTIPLE CHOICE QUESTIONS

1. (c) 2. (a) 3. (a) 4. (c) 5. (a)

12 Network Synthesis

Chapter Outline

- Definition of Hurwitz polynomial and the methods to determine it
- Exploration of positive real functions and the methods to evaluate them
- Foster I & II form using LC functions
- Cauer forms (I & II) using LC functions
- Realisation of RL, RC using foster and cauer methods
- Foster's reactance theorem

12.1 INTRODUCTION

Network synthesis is the study of synthesis of various networks consisting of active elements like resistors and passive elements like capacitors and inductors.

12.2 HURWITZ POLYNOMIAL

Probe

1. Define Hurwitz polynomial.
2. What are the properties of Hurwitz polynomial?

Hurwitz polynomial is a polynomial whose roots lie in the left half plane or in the imaginary axis, that is, real part of every root is zero or negative.

Consider the polynomial $F(s) = \dfrac{P(s)}{Q(s)}$

In which $Q(s)$ is a Hurwitz polynomial when the degree of $P(s)$ does not exceed the degree of $Q(s)$ by more than unity, and the polynomial should not contain multiple poles on $j\omega$ axis.

1. In the polynomial all the quotients should be positive.
2. In the polynomial should not contain any missing terms or else all even or odd terms are missing.
3. The roots of a Hurwitz polynomial either it is odd and even lie in $j\omega$ axis.

4. The polynomial is considered to be Hurwitz polynomial when all the quotients of continued fraction expansion are positive.

Example 12.1

Determine whether the polynomial $P(x) = x^4 + 10x^3 + 8x^2 + 7$ is a Hurwitz polynomial or not. ○○●

Solution The polynomial is not Hurwitz polynomial because the first term is missing.

Example 12.2

State whether the polynomial $f(s) = x^2 + 5x + 6$ is a Hurwitz polynomial. ○●●

Solution Yes, the given polynomial is a Hurwitz polynomial.

The roots of $x^2 + 5x + 6$

$$x^2 + 5x + 6$$

$$x^2 + 2x + 3x + 6$$

$$(x + 2)(x + 3)$$

$$x = -2, -3.$$

As the roots of the polynomial lie in the left half plane, it is a Hurwitz polynomial.

Example 12.3

Determine whether the polynomial is Hurwitz polynomial $P(x) = x^5 + x^3 + x$. ●●●

$$P(x) = x^5 + x^3 + x$$

$$P'(x) = 5x^4 + 3x^2 + 1$$

Solution:

$$\text{Even part} = 5x^4 + 3x^2 + 1$$

$$\text{Odd part} = x^5 + x^3 + x$$

Note: Difficulty Level ⟶ ○○● — Easy; ○●● — Medium; ●●● — Difficult

$$5x^4+3x^2+1)x^5+x^3\;\;+x(\frac{x}{5}$$

$$x^5+\frac{3}{5}x^3+\frac{x}{5}$$

$$\frac{2}{5}x^3+\frac{4x}{5})5x^4+3x^2+1(\frac{25x}{2}$$

$$5x^4+10x^2$$

$$-7x^2+1)\frac{2}{5}x^3+\frac{4x}{5}(\frac{-2x}{35}$$

$$\frac{2}{5}x^3-\frac{2x}{35}$$

$$\frac{30x}{35}$$

As the quotients of the polynomial are negative, it is not a Hurwitz polynomial.

12.3 POSITIVE REAL FUNCTIONS

The Function $F(s)$ is termed as Positive real function when it satisfies the properties of Positive real functions such as

1. The real part of the polynomial should be greater than unity.
2. The poles and zeros of the polynomial should lie in left half of the plane.

University Questions

1. What are the properties of Positive real functions?
2. Define Positive real functions?

[PTU, 2009-2010]

Example 12.4

Check the positive realness of the following function: **[BPUT, 2007]** ○○●

Solution

$$F(x)=\frac{(x+2)}{(x+1)}$$

$$F(x)=\frac{P(x)}{Q(x)}$$

The coefficients are real.

Poles of $F(x)$ are $(x+1)$ $\quad x=-1$

Zeros of $F(x)$ is $(x+2)$ $\quad x=-2$

As all the poles and zeros lie in left half of s plane, the given function is a positive real function.

Example 12.5

$$F(x) = \frac{x^2 - x - 8}{x^2 + 2x - 2}$$

F(*x*) is not real function because real par of numerator and denominator is less than zero.

Solution Poles of *F*(*x*)

$$x^2 + 2x - 2 = 0$$

$$= \frac{-2 \pm \sqrt{(4+8)}}{2} = \frac{-2 \pm 3.46}{2} = -2.732, 0.73$$

Zeros of *F*(*x*)

$$x^2 - x - 8 = 0$$

$$= \frac{1 \pm \sqrt{(1+(4 \times 8)}}{2} = \frac{1 \pm 5.74}{2} = -2.37, 3.37$$

As all the poles and zeros do not lie in left half of *s* plane, the given function is not a positive real function.

Example 12.6

$$F(x) = \frac{(2x+8)}{(x+8)}$$

Solution Poles of *F*(*s*) is $(x + 8)$, $x = -8$

Zeros of *F*(*s*) is $(2x + 8)$, $x = -4$

As all the poles and zeros lie in left half of *s*-plane, the given function is a positive real function.

12.4 FOSTER'S ONE AND TWO FORM FOR LC NETWORK

Foster's network is of two forms:

1. Foster first form or impedance form
2. Foster second form or admittance form

In the Foster's first form, or impedance form, there is a parallel LC circuit which is in series combination with capacitance C_0 and inductance L_∞ as shown in Figure 12.1.

The general equations for the Foster's first form is given by

Probes

1. What are the two forms of Foster's network?
2. Explain the Foster's first form or impedance form with a network diagram.
3. Explain the Foster's second form or admittance form with a network diagram.
4. What is the formula for determining the value of capacitor and inductor for the Foster's first form?
5. What is the formula for determining the value of capacitor and inductor for the Foster's second form?

$$Z(s) = \frac{P_0}{s} + \frac{2P_2 s}{s^2 + \omega_2^2} + \frac{2P_4 s}{s^2 + \omega_4^2} + \cdots + Hs$$

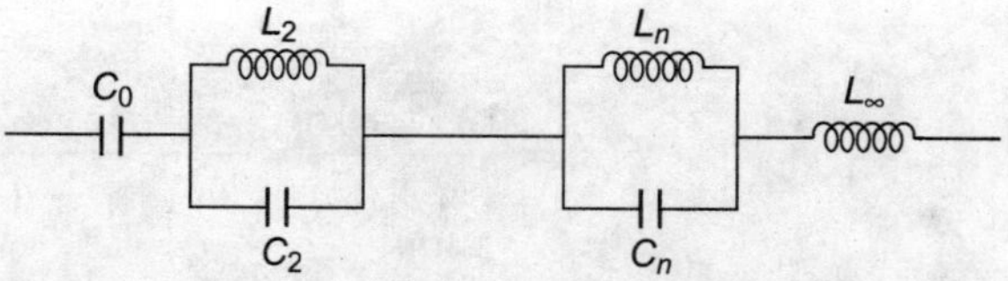

Figure 12.1 *Foster's first form or impedance form*

The value of capacitor $C_0 = \dfrac{1}{P_0}$

The value of inductor $L_\infty = H$

$$C_n = \frac{1}{2P_n} \text{ and } L_n = \frac{2P_n}{\omega_n^2}.$$

By comparing with the general equation to determine the middle terms of capacitor and inductor

In the Foster's second form or admittance form there is a parallel combination of series LC circuits with capacitance C_∞ and inductance L_0.

The general equations for the Foster's second form is given by (Figure 12.2):

$$Y(s) = \frac{P_0}{s} + \frac{2P_2 s}{s^2 + \omega_2^2} + \frac{2P_4 s}{s^2 + \omega_4^2} + \cdots + Hs$$

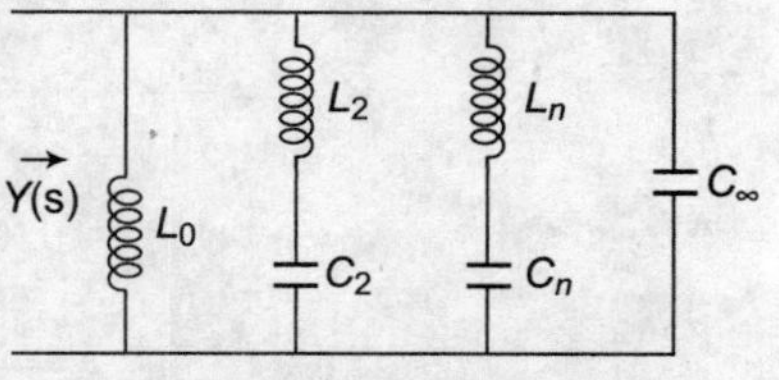

Figure 12.2 *Foster's second form or admittance form*

The value of capacitor $L_0 = \dfrac{1}{P_0}$

The value of inductor $C_\infty = H$

By comparing with the general equation to determine the middle terms of capacitor and inductor $L_n = \dfrac{1}{2P_n}$ and $C_n = \dfrac{2P_n}{\omega_n^2}$.

Example 12.7

Find the foster first and second forms for the function.

$$F(x) = \frac{(x^2+1)(x^2+16)}{x(x^2+4)}$$

Solution **Foster first form**

$$F(x) = \frac{(x^4+17x^2+16)}{(x^3+4x)}; \qquad Z(x) = \frac{(x^4+17x^2+16)}{(x^3+4x)}$$

Since extra term is present in the numerator compared to denominator the two poles exist at $\omega = 0$ and $\omega = \infty$ therefore L_∞ and C_0 are present.

$$x^3+4x)x^4+17x^2+16(x$$

$$\underline{x^4+4x^2}$$

$$13x^2+16$$

$$\frac{(x^4+17x^2+16)}{(x^3+4x)} = x + \frac{13x^2+16}{(x^3+4x)}$$

$$F(x) = \frac{13x^2 + 16}{(x^3 + 4x)} = \frac{A}{x} + \frac{Bx + C}{x^2 + 4}$$

$$13x^2 + 16 = A(x^2 + 4) + Bx^2 + Cx$$

To determine A, substitute $x = 0$

$$16 = 4A, \text{ so } A = 4.$$

Equating x^2: $A + B = 13 \Rightarrow B = 13 - 4 = 9$

$$C = 0$$

$$Z(x) = x + \frac{4}{x} + \frac{9x}{x^2 + 4}$$

$$Z(x) = \frac{P_0}{x} + \frac{2P_2 x}{x^2 + \omega_2^{\,2}} + \text{H}x$$

$$C_0 = 1/P_0 = 1/4 \text{ F}; L_\infty = 1 \text{ H}$$

$$C_2 = \frac{1}{2P_n} = \frac{1}{2P_2} = \frac{1}{9}$$

$$L_2 = \frac{2P_2}{\omega_2^2} = \frac{9}{4}$$

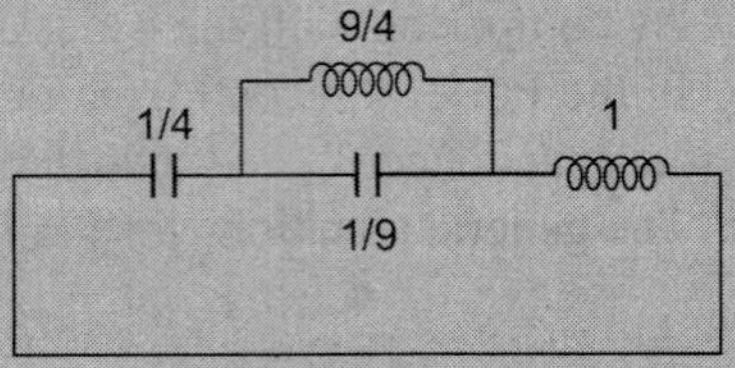

Figure 12.3 (a)

Foster second form

$$F(x) = \frac{(x^2 + 1)(x^2 + 16)}{x(x^2 + 4)}$$

$$Y(x) = \frac{x(x^2 + 4)}{(x^2 + 1)(x^2 + 16)}$$

$$Y(x) = \frac{Ax + B}{x^2 + 1} + \frac{Cx + D}{x^2 + 16}$$

$$x(x^2 + 4) = Ax + B(x^2 + 16) + Cx + D(x^2 + 1)$$

Equating the terms

x^3: $A + C = 1$;

x: $16A + C = 4$

$$A = 1/5 \text{ and } C = 4/5$$

x^2: $B + D = 0$

Const: $16B + D = 0 \Rightarrow B = D = 0$

$$Y(x) = \frac{x/5}{x^2+1} + \frac{4x/5}{x^2+16}$$

$$Z(x) = \frac{P_0}{x} + \frac{2P_2x}{x^2+\omega_2^{\,2}} + \frac{2P_4x}{x^2+\omega_4^{\,2}} + \text{Hx}$$

$$P_0 = H = 0$$

$$2P_2 = 1/5;\ \omega_2^2 = 1;\ 2P_4 = 4/5;\ \omega_4^2 = 16$$

$$L_2 = \frac{1}{2P_n} = \frac{1}{2P_2} = 5\,\text{H}$$

$$L_4 = \frac{1}{2P_n} = \frac{1}{2P_4} = \frac{5}{4}\,\text{H}$$

$$C_2 = \frac{2P_2}{\omega_2^2} = \frac{1}{5}$$

$$C_4 = \frac{2P_4}{\omega_4^2} = \frac{1}{20}$$

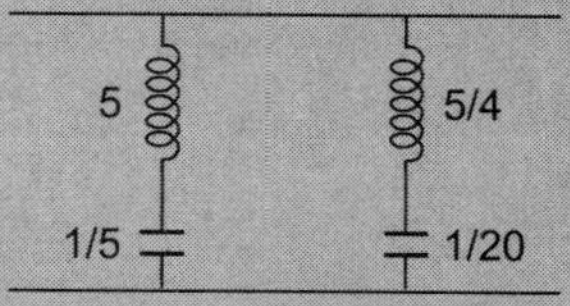

Figure 12.3 (b)

Example 12.8

Find the foster second forms for the function.

$$F(x) = \frac{(x^2+9)(x^2+49)}{x(x^2+36)}$$

Solution **Foster second form**

$$Y(x) = \frac{x(x^2+36)}{(x^2+9)(x^2+49)}$$

$$Y(x) = \frac{Ax+B}{x^2+9} + \frac{Cx+D}{x^2+49}$$

$$x(x^2+36) = Ax + B(x^2+49) + Cx + D(x^2+9)$$

Equating the terms

x^3: $A + C = 1;$

x: $49A + 9C = 36$

$A = 27/40$ and $C = 13/40$

x^2: $B + D = 0$

Const: $49B + 9D = 0$

$$B = D = 0$$

$$Y(x) = \frac{27x/40}{x^2+9} + \frac{13x/40}{x^2+49}$$

$$Z(x) = \frac{P_0}{x} + \frac{2P_2 x}{x^2+\omega_2^2} + \frac{2P_4 x}{x^2+\omega_4^2} + \text{Hs}$$

$$P_0 = H = 0$$

$$2P_2 = 27/40;\ \omega_2^2 = 9;\ 2P_4 = 27/40;\ \omega_4^2 = 49$$

$$L_2 = \frac{1}{2P_n} = \frac{1}{2P_2} = \frac{40}{27}\text{H}$$

$$L_4 = \frac{1}{2P_n} = \frac{1}{2P_4} = \frac{40}{13}\text{H}$$

$$C_2 = \frac{2P_2}{\omega_2^2} = \frac{27}{360}$$

$$C_4 = \frac{2P_4}{\omega_4^2} = \frac{13}{1960}$$

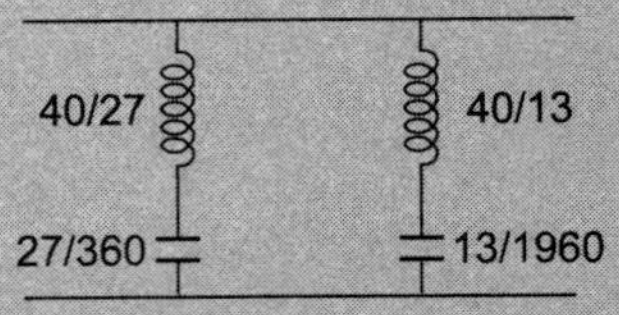

Figure 12.4

12.5 CAUER ONE AND TWO FORM FOR LC NETWORK

In the Cauer's first form (Figure 12.5), series arms are inductors and shunt arms are capacitors which is a ladder network.

In this method of continued fraction, when the driving point function consisting of poles are located at infinity, the first element is inductor and second element is capacitor. The fraction expansion of Cauer's first form is given by:

$$Z(s) = L_1 s + \cfrac{1}{C_1 s + \cfrac{1}{L_2 s + \cfrac{1}{C_2 s + \cdots}}}$$

Probes

1. Explain the Cauer's first form with a network diagram?
2. Explain the Cauer's second form with a network diagram?
3. What is the continued fraction expansion for Cauer first and second form?

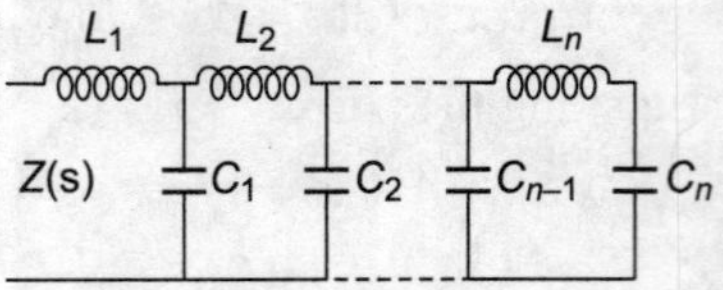

Figure 12.5 *Cauer's first form*

In the Cauer's second form (Figure 12.6), series arms are capacitors and shunt arms are inductors which is a ladder network.

In this method of continued fraction, when the driving point function consisting of poles are located at zero, the first element is inductor and second element is capacitor. The fraction expansion of Cauer's second form is given by:

$$Z(s)=\frac{1}{C_1 s}+\cfrac{1}{\cfrac{1}{L_1 s}+\cfrac{1}{\cfrac{1}{C_2 s}+\cfrac{1}{\cfrac{1}{L_2 s+\cdots}}}}$$

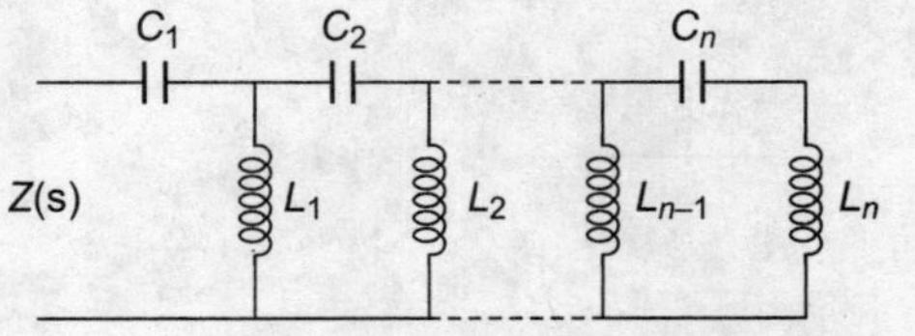

Figure 12.6 *Cauer's second form*

Example 12.9

Find the Cauer's first form for the function.

$$F(x)=\frac{10x^4+12x^2+1}{2x^3+2x}$$

Solution We can expand the function for Cauer's first form

$$2x^3+2x)10x^4+12x^2+1(5x \qquad L_1$$

$$\underline{10x^4+10x^2}$$

$$2x^2+1)2x^3+2x(x \qquad C_1$$

$$\underline{2x^3+x}$$

$$x)2x^2+1(2x \qquad L_2$$

$$\underline{2x^2}$$

$$1)\ x\ (x \qquad C_2$$

$$\underline{x}$$

$$0$$

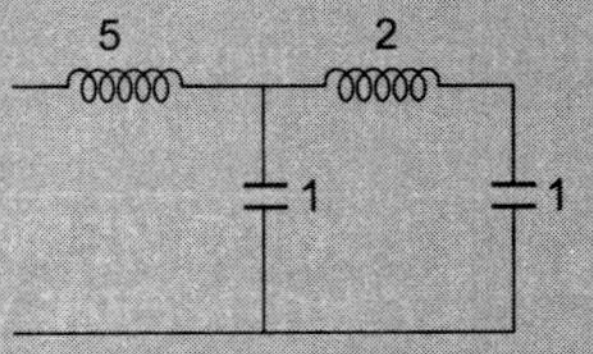

Figure 12.7

Example 12.10

Find the Cauer's second form for the function.

$$F(x)=\frac{2x^4+20x^2+16}{x^3+4x}$$

Solution

$$4x + x^3)16 + 20x^2 + 2x^4(\frac{4}{x} \qquad C_1$$

$$16 + 4x^2$$

$$16x^2 + 2x^4)4x + x^3(\frac{1}{4x} \qquad L_1$$

$$4x + \frac{x^3}{2}$$

$$\frac{x^3}{2})16x^2 + 2x^4(\frac{32}{x} \qquad C_2$$

$$16x^2$$

$$2x^4)\frac{x^3}{2}(\frac{1}{4x} \qquad L_2$$

$$\frac{x^3}{2}$$

$$0$$

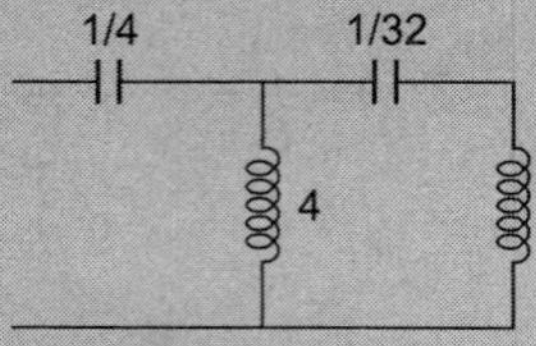

Figure 12.8

12.6 || REALISATION OF RL, RC USING FOSTER AND CAUER METHODS

1. Draw the RL network by Foster method.

(a) Foster first form

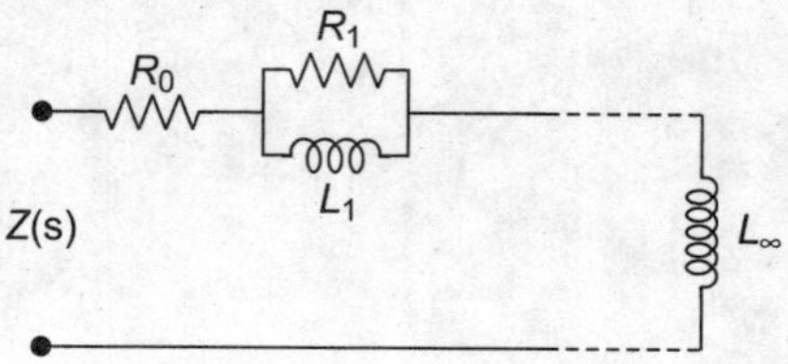

Figure 12.9

(b) Foster second form

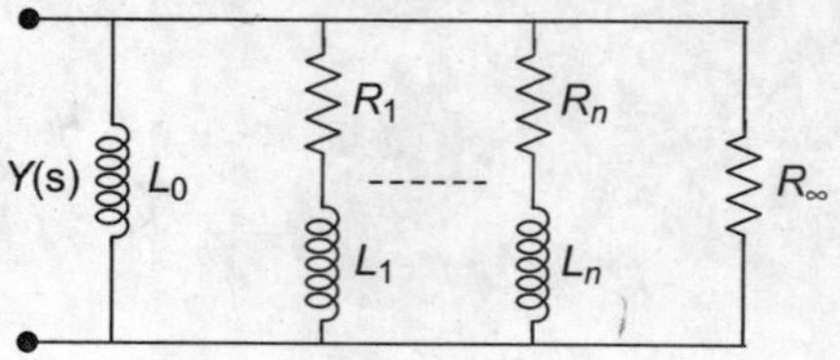

Figure 12.10

2. Draw the RC network by Foster method.

(a) Foster first form

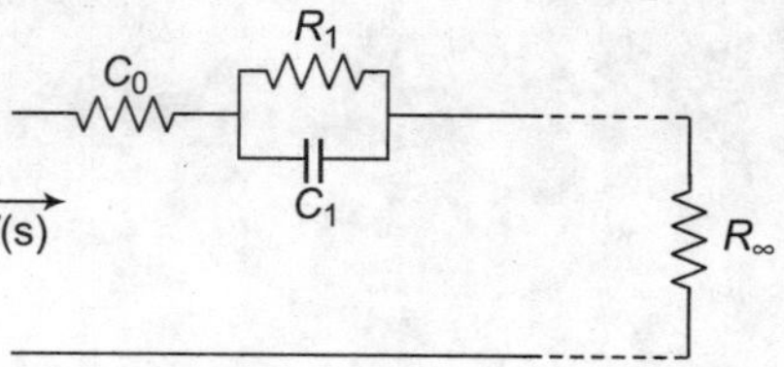

Figure 12.11

(b) Foster second form

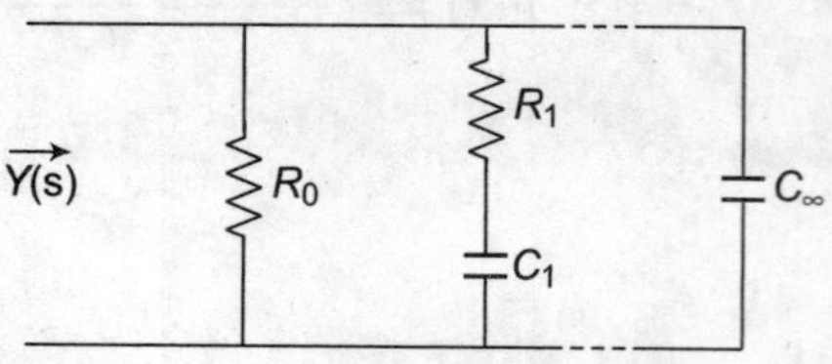

Figure 12.12

3. Draw RL network by Cauer method.

(a) Cauer first form

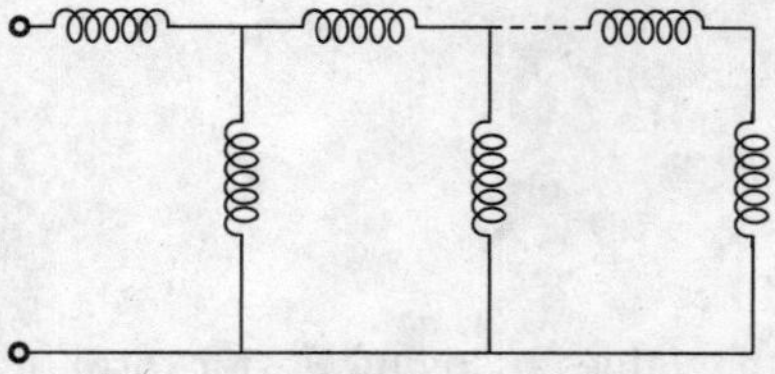

Figure 12.13

(b) Cauer second form

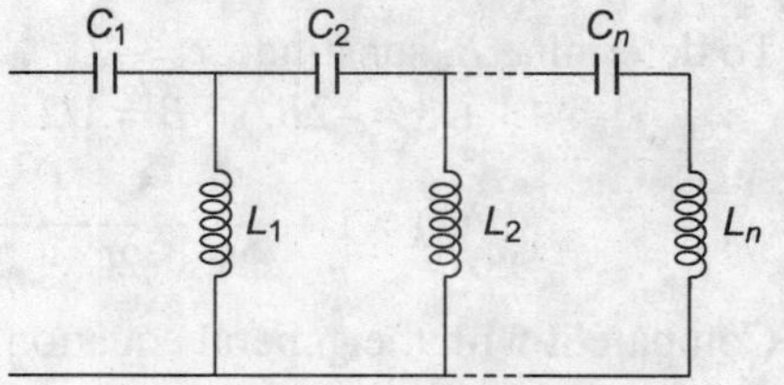

Figure 12.14

4. Draw the RC network by Cauer method.

(a) Cauer first form

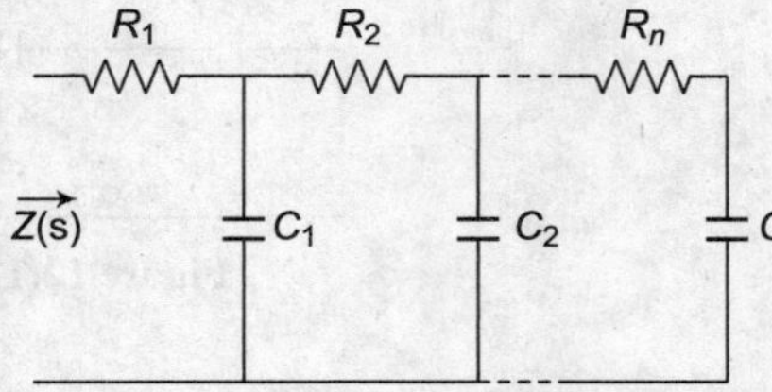

Figure 12.15

(b) Cauer second form

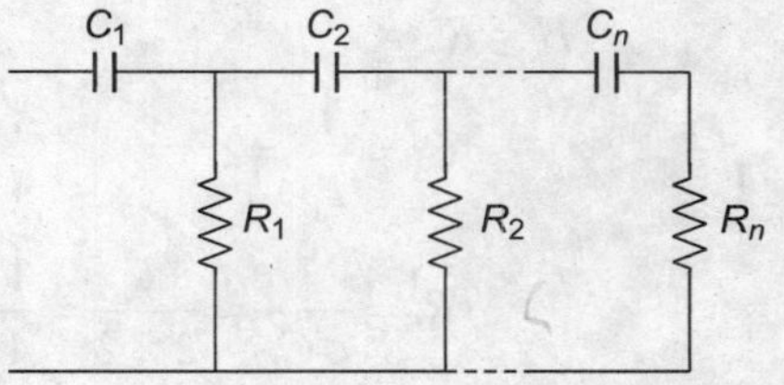

Figure 12.16

Example 12.11

Determine the foster forms for the function

$$F(x) = \frac{x^2 + 4x + 3}{x^2 + 2x}$$

Solution For Foster first form or impedance form

$$Z(x) = \frac{x^2 + 4x + 3}{x^2 + 2x}$$

Step 1: Take partial fraction expansion.

$$\begin{array}{r} x^2 + 2x)\,x^2 + 4x + 3\,(1 \\ \underline{x^2 + 2x} \\ 2x + 3 \end{array}$$

$$F(x) = 1 + \frac{2x + 3}{x(x + 2)} = 1 + \frac{A}{x} + \frac{B}{x + 2}$$

$$2x + 3 = A(x + 2) + Bx$$

To determine A, substitute $x = 0$

$$3 = 2A, \text{ so } A = 3/2.$$

To determine B, substitute $x = -2$

$$-4 + 3 = -2B, \text{ so } B = 1/2.$$

$$F(x) = 1 + \frac{3}{2x} + \frac{1}{2(x+2)}$$

Compare it with the general equation we obtain the values by using Foster form of RC network.

$$H = 1, P_0 = 3/2, \ P_1 = 1/2, \ \sigma = 2$$

Substituting these values, we obtain the value of capacitor and resistance.

$$C_0 = \frac{1}{P_0} = \frac{2}{3}$$

$$H = R_\infty = 1$$

$$C_1 = \frac{1}{P_1} = 2$$

$$R_1 = \frac{1}{\sigma C_1} = \frac{1}{2 \times 2} = \frac{1}{4}$$

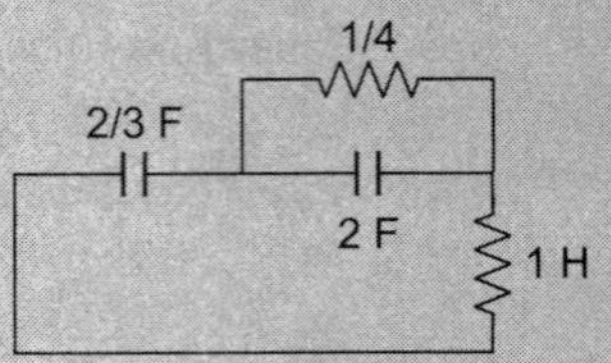

Figure 12.17 (a)

For Foster second form or admittance form

$$Y(x) = \frac{x^2 + 2x}{x^2 + 4x + 3}$$

Step 2: Take partial fraction expansion.

$$x^2 + 4x + 3)x^2 + 2x\,(1$$
$$\underline{x^2 + 4x + 3}$$
$$-2x - 3$$

$$F(x) = 1 - \frac{2x + 3}{x^2 + 4x + 3}$$

Since there negative quotient appears, we have to expand the equation as $\frac{Y(x)}{x}$.

$$\frac{Y(x)}{x} = \frac{(x+2)}{(x+1)(x+3)}$$

$$\frac{(x+2)}{(x+1)(x+3)} = \frac{A}{x+1} + \frac{B}{x+3}$$

$$x + 2 = A(x+3) + B(x+1)$$

To determine A, substitute $x = -1$

$$-1 + 2 = A(-1 + 3) \text{ so } A = 1/2.$$

To determine B, substitute $x = -3$

$$-3 + 2 = -2B \text{ so } B = 1/2.$$

$$Y(x) = \frac{x}{2(x+1)} + \frac{x}{2(x+3)}$$

Compare it with the general equation we obtain the values by using Foster form of RC network.

$$H = 0,\ P_1 = 1/2,\ P_2 = 1/2,\ \sigma_1 = 1,\ \sigma_1 = 3$$

Substituting these values we obtain the value of capacitor and resistance.

$$C_1 = \frac{1}{\sigma_1 R_1} = \frac{1}{2}; \qquad C_2 = \frac{1}{\sigma_2 R_2} = \frac{1}{6}$$

$$R_1 = \frac{1}{P_1} = 2; \qquad R_2 = \frac{1}{P_2} = 2$$

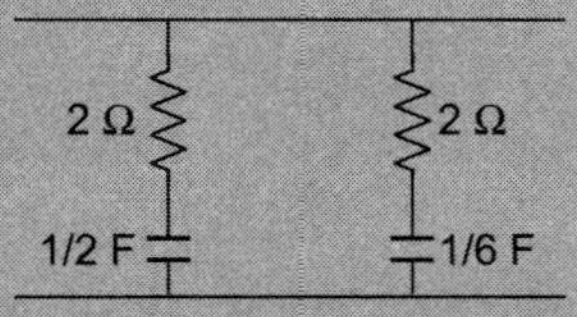

Figure 12.17 (b)

Example 12.12

Find the first and second Cauer form for the function.

$$F(x) = \frac{x^2 + 4x + 3}{x^2 + 2x}$$

Solution **Cauer first form**

$$x^2 + 2x)x^2 + 4x + 3\,(1$$

$$\underline{x^2 + 2x}$$

$$2x + 3)x^2 + 2x\,(\frac{x}{2}$$

$$\underline{x^2 + \frac{3}{2}x}$$

$$\frac{1}{2}x)2x + 3\,(4$$

$$\underline{2x}$$

$$3)\frac{x}{2}\,(\frac{x}{6}$$

$$\underline{\frac{x}{2}}$$

$$0$$

$$Z(x) = 1 + \cfrac{1}{\cfrac{x}{2} + \cfrac{1}{4 + \cfrac{1}{\cfrac{x}{6}}}}$$

$$= R_1 + \cfrac{1}{C_1 s + \cfrac{1}{R_2 + \cfrac{1}{C_2 s + \cdots}}}$$

By comparing with the standard equations, we decided as $Z(x)$ is constant at $x = \infty$, the first element is R_1.

$$R_1 = 1$$

$$C_1 = \frac{1}{2}$$

$$R_2 = 4$$

$$C_2 = \frac{1}{6}$$

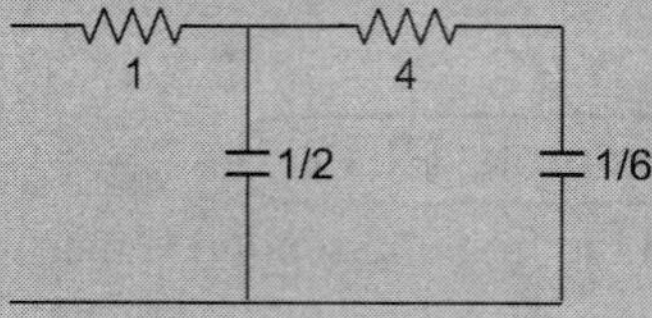

Figure 12.18 (a)

Cauer second form

$$2x + x^2)3 + 4x + x^2\left(\frac{3}{2x}\right.$$

$$\underline{3 + \frac{3}{2}x}$$

$$\frac{5}{2}x + x^2)2x + \quad x^2\left(\frac{4}{5}\right.$$

$$\underline{2x + \frac{4}{5}x^2}$$

$$\frac{1}{5}x^2)\frac{5}{2}x + x^2\left(\frac{25}{2x}\right.$$

$$\underline{\frac{5}{2}x}$$

$$x^2)\frac{1}{5}x^2\left(\frac{1}{5}\right.$$

$$\underline{\frac{1}{5}x^2}$$

$$0$$

$$Z(x) = \frac{3}{2x} + \cfrac{1}{\frac{4}{5} + \cfrac{1}{\frac{25}{2x} + \cfrac{1}{\frac{1}{5}}}}$$

$$Z(s) = \frac{1}{C_1 s} + \cfrac{1}{\cfrac{1}{\frac{1}{R_1} + \cfrac{1}{\frac{1}{C_2 s} + \cfrac{1}{\frac{1}{R_2} + \cdots}}}}$$

By comparing with the standard equations we decided as $Z(x)$ has pole at $s = 0$, the first element is C_1.

$$C_1 = \frac{2}{3}$$

$$R_2 = \frac{5}{4}$$

$$C_3 = \frac{2}{25}$$

$$R_4 = 5$$

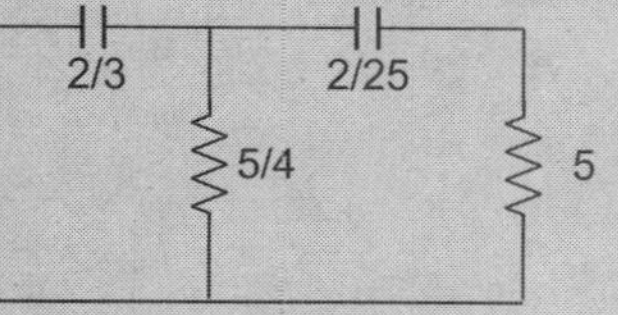

Figure 12.18 (b)

12.7 || FOSTER REACTANCE THEOREM

Foster Reactance Theorem states that the passive elements such as inductors and capacitors increase with frequency. The passive elements are frequency dependent.

Consider the impedance equation in which X changes with frequency

$$Z = ix$$

Consider the admittance equation in which X changes with frequency

$$Y = \frac{1}{ix}$$

Probe

1. What is Foster Reactance Theorem?

POINTS TO REMEMBER

☞ **In Hurwitz polynomial**

- All term should be in a polynomial.
- The quotients should be positive.
- All the roots lie in the left half plane of the axis, i.e the roots should be negative.

☞ **In positive real functions**

- All the poles and zeros lie in left half of *s* plane.
- Real part should be greater than unity.

☞ **In Foster method**

First form

- If pole is at $\omega = 0$ the first element is C_0
- If pole is at $\omega = \infty$ the last element is L_∞

Second form

- If pole is at $\omega = 0$ the first element is L_0
- If pole is at $\omega = \infty$ the first element is C_∞

☞ **In Cauer method**

First form

- The first element is series inductor when pole is at $\omega = \infty$.
- The first element is shunt capacitor when zero is at $\omega = \infty$.
- The last element is series inductor when zero is at $\omega = 0$.
- The last element is shunt capacitor when pole is at $\omega = 0$.

Second form

- The first element is series capacitor when pole is at $\omega = 0$.
- The first element is shunt inductance when zero is at $\omega = 0$.
- The last element is series capacitor when pole is at $\omega = \infty$.
- The last element is shunt inductance when zero is at $\omega = \infty$.

☞ **Foster method**

RL method

- First form

$$Z(s) = P_0 + \frac{P_i s}{s+\sigma_i} + \cdots + Hs$$

- Second form

$$Y(s) = \frac{P_0}{s} + \frac{P_i}{s+\sigma_i} + \cdots + H$$

RC method

- First form

$$Z(s) = \frac{P_0}{s} + \frac{P_i}{s+\sigma_i} + \cdots + H$$

- Second form

$$Y(s) = P_0 + \frac{P_i s}{s+\sigma_i} + \cdots + Hs$$

☞ **Cauer method**

RL method

- First form

$$Z(s) = sL_1 + \cfrac{1}{\cfrac{1}{R_1} + \cfrac{1}{sL_2 + \cfrac{1}{\cfrac{1}{R_2} + \cdots}}}$$

- Second form

$$Z(s) = R_1 + \cfrac{1}{\cfrac{1}{sL_1} + \cfrac{1}{R_2 + \cfrac{1}{\cfrac{1}{sL_2} + \cfrac{1}{R_3 + \cdots}}}}$$

RC method

- First form

$$Z(s) = R_1 + \cfrac{1}{C_1 s + \cfrac{1}{R_2 + \cfrac{1}{C_2 s + \cdots}}}$$

- Second form

$$Z(s) = \frac{1}{C_1 s} + \cfrac{1}{\cfrac{1}{R_1} + \cfrac{1}{\cfrac{1}{C_2 s} + \cfrac{1}{\cfrac{1}{R_2} + \cdots}}}$$

PRACTICE PROBLEMS

1. Determine whether the following polynomial functions are Hurwitz polynomial. ○○●
   (1) $P(x) = x^5 + x^3 + x^1$
   (2) $P(x) = x^4 + 6x^3 + 8x^2 + 10$
2. State whether the polynomial $f(s) = x^2 - x - 12$ is a Hurwitz polynomial. ○●●
3. Determine whether the polynomial $P(x) = 10x^4 + 2x^3 + 12x^2 + 2x + 1$ is a Hurwitz polynomial. ●●●
4. Check the positive realness of the following function. ○○●
   $$F(x) = \frac{(x+3)}{(x-1)}$$
5. Check the positive realness of the following function. ●●●
   $$F(x) = \frac{(x^2+3x+9)}{(x+5)(x+9)}$$
6. Find the foster first forms for the function. ●●●
   $$F(x) = \frac{(x^2+9)(x^2+45)}{x(x^2+49)}$$
7. Find the Cauer's first form for the function: ●●●
   $$F(x) = \frac{2x^4+20x^2+16}{x^3+4x}$$
8. Determine the foster forms for the function ●●●
   $$F(x) = \frac{2x^2+8x+6}{x^2+8x+1}$$
9. Find the second Cauer form for the function ○○●
   $$F(x) = \frac{4x^2+10x+6}{x^2+8x+1}$$
10. Find the first Cauer form for the function ○○●
   $$F(x) = \frac{x^3+6x^2+8x}{x^2+4x+3}$$
11. Determine the foster forms for the function: ●●●
   $$F(x) = \frac{x^2+10x+17}{x^2+7x+6}$$

MULTIPLE CHOICE QUESTIONS

1. Hurwitz polynomial has ○○●
   (a) poles only in the left half of s-plane
   (b) zeros only in the right half of s-plane
   (c) zeros anywhere in s-plane
   (d) poles in $j\omega$ axis only
2. The Cauer method is ○●●
   (a) continued fraction
   (b) partial fraction
   (c) Laplace transform
   (d) numerical method
3. The Foster's method is ○●●
   (a) continued fraction
   (b) partial fraction
   (c) Laplace transform
   (d) numerical method
4. In the first Cauer LC network the first element is series inductor when ●●●
   (a) poles at $\omega = \infty$
   (b) poles at $\omega = 0$
   (c) zeros at $\omega = 0$
   (d) zeros at $\omega = \infty$
5. In the second Cauer LC network the first element is series inductor when ●●●
   (a) poles at $\omega = \infty$
   (b) poles at $\omega = 0$
   (c) zeros at $\omega = 0$
   (d) zeros at $\omega = \infty$

ANSWERS TO MULTIPLE CHOICE QUESTIONS

1. (a) 2. (a) 3. (b) 4. (a) 5. (a)

Filters and Attenuator

13

Chapter Outline

- Characteristics of *T*-network and π-network
- Analysis and design of constant-*k* filters
- Analysis and design of *m*-derived filters
- Explanation of terminating half-sections
- Composite filters design
- Development of attenuators

13.1 || INTRODUCTION

Filter is an electric network used to block unwanted signals so that a signal with very less noise or no nose can be received. Filters are preliminary classified as active and passive filters. A filter designed with passive elements (i.e. R, L and/or C) is known as passive filter. Further classification is done on the basis of the frequency a filter allows to pass through. The chapter explains various types of filters and their characteristic parameters along with filter design methodology. Another important device, attenuator, is discussed in the later stage of chapter. Four primary attenuators have been explained for their working and design.

13.2 || CLASSIFICATION OF FILTERS

University Question

1. Explain how filters are classified. (Figure 13.1). **[PTU, 2008]**

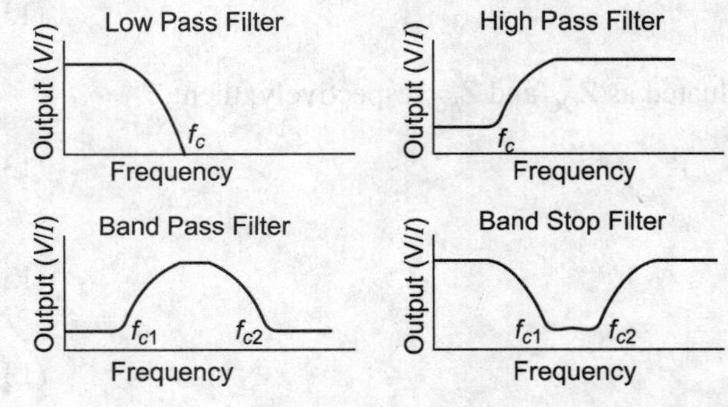

Figure 13.1

Filters are classified into five categories based on frequency bands passed through or rejected.

1. **Band-pass:** A band-pass filter allows passing through the signals of a particular frequency band and rejects signals of all other frequencies.
2. **Notch or Band-reject:** rejects signals of a particular frequency band but allows all other signals.
3. **Low-pass:** passes signals of low frequency, and rejects signals of frequencies above the filter's cut-off frequency.
4. **High-pass:** A high-pass filter passes signals of frequency higher than filter's cut off frequency and rejects low frequency signals.
5. **All-pass:** This type of filter passes thorough signals of all frequencies.

The simplest form of a filter can be realised with using a **Tor π-Network** and this is why, it is called prototype filter.

13.3 || *T*-NETWORK

University Question

1. Derive expression for characteristic impedance for *T*-section in terms of open and short circuit impedances.
[University of Pune, 2015]

A *T*-network is shown in Figure 13.2. We will now discuss its basic terminology

Characteristic Impedance

Suppose, we connect a variable impedance (Z) to the output port of a *T*-network and measure the input impedance (Z_{in}) of the network corresponding to the Z. For a particular value of $Z = Z_0$, the measured input impedance (Z_{in}) is equal to Z_0. This Z_0 is called characteristic impedance of the network.

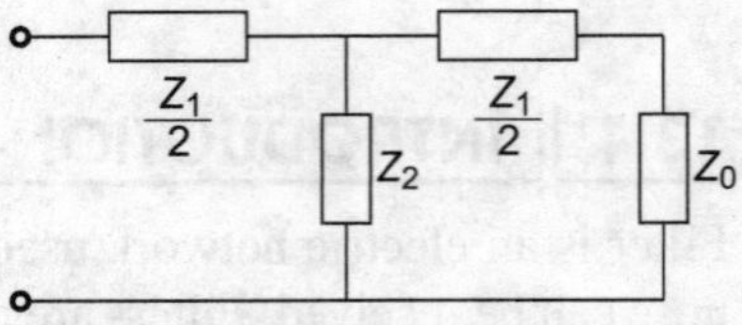

Figure 13.2 *Symmetrical T-Network*

For a *T*-network,

$$Z_0 = Z_{in} = \frac{Z_1}{2} + \frac{Z_2\left(\frac{Z_1}{2} + Z_0\right)}{Z_2 + \left(\frac{Z_1}{2} + Z_0\right)}$$

Solving this for Z_0 gives,

$$Z_0 = \sqrt{\left(\frac{Z_1}{2}\right)^2 + Z_1 Z_2} \tag{13.1}$$

If open and short circuit impedances are evaluated as Z_{OC} and Z_{SC} respectively, then:

$$Z_{OC} = \frac{Z_1}{2} + Z_2 \tag{13.2}$$

$$Z_{SC} = \frac{Z_1(Z_1 + 4Z_2)}{4Z_2 + 2Z_1} \tag{13.3}$$

$$Z_0 = \sqrt{Z_{OC}\, Z_{SC}} \tag{13.4}$$

Propagation Constant

For a two-port network, the propagation constant is defined as:

$$e^{\gamma} = \frac{I_1}{I_2} = \frac{V_1}{V_2} \Rightarrow \gamma = \log\left(\frac{I_1}{I_2}\right) \text{ or } \gamma = \log\left(\frac{V_1}{V_2}\right)$$

By applying KVL in the two loops and using the relations of Eqs (13.2) and (13.3) results:

$$\frac{(e^{\gamma} + e^{-\gamma})}{2} = 1 + \frac{Z_1}{2Z_2} = \cosh\gamma \tag{13.5}$$

$$\sinh\frac{\gamma}{2} = \sqrt{\frac{(\cosh\gamma - 1)}{2}} = \sqrt{\frac{Z_1}{4Z_2}} \tag{13.6}$$

$$(e^{\gamma} - e^{-\gamma})/(e^{\gamma} + e^{-\gamma}) = Z_{SC}/Z_{OC}$$

$$\tanh(\gamma) = Z_{SC}/Z_{OC} \tag{13.7}$$

Example 13.1

Find the characteristic impedance of a *T*-section as shown in Figure 13.3. Verify the value of impedance with the help of open- and short-circuit impedances. ○○●

Solution **Step 1:** Find open circuit impedance:

$$Z_{OC} = 100 + 400 = 500\ \Omega$$

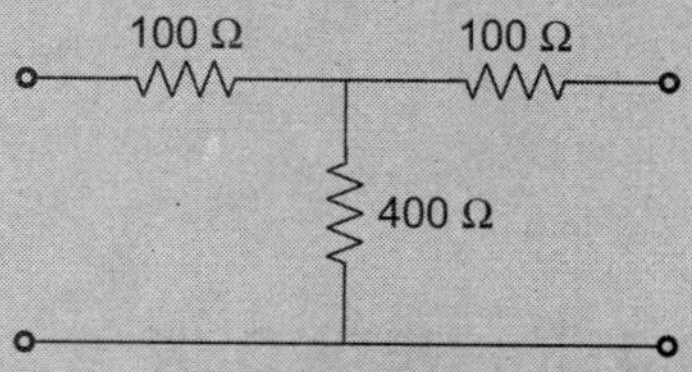

Figure 13.3

Step 2: Find short circuit impedance:

$$Z_{SC} = \frac{200(200 + 4 \times 400)}{4 \times 400 + 2 \times 200} = 180\ \Omega$$

Step 3: Determine Characteristic impedance:

$$Z_0 = \sqrt{Z_{OC} Z_{SC}} = \sqrt{500 \times 180} = 300\ \Omega$$

Step 4: Verify characteristic impedance:

$$Z_0 = \sqrt{\left(\frac{Z_1}{2}\right)^2 + Z_1 Z_2} = \sqrt{\left(\frac{200}{2}\right)^2 + 200 \times 400} = 300\ \Omega$$

Example 13.2

A symmetrical *T*-network consisting of pure resistances has open and short-circuit impedances of $Z_{OC} = 800 \angle 0°$ and $Z_{SC} = 600 \angle 0°$. Design a symmetrical *T*-network. ○●●

Note: Difficulty Level ⟶ ○○● — Easy; ○●● — Medium; ●●● — Difficult

Solution

Step 1: Write the expression for open and short circuit impedances and equate them to the given value:

$$Z_{OC} = 800 = \frac{Z_1}{2} + Z_2$$

$$Z_2 = 800 - \frac{Z_1}{2} \tag{13.8}$$

$$Z_{SC} = 600 = \frac{Z_1(Z_1 + 4Z_2)}{4Z_2 + 2Z_1} \tag{13.9}$$

Step 2: Solve the expressions for Z_2 and Z_1:

Substitute the Z_2 in Eq. (13.9) using Eq. (13.8),

$$600 = \frac{Z_1\left(Z_1 + 4\left(800 - \frac{Z_1}{2}\right)\right)}{4\left(800 - \frac{Z_1}{2}\right) + 2Z_1}$$

$$Z_1^2 - 3200Z_1 + 24 \times 8 \times 10^4 = 0$$

Solving above equation for Z_1

$$Z_1 = 800 \text{ Ohm}$$

and $Z_2 = 800 - 400 = 400$ Ohm

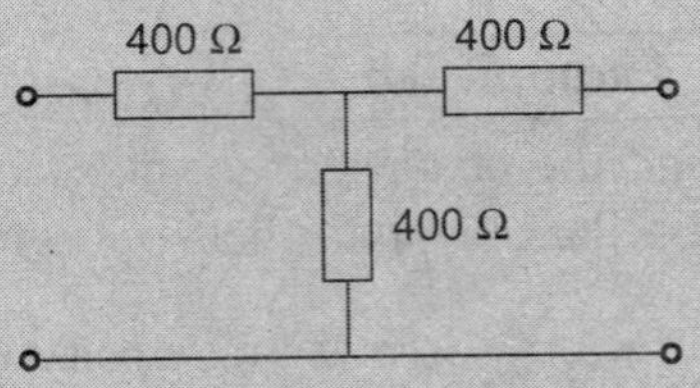

Figure 13.4

13.4 || π-NETWORK

Characteristic Impedance

A π-Network is shown in Figure 13.5. Similar to the *T*-network, Characteristic impedance for a π-Network, can be found by equalising the input impedance of the network to the impedance connected to the output port.

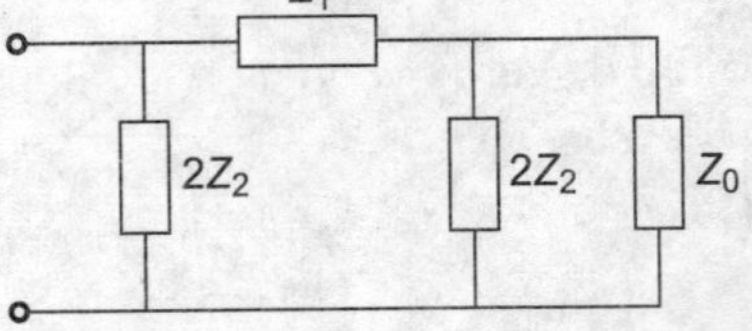

Figure 13.5 *Symmetrical π-Network*

$$Z_0 = Z_{in} = \frac{2Z_2(Z_1 + 2Z_2Z_0/(2Z_2 + Z_0))}{Z_1 + 2Z_2Z_0/(2Z_2 + Z_0) + 2Z_2}$$

Solving this for Z_0 gives,

$$Z_0 = \sqrt{\frac{Z_1Z_2}{1 + \frac{Z_1}{4Z_2}}} \tag{13.10}$$

If open and short circuit impedances are evaluated as Z_{OC} and Z_{SC} respectively, then:

$$Z_{OC} = \frac{2Z_2(2Z_2 + Z_1)}{4Z_2 + Z_1} \tag{13.11}$$

$$Z_{SC} = \frac{2Z_1Z_2}{2Z_2 + Z_1} \tag{13.12}$$

$$Z_0 = \sqrt{Z_{OC}\, Z_{SC}} \tag{13.13}$$

Propagation Constant

Same as of *T*-network as described in Section 13.3 under the heading Propagation Constant.

i.e. $$\cosh y = \frac{1 + Z_1}{2Z_2}$$

13.5 CHARACTERISTIC OF FILTERS

University Question

1. Define following terms: (a) Attenuation constant (b) Phase shift (c) Characteristic Impedance. **[PU, 2011]**

Following are the important parameters of a filter:

1. **Propagation constant:** Ratio of input signal value to the output is determined by propagation constant. It is denoted by γ.

$$e^{\gamma} = \frac{I_1}{I_2} = \frac{V_1}{V_2}$$

$$\gamma = \alpha + j\beta$$

2. **Attenuation (α):** A signal passing through a filter gets attenuated because of impedance of the filter. It depends upon signal frequency. For an ideal filter, attenuation for pass band is equal to **zero.**
3. **Phase shift (β):** Phase of the signal gets changed when it passes through the filter. This is determined by phase shift constant. It also is function of frequency. For an ideal filter, attenuation for pass stop band (attenuation band) is equal to 180°.
4. **Characteristic Impedance (Z_0):** It is the image impedance of filter.

We now will discuss different cases to evaluate the general terms of attenuation and phase shift for different regions. It is already described that for a filter designed with a *T* or a π network,

$$\sinh\left(\frac{\gamma}{2}\right) = \sqrt{\frac{Z_1}{4Z_2}}$$

$$\sinh\left(\frac{\alpha + j\beta}{2}\right) = \sqrt{\frac{Z_1}{4Z_2}}$$

$$\sinh\left(\frac{\alpha}{2}\right)\cos\left(\frac{\beta}{2}\right) + j\cosh\left(\frac{\alpha}{2}\right)\sin\left(\frac{\beta}{2}\right) = \sqrt{\frac{Z_1}{4Z_2}} \tag{13.14}$$

There are two case now:
Case-I: If $\alpha = 0$; i.e. signal is in pass band.
Equation (13.14) becomes

$$j\sin\left(\frac{\beta}{2}\right) = \sqrt{\frac{Z_1}{4Z_2}}$$

Taking the magnitude only, $\sin\left(\frac{\beta}{2}\right) = \sqrt{\left|\frac{Z_1}{4Z_2}\right|}$

$$\beta = 2\sin^{-1}\sqrt{\left|\frac{Z_1}{4Z_2}\right|} \tag{13.15}$$

Equation (13.15) gives phase shift of a signal for pass-band.
Case-II: If $\beta = 180°$; i.e. signal is in attenuation band.
Equation (13.14) becomes

$$j\cosh\left(\frac{\alpha}{2}\right) = \sqrt{\frac{Z_1}{4Z_2}}$$

Taking the magnitude only, $\cosh\left(\frac{\beta}{2}\right) = -\sqrt{\left|\frac{Z_1}{4Z_2}\right|}$

$$\alpha = 2\cosh^{-1}\sqrt{\left|\frac{Z_1}{4Z_2}\right|} \tag{13.16}$$

Equation (13.15) gives attenuation of a signal for attenuation-band.

Condition for Pass-band

Again, from Case-I, for pass band (i.e. $\alpha = 0$), $\sin\left(\frac{\beta}{2}\right) = \sqrt{\left|\frac{Z_1}{4Z_2}\right|}$

Since, $-1 < \sin\left(\frac{\beta}{2}\right) < 1$ and term $\frac{Z_1}{4Z_2}$ is negative, $\Rightarrow -1 < \frac{Z_1}{4Z_2} < 0$ or, $-1 < \frac{Z_1}{4Z_2} < 0$

This is the condition for pass-band.

Example 13.3

For a pass band filter, with series branch impedance $Z_1 = j\omega 5$, what should be the critical value of shunt branch impedance such that cut-off frequency is 2000 Hz. ○●●

Solution Given, $f_c = 2000$ Hz, $\omega_c = 2\pi f_c = 12566.37$ rad/s.

Step 1: Write condition for pass-band:

For pass band, $-1 < \dfrac{Z_1}{4Z_2} < 0$

At cut-off frequency, $\dfrac{Z_1}{4Z_2} = -1$

Or $Z_1 = -4Z_2$

Step 2: Find value of Z_1 at cut-off frequency:

$$Z_1(\omega = \omega_c) = j\omega_c 5 = j62831.85 \text{ Ohm}$$

Step 3: Find Z_2:

$$Z_1 = -4Z_2 \text{ or } Z_2 = -\frac{Z_1}{4} = -j\frac{62831.85}{4} = -j15707.96 \text{ Ohm}$$

(–sign shows that Z_2 should be opposite to Z_1, i.e. capacitive)

Now, since Z_2 is capacitive, $\dfrac{Z_2(\omega)}{Z_2(\omega_c)} = \dfrac{(\omega_c)}{(\omega)}$ or

$$Z_2(\omega) = Z_2(\omega_c)\frac{(\omega_c)}{(\omega)} = -j15707.96 \times \frac{12566.37}{\omega} = \frac{197.4 \times 10^6}{\omega} \text{ Ohm}$$

Example 13.4

For a filter, at certain frequency, if net series and shunt impedances (Z_1 and Z_2) are $j1000$ Ohm and $-j200$ Ohm respectively. Is the frequency in pass-band or reject band. Also, find attenuation if it falls in reject band.

Solution Given: $Z_1 = j1000$ Ohm and $Z_2 = -j200$ Ohm

Step 1: Write condition for pass-band and test given impedances for pass band:

For pass band, $-1 < \dfrac{Z_1}{4Z_2} < 0$

Here, $\dfrac{Z_1}{4Z_2} = \dfrac{j1000}{-j200} = -5$

Since, $-1 > \dfrac{Z_1}{4Z_2}$. It is in not in pass band.

Step 2: Calculate attenuation:

Attenuation, $\alpha = \cosh^{-1}\sqrt{\left|\dfrac{Z_1}{4Z_2}\right|} = \cosh^{-1}\sqrt{|-5|}$

13.6 || CONSTANT-*k* LOW PASS FILTER (LPF)

> **University Questions**
>
> 1. What are low-pass filter? Derive expression for cut-off frequency in terms of *L* and *C*. **[PU, 2015]**
> 2. Discuss how a constant-*k* low pass filter can be designed. **[PTU-EE201]**

Constant *k* filters are the simplest form of filters. These filters consist of *T* or π ladder network of passive elements.

A typical constant *k*-LPF (Low pass filter) can have any of two configurations shown in Figure 13.6.

Since the product of Z_1 and Y_2 of the *T* or π network (shown in Figure 13.6) is constant (real), it is called *Constant k Low pass Filter*. This is possible, if Z_1 is capacitive and Y_2 is inductive or vice versa.

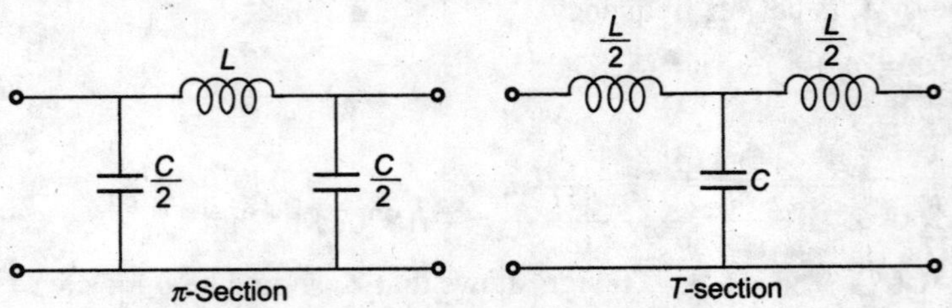

Figure 13.6 *Constant k-LPF*

For low constant *k* type pass filter, shunt arm of the network possess capacitor while series arm an inductor.

13.6.1 Filter Characteristics

Nominal Impedance, $k = \sqrt{Z_1 Z_2} = \sqrt{\dfrac{L}{C}}$

(a) Cut-off Frequencies

Since the pass-band for a *T* or π filter is given by $-1 < \dfrac{Z_1}{4Z_2} < 0$. So, for:

1. Lower Cut-off frequency (ω_{C-1})

$$\frac{Z_1}{4Z_2} = 0 \Rightarrow Z_1 = 0,$$

Z_1 is inductive reactance ($j\omega L$) here, which is zero only at $\omega = 0$ rad/s. $\omega_{C-1} = 0$; $f_{C-1} = 0$

2. Upper Cut-off frequency (ω_{C-2})

$$\frac{Z_1}{4Z_2} = -1 \Rightarrow \frac{j\omega L}{4\left(\dfrac{1}{j\omega C}\right)} = -1,$$

Solving this gives,

$$\omega = \frac{2}{\sqrt{LC}} \text{ rad/s}, \ \omega_{C-2} = \frac{2}{\sqrt{LC}} \Rightarrow f_{C-2} = \frac{1}{\pi\sqrt{LC}}$$

(b) Characteristic Impedance

1. If filter is designed with *T*-network:

$$Z_0 = \sqrt{\left(\frac{Z_1}{2}\right)^2 + Z_1 Z_2} = \sqrt{\left(\frac{j\omega L}{2}\right)^2 + (j\omega L)\left(\frac{1}{j\omega C}\right)} = k\sqrt{1-\left(\frac{f}{f_C}\right)^2}$$

2. If filter is designed with a π-network

$$Z_0 = \frac{Z_1 Z_2}{\sqrt{\left(\frac{Z_1}{2}\right)^2 + Z_1 Z_2}} = \frac{k}{\sqrt{1-\left(\frac{f}{f_C}\right)^2}}$$

(c) Attenuation (α)

$$\alpha = 2\cosh^{-1}\left(\sqrt{\left|\frac{Z_1}{4Z_2}\right|}\right)$$

Putting, $Z_1 = j\omega L$, $Z_2 = 1/j\omega C$ and $\omega_C = \dfrac{2}{\sqrt{LC}}$ in the above expression,

$$\alpha = 2\cosh^{-1}\left(\frac{\omega}{\omega_C}\right) = 2\cosh^{-1}\left(\frac{f}{f_C}\right)$$

(d) Phase Shift (β)

$$\beta = 2\sinh^{-1}\left(\sqrt{\left|\frac{Z_1}{4Z_2}\right|}\right) = 2\sinh^{-1}\left(\frac{f}{f_C}\right)$$

(e) Design Parameters

Value of filter circuit parameters (*L* and *C*) can be found from the cut-off frequency and nominal impedance.

$$k = \sqrt{\frac{L}{C}} \text{ and } \omega_C = \frac{2}{\sqrt{LC}}$$

Solving these for L and C gives,

$$L = \frac{2k}{\omega_C} \text{ and } C = \frac{2}{\omega_C k}$$

Example 13.5

A constant-k low-pass filter is designed to cut off at a frequency of 1000 Hz and the resistance of the load circuit is 50 Ω as shown in Figure 13.7. Find the attenuation constant per section at a frequency of 1500 Hz.

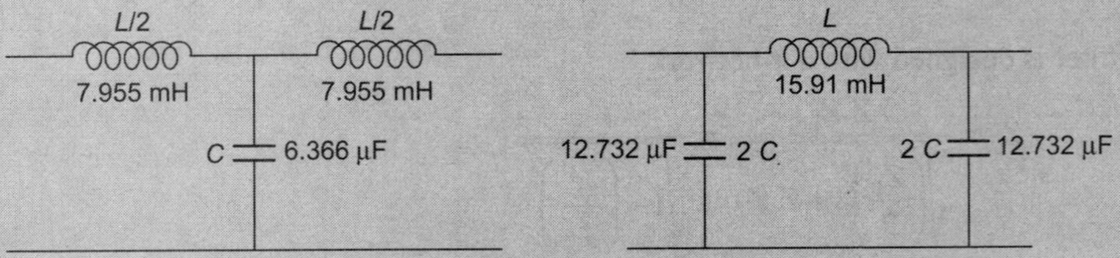

Figure 13.7

Solution Given, $k = 50\ \Omega$ and $f_C = 1000$ Hz, $f = 1500$ Hz

Step 1: Find values of L and C

$$L = k/\pi f = 50/(\pi \times 1500) = 15.91 \text{ mH}$$

$$C = 1/\pi k f = 1/(\pi \times 50 \times 1000) = 6.366 \text{ micro-F}$$

Step 2: Find attenuation coefficient:

$$\text{Attenuation constant, } \alpha = 2\cosh\frac{f}{f_c} = 2\cosh\left(\frac{1500}{1000}\right)$$

$$= 2 \times 0.962 = 1.9245 \text{ Nep}$$

Example 13.6

Design constant-k low-pass T- and π-section filters to be terminated in 600 Ω having cut-off frequency of 3 kHz.

Solution Given data, $R_O = 600\ \Omega$, $f_C = 3$ kHz $= 3000$ Hz

Step 1: Find values of L and C:

$$L = R_O / \pi f = 600/(\pi \times 3000) = 0.064 \text{ H}$$

$$C = 1/\pi R_O f = 1/(\pi \times 600 \times 3000) = 17.69 \text{ micro-F}$$

Step 2: Realise T-network and π-network (Figure 13.8):

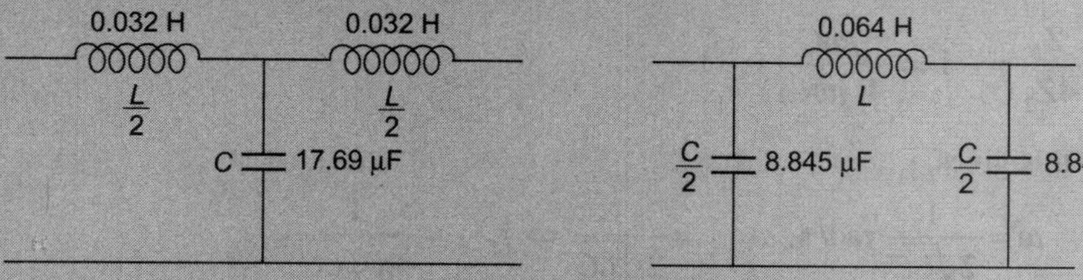

Figure 13.8

13.7 || CONSTANT-*k* HIGH PASS FILTER (HPF)

University Question

1. Give general configuration of constant-k high pass T and π network. Determine attenuation constant, phase shift. **[PTU, 2008]**

A constant k-HPF is shown in Figure 13.9.

Here, series arm has a capacitor while shunt arm has an inductor. So, Z_1 and Z_2 are interchanged. $Z_1 = 1/j\omega C$ and $Z_2 = j\omega L$.

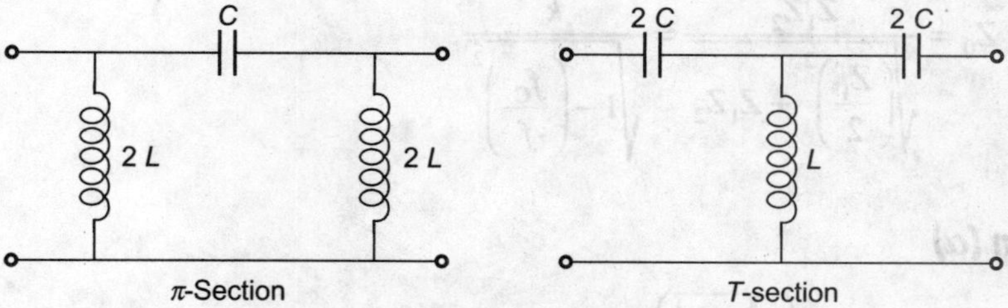

Figure 13.9 *Constant-k-HPF*

Filter Characteristics

$$k = \sqrt{Z_1 Z_2} = \sqrt{\frac{L}{C}}$$

(a) Cut-off Frequencies

Since the pass-band for a T or π filter is given by $-1 < \dfrac{Z_1}{4Z_2} < 0$. So, for:

1. Upper Cut-off frequency (ω_{C-1})

$$\frac{Z_1}{4Z_2} = 0 \Rightarrow Z_1 = 0,$$

Z_1 is capacitive reactance ($1/j\omega C$) here, which is zero only at $\omega = \infty$ rad/s.

$$\omega_{C-1} = \infty \Rightarrow f_{C-2} = \infty$$

2. Lower Cut-off frequency (ω_{C-2})

$$\frac{Z_1}{4Z_2} = -1 \Rightarrow \frac{\frac{1}{j\omega C}}{4(j\omega L)} = -1,$$

Solving this gives,

$$\omega = \frac{1}{2\sqrt{LC}} \text{ rad/ s. } \omega_{C-2} = \frac{1}{2\sqrt{LC}} \Rightarrow f_{C-2} = \frac{1}{4\pi\sqrt{LC}}$$

(b) Characteristic Impedance

1. If filter is designed with *T*-network

$$Z_0 = \sqrt{\left(\frac{Z_1}{2}\right)^2 + Z_1Z_2} = \sqrt{\left(\frac{j\omega L}{2}\right)^2 + (j\omega L)\left(\frac{1}{j\omega C}\right)} = k\sqrt{1 - \left(\frac{f_C}{f}\right)^2}$$

2. If filter is designed with a *π*-network

$$Z_0 = \frac{Z_1Z_2}{\sqrt{\left(\frac{Z_1}{2}\right)^2 + Z_1Z_2}} = \frac{k}{\sqrt{1 - \left(\frac{f_C}{f}\right)^2}}$$

(c) Attenuation (α)

$$\alpha = 2\cosh^{-1}\left(\sqrt{\left|\frac{Z_1}{4Z_2}\right|}\right)$$

Putting, $Z_2 = j\omega L$, $Z_1 = 1/j\omega C$ and $\omega_C = \frac{1}{2\sqrt{LC}}$ in the above expression,

$$\alpha = 2\cosh^{-1}\left(\frac{\omega}{\omega_C}\right) = 2\cosh^{-1}\left(\frac{f_C}{f}\right)$$

(d) Phase Shift (β)

$$\beta = 2\sinh^{-1}\left(\sqrt{\left|\frac{Z_1}{4Z_2}\right|}\right) = 2\sinh^{-1}\left(\frac{f_C}{f}\right)$$

(e) Design Parameters

Value of filter circuit parameters (*L* and *C*) can be found from the cut-off frequency and nominal impedance.

$$k = \sqrt{\frac{L}{C}} \text{ and } \omega_C = \frac{1}{2\sqrt{LC}}$$

Solving these for L and C gives,

$$L = \frac{k}{2\omega_C} \text{ and } C = \frac{1}{2\omega_C k}$$

Example 13.7

Design a constant-k high-pass filter with $f_C = 4$ kHz and design impedance $R_0 = 600\ \Omega$. ○●●

Solution Given data, $R_O = 600\ \Omega$, $f_C = 4$ kHz = 4000 Hz

Step 1: Find values of L and C:

$$L = R_O / 4\pi f = 600/(4\pi \times 4000) = 11.94 \text{ mH}$$

$$C = 1/4\pi R_O f = 1/(4\pi \times 600 \times 4000) = 0.003315 \text{ micro-F}$$

Step 2: Realise T-network and π-network (Figure 13.10):

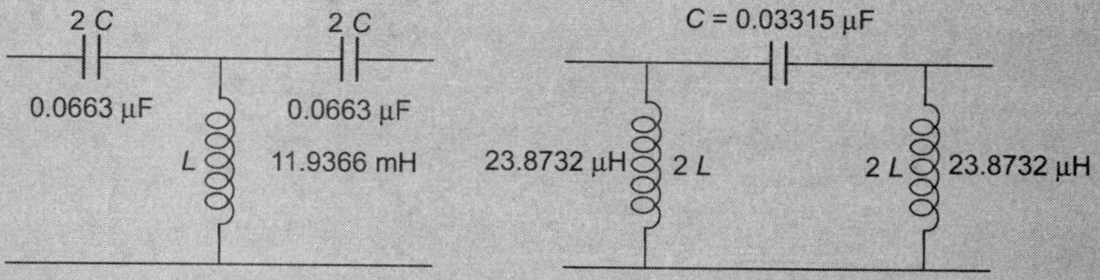

Figure 13.10

Example 13.8

Can you design an LPF and HPF for a cut-off frequency of 50 Hz? If you can, what are the values of the parameters? ○○●

Solution Yes, we can design a filter (HPF/LPF) for 50 Hz cut-off frequency provided the value of the design impedance R_o is being known.

Let us assume that value of design impedance = $R_o\ \Omega$

LPF: $L = R_o/\pi f = R_o/(\pi \times 50)$

$C = 1/\pi R_o f = 1/(\pi \times R_o \times 50)$

HPF: $L = R_o/4\pi f = R_o/4(\pi \times 50)$

$C = 1/4\pi R_o f = 1/(4\pi \times R_o \times 50)$

Example 13.9

A prototype high-pass filter has a cut-off frequency of 10 kHz and design impedance of 600 ohms as shown in Figure 13.11. Find the values of L and C. Also, find attenuation in dB and phase shift in degrees at a frequency of 8 kHz.

Solution $f_C = 10$ kHz, $K = 600\ \Omega$

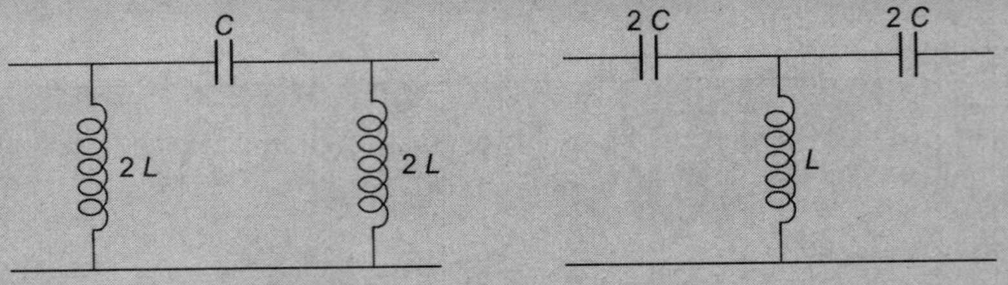

Figure 13.11

Step 1: Find out L and C:

Design Impedance, $K = \sqrt{\dfrac{L}{C}}$

$$K^2 = \frac{L}{C} = 600 \times 600 \tag{13.17}$$

Cut-off frequency, $f_c = \dfrac{1}{4\pi\sqrt{LC}}$

$$10{,}000 = \frac{1}{4\pi\sqrt{LC}}$$

$$LC = \frac{10^{-8}}{16\pi^2} \tag{13.18}$$

Solving Eqs (13.17) and (13.18) for L and C,

$$L = 4.77 \text{ mH and } C = 13.27\ \mu\text{F}$$

Step 2: Determine phase shift and attenuation:

$$\beta = 2\sin^{-1}\frac{f_c}{f} = 2\sin^{-1}\frac{10\,\text{kHz}}{8\,\text{kHz}} = 2\sin^{-1}\frac{10}{8}$$

$$\beta = 2\cosh^{-1}\frac{Z_1}{4Z_2}$$

13.8 || BAND-PASS FILTER (BPF)

University Question

1. Draw and explain constant-*k* '*T*-section band pass filter. [RU, 2006]

A band pass filter (BPF) designed with π-network and T-network is shown in Figure 13.12. Here series and shunt arms have both capacitor and inductor.

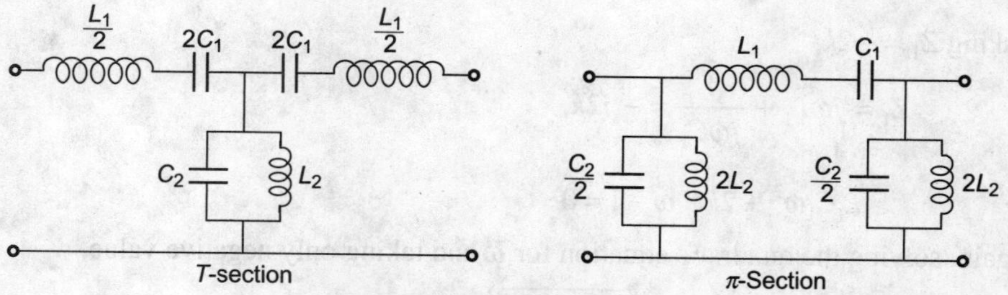

Figure 13.12 *Constant-k BPF*

If the circuit is expressed in terms of Z_1 (net series impedance) and Z_2 (net shunt impedance), then,

$$Z_1 = j\omega L_1 + \frac{1}{j\omega C_1} \text{ and } Z_2 = (j\omega L_2) \parallel \left(\frac{1}{j\omega C_2}\right) = \frac{j\omega L_2}{1-\omega^2 L_2 C_2}$$

For this filter to be a k-type band-pass filter,

$$Z_1 Z_2 = k^2 \Rightarrow \frac{L_2}{C_1} = \frac{L_1}{C_2} = k^2$$

This suggests that resonance frequency of series and shunt branch; $(1/\sqrt{LC})$ must be equal.

(a) Cut-off Frequencies ($\omega_{C-1}, \omega_{C-2}$)

For the pass-band, $-1 < \dfrac{Z_1}{4Z_2} < 0$:

So at cut-off frequency, $-1 = \dfrac{Z_1}{4Z_2} \Rightarrow Z_1 = -4Z_2$

Multiplying both sides by Z_1,

$$Z_1^2 = -4Z_1Z_2 \Rightarrow Z_1^2 = -4k^2$$

$$\Rightarrow \quad Z_1 = \mp j2k$$

1. Taking $Z_1 = + j2k$,

$$Z_1 = j\omega L_1 + \frac{1}{j\omega C_1} = j2k,$$

$$\Rightarrow \quad L_1 C_1 \omega^2 - 2kC_1\omega - 1 = 0$$

Solving the quadratic equation for ω and taking only positive value,

$$\omega = \omega_{C-1} = \frac{k + \sqrt{\left(k^2 + \frac{L_1}{C_1}\right)}}{L_1}$$

2. Taking $Z_1 = -j2k$,

$$Z_1 = j\omega L_1 + \frac{1}{j\omega C_1} = -\,j2k,$$

$$\Rightarrow \qquad L_1C_1\omega^2 + 2kC_1\omega - 1 = 0$$

Again, solving the quadratic equation for ω and taking only negative value,

$$\omega = \omega_{C-2} = -\left(\frac{k + \sqrt{\left(k^2 + \frac{L_1}{C_1}\right)}}{L_1}\right) = -\,\omega_{C-1}$$

(b) Resonant Frequency (f_0)

It is known that, at cut of frequencies, $Z_1 = \mp\, j2k$

This means that, $|Z_1|_{\omega = \omega_{C-1}} = |Z_1|_{\omega = \omega_{C-2}} = 2k$

$$|\,Z_1\,|_{\omega = \omega_{C-1}} = |\,Z_1\,|_{\omega=\omega_{C-2}} \Rightarrow \left|\left(j\omega_{C-1}L_1 + \frac{1}{j\omega_{C-1}C_1}\right)\right| = \left|j\omega_{C-2}L_1 + \frac{1}{j\omega_{C-2}C_1}\right|$$

(Resonance frequency of both series and shunt branch is same and given as, $\omega_0 = \frac{1}{\sqrt{L_1C_1}}$)

Simplifying the above relation with substituting $\frac{1}{\sqrt{L_1C_1}}$ with ω_0,

$$\omega_0 = \sqrt{\omega_{C-1}\,\omega_{C-2}}$$

(c) Design Parameters

We know that, at higher cut of frequencies, $Z_1 = +j2k$

$$j\omega_{C-2}L_1 + \frac{1}{j\omega_{C-2}C_1} = +j2k \tag{13.19}$$

Now, in order to find C_1, L_1 can be replaced with resonant frequency,

$$\omega_0 = \frac{1}{\sqrt{L_1C_1}} \Rightarrow L_1 = \frac{1}{(\omega_0{}^2C_1)}$$

Substituting L_1 now in Eq. (13.19),

$$C_1 = \frac{(\omega_{C-1} - \omega_{C-2})}{k16(\pi\omega_0)^2}$$

$$C_1 = \frac{(f_{C-1} - f_{C-2})}{k4\pi\omega_0^2}$$

And $$L_1 = \frac{1}{\omega_0^2 C_1}$$

L_2, C_2 are found now using the relations: $L_1/L_2 = C_2/C_2 = k^2$

$$C_2 = \frac{1}{k\pi(f_{C-1} - f_{C-2})}$$

$$L_2 = \frac{k(f_{C-1} - f_{C-2})}{4\pi f_0^2}$$

Example 13.10

In a series resonance type band pass filter, L = 60 mH, C = 150 nF, and R = 70 Ω. Determine (a) resonance frequency, (b) bandwidth, and (c) cut-off frequencies. Assume the resistance to be 600 Ω.

Solution

(a) Resonance frequency $f_r = \frac{1}{2\pi\sqrt{LC}} = \frac{1}{2\pi\sqrt{60\times10^{-3}\times150\times10^{-9}}} = 1677.64$ Hz

(b) Bandwidth, BW $= \frac{R}{2\pi L} = \frac{600+70}{2\pi(60\times10^{-3})} = 1777.23$ Hz

(c) Lower frequency limit $= f_1 = f_r - \frac{R}{4\pi L} = 1677.64 - 888.6 = 789$ Hz

Higher frequency limit $= f_2 = f_r + \frac{R}{4\pi L} = 2566.24$ Hz

Example 13.11

For a T-section constant-k BPF, find out: (a) Design Impedance (b) Higher and Lower cut-off frequencies (c) Resonance frequency. Design parameters are: L_1 = 15.915 mH, L_2 = 7.716 mH, C_1 = 0.1929 μF, C_2 = 0.3979 μF.

Solution

(a) Design Impedance $\sqrt{\left(\frac{L_1}{C_2}\right)} = \sqrt{\left(\frac{L_2}{C_1}\right)} = \sqrt{\left(\frac{15.915\times10^{-3}}{0.3979\times10^{-6}}\right)} = 200$ Ohm

(b) Cut-off frequency,

$$\omega_1 = \left(\frac{k + \sqrt{\left(k^2 + \frac{L_1}{C_1}\right)}}{L_1}\right) \Rightarrow f_1 = \frac{1}{2\pi}\left(\frac{k + \sqrt{\left(k^2 + \frac{L_1}{C_1}\right)}}{L_1}\right) = \frac{1}{2\pi}\left(\frac{200 + 350}{0.015915}\right) = 5502 \text{ Hz}$$

Cut-off frequency,

$$\omega_2 = \left(\frac{-k + \sqrt{\left(k^2 + \frac{L_1}{C_1}\right)}}{L_1}\right) \Rightarrow f_2 = \frac{1}{2\pi}\left(\frac{-k + \sqrt{\left(k^2 + \frac{L_1}{C_1}\right)}}{L_1}\right) = \frac{1}{2\pi}\left(\frac{-200 + 350}{0.015915}\right) = 1500.8 \text{ Hz}$$

(c) Resonance frequency, $f_0 = \sqrt{(f_2 f_1)} = f_0 = \sqrt{(5502 \times 1500.8)} = 2873.57$ Hz

13.9 || BAND-STOP FILTER (BSF)

A band stop filter (BSF) designed with π-network and T-network is shown in Figure 13.13.

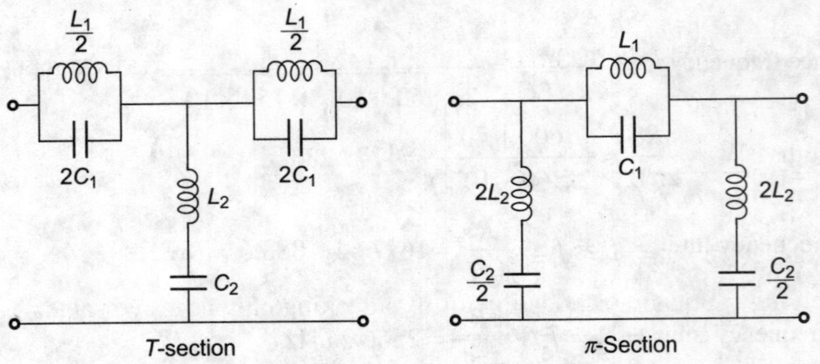

Figure 13.13 *Constant-k BSF*

If the circuit is expressed in terms of Z_1 (net series impedance) and Z_2 (net shunt impedance), then,

$$Z_1 = (j\omega L_1) \,||\, \left(\frac{1}{j\omega C_1}\right) = \frac{j\omega L_1}{1 - \omega^2 L_1 C_1} \quad \text{and} \quad Z_2 = j\omega L_2 + \frac{1}{j\omega C_2}$$

For this filter to be a k-type band-stop filter,

$$Z_1 Z_2 = k^2 \Rightarrow \frac{L_2}{C_1} = \frac{L_1}{C_2} = k^2$$

This suggests that L_1, C_1 and L_2, C_2 are to be selected such that resonance frequency of series and shunt branch; $(1/\sqrt{LC})$ are equal.

(a) Cut-off Frequencies (ω_{C-1}, ω_{C-2}):

For the pass-band, $-1 < \dfrac{Z_1}{4Z_2} < 0$

So at cut-off frequency, $-1 = \dfrac{Z_1}{4Z_2} \Rightarrow Z_1 = -4Z_2$

Similar to Band pass filter, cut-off frequencies are found by:

1. Taking $Z_1 = +j2k$,

$$Z_1 = (j\omega L_1) \,||\, \left(\frac{1}{j\omega C_1}\right) = j2k,$$

$$Z_1 = \frac{j\omega L_1}{1-\omega^2 L_1 C_1} = j2k,$$

$$\Rightarrow \quad 2kL_1C_1\omega^2 + L_1\omega - 2k = 0$$

Solving the quadratic equation for ω and taking only positive value,

$$\omega = \omega_{C-1} = \frac{-1 + \sqrt{\left(1 + 16k^2 \dfrac{C_1}{L_1}\right)}}{8\pi k C_1}$$

2. Taking $Z_1 = -j2k$,

$$Z_1 = \frac{j\omega L_1}{1-\omega^2 L_1 C_1} = -j2k,$$

$$\Rightarrow \quad 2kL_1C_1\omega^2 - L_1\omega - 2k = 0$$

Again, solving the quadratic equation for ω and taking only negative value,

$$\omega = \omega_{C-2} = \frac{1 + \sqrt{\left(1 + 16k^2 \dfrac{C_1}{L_1}\right)}}{8\pi k C_1}$$

(b) Resonant Frequency (f_o)

It is known that, at cut of frequencies, $Z_1 = \mp j2k$

This means that, $|Z_1|_{\omega=\omega_{C-1}} = |Z_1|_{\omega=\omega_{C-2}} = 2k$

$$|Z_1|_{\omega=\omega_{C-1}} = |Z_1|_{\omega=\omega_{C-2}} \Rightarrow \left|\frac{j\omega_{C-1}L_1}{1-\omega_{C-1}{}^2 L_1C_1}\right| = \left|\frac{j\omega_{C-2}L_1}{1-\omega_{C-2}{}^2 L_1C_1}\right|$$

(Resonance frequency of both series and shunt branch is same and given as, $\omega_0 = \frac{1}{\sqrt{L_1 C_1}}$)

Simplifying the above relation with substituting $\frac{1}{\sqrt{L_1 C_1}}$ with ω_0, $\omega_0 = \sqrt{\omega_{C-1}\,\omega_{C-2}}$

(c) Design Parameters

We know that, at lower cut of frequencies, $Z_1 = -j2k$

$$\frac{j\omega_{C-2}L_1}{1-\omega_{C-2}^{\ 2}L_1C_1} = -j2k \tag{13.20}$$

Now, in order to find C_1, L_1 can be replaced with resonant frequency,

$$\omega_0 = \frac{1}{\sqrt{L_1C_1}} \Rightarrow L_1 = \frac{1}{(\omega_0^{\ 2}C_1)}$$

Substituting L_1 now in Eq. (13.20),

$$C_1 = \frac{1}{2k\,(\omega_{C-1}-\omega_{C-2})},\; L_1 = \frac{1}{\omega_0^{\ 2}C_1}$$

L_2, C_2 are found now using the relations:

$$\frac{L_1}{L_2} = \frac{C_2}{C_2} = k^2,\; C_2 = \frac{(f_{C-2}-f_{C-1})}{k\pi f_{C-1}f_{C-2}},\; L_2 = \frac{k}{4\pi(f_{C-2}-f_{C-1})}$$

Example 13.12

Design a passive constant k-type band stop filter having a design impedance of 100 Ω and cut-off frequency 2000 Hz and 5000 Hz.

Solution Given $k = 100\ \Omega$; $f_1 = 2000$ Hz; $f_2 = 5000$ Hz, $f_0 = \sqrt{(f_2 f_1)} = 3162.27$ Hz

Design parameters for a BSF are given as:

$$C_1 = \frac{1}{2k\,(\omega_2-\omega_1)} = \frac{1}{4\pi k(f_2-f_1)} = \frac{1}{4\pi\times 100(5000-2000)} = 0.265\ \mu\text{F}$$

$$L_1 = \frac{1}{\omega_0^{\ 2}C_1} = \frac{1}{4\pi^2\times 3162.27^2\times 0.265\times 10^{-6}} = 9.626\ \text{mH}$$

$$C_2 = \frac{(f_2-f_1)}{k\pi f_1 f_2} = \frac{(5000-2000)}{100\times\pi\times 5000\times 2000} = 0.955\ \mu\text{F}$$

$$L_2 = \frac{k}{4\pi(f_2-f_1)} = \frac{100}{4\pi(5000-2000)} = 2.653\ \text{mH}$$

13.10 || m-DERIVED FILTERS

Probe

1. Explain how *T*-section and π-section of an *m*-derived network are derived from constant-*k* filters.

13.10.1 Limitations of Constant-*k* Type Filters

- Characteristic impedance, Z_0 is function of frequency and hence, even in pass band, load impedance should match with the varying Z_0 for zero voltage or current attenuation.
- Attenuation is not sharp for stop band region.

m-Derived filters are derived from constant-*k* filters by following steps:

1. Multiplying series branch impedances with *m*
2. Dividing shunt branch impedances by *m*
3. Adding extra impedance of opposite sign in series or in parallel to equate the characteristic impedance to that of constant-*k* type filter.

13.10.2 *m*-Derived Filter with *T*-Network

Characteristic impedance of a *T*-network is given by:

$$Z_0 = \sqrt{\left(\frac{Z_1}{2}\right)^2 + Z_1 Z_2}$$

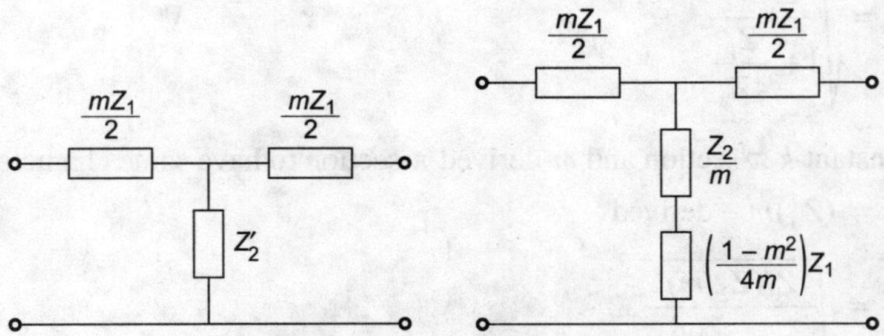

Figure 13.14 *m-derived T-section*

Figure 13.14 shows *T*-sections of both constant-*k* and *m*-derived filters. Both networks have equal characteristic impedances: i.e. (Z_0)constant-k = $(Z_0)m$-derived

$$\sqrt{\left(\frac{Z_1}{2}\right)^2 + Z_1 Z_2} = \sqrt{\left(\frac{mZ_1}{2}\right)^2 + mZ_1 Z_2'}$$

Solving it for Z_2',

$$Z_2' = \frac{Z_2}{m} + \left(\frac{1-m^2}{4m}\right) Z_1$$

Hence, *m*-derived *T*-section can be realised by:

- Multiplying series impedance with *m* and
- Dividing shunt impedance by *m* and
- By adding extra impedance $\left(\frac{1-m^2}{4m}\right)Z_1$ in series with shunt impedance.

13.10.3 *m*-Derived Filter with π-Network

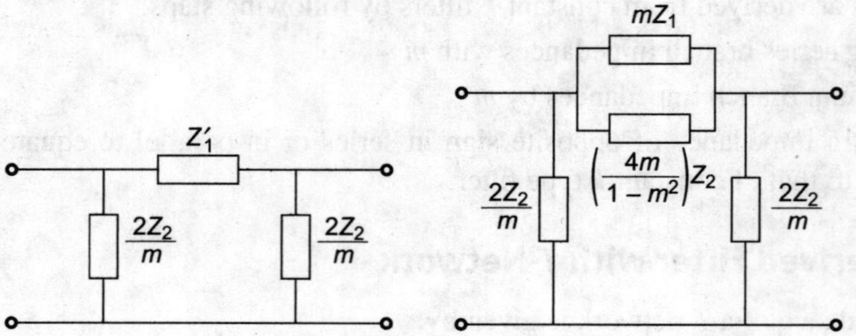

Figure 13.15 *m-Derived π-section*

Characteristic impedance of a π-network is given by

$$Z_0 = \sqrt{\frac{Z_1Z_2}{1+\frac{Z_1}{4Z_2}}}$$

Similarly, for constant-*k* π-section and *m*-derived π-section to have same characteristic impedance:

$$(Z_0)\text{ cons.} - k = (Z_0)m - \text{derived}$$

$$\sqrt{\frac{Z_1Z_2}{1+\frac{Z_1}{4Z_2}}} = \sqrt{\frac{Z_1'(Z_2/m)}{1+\frac{Z_1'}{4(Z_2/m)}}}$$

$$\frac{Z_1}{1+\frac{Z_1}{4Z_2}} = \frac{Z_1'}{m+\frac{Z_1'm^2}{4Z_2}}$$

$$\Rightarrow \qquad Z_1' = \frac{1}{\frac{1}{mZ_1}+\frac{1}{\left(\frac{4m}{1-m^2}\right)Z_2}}$$

Hence, Z_1' is parallel combination of mZ_1 and $\left(\frac{4m}{1-m^2}\right)Z_2$.

1. Multiplying series impedance with m and
2. Dividing shunt impedance by m and
3. By adding extra impedance $\left(\frac{4m}{1-m^2}\right)Z_2$ in parallel with series impedance.

Example 13.13

If an m-derived filter is to be designed with a T-type constant-k filter with $m = 0.6$. If value of series impedance is 200 Ohm, Find the value of additional impedance to be added in series with the shunt branch to match the characteristic impedance. ○●●

Solution Value of additional impedance to be added with shunt branch = $\left(\frac{1-m^2}{4m}\right)Z_1$

$$= \left(\frac{1-0.6^2}{4\times 0.6}\right)200 = 53.33 \text{ Ohm}$$

Example 13.14

An m-derived filter is to be designed with using π-network and $m = 0.6$. If value $Z_1 = 200$ Ohm, $Z_2 = 400$ Ohm. Find the value of impedances of series and shunt branches. ○●●

Solution **Step 1:** Impedance of shunt branch = $2Z_2/m = 2 \times 400/0.6 = 1333.33$ Ohm

Step 2: Impedance to be added in parallel with series branch

$$= \left(\frac{4m}{1-m^2}\right)Z_2 = \left(\frac{4\times 0.6}{1-0.6^2}\right)200 = 750 \text{ Ohm}$$

Step 3: Impedance of series branch = $(m\,Z_1) \parallel \left(\left(\frac{4m}{1-m^2}\right)Z_2\right) = (0.6\times 200) \parallel (750) = \frac{120\times 750}{120+750}$

$$= 103.45 \text{ Ohm}$$

13.11 || m-DERIVED LOW-PASS FILTER

University Question

1. Discuss how a constant-k low pass filter can be designed. [PTU-EE201]

(a) Frequency of Infinite Attenuation (f_∞)

Infinite attenuation for a low-pass occurs if shunt branch gets short circuited or series branch gets open circuited. This happens at resonance:

$$f_\infty = \frac{1}{2\pi}\sqrt{\frac{1}{(mC)\left(\frac{1-m^2}{4m}\right)L}}$$

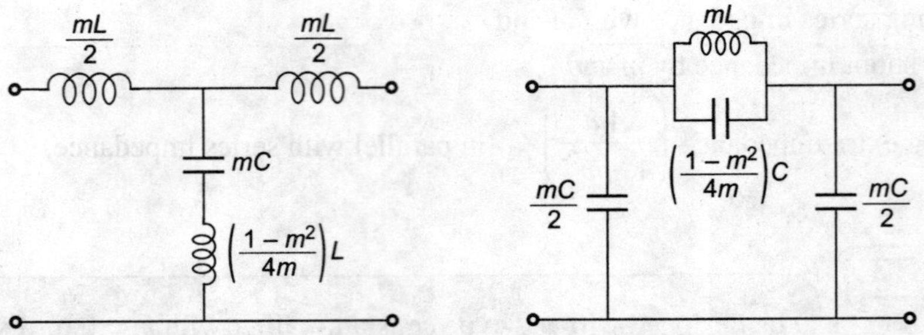

Figure 13.16 *m-derived LPF with T-section and π-section*

$$f_\infty = \frac{1}{\pi}\frac{1}{\sqrt{LC}}\frac{1}{\sqrt{1-m^2}} \tag{13.21}$$

(b) Determination of Value of m

Cut-off frequency for a low-pass filter is given by:

$$f_C = \frac{1}{\pi}\frac{1}{\sqrt{LC}}$$

Substituting this in Eq. (13.21)

$$f_\infty = \frac{f_C}{\sqrt{1-m^2}}$$

$$m = \sqrt{1-\left(\frac{f_C}{f_\infty}\right)^2} \tag{13.22}$$

(c) Design Parameters

Value of L and C remains same as of a constant-*k* type LPF.

Example 13.15

For an *m*-derived LPF, if cut off frequency and frequency of infinite attenuation are 500 Hz and 562 Hz. Find value of *m*.

Solution $f_C = 500$ Hz and $f_\infty = 562$ Hz

$$\text{Value of } m = \sqrt{1-\left(\frac{f_C}{f_\infty}\right)^2} = \sqrt{1-\left(\frac{500}{562}\right)^2} = 0.46$$

Example 13.16

The *T*-section of an *m*-derived LP filter is shown in Figure 13.17. Find value of *k*.

Solution

$$\frac{mL}{2} = 40 \text{ mH} \quad (13.23)$$

$$mc = 0.25\ \mu\text{F} \quad (13.24)$$

Solving Eqs (13.23) and (13.24) $\Rightarrow \dfrac{L}{2C} = 160 \times 10^3$

$$\frac{L}{C} = 320 \times 10^3$$

$$k = \sqrt{\frac{L}{C}} = \sqrt{320 \times 10^3} = 565.68$$

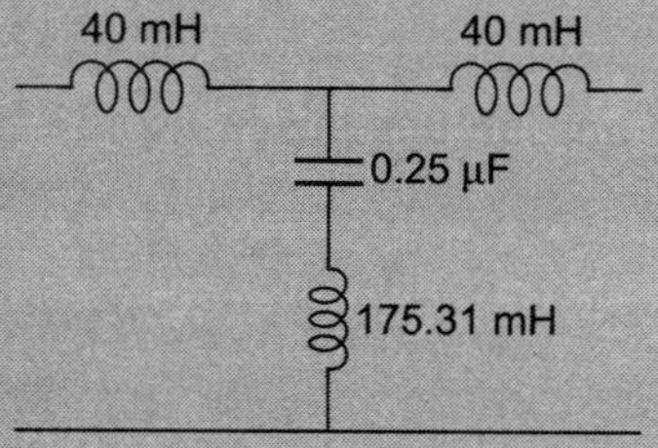

Figure 13.17

13.12 || *m*-DERIVED HIGH-PASS FILTER

University Question

1. Explain and draw *m*-derived high pass filter with π-section. (Figure 13.18) **[RU, 2006]**

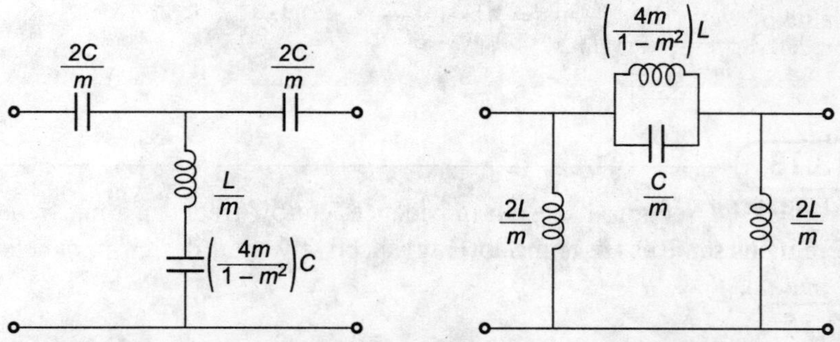

Figure 13.18 *m-derived HPF with T-section and π-section*

(a) Frequency of Infinite Attenuation (f_∞)

Infinite attenuation for a high-pass occurs if shunt branch gets short circuited or series branch gets open circuited. This happens at resonance:

$$f_\infty = \frac{1}{2\pi}\sqrt{\frac{1}{\left(\dfrac{L}{m}\right)\left(\dfrac{4m}{1-m^2}\right)C}}$$

$$f_\infty = \frac{1}{4\pi}\frac{1}{\sqrt{LC}}\sqrt{1-m^2} \quad (13.25)$$

(b) Determination of Value of m

Cut-off frequency for a high-pass filter is given by:

$$f_C = \frac{1}{\pi} \frac{1}{\sqrt{LC}}$$

Substituting this in Eq. (13.25),

$$f_\infty = f_C \sqrt{1 - m^2}$$

$$m = \sqrt{1 - \left(\frac{f_\infty}{f_C}\right)^2} \tag{13.26}$$

(c) Design Parameters

Value of L and C remains same as of a constant-k type HPF.

Example 13.17

For an m-derived HPF, if cut-off frequency and frequency of infinite attenuation are 800 Hz and 700 Hz respectively. Find value of m. ○○●

Solution $f_C = 800$ Hz and $f_\infty = 700$ Hz

$$\text{Value of } m = \sqrt{1 - \left(\frac{f_\infty}{f_C}\right)^2} = \sqrt{1 - \left(\frac{700}{800}\right)^2} = 0.484$$

Example 13.18

For an m-derived HPF T-section, if design impedance, cut-off frequency and frequency of infinite attenuation are 750 Ohm, 700 Hz and 800 Hz respectively, find design parameters (Value of all impedances, L and C). ○○●

Solution Design impedance, $k = 500$ Ohm, $f_C = 800$ Hz and $f_\infty = 700$ Hz

Step 1: Find value of L and C for a constant-k HPF of T-section,

$$L = k/\pi f_C = 500/(\pi \times 800) = 0.199 \text{ H}$$

$$C = 1/\pi k f_C = 1/(\pi \times 500 \times 800) = 79.61\ \mu\text{F}$$

Step 2: Find value of m:

$$m = \sqrt{1 - \left(\frac{f_\infty}{f_C}\right)^2} = \sqrt{1 - \left(\frac{700}{800}\right)^2} = 0.484$$

Step 3:

(a) Value of each series inductance = $mL/2 = 0.484 \times 0.199/2 = 0.048$H

(b) Value of each shunt capacitance = $mC = 0.484 \times 79.61\ \mu$F = 38.53 μF

(c) Value of additional impedance to be connected in series with shunt branch

$$= \left(\frac{1-m^2}{4m}\right)L = 0.079\text{ H}$$

13.13 || TERMINATING HALF SECTIONS

Half section is used when a *T*-network and a *π*-network are to be interconnected. They can be used at both source or load ends. Purpose of half sections is to match the impedance between the two networks.

Half Section with Constant-*k* Filters

A typical constant-*k* half section is shown in Figure 13.19 connecting a *T* and *π* network. For impedance matching,

(a) Image impedance as seen from 1-2 should be equal to characteristic impedance of *T*-network. and

(b) Image impedance as seen from 3-4 should be equal to characteristic impedance of *π*-network.

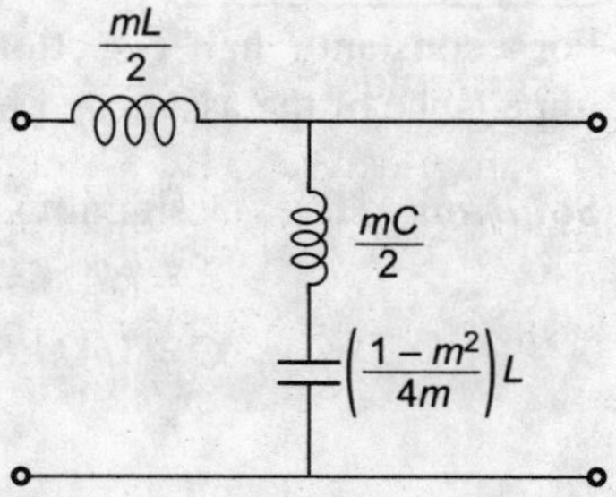

Figure 13.19 *m-derived terminating half-section – T type*

$$Z_{1-2} = \sqrt{Z_{OC}\,Z_{SC}} = \sqrt{(2Z_2)\left(\frac{(2Z_2)(Z_1)}{(2Z_2)+(Z_1)}\right)}$$

$$Z_{1-2} = \sqrt{\frac{4Z_1Z_2^{\ 2}}{Z_1+4Z_2}}$$

This is equal to characteristic impedance of the *π*-network.

$$Z_{3-4} = \sqrt{Z_{OC}\,Z_{SC}} = \sqrt{\left(\frac{Z_1}{2}+2Z_2\right)\left(\frac{Z_1}{2}\right)}$$

$$Z_{3-4} = \sqrt{Z_1Z_2\left(1+\frac{Z_1}{4Z_2}\right)}$$

This is equal to characteristic impedance of the *π*-network.

Half Section with *m*-Derived Filters

Similar analysis can be done for an ***m*-derived** filter shown in Figure 13.20.

If the shown half-section is to be connected between a *T*-network and π-network such that terminals 1-2 are connected to the π-network and terminals 3-4 to the *T*-Network than for impedance matching:

(a) Image impedance as seen from 1-2 should be equal to characteristic impedance of *T*-network. And

(b) Image impedance as seen from 3-4 should be equal to characteristic impedance of π-network.

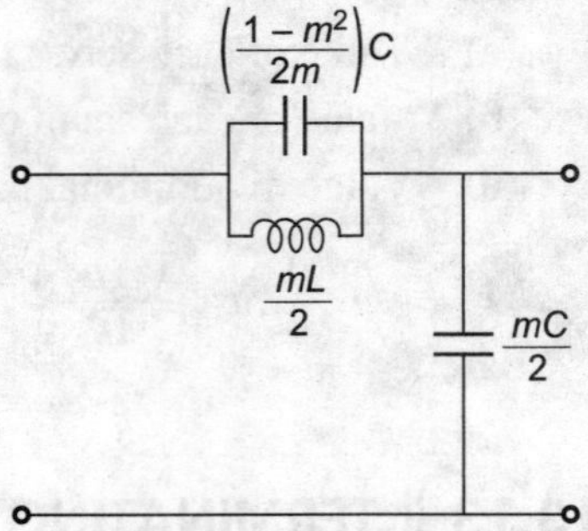

Figure 13.20 *m-derived terminating half-section – π type*

Example 13.19

For a constant-*k* half *T*-section, find the value of design parameters if cut-off frequencies and design impedance of the associated HPF are 5000 Hz and 1000 Ohm respectively.

Solution Here, Design impedance, k = 1000 Ohm, f_c = 5000 Hz

$$L = k/4\pi f = 1000/(4\pi \times 5000) = 15.92 \text{ mH}$$

$$C = 1/4\pi k f = 1/(4\pi \times 1000 \times 5000) = 0.0159 \text{ }\mu\text{F}$$

13.14 COMPOSITE FILTER

University Questions

1. Draw the block diagram of composite filter. **[University of Pune, 2012]**
2. Write short notes on composite filters. **[PTU-EE201]**

A composite filter is designed in order to achieve sharp attenuation even beyond the frequency of infinite attenuation. Block diagram for a typical composite filter is shown in Figure 13.21.

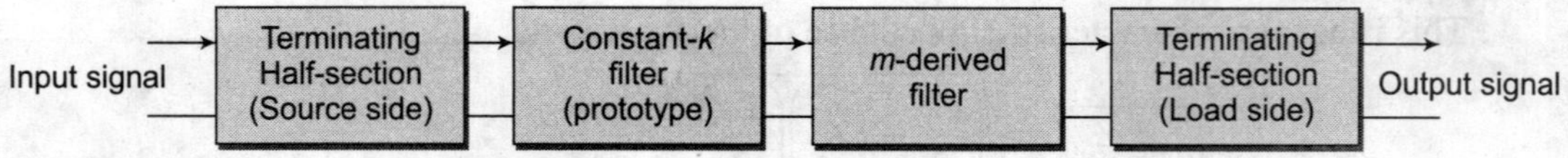

Figure 13.21 *Composite Filter – Block diagram*

Various sections of a composite filter are:

(a) A constant-*k* filter of particular cut-off frequencies.

(b) An *m*-derived filter of desired infinite attenuation frequency for sharp attenuation.

(c) Terminating half-sections at both load and source end for impedance matching (usually with $m = 0.6$).

Composite High-pass filter is shown in Figure 13.22.

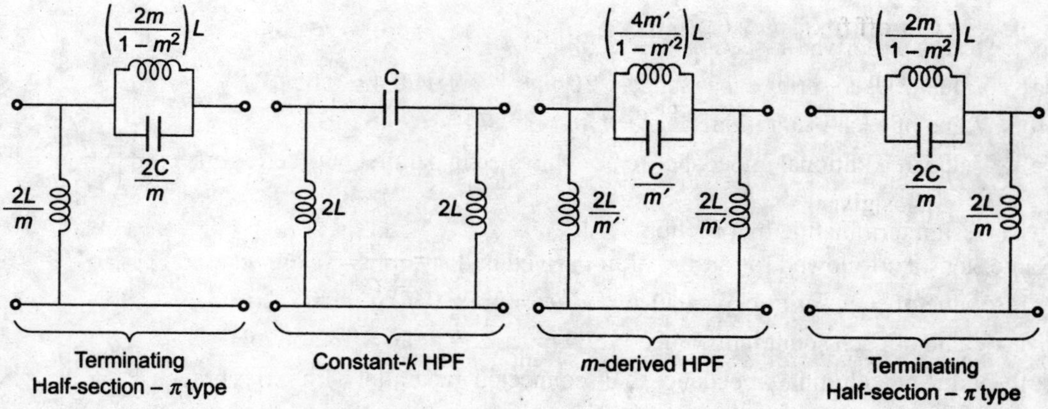

Figure 13.22 *Composite HPF using π-sections*

Composite Low-pass filter is shown in Figure 13.23.

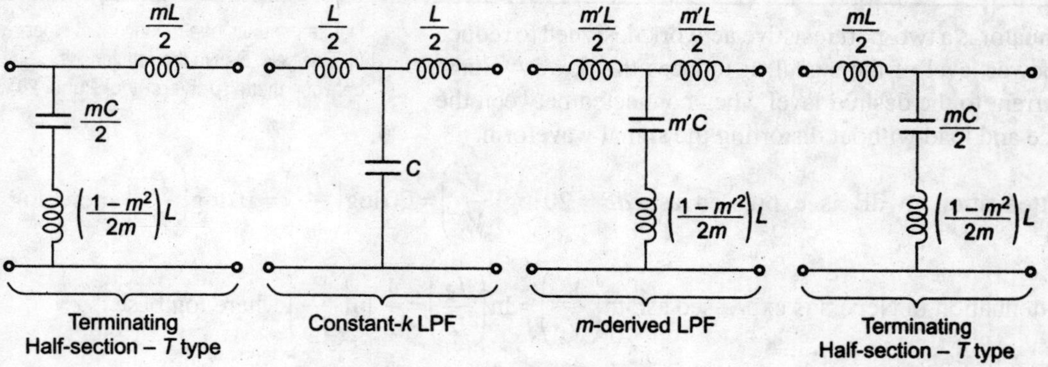

Figure 13.23 *Composite LPF using T-Sections*

Example 13.20

Design a composite high pass filter with:

(a) Characteristic impedance = 1000 Ohm,

(b) Cut-off frequency = 2000 Hz

(c) One *m*-derived *T*-section of $m = 0.4$

(d) *m*-derived *T*-sections at both load and source ends ($m = 0.6$).

Use constant-*k* *T* section as prototype.

Solution **Step 1:** Design prototype constant-*k* *T* section

Given, $k = 1000$ Ohm, $f_c = 2000$ Hz

So, $L = k/\pi f = 1000/(\pi \times 2000) = 159.2$ mH

$C = 1/\pi k f = 1/(\pi \times 1000 \times 2000) = 0.16\ \mu$F

Step 2: Design *m*-derived *T*-section- Given, $m = 0.4$

(a) Value of each series capacitance = $2C/m = 2 \times 0.04/0.4 = 0.05$ µF

(b) Value of each shunt inductance = $L/m = 39.8/0.4 = 99.5$ mH

(c) Value of additional impedance to be connected in parallel with series branch = $\left(\frac{4m}{1-m^2}\right)C =$ 0.076 µF

Step 3: Design terminating half section:

Same steps are followed for design of m-derived half sections. Given, $m = 0.6$

(a) Value of each series capacitance = $2C/m = 2 \times 0.04/0.6 = 0.033$ µF

(b) Value of each shunt inductance = $2L/m = 2 \times 39.8/0.6 = 132.66$ mH

(c) Value of additional impedance to be connected in parallel with series branch = $\left(\frac{2m}{1-m^2}\right)C =$ 0.075 µF

13.15 ATTENUATOR

University Question

1. Define the units of attenuation: (i) Neper (ii) Decibels. Derive the relationship between them. **[University of Pune, 2013]**

Attenuator is a two-port resistive network designed to reduce the power level of the signal. It reduces the power/voltage or current to the desired level when connected between the source and load without distorting the signal waveform.

Attenuation in dB is expressed as: $dB = 20\log\left(\frac{V_1}{V_2}\right) = 20\log\left(\frac{I_1}{I_2}\right) = 10\log\left(\frac{P_1}{P_2}\right)$ here log base is 10.

Attenuation in Nepers is expressed as: $\ln\left(\frac{V_1}{V_2}\right) = \ln\left(\frac{I_1}{I_2}\right) = \frac{1}{2}\ln\left(\frac{P_1}{P_2}\right)$, here log base is *e*.

Since,
$$\log X = \frac{1}{2.303}\ln X$$
$$20\log X = \frac{20}{2.303}\ln X$$
$$20\log X = 8.686\ln X$$

Gain in dB = 8.686 Gain in Nepers.

Example 13.21

For a 40 dB gain, find out the gain in voltage ratio. Also, find the gain in Nepers.

Solution

$$\text{Gain in dB, } D = 20\log\left(\frac{V_1}{V_2}\right) \Rightarrow \frac{V_1}{V_2} = \text{Antilog}\left(\frac{D}{20}\right) \Rightarrow \frac{V_1}{V_2} = 10^{\left(\frac{D}{20}\right)} \Rightarrow \frac{V_1}{V_2} = 10^{\left(\frac{40}{20}\right)} = 100$$

$$\text{Gain in Nepers,} = \frac{1}{8.686}\text{ gain in dB} = \frac{40}{8.686} = 4.60$$

13.16 || LATTICE ATTENUATOR

University Question

1. Write a short note on attenuators. **[PU, 2011]**

Figure 13.24 shows a lattice attenuator. Like π- and T-network, two important parameters of the attenuator are determined here.

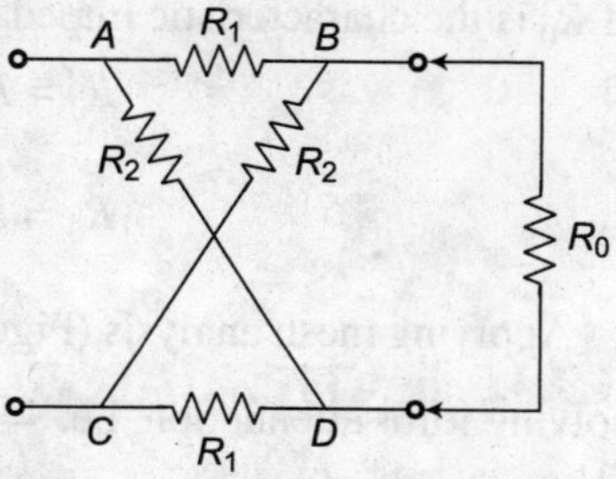

Figure 13.24 *Lattice attenuator*

13.16.1 Characteristic Impedance

$$Z_{1-2} = \sqrt{Z_{OC}\,Z_{SC}} = \sqrt{\left(\frac{R_1 + R_2}{2}\right)\left(\frac{2R_1R_2}{R_1 + R_2}\right)} = \sqrt{R_1R_2} \quad (13.27)$$

13.16.2 Parameter Determination

Attenuation coefficient, $N = e^{\alpha} = \dfrac{I_1}{I_2}$

The circuit can be simplified as:

If the load resistance is equal to the characteristic of attenuator, values of R_1 and R_2 for a desired attenuation (N) are found as described below:

Applying KVL in loops yields,

$$I_1R_0 - I_1R_1 = I_2R_0 + I_2\,R_1$$

$$\frac{I_1}{I_2} = \frac{R_0 + R_1}{R_0 - R_1} = N$$

Solving it for R_1,

$$R_1 = \frac{N-1}{N+1}R_0$$

Using Eq. (13.27), $R_2 = \dfrac{N+1}{N-1}R_0$

Example 13.22

For a lattice attenuator with R_1 = 163.6 Ohm and R_2 = 244.5 Ohm, Find out characteristic resistance and attenuation in dB.

○○●

Solution

(a) Characteristic resistance, $R_0 = \sqrt{R_1\,R_2} = \sqrt{163.6 \times 244.5} = 200$ Ohm

(b) Attenuation, $N = \frac{R_0 + R_1}{R_0 - R_1} = \frac{200 + 163.6}{200 - 163.6} = 10;$

Attenuation in dB = 20 log N = 20 log 10 = 20 dB

13.17 ‖ *T*-TYPE ATTENUATOR

If R_0 is the characteristic impedance then,

$$R_0 = R_1 + (R_2 \parallel (R_1 + R_0))$$

$$R_0 = R_1 + \frac{(R_2(R_1 + R_0))}{R_2 + (R_1 + R_0)} \quad (13.28)$$

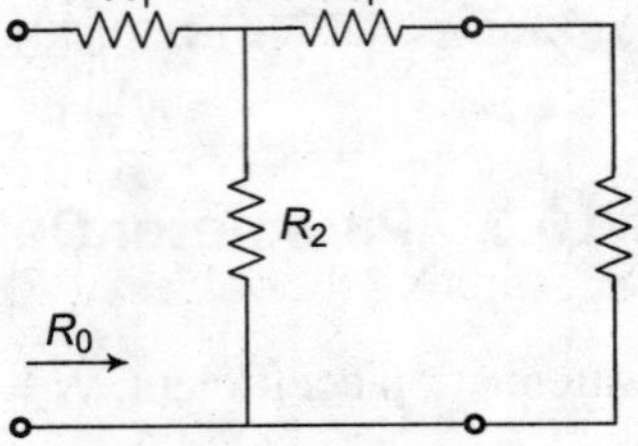

Figure 13.25 *T-type attenuator*

Applying mesh analysis (Figure 13.25), $I_1R_2 + I_1R_2 = I_2R_0 + I_2R_1$

solving it for attenuation, i.e. $\frac{I_1}{I_2}$ yields,

$$\frac{I_1}{I_2} = \frac{R_1 + R_2 + R_0}{R_2} \quad (13.29)$$

Solving Eqs (13.28) and (13.29),

$$R_1 = R_0 \frac{N-1}{N+1} \text{ and } R_2 = R_0 \frac{2N}{N^2 - 1}$$

Example 13.23

Design a symmetrical *T*-attenuator so that it works between a source and load impedance of 260 Ω and 490 Ω respectively and provides an attenuation of 40 dB. ○●●

Solution Given, characteristic impedance, $R_0 = 490\ \Omega$, $D = 40$ dB

Step 1: Find attenuation in terms of current or voltage ratio:

$$\text{N} = \text{Antilog}\left(\frac{D}{20}\right) = \text{Antilog}\left(\frac{40}{20}\right) = 100$$

Step 2: Find values of R_1 and R_2:

$$R_2 = R_0 \frac{2N}{N^2 - 1} = 490 \frac{2 \times 100}{100 \times 100 - 1} = 9.80 \text{ Ohm}$$

$$R_1 = R_0 \frac{N-1}{N+1} = 490 \frac{100 - 1}{100 + 1} = 480.3 \text{ Ohm}$$

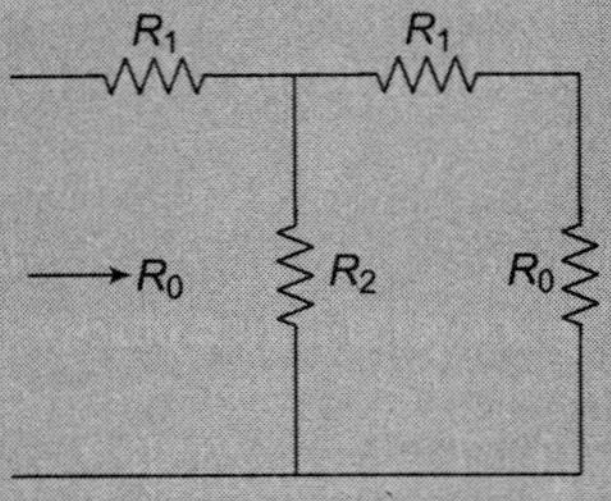

Figure 13.26

13.18 || π-TYPE ATTENUATOR

Using bisection theorem, a lattice equivalent network of a π network can be found using its bisections as shown in Figure 13.27.

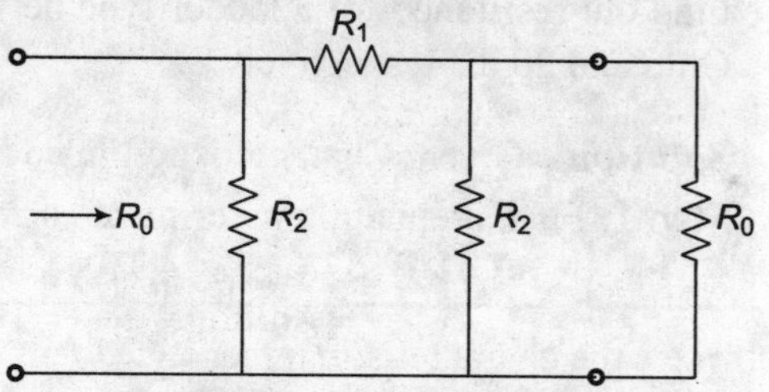

Figure 13.27 *π-type attenuator*

Bisections of the π-network will have series arm of $\frac{R_1}{2}$ and shunt branch of $2R_2$.

Equivalent lattice network will have:

$$R_1' = \left(\frac{R_1}{2} \times 2R_2\right) / \left(\frac{R_1}{2} + 2R_2\right) \text{ and} = R_2' = 2R_2$$

Since for a lattice network,

$$R_1 = \frac{N-1}{N+1} R_0 \;; \quad R_2 = \frac{N+1}{N-1} R_0$$

Substituting the values of R_1 and R_2;

$$R_1' = R_0 \frac{N^2 - 1}{2N}; \quad R_2' = \frac{R_0}{2} \frac{N+1}{N-1}$$

Example 13.24

Design a π-type attenuator to give 20 dB attenuation and to have a characteristic impedance of 100 Ω.

Solution Given, characteristic impedance, $R_0 = 100\ \Omega$, $D = 100$ dB

Step 1: Find values of R_1 and R_2

$$R_1' = R_0 \frac{N^2 - 1}{2N} = 100 \frac{20^2 - 1}{2 \times 20} = 495 \text{ Ohm}$$

$$R_2' = \frac{R_0}{2} \frac{N+1}{N-1} = \frac{100}{2} \frac{20+1}{20-1} = 61.11 \text{ Ohm}$$

$$R_1 = R_1' = 495 \text{ Ohm}$$

Since, $R_2 = 2R_2' = 61.11 \times 2 = 122.22$ Ohm

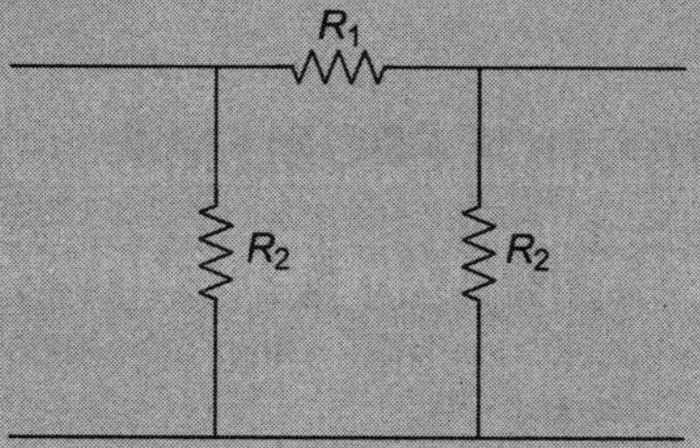

Figure 13.28

13.19 || LADDER-TYPE ATTENUATOR

When attenuation with single step of a T or π network does not match the desired value, multiple units of identical T or π networks are cascaded.

A single unit can be designed following the corresponding formulae of parameter determination and attenuation required per step.

Example 13.25

Find out resistances of a ladder-type network, if load resistance and attenuation per section are 500 Ohm and 20 dB respectively. ○●●

Solution Given, Characteristic Impedance, $R_0 = 500\Omega$, $D = 20$ dB

Step 1: Find attenuation in terms of current or voltage ratio:

$$N = \text{Antilog}\left(\frac{20}{20}\right) = 10$$

Step 2: Find values of R_1 and R_2

$$R_1 = R_0 \frac{N^2 - 1}{2N} = 500 \frac{10 \times 10 - 1}{2 \times 10} = 2475 \text{ Ohm}$$

$$R_2 = \frac{R_0}{2} \frac{N+1}{N-1} = \frac{500}{2} \frac{10+1}{10-1} = 305.55 \text{ Ohm}$$

POINTS TO REMEMBER

- Attenuation coefficient (α) for pass band is zero.
- Phase shift for stop band (attenuation band) is π.
- Condition to get cut off frequency, $\frac{Z_1}{4Z_2} = -1$

PRACTICE PROBLEMS

1. Design a symmetrical resistive *T*-section with open and short circuit impedances equal to 2000 Ohm and 1000 Ohm respectively. ○○●
2. For a π-network having both shunt impedances equal to 200 Ohm and series inductance of 500 Ohm, find characteristic impedance. Assume all impedances to be resistive. ○○●
3. A low pass filter is designed with shunt branch having a capacitor of 0.20 μF and series branch having two inductors each of 15 mH. Calculate (a) Cut-off frequency, Attenuation and Phase shift for (b) $f = 5000$ Hz, and (c) $f = 1000$ Hz. ○●●
4. Find characteristic impedance of a low pass filter at 2000 Hz if cut-off frequency is 5000 Hz. Design impedance = 200 Ohm. ○●●
5. A high pass filter is designed with two series branches each having capacitance of 0.20 μF and a shunt branch having inductance 15 mH. Calculate: (a) Cut-off frequency, Attenuation and Phase shift for (b) $f = 500$ Hz and (c) $f = 5{,}000$ Hz. ○●●
6. For an *m*-derived *T*-section high pass filter, if infinite attenuation is desired at frequency not lower than 10% of cut-off frequency. Find the value of *m*. ○○●
7. For an *m*-derived π-section high pass filter with characteristic impedance of 600 Ohm, ○●●

cut-off frequency of 2 kHz, frequency of infinite attenuation equal to 1.8 kHz, find the value of inductance to be connected in parallel with shunt branch impedance derived from constant-*k* filter.

8. Design a composite low pass filter with: ●●●
(a) Characteristic impedance = 500 Ohm,
(b) Cut-off frequency = 2000 Hz
(c) Frequency of infinite attenuation = 2500 Hz
(d) *m*-derived *T*-sections at both load and source ends ($m = 0.6$).

Use constant-*k* *T* section as prototype.

9. With a lattice attenuator of 150 Ohm characteristic resistance, it is desired to reduce the power level to half. Determine its design parameters. ○●●

MULTIPLE CHOICE QUESTIONS

1. For an ideal low pass filter with cut-off frequency of 2 kHz, value phase shift for a signal of 5 kHz will be ○○●
(a) Zero (b) 90 degree (c) 180 degree (d) 45 degree

2. For a High pass filter designed with π-network, characteristic impedance at cut-off frequency is: ○●●
(a) Zero (b) Infinite (c) Imaginary (d) Negative

3. Value of *m* for an *m*-derived filter with cut-off frequency of 8 kHz and frequency of infinite attenuation of 7.2 kHz will be: ○●●
(a) 0.54 (b) 0.44 (c) 0.60 (d) 0.23

4. Attenuation coefficient for a constant-low pass filter of 1 kHz cut-off frequency at 2 kHz is: ○●●
(a) Infinite (b) Zero (c) $1/e$ (d) e

5. If output power is 1/10 of input power, attenuation in dB will be: ○●●
(a) 10 (b) 20 (c) 10/2.308 (d) 0

ANSWERS TO MULTIPLE CHOICE QUESTIONS

1. (c) 2. (b) 3. (b) 4. (a) 5. (a)